sation of nuclear testing and the prevention of surprise attack; the abortive preparations for a summit meeting; problems relating to military disengagement in Europe (the Rapacki Plan); German unification and the Berlin crisis; questions of trade and cultural relations.

The reader will also find ample documentation of significant developments pertaining to the Cyprus issue, the rise of nationalism in Africa (the Cairo and Accra conferences), the problems of the space age, international scientific cooperation, and many other vital events.

The annual volumes of DOCUMENTS ON AMERICAN FOREIGN RELATIONS provide an authoritative record of America's developing relationships with the other nations of the world.

SOME PUBLICATIONS OF THE
COUNCIL ON FOREIGN RELATIONS

FOREIGN AFFAIRS (quarterly), edited by Hamilton Fish Armstrong.
THE UNITED STATES IN WORLD AFFAIRS (annual). Volumes for 1931, 1932, and 1933, by Walter Lippmann and William O. Scroggs; for 1934-1935, 1936, 1937, 1938, 1939 and 1940, by Whitney H. Shepardson and William O. Scroggs; for 1945-1947, 1947-1948 and 1948-1949, by John C. Campbell; for 1949, 1950, 1951, 1952, 1953 and 1954, by Richard P. Stebbins; for 1955, by Hollis W. Barber; for 1956, 1957 and 1958, by Richard P. Stebbins.
DOCUMENTS ON AMERICAN FOREIGN RELATIONS (annual). Volume for 1952 edited by Clarence W. Baier and Richard P. Stebbins; for 1953 and 1954, edited by Peter V. Curl; for 1955, 1956 and 1957, edited by Paul E. Zinner.
POLITICAL HANDBOOK OF THE WORLD (annual), edited by Walter H. Mallory.
THE SCHUMAN PLAN: A Study in Economic Cooperation, 1950-1958, by William Diebold, Jr.
SOVIET ECONOMIC AID: The New Aid and Trade Policy in Underdeveloped Countries, by Joseph Berliner.
RAW MATERIALS: A Study of American Policy, by Percy W. Bidwell.
FOREIGN POLICY: THE NEXT PHASE, by Thomas K. Finletter.
NATO AND THE FUTURE OF EUROPE, by Ben T. Moore.
AFRICAN ECONOMIC DEVELOPMENT, by William A. Hance.
DEFENSE OF THE MIDDLE EAST: Problems of American Policy, by John C. Campbell.
INDIA AND AMERICA: A Study of Their Relations, by Phillips Talbot and S. L. Poplai.
JAPAN BETWEEN EAST AND WEST, by Hugh Borton, Jerome B. Cohen, William J. Jorden, Donald Keene, Paul F. Langer and C. Martin Wilbur.
NUCLEAR WEAPONS AND FOREIGN POLICY, by Henry A. Kissinger.
MOSCOW-PEKING AXIS: Strengths and Strains, by Howard L. Boorman, Alexander Eckstein, Philip E. Mosely and Benjamin Schwartz.
CLIMATE AND ECONOMIC DEVELOPMENT IN THE TROPICS, by Douglas H. K. Lee.
WHAT THE TARIFF MEANS TO AMERICAN INDUSTRIES, by Percy W. Bidwell.
UNITED STATES SHIPPING POLICY, by Wytze Gorter.
RUSSIA AND AMERICA: Dangers and Prospects, by Henry L. Roberts.
STERLING: Its Meaning in World Finance, by Judd Polk.
KOREA: A Study of U.S. Policy in the United Nations, by Leland M. Goodrich.
FOREIGN AFFAIRS BIBLIOGRAPHY, 1942-1952, by Henry L. Roberts.
AMERICAN AGENCIES INTERESTED IN INTERNATIONAL AFFAIRS, compiled by Ruth Savord and Donald Wasson.
JAPANESE AND AMERICANS: A Century of Cultural Relations, by Robert S. Schwantes.
THE FUTURE OF UNDERDEVELOPED COUNTRIES: Political Implications of Economic Development, by Eugene Staley.
THE UNDECLARED WAR, 1940-1941, by William L. Langer and S. Everett Gleason.
THE CHALLENGE TO ISOLATION, 1937-1940, by William L. Langer and S. Everett Gleason.
MIDDLE EAST DILEMMAS: The Background of United States Policy, by J. C. Hurewitz.
BRITAIN AND THE UNITED STATES: Problems in Cooperation, a joint report prepared by Henry L. Roberts and Paul A. Wilson.
TRADE AND PAYMENTS IN WESTERN EUROPE: A Study in Economic Cooperation, 1947-1951, by William Diebold, Jr.
SURVEY OF AMERICAN FOREIGN RELATIONS (in four volumes, 1928-1931), prepared under the direction of Charles P. Howland.

DOCUMENTS ON AMERICAN FOREIGN RELATIONS
1958

DOCUMENTS ON

AMERICAN

FOREIGN RELATIONS

1958

EDITED BY

PAUL E. ZINNER

Published for the

COUNCIL ON FOREIGN RELATIONS

by

HARPER & BROTHERS

NEW YORK

1960

DOCUMENTS ON AMERICAN FOREIGN RELATIONS, 1958

Copyright, © 1959, by Council on Foreign Relations, Inc.
Printed in the United States of America

All rights reserved, including the right to reproduce
this book or any portion thereof in any form.

For information, address Council on Foreign Relations,
58 East 68th Street, New York 21

SECOND PRINTING

The Colonial Press Inc., Clinton, Mass.

Library of Congress catalog card number: LC 39-28987

Published in Great Britain and the British
Commonwealth, excluding Canada, by
London: Oxford University Press

50309

PREFACE

IN KEEPING with established tradition, this volume of *Documents on American Foreign Relations* seeks to provide concise yet comprehensive documentation of the global foreign relations of the United States in a single calendar year.

In contrast with 1957, which was a year of relative diplomatic quiescence, 1958 witnessed the resurgence of the feverish pace of international relations that has marked the postwar period generally. The year's major crises, centering upon the Middle East, the Formosa Strait, and Berlin, are accorded due prominence in the amplitude of documentation about them. The voluminous public correspondence conducted by the President with Messrs. Bulganin and Khrushchev and other East-West exchanges in the form of notes, memoranda, proposals and—in rare cases—agreements are also treated extensively, despite the long-winded nature of most communications of Soviet origin and the repetitive character of the exchanges in general. The reason for such a thorough treatment even of issues that never came to a head, like the summit meeting, is to provide continuity of documentation of questions of surpassing importance and to show wherever possible even subtle modifications in the views propounded by one or another of the major powers.

In the editor's opinion, the value of presenting complete series of diplomatic exchanges exceeds the virtues of a high degree of selectivity. The serious researcher must always wonder whether a missing document contained anything of potential interest or if perhaps a passage excised from a document cast revealing light upon questions of concern to him. Unfortunately, given the copious raw material from which to select, this year more than ever in the past, there had to be a fair amount of excerpting and only a few problems could be documented fully.

Aside from the headline attractions mentioned above, less prominent but perhaps intrinsically no less significant developments such as the tenth anniversary session of the Colombo Plan organization, the United Nations Conference on the

Law of the Sea and discussions concerning the peaceful uses of outer space are also duly noted in this volume, as is the question of the status of Cyprus. But the internal crisis in France, the closely related problem of Algeria and the continuing ideological struggle between Tito's Yugoslavia and the Communist bloc receive skimpy attention if any at all. This is due to the paucity of important American statements on these issues and to the inevitable limitations of space.

The guiding principle in the selection of documents continues to be their bearing on American policy specifically rather than on world relations generally. Even so, many documents originating from a variety of countries and by no means only from the major powers are featured alongside the pronouncements of the President, the Secretary of State and other leading American public figures. Of particular interest are the documents relating to the rise of African nationalism and the statements of the People's Republic of China.

As with past volumes, the preparation of this volume for publication was greatly facilitated by the generous assistance of various members of the Council staff and the understanding attitude of the business office under Frank D. Caruthers, Jr. Of particular help was the Council's efficient and highly accommodating library staff. Richard P. Stebbins, author of the Council's annual analytical treatise on *The United States in World Affairs,* as usual, provided discreet suggestions for improving the selection and presentation of the material. Finally, thanks are due to the publishers of *Current History* and *The Current Digest of the Soviet Press* for permission to reproduce some of the excellent translations of foreign language documents originally printed by them.

May 1959   PAUL E. ZINNER

CONTENTS

D. Disarmament

1. Exchange of Correspondence between the President and the Chairman of the Council of Ministers of the USSR (Khrushchev)

2. Technical Talks on the Detection of Nuclear Explosions, Geneva, July 1-August 21, 1958

3. Exchange of Views on Negotiations for the Suspension of Nuclear Tests

CHAPTER ONE

THE UNITED STATES: PRINCIPLES AND POLICIES

A. Annual Review.

(1) *Message of the President on the State of the Union, January 9, 1958.*[1]

Mr. President, Mr. Speaker, Members of the 85th Congress: It is again my high privilege to extend personal greetings to the Members of the 85th Congress.

All of us realize that, as this new session begins, many Americans are troubled about recent world developments which they believe may threaten our Nation's safety. Honest men differ in their appraisal of America's material and intellectual strength, and the dangers that confront us. But all know these dangers are real.

The purpose of this message is to outline the measures that can give the American people a confidence—just as real —in their own security.

I am not here to justify the past, gloss over the problems of the present, or propose easy solutions for the future.

I am here to state what I believe to be right and what I believe to be wrong; and to propose action for correcting what I think wrong.

I

There are two tasks confronting us that so far outweigh all others that I shall devote this year's message entirely to them.

The first is to insure our safety through strength.

As to our strength, I have repeatedly voiced this conviction: We now have a broadly based and efficient defensive strength, including a great deterrent power, which is, for the present, our main guaranty against war; but, unless we act wisely and promptly, we could lose that capacity to deter attack or defend ourselves.

[1] House Document 251, 85th Cong., 2d Sess.

My profoundest conviction is that the American people will say, as one man: No matter what the exertions or sacrifices, we shall maintain that necessary strength.

But we could make no more tragic mistake than merely to concentrate on military strength.

For if we did only this, the future would hold nothing for the world but an age of terror.

And so our second task is to do the constructive work of building a genuine peace. We must never become so preoccupied with our desire for military strength that we neglect those areas of economic development, trade, diplomacy, education, ideas, and principles where the foundations of real peace must be laid.

II

The threat to our safety, and to the hope of a peaceful world, can be simply stated. It is Communist imperialism.

This threat is not something imagined by critics of the Soviets. Soviet spokesmen, from the beginning, have publicly and frequently declared their aim to expand their power, one way or another, throughout the world.

The threat has become increasingly serious as this expansionist aim has been reinforced by an advancing industrial, military, and scientific establishment.

But what makes the Soviet threat unique in history is its all-inclusiveness. Every human activity is pressed into service as a weapon of expansion. Trade, economic development, military power, arts, science, education, the whole world of ideas—all are harnessed to this same chariot of expansion.

The Soviets are, in short, waging total cold war.

The only answer to a regime that wages total cold war is to wage total peace.

This means bringing to bear every asset of our personal and national lives upon the task of building the conditions in which security and peace can grow.

III

Among our assets, let us first briefly glance at our military power.

Military power serves the cause of security by making prohibitive the cost of any aggressive attack.

It serves the cause of peace by holding up a shield behind which the patient constructive work of peace can go on.

But it can serve neither cause if we make either of two

mistakes. The one would be to overestimate our strength, and thus neglect crucially important actions in the period just ahead. The other would be to underestimate our strength. Thereby we might be tempted to become irresolute in our foreign relations, to dishearten our friends, and to lose our national poise and perspective in approaching the complex problems ahead.

Any orderly balance sheet of military strength must be in two parts. The first is the position as of today. The second is the position in the period ahead.

As of today: our defensive shield comprehends a vast complex of ground, sea, and air units, superbly equipped and strategically deployed around the world. The most powerful deterrent to war in the world today lies in the retaliatory power of our Strategic Air Command and the aircraft of our Navy. They present to any potential attacker who would unleash war upon the world the prospect of virtual annihilation of his own country.

Even if we assume a surprise attack on our bases, with a marked reduction in our striking power, our bombers would immediately be on their way in sufficient strength to accomplish this mission of retaliation. Every informed government knows this. It is no secret.

Since the Korean armistice, the American people have spent $225 billion in maintaining and strengthening this overall defensive shield.

This is the position as of today.

Now as to the period ahead: Every part of our Military Establishment must and will be equipped to do its defensive job with the most modern weapons and methods. But it is particularly important to our planning that we make a candid estimate of the effect of long-range ballistic missiles on the present deterrent power I have described.

At this moment, the consensus of opinion is that we are probably somewhat behind the Soviets in some areas of long-range ballistic missile development. But it is my conviction, based on close study of all relevant intelligence, that if we make the necessary effort, we will have the missiles, in the needed quantity and in time, to sustain and strengthen the deterrent power of our increasingly efficient bombers. One encouraging fact evidencing this ability is the rate of progress we have achieved since we began to concentrate on these missiles.

The intermediate ballistic missiles, Thor and Jupiter, have

already been ordered into production. The parallel progress in the intercontinental ballistic missile effort will be advanced by our plans for acceleration. The development of the submarine-based Polaris missile system has progressed so well that its future procurement schedules are being moved forward markedly.

When it is remembered that our country has concentrated on the development of ballistic missiles for only about a third as long as the Soviets, these achievements show a rate of progress that speaks for itself. Only a brief time back, we were spending at the rate of only about $1 million a year on long-range ballistic missiles. In 1957 we spent more than $1 billion on the Atlas, Titan, Thor, Jupiter, and Polaris programs alone.

But I repeat, gratifying though this rate of progress is, we must still do more.

Our real problem, then, is not our strength today; it is rather the vital necessity of action today to insure our strength tomorrow.

What I have just said applies to our strength as a single country. But we are not alone. I have returned from the recent NATO meeting[2] with renewed conviction that, because we are a part of a worldwide community of free and peaceful nations, our own security is immeasurably increased.

By contrast, the Soviet Union has surrounded itself with captive and sullen nations. Like a crack in the crust of an uneasily sleeping volcano, the Hungarian uprising revealed the depth and intensity of the patriotic longing for liberty that still burns within these countries.

The world thinks of us as a country which is strong, but which will never start a war. The world also thinks of us as a land which has never enslaved anyone and which is animated by humane ideals. This friendship, based on common ideals, is one of our greatest sources of strength.

It cements into a cohesive security arrangement the aggregate of the spiritual, military, and economic strength of all those nations which, with us, are allied by treaties and agreements.

Up to this point, I have talked solely about our military strength to deter a possible future war.

I now want to talk about the strength we need to win a

[2] *Documents on American Foreign Relations, 1957*, pp. 91-126.

different kind of war—one that has already been launched against us.

It is the massive economic offensive that has been mounted by the Communist imperialists against free nations.[3]

The Communist imperialist regimes have for some time been largely frustrated in their attempts at expansion based directly on force. As a result, they have begun to concentrate heavily on economic penetration, particularly of newly developing countries, as a preliminary to political domination.

This nonmilitary drive, if underestimated, could defeat the free world regardless of our military strength. This danger is all the greater precisely because many of us fail or refuse to recognize it. Thus, some people may be tempted to finance our extra military effort by cutting economic assistance. But at the very time when the economic threat is assuming menacing proportions, to fail to strengthen our own effort would be nothing less than reckless folly.

Admittedly, most of us did not anticipate the psychological impact upon the world of the launching of the first earth satellite. Let us not make the same kind of mistake in another field, by failing to anticipate the much more serious impact of the Soviet economic offensive.

As with our military potential, our economic assets are more than equal to the task. Our independent farmers produce an abundance of food and fiber. Our free workers are versatile, intelligent, and hard working. Our businessmen are imaginative and resourceful. The productivity, the adaptability of the American economy is the solid foundation stone of our security structure.

We have just concluded another prosperous year. Our output was once more the greatest in the Nation's history. In the latter part of the year, some decline in employment and output occurred, following the exceptionally rapid expansion of recent years. In a free economy, reflecting as it does the independent judgments of millions of people, growth typically moves forward unevenly. But the basic forces of growth remain unimpaired. There are solid grounds for confidence that economic growth will be resumed without an extended interruption. Moreover, the Federal Government, constantly alert to signs of weakening in any part of our economy, al-

[3] For background see *Department of State Bulletin*, v. 38 (January 27, 1958), pp. 144-149; also *The Sino-Soviet Economic Offensive in the Less Developed Countries*, Department of State Publication 6632.

ways stands ready, with its full power, to take any appropriate further action to promote renewed business expansion.

If our history teaches us anything, it is this lesson: so far as the economic potential of our Nation is concerned, the believers in the future of America have always been the realists.

I count myself as one of this company.

Our long-range problem, then, is not the stamina of our enormous engine of production. Our problem is to make sure that we use these vast economic forces confidently and creatively, not only in direct military defense efforts, but likewise in our foreign policy, through such activities as mutual economic aid and foreign trade.

In much the same way, we have tremendous potential resources on other nonmilitary fronts to help in countering the Soviet threat: education, science, research, and, not least, the ideas and principles by which we live. And in all these cases the task ahead is to bring these resources more sharply to bear upon the new tasks of security and peace in a swiftly changing world.

IV

There are many items in the administration's program, of a kind frequently included in a state of the Union message, with which I am not dealing today. They are important to us and to our prosperity. But I am reserving them for treatment in separate communications because of my purpose today of speaking only about matters bearing directly upon our security and peace.

I now place before you an outline of action designed to focus our resources upon the two tasks of security and peace.

In this special category I list eight items requiring action. They are not merely desirable. They are imperative.

1. Defense Reorganization

The first need is to assure ourselves that military organization facilitates rather than hinders the functioning of the Military Establishment in maintaining the security of the Nation.

Since World War II, the purpose of achieving maximum organizational efficiency in a modern defense establishment has several times occasioned action by the Congress and by the executive.

The advent of revolutionary new devices, bringing with

them the problem of overall continental defense, creates new difficulties, reminiscent of those attending the advent of the airplane half a century ago.

Some of the important new weapons which technology has produced do not fit into any existing service pattern. They cut across all services, involve all services, and transcend all services, at every stage from development to operation. In some instances they defy classification according to branch of service.

Unfortunately, the uncertainties resulting from such a situation, and the jurisdictional disputes attending upon it, tend to bewilder and confuse the public and create the impression that service differences are damaging the national interest.

Let us proudly remember that the members of the Armed Forces give their basic allegiance solely to the United States. Of that fact all of us are certain. But pride of service and mistaken zeal in promoting particular doctrine has more than once occasioned the kind of difficulty of which I have just spoken.

I am not attempting today to pass judgment on the charge of harmful service rivalries. But one thing is sure. Whatever they are, America wants them stopped.

Recently I have had under special study the never-ending problem of efficient organization, complicated as it is by new weapons. Soon my own conclusions will be finalized. I shall promptly take such executive action as is necessary and, in a separate message, I shall present appropriate recommendations to the Congress.[4]

Meanwhile, without anticipating the detailed form that a reorganization should take, I can state its main lines in terms of objectives:

A major purpose of military organization is to achieve real unity in the Defense Establishment in all the principal features of military activity. Of all these, one of the most important to our Nation's security is strategic planning and control. This work must be done under unified direction.

The defense structure must be one which, as a whole, can assume, with top efficiency and without friction, the defense of America. The Defense Establishment must therefore plan for a better integration of its defensive resources, particularly with respect to the newer weapons now building and under

[4] See *Public Law* no. 85-599, 85th Cong., 2d Sess. (Department of Defense Reorganization Act of 1958, August 6, 1958).

development. These obviously require full coordination in their development, production, and use. Good organization can help assure this coordination.

In recognition of the need for single control in some of our most advanced development projects, the Secretary of Defense has already decided to concentrate into one organization all the antimissile and satellite technology undertaken within the Department of Defense.

Another requirement of military organization is a clear subordination of the military services to duly constituted civilian authority. This control must be real; not merely on the surface.

Next there must be assurance that an excessive number of compartments in organization will not create costly and confusing compartments in our scientific and industrial effort.

Finally, to end interservice disputes requires clear organization and decisive central direction, supported by the unstinted cooperation of every individual in the Defense Establishment, civilian and military.

2. Accelerated Defense Effort

The second major action item is the acceleration of the defense effort in particular areas affected by the fast pace of scientific and technological advance.

Some of the points at which improved and increased effort are most essential are these:

We must have sure warning in case of attack. The improvement of warning equipment is becoming increasingly important as we approach the period when long-range missiles will come into use.

We must protect and disperse our striking forces and increase their readiness for instant reaction. This means more base facilities and standby crews.

We must maintain deterrent retaliatory power. This means, among other things, stepped-up long-range missile programs; accelerated programs for other effective missile systems; and, for some years, more advanced aircraft.

We must maintain freedom of the seas. This means nuclear submarines and cruisers; improved antisubmarine weapons; missile ships; and the like.

We must maintain all necessary types of mobile forces to deal with local conflicts, should there be need. This means further improvements in equipment, mobility, tactics, and firepower.

Through increases in pay and incentive, we must maintain in the Armed Forces the skilled manpower modern military forces require.

We must be forward looking in our research and development to anticipate and achieve the unimagined weapons of the future.

With these and other improvements, we intend to assure that our vigilance, power, and technical excellence keep abreast of any realistic threat we face.

3. Mutual Aid

Third: We must continue to strengthen our mutual security efforts.

Most people now realize that our programs of military aid and defense support are an integral part of our own defense effort. If the foundations of the free world structure were progressively allowed to crumble under the pressure of Communist imperialism, the entire house of freedom would be in danger of collapse.

As for the mutual economic assistance program, the benefit to us is threefold. First, the countries receiving this aid become bulwarks against Communist encroachment as their military defenses and economies are strengthened. Nations that are conscious of a steady improvement in their industry, education, health, and standard of living are not apt to fall prey to the blandishments of Communist imperialists.

Second, these countries are helped to reach the point where mutually profitable trade can expand between them and us.

Third, the mutual confidence that comes from working together on constructive projects creates an atmosphere in which real understanding and peace can flourish.

To help bring these multiple benefits, our economic aid effort should be made more effective.

In proposals for future economic aid, I am stressing a greater use of repayable loans, through the development loan fund, through funds generated by sale of surplus farm products, and through the Export-Import Bank.

While some increase in Government funds will be required, it remains our objective to encourage shifting to the use of private capital sources as rapidly as possible.

One great obstacle to the economic aid program in the past has been, not a rational argument against it on the merits, but a catchword: "give-away program."

The real fact is that no investment we make in our own

security and peace can pay us greater dividends than necessary amounts of economic aid to friendly nations.

This is no "giveaway."

Let's stick to facts.

We cannot afford to have one of our most essential security programs shot down with a slogan.

4. Mutual Trade

Four: Both in our national interest, and in the interest of world peace, we must have a 5-year extension of the Trade Agreements Act with broadened authority to negotiate.[5]

World trade supports a significant segment of American industry and agriculture. It provides employment for 4½ million American workers. It helps supply our ever-increasing demand for raw materials. It provides the opportunity for American free enterprise to develop on a world-wide scale. It strengthens our friends and increases their desire to be friends. World trade helps to lay the ground work for peace by making all free nations of the world stronger and more self-reliant.

America is today the world's greatest trading nation. If we use this great asset wisely to meet the expanding demands of the world, we shall not only provide future opportunities for our own business, agriculture, and labor, but in the process strengthen our security posture and other prospects for a prosperous, harmonious world.

As President McKinley said, as long ago as 1901: "Isolation is no longer possible or desirable. . . . The period of exclusiveness is past."

5. Scientific Cooperation with Our Allies

Fifth: It is of the highest importance that the Congress enact the necessary legislation to enable us to exchange appropriate scientific and technical information with friendly countries as part of our effort to achieve effective scientific cooperation.

It is wasteful in the extreme for friendly allies to consume talent and money in solving problems that their friends have already solved—all because of artificial barriers to sharing. We cannot afford to cut ourselves off from the brilliant talents and minds of scientists in friendly countries. The task ahead will be hard enough without handcuffs of our own making.

[5] Document 3, below.

The groundwork for this kind of cooperation has already been laid in discussions among NATO countries. Promptness in following through with legislation will be the best possible evidence of American unity of purpose in cooperating with our friends.

6. Education and Research

Sixth: In the area of education and research, I recommend a balanced program to improve our resources, involving an investment of about a billion dollars over a 4-year period. This involves new activities by the Department of Health, Education, and Welfare designed principally to encourage improved teaching quality and student opportunities in the interests of national security. It also provides a fivefold increase in sums available to the National Science Foundation for its special activities in stimulating and improving science education.

Scrupulous attention has been paid to maintaining local control of educational policy, spurring the maximum amount of local effort, and to avoiding undue stress on the physical sciences at the expense of other branches of learning.

In the field of research, I am asking for substantial increases in basic research funds, including a doubling of the funds available to the National Science Foundation for this purpose.

But Federal action can do only a part of the job. In both education and research, redoubled exertions will be necessary on the part of all Americans if we are to rise to the demands of our times. This means hard work on the part of State and local governments, private industry, schools and colleges, private organizations and foundations, teachers, parents, and—perhaps most important of all—the student himself, with his bag of books and his homework.

With this kind of all-inclusive campaign, I have no doubt that we can create the intellectual capital we need for the years ahead, invest it in the right places—and do all this, not as regimented pawns, but as free men and women.

7. Spending and Saving

Seventh: To provide for this extra effort for security, we must apply stern tests of priority to other expenditures, both military and civilian.

This extra effort involves, most immediately, the need for a supplemental defense appropriation of $1.3 billion for fiscal year 1958.

In the 1959 budget, increased expenditures for missiles, nuclear ships, atomic energy, research and development, science and education, a special contingency fund to deal with possible new technological discoveries, and increases in pay and incentives to obtain and retain competent manpower add up to a total increase over the comparable figures in the 1957 budget of about $4 billion.

I believe that, in spite of these necessary increases, we should strive to finance the 1959 security effort out of expected revenues. While we now believe that expected revenues and expenditures will roughly balance, our real purpose will be to achieve adequate security, but always with the utmost regard for efficiency and careful management.

This purpose will require the cooperation of Congress in making careful analysis of estimates presented, reducing expenditure on less essential military programs and installations, postponing some new civilian programs, transferring some to the States, and curtailing or eliminating others.

Such related matters as the national debt ceiling and tax revenues will be dealt with in later messages.

8. Works of Peace

My last call for action is not primarily addressed to the Congress and people of the United States. Rather, it is a message from the people of the United States to all other peoples, especially those of the Soviet Union.

This is the spirit of what we would like to say:

"In the last analysis, there is only one solution to the grim problems that lie ahead. The world must stop the present plunge toward more and more destructive weapons of war, and turn the corner that will start our steps firmly on the path toward lasting peace.

"Our greatest hope for success lies in a universal fact: the people of the world, as people, have always wanted peace and want peace now.

"The problem, then, is to find a way of translating this universal desire into action.

"This will require more than words of peace. It requires works of peace."

Now, may I try to give you some concrete examples of the kind of works of peace that might make a beginning in the new direction.

For a start our people should learn to know each other better. Recent negotiations in Washington have provided a basis in principle for greater freedom of communication and exchange of people. I urge the Soviet Government to co-operate in turning principle into practice by prompt and tangible actions that will break down the unnatural barriers that have blocked the flow of thought and understanding be-tween our people.

Another kind of work of peace is cooperation on projects of human welfare. For example, we now have it within our power to eradicate from the face of the earth that age-old scourge of mankind: malaria. We are embarking with other nations in an all-out 5-year campaign to blot out this curse forever. We invite the Soviets to join with us in this great work of humanity.

Indeed, we would be willing to pool our efforts with the Soviets in other campaigns against the diseases that are the common enemy of all mortals—such as cancer and heart dis-ease.

If people can get together on such projects, is it not possible that we could then go on to a full-scale cooperative program of science for peace?

We have as a guide and inspiration the success of our atoms-for-peace proposal, which in only a few years, under United Nations auspices, became a reality in the Interna-tional Atomic Energy Agency.

A program of science for peace might provide a means of funneling into one place the results of research from scien-tists everywhere and from there making it available to all parts of the world.

There is almost no limit to the human betterment that could result from such cooperation. Hunger and disease could increasingly be driven from the earth. The age-old dream of a good life for all could, at long last, be translated into reality.

But of all the works of peace, none is more needed now than a real first step toward disarmament.

Last August [November] the United Nations General As-sembly, by an overwhelming vote, approved a disarmament plan that we and our allies sincerely believed to be fair and practical.[6] The Soviets have rejected both the plan, and the negotiating procedure set up by the United Nations. As a result, negotiation on this supremely important issue is now at a standstill.

But the world cannot afford to stand still on disarmament.

[6] *Documents on American Foreign Relations, 1957,* pp. 446-449.

We must never give up the search for a basis of agreement.

Our allies from time to time develop differing ideas on how to proceed. We must concert these convictions among ourselves. Thereafter, any reasonable proposal that holds promise for disarmament and reduction of tension must be heard, discussed, and, if possible, negotiated.

But a disarmament proposal, to hold real promise, must at the minimum have one feature: reliable means to insure compliance by all. It takes actions and demonstrated integrity on both sides to create and sustain confidence. And confidence in a genuine disarmament agreement is vital, not only to the signers of the agreement, but also to the millions of people all over the world who are weary of tensions and armaments.

I say once more, to all peoples, that we will always go the extra mile with anyone on earth if it will bring us nearer a genuine peace.

Conclusion

These, then, are the ways in which we must funnel our energies more efficiently into the task of advancing security and peace.

These actions demand and expect two things of the American people: sacrifice, and a high degree of understanding. For sacrifice to be effective it must be intelligent. Sacrifice must be made for the right purpose and in the right place— even if that place happens to come close to home.

After all, it is no good demanding sacrifice in general terms one day, and the next day, for local reasons, opposing the elimination of some unneeded Federal facility.

It is pointless to condemn Federal spending in general, and the next moment condemn just as strongly an effort to reduce the particular Federal grant that touches one's own interest.

And it makes no sense whatever to spend additional billions on military strength to deter a potential danger, and then, by cutting aid and trade programs, let the world succumb to a present danger in economic guise.

My friends of the Congress: The world is waiting to see how wisely and decisively a free representative government will now act.

I believe that this Congress possesses and will display the wisdom promptly to do its part in translating into law the actions demanded by our Nation's interests. But, to make law effective, our kind of government needs the full voluntary support of millions of Americans for these actions.

I am fully confident that the response of the Congress and of the American people will make this time of test a time of honor. Mankind then will see more clearly than ever that the future belongs, not to the concept of the regimented atheistic state, but to the people—the God-fearing peace-loving people of all the world.

B. The Defense of the Nation and of the Free World.

(2) Budget Message of the President, January 13, 1958.[1]

(Excerpts)

To the Congress of the United States:

The budget for the fiscal year 1959 which I am transmitting with this message reflects the swiftly moving character of the time in which we live. It is clearly a time of growing opportunity as technology and science almost daily open wholly new vistas to all mankind. Yet it is also a time of growing danger. The progress of the Soviets in long-range missiles and other offensive weapons, together with their continuing rejection of a workable disarmament, compels us to increase certain of our defense activities which we have only recently expanded many fold.

We know that we are sturdy today in the many strengths that keep the peace. This budget reflects our determination to remain so in the future.

This budget reflects another determination—that of adhering to those principles of governmental and fiscal soundness that have always guided this administration—economy in expenditures, efficiency in operations, promotion of growth and stability in a free-enterprise economy, a vigorous Federal-State system, concern for human well-being, priority of national security over lesser needs, revenues adequate to cover expenditures and permit debt reduction during periods of high business activity, and revision and reduction of taxes when possible.

To meet the responsibilities imposed on us by world conditions and by the fiscal principles to which we adhere, the budget for 1959 contains recommendations to provide:

(1) An immediate increase for 1958 of $1.3 billion in

[1] House Document 266, 85th Cong., 2d Sess.

spending authority for the Department of Defense, and a further increase of $2.5 billion in 1959 over 1958, to be applied principally to accelerate missile procurement, to strengthen our nuclear retaliatory power, and to spur military research and development programs;

(2) A resulting increase of $2.8 billion in estimated 1959 expenditures over 1957 for missiles, nuclear armed or powered ships, atomic energy, research and development, science and education, plus a further provision of $0.5 billion for defense purposes, if needed; in addition, authority to transfer up to $2 billion between military appropriations, in order to take prompt advantage of new developments;

(3) A decrease of $1.5 billion in 1959 expenditures below 1957 for other military arms and equipment and aircraft of declining importance, in favor of the newer weapons;

(4) Curtailments, revisions, or eliminations of certain present civil programs, and deferments of previously recommended new programs, in order to restrain nonmilitary spending in 1959 and to provide the basis for budgetary savings of several billion dollars annually within a few years;

(5) Continuation of present tax rates to help achieve a balanced budget in 1959.

I believe that this budget adequately provides for our Federal responsibilities in the year ahead.

The estimated budget totals for the current fiscal year and for the fiscal year 1959 are compared with actual results of earlier years in the following table:

BUDGET TOTALS

[Fiscal years. In billions]

	1956 actual	1957 actual	1958 estimate	1959 estimate
Budget receipts	$68.1	$71.0	$72.4	$74.4
Budget expenditures	66.5	69.4	72.8	73.9
Budget surplus (+) or deficit (−)	+1.6	+1.6	−.4	+.5
New obligational authority	63.2	70.2	74.4 [1]	72.5

[1] Includes $6.6 billion of anticipated supplemental requests.

DEFENSE, SCIENCE, AND THE BUDGET

Americans are determined to maintain our ability to deter war and to repel and decisively counter any possible attack.

Today we possess military superiority over any potential aggressor or aggressors. Every American should clearly understand that the vast defense programs undertaken during the past several years have greatly advanced our military preparedness and developed and harnessed impressive new scientific achievements. We have sharply increased the numbers of scientists and engineers assigned to top priority defense programs. We have expanded many fold the expenditures for the development of missiles, both defensive and counteroffensive. We have accelerated development of advanced guidance systems, new fuels, and heat-resistant materials. We have greatly enlarged our network of warning devices and communications.

Our longer-range ballistic missile development, in particular, has long had the highest national priority. The result is striking. Whereas in 1953 we spent only $1 million on these programs, we spent $1 billion in 1957 and will spend more in 1958 and still more in 1959.

Our defenses are strong today, both as a deterrent to war and for use as a crushing response to any attack. Now our concern is for the future. Certain elements of our defense program have reached the point where they can be further accelerated. I will transmit to the Congress, immediately, a supplemental appropriation request of $1.3 billion for the Department of Defense for the fiscal year 1958. Further increases in new obligational authority are requested for the fiscal year 1959. The recommended authority for the military functions of the Department of Defense is $39.1 billion, which is $0.6 billion more than was requested in last year's budget for 1958 and $3.8 billion more than the amount the Congress has thus far enacted for 1958. Spending for military functions of the Department of Defense in 1959 is estimated to total $39.8 billion.

The development of longer-range ballistic missiles, construction of missile sites and detection systems, and other missile programs including guided missile ships will be subtantially augmented. The total expenditures for missile research, development and procurement, for guided missile ships, and for missile-related construction will be $4.3 billion in 1958 and $5.3 billion in 1959, compared with $3 billion spent in 1957, $1.7 billion in 1956, and $1.2 billion in 1955. Commencing in 1958, we will procure a number of new missiles which have been recently developed and have now become operational.

As an indispensable part of our efforts to maintain an adequate defense, the budget recommendations for 1959 call for continued contributions to the efforts of free world nations to promote the collective defense and economic growth. The Soviet threat to freedom is far more than military power alone. Poverty and ignorance, and the despair, fear, and unrest that flow from them, have always been enemies to liberty. The Communists well know this and unceasingly exploit these factors to extend their influence and control. This Soviet economic assault on freedom is rapidly growing. Conquest by this route is no less menacing to us and other free nations than conquest by military force. We must, accordingly, vigorously advance our programs to assist other peoples in their efforts to remove poverty and ignorance. As we succeed in these military and economic efforts, our own freedom and security are strengthened, and the prospects for peace are improved.

Scientific and research efforts throughout the Nation must be expanded. This is a task not only for the Government but also for private industry, foundations, and educational institutions. The Government, on its part, will increase its efforts in this area. Supplemental appropriations for 1958 will be requested for the National Advisory Committee for Aeronautics and the National Science Foundation, as well as the Department of Defense. For 1959, new programs to promote education in science are being recommended and basic research activities are being generally expanded.

Changes in Emphasis

Total Government expenditures (1) for all procurement to equip our forces and those of our allies with weapons, ships, planes, and missiles, (2) for atomic energy, and (3) for all scientific research and education will be approximately $21.1 billion in 1958 and $21.6 billion in 1959, compared with $20.5 billion in 1957.

Within these totals for procurement and science, we have gradually but substantially changed our emphasis. This administration's continuing attention in recent years to new concepts of defense is shown by the fact that more than 75% of the total funds for procurement in the 1959 budget and 1958 supplemental requests is programed for new types of equipment which had not been developed in the fiscal year 1955 or were not being bought in production quantities in that year—the first full year following the Korean conflict.

In 1953, missiles alone took less than 2 cents of each dollar spent for major procurement; in 1957, missiles took about 15 cents of every procurement dollar; and in 1959 will take about 24 cents.

The greatly increased firepower of modern weapons and the continuing increase in efficiency permit a further reduction in the numbers of military personnel. Procurement of older types of weapons and equipment is also being reduced. Other defense expenditures will be reduced by closing installations that are outmoded or are of limited use, and by tightening maintenance standards, procurement practices, and supply management.

* * *

ANALYSIS OF MAJOR PROGRAMS
AND BUDGETARY ISSUES

For purposes of summarization and discussion, budget expenditures are grouped into the categories of protection, civil benefits, interest and general government.

Expenditures for major national security and for international affairs and finance, which together make up the category of "protection," will require 64% of estimated total 1959 budget expenditures. The $47.1 billion estimated to be spent on protection in the fiscal year 1959 is more than in any year since 1955.

An estimated 22% of budget expenditures in 1959 will be for civil benefit programs. These programs are grouped under the headings: Labor and welfare; commerce and housing; veterans services and benefits; agriculture and agricultural resources; and natural resources. The estimated $16.4 billion to be spent on civil benefits in 1959 is $0.6 billion less than the comparable amount for the current year.

The estimate of 1959 expenditures for interest is $7.9 billion, the same as in 1958. Expenditures for general government will require an estimated $1.4 billion in 1959, also about the same as in 1958.

The budget also includes estimated expenditures of $1.1 billion for the fiscal year 1959 as an allowance for proposed legislation and contingencies not included in the categories above. Within this allowance $500 million is estimated specifically for defense contingencies, $339 million is estimated for proposed pay adjustments for postal and other civilian employees not in the Department of Defense, and $300 million is for other contingencies. The cost of proposed pay adjustments for military and civilian personnel of the Department of Defense is included in the estimates for that Department.

PROTECTION

Our security is an integral part of the security of the entire free world. In addition to strengthening our own defenses, we must improve the effectiveness of our partnership with our allies. This requires a greater pooling of scientific resources, a freer exchange of technological information, and closer military cooperation. Preliminary steps to accomplish these objectives were taken at the recent Paris meeting of the North Atlantic Treaty Organization.[2]

This budget reflects coordinated plans for strengthening our own and allied defenses. The composition of free world forces, and the equipment with which they are provided, must be designed for the needs of an era of increasingly destructive weapons with far-reaching range. Our Government's research and development will be generally expanded with particular emphasis on developing and improving missiles both for defensive and for counteroffensive purposes.

An effective system of military security requires closer economic cooperation through trade, investment, loans, and technical assistance with nations throughout the free world so that they can develop their resources and raise their living standards. To the degree that this economic cooperation strengthens the internal stability and ability of those nations to preserve their independence, the cause of a just and lasting peace will be advanced.

Major National Security

New obligational authority recommended for major national security programs for 1959 is $44.3 billion, compared to $41.0 billion estimated for 1958 and $41.3 billion enacted for 1957.

Expenditures for these programs are estimated to be $45.8 billion in the fiscal year 1959, $1 billion more than in 1958 and $1.4 billion more than in 1957. Increases are anticipated for the military functions of the Department of Defense and for atomic energy development. Expenditures for military assistance and defense support will be about the same as in the current year, but appropriations will increase to finance the

[2] *Documents on American Foreign Relations, 1957,* pp. 91-126.

lead-time for newer-type weapons. Expenditures for the stock-piling of strategic and critical materials and for the defense production expansion program will decline.

DEPARTMENT OF DEFENSE, MILITARY FUNCTIONS

To accelerate the adaptation of our defenses to changing conditions, a request for supplemental appropriations of $1.3 billion for the Department of Defense in the fiscal year 1958 is being transmitted to the Congress. The result will be to increase total new obligational authority for 1958 for the military functions of the Department of Defense to $36.6 billion. A further increase of $2.5 billion is recommended for the fiscal year 1959, bringing the total for that year to $39.1 billion.

It is essential that we be able promptly to modify and accelerate programs when and as important discoveries or technological developments in weapons indicate such action to be desirable. To accomplish this end, the budget includes a contingency reserve of $500 million for defense purposes only. It also proposes that the Congress authorize the President to transfer up to $2 billion between appropriations available for military functions of the Department of Defense. This transfer authority is important and I will not hesitate to use it.

I have already discussed the urgent problem of reorganization of the Department of Defense in the State of the Union message. In the interest of the taxpayer, improved operating and fiscal controls must accompany larger appropriations.

Expenditures in 1958 are now estimated to be $38.9 billion compared with the original 1958 budget estimate of $38 billion. Estimated expenditures for 1959 are $39.8 billion, an increase of $0.9 billion over the current estimate for 1958, $1.3 billion higher than in 1957, and $4 billion more than in 1956.

These increased appropriations and expenditures are neces-sary for a speedup in the adjustment of military strategy, forces, techniques, and organization to keep pace with the rapid strides in science and technology. Since the end of the Korean conflict, new weapons systems of vastly increased combat effectiveness have been provided for our military forces, while numbers of military units and personnel have been gradually reduced. We can expect new developments at an ever-increasing pace.

The rapidly changing character of the military program

is strikingly evident when the weapons and equipment we propose to buy in 1959 are compared with those bought as recently as 1955—the first full fiscal year after the Korean conflict.

There is hardly a production model aircraft on the Air Force's proposed list for procurement with 1959 funds that was included in its 1955 program. All the fighters and bombers proposed for procurement with 1959 appropriations will be capable of supersonic speeds and of using guided missiles and nuclear weapons. Of the $1.5 billion of aircraft, engines, and aeronautical equipment proposed to be bought by the Navy in 1959, about 80% will be for models which had not reached the point of being bought in production quantities in 1955.

Even in the new field of missile technology, there will be a very marked shift of emphasis from the earlier, initial weapons systems to the much more advanced systems of the future. The longer range ballistic missiles—Atlas, Titan, Thor, Jupiter, Polaris—only one of which was beyond the technical study stage $2\frac{1}{2}$ years ago, will account for nearly half of the missile program for 1959. For the total missile program, about 90% of the dollars planned for procurement in 1959 are for weapons which were not in production in operational quantities in 1955.

Most of the ships in the proposed 1959 construction program are entirely new types not to be found in the 1955 shipbuilding list. These include guided missile destroyers and the first nuclear-powered frigate. The first three ballistic missile submarines for the fleet are included in the 1958 supplemental request.

Fully half of the proposed 1959 program of military construction is for facilities for the Strategic Air Command and for weapons systems and equipment which will have been brought into operational use since 1955.

Research and the operation of facilities or research, development, and testing of missiles will take a much greater proportion of the research and development budget in 1959 than in 1955. In the 4 fiscal years 1956-59, roughly $20 billion of research and development, procurement, military personnel, and construction funds will have been programed for the research, development, test, and evaluation of new weapons systems to bring them to operational status.

Programs requiring greater emphasis.—The budget provides funds for a still greater expansion of the swiftly progressing intercontinental and intermediate range ballistic missile programs. The Jupiter and Thor intermediate range ballistic missiles are being placed in production. Work on the Atlas intercontinental ballistic missile will be accelerated.

Funds are also provided to speed up the operational availability of the Polaris intermediate range ballistic missile and the first three submarines designed to employ this weapon.

Expansion and further improvement of the continental defense early warning network will be undertaken and construction of a new ballistic missile detection system started, including the necessary facilities for communication with the North American Defense Command and the Strategic Air Command.

This budget includes funds for accelerating the dispersal of Strategic Air Command aircraft to additional bases and for the construction of "alert" facilities. The readiness of these retaliatory forces must be measured in minutes. Not only must planes be kept constantly in the air, but also additional combat air crews must be able to take off almost instantly upon receipt of warning of an impending enemy attack. Takeoff time will be appreciably shortened by constructing additional runways, fueling stations, and quarters for the crews at the runway. Within the total appropriations for the fiscal years 1958 and 1959, about $0.5 billion is provided for the dispersal and increased readiness of the Strategic Air Command.

Funds are provided for an expanded research and development effort on military satellites and other outer space vehicles, and on antimissile missile systems, to be carried out directly under the Secretary of Defense. An increase is also included for basic and applied research in other areas.

Antisubmarine warfare capabilities will be increased to counter potential enemy submarine threats.

While greater attention is given in this budget to the foregoing areas, conventional warfare capabilities of all the military services are also being improved. For example, funds are provided to initiate production of new models of small arms and ammunition, standardized for use by all members of the North Atlantic Treaty Organization.

*   *   *

DEVELOPMENT AND CONTROL OF ATOMIC ENERGY

Expenditures by the Atomic Energy Commission in the fiscal year 1959 will increase to $2,550 million. $250 million more than estimated for 1958, which in turn was $310 million over 1957. These increases reflect our determination both to increase the tempo of progress in achieving a greater nuclear military capability and to press ahead in our successful development of the peaceful applications of atomic energy.

From year to year we have hoped that success would finally crown our efforts to reach an international agreement which would permit, if not general disarmament, at least some reduction in the production of nuclear armaments. Again we find ourselves in a situation that leaves us no choice but to test and produce further quantities of such armaments for the defense of the free world. The substantial increase in the availability of uranium concentrates and the expanded capacity of the Atomic Energy Commission's production plants will result in greater production and larger operating expenditures in 1959.

During the last several years, the Atomic Energy Commission's research and development in both peaceful and military applications of atomic energy have grown rapidly to the highest levels ever attained. Continuing emphasis will be given to basic research, and construction will continue on four additional high-energy particle accelerators in the multi-billion electron-volt range.

Applied research and development activities will be increased in 1959 and concentrated on those aspects which appear most likely to result in reaching technical goals. In particular, there will be continuing emphasis on naval and other military nuclear propulsion reactors, and on the more promising approaches to development of reactors to produce safe and economic electrical energy for civilian use.

STOCKPILING AND DEFENSE PRODUCTION EXPANSION

Expenditures for stockpiling and expansion of defense production are estimated to be $565 million in 1958 and $422 million in 1959. The stockpile objectives on all but a few scarce materials will be substantially completed under contracts now in force. In October 1957, an advisory committee was established to work with the Office of Defense Mobilization on a study of stockpiling policies and programs in the light of current concepts of war and defense.

The Defense Production Act of 1950 has provided much of the basic authority required to bring about needed expansion of production capacity, to provide controls over the use of scarce materials, and to initiate other measures essential to enhance our military strength. It should be extended another 2 years beyond its present expiration date of June 30, 1958. I do not now anticipate any specific new programs which will require financial assistance under this legislation, but accelerated research and development in certain military programs may require further expansion of production potentials for key materials. The authority to set priorities and allocate materials, currently being used for critical materials for direct military and atomic energy procurement, will continue to be needed.

MUTUAL SECURITY PROGRAM

Soviet ambition poses a threat to the free countries that takes several forms: open armed attack, internal subversion, and economic domination. Mutual security helps to meet all forms of this threat. For the fiscal year 1959, I am recommending new obligational authority of $3,940 million for the mutual security program. Expenditures are estimated to be $3,868 million.

Two portions of the mutual security program—military assistance and defense support—are primarily related to our military defense effort and, therefore, are discussed in this section of the message. The other portions of the mutual security program, while they contribute to security and defensive strength, are primarily designed to promote the economic development and political stability of less developed countries. They are discussed in the international affairs and finance section of this message. The two parts of the mutual security program are combined in the following table: [see p. 26.]

Mutual security, military assistance.—The nature of military assistance varies by country and area, taking into account military need, technological abilities, and division of defense responsibility among the United States and other countries. Countries which have received military assistance maintain for the common defense of the free world the equivalent of 200 army divisions, and some 23,000 aircraft and 2,300 naval vessels. From 1950 through 1957 our assistance has augmented by about 17% the total defense expenditures of these countries.

MUTUAL SECURITY PROGRAM

[Fiscal years. In millions]

Function and program	Budget expenditures			Recommended new obligational authority for 1959
	1957 actual	1958 estimate	1959 estimate	
Major national security:				
Military assistance:				
Present program	$2,352	$2,200	$1,846	....
Proposed legislation	....	....	354	$1,800
Defense support:				
Present program	1,143	945	575	....
Proposed legislation	....	....	310	865
Subtotal	3,495	3,145	3,085	2,665
International affairs and finance:				
Development loan fund	....	20	174	625
Technical cooperation:				
Present program	114	136	103	....
Proposed legislation	....	....	47	164
Special and other assistance:				
Present program	341	448	266	....
Proposed legislation	....	....	193	486
Subtotal	455	604	783	1,275
Total, mutual security	3,950	3,749	3,868	3,940 [1]

[1] Compares with new obligational authority of $3,807 million for 1957 and $2,764 million for 1958.

In Europe, this assistance is programed according to the defensive strategy for the whole North Atlantic Treaty Organization.

Military assistance for certain other countries, particularly in the Middle East and Asia, will continue to give special emphasis to the threat of internal subversion while also contributing to the deterrence of foreign attack.

In addition to missiles and other advanced weapons, the military assistance program provides for necessary conventional equipment, supplies, construction, and training for ground, sea, and air defense of friendly countries.

Continuing efforts are being made to maintain the forces needed for international defense purposes at the lowest possible cost. The strength of forces in assisted countries has been and will continue to be reviewed to insure that our support is related to current military requirements and technology. We are financing military equipment wherever possible on a basis of sales for cash and credit rather than by grants.

Recommended new obligational authority for military assistance in the fiscal year 1959 is $1,800 million. To fulfill probable needs growing out of agreements at recent NATO meetings, an additional amount of up to $200 million for procurement of more missiles and other new equipment is covered by the allowance for proposed legislation and contingencies for the fiscal year 1958. Expenditures for military assistance in 1959, which will be made primarily from obligational authority enacted in previous years, are estimated to be $2,200 million, the same amount estimated for 1958.

I firmly believe that the current United States outlay for protection would have to be substantially larger were it not for the military assistance program which enables other countries to contribute more to collective defense. Without our military assistance program the same degree of protection might not be obtainable at any cost.

Mutual security, defense support.—Our military assistance is extended to many countries that are maintaining collective defense forces beyond their economic means. Therefore, we supply economic assistance under the appropriations for defense support so that these countries can provide for their defense forces and at the same time maintain economic and political stability.

New obligational authority of $865 million is requested for defense support. Expenditures in 1959 are estimated at $885 million or $60 million below the estimate for 1958.

In determining these amounts, account has been taken of the most effective use of local currencies obtained as counterpart for assistance dollars and from sales of surplus United States farm products. The local currencies, which are in addition to dollar grants, are used to help channel the countries' own economic resources to the most desirable objectives. However, these currencies cannot replace the dollars needed for materials and equipment that must be imported, mainly from the United States.

International Affairs and Finance

The major objective of our international economic policies and programs is to help build the free world's economic strength in the interest of mutual well-being and the maintenance of peace. Expanded production, improved efficiency, and greater economic progress for ourselves and other peoples of the free world will depend to a considerable extent on an increase in the flow of international trade and investment. To aid in this worldwide objective and at the same time to expand our markets abroad and thus create new jobs at home, I am recommending the extension with broadened authority of the Reciprocal Trade Agreements program. I am also recommending an expansion of the lending authority of the Export-Import Bank, an increase in new obligational authority for developmental and technical assistance under the mutual security program, and the authorization of funds to assist in the completion of the Inter-American Highway.

International affairs and finance are estimated to require $1.3 billion of expenditures in the fiscal year 1959, $156 million less than in 1958. The decline reflects primarily the fact that in 1958 the Export-Import Bank has made a substantial disbursement under a previously authorized loan to the United Kingdom.

Reciprocal trade.—In order to pay for imports of goods and services from the United States other countries must be able to export to us. Progress for them and for us will receive its greatest impetus by development of the most favorable fields of production coupled with a gradual but steady reduction of unjustifiable trade barriers. We welcome the proposed European common market and free trade area as steps toward these broad goals.

We live in a world of economic, no less than political, interdependence. As the greatest producer, consumer, and exporter in the world, the United States must be a dependable market for foreign goods if mutually beneficial trade is to grow and prosper. The Reciprocal Trade Agreements Act should be extended for 5 years beyond its expiration date of June 30, 1958, with certain new authority for the President to negotiate gradual and selective tariff reductions. Legislation should also be enacted to authorize United States membership in the Organization for Trade Cooperation to improve the administrative efficiency of our trade agreements with other countries. To provide coordinated Cabinet level direction of this program at home, I have recently established the Trade Policy Committee under the chairmanship of the Secretary of Commerce.[3]

In addition, I recommend that the Congress delete a

[3] *Department of State Bulletin*, v. 37 (December 16, 1957), p. 957.

rider which in past years has been attached to the Defense Appropriation Act and which virtually prohibits normal competitive bidding by other countries on many defense contracts. The rider is clearly inconsistent with policies designed to expand international trade and makes our heavy defense costs even more burdensome.

Export-Import Bank.—The Export-Import Bank has had a steadily increasing role in promoting United States exports and imports and in financing economic development projects abroad through loans to United States and foreign firms and to foreign countries. Since the Bank requires repayment in dollars, its loans for economic development are made for projects that will earn or save dollars for the borrowing country, or for projects in countries with adequate prospects of earning dollars from other sources. It is now estimated that the lending authority provided the Bank in 1955 will be entirely committed sometime during 1959. To assure continuity in the Bank's operation and to provide for possible emergencies, I am requesting $2 billion in new obligational authority to expand the Bank's lending capacity. This new authorization should be made available before the end of the current fiscal year.

Nonmilitary mutual security.—While strengthened trade legislation and additional lending authority for the Export-Import Bank will help substantially in promoting world commerce and economic development, these actions are insufficient in themselves to accomplish our international objectives.

Few national desires are stronger today than the wish of the peoples of less developed countries to improve their living standards. It is our national policy to encourage and assist this aspiration. As a country blessed with great natural resources, modern industry, and high productivity, we recognize the compelling humanitarian reasons for helping less fortunate people abroad as we help them at home.

The progress of some less developed countries will be dangerously slow without outside help, despite their best efforts. The people of these countries are conscious of the technological advances made and the levels of living enjoyed beyond their borders, and are understandably impatient for similar achievements. If Western help is unavailable or inadequate, these countries may become dependent upon the Communist bloc. We are concerned that they strengthen their independence and find prospects for improved living standards within a free society. It is my earnest hope that other free governments will also enlarge their efforts in advancing the development, trade, and well-being of less developed countries.

In addition, without economic progress, military security may prove illusory. People who see little improvement in their economic conditions may question the value of the freedom that our mutual defense efforts are intended to preserve. The events of the cold war reemphasize the importance of our helping to insure that peoples of less developed countries have faith in their future.

For these various reasons, it is critically necessary to carry forward our development loans, technical assistance, and other special types of assistance under the mutual security program.

Mutual security, development loan fund.—In many cases, urgent needs for economic development in less developed countries cannot be financed by the Export-Import Bank or by other sources such as the International Bank for Reconstruction and Development or private institutions. To meet such needs for financing economically and technically sound projects, the development loan fund was authorized in the Mutual Security Act of 1957.[4] Loans from this fund may be made on less stringent terms than Export-Import Bank or other such loans, with repayments in local currencies as well as dollars.

Projects are now being considered and negotiations are being started with a number of countries which will result in the commitment of an appreciable volume of loans by the end of the fiscal year 1958. To make possible the continuation and expansion of such development loans, I am requesting provision of $625 million in new obligational authority for 1959, as authorized by the Congress in basic legislation last year.

Mutual security, technical cooperation.—Because of technical assistance extended under the mutual security program, millions of people today are better off than before and productivity has been significantly increased. For example, disease has been lessened in many countries as people have been taught water purification techniques. Illiteracy has been greatly reduced. Farmers in many countries have learned how to diversify crops and improve livestock strains.

[4] *Documents on American Foreign Relations, 1957,* p. 59.

This budget requests $164 million of new obligational authority in 1959 to carry forward the United States program of technical assistance and also to provide for our joining with other nations to increase the financial resources of the United Nations program of technical assistance. This increase will help to broaden the scope of multilateral cooperation through a new program for regional surveys of resources and for regional training institutes approved last December by the United Nations General Assembly. I am convinced of the need for our own technical assistance program and I am equally convinced of the need for multilateral technical assistance programs, in which our contribution is multiplied by the funds and experts of many nations.

Mutual security, special and other assistance.—The budget for the mutual security program provides for certain additional special activities, such as support vital to the stability of a number of friendly countries not covered by other categories of aid, our contributions to the United Nations International Children's Fund, and our refugee programs.

It is obviously impossible to predict today all of the problems which the free world will face during 1959. In order to help meet the emergencies that experience shows inevitably arise, I believe it necessary that a special contingency fund again be provided in the mutual security appropriation. For this purpose, $200 million is recommended for 1959.

Diplomacy, informational and cultural programs, and exchange of persons.—Greater understanding among nations, on a people-to-people as well as a government-to-government basis, is a necessary part of our efforts to remove the misunderstandings that hinder disarmament, the building of a safeguarded peace, and the strengthening of freedom. It is especially important that Americans and peoples who have recently gained, or are approaching, independence come to appreciate each other's problems and aspirations. It is similarly important that Americans and Eastern Europeans renew the contacts that once were an important strand in friendly international relations.

The budget recommends $183 million in new obligational authority in 1959 for the conduct of foreign affairs, primarily for the operation of the Department of State. This amount includes provision for additional foreign service posts in Africa and for the strengthening of consular, economic, and political work in the Middle East and the Far East. New obligational authority requested for the United States Information Agency, and for exchange of persons, cultural presentations, and international trade fairs amounts to $139 million; within this total, there is provision for more exchanges of leaders, scientists, and students with Eastern Europe and other areas.

I wish here to call attention specifically to the need for a supplemental appropriation for the Brussels Fair. Congressional action on this important activity last year left United States participation badly hampered in comparison with programs of other nations, especially the Soviet Union. I consider this item of particular importance to our country and urge the Congress to expedite its approval.

*   *   *

C. Foreign Economic Policy.

1. *The Reciprocal Trade Agreements Program.*

(3) *Message of the President Recommending Renewal of the Trade Agreements Act, January 30, 1958.*[1]

To the Congress of the United States:

I request the Congress to enact legislation that will permit a continuation of the reciprocal trade agreements program on an effective basis for a minimum of 5 additional years past June 30, 1958.

The enactment of this legislation—unweakened by amendments of a kind that would impair its effectiveness—is essential to our national economic interest, to our security, and to our foreign relations.

The high importance of trade to our economy is evident. The income of our people arising from export trade alone approximates or exceeds that arising from many major segments of our economy. The development of a healthy export trade has created a significant number of jobs for our working men and women. Imports furnish our industries with essential raw materials and the benefits of technological advances, add to the variety of goods available to our consumers, and also create jobs for our workers. Moreover, important geographical areas within our country, as well as many of our key industries in both manufacturing and agriculture, look to

[1] House Document 320, 85th Cong., 2d Sess.

expanding world trade as an essential ingredient of their future prosperity.

Reciprocal trade agreements negotiated since the advent of the Trade Agreements Act have helped bring a more vigorous, dynamic growth to our American economy. Our own economic self-interest, therefore, demands a continuation of the trade agreements program. Under this program sound two-way trade can be further developed to assure to our industries widening opportunities for participation in world markets, and to provide foreign nations the opportunity to earn the dollars to pay for the goods we sell. We can either receive the benefits of the reciprocal lowering of trade barriers or suffer the inevitable alternative of increasingly high barriers against our own commerce which would weaken our economy and jeopardize American jobs.

Important as growing international trade is to our country, it is equally important to our Allies and trading partners. For them it is indeed vital to the health and growing strength of their economies, on which their political stability and military power heavily depend. The assured future of the reciprocal trade program is necessary for our national security and for our entire foreign policy.

In particular, it is essential to enable us to meet the latest form of economic challenge to the free world presented by communism. In the state of the Union message, I spoke of the economic offensive that has been mounted against free nations by the Communist imperialists. The Soviet Union is engaged in an intensive effort, through combined programs of trade and aid, to divide the countries of the free world, to detach them one by one and swing them into the orbit of Communist influence.

We must recognize the growing capacity of the Soviet Union in the economic field. Their advances in technology and industrialization, together with their continuing repression of domestic consumption, enable them to supply, better than ever before, the machinery, manufactures, and other goods which are essential to the economic life of many countries.

The Soviet capacity to export is matched by its capacity and willingness to import. It is increasingly offering to import the surpluses of non-Communist states. In this way it seeks to tie such states to the Soviet orbit, and to exploit the trade difficulties of the free world.

This challenge in the economic field cannot be ignored without the gravest risk to our way of life. This fact alone makes it imperative that previous positions be reexamined, and that particular interests be reappraised in the light of overriding national needs.

The question is whether the system of free competitive enterprise for which we stand will meet successfully in the international economic arena the challenge hurled by the Soviet leaders.

We will fail in this endeavor if the free countries do not continue their reduction of the barriers which they themselves impose on their trade with each other. We will fail if closed markets and foreign exchange shortages force free world countries into economic dependence upon the Communist bloc. We will fail if the United States should now abandon the task of building a world trading system from which all free world countries can gain strength and prosperity in a free economic society.

If our Government is to play its decisive part in protecting and strengthening the free economic system against the Communist threat, the trade agreements legislation which the administration is requesting of Congress must be enacted.

The Secretary of Commerce, who is Chairman of the Trade Policy Committee which I recently established to advise and assist me in the administration of the trade agreements program, including review of recommendations of the United States Tariff Commission, will transmit to the Congress the administration's legislative proposals. These proposals, including the various safeguards for domestic industry, will generally follow the pattern set by the Trade Agreements Extension Act of 1955.

The amount of tariff reduction authority to be requested is essential to the continuing success of the program, as is the 5-year period of the proposed extension to the continuity in our trade relations.

There is a further and very specific factor necessitating a minimum extension of 5 years. Six European nations, which purchased nearly $3 billion of our exports last year, have established a European Economic Community which will become a common market with a population nearly as large as our own. These countries will ultimately have a common tariff applying to imports from the rest of the world. It is anticipated that important steps toward this common tariff will become effective during 1962—up to 4½ years from the renewal date of our trade agreements legislation. This period must be devoted to negotiations with the new Economic Community and these negotiations must be preceded by painstaking preparations. Both preparation and negotiation must be based on a clear grant of adequate authority. This timetable requires an extension of the legislation for a minimum of 5 years. Such an extension, with the tariff reduction authority to be requested, is necessary to carry the trade agreements program through the early formative years of the European Economic Community and strengthen our ability to further vital American interests there and elsewhere in the world.

The 5-year extension of the Trade Agreements Act with broadened authority to negotiate is essential to America's vital national interests.[2] It will strengthen our economy which is the foundation of our national security. It will enhance the economic health and strength of the free world. It will provide a powerful force in waging total peace.

Dwight D. Eisenhower

2. The Mutual Security Program.

(4) *Message of the President on the Mutual Security Program for Fiscal Year 1959, February 19, 1958.*[3]

To the Congress of the United States:

The state of the Union message this year set forth an eight-point program required to focus the resources of America upon the urgent tasks of security and peace. As an essential element of that effort, I recommended the vigorous continuation of our mutual security program. I now ask enactment of the legislation that will accomplish this.

It is my duty to make clear my profound conviction that the vigorous advancement of this program is our only logical course. An alternative there is, to discontinue or sharply reduce the program, but the consequences would be—

A severe dislocation and basic impairment of free world power;

A certain crumbling, under Sino-Soviet pressures, of our strategic overseas positions and a forcing of these positions progressively back toward our own shores;

A massive increase in our own defense budget, in amounts far exceeding mutual security appropriations, necessitating increases in taxes;

[2] The Trade Agreements Extension Act of 1958 (*Public Law* no. 85-686, 85th Cong., 2d Sess., August 20, 1958) extends the President's authority to enter into foreign trade agreements until June 30, 1962.
[3] House Document 338, 85th Cong., 2d Sess.

A heavy increase in inductions of American youth into our own Armed Forces; and

Ultimately a beleaguered America, her freedoms limited by mounting defense costs, and almost alone in a world dominated by international communism.

Those who would consider this alternative to support of our mutual security program must measure well these consequences.

Since the mutual security program was initiated 10 years ago, its essentials have remained the same: Its means are military, economic, and technical cooperation with other nations. Its object is to preserve peace and freedom for our Nation and for other nations of the free world. Its achievement is what its name declares—the mutual security of our own and other free nations.

It is easy to forget our fears of only a decade ago that France, Italy, and other nations of Europe devastated by war would be engulfed by the Red tide. Due in major measure to this great program, these and other nations of Asia and the Middle East are free today and stand with us against Communist domination.

It is also our mutual security program which has afforded the critical margin of assistance required by still other nations, great and small, in order to make the economic progress essential to their survival.

The accomplishments under this program in building the military strength of the free world have been dramatic. Since 1950, when the military assistance program was inaugurated, the ground forces of countries associated with us for collective defense have grown to include nearly 5 million well trained and equipped fighting men situated at strategic locations around the world. Naval forces have increased by over 100 percent, and the air forces of these nations now include 32,000 aircraft, of which over 14,000 are jets. In the buildup of their forces, the nations associated with us have spent over five times as much as we have expended on military assistance.

The value of the mutual security program to our national safety and to freedom throughout the world is many times greater than its cost.

I. MUTUAL SECURITY IN THE NUCLEAR ERA

The United States will keep its own military forces strong and ready. But we must not allow concentration on our military might to divert us from other essential objectives of our national security program.

The major objectives of our security effort are to provide opportunities for the advancement of peace and freedom: First, by deterring general nuclear war; second, by preventing local Sino-Soviet aggression; and, third, by forestalling Communist subversion or massive economic penetration of other nations.

In achieving these major objectives of our national security effort, the mutual security program is indispensable.

Deterring Total War

All mankind has a revulsion against nuclear war. We prayerfully hope that this sentiment will ultimately persuade the Soviet Government to participate in a plan of genuine disarmament. Until then, however, we must maintain the deterrent power of our Armed Forces. This power is immeasurably increased by the cooperation of nations friendly to us—in Europe, Africa, the Near East, and Far East, and in our own hemisphere—and by the forward bases there maintained.

The mutual security program plays a direct part in the availability of bases from which strategic striking forces can be staged and fueled. Similarly, it makes possible the logistic, warning, and defense facilities essential to the operation of these bases.

The importance of these facts increases as intermediate range ballistic missiles provide this supplement to our striking power.

Preventing Local Aggression

Our defensive power must be directed as well toward deterring local aggressions which could lead to global war or to piecemeal absorption of the free world by Communist imperialism. It is imperative that the free world maintain strong conventional forces capable of dealing effectively with such aggressions whenever and wherever they may occur. America alone cannot maintain such forces on the scale required. They must be developed by the threatened nations themselves.

Those nations are anxious to provide for their own defense. They can supply the men and much of the needed facilities and support. But many of them lack the modern industries necessary to provide military equipment or they lack the economic strength needed to bear the full burden of the agreed military effort. To maintain this effort they must have help.

We provide this help—arms through military assistance and economic aid through defense support.

In short, our own military strength, great as it is, is vastly increased by the power of our allies, by the bases we have jointly established and by the whole fabric of our collective security system.

Prevention of Communist Subversion and Penetration

It is not enough, however, that our military assistance and defense support help to prevent Communist expansion by force of arms. We are equally concerned by the danger of Communist absorption of whole nations by subversion or economic penetration.

Military strength alone is not an adequate barrier to this insidious process.

To defeat the spread of communism by these means, economic progress is essential.

Our technical assistance and economic development programs serve this larger purpose. They are addressed for the most part to the less developed countries of the free world, because it is in these countries that freedom now hangs most precariously in the balance.

More than 1 billion people live in these newly developing nations. These people want economic as well as political independence; they want education and the enriched life it will bring; they want a voice in world affairs; and they want urgently to have the material advances made possible by modern technology.

The governments of these newly developing countries are now under pressure from within to fulfill the hopes and needs of their people for education and economic betterment. They are exposed to Communist enticements and threats. Against a background of massive social and economic problems, solid steps toward solving these problems have been taken.

But even with the most determined local effort, in many countries the prospects for economic growth, unassisted, are not promising. If free institutions are to survive in these countries they must have external help. They must have technical assistance to train their manpower, to explore their resources and use them productively. They must have supplementary capital from abroad for investment in agriculture, power, transportation, and industry. They must have help to tide them over economic difficulties that threaten their stability and cohesion. They must have increasing trade with availability of necessary imports and growing markets over a long term.

It is the purpose of our economic and technical assistance programs to enlarge the community of nations that can meet the aspirations of their people for economic and social improvement. We can help to demonstrate that growth can be achieved more readily in conditions of freedom, that it is not necessary to sacrifice liberty for bread.

It is also in our interest to establish a sound basis for effective international cooperation. Poverty is a divisive force in the world. Working together with the people of less developed countries in a common attack on poverty, we talk a common language that all men understand and we help to establish the basis for better relations and more enduring cooperation among free nations.

We also have an economic interest in promoting the development of the free world. In the years to come, the increased economic strength of less developed countries should prove mutually beneficial in providing growing markets for exports, added opportunities for investment, and more of the basic materials we need from abroad.

The leaders of the Communist bloc are acutely aware that the economic needs of many independent nations offer communism a valuable opportunity to influence the political direction in which those nations will move. For the past 3 years, the Soviet Union, Communist China, and the satellite nations have been offering increasing amounts of economic and technical aid to countries of the free world, often under conditions that, on the surface, are appealing. They have already concluded agreements for aid involving substantial sums, and additional offers are outstanding. In several free nations, the aid pledged by the Communist bloc equals or exceeds that made available to them from free world nations in the same period.

If the purpose of Soviet aid to any country were simply to help it overcome economic difficulties without infringing its freedom, such aid could be welcomed as forwarding the free world purpose of economic growth. But there is nothing in the history of international communism to indicate this can be the case. Until such evidence is forthcoming, we and other free nations must assume that Soviet bloc aid is a new, subtle, and longrange instrument directed toward the same old purpose of drawing its recipient away from the community of free nations and ultimately into the Communist orbit.

The newly independent countries will not knowingly choose subordination. They are proud of their sovereignty. They know recent history which shows plainly that whenever the opportunity has arisen, the Soviet Union has swallowed up its neighbors and is willing to use tanks to crush attempts to gain freedom from Soviet domination.

Yet if newly developing countries are forced to choose between abandoning development programs demanded by their people or achieving them through Communist bloc assistance, the opportunity for Communist economic penetration will be greatly enhanced.

The United States provided economic and technical help for development for many years before the Soviet economic offensive began. It is now all the more important than we and other developed nations of the free world should continue and increase effective programs of aid which may be relied on by the less developed countries to give them timely and substantial help.

So long as the uncommitted countries know that the rest of the free world shares their aspirations and is prepared to help them achieve economic and social progress in independence and freedom, we can be confident that the cause of the free world will prevail.

II. THE PROGRAM FOR FISCAL YEAR 1959

The mutual security program which I recommend for fiscal year 1959 contains essentially the same component parts as authorized by the Congress last session. To carry out this program I request $3,942,100,000.[4]

Military Assistance

Military assistance continues to be the essential program by which we join with our allied and associated nations in

---

[4] The Congress enacted an appropriation of $3,298,092,500. See *Public Law* no. 85-853, 85th Cong., 2d Sess. (Mutual Security Appropriation Act, 1959. August 28, 1958).

maintaining well-armed forces in NATO, the Baghdad Pact, the Southeast Asia Treaty Organization, and in other key nations in the Far East and Southeast Asia. Through this program we also supply advanced weapons to our allies in Europe and elsewhere for their effective defense.

The mutual defense assistance which we have furnished, and are proposing to furnish, to nations, organizations, and areas of the free world will continue to make them more able to defend themselves, and will thereby strengthen the security of the United States and promote world peace.

I ask for $1,800 million for military assistance. This sum will be sufficient to maintain during fiscal year 1959 the level of deliveries carried out in fiscal year 1957 and projected for fiscal year 1958.

Defense Support

For defense support I request $835 million, to go to 12 countries that are supporting substantial military forces. These funds are needed to enable the recipient countries to make a mutually agreed contribution to our common military effort. This amount is substantially what I requested last year for support to these same 12 countries. Of the total amount, 70 percent would be used in 4 countries—Korea, the Republic of China, Vietnam, and Turkey.

Special Assistance

Several of our mutual security needs, some closely related to our collective security effort, cannot be met through other categories of assistance. For these we shall need to provide special assistance. I request $212 million for special assistance. This will serve two main interests.

First, special assistance helps maintain political and economic stability in certain nations where we do not support substantial military forces. Among such nations are Morocco and Libya where we have Strategic Air Command bases of great importance. In fiscal year 1958 assistance of this nature was included within the category of defense support. It will help clarify the purpose of this assistance if it is now provided as special assistance.

Second, special assistance supports another group of activities not falling properly under other categories of the act; for example, a continuation of the worldwide malaria-eradication program, the European technical exchange program, and a program in Latin America to provide training and civilian type equipment to military engineer units for construction of useful public projects.

Development Loan Fund

This Congress in its first session established the development loan fund to help friendly nations strengthen themselves by encouraging the development of their economies on the basis of self-help and mutual cooperation.

This action was taken to place our economic development assistance on the long-term basis essential for sound planning and execution of development programs. The Congress appropriated initial capital of $300 million. The fact that the fund has already received applications totaling well over $1 billion is a measure of the hopes which these newly developing nations place in it.

I request that the $625 million already authorized to be made available beginning in fiscal year 1959 be appropriated in full. This full amount is needed as additional capital for the fund in order that its basic objectives may be realized.

The fund's long-term character set it apart from economic assistance elsewhere provided in the mutual security program. I believe it is wise, therefore, to identify the fund as a separate entity. I am accordingly requesting incorporation of the fund with a board of directors which will both act as the governing body of the fund and assure coordination with our foreign policy objectives, with other mutual security activities and with lending activities of the Export-Import Bank and the International Bank.

Technical Cooperation

Our technical cooperation program is well established and has wide support of the American people. It should be gradually increased as additional able, well-trained technicians can be prepared to work abroad. For this program I ask $142 million for fiscal year 1959.

I also ask $20 million for the United States contribution to the United Nations technical assistance program. At the recent meeting of the General Assembly, the United States took the lead in proposing an expansion of this program, including the establishment of a special projects fund, in order to meet repeated and urgent requests from the newly developing nations for forms of technical development not now available from the United Nations. The proposal, if fully implemented by contributions from United Nations members, would ultimately result in a United Nations program of $100 million a year. I anticipate that an appropriation of $20 million will be sufficient to meet our obligations under this arrangement during the coming fiscal year.

In addition I request $1.5 million to continue our contribution to the work of the Organization of American States.

Contingency Fund

Past experience has proven time and again that, as the fiscal year develops, contingencies will arise for which funds will be needed. Some of these can be foreseen but without certainty as to the amounts; some cannot now be foreseen. Considering the turbulent state of the world today, I believe a fund of $200 million for contingencies is the minimum that will be needed for these purposes. Funds in the same amount were requested for fiscal year 1958 as a clearly distinguished part of special assistance. The important need for such funds can more clearly be identified through a separate appropriation to be used as required under the established categories of assistance.

Other Programs

For other programs I ask the appropriation of $106.6 million. As in past years these funds will provide for our contribution to the United Nations Children's Fund, certain refugee programs, the atoms-for-peace program, and for the cost of administering the economic programs. This administrative cost includes initial funds for bringing about an increase in the training of employees to speak the language of the countries in which they will serve. This is increasingly important because many of the newly independent nations speak languages in which we have few experts.

III. CONCLUSION

In recommending to you the vigorous continuation of our mutual security program, I am conscious of the feeling of some that desirable developments should be accomplished in this country before funds are used for development abroad.

This feeling springs in large part from the kind of misunderstandings typified by the name so often attached to this program: "foreign aid." This name is often used as though the program were some sort of giveaway or handout to foreigners, without benefit to ourselves.

For all the reasons I have discussed, the very opposite is true. Our mutual security program is of transcendent importance to the security of the United States.

No one would seriously argue that funds for our own military forces should be denied until desirable civilian projects had been provided for. Yet our expenditures for mutual security are fully as important to our national defense as expenditures for our own forces, and dollar for dollar buy us more in security.

For the safety of our families, the future of our children and our continued existence as a nation, we cannot afford to slacken our support of the mutual security program. The program I have recommended represents the smallest amount we may wisely invest in mutual security during the coming year.

(5) Exchange of Correspondence between Members of the Senate Committee on Foreign Relations and the President.[5]

LETTER FROM MEMBERS OF THE SENATE COMMITTEE ON FOREIGN RELATIONS TO THE PRESIDENT

AUGUST 25, 1958

THE PRESIDENT,

The White House

DEAR MR. PRESIDENT: On August 23, the Mutual Security Appropriations Bill for 1959 was approved by the Congress.[6] The undersigned members of the Committee on Foreign Relations voted in favor of this bill as they had previously done with respect to the authorizing legislation.

The experience was not a new one for us. Every member who has affixed his signature to this letter has generally supported Mutual Security legislation throughout the years of your Administration as well as of the previous Administration. We have been aware of the great monetary cost to the people of the United States which the policy of mutual

[5] *Department of State Bulletin*, v. 39 (October 6, 1958), pp. 546-549.
[6] *Public Law* no. 85-853, 85th Cong., 2d Sess. (Mutual Security Appropriation Act, 1959, August 28, 1958).

security has involved. We have measured that cost, however, against the even greater cost of a spread of totalitarianism and the ultimate cost of another war to the United States. On balance, it has been clear to us that the monetary cost of mutual security has been warranted by the service which that policy has heretofore performed in strengthening the resistance of other nations to totalitarianism and thereby reducing the danger of another great war.

In writing you concerning the Mutual Security Program, we do so with a sense of non-partisanship in matters which concern the vital interests of the nation. This is why we have delayed this letter until after the completion of the legislative process on this program. We write now to inform you of our deep concern over the present concept and administration of the program. We do not presume to trespass on your authority as President of the United States to administer the law of the United States. We do believe, however, as individual members of the Senate with some experience and understanding of the program and a full appreciation of its importance, that with respect to the less developed countries there is a serious distortion in the present relative importance which is attached to military and related aid on the one hand and technical assistance and self-liquidating economic development assistance on the other. For several years, we have received testimony and otherwise obtained information which tends to support this opinion. Furthermore, we have seen of late many statements in the press by members of your Administration which suggest that the primary threat of Soviet totalitarianism lies in the political and economic realm. Yet the Mutual Security Program which the Administration presented to the Congress reflects little responsiveness to these observations.

Overemphasis on military assistance has tended unavoidably to involve the United States in situations in which our aid may have contributed to the maintenance in power of regimes which have lacked broad support within the countries we have assisted. It has helped to create abroad a militaristic image of the United States which is a distortion of our national character. It has distracted attention, energy and perhaps economic aid, from more pressing problems. And finally, we believe military assistance by its very nature tends to create and then to perpetuate military hierarchies which even in the most well-developed countries may endanger the

very values of individual freedom which we seek to safeguard.

In support of these views, we refer to the unanimous report last year of the Special Committee to Study the Foreign
Aid Program,[7] in which it was recommended that although
"military aid should be continued," "efforts consistent with
national security should be made to reduce the rate of expenditures." That same report drew attention to three
specific questions which the Committee felt required careful
examination, namely: "(1) The suitability of the level of
military aid and the types of arms being provided to less
developed countries; (2) the possibility that competition for
arms aid among recipients is adding unduly to the cost of
the program; (3) the possibility that, in planning foreign aid
programs, insufficient consideration is given to the impact
of arms aid as a factor in generating increased needs for supporting aid."

While we know you have had considerations of this kind
in mind in preparing annual presentations of the Mutual
Security Program, we believe that there may have been a
tendency to believe that Congress blindly supports military
assistance but looks with disfavor on economic assistance. So
far as the undersigned are concerned that is not the case.
Indeed, during consideration this year of the Mutual Security
legislation, various of the undersigned gave serious consideration, or urged, or voted for substantial reductions of the
funds available for military assistance. Such reductions either
were not proposed or were not adopted because of the possibility of serious foreign policy repercussions unless reductions
in military assistance can be carefully planned and phased
into being over a period of time.

It seems to us of the greatest national importance that
you give personal attention to this matter in the time which
will elapse before the Mutual Security legislation is again
presented to the Congress. We urge most respectfully that you
study the Mutual Security Program in the light of the views
of members of your Administration, of members of Congress
and many others who have stressed that it is in the political
and economic realm that the concepts of freedom are now
undergoing a universal trial. It may be that such a study
will lead you, Mr. President, as it has led us to the conclusion
that the principal and most costly shortcoming in the Mutual
Security Program remains as it has been for some time—the

[7] S.Rept. 300, 85th Cong., 1st Sess.

failure to emphasize military aid less and to stress economic aid and technical assistance more. It may be that such a study will reveal that the military and non-military portions of the program are drawn up independently to an undue extent and then put together automatically in the same package.

We are anxious to do what is necessary for the welfare of the nation. So long as an aid program serves the enlightened self-interest of the people of the United States, we shall support it. We can do so, however, only if it is reasonably clear that it is administered in a fashion which does, in fact, contribute to that end. Therefore, we express to you our concern that we may be pursuing a pattern of foreign aid drawn by force of habit rather than one adjusted to current international realities.

We write you at this time because we are aware that budgets for the Mutual Security Program are prepared many months in advance. If there is to be an adjustment in this program in 1959, then the most appropriate time to act is now. We hope that before this program is again presented to Congress you will have had opportunity to re-appraise the relationship between the military and economic assistance aspects of the Mutual Security Program.

Yours respectfully,

THEODORE FRANCIS GREEN
J. W. FULBRIGHT
JOHN J. SPARKMAN
HUBERT H. HUMPHREY
MIKE MANSFIELD
WAYNE MORSE
JOHN F. KENNEDY
WILLIAM LANGER

ENCLOSURES

LETTER FROM SENATOR SMITH TO SENATOR FULBRIGHT

AUGUST 21 1958

DEAR BILL: I apologize for my delay in answering your letter of August 13th.

On reflection, while I feel that your emphasis on economic aid rather than military aid is a sound approach, I would prefer not to join in a letter from the entire Committee which would seem to imply that the operations of the Administration were open to criticism.

My own feeling is that while I would favor less military aid, nevertheless we have been compelled to think of the security of our country in light of the Soviet threat. These security needs must be balanced with our consideration of what might be called the wider range of our activities in supporting a positive program for the betterment of the other countries of the world.

My hope is that we can ultimately work out disarmament movements and UN responsibilities so that by degrees the military side can be substantially reduced. As rapidly as this can be accomplished we can move into the constructive build-up side in order that there may be a broad area of cooperation between the better-to-do nations of the world, and the underdeveloped areas, in terms of insuring the freedom, independence and self-determination, and especially economic stability of the latter.

This is doubtless along the same lines as your thinking, but just as I am leaving the Senate I do not wish to join in what might be construed to be a criticism of the Administration's policies which I have been defending vigorously since the mutual security concept was inaugurated.

Should you and your colleagues decide to forward the leter you have sent to us, I would be glad to have you enclose this letter with it, indicating that I am in agreement with your thoughts of moving more and more towards the constructive, posititve side and ultimately reducing the defensive, negative side.

Always cordially yours,

H. ALEXANDER SMITH, U.S.S.

The Honorable J. W. FULBRIGHT
United States Senate
Washington, D.C.

LETTER FROM SENATOR CAPEHART
TO SENATOR FULBRIGHT

AUGUST 22, 1958

DEAR BILL: I am sorry that I have delayed so long in replying to your letter of August 13th with reference to your proposal to forward a letter on the subject of mutual security appropriations to President Eisenhower.

But I would say frankly that I am not in a position to join as a co-signer of the proposed letter which you enclosed. My position on the matter of military and economic aid is well known and I feel that it would be inappropriate for me to join as co-signer of a communication which might be interpreted to contain implications of criticism to the Administration.

I am sure you know, because you have heard me say so many, many times, that I favor theappropriation of military aid funds directly to our own military to be administered by our own military establishment. I likewise have favored converting whatever economic aid program is dictated by the circumstances of the moment into a loan program.

I hope with you that the day will come when the necessity for military aid is reduced or eliminated entirely. I do not see that possibility at the moment in the light of continuing Soviet threats.

While I am sure that you and I are in complete agreement on the objectives of the mutual security program, I do not feel that I can completely endorse the views expressed in the proposed draft of your letter at this time. Thus, if you and other members of the committee do decide to send your letter to the President, I hope you will feel that it is appropriate to include this letter as an expression of my own views on the subject.

I very much appreciate your giving me the opportunity to express my views with respect to this very, very important matter.

Regards.

Sincerely,

HOMER E. CAPEHART

Honorable J. WILLIAM FULBRIGHT
Room 409
United States Senate
Washington, D.C.

LETTER FROM THE PRESIDENT TO THE CHAIRMAN OF THE SENATE FOREIGN RELATIONS COMMITTEE (GREEN)

SEPTEMBER 11, 1958

DEAR MR. CHAIRMAN: I appreciate your August 25 letter, co-signed by several of your colleagues, and also the separate comments of Senators Smith and Capehart. Certainly we agree fully as to the already great and steadily growing importance of our economic assistance programs. For a considerable time I have urged their expansion and have been gratified by your Committee's support, but unfortunately the Congress as a whole has sharply reduced the appropriations. Additional emphasis on these programs is being considered, and I judge from your letter that in this effort I can continue to count on your Committee's support.

As for the military part of mutual security, I am acutely conscious of its world-wide implications. Not only have requests for funds for the military programs been reduced appreciably since this Administration took office, but the percentage of the total effort devoted to military and related aid has been also substantially decreased. Enlargement of our economic programs next year would of course further decrease the military proportion.

Because both of these programs—the military as well as the economic—serve our national interests, an increasing of one at the expense of the other could have very harmful effects. Without prejudging the matter, I must say that the threatening posture of the Sino-Soviet Bloc, the importance of our collective security relationships, and the increasing cost of weapons will require a most careful weighing of the security impact of further reductions in military programs before they can be seriously contemplated.

I have sent copies of your letter to Secretary Dulles and Secretary McElroy. Please give your colleagues my assurance that their views will have thoughful attention as next year's program is readied for submission to Congress.[8]

Sincerely,

Dwight D. Eisenhower

The Honorable Theodore Francis Green
*Chairman, Committee on Foreign Relations,
United States Senate,
Washington, D.C.*

3. The International Monetary Fund and International Bank for Reconstruction and Development.

(6) Letter from the President to the Secretary of the Treasury (Anderson), August 26, 1958.[9]

Dear Mr. Secretary: I have read with great interest your letter concerning the adequacy of the present resources of the International Monetary Fund and the International Bank for Reconstruction and Development.[10]

I thoroughly agree with you that the well-being of the free world is vitally affected by the progress of the nations in the less developed areas as well as the economic situation in the more industrialized countries. A sound and sustainable rate of economic growth in the free world is a central objective of our policy.

It is universally true, in my opinion, that governmental strength and social stability call for an economic environment which is both dynamic and financially sound. Among the principal elements in maintaining such an economic basis for the free world are (1) a continuing growth in productive investment, international as well as domestic; (2) financial policies that will command the confidence of the public, and assure the strength of currencies; and (3) mutually beneficial international trade and a constant effort to avoid hampering restrictions on the freedom of exchange transactions.

During the past year, as you know, major advances have been made in our own programs for dealing with these problems. These include an increase in the lending authority

[8] On November 24, 1958 the President appointed a committee to study the United States Military Assistance Program and named William H. Draper, Jr. as its chairman. *Department of State Bulletin*, v. 39 (December 15, 1958), p. 954.
[9] *Ibid.* (September 15, 1958), pp. 412-414.
[10] *Ibid.*, pp. 414-415.

of the Export-Import Bank; establishment of the Development Loan Fund on a firmer basis through incorporation and enlargement of its resources; extension and broadening of the Reciprocal Trade Agreements Act; and continuation of the programs carried forward under the Agricultural Trade Development and Assistance Act.

Our own programs, however, can do only a part of the job. Accordingly, as we carry them forward, we should also seek a major expansion in the international programs designed to promote economic growth with the indispensable aid of strong and healthy currencies.

As you have pointed out, the International Bank for Reconstruction and Development and the International Monetary Fund are international instruments of proved effectiveness already engaged in this work. While both institutions still have uncommitted resources, I am convinced that the time has now come for us to consider, together with the other members of these two agencies, how we can better equip them for the tasks of the decade ahead.

Accordingly, I request, assuming concurrence by the interested members of the Congress with whom you will consult, that you take the necessary steps in conjunction with the National Advisory Council on International Monetary and Financial Problems, to support a course of action along the following lines:

First: In your capacity as United States Governor of the International Monetary Fund, I should like to have you propose, at the Annual Meeting of the Fund at New Delhi in October, that prompt consideration be given to the advisability of a general increase in the quotas assigned to the member governments.[11]

The past ten years testify to the important role played by the International Monetary Fund in assisting countries which, from time to time, have encountered temporary difficulties in their balance of payments. We are now entering a period when the implementation of effective and sound economic policies may be increasingly dependent in many countries upon the facilites and technical advice which the Fund can make available as they meet temporary external financial difficulties. This is particularly true of the less developed countries with the great variability in foreign exchange receipts to which they are subject from time to time. It also applies to industrialized countries which are

[11] *Ibid.* (November 17, 1958), pp. 793-798.

dependent on foreign trade. Through its growing experience and increasingly close relations with its members, the Fund can also help see to it that countries are encouraged to pursue policies that create stable financial and monetary conditions while contributing to expanding world trade and income. The International Monetary Fund is uniquely qualified to harmonize these objectives but its present resources do not appear adequate to the task.

Second: In your capacity as United States Governor of the International Bank for Reconstruction and Development, I should like to have you propose, at the Annual Meeting of the Bank, that prompt consideration be given to the advisability of an increase in the authorized capital of the Bank and to the offering of such additional capital for subscription by the Bank's member governments. Such additional capital subscriptions, if authorized, would not necessarily require additional payments to be made to the Bank; they would, however, ensure the adequacy of the Bank's lending resources for an extended period by strengthening the guarantees which stand behind the Bank's obligations.

The demands upon the Bank for development loans have been increasing rapidly, and it is in a position to make a growing contribution to the economic progress of the free world in the period which lies ahead. Moreover, it can do this by channeling the savings of private investors throughout the world into sound loans, repayable in dollars or other major currencies. But to meet the rising need for such sound development loans, it must be able to raise the funds in the capital markets of the free world. An increase in the Bank's subscribed capital, by increasing the extent of the responsibility of member governments for assuring that the Bank will always be in a position to meet its obligations, would enable the Bank to place a larger volume of its securities in a broader market, while still maintaining the prime quality of its securities and hence the favorable terms on which it can borrow and re-lend funds.

Third: With respect to the proposal for an International Development Association, I believe that such an affiliate of the International Bank, if adequately supported by a number of countries able to contribute, could provide a useful supplement to the existing lending activities of the Bank and thereby accelerate the pace of economic development in the less developed member countries of the Bank. In connection with the study of this matter that you are undertaking in the

National Advisory Council pursuant to the Senate Resolution, I note that you contemplate informal discussions with other member governments of the Bank with a view to ascertaining their attitude toward an expansion of the Bank's responsibilities along these lines. If the results indicate that the creation of the International Development Association would be feasible, I request that, as a third step, you initiate promptly negotiations looking toward the establishment of such an affiliate of the Bank.

The three-point program I have suggested for consideration would require intensified international cooperation directed to a broad attack upon some of the major economic problems of our time. A concerted and successful international effort along these lines would, I feel certain, create a great new source of hope for all those who share our conviction that with material betterment and free institutions flourishing side by side we can look forward with confidence to a peaceful world.

Sincerely,
DWIGHT D. EISENHOWER

4. *Export Controls.*

(7) *Department of Commerce Announcement of Changes in Export Controls Applied to the Sino-Soviet Bloc, August 14, 1958.*[12]

The Department of Commerce on August 14 announced that significant changes are being made in U.S. export controls as a result of agreements reached in recent consultations between the United States and friendly foreign countries.

These changes will lead to a net reduction of U.S. controls. There will also be additions to the list of controlled commodities as a result of freeworld scientific and technological progress. The agreements reached are recommendations to the participating governments for minimum levels of control. Decisions as to the level of U.S. controls will take additional time. These new agreements followed a review of international strategic controls, which took place at Paris during the past 5 months between the United States and 14 other nations of the free world. The international controls apply to all countries of the Sino-Soviet bloc.

The principal aim of U.S. export controls is to prevent export of goods which would build up the Sino-Soviet war

[12] *Ibid.* (September 8, 1958), p. 392.

machine. This policy will continue, and the total U.S. embargo against shipments to Communist China, north Korea, and north Viet-Nam remains unchanged.

Up to now, the Department's Bureau of Foreign Commerce generally has denied Soviet-bloc applications to export goods listed on its Positive List of Commodities. Since the list is currently being revised, BFC is not now able to advise exporters specifically in advance as to which items are likely to be approved for export to Eastern Europe.[13]

[13] On September 3, 1958 the Department of State published the revised unclassified title I, category A, Battle Act (Mutual Defense Assistance Control Act of 1951) list of embargoed items, consisting of arms, ammunition, implements of war and atomic energy materials. *Ibid.* (September 22, 1958), pp. 467-469.

CHAPTER TWO

THE WESTERN COMMUNITY

A. The North Atlantic Treaty Organization.
   1. *Ministerial Session of the North Atlantic Council, Copenhagen, May 5-7, 1958.*
   (8) *Final Communiqué, Copenhagen, May 7, 1958.*[1]

The North Atlantic Council held its spring ministerial meeting in Copenhagen from May 5 to 7, 1958.

2. The Foreign Ministers of the fifteen NATO countries have deepened and strengthened their mutual understanding and their unity of purpose. NATO, a defensive organization, is now much more than merely a military alliance. It is becoming a true community of free nations. Within this community, to a degree unprecedented in history, countries are carrying out a policy of close cooperation in peacetime without abandoning their independence. This development is one of the most significant and promising events of our time.

3. The Council reviewed the activities of the alliance and examined the international situation. For the first subject of discussion, the Council had before it the report submitted by the Secretary General. The Council was in agreement with this analysis of the work of the alliance in the past year. They agreed in particular that the outstanding achievement had been the remarkable progress made in the strengthening of political consultation. This has been successfully applied to an increasing number of problems and has led to coordination of policy on major questions of common interest. The Council also expressed its satisfaction with the results of the recent conference of Defence Ministers[2] and with the good start made in the field of scientific cooperation.

4. The Ministers recognized that political unity and the efficient organization of defence were not enough. Economic cooperation is also essential between the members of the alliance. Every effort should be made to ensure economic prosperity, notably by the expansion of international trade

[1] *Department of State Bulletin*, v. 38 (May 26, 1958), pp. 850-851.
[2] *Ibid.* (May 5, 1958), pp. 729-730.

and by aid to underdeveloped countries. Consultations on methods and machinery for such cooperation will take place within the alliance. The Ministers attach special importance to the successful conclusion of the economic negotiations now being undertaken and to the establishment of close ties between the European countries and the whole free world.

5. During their consideration of the international situation the Ministers had a discussion on the question of a possible summit conference. The Council believes that summit meetings are desirable if they offer prospects of reaching settlement on important questions. The Council considers that conferences at the summit are not the only way, or necessarily the best way, of conducting negotiations or reducing international tensions. In any event, such conferences must be properly prepared and take place in a favorable atmosphere.

6. The Ministers regretted that during the last few weeks the Soviet Union has made the preparations for a possible summit conference more difficult by posing unreasonable conditions. The Soviet Union has recently aggravated international tension by its veto in the Security Council of the United States proposals to reduce the risks of surprise attack over the Arctic.[3]

7. Despite the disappointment and doubts to which the Soviet attitude gives rise, the NATO Governments will not be discouraged nor give up their attachment to the principle of negotiation.

8. Should a summit conference take place at this time it should consider certain important problems, among others the German problem, which were identified by the Heads of Governments meeting at Geneva in 1955 and on which, unfortunately, little or no progress towards a solution has been made. Controlled disarmament, desired so ardently by all peoples, should be one of the main questions on the agenda. The proposals made by the Western Powers on 29th August, 1957 and approved by a large majority in the United Nations could afford a reasonable basis for this discussion.[4]

9. The Council expressed the hope that it might yet prove possible, in spite of repeated Soviet refusal, to inaugurate expert technical discussions, between representatives of the Soviet Union and of the Western Powers principally concerned, on detailed measures on control over disarmament.

[3] Documents 162 and 163, below.
[4] *Documents on American Foreign Relations, 1957*, pp. 439-446.

Agreement on measures necessary, for example, to prevent surprise attack or to detect nuclear explosions might go far towards demonstrating the possibility of agreement on disarmament, improving its prospects and accelerating its application when reached. In order to prepare the way for such agreement the Council will consider the possibility of carrying out studies and experiments on the technical problems of inspection and control.

10. In conclusion, the Ministers confirmed the full agreement of their governments on the basic principles of the alliance, its goals and the methods of obtaining them.

2. Ministerial Session of the North Atlantic Council, Paris, December 16-18, 1958.

(9) Final Communiqué, Paris, December 18, 1958.[5]

The North Atlantic Council held its regular Ministerial Session in Paris from 16th to 18th December, 1958.

International Situation

In a comprehensive survey of the international situation, the Council gave first place to the question of Berlin. The member countries made clear their resolution not to yield to threats. Their unanimous view on Berlin was expressed in the Council's Declaration of 16th December.[6]

The Council will continue to follow this question with close attention and will shortly discuss the replies to be sent to the Soviet notes of 27th November.

The member states of NATO sincerely believe that the interests of peace require equitable settlements of the outstanding political issues which divide the free world from the Communist world. A solution of the German question, linked with European security arrangements, and an agreement on controlled disarmament remain in their view essential. The NATO Governments will continue to seek just settlements of these problems, but regret that Western proposals on these questions have so far been ignored by the Soviet Government.

The Council heard reports on the Geneva discussions on the discontinuance of nuclear weapons tests, and on measures helpful in preventing surprise attack.

The Council's review of the international situation, on

[5] Department of State Bulletin, v. 40 (January 5, 1959), pp. 3-4.
[6] Document 59, below.

the basis of reports prepared by the Political Committee, covered a wide range of problems.

Special attention was given to the efforts of the Communist bloc to weaken the positions of the free world in different areas.

Political Cooperation

The Council had before it a report by the Secretary General on political cooperation in the Alliance. The Ministers consider that important progress has been made in this field during 1958. They examined the problems inevitably created by the widening of political consultation. There was general agreement that the existing machinery of NATO is well suited to the needs of the Alliance, and that flexible methods would produce better results than any codification of rules. The Ministers agreed that the preparation of political consultation in the Council could be improved, in particular by more systematic study of long-term political questions. The Council paid tribute to the efforts of the Secretary General in the field of conciliation between member countries.

Economic Questions

The Ministers reaffirmed the importance they attach to the measures taken both individually and collectively by member countries to stimulate economic activity and to ensure continuing expansion without inflation.

The Council noted the difficulties encountered in the negotiations undertaken for the Organization of Economic Cooperation between the European members of the Alliance who are in the Common Market and those who are not.

It considers it necessary that a multilateral association should be established at the earliest possible date and expresses the hope that the efforts now being undertaken with a view to a solution will be successful.

The Council heard a joint statement by the Greek and Turkish Foreign Ministers on the problems of the less developed member countries, and instructed the Permanent Council to undertake a study of this matter.

Military Questions

The Council examined the military situation of the Alliance. After hearing reports by the Standing Group and the Supreme Allied Commanders, the Ministers emphasized the vital need, in view of the continuing increase in Soviet armaments, to sustain without relaxation the effort of member countries to improve the defensive power of the Alliance.

The Council reaffirmed that NATO defensive strategy continues to be based on the existence of effective shield forces and on the manifest will to use nuclear retaliatory forces to repel aggression.

The Ministers examined the report of the 1958 Annual Review and approved its conclusions. The implementation of the plans agreed in December 1957 by the Heads of Government is being actively pursued, and methods for accelerating their realization were agreed.

The next regular Ministerial Meeting of the Council will be held in Washington on April 2nd to 4th, 1959, at the invitation of the United States Government, on the occasion of the tenth anniversary of the signing of the North Atlantic Treaty.

B. The European Atomic Energy Community (EURATOM).

(10) *Message of the President Recommending Approval of an International Agreement between the United States and EURATOM, June 23, 1958.*[1]

To the Congress of the United States:

I am transmitting today for approval by the Congress an international agreement between the Government of the United States and the European Atomic Energy Community which will be a first step toward mutually beneficial cooperation in the peaceful applications of atomic energy between this new European Community and the United States.[2] The specific program which I am asking the Congress to consider and approve on an urgent basis is a joint undertaking by the United States and Euratom to foster the construction in Europe by 1963 of approximately 6 major nuclear power reactors which would produce about 1 million kilowatts of electricity.

This international agreement is being submitted pursuant to the provisions of sections 11 (L) and 124 of the Atomic

[1] House Document 411, 85th Cong., 2d Sess.
[2] The agreement transmitted by the President was a preliminary agreement signed at Brussels on May 25, 1958 and at Washington on June 18, 1958. The final agreement, embodying the features listed in the outline printed as document 19 below, was signed at Brussels on November 8, 1958. See *Department of State Bulletin*, v. 40 (January 12, 1959), pp. 69-74.

Energy Act of 1954, as amended. The cooperation to be undertaken after approval of the international agreement will be pursuant to the terms and conditions of an agreement for cooperation entered into in accordance with section 123 of that act.

The elements which combine to make such a joint program possible are the same that led to the first great breakthrough in the development of atomic energy 15 years ago: the intimate association of European and American scientists and close association between European and American engineers and industries. While the joint nuclear power program draws heavily on the history of atomic energy development there are important new elements which reflect the changing world scene.

The first is the changing face of Europe symbolized by the European Atomic Energy Community, which now takes its place beside the Coal and Steel Community and the European Economic Community (Common Market) in a further major step toward a united Europe. The inspiration of European statesmen which has now come to fruition in Euratom is the simple but profoundly important idea that through concentration of the scientific and industrial potentialities of the six countries it will be possible to develop a single major atomic energy complex, larger than the sum of the parts, and designed to exploit the peaceful potential of atomic energy. One motivation which has therefore led to the creation of this new Community is the growing sense of urgency on the part of Europeans that their destiny requires unity and that the road toward this unity is to be found in the development of major common programs such as Euratom makes possible. Another important motivation is the present and growing requirement of Europe for a new source of energy in the face of rapidly increasing requirements and the limited possibilities of increasing the indigenous supply of conventional fuels. The Europeans see atomic energy not merely as an alternative source of energy but as something which they must develop quickly if they are to continue their economic growth and exercise their rightful influence in world affairs. The success of this undertaking, therefore, is of vital importance to the United States, for the 160 million people on the Continent of Europe are crucial to North Atlantic strength.

It is therefore gratifying that the reactor research, development, testing, and construction program in the United States has progressed to the point that United States reactors of proven types are available and will be selected for commercial exploitation in the joint program of large-scale nuclear reactors.

The abundance of conventional fuel in the United States and hence our lower cost of electricity as contrasted with higher energy costs in Europe means that it is possible for nuclear power reactors to produce economic electrical energy in Europe before it will be possible to do so in most parts of the United States.

The basic arrangements which have been worked out with Euratom are designed to take advantage of many favorable factors and circumstances. They promise to result in a program that will initially be of great benefit to Euratom and the United States, and thereafter to nations everywhere that choose to profit from Euratom's experience. American knowledge and industrial capacity will be joined with the scientific and industrial talents of Europe in an accelerated nuclear power program to meet Europe's presently urgent need for a new source of energy.

The plants to be built will be paid for and operated by the existing public and private utilities in the six countries; components will be manufactured by American and European industry. Through this association the basis will be laid for future mutually beneficial commercial collaboration in the atomic energy business. The major portion of the fund for the construction of the plants will come from European sources of capital. The United States, through the Export-Import Bank, is prepared to supplement these funds by making available to the new Community a long-term line of credit.

A central purpose of the proposed joint program is for Euratom and the United States Government to create an institutional and economic environment which will encourage the European utilities to embark quickly upon a large-scale nuclear power program. As this program goes forward, it will make possible significant progress in the development of atomic power elsewhere in the world.

The expectation that nuclear power will be economic rests on the inherent promise of achieving substantially lowered fuel costs which will more than compensate for the higher capital costs of nuclear plants. The principal immediate problem is to limit during this developmental phase the economic uncertainties connected with the burning of nuclear fuel in these reactors. To assist in meeting this problem the United States will provide certain special and limited guaranties and incentives to permit American fuel fabricators and the European utilities and industries to enter into firm contractual arrangements with greater certainty as to the actual costs of nuclear energy from the reactors than is now possible.

Of major importance, the new European Community and the United States will establish a jointly financed research and development program, the purpose of which will be to improve the performance of these reactors and thus to further the economic feasibility of nuclear power. Information developed under the joint program will be made available to American and European industry for the general advancement of power reactor technology.

In addition to the international agreement submitted herewith, the necessary requests for congressional action required to carry out the program will be submitted shortly.

I believe that the initiation of this program of cooperation with Euratom represents a major step in the application of nuclear technology for the benefit of mankind.

The United States and Euratom have reaffirmed their dedication to the objectives of the International Atomic Energy Agency and intend that the results of this program will benefit the Agency and the nations participating in it. Consideration is now being given to ways in which the United States can work with the Agency in carrying forward its functions. A proposed agreement for cooperation with the International Atomic Energy Agency is now being negotiated and is under review by the Agency. This agreement provides principally for the transfer of the special nuclear material already offered to the Agency by the United States for certain services, such as chemical processing, and for the broad exchange of unclassified information in furtherance of the Agency's program.

In recognition of the importance of the joint United States-Euratom program, I must stress its urgency. It was only on the 1st of January of this year that the new Community came into being, determined to fulfill its obligation to create the conditions which will permit the earliest development of nuclear power on a major scale. The Community is determined, as are we, that the joint program should be initiated this year. I am sure that the Congress, having in mind the political and economic advantages which will accrue to us and our European friends from such a joint endeavor, will wish to consider quickly and favorably the proposed program.[3]

DWIGHT D. EISENHOWER

(11) Outline of Proposed United States—EURATOM Program, June 23, 1958.[4]

A. Objectives

1. The aim of the joint program will be to bring into operation in the Community by 1963 about one million electric kilowatts of installed nuclear capacity, in reactors of proven types developed in the United States, and to initiate immediately a joint research and development program centered on those reactors. The program would be conducted so as to obtain maximum support of the industries of the Community and of the United States. Their active participation is indispensable to the success of the program.

B. Major Features

1. The total capital cost, exclusive of fuel, is estimated not to exceed $350 million. These funds will be provided for by the participating utilities and other European sources of capital, such financing to be arranged with the appropriate assistance of EURATOM. Up to $135 million would be provided by the United States Government to EURATOM in the form of a long-term line of credit from the Export-Import Bank. These funds will be re-lent by EURATOM for the construction of nuclear power plants under the program.

2. The nuclear power plants under the program will be built, owned, and operated by utilities in the member states. All risks due to uncertainties in construction, maintenance, and operating costs and load factors will be borne directly by these utilities. In the course of the negotiation it was determined that the economic risks associated today with the reactor fuel cycle must be minimized if participation by the European utility industry is to be reasonably assured. To this end the United States, for a 10-year period of operation, will guarantee ceiling costs for the fabrication of the fuel elements required, as well as a fixed life for these elements.

[3] Public Law no. 85-846, 85th Cong., 2d Sess. (Euratom Cooperation Act of 1958, August 28, 1958). The act sets forth the terms of cooperation between the United States and EURATOM.
[4] Department of State Bulletin, v. 39 (July 14, 1958), pp. 71-72.

3. A proposed research and development program established for a 10-year period will be centered on the improvement in the performance of the reactors involved in the program and the lowering of fuel cycle costs. During the first 5 years the financial contribution of the Community and the United States will amount to about $50 million each, with the sum required for the second 5-year period to be determined at a later date.

4. Under the arrangements proposed the United States would sell to the Community a net quantity of 30,000 kilograms of contained U-235 in uranium to cover the fueling and other requirements of the program for such material over a 20-year operating period. The initial operating inventory, which amounts to approximately 9,000 kilograms of contained U-235 would be sold to the Community on a deferred payment basis. The balance of about 20,000 kilograms, which represents estimated burnup and process losses over the 20-year operating period, and 1,000 kilograms to provide for research and test reactors associated with the programs, would be paid for on a current basis.

5. The U.S. Atomic Energy Commission will process in its facilities, at established U.S. domestic prices, spent fuel elements from the reactors to be included in the program.

6. With respect to any special nuclear material produced in reactors fueled with materials obtained from the United States under this joint program, which is in excess of the need of the Community for such material for the peaceful uses of atomic energy, the International Atomic Energy Agency would have the right of first option to purchase such material at the announced fuel value price in effect in the United States at the time of purchase. In the event this option is not exercised by the Agency, the United States would be prepared during the first 10 years of reactor operation to purchase such material at the U.S.-announced fuel value price in effect at the time of purchase.

7. Technological and economic data developed under the program would be made available to the industries within the Community and the United States under provisions designed to assure the widespread dissemination of the information developed in the course of the program.

8. Under the program the Community will assume responsibility for the establishment of a safeguards system which will be formulated in accordance with agreed-upon principles. This system will be designed to assure that the

materials received from the United States, as well as special nuclear material produced therefrom, will be used for peaceful purposes only. The proposed agreement for cooperation with the Community provides for frequent consultation between parties on the operation of the system and that the Community will establish a mutually satisfactory safeguards system based on these principles. By exchange of letters both parties have agreed that the terms of the agreement include permission for verification, by mutually approved scientific methods, of the effectiveness of the safeguards and control systems applied to nuclear materials received from the other party or derived therefrom in connection with the joint program. Continuation of the cooperative program will be contingent upon the Community's establishing and maintaining a mutually satisfactory safeguards system. The Community also has agreed to consult with the International Atomic Energy Agency to assure the development of a safeguards system reasonably compatible with that of the Agency. The agreement for cooperation, which has been negotiated, will contain all of the guaranties required by section 123 of the Atomic Energy Act of 1954, as amended. In addition, in the event of the establishment of an international safeguards and control system by the International Atomic Energy Agency, the United States and EURATOM will consult regarding assumption by that Agency of the safeguards and control over fissionable material utilized and produced in implementation of the joint program.

C. The United Kingdom.

1. *Exchange of Notes Concerning an Agreement for the Supply of Intermediate-Range Ballistic Missiles to the United Kingdom.*

   (12) *United States Note and Memorandum, February 22, 1958.*[1]

EXCELLENCY: I have the honor to refer to discussions which have taken place between representatives of the Government of the United Kingdom of Great Britain and Northern Ireland and of the Government of the United States of America on the subject of the supply by the United States Government to the United Kingdom Government of intermediate range ballistic missiles.

[1] *Department of State Bulletin*, v. 38 (March 17, 1958), pp. 418-419.

I also have the honor to record that, pursuant to the agreement in principle reached between the Prime Minister of the United Kingdom and the President of the United States at Bermuda on March 22, 1957,[2] and in support of the purposes of the North Atlantic Treaty and the obligations of the parties thereto, the representatives of the two Governments have agreed to the terms set out in the memorandum annexed hereto regarding the proposed supply of intermediate range ballistic missiles.

Accordingly, I have the honor to propose that this Note and Your Excellency's reply to that effect shall be regarded as constituting an Agreement between the two Governments in the terms set out in the annexed memorandum and that such Agreement shall have effect from the date of Your Excellency's reply.

Accept, Excellency, the renewed assurances of my highest consideration.

For the Secretary of State:

CHRISTIAN A. HERTER

His Excellency
Sir HAROLD CACCIA, K. C. M. G., K. C. V. O.,
   British Ambassador.

MEMORANDUM

1. The Government of the United States shall supply to the Government of the United Kingdom an agreed number of intermediate range ballistic missiles and their related specialized equipment and make available training assistance in order to facilitate the deployment by the Government of the United Kingdom of the said missiles. The missiles shall be located only in the United Kingdom at such sites and under such conditions as may be agreed upon between the two Governments.

2. The United Kingdom Government shall provide the sites and supporting facilities required for the deployment of the missiles.

3. Ownership of the missiles and related equipment shall pass to the United Kingdom Government under established United States Mutual Assistance Program procedures as soon as the United Kingdom Government is in a position to man and operate the missiles.

4. The missiles will be manned and operated by United

[2] *Documents on American Foreign Relations, 1957*, pp. 130-132.

Kingdom personnel, who will be trained by the United States Government for the purposes of this project at the earliest feasible date.

5. For the purposes of this Agreement, training and test-firing of missiles will normally take place on United States instrumented ranges but by agreement with the United States Government the United Kingdom Government may arrange with the Government of the Commonwealth of Australia for missiles to be test-fired on the Woomera Range in Australia.

6. Material, equipment, and training provided by the United States Government to the United Kingdom Government pursuant to the arrangements recorded herein will be furnished pursuant to the United States Mutual Security Act of 1954, as amended, acts amendatory or supplementary thereto, appropriations acts thereunder or any other applicable United States legislative provisions.

7. The decision to launch these missiles will be a matter for joint decision by the two Governments. Any such joint decision will be made in the light of the circumstances at the time and having regard to the undertaking the two Governments have assumed in Article 5 of the North Atlantic Treaty.

8. References to intermediate range ballistic missiles in this Agreement do not include the nuclear warheads for such missiles. The United States Government shall provide nuclear warheads for the missiles transferred to the United Kingdom Government pursuant to this Agreement. All nuclear warheads so provided shall remain in full United States ownership, custody and control in accordance with United States law.

9. The arrangements recorded herein are made in consonance with the North Atlantic Treaty and in pursuance of the Mutual Defense Assistance Agreement between the United Kingdom Government and the United States Government, signed January 27, 1950, as supplemented, and related agreements, and are subject to the applicable provisions thereof.

10. This Agreement shall be subject to revision by agreement between the two Governments and shall remain in force for not less than five years from the date of the Agreement but may thereafter be terminated by either Government upon six months' notice.

68   DOCUMENTS ON AMERICAN FOREIGN RELATIONS

(13) *United Kingdom Note, February 22, 1958.*[3]

SIR, I have the honour to acknowledge receipt of your Note of today's date with reference to discussions which have taken place between representatives of the Government of the United States of America and of the Government of the United Kingdom of Great Britain and Northern Ireland on the subject of the supply to the United Kingdom of intermediate range ballistic missiles, which Note reads as follows:

[Here is repeated the full text of the U.S. note.]

I have the honour to inform you that the proposal made in your Note is acceptable to the Government of the United Kingdom and to confirm that your Note, together with this reply, shall constitute an Agreement between the two Governments in the terms set out in the memorandum annexed to your Note, a copy of which memorandum is enclosed, such Agreement to have effect from the date of this Note.

I avail myself of this opportunity to renew to you the assurance of my highest consideration.

HAROLD CACCIA

2. *Agreement for Cooperation on the Uses of Atomic Energy for Mutual Defense Purposes.*

(14) *Text of Agreement, July 3, 1958.*[4]

The Government of the United States of America and the Government of the United Kingdom of Great Britain and Northern Ireland on its own behalf and on behalf of the United Kingdom Atomic Energy Authority.

Considering that their mutual security and defense require that they be prepared to meet the contingencies of atomic warfare;

Considering that both countries have made substantial progress in the development of atomic weapons;

Considering that they are participating together in international arrangements pursuant to which they are making substantial and material contributions to their mutual defense and security;

Recognizing that their common defense and security will be advanced by the exchange of information concerning

[3] *Department of State Bulletin,* v. 38 (March 17, 1958), p. 419.
[4] *Ibid.,* v. 39 (July 28, 1958), pp. 161-164.

atomic energy and by the transfer of equipment and materials for use therein;

Believing that such exchange and transfer can be undertaken without risk to the defense and security of either country; and

Taking into consideration the United States Atomic Energy Act of 1954, as amended, which was enacted with these purposes in mind.[5]

Have agreed as follows:

ARTICLE I

General Provision

While the United States and the United Kingdom are participating in an international arrangement for their mutual defense and security and making substantial and material contributions thereto, each Party will communicate to and exchange with the other Party information, and transfer materials and equipment to the other Party, in accordance with the provisions of this Agreement provided that the communicating or transferring Party determines that such cooperation will promote and will not constitute an unreasonable risk to its defense and security.

ARTICLE II

Exchange of Information

A. Each Party will communicate to or exchange with the other Party such classified information as is jointly determined to be necessary to:

1. the development of defense plans;

2. the training of personnel in the employment of and defense against atomic weapons and other military applications of atomic energy;

3. the evaluation of the capabilities of potential enemies in the employment of atomic weapons and other military applications of atomic energy;

4. the development of delivery systems compatible with the atomic weapons which they carry; and

5. research, development and design of military reactors to the extent and by such means as may be agreed.

B. In addition to the cooperation provided for in paragraph A of this Article each Party will exchange with the

[5] *Public Law* no. 85-479, 85th Cong., 2d Sess. (July 2, 1958).

other Party other classified information concerning atomic weapons when, after consultation with the other Party, the communicating Party determines that the communication of such information is necessary to improve the recipient's atomic weapon design, development and fabrication capability.

ARTICLE III

Transfer of Submarine Nuclear Propulsion Plant and Materials

A. The Government of the United States will authorize, subject to terms and conditions acceptable to the Government of the United States, a person to transfer by sale to the Government of the United Kingdom or its agent one complete submarine nuclear propulsion plant with such spare parts therefor as may be agreed by the Parties and to communicate to the Government of the United Kingdom or its agent (or to both) such classified information as relates to safety features and such classified information as is necessary for the design, manufacture and operation of such propulsion plant. A person or persons will also be authorized, for a period of ten years following the date of entry into force of this Agreement and subject to terms and conditions acceptable to the Government of the United States, to transfer replacement cores or fuel elements for such plant.

B. The Government of the United States will transfer by sale agreed amounts of U-235 contained in uranium enriched in the isotope U-235 as needed for use in the submarine nuclear propulsion plant transferred pursuant to paragraph A of this Article, during the ten years following the date of entry into force of this Agreement on such terms and conditions as may be agreed. If the Government of the United Kingdom so requests, the Government of the United States will during such period reprocess any material sold under the present paragraph in facilities of the Government of the United States, on terms and conditions to be agreed, or authorize such reprocessing in private facilities in the United States. Enriched uranium recovered in reprocessing such materials by either Party may be purchased by the Government of the United States under terms and conditions to be agreed. Special nuclear material recovered in reprocessing such materials and not purchased by the Government of the United States may be returned to or retained by the

Government of the United Kingdom and any U-235 not purchased by the Government of the United States will be credited to the amounts of U-235 to be transferred by the Government of the United States under this Agreement.

C. The Government of the United States shall be compensated for enriched uranium sold by it pursuant to this Article at the United States Atomic Energy Commission's published charges applicable to the domestic distribution of such material in effect at the time of the sale. Any purchase of enriched uranium by the Government of the United States pursuant to this Article shall be at the applicable price of the United States Atomic Energy Commission for the purchase of enriched uranium in effect at the time of purchase of such enriched uranium.

D. The Parties will exchange classified information on methods of reprocessing fuel elements of the type utilized in the propulsion plant to be transferred under this Article, including classified information on the design, construction and operation of facilities for the reprocessing of such fuel elements.

E. The Government of the United Kingdom shall indemnify and hold harmless the Government of the United States against any and all liabilities whatsoever (including third-party liability) for any damage or injury occurring after the propulsion plant or parts thereof, including spare parts, replacement cores or fuel elements are taken outside the United States, for any cause arising out of or connected with the design, manufacture, assembly, transfer or utilization of the propulsion plant, spare parts, replacement cores or fuel elements transferred pursuant to paragraph A of this Article.

ARTICLE IV

Responsibility for Use of Information, Material, Equipment and Devices

The application or use of any information (including design drawings and specifications), material or equipment communicated, exchanged or transferred under this Agreement shall be the responsibility of the Party receiving it, and the other Party does not provide any indemnity, and does not warrant the accuracy or completeness of such information and does not warrant the suitability or completeness of such information, material or equipment for any particular use or application.

ARTICLE V

Conditions

A. Cooperation under this Agreement will be carried out by each of the Parties in accordance with its applicable laws.

B. Under this Agreement there will be no transfer by either Party of atomic weapons.

C. Except as may be otherwise agreed for civil uses, the information communicated or exchanged, or the materials or equipment transferred, by either Party pursuant to this Agreement shall be used by the recipient Party exclusively for the preparation or implementation of defense plans in the mutual interests of the two countries.

D. Nothing in this Agreement shall preclude the communication or exchange of classified information which is transmissible under other arrangements between the Parties.

ARTICLE VI

Guaranties

A. Classified information, materials and equipment communicated or transferred pursuant to this Agreement shall be accorded full security protection under applicable security arrangements between the Parties and applicable national legislation and regulations of the Parties. In no case shall either Party maintain security standards for safeguarding classified information, materials or equipment made available pursuant to this Agreement less restrictive than those set forth in the applicable security arrangements in effect on the date this Agreement comes into force.

B. Classified information communicated or exchanged pursuant to this Agreement will be made available through channels existing or hereafter agreed for the communication or exchange of such information between the Parties.

C. Classified information, communicated or exchanged, and any materials or equipment transferred, pursuant to this Agreement shall not be communicated, exchanged or transferred by the recipient Party or persons under its jurisdiction to any unauthorized persons, or, except as provided in Article VII of this Agreement, beyond the jurisdiction of that Party. Each Party may stipulate the degree to which any of the information, materials or equipment communicated, exchanged or transferred by it or persons under its jurisdiction pursuant to this Agreement may be disseminated or distributed; may specify the categories of persons who may have access to such information, materials or equipment; and may impose such other restrictions on the dissemination or distribution of such information, materials or equipment as it deems necessary.

ARTICLE VII

Dissemination

Nothing in this Agreement shall be interpreted or operate as a bar or restriction to consultation or cooperation in any field of defense by either Party with other nations or international organizations. Neither Party, however, shall communicate classified information or transfer or permit access to or use of materials, or equipment, made available by the other Party pursuant to this Agreement to any nation or international organization unless authorized to do so by such other Party, or unless such other Party has informed the recipient Party that the same information has been made available to that nation or international organization.

ARTICLE VIII

Classification Policies

Agreed classification policies shall be maintained with respect to all classified information, materials or equipment communicated, exchanged or transferred under this Agreement. The Parties intend to continue the present practice of consultation with each other on the classification of these matters.

ARTICLE IX

Patents

A. With respect to any invention or discovery employing classified information which has been communicated or exchanged pursuant to Article II or derived from the submarine propulsion plant, material or equipment transferred pursuant to Article III, and made or conceived by the recipient Party, or any agency or corporation owned or controlled thereby, or any of their agents or contractors, or any employee of any of the foregoing, after the date of such communication, exchange or transfer but during the period of this Agreement:

1. in the case of any such invention or discovery in which rights are owned by the recipient Party, or any agency or corporation owned or controlled thereby, and not included in subparagraph 2 of this paragraph, the recipient Party shall, to the extent owned by any of them:

(a) transfer and assign to the other Party all right, title and interest in and to the invention or discovery, or patent application or patent thereon, in the country of that other Party, subject to the retention of a royalty-free, non-exclusive, irrevocable license for the governmental purposes of the recipient Party and for the purposes of mutual defense; and

(b) grant to the other Party a royalty-free, non-exclusive, irrevocable license for the governmental purposes of that other Party and for purposes of mutual defense in the country of the recipient Party and third countries, including use in the production of material in such countries for sale to the recipient Party by a contractor of that other Party;

2. in the case of any such invention or discovery which is primarily useful in the production or utilization of special nuclear material or atomic energy and made or conceived prior to the time that the information it employs is made available for civil uses, the recipient Party shall:

(a) obtain, by appropriate means, sufficient right, title and interest in and to the invention or discovery, or patent application or patent thereon, as may be necessary to fulfill its obligations under the following two subparagraphs:

(b) transfer and assign to the other Party all right, title and interest in and to the invention or discovery, or patent application or patent thereon, in the country of that other Party, subject to the retention of a royalty-free, non-exclusive, irrevocable license, with the right to grant sublicenses, for all purposes; and

(c) grant to the other Party a royalty-free, non-exclusive, irrevocable license, with the right to grant sublicenses, for all purposes in the country of the recipient Party and in third countries.

B. 1. Each Party shall, to the extent owned by it, or any agency or corporation owned or controlled thereby, grant to the other Party a royalty-free, non-exclusive, irrevocable license to manufacture and use the subject matter covered by any patent and incorporated in the submarine propulsion plant and spare parts transferred pursuant to paragraph A of Article III for use by the licensed Party for the purposes set forth in paragraph C of Article V.

2. The transferring party neither warrants nor represents that the submarine propulsion plant or any material or equipment transferred under Article III does not infringe any patent owned or controlled by other persons and assumes no liability or obligation with respect thereto, and the recipient Party agrees to indemnify and hold harmless the transferring Party from any and all liability arising out of any infringement of any such patent.

C. With respect to any invention or discovery, or patent thereon, or license or sublicense therein, covered by paragraph A of this Article, each Party:

1. may, to the extent of its right, title and interest therein, deal with the same in its own and third countries as it may desire, but shall in no event discriminate against citizens of the other Party in respect of granting any license or sublicense under the patents owned by it in its own or any other country;

2. hereby waives any and all claims against the other Party for compensation, royalty or award, and hereby releases the other Party with respect to any and all such claims.

D. 1. No patent application with respect to any classified invention or discovery employing classified information which has been communicated or exchanged pursuant to Article II, or derived from the submarine propulsion plant, material or equipment transferred pursuant to Article III, may be filed:

(a) by either Party or any person in the country of the other Party except in accordance with agreed conditions and procedures; or

(b) in any country not a party to this Agreement except as may be agreed and subject to Articles VI and VII.

2. Appropriate secrecy or prohibition orders shall be issued for the purpose of giving effect to this paragraph.

ARTICLE X

Previous Agreements for Cooperation

Effective from the date on which the present Agreement enters into force, the cooperation between the Parties being carried out under or envisaged by the Agreement for Cooperation Regarding Atomic Information for Mutual Defense Purposes, which was signed at Washington on June 15, 1955,[6] and by paragraph B of Article I bis of the Agreement

[6] *Department of State Bulletin*, v. 33 (July 11, 1955), pp. 63-64.

for Cooperation on Civil Uses of Atomic Energy, which was signed at Washington on June 15, 1955,[7] as amended by the Amendment signed at Washington on June 13, 1956,[8] shall be carried out in accordance with the provisions of the present Agreement.

ARTICLE XI

Definitions

For the purposes of this Agreement:

A. "Atomic weapon" means any device utilizing atomic energy, exclusive of the means of transporting or propelling the device (where such means is a separable and divisible part of the device), the principal purpose of which is for use as, or for development of, a weapon, a weapon prototype, or a weapon test device.

B. "Classified information" means information, data, materials, services or any other matter with the security designation "Confidential" or higher applied under the legislation or regulations of either the United States or the United Kingdom, including that designated by the Government of the United States as "Restricted Data" or "Formerly Restricted Data" and that designated by the Government of the United Kingdom as "ATOMIC".

C. "Equipment" means any instrument, apparatus or facility and includes any facility, except an atomic weapon, capable of making use of or producing special nuclear material and component parts thereof, and includes submarine nuclear propulsion plant, reactor and military reactor.

D. "Military reactor" means a reactor for the propulsion of naval vessels, aircraft or land vehicles and military package power reactors.

E. "Person" means:

1. any individual, corporation, partnership, firm, association, trust, estate, public or private institution, group, government agency or government corporation other than the United States Atomic Energy Commission and the United Kingdom Atomic Energy Authority; and

2. any legal successor, representative, agent or agency of the foregoing.

[7] Department of State, Treaties and Other International Acts Series 3321.
[8] *Ibid.*, 3608.

F. "Reactor" means an apparatus, other than an atomic weapon, in which a self-supporting fission chain reaction is maintained and controlled by utilizing uranium, plutonium or thorium, or any combination of uranium, plutonium or thorium.

G. "Submarine nuclear propulsion plant" means a propulsion plant and includes the reactor, and such control, primary, auxiliary, steam and electric systems as may be necessary for propulsion of submarines.

H. References in this Agreement to the Government of the United Kingdom include the United Kingdom Atomic Energy Authority.

ARTICLE XII

Duration

This Agreement shall enter into force on the date on which each Government shall have received from the other Government written notification that it has complied with all statutory and constitutional requirements for the entry into force of this Agreement,[9] and shall remain in force until terminated by agreement of both Parties, except that, if not so terminated, Article II may be terminated by agreement of both Parties, or by either Party on one year's notice to the other to take effect at the end of a term of ten years, or thereafter on one year's notice to take effect at the end of any succeeding term of five years.

IN WITNESS WHEREOF, the undersigned, duly authorized, have signed this Agreement.

DONE at Washington this third day of July, 1958, in two original texts.

For the Government of the United States of America:

JOHN FOSTER DULLES
Secretary of State

For the Government of the United Kingdom of Great Britain and Northern Ireland:

HOOD
Her Majesty's Chargé d'Affaires a. i.

[9] The treaty entered into force on August 4, 1958.

D. France.

(15) Joint Announcement by the Treasury Department, the Department of State and the Export-Import Bank, January 30, 1958.[1]

Discussions on the French financial situation have been held in Washington during the past two weeks between officials and agencies of the Government of the United States and a French financial mission headed by M. Jean Monnet.

The United States has been represented in these talks by the Secretary of the Treasury, Mr. Robert B. Anderson; the Deputy Under Secretary of State for Economic Affairs, Mr. C. Douglas Dillon; and the President of the Export-Import Bank, Mr. Samuel C. Waugh.

The representatives of the French Government have simultaneously conducted similar discussions with the International Monetary Fund, in Washington, and the European Payments Union, in Paris.

All of these discussions were completed today.

During the discussions the French representatives have described the financial program which has been adopted by the French Government and Parliament for the purpose of eliminating inflation, achieving equilibrium in the French balance-of-payments, and restoring financial stability. This program is described in the statement which has been issued today by the French Government.

In view of the financial program adopted by France, the European Payments Union will extend to France credits equivalent to $250,000,000;[2] the International Monetary Fund has agreed to make available to France the equivalent of $131,250,000;[3] and the United States has agreed to extend to France certain financial facilities amounting to $274,000,-000.

The amounts to be provided by these three sources total $655,250,000, which will assist the French Government in carrying through the financial program it has adopted.

The financial facilities being extended to France by the Government of the United States consist of the following arrangements:

[1] *Department of State Bulletin*, v. 38 (February 17, 1958), pp. 269-270.
[2] *Ibid.* p. 271.
[3] *Ibid.*

Agreement relating to the refunding, at maturity date, of the
next four semi-annual installments of principal on prior Export-Import Bank loans $96 million
Agreement relating to the postponement of 3 annual installments, as to principal and interest, on prior Lend-lease and
Surplus Property credits $90 million
Agreements for the shipment to France of cotton under Pub-
lice Law 480 and Section 402 of the Mutual Security Act (to
be completed) $43 million
Agreement for the sale, for francs, of United States military
supplies and equipment for French NATO forces in Europe,
up to $45 million

$274 million

The details of the arrangements provided through the
European Payments Union and the International Monetary
Fund are being announced by the two international institu-
tions.

E. Italy.

(16) *Joint Statement on Talks Held between the
President and the President of the Council of
Ministers of Italy (Fanfani), July 30, 1958.*[1]

The President of the United States, the President of the
Council of Ministers of the Italian Republic, who is also
Minister of Foreign Affairs, and the Secretary of State of the
United States have concluded two days of discussion on a wide
range of topics of mutual interest to their two countries.
Other governmental representatives on both sides took part
in particular phases of the discussions. In an atmosphere of
friendship and understanding they examined the present
world situation, including the Middle East and the problems
surrounding a possible meeting of Heads of Government
within the framework of the United Nations.

The President, the Secretary of State and the Prime Minister exchanged views on the recent developments in the Middle East and found themselves in satisfactory accord. They
also agreed on the importance of the position of Italy with
respect to its interest in the Mediterranean and in the Middle East, and hence on the importance of insuring means
whereby Italy's views may be taken into account on a continuing basis. They arranged to remain in close contact.

The President and the Italian Prime Minister reaffirmed
the dedication of their countries to the North Atlantic Alliance and to the United Nations established to defend the

[1] *Department of State Bulletin*, v. 39 (August 18, 1958), p. 287.

peace and to protect the right of peopels to live in freedom under governments of their own choosing. They reiterated their firm conviction that the combined strength and coordinated action of the free and independent countries of the North Atlantic Alliance are vital to their peace and security, and will remain a cornerstone of their foreign policies.

The President and the Secretary of State expressed full recognition of the contribution being made by Italy in the development of closer political and economic association between the countries of Europe for the purpose of improving the well-being of their peoples.

The Prime Minister outlined the program he proposes with regard to his country's economic problems, including foreign trade. The representatives of the United States expressed their appreciation and their confidence that increased economic ties between the United States and Italy might contribute favorably to this program.

In conclusion the President expressed his gratification with the Prime Minister's visit to Washington and for the opportunity thus provided for a friendly and constructive exchange of views. The Prime Minister in turn voiced his satisfaction at being able, following the assumption of his high offices, to renew his acquaintance with the President and the Secretary of State.

F. Turkey.

(17) *Joint United States-Turkish Statement Concerning Financial Assistance to Turkey, Paris, July 31, 1958.*[1]

Representatives of the United States and Turkey, meeting in Paris, today completed discussions relating to financial assistance to Turkey.

The Government of the United States was represented by Ambassador W. Randolph Burgess, U.S. Representative to the Organization for European Economic Cooperation, and Assistant Secretary of the Treasury Laurence B. Robbins. The Government of Turkey was represented by the Minister of Foreign Affairs F. R. Zorlu and the Minister of Finance H. Polatkan.

During these discussions the Turkish Government informed the Government of the United States that Turkey had

[1] *Ibid.* (August 25, 1958), pp. 322-323.

advised the International Monetary Fund and the Organization or European Economic Cooperation of the decision of the Turkish Government to adopt a comprehensive financial program designed to eliminate inflation and restore financial stability.

As a consequence of the financial program undertaken by Turkey, Government members of the OEEC and the European Payments Union, acting under the aegis of the OEEC, intend to extend to Turkey credits equivalent to $100,000,000.[2] The International Monetary Fund has agreed to make available to Turkey the equivalent of $25,000,000,[3] and the United States has agreed to extend to Turkey certain financial facilities amounting to $234,000,000.

The total of $359,000,000 in financial facilities to be provided Turkey from these three sources is designed to take account of the Turkish balance-of-payments situation, particularly during the next twelve months, and to enable the Turkish Government to carry into effect the financial program which it has decided upon.

Also, the Governments concerned have agreed to confer at an early date, under the aegis of the OEEC, with a view to rearranging Turkey's short-term debt so that repayment of this debt will be spread over a period in the light of Turkey's ability to pay.

The financial facilities to be provided Turkey by the United States would consist of the following:

1. Special grant assistance to Turkey in meeting immediate balance-of-payments needs[4]	$ 25,000,000
2. Development assistance to be extended by lending institutions of the United States Government for loans on agreed projects in such fields as solid fuels, power, minerals, manufacturing industries and transportation[4]	75,000,000
3. Defense support assistance during fiscal year 1959[4]	75,000,000
4. Postponement of 20 semi-annual installments as to principal and interest, on 3 ECA-MSA loans to Turkey of 1948, 1949 and 1952	44,000,000
5. Sale to Turkey, for payment in liras, of agricultural products to be agreed upon (subject to the extension by Congress of the Agricultural Trade Development and Assistance Act), estimated at an export value of not less than	15,000,000
	$234,000,000

[2] The OEEC announcement of the extension of credit was made on August 4, 1958. *Ibid.,* p. 323.
[3] The IMF announcement of the extension credit was made on August 3, 1958. *Ibid.*
[4] It is understood that that part of the assistance described in these headings that is to be provided under the Mutual Security Act would be subject to Congressional appropriations for Mutual Security for use beginning in fiscal year 1959 [footnote in original].

G. Cyprus.

(18) *Statement by the Prime Minister of the United Kingdom (Macmillan) in the House of Commons Outlining Policy Proposals for Cyprus, June 19, 1958.*[1]

(Excerpt)

*   *   *

The policy of Her Majesty's Government in Cyprus has had four main purposes:

(a) To serve the best interests of all the people of the island;

(b) To achieve a permanent settlement acceptable to the two communities in the island and to the Greek and Turkish Governments;

(c) To safeguard the British bases and installations in the island, which are necessary to enable the United Kingdom to carry out her international obligations;

(d) To strengthen peace and security, and cooperation between the United Kingdom and her allies, in a vital area.

These are the aims which Her Majesty's Government have consistently pursued and which have guided their efforts in recent months to find common ground on which an agreed settlement might be reached. It is deeply regretted that all attempts in this direction have hitherto proved unsuccessful.

In view of the disagreement between the Greek and Turkish Governments and between the two communities in Cyprus, and of the disastrous consequences for all concerned if violence and conflict continue, an obligation rests with the United Kingdom Government, as the sovereign power responsible for the administration of the island and the well-being of its inhabitants, to give a firm and clear lead out of the present deadlock. They accordingly declare a new policy which represents an adventure in partnership—partnership between the communities in the island and also between the Governments of the United Kingdom, Greece and Turkey.

The following is an outline of the partnership plan:

[1] House of Commons, Parliamentary Debates, *Weekly Hansard*, No. 427 (June 13-19, 1958), cols. 1321-1324.

I. Cyprus should enjoy the advantages of association not only with the United Kingdom, and therefore with the British Commonwealth, but also with Greece and Turkey. II. Since the three Governments of the United Kingdom, Greece and Turkey all have an interest in Cyprus, Her Majesty's Government will welcome the co-operation and participation of the two other Governments in a joint effort to achieve the peace, progress and prosperity of the Island. III. The Greek and Turkish Governments will each be invited to appoint a representative to co-operate with the Governor in carrying out this policy. IV. The Island will have a system of representing Government with each community exercising autonomy in its own communal affairs. V. In order to satisfy the desire of the Greek and Turkish Cypriots to be recognized as Greeks and Turks, Her Majesty's Government will welcome an arrangement which gives them Greek or Turkish nationality, while enabling them to retain British nationality. VI. To allow time for the new principle of partnership to be fully worked out and brought into operation under this plan in the necessary atmosphere of stability, the international status of the Island will remain unchanged for seven years. VII. A system of representative government and communal autonomy will be worked out by consultation with representatives of the two communities and with the representatives of the Greek and Turkish Governments. VIII. The essential provisions of the new constitution will be:

(a) There will be a separate House of Representatives for each of the two communities, and these Houses will have final legislative authority in communal affairs.
(b) Authority for internal administration, other than communal affairs and internal security, will be undertaken by a Council presided over by the Governor and including the representatives of the Greek and Turkish Governments and six elected Ministers drawn from the Houses of Representatives, four being Greek Cypriots and two Turkish Cypriots.
(c) The Governor, acting after consultation with the representatives of the Greek and Turkish Govern-

ments, will have reserve powers to ensure that the interests of both communities are protected.

(d) External affairs, defence and internal security will be matters specifically reserved to the Governor acting after consultation with the representatives of the Greek and Turkish Governments.

(e) The representatives of the Greek and Turkish Governments will have the right to require any legislation which they consider to be discriminatory to be reserved for consideration by an impartial tribunal.

IX. If the full benefits of this policy are to be realized, it is evident that violence must cease. Subject to this, Her Majesty's Government intend to take progressive steps to relax the Emergency Regulations and eventually to end the State of Emergency. This process would include the return of those Cypriots at present excluded from the Island under the Emergency Regulations.

X. A policy based on these principles and proposals will give the people of the Island a specially favoured and protected status. Through representative institutions they will exercise authority in the management of the Island's internal affairs, and each community will control its own communal affairs. While the people of the Island enjoy these advantages, friendly relations and practical co-operation between the United Kingdom, Greece and Turkey will be maintained and strengthened as Cyprus becomes a symbol of co-operation instead of a cause of conflict between the three Allied Governments.

Her Majesty's Government trust that this imaginative plan will be welcomed by all concerned in the spirit in which it is put forward, and for their part they will bend all efforts to ensuring its success. Indeed, if the Greek and Turkish Governments were willing to extend this experiment in partnership and co-operation, Her Majesty's Government would be prepared, at the appropriate time, to go further and, subject to the reservation to the United Kingdom of such bases and facilities as might be necessary for the discharge of her international obligations, to share the sovereignty of the Island with their Greek and Turkish allies as their contribution to a lasting settlement.[2]

[2] Following consultations with the Greek and Turkish Prime Ministers, the Prime Minister of the United Kingdom (Macmillan) modified the policy proposals for Cyprus on August 15, 1958.

(19) *Statement by the Prime Minister of the United Kingdom (Macmillan) in the House of Commons, December 10, 1958.*[3]

(Excerpt)

*   *   *

After two weeks of debate on the Cyprus question the General Assembly of the United Nations has passed a short resolution in very general terms.[4] At one time there were seven different draft resolutions before the Political Committee. Some of these would have been acceptable to us, others we thought, pointed too much in the direction of a particular final solution.

The Minister of State for Foreign Affairs took the opportunity of the debate in the United Nations to give a full explanation of our policy. He described in detail the British Plan with which the House is familiar. He also explained the lengths to which Her Majesty's Government have gone in their endeavors to reach an agreement for the holding of a conference at which the British Plan could be discussed and amendments to it agreed, and at which the final solution could also be discussed. We still believe that useful progress could be made through a conference either confined to the parties directly concerned—including of course Cypriot representatives—or with the assistane of others chosen by agreement.

The proceedings in the General Assembly revealed a wide measure of understanding of the complexity of the Cyprus problem and not a little sympathy for the efforts which Her Majesty's Government have made to deal with it. They also, I think, revealed some reluctance on the part of many of those not directly concerned with the problem to try to lay down the conditions on which a settlement should be sought. The resolution finally adopted avoided this and simply expressed confidence that continued efforts would be made by the parties to reach a peaceful, democratic, and just solution

[3] House of Commons, Parliamentary Debates, *Weekly Hansard*, No. 440 (December 5-11, 1958), cols. 345-347.
[4] General Assembly Resolution 1287 (XIII), United Nations General Assembly, *Official Records, Thirteenth Session*, Supplement No. 18(A/4090), p. 5.

in accordance with the Charter of the United Nations. That is certainly our hope.

It is right that a little time should now be allowed for the Governments concerned to consider their position in the light of the United Nations debate. Next week, in Paris, there is a Ministerial Meeting of the North Atlantic Council which will be attended by My Right Honorable and Learned Friend, the Foreign Secretary and I have every expectation that the Foreign Ministers of Greece and Turkey will be present. No doubt advantage will be taken of this occasion for confidential discussions between those who have been principally concerned. I feel sure that this approach is the most likely to be fruitful.

As we have already made clear, we are ready to discuss with our Greek and Turkish allies the interim arrangements for the administration of Cyprus described in my statements of the 19th of June and the 15th of August and we are willing, as we have said, to put into effect any amendments to our announced policy on which agreement can be reached. These offers remain open and can be taken up at any time. We regretted that the Greek Government did not feel able to agree to a conference on the lines discussed in N.A.T.O. last October. But the position may now have changed. In any case, we continue to hope that, in time, the Greek Government will see the advantages to the Greek Cypriots and to Greece of the offers which we have made to them.

Whatever the difficulties, progress has been made in narrowing the area of dispute. For our part we shall do our utmost to reach agreement.

CHAPTER THREE

EAST-WEST RELATIONS: DISARMAMENT, EUROPEAN SECURITY, GERMANY

A. Exchange of Correspondence between the President and the Chairman of the Council of Ministers of the USSR (Bulganin).

(20) Letter from the President, January 12, 1958.[1]

DEAR MR. CHAIRMAN: When on December 10 I received your communication, I promptly acknowledged it with the promise that I would in due course give you a considered reply.[2] I now do so.

Your communication seems to fall into three parts: the need for peace; your contention that peace is endangered by the collective self-defense efforts of free world nations; and your specific proposals. I shall respond in that same order and make my own proposals.

I.

Peace and good will among men have been the heartfelt desire of peoples since time immemorial. But professions of peace by governmental leaders have not always been a dependable guide to their actual intentions. Moreover, it seems to me to be profitless for us to debate the question of which of our two governments wants peace the more. Both of us have asserted that our respective peoples ardently desire peace and perhaps you and I feel this same urge equally. The heart of the matter becomes the determination of the terms on which the maintenance of peace can be assured, and the confidence that each of us can justifiably feel that these terms will be respected.

In the United States the people and their government desire peace and in this country the people exert such constitutional control over government that no government could possibly initiate aggressive war. Under authority already given by our Congress, the United States can and would respond at once if we or any of our allies were attacked. But the United States cannot initiate war without the prior

[1] *Department of State Bulletin*, v. 38 (January 27, 1958), pp. 122-127.
[2] *Documents on American Foreign Relations, 1957*, pp. 81-90.

approval of the peoples' representatives in the Congress. This
process requires time and public debate. Not only would our
people repudiate any effort to begin an attack, but the element of surprise, so important in any aggressive move, would
be wholly lacking. Aggressive war by us is not only abhorrent;
it is impractical and impossible.

The past forty years provide an opportunity to judge the
comparative peace records of our two systems. We gladly
submit our national record for respecting peace to the impartial judgment of mankind. I can assure you, Mr. Chairman, that in the United States the waging of peace has priority in every aspect, and every element, of our national life.

II.

You argue that the danger of war is increased because the
United States and other free world nations seek security on
a collective basis and on the basis of military preparedness.
Three times in this century wars have occurred under circumstances which strongly suggest, if indeed they do not prove,
that war would not have occurred had the United States been
militarily strong and committed in advance to the defense
of nations that were attacked.

On each of these three occasions when war came, the
United States was militarily unprepared, or ill-prepared, and
it was not known that the United States would go to the aid
of those subjected to armed aggression. Yet now it appears,
Mr. Chairman, that you contend that weakness and disunity
would make war less likely.

I may be permitted perhaps to recall that in March 1939,
when the Soviet Union felt relatively weak and threatened by
Fascist aggression, it contended that aggression was rife because "the majority of the non-aggressive countries, particularly England and France, have rejected the policy of
collective security," and Stalin went on to say that the policy
of "Let each country defend itself as it likes and as best it
can . . . means conniving at aggression, giving free rein to
war."

Now the Soviet Union is no longer weak or confronted by
powerful aggressive forces. The vast Sino-Soviet bloc em-
braces nearly one billion people and large resources. Such a
bloc would of course be dominant in the world were the free
world nations to be disunited.

It is natural that any who want to impose their system on
the world should prefer that those outside that system should

be weak and divided. But that expansionist policy cannot be sanctified by protestations of peace.

Of course the United States would greatly prefer it if collective security could be obtained on a universal basis through the United Nations.

This was the hope when in 1945 our two governments and others signed the Charter of the United Nations, conferring upon its Security Council primary responsibility for the maintenance of international peace and security. Also, by that Charter we agreed to make available to the Security Council armed forces, assistance and facilities so that the Council could maintain and restore international peace and security.

The Soviet Union has persistently prevented the establishment of such a universal collective security system and has, by its use of the veto—now 82 times—made the Security Council undependable as a protector of the peace.

The possibility that the Security Council might become undependable was feared at the San Francisco Conference on World Organization, and accordingly the Charter recognized that, in addition to reliance on the Security Council, the nations possessed and might exercise an inherent right of collective self-defense. It has therefore been found not only desirable but necessary, if the free nations are to be secure and safe, to concert their defensive measures.

I can and do give you, Mr. Chairman, two solemn and categorical assurances.

(1) *Never* will the United States lend its support to any aggressive action by any collective defense organization or any member thereof;

(2) *Always* will the United States be ready to move toward the development of effective United Nations collective security measures in replacement of regional collective defense measures.

I turn now to consider your specific proposals.

III.

I am compelled to conclude after the most careful study of your proposals that they seem to be unfortunately inexact or incomplete in their meaning and inadequate as a program for productive negotiations for peace.

You first seem to assume that the obligations of the Charter are non-existent and that the voice of the United Nations is nothing that we need to heed.

You suggest that we should agree to respect the independ-

ence of the countries of the Near and Middle East and renounce the use of force in the settlement of questions relating
to the Near and Middle East. But by the Charter of the
United Nations we have already taken precisely those obligations as regards all countries, including those of the Near and
Middle East. Our profound hope is that the Soviets feel themselves as bound by the provisions of the Charter, as, I assure
you, we feel bound.

You also suggest submitting to the member states of NATO
and the Warsaw Pact some form of non-aggression agreement.
But all of the members of NATO are already bound to the
United Nations Charter provision against aggression.

You suggest that the United States, the United Kingdom
and the Soviet Union should undertake not to use *nuclear*
weapons. But our three nations and others have already undertaken, by the Charter, not to use *any* weapons against the
territorial integrity or political independence of any state.
Our profound hope is that no weapons will be used by any
country for such an indefensible purpose and that the Soviet
Union will feel a similar aversion to any kind of aggression.

You suggest that we should proclaim our intention to
develop between us relations of friendship and peace cooperation. Such an intention is indeed already proclaimed
as between ourselves and others by the Charter of the United
Nations to which we have subscribed. The need is, not to
repeat what we already proclaim, but, Mr. Chairman,
to take concrete steps under the present terms of the Charter,
that will bring about these relations of friendship and peaceful cooperation. As recently as last November, the Communist Party of the Soviet Union signed and proclaimed to
the world a declaration which was designed to promote the
triumph of Communism throughout the world by every means
not excluding violence, and which contained many slanderous
references to the United States.[3] I am bound to point out
that such a declaration is difficult to reconcile with professions of a desire for friendship or indeed of peaceful co-
existence. This declaration makes clear where responsibility
for the "Cold War" lies.

You propose that we broaden the ties between us of a
"scientific, cultural and athletic" character. But already our
two countries are negotiating for peaceful contacts even
broader than "scientific, cultural and athletic." We hope for

[3] *Ibid.*, pp. 150-157.

a positive result, even though in 1955, after the Summit Conference, when negotiations for such contacts were pressed by our Foreign Ministers at Geneva, the accomplishments were zero. It is above all important that our peoples should learn the true facts about each other. An informed public opinion in both our countries is essential to the proper understanding of our discussions.

You propose that we develop "normal" trade relations as part of the "peaceful cooperation" of which you speak. We welcome trade that carries no political or warlike implications. We do have restrictions on dealings in goods which are of war significance, but we impose no obstacles to peaceful trade.

Your remaining proposals relate to armament. In this connection, I note with deep satisfaction that you oppose "competition in the production of ever newer types of weapons." When I read that statement I expected to go on to read proposals to stop such production. But I was disappointed.

You renew the oft-repeated Soviet proposal that the United States, the United Kingdom and the Soviet Union should cease for two or three years to test nuclear weapons; and you suggest that nuclear weapons should not be stationed or produced in Germany. You add the possibility that Poland and Czechoslovakia might be added to this non-nuclear weapons area.

These proposals do not serve to meet the real problem of armament. The heart of that problem is, as you say, the mounting *production*, primarily by the Soviet Union and the United States, of new types of weapons.

Your proposal regarding Central Europe will of course be studied by NATO and the NATO countries directly involved from the standpoint of its military and political implications. But there cannot be great significance in denuclearizing a small area when, as you say, "the range of modern types of weapons does not know of any geographical limit," and when you defer to the indefinite future any measures to stop the production of such weapons.

I note, furthermore, that your proposal on Germany is in no way related to the ending of the division of that country but would, in fact, tend to perpetuate that division. It is unrealistic thus to ignore the basic link between political solutions and security arrangements.

Surely, Mr. Chairman, at a time when we share great responsibility for shaping the development of the international situation, we can and must do better than what you propose.

In this spirit, I submit some proposals of my own.

IV.

(1) I propose that we strengthen the United Nations.

This organization and the pledges of its members embodied in the Charter constitute man's best hope for peace and justice. The United States feels bound by its solemn undertaking to act in accordance with the Principles of the Charter. Will not the Soviet Union clear away the doubt that it also feels bound by its Charter undertakings? And may we not perhaps go further and build up the authority of the United Nations?

Too often its recommendations go unheeded.

I propose, Mr. Chairman, that we should rededicate ourselves to the United Nations, its Principles and Purposes and to our Charter obligations. But I would do more.

Too often the Security Council is prevented, by veto, from discharging the primary responsibility we have given it for the maintenance of international peace and security. This prevention even extends to proposing procedures for the pacific settlement of disputes.

I propose that we should make it the policy of our two governments at least not to use veto power to prevent the Security Council from proposing methods for the pacific settlement of disputes pursuant to Chapter VI.

Nothing, I am convinced, would give the world more justifiable hope than the conviction that both of our governments are genuinely determined to make the United Nations the effective instrument of peace and justice that was the original design.

(2) If confidence is to be restored, there needs, above all, to be confidence in the pledged word. To us it appears that such confidence is lamentably lacking. That is conspicuously so in regard to two areas where the situation is a cause of grave international concern.

I refer first of all to Germany. This was the principal topic of our meeting of July 1955 and the only substantive agreement which was recorded in our agreed Directive was this:[4]

"The Heads of Government, recognizing their common responsibility for the settlement of the German question and the re-unification of Germany, have agreed the settle-

[4] *Ibid., 1955,* pp. 225-227.

ment of the German question and the re-unification of Germany by means of free elections shall be carried out in conformity with the national interests of the German people and the interests of European security."

In spite of our urging, your government has, for now two and one half years, taken no steps to carry out that agreement or to discharge that recognized responsibility. Germany remains forcibly divided.

This constitutes a great error, incompatible with European security. It also undermines confidence in the sanctity of our international agreements.

I therefore urge that we now proceed vigorously to bring about the reunification of Germany by free elections, as we agreed, and as the situation urgently demands.

I assure you that this act of simple justice and of good faith need not lead to any increased jeopardy of your nation. The consequences would be just the opposite and would surely lead to greater security. In connection with the re-unification of Germany, the United States is prepared, along with others, to negotiate specific arrangements regarding force levels and deployments, and broad treaty undertakings, not merely against aggression but assuring positive reaction should aggression occur in Europe.

The second situation to which I refer is that of the countries of Eastern Europe. The Heads of our two Governments, together with the Prime Minister of the United Kingdom, agreed in 1945 that the peoples of these countries should have the right to choose the form of government under which they would live, and that our three countries had a responsibility in this respect. The three of us agreed to foster the conditions under which these peoples could exercise their right of free choice.

That agreement has not as yet been fulfilled.

I know that your government is reluctant to discuss these matters or to treat them as a matter of international concern. But the Heads of Governments did agree at Yalta in 1945 that these matters *were* of international concern and we specifically agreed that there could appropriately be international consultation with reference to them.

This was another matter taken up at our meeting in Geneva in 1955. You then took the position that there were no grounds for discussing this question at our conference and that it would involve interference in the internal affairs of the Eastern European states.

But have not subsequent developments shown that I was justified in my appeal to you for consideration of these matters? Surely the Hungarian developments and the virtually unanimous action of the United Nations General Assembly in relation thereto show that conditions in Eastern Europe are regarded throughout the world as much more than a matter of purely domestic scope.

I propose that we should now discuss this matter. There is an intrinsic need of this in the interest of peace and justice, which seems to me compelling.

(3) I now make, Mr. Chairman, a proposal to solve what I consider to be the most important problem which faces the world today.

(a) I propose that we agree that outer space should be used only for peaceful purposes. We face a decisive moment in history in relation to this matter. Both the Soviet Union and the United States are now using outer space for the testing of missiles designed for military purposes. The time to stop is now.

I recall to you that a decade ago, when the United States had a monopoly of atomic weapons and of atomic experience, we offered to renounce the making of atomic weapons and to make the use of atomic energy an international asset for peaceful purposes only. If only that offer had been accepted by the Soviet Union, there would not now be the danger from nuclear weapons which you describe.

The nations of the world face today another choice perhaps even more momentous than that of 1948. That relates to the use of outer space. Let us this time, and in time, make the right choice, the peaceful choice.

There are about to be perfected and produced powerful new weapons which, availing of outer space, will greatly increase the capacity of the human race to destroy itself. If indeed it be the view of the Soviet Union that we should not go on producing ever newer types of weapons, can we not stop the production of such weapons which would use or, more accurately, misuse, outer space, now for the first time opening up as a field for man's exploration? Should not outer space be dedicated to the peaceful uses of mankind and denied to the purpose of war? That is my proposal.

(b) Let us also end the now unrestrained production of nuclear weapons. This too would be responsive to your urging against "the production of ever newer types of weapons". It is possible to assure that newly produced fissionable material should not be used for weapons purposes. Also existing weapons stocks can be steadily reduced by ascertainable transfers to peaceful purposes. Since our existing weapons stocks are doubtless larger than yours we would expect to make a greater transfer than you to peaceful purposes stocks. I should be glad to receive your suggestion as to what you consider to be an equitable ratio in this respect.

(c) I propose that, as part of such a program which will reliably check and reverse the accumulation of nuclear weapons, we stop the testing of nuclear weapons, not just for two or three years, but indefinitely. So long as the accumulation of these weapons continues unchecked, it is better that we should be able to devise weapons which will be primarily significant from a military and defensive standpoint and progressively eliminate weapons which could destroy, through fall-out, vast segments of human life. But if the production is to be stopped and the trend reversed, as I propose, then testing is no longer so necessary.

(d) Let us at the same time take steps to begin the controlled and progressive reduction of conventional weapons and military manpower.

(e) I also renew my proposal that we begin progressively to take measures to guarantee against the possibility of surprise attack. I recall, Mr. Chairman, that we began to discuss this at our personal meeting two and a half years ago, but nothing has happened although there is open a wide range of choices as to where to begin.

The capacity to verify the fulfillment of commitments is of the essence in all these matters, including the reduction of conventional forces and weapons, and it would surely be useful for us to study together through technical groups what are the possibilities in this respect upon which we could build if we then decide to do so. These technical studies could, if you wish, be undertaken without commitment as to ultimate acceptance, or as to the interdependence, of the propositions involved. It is such technical studies of the possibilities of verification and supervision that the United Nations has proposed as a first step. I believe that this is a first step that would promote hope in both of our countries and in the world. Therefore I urge that this first step be undertaken.

V.

I have noted your conclusion, Mr. Chairman, that you attach great importance to personal contact between statesmen and that you for your part would be prepared to come to an agreement on a personal meeting of state leaders to discuss both the problems mentioned in your letter and other problems.

I too believe that such personal contacts can be of value. I showed that by coming to Geneva in the summer of 1955. I have repeatedly stated that there is nothing I would not do to advance the cause of a just and durable peace.

But meetings between us do not automatically produce good results. Preparatory work, with good will on both sides, is a prerequisite to success. High level meetings, in which we both participate, create great expectations and for that reason involve a danger of disillusionment, dejection and increased distrust if in fact the meetings are ill-prepared, if they evade the root causes of danger, if they are used primarily for propaganda, or if agreements arrived at are not fulfilled.

Consequently, Mr. Chairman, this is my proposal:

I am ready to meet with the Soviet leaders to discuss the proposals mentioned in your letter and the proposals which I make, with the attendance as appropriate of leaders of other states which have recognized responsibilities in relation to one or another of the subjects we are to discuss. It would be essential that prior to such a meeting these complex matters should be worked on in advance through diplomatic channels and by our Foreign Ministers, so that the issues can be presented in form suitable for our decisions and so that it can be ascertained that such a top-level meeting would, in fact, hold good hope of advancing the cause of peace and justice in the world. Arrangements should also be made for the appropriate inclusion, in the preparatory work, of other governments to which I allude.

I have made proposals which seem to me to be worthy of our attention and which correspond to the gravity of our times. They deal with the basic problems which press upon us and which if unresolved would make it ever more difficult to maintain the peace. The Soviet leaders by giving evidence of a genuine intention to resolve these basic problems can make an indispensable contribution to clearing away the obstacles to those friendly relations and peaceful pursuits which the peoples of all the world demand.

Sincerely,

DWIGHT D. EISENHOWER

(21) *Letter from the Chairman of the Council of Ministers of the USSR (Bulganin), February 1, 1958.*[5]

DEAR MR. PRESIDENT: I received your reply to my message of December 10 last as well as your communication to the effect that you had received my message of January 8, 1958.[6] While awaiting your reply with regard to the substance of my message of January 8 and of the proposals of the Soviet Government on matters pertaining to the lessening of international tension, I shall take the liberty to present certain considerations which have arisen in connection with your message.

First of all, I should like to inform you that we in Moscow have received with gratification your agreement with our opinion concerning the usefulness of personal contacts between statesmen of various countries which you have expressed, as well as your readiness to meet with Soviet leaders and the leaders of other appropriate states concerned for the purpose of conducting negotiations.

We also note that you share our opinion that its is desirable that the proposed summit meeting be successful. It is from these considerations, as I have already informed you, that the Soviet Government proceeded in developing concrete proposals to conduct the meeting. We propose that the attention of participants at the top level be concentrated on the most urgent problems, with regard to which the known positions of states provide a certain degree of assurance as to their positive solution at this time. This is why the Soviet Government proposes, as you know, that such problems as the following be discussed at the meeting:

Immediate suspension of atomic and hydrogen weapons tests; renunciation by the U.S.S.R., the United States, and the United Kingdom of the use of nuclear weapons;

Creation in Central Europe of a zone free of atomic weapons;

Conclusion of a nonaggression pact between the NATO member states and states party to the Warsaw Treaty;

Reduction in the number of foreign troops stationed in the territory of Germany and within the borders of other European states;

---

[5] *Department of State Bulletin,* v. 38 (March 10, 1958), pp. 376-380.
[6] Not printed.

Development of an agreement on question pertaining to the prevention of sudden attack;

Measures to expand international trade ties;

Discontinuation of propaganda for war; and

Ways and means for lessening the tension in the Near and Middle East area.

In addition, as is indicated in the proposals of the Soviet Government of January 8, the meeting could discuss other constructive proposals directed towards terminating the "cold war" which may be presented by other participants in the meeting. It is obvious that there must be unanimous agreement of all participants as to the necessity for considering such proposals.

As to problems with regard to which there is, at this time, little foundation for counting on their mutually acceptable solution, the meeting could agree on the procedure for their consideration at the next stage of negotiations between states. It is our profound conviction that such a method of gradually solving international problems is, under present conditions, where the necessary trust in the relations between states is still lacking, the most realistic and promising. There is no doubt that the reaching of agreements, initially at least on individual problems, would creat favorable premises for setting other unsolved international problems also.

Let us take as an example the proposal for an immediate suspension of atomic and hydrogen weapons tests even for a period of two or three years. The urgency of the solution of this matter is obvious. It was again most forcefully emphasized in the petition of 9,235 scientists from 44 countries, which was addressed to the Secretary General of the United Nations, Mr. Hammarskjold, a few days ago and which calls for an immediate suspension of nuclear weapons tests. This petition, which was signed, in particular, by 101 members of the National Academy of Science of the United States and 216 Soviet scientists, states that each nuclear bomb test increases the amount of radioactive particles which are harmful to the health of people on the entire globe.

At the same time it is known that the majority of states, including powers possessing nuclear weapons, recognize in principle the necessity of reaching agreement on this matter. If we take into account the fact that the implementation of control over the fulfillment by states of commitments undertaken by them with regard to a suspension of nuclear weapons tests is comparatively easy and that such a step gives none of the states possessing nuclear weapons any advantage which would prejudice the interests of other states, then it would become clear that the reaching of an agreement on this subject is fully possible at this time and depends exclusively on the states possessing nuclear weapons. As to the Soviet Union, it is, as has been repeatedly stated, prepared to suspend the testing of such weapons if other powers agree to do the same.

Are the doubts as to the significance of such an agreement justified? In our opinion they are not. In this respect we fully share the opinion of scientists who state in the above-mentioned petition that an international agreement on suspension of nuclear bomb tests at this time could serve as a first step towards more extensive disarmament and towards an ultimate effective prohibition of nuclear weapons.

We also consider the other above-mentioned problems no less important and ripe to the same degree for consideration and successful solution at this time.

In your message, Mr. President, while expressing your agreement to discuss at a summit meeting the proposals of the Soviet Government, you, on your part, propose that a number of other matters be discussed.

It is obvious that in any negotiations, the more so in negotiations at the highest possible level, only those problems which all the participants are prepared to consider should be discussed. There is hardly anyone who would object to this. However, I cannot help noting the following circumstance. While expressing your agreement to discuss at the meeting the matters suggested by the Soviet Union, you make it understood in advance that from your point of view it is not useful or necessary to reach an agreement on such matters as the proposal for a renunciation by the United States, the United Kingdom, and the U.S.S.R. of the use of nuclear weapons, the proposal to conclude a nonaggression pact between NATO member states and the states party to the Warsaw Treaty, or the proposal to renounce the use of force in solving the problems connected with the Near and Middle East. In this connection references are made to the fact that the commitments envisaged in the said proposals are covered by the commitments which are imposed by the U.N. Charter on the members of that organization.

The same argument is advanced to provide the foundation for the negative attitude, expressed in your reply message, toward the Soviet proposal that our states proclaim their firm intention to develop between themselves relations of friendship and peaceful co-operation. If the United States Government does not consider it possible or desirable to accept such a proposal, then this fact can only cause our deep regret, since the Soviet Government, which is striving consistently for peaceful coexistence and friendly cooperation with all countries, attaches in this connection an especially great significance to the improvement or relations between the USSR and the United States. In doing so we believe that the present unsatisfactory status of these relations is by no means dictated by necessity and that there are sufficient practical possibilities for a change for the better, which is in fact proven by the Agreement on Exchanges in the Fields of Culture, Technology and Education, signed by our representatives a few days ago.[7] We are convinced that an improvement in relations between our states requires active efforts by both sides and we cannot, of course, help experiencing disappointment that our proposal for making a new important step along this path is rejected by reference again to the Charter of the United Nations—a reference, the artificial nature of which is obvious.

I need not, Mr. President, put particular emphasis on the fact that the proposals of the Soviet Government advanced for the consideration of states are directed towards strengthening universal peace and are in full accord with the principles and objectives of the United Nations Charter. The implementation of the measures proposed by us would contribute to the strengthening of the United Nations, would assist it in becoming a really effective organ, protecting the cause of peace. And so far the trouble has not been in the fact that such measures were taken but rather in the fact that, contrary to the principles and objectives of the Charter of the United Nations, agreements were concluded and such organizations were created as NATO, SEATO, and the Baghdad bloc, which undermine the authority of the United Nations and in no way contribute to the lessening of international tension. If one wishes to be consistent and take the position of the United Nations Charter, then first of all it is necessary to liquidate such military grouping. However, since on the part of the Western powers there is no readiness to take such a step at this time, the Soviet Government proposes that joint decisions be made in which there would be confirmed our firm intention to support the United Nations Charter and

[7] Document 61, below.

to execute persistently such measures as would ensure the security of peoples.

We should like to emphasize that the U.N. Charter, as you well know, does not forbid and does not exclude agreements between states directed toward the realization of its principles. On the contrary, the U.N. Charter requires of all states that they strengthen and bring into existence through various acts the principles of maintaining and strengthening peace proclaimed in the Charter. As you know, with the Charter in existence, the U.N. itself adopts a number of resolutions, declarations, appeals, and other decisions, and this is very natural, as is also natural the presence of a whole series of interstate agreements directed toward guaranteeing various forms of peaceful co-operation among U.N. members.

In this connection I should like to refer also to your proposal regarding measures for strengthening the U.N. We, Mr. President, do not disagree with you that it is necessary to strengthen the U.N. and make it an effective organ of international co-operation. In our opinion, much could be done in this respect through the joint efforts of all states, primarily the great powers which are permanent members of the Security Council.

But what does your message propose? It proposes, in essence, one thing: to depart from the principle of unanimity of the great powers in the Security Council, a unanimity which is the basic pivot on which hinges the very existence of the U.N. Twelve years' experience of the activity of the U.N. has shown with all certainty that this very right of unanimity of the great powers in the Security Council ("veto") makes possible the very existence of the U.N. as an international organization for the maintenance of universal peace and prevents the adoption of important political decisions in the Security Council which would not take into account the interests of states which find themselves in the minority. The U.N. is not some kind of world government which could enact laws and adopt decisions that would be binding on all states. In the creation of the U.N. it was kept in mind, and this has been stated with full clarity in the Charter, that states become members of it voluntarily and voluntarily assume obligations to execute the demands of the Charter, while fully maintaining their independence and integrity. The U.N. Charter provides that this organization must be a center for coordinating the actions of nations and for working out mutually acceptable decisions. These ends are also served by the rule of unanimity of the great powers. The abolition of this rule would lead to abuses, to the violation of the interests of the minority, and to attempts to use this organization to the advantage of some one power or group of powers. Is it possible to forget that states which are members of the U.N. are sovereign and independent states and cannot permit themselves to be saddled with decisions which are incompatible with their sovereignty?

It is absolutely obvious, Mr. President, that departure from the rule of unanimity of the great powers would not only fail to strengthen the U.N. but, on the contrary, such a step would weaken this organization and would in the last analysis lead to its disintegration. This cannot be permitted if we are really striving to transform the U.N. into an effective organ of international co-operation and not into an instrument in the hands of supporters of a policy "from out of a position of strength." To identify the U.N. with the interests of a group of states, and actually with those of a single power, means canceling the U.N. Charter for purposes which have nothing in common with those high principles and tasks for the sake of which this international organization was created.

In your message of January 12 you also touch on the German question and that of the situation in countries of Eastern Europe. Our position on the German question is generally known; the substance of it was set forth in my message to you of January 8, where it is stressed that both at the Geneva Meeting of the Heads of Government and also thereafter we have clearly and unambiguously stated that in the light of the actual situation that has developed in Germany its reunification cannot be achieved without a rapprochement and understanding between both sovereign German states. It is in this very direction that the proposal is intended on the part of the Government of the German Democratic Republic for a German confederation, and therefore we fully support it. One cannot fail to see that under present conditions any approach which does not take all this into account will not only fail to contribute to the solution of the German problem but will also lead to an increase in tension in relations between states.

As for the question of the situation in the countries of Eastern Europe, the position of the Soviet Government does not require any kind of clarification, and I consider that any kind of polemics on this question would not be of any benefit. However, is it permissible to inquire how it is possible, while having normal diplomatic relations with the people's democractes or with some of them and consequently recognizing the sovereignty and the independence of these counties, to propose to other states to discuss questions dealing with the internal situation in these countries? The Soviet Union cannot be a party to any such dealings which we can consider only as inadmissible interference in the internal affairs of sovereign states. I could also ask another question: are there any grounds for any country to assume the part of an arbiter and presume to decide as to what social and economic regime should be established in any given country? It is precisely for that reason that my colleagues and I declared with the utmost firmness at the Meeting of the Heads of Government at Geneva in 1955 that such questions cannot be the subject of international negotiations.

In indicating the motives for your proposal for the discussion of this question you refer, in particular, to the events in Hungary. But is it not a fact that the events in Hungary have proven above all that the Hungarian people knew how to properly resist those elements which, acting on directives and with the support of certain circles from abroad, made an assault against the social system chosen by the people of Hungary?

For our part, we are firmly convinced that the cause of strengthening universal peace demands of us all that we direct our energies toward those problems the solution of which would create conditions for the development of peaceful cooperation among nations and that we not permit relations to be poisoned by raising such questions as might lead us away from questions of real importance for the preservation of peace. In this respect I think that you will agree that if we are to proceed from a sincere desire to carry out fruitful negotiations, then persistence in advancing, in fact imposing questions which do not meet the approval of other participants in the negotiations, will be of little benefit.

Your message, Mr. President, makes it clear that you, like ourselves, attach great importance to the consideration of the problem of disarmament at a summit meeting. We hope that agreement between us in this respect will allow us to find an element in the problem of disarmament, on which we can reach the same opinion and finally break the deadlock with regard to this entire problem, the solution of which is indispensable for the preservation of peace.

We think as before, that the proposals presented by us in respect to individual aspects of this problem take into consideration the situation as it exists in respect to disarmament and correspond to the needs of the present moment. I would like to make some remarks concerning the considerations presented on this question in your message. We, of course, do not deny the importance of the question of using outer space for peaceful purposes exclusively, i.e., first of all, of the question of the prohibition of intercontinental ballistic missiles with nuclear warheads. I hope, however, Mr. President, that you will agree that this question can be considered only as a part of the general problem of the prohibition of nuclear and rocket weapons. It is for that very reason that the Soviet Union, in the interest of strengthening peace and reaching agreement on questions of disarmament, is also prepared to discuss the question of intercontinental missiles, provided the Western powers are prepared to agree on the prohibition of nuclear and hydrogen weapons, the cessation of tests of such weapons and the liquidations of foreign military bases in the territories of other states. There can be no doubt that in such a case the reaching of an agreement on the use of cosmic space for peaceful purposes exclusively would not meet with any difficulties.

Is it necessary to argue that a realistic approach to the problem of disarmament requires that the interests of the security of all countries be taken into account rather than of a single country? It can be directly stated that if any of the participants in the negotiations on disarmament is concerned about his own security alone and strives to ensure for himself strategic or other advantages in the course of negotiations, then such negotiations can certainly not lead to any positive results.

I should also like to touch here upon another aspect of this question. Would it be right, Mr. President, if we were to start discussing the problems of cosmic space alone, while setting aside such "earthly" international problems requiring solution as, for instance, the question of the prohibition of atomic and hydrogen weapons? What would be the reaction of the peoples now living in dire anxiety because of the "cold war," the intensification of the armaments race, and the threat of a new war? They would be justified in saying that we do not do what we should and that our first task and duty to mankind must be the elimination of the threat of a new war and the strengthening of peace among the peoples of the earth. Let us then use our joint efforts to achieve these noble goals.

Speaking of the danger of a new war, I must again bring to your attention the great harm done to the cause of peace by the unrestrained propaganda for war being conducted in several Western countries. After all, the situation is such that some rabid partisans of a policy of "positions of strength" openly utter the dangerous call for a preventive war. It is our deep conviction that it is necessary to put an end to this intolerable situation, and the sooner the better. As a matter of fact if we are all really striving to preserve peace, then why should we not unequivocally and decisively condemn propaganda for war and the attempts to cloak warmongering with hypocritical references to freedom of speech and of the press? I am convinced that if all the governments which are to participate in our negotiations take such a position, this alone will, without doubt, contribute to the establishment of a healthier international situation and will create more favorable conditions for the settlement of international problems, which now at times appear to be insoluble.

At the beginning of your message you said, Mr. President, that peace and good will among men have been the sincere desire of all peoples from time immemorial. This cannot be denied. That is precisely why we proposed to other governments to jointly take concrete steps which would show in action our common readiness to strive for the strengthening of peace and for an improvement in international relations. It is upon the statesmen of all nations, and primarily of the great powers, that now depends to a great extent the answer to the main question which so deeply agitates humanity: Will it be possible to avert the senseless drift toward the catastrophe of war and to reverse the trend of events in the direction of strengthening peace and friendly co-operation among nations?

Our responsibility for the fate of the present and the future generations is indeed great, but our opportunities are no less great. It is obvious that a readiness on the part of the governments of the U.S.S.R. and the U.S.A., as well as that of other great powers, to combine their efforts for ensuring peace throughout the world would be a reliable guarantee that the clouds hovering over the would would be dispersed, and that peoples will at last be able to breathe freely and turn without fear to the creative labors of peace. I do not doubt that a high-level meeting of leading statesmen, such as we propose, with the participating of the heads of government, may become an important step in this very direction, provided all of the participants display the necessary respect for the interest of one another and that they recognize as their principal and noble purpose the strengthening of universal peace.

In my message of January 8 I placed before you the motives by which the Soviet Government is guided in its opinion that the proposed negotiations should take place at the highest level with the participation of the heads of governments. Judging from your reply, you are of the opinion that a summit meeting should be preceded by a meeting of foreign ministers who would consider problems in substance, and thus the summit meeting is made contingent on the results of the meeting of ministers.

It is hardly necessary to repeat why we should like to avoid this. I merely wish to note that if we take into consideration the prejudiced position of some of the possible participants in a meeting of ministers, then we see that there is no assurance that a meeting with such participants would not erect additional obstacles to the preparation of a meeting at the highest level, thus destroying at the very outset this important and urgent undertaking.

It seems to me that the experiences of the past meetings of foreign ministers speak for themselves. Very recently the NATO members held a high-level conference, with the participation of the heads of government, devoted almost exclusively to the discussion of further military preparations within NATO. How should one interpret in this connection the position of those who oppose a meeting at the same high level, the purpose of which would be to discuss a program of peace, a program for the elimination of the threat of a new war, and easing of international tensions. As to the preparation of a summit meeting we are certain that if accord is reached on having such a meeting, then the procedural and other questions bearing on the practical implementation of such an accord could be solved, in our opinion, without any special difficulties. These questions could be agreed upon through the usual diplomatic channels.

Permit me to express the hope that you will give due attention to my remarks, which derive from a sincere desire to promote the earliest possible convening of a summit meeting, which would be an important step toward the liquidation of the "cold war" and toward the strengthening of universal peace.

The historical moment in which we live urgently demands that we all be imbued with a feeling of special responsibility and that we set aside all secondary considerations and all the prejudices which so often hinder successful work for strengthening peace. This is required by the highest interests of our peoples and of all humanity. We are deeply convinced that the joint efforts of our countries together with the efforts of other governments, can mark the beginning of a new chapter in the development of mankind, that of peaceful co-operation and friendship among nations.

With sincere respect,

N. BULGANIN

(22) Letter from the President, February 15, 1958.[8]

MY DEAR MR. CHAIRMAN: I am in receipt of your communication of February 1. I note that it is a slightly abbreviated and moderated edition of the lengthy and rather bitter speech which Mr. Khrushchev made at Minsk on January 22.[9]

I begin to wonder, Mr. Chairman, whether we shall get anywhere by continuing to write speeches to each other? As I read your successive lengthy missives of December 10, January 8, and February 1, I cannot avoid the feeling that if our two countries are to move ahead to the establishment of better relations, we must find some ways other than mere prolongation of repetitive public debate. In this connection, I have some thoughts to offer.

But first I comment briefly on your latest note.

II.

I tried in my letter to you of January 12 to put forward some new ideas. For example, I proposed strengthening the United Nations by rededication of our nations to its purposes and principles, with the accompaniment of some reduction in the use of the veto power in the Security Council.

That proposal you reject, alleging that it would give to the

[8] Department of State Bulletin, v. 38 (March 10, 1958), pp. 373-376.
[9] See Pravda, January 26, 1958, pp. 1-3. A complete English translation appears in The Current Digest of the Soviet Press, v. 10 (March 5, 1958), pp. 15-22 and 51.

Security Council a power to "adopt decisions that would be binding on all States" and make it in effect a "world government." That argument is directed to a misrepresentation of my proposal. I suggested that our two nations should, as a matter of policy, avoid vetoing Security Council recommendations as to how nations might proceed toward the peaceful solution of their disputes. Surely authority to *recommend*, and that only as to *procedures*, is not to impose binding decisions. Already, the General Assembly can, free of veto, recommend procedures for peaceful settlement. Would it really be catastrophic for the Security Council to exercise that same facility?

III.

Another new idea was that outer space should be perpetually dedicated to peaceful purposes. You belittle this proposal as one made to gain strategic advantages for the United States. Mr. Khrushchev in his Minsk speech said, "This means they want to prohibit that which they do not possess."

Since the record completely disproves that uncalled for statement, may we now hope between us to consider and devise cooperative international procedures to give reality to the idea of use of outer space for peace only.

When the United States alone possessed atomic weapons and the Soviet Union possessed none, the United States proposed to forego its monopoly in the interest of world peace and security. We are prepared to take the same attitude now in relation to outer space. If this peaceful purpose is not realized, and the worse than useless race of weapons goes on, the world will have only the Soviet Union to blame, just as it has only the Soviet Union to blame for the fact that atomic and nuclear power are now used increasingly for weapons purposes instead of being dedicated wholly to peaceful uses as the United States proposed a decade ago.

The Soviet Union refused to cooperate in tackling the problem of international control of atomic energy when that problem was in its infancy. Consequently, it has now become too late to achieve totally effective control although there can be, as we propose, a controlled cessation of further weapons testing and of the manufacture of fissionable material for weapons purposes. But, as your Government said on May 10, 1955,[10] a total "ban" on atomic and hydrogen weapons could not now be enforced because "the possibility

[10] *Documents on American Foreign Relations, 1955*, pp. 417-430.

would be open to a potential aggressor to accumulate stocks of atomic and hydrogen weapons for a surprise atomic attack on peace-loving states."

A terrible new menace can be seen to be in the making. That menace is to be found in the use of outer space for war purposes. The time to deal with that menace is now. It would be tragic if the Soviet leaders were blind or indifferent toward this menace as they were apparently blind or indifferent to the atomic and nuclear menace at its inception a decade ago.

If there is a genuine desire on the part of the Soviet leaders to do something more than merely to talk about the menace resulting from what you described as "the production of ever newer types of weapons," let us actually do what even now would importantly reduce the scope of nuclear warfare, both in terms of checking the use of fissionable material for weapons purposes and in wholly eliminating the newest types of weapons which use outer space for human destruction.

IV.

With respect to the meeting of Heads of Government, the cumulative effect of your last three missives is to leave considerable puzzlement as to what you think another such meeting could contribute to a genuine settlement of our problems.

You have proposed, and insisted on, about ten topics which you want to have discussed at such a meeting. I, in turn, suggested some eight topics which I thought should be discussed—strengthening the United Nations, dedicating outer space to peaceful purposes, the reunification of Germany, the right of the peoples of Eastern Europe to choose the form of government under which they would live, and a number of specific proposals in the disarmament field.

I wrote that, if there were to be a top-level meeting, I would be willing to discuss your proposals in good faith if you would so discuss mine. Your answer is that I must be prepared to discuss your proposals but that as regards mine there must, you said "be unanimous agreement of all participants as to the necessity for considering such proposals." In other words, you demand the right to veto discussion of the matters I believe to be vital to peace.

I noted that Mr. Khrushchev devoted a considerable part of his Minsk speech to a discussion of conditions in Hungary, Poland, and East Germany. Does the Soviet Union claim such a proprietary interest in these lands and people that to discuss them is solely a matter of Soviet domestic concern? If not, and if these lands and people can be discussed by Soviet leaders as an international problem, why cannot we both discuss them?

If indeed a top-level conference were to apply the formula that no one is to say anything except what all the rest agree they would like to hear, we would, as I said in my last press conference, end up in the ludicrous posture of our just glaring silently at each other across the table.

Perhaps the impasse to which we seem to have come can be broken by less formal and less publicized contacts through which we would continue to seek to find out whether there can be a top-level meeting which, in the words of my letter to you of January 12, 1958, "would hold good hope of advancing the cause of peace and justice in the world." Exchanges of views effected through our Ambassadors or Foreign Ministers may serve better than what Mr. Khrushchev referred to at Minsk as "polemics" between Heads of Government. The United States is accordingly consulting with some other interested nations as to the desirability of exploring, through more normal channels, the prospects of a top-level meeting which would be adequate as to subjects, and as to which preliminary exchanges would indicate good prospect of an accord. You will understand, of course, that, whatever be the preparatory procedures, these would, as far as the United States was concerned, require the participation of our Secretary of State.

V.

"Polemics" will not, I fear, advance us along the path of better relations which is my nation's goal. Indeed, I deplore the constantly mounting accusations within the Soviet Union that the United States is a nation ruled by aggressive war-minded imperialists. Mr. Khrushchev's speech of January 22 is an outstanding example of such charges and indeed they are to be found in your February 1 note.

What is the explanation of such charges? They seem to fly in the face of established history.

Until the end of the First World War, war was generally accepted as a lawful means of conducting foreign policy. But after World War I showed the terrible consequences of such toleration of war, the United States took the initiative in bringing about the Pact of Paris whereby the nations of the world renounced war as an instrument of national policy. An even broader renunciation of force is now found in the United Nations Charter. The United States, which initiated the concept of the international renunciation of force, has sought to adhere scrupulously to that concept.

I am really amazed now to be told by Soviet leaders, who have never even been near this country, that there are in the United States those who, in your words "utter the dangerous call for preventive war"; and conduct "unrestrained propaganda for war." If any such persons exist in the United States, I do not know of them; nor do I know of any "imperialist ruling circles" that are supposedly eager to plunge the world into war in order to make financial gains.

These allegations do not provide the real facts of American life. The real facts are the intense longing of the American people for peace; the working of the American constitutional system which assures that government shall be responsive to the peaceful will of the people; our "built-in" guarantees against the possibiltiy of any United States Government suddenly initiating war; our national dedication to the international renunciation of force as an instrument of national policy; the decisive influence for peace of American religious, labor, intellectual and political leaders and of their organizations.

It is, of course, quite true that our people are flatly opposed to regimes which hold people against their will and which deny the principle on which our nation was founded, that governments derive their just powers from the consent of the governed and can never rightly deprive the governed of their inalienable right to life, liberty and the pursuit of happiness. Our people's rejection of many foreign and domestic aspects of Soviet methods and policies is, however, demonstrably not a moving cause to war. Otherwise we would have struck when we had atomic weapons and the Soviet Union had none; or when we had thermonuclear bombs and the Soviet Union had none.

VI.

When I contrast the actual facts of American life with such portrayals as those of Mr. Khrushchev at Minsk, and indeed of your latest communication to me, I am impressed more than ever before with the enormous difficulties besetting us in attempting to move toward better relations and with the greater necessity than ever before of doing so.

It is possible that Soviet leadership feels it necessary deliberately to misrepresent the American viewpoint. If so, one effect would be to confuse their own people and the people of those Eastern European countries under their domination, who are denied access to world information except as the Soviet leaders permit. Another effect would be to make true cooperation more difficult. Possibly also these misrepresentations constitute blind adherence to what was one of the early tenets of orthodox Communism, namely, that capitalistic societies are by their very nature warlike.

I prefer, however, to assume that these misrepresentations are not wilful but result from genuine misconceptions which could be done away with.

VII.

Our two nations are both now exploring and seeking to learn the truth about outer space. But is it not more important to learn the truth about each other? The ambassadorial agreement concluded between our Governments on January 27, 1958,[11] points in this direction. It contemplates exchanges that, it is said, "will contribute significantly to the betterment of relations between the two countries, thereby contributing to a lessening of international tension." I hope that we shall make full use of that agreement. But, for the most part, it deals with exchanges of technicians and specialists in various fields. Would it not be well if, in addition, leaders of thought and influential citizens within the Soviet Union should come to visit the United States, not to acquire technical knowledge but rather to learn at first hand the feeling of our people toward peace and the working of our popular institutions as they affect our conduct of foreign relations. Most of the Soviet citizens who exert an influence are strangers to this country with, I fear, totally false conceptions. These misconceptions I should like to see corrected in the interests of better relations. I can assure you that groups of qualified citizens of the U.S.S.R. coming here for the purpose I describe would receive every facility to learn about our country and our people and the working of our political institutions.

I feel also that we need particularly to be thinking not only of the present but also of the future and of those, now young, who in a few years will be carrying heavy responsibilities that our generation will pass on to them. I think our young peo-

[11] Document 61, below.

ple should get to know more about each other. I strongly feel that the recent agreement for the exchange of 20 to 30 students a year is a small step in the right direction, but woefully inadequate. I may write you further on this topic.

VIII.

In the meantime, I reaffirm what has been so often said by Secretary Dulles and by myself. The American nation wants nothing more than to cooperate wholeheartedly with any Soviet Government which is genuinely dedicated to advancing, by peaceful means, the welfare of the people of the Soviet Union. It should, however, be appreciated how difficult it is to generate here the good will which the Soviet leaders claim they want, so long as there remains between our two countries the vast gulf of misunderstanding and misrepresentation that is again revealed by both speeches and written communications of Soviet leaders. If the Soviet leaders sincerely desire better relations with us, can they truly think it helpful for the Soviet Union to continue to pursue the objectives of International Communism, which include the overthrow of other governments? The Moscow Manifesto made last November by the representatives of Communist Parties from 64 nations, and the Soviet Government's official endorsement of the results of the recent Afro-Asian Conference in Cairo could not fail to raise in the minds of our people the question of the real purposes of the Soviet leaders.

We shall nevertheless go on seeking such good relations. And I hope that, if there is a positive response to the concrete suggestion here made, we may perhaps do something toward ushering in a new and better era.

Sincerely,

DWIGHT D. EISENHOWER

(23) *Letter from the Chairman of the Council of Ministers of the USSR (Bulganin) March 3, 1958.*[12]

(Excerpts)

* * *

In our letters to each other during recent months we have exchanged views in regard to the holding of a summit conference, and I consider that this exchange of views has had

[12] *Department of State Bulletin*, v. 38 (April 21, 1958), pp. 648-652.

a positive significance and has played a definite role in the preparation of such a meeting. Above all, our correspondence has shown that the governments of our two countries hold the general opinion that a conference of top government officials is desirable and that its successful outcome can exert a favorable influence on the entire international situation. Furthermore, we have had an opportunity to present in a preliminary way our views with regard to a number of specific problems, which is useful in itself, since it facilitates the search for a mutually acceptable basis of negotiations.

*　　*　　*

We, by no means believe, nor have we ever stated, that only the topics proposed for discussion by the Soviet Union can be considered at a summit meeting. I should like to remind you that in our proposals of January 8 there was a direct statement concerning the willingness of the Soviet Government also to discuss, by mutual agreement, such additional constructive proposals contributing to a termination of the "cold war" as might be presented by the other participants in the meeting.

However, this does not mean that we can agree to discuss matters that are in the sphere of internal affairs of other states, the consideration of which could have no results other than a still further aggravation of the relations between states. Precisely in this category belong such matters as the situation in the countries of Eastern Europe and the unification into a single state of the German Democratic Republic and the Federal Republic of Germany.

*　　*　　*

My colleagues and I have closely studied the considerations contained in your messages. The Soviet Government agrees to discuss the following questions as well at a summit conference:

We are prepared to discuss the questions of prohibiting the use of outer space for military purposes and the liquidation of alien military bases on foreign territories. I think you will agree that the reaching of an agreement on this important question would greatly reduce the danger of a sudden outbreak of war and would be an important step toward ensuring conditions for a tranquil and peaceful life among nations.

The Soviet Government also considers it possible to discuss the matter of concluding a German peace treaty. We propose that the governments of the German Democratic Republic and the Federal Republic of Germany be invited to participate in the discussion of this problem. Of course, the problem of uniting the G.D.R. and the F.R.G. in a single state, which falls completely within the competence of these two German states, cannot, as the Soviet Government has already stated repeatedly, be the subject of discussion at the forthcoming summit conference.

We agree that at a summit conference there should also be a discussion of the questions of developing ties and contacts among countries. The Soviet Government has invariably been in favor of every possible development of such contacts. It shares the views expressed in your message of February 15 concerning the importance of such contacts. I should like to emphasize that for its part the Soviet Government attaches great significance to the maintenance of systematic personal contacts between top government officials for the exchange of views concerning current international problems in the interests of improving relations between states and of strengthening mutual trust and consolidating universal peace.

Likewise, we are not opposed to having an exchange of views regarding ways of strengthening the U.N.; we have merely expressed certain considerations of principle which we have in this respect.

I have already had occasion to explain why we consider unacceptable the proposal that our two governments renounce the principle of unanimity of the permanent members of the U.N. Security Council in deciding certain questions in that body. We cannot agree at all with the claim that the only thing in question is the procedural aspect of the matter, although, as is well known, this aspect also has important significance in settling great political problems.

*   *   *

As to the method of preparation for the conference, the necessity for which has now been expressed by the heads of the governments of all the largest states, the Soviet government feels that all ways and means should be used that might expedite such preparations.

*   *   *

I must say, Mr. President, that the present state of preparation of the summit conference causes us definite concern. The lack of a reply from the Government of the United

States to a number of concrete proposals from the Soviet Government concerning preparations for the conference, and also the fact that the Government of the United States continues knowingly to submit unacceptable questions, all of this obviously delays the convening of the conference.

We are all the more alarmed since, in addition to delaying a decision on the question of convening the conference, the governments of the United States and of certain other NATO member states are stepping up the tempo of practical measures in the sphere of military preparations, which cannot but aggravate international tension. I have in mind particularly a recently signed agreement between the United States and Great Britain on the establishment of bases in the territory of the latter for launching American medium-range rockets,[13] and also the announcement of the convening in Paris, in April of this year, of a conference of Defense Ministers of the NATO nations for the purpose of studying such questions as setting up rocket bases in the territories of NATO member countries, stockpiling atomic weapons in those countries, and the transfer of atomic weapons to NATO members.

We note that the press of certain Western powers has recently stated openly that the United States will not consent to a summit conference until agreements have been reached concerning the establishment of American rocket bases in the territory of the West European NATO member countries.

All of this results in a very strange situation: on the one hand, assertions are being made regarding readiness to make efforts toward relaxing international tension and lessening the danger of war; on the other hand, military preparations are being made with feverish haste, which can only increase international tension and the danger of war.

* * *

B. **Further Exchange of Correspondence between the President and the Chairman of the Council of Ministers of the USSR (Khrushchev).**

　1. *Disarmament and Related Problems (See Documents 32-39 and 44.)*
　2. *Preparing for a Summit Meeting (See Documents 30 and 31.)*
　3. *The Middle East Crisis (See Documents 89, 90, 93-95, 98, 99.)*

[13] Documents 12 and 13, above.

4. *The Crisis in the Taiwan Strait* (*See Documents 128 and 131.*)

5. *Improving Trade Relations* (*See Document 62.*)

C. Preparing for a Summit Meeting.

(24) *Western Three Power Declaration, March 31, 1958.*[1]

The present international situation requires that a serious attempt be made to reach agreement on the main problems affecting attainment of peace and stability in the world. In the circumstances a summit meeting is desirable if it would provide opportunity for conducting serious discussions of major problems and would be an effective means of reaching agreement on significant subjects.

It is clear that, before a summit meeting can meet in these conditions, preparatory work is required.

This preparatory work could best be performed by exchanges through diplomatic channels leading to a meeting between foreign ministers.

The main purpose of this preparatory work should be to examine the position of the various governments on the major questions at issue between them and to establish what subjects should be submitted for examination by heads of government. It would not be the purpose of these preparatory talks to reach decisions but to bring out, by general discussion, the possibilities of agreement.

The foreign ministers, assuming they have concluded the preparatory work to their satisfaction, would reach agreement on the date and place of the summit meeting and decide on its composition.

If this procedure is acceptable to the Soviet Government, it is suggested that diplomatic exchanges should start in Moscow in the second half of April.

(25) *Soviet Aide Memoire, April 11, 1958.*[2]

(Excerpt)

*   *   *

With a view to the speediest completion of preparatory work regarding the convocation of the summit conference the Soviet Government deems it necessary at present to reach

[1] *Department of State Bulletin,* v. 38 (April 21, 1958), p. 648.
[2] *Ibid.* (May 5, 1958), p. 728.

agreement on, first of all, the question of holding the meeting of ministers of foreign affairs not later than the end of April or the middle of May 1958. In this connection it is borne in mind that all preparatory work through diplomatic channels must be completed by that time. For this reason, the Soviet Government deems it expedient to restrict the exchange of views through diplomatic channels to a minimum of questions relating directly to the organization of a meeting of ministers of foreign affairs, that is, questions of the date and place of the ministers meeting and the composition of its participants.

Striving for a most rapid completion of preparatory work for the summit conference, the Soviet Union, as is known, long ago submitted for consideration by the Governments of the United States, Great Britain, and France, its proposals on the question of a summit conference agenda, the composition of its participants, and the place and date of holding it. The Soviet Government expects that the Governments of the United States, Great Britain, and France will give in the near future a definite reply to these concrete proposals.

As regards the meeting of ministers of foreign affairs, these ministers—in the opinion of the Soviet Government—must reach agreement on the question of date, venue, and composition of a high level conference, and determining the range of questions which will be considered at the conference.

In this connection it is not excluded that while attending to preparations for the high level conference, the ministers may if necessary and if generally agreed, exchange opinions on certain of the problems proposed by the parties for inclusion in the agenda of the summit conference, for the purpose of determining whether it is expedient to include a given question in the summit conference agenda.

It is self-evident that the question of the convocation of a high level conference cannot be linked with the results of the meeting of ministers of foreign affairs. The Soviet Government, on its part, will do everything possible for this aim to be achieved. However, if the ministers are unable to reach the necessary agreement on questions of preparations for a summit conference, this would not signify in any way that the necessity of having such a conference has become less pressing.

The present tense international situation demands the speedy settlement of ripe international problems; in these conditions it would be incorrect to make the convocation of a high level conference depend on the results of a meeting of ministers of foreign affairs. It is perfectly obvious that difficulties which may appear during the ministers conference can and must be overcome at a conference of statesmen invested with wider powers.

Guided by the aforesaid, the Soviet Government expresses readiness to begin in Moscow on Apr. 17 the exchange of views about preparations for a meeting of ministers of foreign affairs.

(26) Soviet Memorandum, May 5, 1958.[3]

PROPOSALS OF THE SOVIET GOVERNMENT AS TO QUESTIONS TO BE CONSIDERED AT THE CONFERENCE WITH PARTICIPATION OF THE HEADS OF GOVERNMENT

On January 8, 1958, the Soviet Government presented for consideration by other Governments its concrete proposals on problems of easing international tension.[4] These proposals provide for a high-level conference of top government officials with the participation of the Heads of Government to discuss issues the settlement of which would promote the easing of international tension and the creation of trust in relations between states.

As before, the Soviet Government considers that a series of pressing international problems can be solved even at the present time. Its position is that it is necessary and possible to achieve agreement among states on outstanding issues in international relations. The Soviet Union, for its part, has listed a number of such issues and is prepared to participate in the consideration of other problems which might be proposed by the participants in the conference at the summit provided, of course, that these questions are within the competence of the international meeting and are directed toward strengthening peace.

The Soviet Government is firmly convinced that if the Heads of Government firmly resolve to devote their efforts to seeking mutually acceptable solutions for pressing international problems, then it is possible to say with certainty that the forthcoming conference at the summit will ensure the necessary turning point in the development of relations between states in the direction of improving the entire international situation and the liquidation of the "cold war."

[3] Ibid., v. 39 (July 7, 1958), pp. 17-22.
[4] Not printed.

Taking into account the exchange of views which has occurred on the question of convening a conference at the summit and seeking to facilitate the completion of the prepatory work for this conference in as short a period as possible, the Soviet Government for its part submits for consideration at the conference the following questions and at the same time sets forth some views on these questions:

1. *Immediate cessation of atomic and hydrogen weapons tests*

Cessation of tests of all types of atomic and hydrogen weapons is a pressing problem for which it is possible to find a practical solution. Universal cessation of tests of such weapons would have beneficial results in strengthening the cause of peace and putting an end to the armaments race. Agreement on this question would be a definite barrier to the creation of new and still more destructive types of atomic and hydrogen weapons and would be a practical step on the road to complete prohibition of such weapons of mass destruction.

The necessity for an immediate solution of this question is dictated also by the fact that continued tests of atomic and hydrogen weapons are, according to the testimony of the most prominent scientists, increasing the concentration of atomic radiation in the atmosphere, the soil, and the water, which are already creating a serious danger to the health and life of people now living and threatening the normal development of future generations. This danger will increase still more in the future if an end is not put to experimental explosions of nuclear weapons.

At the present time, nuclear weapons are being produced by only three states—the USSR, the USA, and the United Kingdom,—and the cessation of tests of such weapons now depends, since the Soviet Union has already unilaterally ceased its tests, upon only two powers—the USA and the United Kingdom. The Soviet Government expects that the USA and the United Kingdom will cease without delay their testing of nuclear weapons, so that it may be possible to agree at the conference, with the participation of the Heads of Government, on the consolidation of such decisions by the three powers by means of appropriate agreements.

Although modern technical devices for detecting nuclear explosions can record any explosions of atomic and hydrogen weapons, no matter where they are carried out, and each power concerned can itself determine whether the other parties are complying with the agreement to cease the tests, the Soviet Government reiterates its consent to the establishment of international control over the cessation of nuclear weapons tests by means of international control posts, as it already proposed in June 1957.[5] It considers that it will not be difficult to agree on concrete measures for such control as soon as the Governments of the USA and the United Kingdom also cease testing such weapons. Otherwise, any negotiations concerning questions of control, whether they be on the level of experts or any other level, will inevitably become fruitless discussions and will, naturally, have no real results.

To make the cessation of tests of atomic and hydrogen weapons contingent upon the solution of other disarmament questions, concerning which there are still serious differences of opinion and the solution of which is a more complex matter, would be tantamount to an actual refusal to cease the atomic and hydrogen weapon tests. Although the immediate cessation of nuclear weapons tests by all the powers possessing such weapons would place the Warsaw Pact member nations in an unfavorable position in comparison with the NATO nations, since the Soviet Union has carried out considerably fewer experimental explosions of atomic and hydrogen weapons than the USA and the United Kingdom, nevertheless the Soviet Union has consented to this in the desire to make a practical beginning for the cessation of the atomic arms race. The acceptance of this proposal by the United States of America and the United Kingdom would put an end to tests of atomic and hydrogen weapons everywhere and forever.

2. Renunciation of the use of all types of atomic, hydrogen, and rocket weapons

The Soviet Government considers that the achievement of agreement on the joint renunciation by the states possessing nuclear weapons—the USSR, the USA, and the United Kingdom—of the use of all types of such weapons, including air bombs, rockets, of any range, with atomic and hydrogen warheads, atomic artillery, etc., would be an important step toward eliminating the danger of atomic war and reducing tension in relations between states. In case agreement is reached to renounce the use of nuclear weapons, any government that would dare to violate such an agreement would reveal itself to the eyes of the peoples as an aggressor, as an enemy of peace.

[5] *Documents on American Foreign Relations, 1957*, p. 424.

The great significance of such an agreement is confirmed by historical experience. As is known, the Geneva Protocol of 1925 on the prohibition of the use of chemical and bacteriological weapons played an important role in the matter of preventing the utilization of such types of weapons during the Second World War. In the opinion of the Soviet Government, the decision to renounce the use of atomic, hydrogen, and rocket weapons could be legalized by means of extending the Geneva Protocol of 1925 to nuclear and rocket weapons.

The Soviet Government considers that an agreement of the powers now, at this stage, to renounce the use of nuclear and rocket weapons would create an auspicious basis for the achievement, at the next stage, of such measures as the complete and unconditional prohibition of nuclear weapons, the cessation of their production, with their elimination from the armaments of states, and the liquidation of all stockpiles of such weapons.

3. *Creation in Central Europe of a zone free of atomic, hydrogen and rocket weapons*

At the present time, two groups of states oppose each other in Central Europe and armed forces and armaments of various types, in quantities abnormal for peacetime, are concentrated there. This one circumstance alone creates a serious threat to peace and it is impossible to ignore the fact that in such a situation, by evil intent or by chance, the fires of a new war can break out with the use of the most modern means of destruction, that is, nuclear and rocket weapons.

In order to preclude the danger of such a turn of events, the Soviet Government deems it expedient to examine at the conference the proposal of the Government of the Polish People's Republic concerning the creation in Europe of a zone free of atomic, hydrogen, and rocket weapons, which would include the territories of the Polish People's Republic, the Czechoslovak Republic, the German Democratic Republic, and the Federal Republic of Germany.[6] Assumption by these states of the obligation not to produce or to permit the stationing on their territories of nuclear weapons of all possible types, and also the establishment of sites for the launching of rockets capable of carrying nuclear warheads, would undoubtedly help to prevent the possibility of military conflicts breaking out in the center of Europe. In as much as the Governments of the Polish People's Republic, the Czechoslovak

6 Document 46, below.

Republic, and the German Democrat Republic have already declared their agreement to be included in a zone free of atomic weapons, the creation of such a zone now depends only on the agreement of the Government of the Federal Republic of Germany.

Agreement among the Governments of the USSR, the USA, the United Kingdom, and France on the advisability of creating a zone free of atomic weapons in this area of Europe would undoubtedly facilitate reaching an agreement with the Government of the Federal Republic of Germany with regard to the Federal Republic of Germany's joining this zone.

Agreement on the creation of a zone free of atomic weapons in Europe will be effective if, along with the corresponding obligations of the states included in the said zone, the powers that include nuclear and rocket weapons among the armaments of their forces would, for their part, assume an obligation to respect the status of this zone and consider the territory of the states included in it as excluded from the sphere of use of atomic, hydrogen, and rocket weapons. As for the Soviet Union, it has already declared its readiness to assume the above-mentioned obligations if the Governments of the US, the United Kingdom, and France do the same.

The obligations of the states included within the zone and the obligations of the Great Powers could be legalized both in the form of an appropriate international treaty and also in the form of appropriate unilateral declarations.

For the purpose of ensuring the effectiveness of the obligations and their fulfillment, the states concerned would be obligated to establish in the territory of the zone free of atomic weapons a system of broad and effective control, both on land and in the air, with the establishment of control points by agreement of the states concerned. The creation in the center of Europe of a zone free of atomic weapons would be an important step on the road toward cessation of the dangerous arms race and removal of the threat of atomic war.

4. Non-aggression pact

Seeking to further the easing of international tension, the Soviet Government considers that it would be in the interests of cessation of the "cold war" and of the arms race to conclude in one or another form a non-aggression pact (or agreement) between the states members of NATO and the states participating in the Warsaw Pact. Conclusion of such a pact would be an important step on the road toward the creation of an all-European system of security and the strengthening of mutual trust and cooperation between states.

If the Western powers display a desire to conclude such a pact or agreement, then in the opinion of the Soviet Government it would not be difficult to come to an agreement on its form on the basis of a multilateral agreement among all countries included in the Warsaw Pact organization and the North Atlantic Alliance, or among certain countries belonging to these groups, or, lastly, in the form of non-aggression agreements on a bilateral basis between separate members of these groups.

The Soviet Government considers that the basis for such an agreement must be the mutual renunciation by the contracting parties of the use of force or threat of force and the obligation to settle disputes which may arise between the parties to the agreement by peaceful means alone. The desirability of mutual consultations among the parties to the agreement, in connection with the fulfillment of the obligations undertaken by them under the agreement, should also be envisaged.

Such a pact could be open to accession by all the other states of Europe in order to facilitate the creation at a later stage of a system of all-European security and the gradual liquidation of existing military-political groups.

In proposing the conclusion of a non-aggression pact, the Soviet Government regards it as the first step toward a radical improvement in the relations among the states included in the North Atlantic Alliance and the Warsaw Pact organization and as a prerequisite for the conclusion at a later stage of a broader treaty on European security.

5. *Prohibition of the use of outer space for military purposes; liquidation of foreign military bases in foreign territories; international cooperation in the study of outer space*

Scientific-technical progress in the realm of rocket technology has raised the question of what direction the use of the latest scientific achievements will take: Will they serve peaceful purposes or will they be used for furthering the arms race, increasing the danger of the outbreak of an atomic war?

An effective measure, which would completely exclude the possibility of using outer space for military purposes and which would ensure application of the tremendous achievements in the creation of rocket and artificial earth satellites exclusively for peaceful purposes, would be a complete and unconditional ban on atomic and hydrogen weapons, together with their exclusion from armaments and the destruction of stockpiles. Since this is difficult at the present time, owing to the position of the Western powers, and must obviously be realized at a later stage, the Soviet Government proposes that at the present stage agreement be reached on a ban on the use of outer space for military purposes with, at the same time, the liquidation of military bases in foreign territories, first of all in the territory of the countries of Europe, the Near and Middle East, and North Africa. Such a measure would be in the interest of the security of all states. As for the states in whose territory such military bases are situated, such a decision would only be to their advantage, as the liquidation of military bases would remove the threat to which they subject themselves by making their territory available for the establishment of foreign military bases.

Guided by these considerations, the Soviet Government proposes a discussion of the question of concluding an international agreement on the use of outer space for peaceful purposes, which would include the following basic provisions:

A ban on the use of outer space for military purposes and an obligation on the part of states to launch rockets into outer space only in accordance with an agreed international program.

Liquidation of foreign military bases in the territory of other states, first of all in Europe, the Near and Middle East, and North Africa.

Establishment, within the framework of the UN, of appropriate international control of the fulfillment of the above obligations.

Creation of a UN agency for international cooperation in the field of the study of outer space.

Conclusion of such an agreement would lead toward broad international cooperation in the peaceful use of outer space and would initiate joint research by scientists of all countries in problems connected with the cosmos.

6. *Reduction in the number of foreign troops stationed in the territory of Germany and within the borders of other European states*

Consistently seeking the necessary agreement with other powers, the Soviet Union more than once has introduced concrete proposals on disarmament, and has also carried out a series of unilateral measures for reducing its own armed forces and armaments, proceeding from the premise that the other Great Powers will, for their part, follow this example. The Soviet Union is an advocate of a radical solution of the disarmament problem, a substantial reduction in the armed forces and armaments of states, the complete withdrawal of foreign armed forces from the territory of European states members of both military groups, including Germany, and the liquidation of all foreign military bases on foreign territories.

However, inasmuch as the Western powers have hitherto not displayed their readiness to come to an agreement on all these questions, the Soviet Union proposes, at this stage, that a start be made toward the solution of those questions on which there already exists a complete possibility of reaching an agreement. The Soviet Government proposes a gradual reduction of foreign troops in foreign territories and submits the proposal, in the nature of a first step, to reduce during 1958 the armed forces of the USSR, the US, the United Kingdom, France, and other states having troops in the territory of Germany, by one-third or to any other agreed extent. The reduced contingents of these troops must be withdrawn from the territory of Germany inside their own national frontiers.

The question of a substantial reduction in the armed forces and armaments of states and the conclusion of an appropriate international agreement with this objective, as well as the complete withdrawal of foreign armed forces from the territories of the states members of NATO and the Warsaw Treaty could be discussed during the following stage of negotiations.

7. Conclusion of a German peace treaty

All the peoples of Europe, which were drawn into the war on the side of Hitlerite Germany, have long been enjoying the fruits of a peaceful situation and have been building their life independently, whereas the German people are still deprived of the conditions for the peaceful development of their country and existence on equal terms with other peoples. The absence of a peace treaty also has a negative effect on the solution of its national task of unifying the country. Furthermore, the lack of a solution for questions connected with a peaceful settlement in Germany is used by those who do not value the fate of peace in Europe for drawing the Western part of Germany into preparation for atomic war.

Under these conditions, the Soviet Government considers that the powers responsible for the development of Germany in a peaceful manner should strive to attain a peaceful settlement with Germany as soon as possible. Being an advocate of such a settlement, the Soviet Government reiterates its proposal for a discussion at a summit conference of the question concerning the preparation and conclusion of a German peace treaty.

However, taking into consideration the attitude of the Governments of the US and other Western powers toward this proposal, the Soviet Government would be ready at the forthcoming meeting to come to an agreement at least on the first steps toward the solution of this question, namely, to agree, at the present stage, on the basic principles of a German peace treaty and the manner of its preparation. In this, the Soviet Government proceeds from the premise that preparatory work toward conclusion of a German peace treaty, with the participation of German representatives from the GDR and the FRG, would give impetus to the unification of the efforts of the German Democratic Republic and the Federal Republic of Germany toward their rapprochement and restoration of the unity of the German people.

8. *Prevention of surprise attack against one state by another*

Inasmuch as it still does not appear possible at the present time to resolve the problem of disarmament in full and there is talk of reaching an agreement regarding partial measures of disarmament, the Soviet Government proposes that the question of the prevention of surprise attack be gradually resolved, according to the nature of the measures, in the field of disarmament in the first stage. It would be necessary to come to an understanding concerning the establishment of control posts at railroad junctions, in large ports, and on main highways, and concerning the taking of aerial photographs in the zones of demarcation of the principal armed forces of the military groups in Europe, at the present stage in definite limited areas, which will be considered as the most important from the point of view of eliminating the danger of surprise attack.

In proposing such an approach to the solution of this problem, the Soviet Government proceeds from the premise that the Western powers have recognized the practical value of the Soviet proposal concerning the establishment of control posts as a means of preventing surprise attack. This gives a basis for hope that the conference can come to an agreement on this question.

The Soviet Government reiterates its proposal on the establishment in Europe of a zone of aerial inspection to a distance of 800 kilometers east and west of the line of demarcation of the armed forces of the NATO and Warsaw Pact military groups.

As for the proposal for carrying out aerial photography of vast regions or of the whole territory of the USSR and the USA, this question cannot be considered apart from measures for easing international tension and strengthening trust between states, especially between the Great Powers. In the present international situation, with the continuing arms race, which causes international tension as well as distrust and suspicion in the relations between states, with the "cold war" casting its black shadow over the whole international situation, the proposal concerning reciprocal flights over the entire territories of both countries is unrealistic. The Soviet Government considers, however, that this step can be carried out at the concluding stage of the problem of disarmament, that is, when the question concerning the complete ban on atomic and hydrogen weapons, with their elimination from armaments, concerning the substantial reduction of the armed forces and armaments of states, and concerning the liquidation of military bases in foreign territories is settled, that is, when relations of trust between states are actually established.

9. *Measures to expand international trade relations*

The Soviet Government considers that at the present time there are real opportunities for taking a number of steps to expand international trade relations as the natural and most dependable basis for peaceful cooperation among all states independently of the differences in their social systems. For the restoration and expansion of the trade of the Western countries with the enormous market of the East, where about a billion people live, it is essential above all to remove the discrimination and barriers hitherto existing, which hinder the expansion of international trade.

At the present time, as a result of the industrial slump and the decline in trade, a number of Western countries are experiencing serious economic difficulties, the remedy for which should also be sought by means of the development of international trade and not by means of an armaments race, or the intensification of economic war and blockade.

As concrete measures for the expansion of international trade, the Soviet Government proposes the adoption of a declaration of the basic principles of international economic cooperation, in which it would be desirable to include clauses on the observance of full equality; mutual benefit; the inadmissibility of any sort of discrimination in economic and trade relations between states; respect for the sovereign right of each state to dispose of its own wealth and natural resources; mutual assistance and aid to underdeveloped countries in their economic growth without the presentation of any sort of demand of a political, military, or other character incompatible with the national sovereignty of those countries.

There is also an urgent need to hold an international economic conference at which it would be desirable to discuss the question of the further development of international trade on a long-term basis so as to establish confidence and stability among trading countries, and also to discuss the question of the creation, within the framework of the UN, of an international trade organization open to all countries.

It would likewise be necessary to discuss such urgent questions as the rational utilization of world economic resources and the granting of aid to underdeveloped countries. For such aid, it would be possible to find additional funds by means of the reduction of expenditures for armaments.

10. Development of ties and contacts between states

The Soviet Government attaches great importance to the development of international contacts, and stands immutably for the development of contacts between East and West. The establishment of broader political, economic, and cultural ties between countries, independent of their social system, on the basis of mutual respect for sovereign rights and noninterference in their internal affairs satisfies the vital interests of peoples, and promotes the strengthening of friendship and of economic cooperation among them. This is confirmed, in particular by the successful completion of bilateral negotiations and the signing in Washington of a Soviet-American agreement in the fields of culture, technology, and education, as well as by the successful collaboration of the scientists of many countries in the program of the International Geophysical Year.

The Soviet Government also attaches great importance to the establishment and expansion of regular personal contacts between government and public figures of the countries of the East and the West for an exchange of opinions on current international questions. The expansion of such ties and contacts in the near future could be realized by means of the mutual exchange of parliamentary delegations and delegations of public entities; mutual exchange of delegations of scientific, technical, and cultural workers; mutual exchange of artists, theater troupes, symphony orchestras, etc.; mutual exchange of scientific and technical literature and documents, including designs and blueprints of machines and equipment, descriptions of technological processes, etc.; free access to industrial exhibitions; mutual exchange of students, professors, and university delegations; every kind of encouragement for tourism, sporting events, etc.

11. *Cessation of propaganda for war, hostility, and hatred between peoples*

Notwithstanding the fact that ten years have already passed since the adoption in October 1947 of the resolution of the UN General Assembly on the banning of propaganda for war, this unanimous resolution of the assembly is not being implemented in a number of countries. The idea of inevitability of a new war is being continually suggested to the peoples of these countries in the press, by radio and television, and by other means; the necessity of a race in nuclear armaments and of a further increase in military budgets and taxes on the population is being urged.

There is no doubt that, with good will and a mutual desire on the part of all participants in the summit conference, it would not be difficult to reach an understanding on the question of ceasing propaganda for war and carrying on instead a propaganda for friendship among peoples.

A settlement of this question could be achieved by means of the adoption of a joint declaration whereby the governments participating in the conference would confirm their intention to carry out faithfully the resolution of the UN General Assembly of October 1947 on the banning of all kinds of propaganda for war inimical to the cause of peace and mutual understanding and would undertake to adopt effective measures for the suppression of such propaganda in their own countries.

12. *Ways to ease the tension in the Near and Middle East*

In recent years in the Near and Middle East there have periodically come into being centers of tension containing the seeds of dangerous international conflicts capable of leading to a breach of world peace. In order to reduce tension in the Near and Middle East, it is necessary to create in the countries of that region the assurance that any breach of peace in the Near and Middle East on the part of any aggressive forces whatsoever will be decisively condemned and stopped. One of the measures could be a joint declaration of powers condemning the use of force in the settlement of disputes in the Near and Middle East, as well as interference in the internal affairs of the countries of that region. It would also be possible to come to an understanding on the mutual obligations of the countries participating in the conference not to supply weapons to the countries of the Near and Middle East, and also not to station nuclear and rocket weapons in those countries.

Considering the economic difficulties being experienced by the countries of the Near and Middle East, and their aspiration to consolidate their independence, the necessity arises of also considering the question of economic collaboration with the countries of the Near and Middle East, especially in the field of assistance for the creation in them of a national industry, proceeding from the principles of full equality and mutual benefit without the imposition upon them of any political, military, or other conditions whatsoever that are incompatible with the principles of independence and sovereignty.

(27) *Western Three Power Memorandum, May 28, 1958.*[7]

The Governments of the US, UK and France believe that the present international situation requires that a serious attempt be made to reach agreement on the main problems affecting the attainment of peace and stability in the world. They consider that, in the circumstances, a Summit meeting would be desirable if it would provide the opportunity for serious discussions of major problems and would be an effective means of reaching agreement on significant subjects.

[7] *Department of State Bulletin*, v. 39 (July 7, 1958), pp. 12-16.

They regard such settlements as constituting effective means for developing a spirit of confidence in their relations with the Soviet Union which could lead to cooperation among nations in the pursuit of a just and lasting peace.

Such settlements, if they are to serve this purpose, must take into account the legitimate interests of all the parties concerned and must embrace the necessary elements to assure their implementation.

In his letter of January 12, 1958, President Eisenhower put forward a series of proposals to Premier Bulganin. The Governments of the US, UK and France consider that they form the basis for mutually beneficial settlements at a meeting of Heads of Government. Some of the considerations which underlie this view are set forth below. In making their proposals in the field of disarmament, the three governments recall their obligations, undertaken in the UN Charter, not to use any weapons against the territorial integrity or political independence of any state. While a comprehensive disarmament remains their ultimate aim, they propose certain practical balanced and interdependent measures which would mark significant progress toward controlling the arms race and thus reducing the danger of war. Progress of this sort would also create an atmosphere of confidence which could facilitate settlement of the political controversies that disturb relations between the Western Powers and the Soviet Union. Reduction in both nuclear weapons and conventional armed forces and armaments are vital for this purpose. The three Governments therefore consider it desirable to make clear once again what were the reasons which led them to put forward far reaching proposals for partial disarmament in 1957.

1. *Measures to control production of fissionable materials for nuclear weapons and to reduce existing military stocks of such materials*

As for the nuclear problem, the heart of the matter is not the mere testing, but the weapons themselves. The Western Powers seek a dependable ending to the accumulation of nuclear weapons and a dependable beginning of the steady reduction of existing weapons stockpiles. Since there is no known reliable means for detecting the weapons already made, the most effective and feasible way to work toward the reduction and elimination of nuclear weapons is to halt production of fissionable materials for making them and to begin reducing weapons stockpiles by equitable transfers to peaceful uses. The Western Powers are prepared to discuss these measures and the ratios of materials to be transferred from existing weapons stocks to peaceful uses with a view to arriving at equitable proportions for such transfers by the states concerned.

2. *Suspension of nuclear tests*

If there is agreement to put an end to the production of new fissionable materials for nuclear weapons, the way lies open to an immediate solution of the problem of nuclear testing. So long as unrestricted manufacture of nuclear weapons continues, and new means are being developed for delivering nuclear weapons rapidly and surely the suspension of nuclear testing does not constitute disarmament. It is relevant to underline the fact that the existence of nuclear stocks, which are constantly growing, constitutes a much more serious dnager than nuclear tests. Thus, the Western Powers propose not only the suspension of nuclear tests but the stopping of production of new fissionable materials for weapons purposes and the progressive conversion of stocks of these materials to peaceful uses. Testing could be stopped indefinitely if the necessary inspection system is installed and the production of fissionable materials for weapons is also effectively ended. Both would be carried out under effective measures of international control.

3. *The reduction and limitation of conventional arms and manpower*

An agreement on initial verifiable reductions of armed forces and their stocks of arms could ease the way toward settlement of problems which create international friction. In their turn, such settlements could set the stage for further reductions. This is a sound approach for developing confidence in relations between the countries. On the other hand, unverified and uncontrolled unilateral measures can well be merely shifts in deployment or temporary reductions. They do not inspire confidence.

With these considerations in mind, the Western Governments propose that the Soviet Union join them in agreeing on an initial limitation of their armed forces; and on placing in storage depots, within their own territories, and under the supervision of an international control organization, specific quantities of designated types of armaments. They will be prepared also to negotiate on a further limitation of their armed forces and armaments provided that compliance with commitments above has been verified to mutual satisfaction, that there has been progress toward the solution of political issues, and that other essential states have accepted equitable levels for their armed forces and armaments.

4. *Measures to guard against surprise attack*

Until general controlled disarmament becomes a reality, the surest way toward the development of confidence lies in lifting fears of surprise attack. Growing capabilities of surprise attack on a massive scale underscore the importance of a prompt beginning on measures to deal with this problem. The Western Powers want to meet it on the broadest scale possible. The Governments of the US, UK and France express their readiness to enter into discussion of this subject both from the standpoint of technical considerations of ways and means of achieving this end in the most practical way and from the standpoint of initial areas to be included in the progressive installation of such a system. In this connection the three Governments reaffirm their willingness as expressed in the United Nations Disarmament Subcommittee on August 29, 1957,[8] to consider the installation of a system of air and ground inspection as a safeguard against surprise attack on a comprehensive scale embracing all of the US, USSR, Canada, and with the consent of the countries involved, the greater part of Europe as well. If this proposal is not acceptable to the USSR, the three Governments are also prepared to consider the establishment in the first instance of smaller zones in the Arctic and European regions, provided that the latter also included a significant part of the territory of the Soviet Union. As the US indicated at Geneva in 1955, if agreement is reached on the installation of measures of air and ground inspection on the comprehensive scale outlined above, negotiations could be undertaken promptly both with other sovereign states involved and with the Soviet Union for the appropriate extension of such inspection, on a reciprocal, equitable basis and subject to the consent of any governments concerned, to bases outside of national territory.

5. *Use of outer space for peaceful purposes*

An opportunity to stop the development of new and more powerful weapons was tragically lost a decade ago when the US offer to renounce making atomic weapons and to make

[8] *Documents on American Foreign Relations, 1957*, pp. 439-446.

the use of atomic energy an international asset for peaceful purposes only was not accepted. A great step forward in building confidence among peoples and in reducing the danger to humanity from new and powerful weapons would have been made if this offer had been accepted. The responsible countries are faced once more with a similar decision, laden with serious consequences for mankind. The three governments propose that the Soviet Union join in the establishment of a group of experts who would make the necessary technical studies for determining what measures are required to assure that outer space is used for peaceful purposes only.

6. *Reunification of Germany in accordance with the terms of the 1955 Directive of the four Heads of Government to the Ministers of Foreign Affairs*

The continued division of Germany is a major obstacle to the restoration of confidence and the creation of conditions of genuine peace and stability in Europe. Thirteen years have passed since the end of the war in Europe, yet no peace settlement has been made with Germany. A necessary prerequisite for such a settlement is the creation of a government which truly reflects the will of the German people. Only a government created on such a basis can undertake obligations which will inspire confidence on the part of other countries and which will be considered just and binding by the people of Germany themselves.

The Heads of Government in Geneva recognized the common responsibility of the four powers for the settlement of the German question and the reunification of Germany. They agreed that the settlement of the German question and the reunification of Germany through free elections should be carried out in conformity with the national interests of the German people and the interests of European security. The Western Powers propose that the Soviet Union join with them in immediate steps to carry out their responsibility by agreeing to permit an all-German Government to be formed by free elections and enabling it to carry out its functions. Such an agreement would give tangible evidence of a common desire on the part of the four governments to create the conditions of trust on which a lasting peace can be based.

7. *European security arrangements*

The Western Powers are aware of the fact that the Soviet Union has expressed concern that the creation of a freely-chosen all-German Government with the full attributes of sovereignty would bring about changes in the present situation in Europe which the Soviet Union would consider detrimental to its security interests. The three governments are prepared to enter into arrangements concerning European security which would give assurances to the Soviet Union in this regard. The arrangements they envisage would involve limitations on forces and armaments. They would also involve assurances designed to prevent aggression in Europe by the exchange of undertakings to take appropriate action in the event of such aggression.

The three governments seek no one-sided advantage in such arrangements, nor do they contemplate entering into arrangements which would give a one-sided advantage to the Soviet Union to the prejudice of their essential security interests. Confidence can be created by international agreements only if the agreements take equally into account the legitimate security interests of all the parties concerned.

The Western Powers call on the Soviet Union to enter into negotiations on the subject of European security in this spirit, with a view to concluding a treaty which would enter into force in conjunction with an agreement on the reunification of Germany. This would recognize the close link which the powers concerned have agreed exists between the two subjects. The linked settlement of these two questions and the confidence created thereby would also permit further progress to be made in the limitation of armaments generally.

8. *International exchanges*

Lasting peace requires a satisfactory settlement of the problems which concern the general relationship between the peoples of Eastern Europe and those of the Western countries. An important step forward along the path of mutual understanding would be made if the interested governments agreed to remove the obstacles which still prevent peoples from knowing each other and to satisfy the common aspirations of all men by guaranteeing them objective and complete information and by promoting closer cultural ties and human relations.

In July 1955, at the Geneva Conference, the four Heads of Government included this question in the directives given to the Ministers of Foreign Affairs. While some progress has been made in certain fields since that date, much remains to be done to eliminate the obstacles which still hinder mutual acquaintance and understanding, the conditions for a durable and genuine peace.

9. *Means of strengthening the United Nations*

The peoples of the world look upon the UN organization
and the pledges of its members embodied in its Charter as
man's best hope for peace and justice. Thus, the Western
governments cannot but welcome the recent assertion of the
Soviet Union that it believes in the importance of the United
Nations and its role in the maintenance of peace and security
as well as in the peaceful settlement of international issues.
Like the USSR, they deem that efforts should be made to
strengthen the United Nations by every means, so that it
should be able to fulfill its tasks more effectively. One practical way in which this can be done now is through an undertaking by the Governments of the US, UK, France and USSR
that they will, as a matter of policy, avoid vetoing Security
Council recommendations as to how nations might proceed
toward the peaceful solution of their disputes.

10. *Ways of easing tensions in Eastern Europe*

The creation of conditions of stability in Eastern Europe
based on relations of independence and friendship among the
countries of the area would greatly contribute to the cause
of promoting a just and lasting world peace. That this should
come about is thus not an aspiration of neighboring Western
Europe alone, but of all the world. This international interest found its expression in the international agreements concerning the right of the peoples of the area to chose their
own governments; the peace treaties with their provisions
designed to safeguard human rights; the efforts of many
countries to improve the economic welfare of the people;
and efforts to eliminate interference in their internal affairs.

The Western Powers believe that a serious discussion of
the problem posed by the existence of tensions in Eastern
Europe should be held with the aim of eliminating interference in the internal affairs of the countries of that region
and the use of force in the settlement of disputes there.

The Western governments believe that the proposals set
forth above are feasible and could be put into effect now.
They believe their implementation is verifiable. The proposals take into account the legitimate interests and security
needs of the countries concerned. Their adoption could
create a basis for the development of an atmosphere of confidence and trust that would favor the growth of more active
mutually beneficial relations between our peoples and governments.

(28) *Western Three Power Aide Memoire, May 28, 1958.*[9]

The Governments of the US, UK and France after consideration of the Soviet Government's Aide Memoire of May 5, have concluded that the positions of the governments with regard to the purpose of the talks between the three Western Ambassadors and the Soviet Foreign Minister and of a subsequent Foreign Ministers' meeting are sufficiently close to permit the substantive preparatory work for a possible Summit meeting to proceed without delay. It is their understanding that this work should go forward along the following lines:

The purpose of the preparatory work shall be to examine the position of the various governments on the major questions at issue between them and to establish what subjects should be submitted for examination by Heads of Government. It is understood that it would not be the purpose of the preparatory work to reach decisions, but to bring out, by general discussion, the possibilities of agreement. When they have made progress in these talks the Ambassadors and the Soviet Foreign Minister will also have the task of agreeing on the time, place and composition of a Foreign Ministers' meeting.

The special tasks assigned to the Foreign Ministers themselves shall be to establish whether they are satisfied that the preparatory work affords the prospect that a Summit meeting would, in fact, provide the opportunity for conducting serious discussions of major problems and be the means for reaching agreement on significant subjects. If and when this has been established to their satisfaction, the Foreign Ministers will then reach agreement on the date, place and composition of a Summit meeting.

(29) *Western Three Power Agenda Items, May 31, 1958.*[10]

[With only Western items listed as examples]

Disarmament

(a) Measures to control the production of fissionable material for nuclear weapons and to reduct existing military stocks of such materials;

[9] *Department of State Bulletin,* v. 39 (July 7, 1958), p. 16.
[10] *Ibid.,* pp. 16-17.

(b) The suspension of nuclear tests;

(c) The reduction and limitation of conventional arms and manpower;

(d) Measures to guard against surprise attack;

(e) The use of outer space for peaceful purposes.

European Security and Germany

(a) Reunification of Germany in accordance with the terms of the 1955 Directive of the four Heads of Government to the Ministers of Foreign Affairs;

(b) European security arrangements.

International Exchanges

(a) Cessation of jamming of foreign broadcasts;

(b) Censorship;

(c) Free distribution and sale to the public of books and publications;

(d) Free distribution and sale of foreign newspapers and periodicals;

(e) Freedom of travel.

Methods of Improving International Cooperation

Means of strengthening the United Nations.

Other Topics

Ways of easing tension in Eastern Europe.

> (30) *Letter from the Chairman of the Council of Ministers of the USSR (Khrushchev) to the President, June 11, 1958.*[11]

(Excerpts)

Dear Mr. President,

I feel compelled to address this message to you in view of the situation that has arisen in the negotiations on preparation of a Summit Meeting.

It is now nearly two months since the preliminary diplomatic negotiations on preparation of this meeting began at the suggestion of the Western Powers. When the Western Powers first raised the question of preliminary diplomatic negotiations, the Soviet Government expressed serious doubt as to whether this procedure would facilitate the convening of a Summit Meeting. We did not conceal our apprehension

[11] *New Times*, no. 26 (June 1958), Supplement, pp. 2-6.

that, having embarked on these talks, we might find our-selves on a slippery path that would delay matters and put off the Heads of Government Conference. Nonetheless, the So-viet Government consented to these talks inasmuch as the Western Powers insisted on this method of preparing the meeting.

Unfortunately, our apprehensions about the preliminary talks are being justified. We are still marking time in prepa-rations for the meeting, and on a number of questions are, in effect, moving backwards. That being the situation, many —and not only in the Soviet Union—are beginning to won-der whether the very proposal to hold these preliminary talks was not calculated to create additional impediments to a top-level conference.

When, six months ago, the Soviet Government invited the United States and other Governments to convene a broad international conference of leading statesmen, we were ani-mated by the desire to find, through joint effort, ways and means of radically changing the present state of international relations. We believed, as we do now, that this meeting should lead to agreement on easing the strain in international relations, ending the cold war, providing conditions for the peaceful co-existence of nations and renouncing war as a method of resolving controversial questions. The dangerous trend international relations have now taken, particularly relations between the Great Powers, must not be allowed to continue. Now that the Powers possess weapons of limitless destructive force, passivity would be a crime. The time has come for vigorous joint intervention by responsible states-men to remove the terrible danger, free mankind of the op-pressing menace of atomic war and give the people what they need most of all—stable peace and confidence in the morrow.

Mr. President, in January you responded to the proposal for a Summit Conference, stating that you were prepared to meet with the leaders of the Soviet Union and other coun-tries. The Governments of Great Britain and France like-wise responded to our proposal. All this reinforced our hopes for an early Summit Meeting and was welcomed by the Gov-ernments and peoples of all countries.

It was, therefore, natural to expect that in the course of the preliminary talks the parties would endeavour to submit for consideration at the Summit such pressing international problems on which, given the good will of the negotiators, there was a practical possibility of achieving positive results already at this stage and thus bring about a healthier international climate. We continue to hold that view, notably with regard to the agenda for a Summit Meeting.

*   *   *

As you know, Mr. President, in the proposals submitted to your Ambassador in Moscow on May 5, the Soviet Government set forth its views on the questions that might be discussed at the Summit Conference. This was done with the object of facilitating agreement on convocation of the conference. We took into account the views of the Western Governments, notably the U.S. Government, as expressed in the course of the discussions on preparation of the conference. The text of the Soviet proposals is appended to this message.[12]

In advancing its proposals for a Summit agenda, the Soviet Union announced from the very start that it was prepared to examine, by common consent, any other suggestions likely to end the cold war and arms drive.

*   *   *

The Soviet Government continues to consider it its duty to do everything it can to expedite solution of the disarmament problem. That is the aim of the recent decisions on substantial reduction of our armed forces and unilateral termination of testing of all types of atomic and hydrogen weapons. Eager to expedite agreement on universal cessation of the tests, the Soviet Government has agreed, in deference to the wishes of the United States and British Governments, for experts to study methods of detecting possible violation of a test ban.

We hope that this new step by the Soviet Union will be properly received by the Western Powers and will result in a more favourable atmosphere for an early Summit Meeting.

Mr. President, I think the time has come fully and frankly to clarify the attitude of the parties on the cardinal question: do all the parties really want a Summit Meeting? I must say that the documents we have received from the Western Powers inspire grave doubts on this score. It is hard to get away

[12] The enclosure was the Soviet memorandum of May 5 (for text, see Document 26, above) with the addition of a final paragraph which reads as follows:

"The Soviet Government is convinced that good will and readiness to seek mutually acceptable solutions, with due regard for the interest of the parties concerned, can ensure the success of a summit conference and can cause the necessary shift in the development of the international situation in the interest of strengthening peace among nations."

from the thought that the authors of the proposals set forth in them were animated not by a desire to find solutions acceptable to all concerned, but, on the contrary, sought out issues for the solution of which conditions have not yet matured, in order to be able to say later that they were right in predicting the failure of a Heads of Government Meeting.

All this has impelled us to address this letter to you. We would like to know definitely whether the Western Powers have serious intentions regarding the organization and conduct of Summit talks, the results of which are awaited by virtually the whole of mankind. Or is this merely an attempt to lull public attention, create the impression that contact has been established and negotiations are in progress, while in actual fact issues are advanced that cannot only torpedo preparation of the meeting, but prevent it being held, so that later on the Soviet Union could be accused of "intransigence." That tactic is all to well known to us from the experience of certain earlier negotiations.

The Soviet Government has closely studied the proposals for a Summit agenda set forth in your messages, Mr. President. We have stated our views on them in detail, declaring that several of the items suggested by the Western Powers we consider to be acceptable for discussion. We are prepared to examine also ways and means of strengthening the United Nations, a question touched upon in the correspondence between our Governments, for we, too, have something to say on this score.

Mr. President, I have stated with full frankness my views on the situation that has arisen in the preparation of a Summit Meeting. It is a situation in which special responsibility devolves on the Governments of the Great Powers. To appreciate the gravity of that responsibility, we have only to visualize how depressed the peoples would feel if we failed to find a common language. No one would understand or justify statesmen who could not agree even on how to begin negotiations. And this at a time when the world is in a state of agitation, caused by intensification of the arms drive, and when there is no place on earth where the people are free of the oppressive fear engendered by the war danger.

We are convinced that the joint efforts of the nations, and primarily the joint efforts of the United States of America and the Soviet Union, can transform the international situation. An important step in that direction would be a conference of leading statesmen, with the Heads of Government participating. I express the hope that the Government of the United States of America will give due consideration to this message and, for its part, will take the necessary steps to prevent disruption of the Summit Conference and clear the way to it of artificial obstacles.

I am sending messages on the subject also to the Prime Minister of Great Britain and the President of the Council of Ministers of France.

Sincerely,

N. KHRUSHCHEV

(31) *Letter from the President to the Chairman of the Council of Ministers of the USSR (Khrushchev), July 1, 1958.*[13]

DEAR MR. CHAIRMAN: I was frankly surprised by your letter of June 11. You complain about delay in preparations for a Summit meeting precisely at the moment when the Western powers have submitted a proposal for a serious and effective procedure for conducting these preparations. This refutes the allegation contained in your letter that the three Western powers are creating obstacles and impeding progress toward a Summit meeting.

The position of the Western powers concerning holding of a meeting of Heads of Government has been clear from the outset. They consider such a meeting desirable if it would provide an opportunity for conducting serious discussions of major problems and would be an effective means of reaching agreement on significant subjects. From the known positions of the Soviet Government, there is no evidence so far that such is the case. That is why the Western powers insist on adequate preparatory work and why they have put forward their proposal to facilitate satisfactory completion of this work.

The Soviet Government instead has disrupted the discussions in Moscow by taking upon itself to publish with bare hours of warning and no attempt at consultation the documents exchanged between it and the Western powers, including diplomatic documents originating from the Western powers.[14] This action is scarcely consonant with the spirit of serious

[13] *Department of State Bulletin*, v. 39 (July 21, 1958), pp. 95-96.
[14] On June 16, 1958 the Soviet government released to the public a number of documents, including its memorandum of May 5, 1958 and the Western Three Power memorandum of May 28, 1958 (Documents 26 and 27 above). See *New Times*, no. 26 (June 1958), Supplement, pp. 7-16.

preparation in which the Western powers entered into these diplomatic exchanges. It cannot but cast doubt on the intentions of the Soviet Government concerning the proper preparations for a Summit meeting.

Following receipt of the Soviet agenda proposals on May 5 the three Ambassadors in interviews on May 28, 31 and June 2 presented in return the Western agenda proposals. They also outlined to Mr. Gromyko a suggested procedure for overcoming the difficulty caused by the fact that the two sets of proposals were widely divergent. The Western Ambassadors are quite ready to offer comments on the Soviet agenda proposals and to clarify certain points in their own proposals on which the Soviet Government seems to have misconceptions. But the Western Governments cannot agree that the discussions between their Ambassadors and Mr. Gromyko should be based exclusively on the Soviet list any more than they would expect the Soviet Government to agree to base the discussions solely on the Western list. Since the topics in both lists fall under certain general headings, the Western proposal was that preparatory discussion of the individual topics put forward by the two sides should take place within the framework of these general headings. Had this been accepted by the Soviet Government, the Soviet Foreign Minister and the Ambassadors could have proceeded to examine the positions of the various governments on the topics in both lists and establish what subjects should be submitted for examination by the Heads of Government. Neither side would, during the preparatory stage, have been able to veto the inclusion of any topic for discussion and an opportunity would have been afforded to find some common ground, for later consideration by Heads of Government.

Mr. Gromyko promised an official reply to the above proposal. Instead, however, the Soviet Government has now addressed communications to the Heads of Government of the three Western powers, in the form of your letters of June 11, which repeat the arguments in favor of the Soviet set of proposals of May 5 and criticize some of the Western proposals which it happens not to like. The procedural proposal put forward by the Ambassadors has been ignored altogether.

You allege in your letters that the Western powers by including, as possible subjects of discussion at a meeting of Heads of Government, some of the great political issues that create grave tension are trying to prevent the holding of a Summit meeting. There is no warrant for this allegation. A meeting of Heads of Government would not respond to the hopes and aspirations of mankind if they met under an injunction that seals their lips so that they could not even mention the great political issues that gravely trouble their relations and endanger world peace.

In spite of the arbitrary action of the Soviet Government and its apparent unwillingness to negotiate seriously on concrete points at issue, the Western powers do not propose to abandon hope or to relax their efforts to seek solutions of the major outstanding problems. If the Soviet Government is equally serious in pursuing this goal, it will accept the procedural proposal put forward by the Western powers or advance some equally effective and workable alternative.

Sincerely,

DWIGHT D. EISENHOWER

D. Disarmament.

1. *Exchange of Correspondence between the President and the Chairman of the Council of Ministers of the USSR (Khrushchev).*

(32) *Letter from the Chairman of the Council of Ministers (Khrushchev), April 4, 1958.*[1]

DEAR MR. PRESIDENT: One of the most urgent problems in present international relations which very deeply agitates millions of people in all countries of the world is that of the necessity of the immediate discontinuance of tests of atomic and hydrogen weapons of various kinds. It is easy to understand the deep alarm which the continuing experimental explosions of nuclear weapons arouse among all strata of society, from political personages, scientists, and specialists to ordinary people, the rank-and-file workers of city and village, to mothers of families. These tests stimulate the armaments race and promote the development of new and ever more destructive and deadly kinds of nuclear weapons, and thereby still further intensify the threat of atomic war which hangs over mankind.

Moreover, systematic explosions of atomic and hydrogen weapons for experimental purposes even now, in peacetime, are causing damage to the health of peaceful, unsuspecting, and entirely innocent inhabitants of various countries. In

[1] *Department of State Bulletin*, v. 38 (April 28, 1958), pp. 680-681.

the petition signed by 9235 scientists of 44 countries, including many prominent scientists of the United States of America and of the Soviet Union, and delivered in January of this year to the Secretary General of the United Nations, it is stated that each test of a nuclear bomb increases the quantity of radioactive fallout, thereby causing harm to the health of people throughout the entire world and threatening the normal development of coming generations.

Taking all this into account, the Soviet government has come to the conclusion that it is impossible to postpone any longer the solution of the question concerning the discontinuance of nuclear weapon tests because it is impossible to allow the health of the people to be irreparably harmed.

Today only three powers so far—the U.S.S.R., the U.S.A., and Great Britain—possess nuclear weapons, and therefore an agreement on the discontinuance of nuclear weapon tests is comparatively easy to reach. However, if the tests are not now discontinued, then after some time other countries may become possessors of nuclear weapons and under such conditions it will of course be a more complicated matter to reach an agreement on the discontinuance of the tests.

During the last three years the Soviet government has repeatedly approached the governments of the United States of America and of Great Britain with proposals to discontinue tests of atomic and hydrogen weapons. In as much as both the Government of the United States and the Government of Great Britain have not wished to agree to discontinue nuclear tests without specifying a time limit, the Soviet Union advanced a proposal of its own, that is, to discontinue these tests, at first even for a limited time, for two or three years, for example. The proposals of the U.S.S.R. on this question provide for the establishment of the necessary international control for the discontinuance of tests.

Despite all this, it has unfortunately been impossible up to now to come to an agreement for settling the question concerning an unconditional and immediate discontinuance of nuclear tests, or even concerning a temporary suspension.

Guided by the desire to make a practical beginning to the discontinuance of tests of atomic and hydrogen weapons everywhere and thereby take the first step in the direction of a final liberation of mankind from the threat of a destructive atomic war, the Supreme Soviet of the Union of Soviet Socialist Republics has decreed the discontinuance in the

Soviet Union of tests of all kinds of atomic and hydrogen weapons.[2]

The Soviet Government, implementing this decree of the Supreme Soviet of the U.S.S.R., *decided to discontinue unilaterally, as of March 31, 1958, tests of any kind of atomic and hydrogen weapons.*

The Soviet Government addresses to the Government of the United States of America, and also to the Government of Great Britain, a proposal to join in these measures.

If the governments of the countries which now have nuclear weapons at their disposal support this proposal of the U.S.S.R. and in their turn adopt a decision to renounce further tests, then the question which so deeply agitates the peoples of the whole world will finally be resolved and a great step will thereby be taken toward the establishment of genuine trust among states and toward the strengthening of peace.

However, if the governments of the countries with the nuclear weapons at their disposal do not wish to respond to this decision of the Soviet Government and prefer to leave things as they were before and continue experiments with atomic and hydrogen weapons, then in such case the Soviet Union, in the interests of ensuring its own safety, will of course have no alternative other than that of considering itself freed from any obligation undertaken by it in regard to the discontinuance of nuclear tests. The Soviet Government would not like to see matters take such a course.

The Government of the U.S.S.R. expresses the sincere hope that the Government of the United States of America will join in the initiative of the Soviet Union and will thereby make possible the discontinuance forever of nuclear weapon tests everywhere.

In the opinion of the Soviet Government it would be appropriate if our two countries—the U.S.S.R. and the U.S.A., which were the first to create atomic and hydrogen weapons and to possess considerable stocks of these weapons—would come forth as leaders in the noble cause of the immediate cessation of nuclear tests.

This first practical step on the path toward the protection of mankind against the calamities with which it is threatened by modern nuclear weapons would enormously facilitate the advance toward a solution of the problem, that is, the com-

[2] The text of the decree is reprinted in the *Department of State Bulletin,* v. 38 (April 21, 1958), pp. 646-647.

plete liberation of peoples from the threat of an atomic war. Hardly anyone will deny that the discontinuance of experiments with atomic and hydrogen weapons would greatly improve the international political atmosphere as a whole and would create more favorable conditions for the settlement of other unsolved international problems.

Permit me, Mr. President, to express the hope that the proposals of the Soviet Government stated above will meet with a favorable attitude on the part of the Government of the United States of America.

With sincere esteem,

N. KHRUSHCHEV

(33) Letter from the President, April 8, 1958.[3]

DEAR MR. CHAIRMAN: I have your communication of April 4 repeating, in substance, the already widely publicized statement of the Soviet Government with reference to the suspension of nuclear testing.

It seems peculiar that the Soviet Union, having just concluded a series of tests of unprecedented intensity, should now, in bold headlines, say that it will not test again, but add, in small type, that it may test again if the United States carries out its already long announced and now imminent series of tests.

The timing, wording, and manner of the Soviet declaration cannot but raise questions as to its real significance.

The position of the United States on this matter of testing is well-known. For several years we have been seeking a dependable ending to the accumulation of nuclear weapons and a dependable beginning of the steady reduction of existing weapons stockpiles. This was my "Atoms for Peace" proposal, made in 1953 before the United Nations. Surely, the heart of the nuclear problem is not the mere testing of weapons, but the weapons themselves. If weapons are dependably dealt with, then it is natural to suspend their testing. However, the Soviet Union continues to reject the concept of an internationally supervised program to end weapons production and to reduce weapons stocks. Under those circumstances of the Soviet's making, the United States seeks to develop the defensive rather than the offensive capabilities of nuclear power and to learn how to minimize the fissionable fallout.

[3] *Ibid.* (April 28, 1958), pp. 679-680.

It goes without saying that these experiments, so far as the United States is concerned, are so conducted that they cannot appreciably affect human health.

Perhaps, Mr. Chairman, you recall the Joint Declaration made by the Governments of the United Kingdom and the United States at Bermuda on March 24, 1957.[4] We then declared that we would conduct nuclear tests only in such a manner as would keep world radiation from rising to more than a small fraction of the levels that might be hazardous. We went on to say that we would continue publicly announcing our test series well in advance of their occurrence with information as to their location and general timing.

We further said that we would be willing to register with the United Nations advance notice of our intention to conduct future nuclear tests and to permit limited international observation of such tests if the Soviet Union would do the same.

The Soviet Union has never responded to that invitation. Its latest series of tests was conducted behind a cloak of secrecy, so far as the Soviet Union could make it so. Nevertheless, as I recently stated,[5] it is the intention of the United States to invite observation by the United Nations of certain of our forthcoming tests.

Not only did the Soviet Union ignore our Bermuda proposal on testing, but it has persistently rejected the substance of my "Atoms for Peace" proposal. It refuses to agree to an internationally supervised cut-off of the use of new fissionable material for weapons purposes and the reduction of existing weapons stocks by transfers to peaceful purposes. During the five years since I first proposed "Atoms for Peace," the destructive power in our nuclear arsenals has steadily mounted, and a dependably controlled reduction of that power becomes ever more difficult.

Mr. Chairman, now that you have become head of the Soviet Government, will you not reconsider your Government's position and accept my proposal that fissionable materials henceforth be manufactured only for peaceful purposes?

If the Soviet Union is as peace-loving as it professes, surely it would want to bring about an internationally supervised

[4] *Documents on American Foreign Relations, 1957,* pp. 130-132.
[5] *Department of State Bulletin,* v. 38 (April 14, 1958), p. 601. The test demonstrations were subsequently canceled because of inclement weather. See *ibid.* v. 39 (August 11, 1958), p. 237.

diversion of fissionable material from weapons purposes to peace purposes.

If the Soviet Union is unwilling to accept "Atoms for Peace," there are other outstanding proposals by which the Soviet Union can advance the cause of peace. You will recall, Mr. Chairman, my "Open Skies" proposal made to you and Chairman Bulganin in Geneva in 1955.[6] You will also recall my proposals for the international use of outer space for peaceful purposes emphasized in my recent correspondence with Chairman Bulganin. These proposals await Soviet acceptance.

The United States is also prepared, in advance of agreement upon any one or more of the outstanding "disarmament" propositions, to work with the Soviet Union, and others as appropriate, on the technical problems involved in international controls. We both recognize that international control would be necessary. Indeed, your present letter to me speaks of "the establishment of the necessary international control for the discontinuance of tests."

What is "necessary"? The question raises problems of considerable complexity, given the present possibility of conducting some types of tests under conditions of secrecy.

If there is ever to be an agreed limitation or suspension of testing, and the United States hopes and believes that this will in due course come about as part of a broad disarmament agreement, plans for international control should be in instant readiness. Why should we not at once put our technicians to work to study together and advise as to what specific control measures are necessary if there is to be a dependable and agreed disarmament program?

The United Nations General Assembly has called for technical disarmament studies, in relation both to nuclear and conventional armaments. The United States says "yes". I urge, Mr. Chairman, that the Soviet Union should also say "yes". Then we can at once begin the preliminaries necessary to larger things.

Sincerely,

DWIGHT D. EISENHOWER

[6] Documents on American Foreign Relation, 1955, pp. 213-216.

(34) *Letter from the Chairman of the Council of Ministers of the USSR (Khrushchev), April 22, 1958.*[7]

(Excerpts)

DEAR MR. PRESIDENT: I have received your message of April 8, containing a reply to my message to you in which, on behalf of the Soviet Government, I called upon the Government of the United States of America to join in the decision of the Soviet Union to terminate the testing of atomic and hydrogen weapons.

*　　*　　*

Your negative reply to my message has caused profound disappointment among us. I shall not speak of the tone of the message or of the inclusion in it of a number of assertions in which the position of the U.S.S.R. on the problem of disarmament is knowingly distorted.

The main point is that in your reply we have found no statement concerning the willingness of the United States of America to follow the example of the Soviet Union and to terminate, in its turn, the testing of nuclear and hydrogen weapons.

Moreover, in your message an attempt is made to cast doubt on the sincerity of the step taken by the Soviet Union. To be frank, I became perplexed when I learned that in a statement at your press conference of April 2 you evaluated the decision of the supreme organ of the Soviet state as a "propaganda gesture." [8] How can an act aimed at erecting the first barrier against the nuclear armaments race and at protecting the life and health of mankind from the danger of atomic radiation be called propaganda?

In your message you deemed it necessary to state that the Soviet Union had adopted this decision after having conducted tests of atomic and hydrogen weapons. But is it not a fact that the United States of America has conducted a considerably greater number of tests of nuclear weapons than has the Soviet Union? Did not the United States of America have the opportunity after any of these tests to display initiative in the matter of terminating further tests? I can assure you, Mr. President, that if the United States had been the

[7] *Department of State Bulletin*, v. 38 (May 19, 1958), pp. 812-815.
[8] *New York Times*, April 3, 1958.

first to take such a step, we would have welcomed it sincerely.

It is well known that negotiations among states on the question of terminating nuclear weapons tests have not yet resulted in any agreement. But does this mean that we must resign ourselves to the present situation and undertake no steps to achieve a solution of this problem? Of course not. Peoples demand of us practical steps, and it is the duty of statesmen to do everything in their power to bring about a realization of the aspirations of peoples.

In such an important matter as the cessation of atomic and hydrogen weapons tests someone had to take the first step. We have taken that step, and we are waiting for the Government of the United States of America to follow our example. If we proceed on the principle of strengthening peace and preventing the threat of nuclear war, it should be stated directly that there are no reasons which would prevent the Government of the United States of America from taking such a step.

Indeed, can a cessation of atomic and hydrogen weapons tests by the United States, following a similar step by the Soviet Union, really prejudice in any way the interests of security or the prestige of the United States? Unquestionably, it cannot. If the point is that the United States needs tests to perfect atomic and hydrogen weapons, then, since the United States has already conducted a considerably greater number of these tests than has the Soviet Union, it follows that in this respect also the United States would lose nothing at all by terminating the testing of nuclear and hydrogen weapons in a situation where the Soviet Union has already ceased such tests.

With the testing of atomic weapons terminated, all parties would find themselves in an equal position, from the standpoint of their security interests. One could object to terminating nuclear weapons tests in the event, for instance, that one of the parties would like to obtain military or strategic advantages over the other party. However, I believe that you, Mr. President, agree that none of the parties should strive toward such an objective.

As to the matter of prestige, I believe that you will agree with me that a power acting in the interest of strengthening peace will never impair its prestige. On the contrary, peoples will only be grateful to any state if it undertakes actions directed toward strengthening peace. It is never too late for good deeds.

In your reply you speak of the possibility of conducting certain types of tests in secrecy, thereby giving us to understand that it will be impossible to verify the suspension of tests and that deception is possible here. We cannot agree with this appraisal, for in reality the situation is quite different. It is a known fact that at the present time there do exist such apparatus, such instruments, and such methods of detection as to make it possible to record any explosions of atomic and hydrogen weapons, wherever they may be detonated. You have even spoken of this yourself. Thus, no state can violate its commitment to cease testing atomic and hydrogen weapons without other states becoming apprised of this violation.

It should be added to the foregoing that the Soviet Government not only does not object to the establishment of a system of control over the cessation of atomic and hydrogen weapons tests but has even introduced its own specific proposals in this regard. Unfortunately, the Western Powers have not accepted the proposal of the Soviet Union, and it has not yet been possible to reach an agreement on the matter of control over the cessation of atomic and hydrogen weapons tests.

There is no need for me to put particular emphasis here on the enormous moral and political responsibility which would be assumed by states declaring a cessation of atomic and hydrogen weapons tests. Is it conceivable that in time some state might violate the obligations assumed, knowing beforehand that it would thus expose itself in the eyes of nations?

You also say that the cessation of nuclear weapons tests must be part of a broad agreement on disarmament. It is entirely impossible to agree with this statement, considering the many years of experience of essentially fruitless negotiations on problems of disarmament. Authoritative scientists are already giving warnings concerning the dangerous consequences of radio-active fallout for the health of people throughout the entire globe.

What then, Mr. President, awaits us in the future, if along with conversations about disarmament the testing of ever more powerful means of destruction continues? Is it not obvious that the baneful character of radioactive particles which fall out in nuclear weapons tests will not be diminished at all by the fact that the conducting of these or other tests will be announced in advance and that representatives of various countries will be present at these tests?

Only one thing can put an end to the increasing threat to the health of human beings, and that is the cessation of tests of any kind of atomic and hydrogen weapons. Such a decision by three powers in possession of these weapons would be, at the same time, a great practical contribution to the cause of lessening international tension and strengthening trust and confidence in relations between states. There is no doubt that if the U.S.A. and Great Britain would follow the example of the Soviet Union and cease testing atomic and hydrogen weapons, this would also undoubtedly contribute to the settlement of other unsolved international problems, including that of disarmament.

These are my observations on the matter of ceasing the testing of atomic and hydrogen weapons.

In your message, Mr. President, you recall, as if to counterbalance the proposal of the U.S.S.R. to cease testing atomic and hydrogen weapons, your previous proposals regarding "open skies," the use of outer space for peaceful purposes, and the cessation of production of fissionable materials for military purposes.

In this connection I should like to state that the position of the Soviet Union on all these questions is well known.

We have already stated repeatedly, and we do so again, that the flights of aircraft of one country over the territory of another, provided for by the "open sky" plan, would contribute nothing to the solution of the problem of disarmament.

The peoples of our countries will hardly feel more secure or acquire peace and tranquillity from the fact that American aircraft will be flying over our country from one end to the other and that Soviet aircraft will be plowing through American skies under circumstances where attitudes of tension and mistrust prevail. Is it not more correct to assume the opposite?

Under conditions where all our proposals to prohibit atomic and hydrogen weapons or at least to renounce their use are categorically rejected, where preparation is being made for atomic warfare, as is proven by decisions of the December session of NATO and by the continuing, intensive construction of newer and newer military bases which, according to the candid admission of certain political and military figures of the U.S.A. and other countries belonging to NATO, are designed for inflicting an "atomic blow" against the Soviet Union—under these conditions aerial photography might increase international tension and suspicion among nations. This would not only fail to contribute to the liquidation of the "cold war" and the establishment of friendly relations among states but would play into the hands of forces which are attempting to find a pretext to engulf humanity in a destructive atomic war.

In this connection I should like to state that the Soviet Union could not fail to note the report that the military command of the U.S.A. has already repeatedly sent aircraft of the Strategic Air Command with a hydrogen bomb load in the direction of the U.S.S.R.[9] According to these reports, the orders for the flight of the aircraft were issued in connection with reports from American radar stations to the effect that Soviet guided missiles were allegedly approaching the territory of the U.S.A. Of course, no Soviet missiles have threatened or do threaten the U.S.A., and the American radar stations' signals were in error, as was to be expected.

There is no special need for me to speak of what a serious danger to the cause of peace is represented by such flights of American aircraft with a hydrogen bomb load toward the borders of the Soviet Union. Is it not clear that in such a situation a simple error in transmitting signals may cause a world catastrophe?

Imagine for a minute, Mr. President, what would happen if the Soviet command, acting in a manner similar to that in which the American military command is now acting, should send aircraft with an atomic and hydrogen bomb load in the direction of the U.S.A., citing the fact that radar stations are sending signals of the approach of American military aircraft, or if the Soviet military command, in reply to the provocative flights of American aircraft, should in its turn decide to send Soviet military aircraft with a hydrogen bomb load in the direction of the United States of America. And yet such flights of Soviet aircraft under these conditions would be absolutely justified.

It suffices to present the problem in this manner to make it clear how dangerous such actions of the American command are. You may say that I am too sharp in my description when I speak of these irresponsible and provocative actions of the American military command. However, I speak of this in this way only because I am compelled to do so by my alarm when I think that, in the atmosphere of the military

[9] Document 162, below.

psychosis which is so characteristic of certain circles in your country, a world tragedy, with millions and millions of human victims, could develop, unexpected by any of us.

We expect from the Government of the United States that it will put an immediate end to this dangerous playing with fire.

Furthermore, I should like to touch upon the matter of the use of outer space for peaceful purposes.

In the course of the exchange of views in connection with the preparations for convening a summit conference, you proposed that the question of the prohibition of the use of outer space for military purposes be discussed at that meeting. We seriously considered this proposal of yours, and we stated that we were prepared to consider at a summit meeting the question of the prohibition of the use of outer space for military purposes and the liquidation of military bases in foreign territories. In this connection we proceed from the premise that any solution of this problem must take into account the security of the Soviet Union, the United States of America, and other countries. The proposal of the Soviet government for the prohibition of the use of outer space for military purposes, the liquidation of bases in foreign territories, and international cooperation in the field of the study of outer space meets this objective. We are prepared to conclude an agreement which would provide for the prohibition of the use of outer space for military purposes and would permit the launching of rockets into outer space only in accordance with an agreed international program of scientific research. At the same time, we cannot ignore the fact that atomic and hydrogen weapons can be delivered to the target not only by means of intercontinental rockets but also by means of intermediate and short-range rockets, as well as by means of conventional bombers stationed at the numerous American military bases located in areas adjacent to the Soviet Union.

Your proposal for the use of outer space for peaceful purposes provides, in fact, for the prohibition of intercontinental ballistic missiles alone, leaving aside the other important aspects of this problem. It is easy to see that you propose such a solution of the question as would correspond to the interests of the security of the United States alone, but would not provide any measures that would remove the threat to the security of the Soviet Union or to that of many other states created by the existence of numerous American military bases in foreign territories. The essence of your proposal is to prevent, through the prohibition of intercontinental ballistic missiles, a nuclear counterblow through outer space from being delivered against yourselves. Of course, it is impossible to agree to such an inequitable solution, which would put one side in a privileged position with regard to the other. Therefore we stated that an agreement on the prohibition of the use of outer space for military purposes must also provide for the liquidation of military bases located in foreign territories, and primarily in Europe, in the Near and Middle East, and in North Africa.

Such a solution of the problem, in our opinion, is equitable because it fully meets the interests of security of the United States, of the Soviet Union, and of other countries, and offers no advantage to any of them. As for the states on the territories of which American military bases are located, it may be said with assurance that they would only profit from such a solution of the problem, in as much as a liquidation of bases would fully meet the interests of the national security of these states by averting the deadly peril which could threaten their populations in case of war.

In your message, Mr. President, you pass over our proposal in complete silence and state that you await the acceptance of your proposal by the Soviet Government. An impression is created that it is desired to impose upon us a solution of the problem of the use of outer space such as would correspond to the interests of the United States alone and would completely ignore the interests of the Soviet Union. Such a one-sided approach is absolutely inadmissible in negotiations between independent states and, of course, cannot lead to the achievement of an agreement.

In your letter, Mr. President, in touching upon the question of the peaceful use of atomic energy, you attempt to present the matter in such a way as to create the impression that the United States of America is the champion of the peaceful use of atomic energy. However, the actual facts do not bear this out. Indeed, on the basis of facts, one cannot fail to recognize that the Soviet Union is a resolute advocate of the idea that atomic energy must not serve the purpose of exterminating human beings but should rather be fully directed toward serving the peaceful needs of humanity. Since the early days of this problem the Soviet Government has consistently striven in the United Nations for a prohibition of the use of all kinds of atomic and hydrogen weapons, for the elimination of these arms from the armaments of states, for the destruction of the stockpiles thereof, and for the discontinuance of the manufacture of such weapons and the establishment of international control over the execution of these measures.

What has prevented the acceptance of this proposal, the aim of which was to lay a foundation for the use of atomic energy exclusively for peaceful purposes? As is well known, the United States, together with its Western allies, also since the early days of this problem, has objected to these proposals and has prevented their acceptance, continuing to build its foreign policy on the use of nuclear arms. Thus, a deep abyss has appeared between the words of the United States about its desire to direct its atomic energy toward peaceful purposes, and its deeds.

It is understandable that the Soviet Union, which considers it its sacred duty to rescue mankind from the threat of a destructive atomic war, could not and cannot agree to such proposals, which would lead away from the prohibition of atomic and hydrogen weapons and would play into the hands of those forces which strive to have the threat of atomic war constantly hang over mankind like the sword of Damocles.

Unfortunately, your letter of April 8 also contains no proposals directed toward the solution of the problem of disarmament and removal of the threat of nuclear war. Instead of that you proposed that we engage in a study of the question concerning the necessary measures of control by appointing appropriate experts for this purpose. But is it possible for technical experts to contribute anything to the solution of the problem of disarmament if no agreement between Governments has been reached on this point? During the thirteen years of negotiations on disarmament hundreds of speeches were delivered and mountains of paper were written on the subject of control, but this did not bring us one step closer to the solution of the problem of disarmament. It is impossible to permit the solution of the problem of disarmament itself to be endlessly delayed under the pretext of studying the problems of control.

The Soviet Union has not only never objected to control but also repeatedly introduced proposals itself concerning the establishment of a reliable system of control over the execution of specific measures for disarmament. However, the refusal of the Western Powers to take any practical disarmament steps made the problem of control aimless, because it is of course, impossible to control the execution by states of commitments which do not exist.

The present international situation demands of all states— and, above all, of the great powers, which bear the main responsibility for the destinies of the world—not general phrases about the desirability of disarmament but concrete action in this field.

The Soviet Union has made its contribution to the cause of lessening international tension, to the cause of peace. From now on not a single atomic bomb nor a single hydrogen bomb will be exploded by the Soviet Union unless the United States and United Kingdom compel us to do so. We address the Governments of the United States and Great Britain with the appeal: do not commence a chain reaction of experimental explosions of atomic and hydrogen bombs.

The solution of the problem of whether an end will be put to nuclear tests forever or whether these tests will continue poisoning the air and increasing the threat of the outbreak of a destructive atomic war now depends on two powers only, the United States of America and Great Britain, and the governments of the United States and the United Kingdom bear a great responsibility before the entire world.

Perhaps, Mr. President, you do not share all the considerations presented by me, but I should still like to express a desire: would it not be possible to put an end to polemics on this subject, close the book on the past, and agree that the United States of America and Great Britain will discontinue atomic and hydrogen weapons test, just as the Soviet Union has done?

I assure you that humanity would breathe a deep sigh of relief if all three powers which manufacture atomic and hydrogen weapons would stop the tests of such weapons.

It is our profound hope, Mr. President, that you will use all your authority and influence for these noble aims.

With sincere respect,

N. KHRUSHCHEV

(35) Letter from the President, April 28, 1958.[10]

DEAR MR. CHAIRMAN: I have your communication of April twenty-second in reply to mine of April eighth. I regret that it is not an affirmative response to my proposal.

You refer in your letter to the question raised recently by

[10] Department of State Bulletin, v. 38 (May 19, 1958), pp. 811-812.

the Soviet Union in the United Nations Security Council
which also touches upon the disarmament question. I am
sure that you would agree that with the growing capabilities
in the Soviet Union and the United States of massive surprise
attack it is necessary to establish measures to allay fears. The
United States has just asked the Security Council to recon-
vene in order to consider the establishment of an international inspection system for the Arctic zone.[11] The United
States has submitted a constructive proposal to this end. I
urge you to join with us in supporting the resolution of the
United States now before the Council. Your support of this
proposal and subsequent cooperation would help to achieve
a significant first step. It would help to reduce tensions, it
would contribute to an increase of confidence among states,
and help to reduce the mutual fears of surprise attack.

The United States is determined that we will ultimately
reach an agreement on disarmament. In my letter of April
eighth, I again proposed an internationally supervised cutoff
of the use of new fissionable materials for weapons purposes
and the reduction of existing weapons stocks by transfer to
peaceful purposes; an agreed limitation or suspension of testing; "open skies," and the international use of outer space
for peaceful purposes.

As an effective means of moving toward ultimate agreement
on these matters and other disarmament matters, I proposed
that we start our technical people to work immediately upon
the practical problems involved. These studies were called for
by the United Nations General Assembly. They would include the practical problems of supervision and control
which, you and I agree, are in any event indispensable to
dependable disarmament agreements.

The solution of these practical problems will take time.
I am unhappy that valuable time is now being wasted.

You say that we must first reach a final political agreement
before it is worthwhile even to initiate the technical studies.
But such studies would, in fact, facilitate the reaching of the
final agreement you state you desire.

For example, why could not designated technical people
agree on what would be required so that you would know
if we violated an agreement to suspend testing and we would
know if you should commit a violation?

Would not both sides be in a better position to reach
agreements if we had a common accepted understanding as

[11] Document 163, below.

to feasibility of detection or as to method of inspecting against surprise attack?

Studies of this kind are the necessary preliminaries to putting political decisions actually into effect. The completion of such technical studies in advance of a political agreement would obviate a considerable period of delay and uncertainty. In other words, with the practicalities already worked out, the political agreement could begin to operate very shortly after it was signed and ratified.

I re-emphasize that these studies are without prejudice to our respective positions on the timing and interdependence of various aspects of disarmament.

Mr. Chairman, my offer to you still and always will remain open. I hope you will reconsider and accept it. In that way we both can make an important contribution to the cause of just and lasting peace.

Sincerely,

DWIGHT D. EISENHOWER

(36) *Letter from the Chairman of the Council of Ministers of the USSR (Khrushchev), May 9, 1958.*[12]

(Excerpts)

DEAR MR. PRESIDENT: I have received your message of April 28. Unfortunately, I have found in it no answer by the United States Government to our statement on the question of the cessation of atomic and hydrogen weapons tests, which was the subject of my letter of April 22. However, the necessity of solving this question is now all the more urgent because attempts are already being made to disrupt the efforts toward terminating nuclear weapons tests universally and forever. I refer to the nuclear bomb tests recently carried out by the United States of America and the United Kingdom.

*   *   *

The problems of control of the cessation of atomic and hydrogen weapons tests in no way represent an obstacle to an immediate cessation of such tests.

We believe that in the first instance it is necessary that the United States of America and the United Kingdom cease

[12] *Department of State Bulletin,* v. 38 (June 9, 1958), pp. 940-942.

testing atomic and hydrogen weapons, as has already been done by the Soviet Union, and that this basic problem be solved without delay. One cannot fail to see that this is the shortest way toward a solution of the problem of ceasing experimental explosions of nuclear weapons. In my correspondence with you I have already expressed fears that— under present conditions, where, among States possessing nuclear weapons, no unity of opinion exists with regard to the basic question of the necessity of ceasing without delay the testing of atomic and hydrogen bombs—the transfer of this problem to technical experts for study might entail a delay in the solution of this urgent matter. One must not close one's eyes to the fact that such a situation could be exploited by those who are interested in such a delay. On the contrary, if the United States and the United Kingdom should also decide to cease the testing of nuclear weapons, then this very fact would create conditions under which each party would be interested in having all other States which ceased the testing of atomic and hydrogen weapons fulfill the obligations assumed by them.

Your messages indicate that you attach great importance to having experts study the technical details connected with the control of the execution of an agreement on the cessation of atomic and hydrogen weapons tests. Taking this into account, we are prepared, in spite of the serious doubts on our part, of which I have spoken above, to try even this course. The Soviet Government agrees to having both sides designate experts who would immediately begin a study of methods for detecting possible violations of an agreement on the cessation of nuclear tests with a view to having this work completed at the earliest possible date, to be determined in advance.

At the same time I once again appeal to you, Mr. President, to support the initiative of the Soviet Union in the matter of ceasing atomic and hydrogen tests and thus make possible a final solution of this problem, which is ardently hoped for by the peoples of all countries.

*   *   *

I must touch upon one other matter concerning which we should like to have complete clarity between us. The Soviet Union has recently been reproached for not agreeing to the American proposal to establish an inspection zone in the

Arctic region even though the majority of the members of the Security Council voted for this proposal. Let me say frankly: the method to which the U.S.A. resorted in the Security Council in the consideration of the question raised by the Soviet Union of the necessity of putting an end to flights of American military aircraft armed with atomic and hydrogen bombs in the direction of the borders of the U.S.S.R. does not, in our opinion, indicate any serious intention of reaching an agreement on a mutually acceptable basis but is, rather, an indication of attempts to exert pressure on the Soviet Union through the use of a majority of the votes in the Security Council. It is very well known that this majority in the Security Council has been formed by the votes of countries which are in various degrees dependent on the U.S.A., primarily from an economic standpoint. Thus the Security Council, in its present composition, cannot be considered an impartial arbiter, and this is the reason why at the present time it does not play the important role in the matter of maintaining international peace and security with which it was entrusted by the U.N. Charter. The Soviet Government is sincerely striving for an equitable and mutually acceptable agreement with the U.S.A. and other Western powers. We are striving to establish peaceful relations between our countries and improve these relations day by day. We were also guided by such aspirations in taking such a step as unilateral cessation of nuclear weapons tests and in making our proposals for calling a meeting with the participation of heads of government.

* * *

(37) *Letter from the President, May 24, 1958.*[13]

DEAR MR. CHAIRMAN: I have your letter of May 9, 1958. I note with satisfaction that you accept, at least partially, my proposal that technical persons be designated to ascertain what would be required to supervise and control disarmament agreements, all without prejudice to our respective positions on the timing and interdependence of various aspects of disarmament.

Your letter of May ninth states that "the Soviet Government agrees to have both sides designate experts who would immediately begin a study of methods for detecting possible

[13] *Ibid.*, p. 939.

violations of an agreement on the cessation of nuclear tests with a view to having this work completed at the earliest possible date, to be determined in advance."

Experts from our side will be prepared to meet with experts from your side at Geneva, if the Swiss Government agrees, within three weeks of our learning whether these arrangements are acceptable to you. On our side, experts would be chosen on the basis of special competence. I have in mind, for example, experts who might be contributed not only from the United States, but from the United Kingdom which, like the Soviet Union and the United States, has conducted nuclear tests, and from France, which has advanced plans for testing, and possibly from other countries having experts who are advanced in knowledge of how to detect nuclear tests. We assume that the experts on the side of the Soviet Union would be similarly chosen on the basis of special competence, so as to assure that we get scientific, not political, conclusions.

I also suggest that the experts should be asked to make an initial progress report within thirty days after convening and to aim at a final report within sixty days or as soon thereafter as possible.

In view of the Charter responsibilities of the General Assembly and the Security Council of the United Nations in the field of disarmament, we would propose to keep the United Nations and its appropriate organs informed of the progress of these talks through the intermediary of the Secretary General.

I will write you further shortly regarding your statements on the problem of surprise attack and the Arctic Zone of inspection which we have proposed.

Sincerely,

DWIGHT D. EISENHOWER

(38) *Letter from the Chairman of the Council of Ministers of the USSR (Khrushchev), May 30, 1958.*[14]

DEAR MR. PRESIDENT: I have received your message dated May 24 in reply to my letter of May 9.

As in your preceding messages, I have, unfortunately, found no answer to such an urgent problem as that of immediate cessation of atomic and hydrogen weapons tests,

[14] *Ibid.* (June 30, 1958), pp. 1083-1084.

which was the subject of my previous messages to you. There is no need to speak once again of the fact that, under present conditions, with no agreement among states possessing nuclear weapons as to the basic question—the necessity to cease without delay the testing of atomic and hydrogen bombs—a study by technical experts of the methods of detection of possible violations of an agreement on the cessation of nuclear tests may lead to a delay in the solution of the main problem, namely, that of a cessation of tests. This is a matter of serious concern to us. At this time, therefore, when we are agreeing on convening a meeting of experts, it would be necessary to take steps toward having the work of the experts completed at the earliest possible date, to be established in advance.

We agree to your proposal that the experts should undertake their task within the next three weeks with a view to beginning the work as soon as possible.

In your reply you also express yourself in favor of instructing the experts to prepare a report on the first results of their work within 30 days, or as soon as possible after the expiration of that period.

The Soviet Government considers that in the interests of the earliest possible universal cessation of nuclear weapons tests it would be advisable to agree that the entire work of the experts be concluded within three or four weeks after the date of the beginning of the work of the conference and that within this period a final report of the experts, with their conclusions and findings, be submitted to the governments of those states whose experts take part in the conference.

Furthermore, you state that experts not only from the USSR and the USA might be designated but also from Great Britain and France and, possibly, from other countries which have specialists with a thorough knowledge in the field of detecting nuclear tests. The Soviet Government has no objection to this, and it proposes that experts from Czechoslovakia and Poland likewise take part in the work of the conference.

Nor does the Soviet Government consider that the work of the experts should be confined to this group of countries. Therefore it seems advisable to invite experts from India also, and possibly from certain other countries, to participate in the conference.

As to the site of the conference of experts, we do, of course, share the opinion that Geneva is a suitable place. However, we would prefer that this conference be held in Moscow. I can assure you, Mr. President, that all the facilities necessary for the experts to conduct their work will be provided in Moscow. The Soviet Government agrees to the proposal that the Security Council, as well as the UN General Assembly, be kept informed through the Secretary General as to the progress of the work of the conference of experts.

I hope, Mr. President, that the considerations I have presented will meet with a favorable attitude on your part.

Upon receiving a reply from you, the Soviet Government will communicate the list of experts from the Soviet Union who will participate in the said conference.

With sincere respect,

N. KHRUSHCHEV

(39) *Letter from the President, June 10, 1958.*[15]

DEAR MR. CHAIRMAN: I have your letter of May 30 and am glad to note you have accepted my proposal that technical experts meet to study the possibility of detecting violations of a possible agreement on suspension of nuclear tests. These talks would be undertaken without commitment as to the final decision on the relationship of nuclear test suspension to other more important disarmament measures I have proposed.

I propose that these discussions begin on or about July 1 in Geneva. While we appreciate your offer to hold these talks in Moscow, we believe that Geneva would be preferable from our standpoint, and note that it would be acceptable to you. The Swiss Government has agreed to this location.

With respect to participation I suggest that initially at least we adhere to the concept expressed in your letter of May 9, 1958, where you say, "the Soviet Government agrees to having both sides designate experts." As indicated in my letter of May 24, 1958, our side at this discussion will include experts from the United States, United Kingdom, France and possibly from other countries which have specialists with a thorough knowledge in the field of detecting nuclear tests, and we note that you have no objection to this. With regard to the inclusion on your side of experts from Czechoslovakia and Poland, we have no objection to this. With respect to experts of nationalities not identified with either side, we have no objection in principle to their joining later in the

[15] *Ibid.*, p. 1083.

discussions if it is agreed during the course of the talks that this is necessary or useful from the point of view of the purposes of the technical talks.

It may be possible for the experts to produce a final report within three or four weeks as you suggest. However, I believe that there should be enough flexibility in our arrangements to allow a little longer time if it is needed to resolve the complex technical issues involved.

I propose that further arrangements for the meeting be handled through normal diplomatic channels.[16]

Sincerely,

DWIGHT D. EISENHOWER

2. Technical Talks on the Detection of Nuclear Explosions, Geneva, July 1–August 21, 1958.

(40) Report of the Conference of Experts to Study the Possibility of Detecting Violations of a Possible Agreement on the Suspension of Nuclear Tests, Geneva, August 21, 1958.[17]

I. INTRODUCTION

A. In accordance with an agreement reached as a result of an exchange of letters between the Chairman of the Council of Ministers of the Union of Soviet Socialist Republics, N. S. Khrushchev, and the President of the United States of America, Dwight D. Eisenhower, regarding the calling of a conference of experts to study the possibility of detecting violations of a possible agreement on the suspension of nuclear tests, there began on 1 July 1958, in Geneva, in the Palais des Nations, a conference of, on the one hand, experts from Western countries and, on the other hand, delegations of experts of the Union of Soviet Socialist Republics, the Polish People's Republic, the Czechoslovak Republic and the People's Republic of Romania.

B. The Secretary-General of the United Nations was represented at the Conference by his Personal Representative, Mr. T. G. Narayanan. Conference facilities and Secretariat service were provided by the United Nations. The Experts express their appreciation for the good offices of the Secretary-General

---

[16] For an exchange of diplomatic notes preceding and accompanying the meeting of technical experts see the *Department of State Bulletin*, v. 39 (July 7, 1958), pp. 11-12; (July 14, 1958), pp. 47-48; (July 21, 1958), pp. 101-102, and (August 11, 1958), pp. 235-237.

[17] *Ibid.* (September 22, 1958), pp. 453-461.

and his Personal Representative, and for the services of the Secretariat staff attached to the Conference.

C. The agenda for the Conference, adopted on 4 July, included the following main questions:

1. Exchange of opinions on the problem of the various methods for detecting atomic explosions and on other general problems of the Conference deliberations.

2. Determination of a list of basic methods of systematic observations for phenomena indicative of an explosion.

3. A system for controlling the observance of an agreement on the cessation of nuclear tests.

4. Drawing up a report of experts to the governments of those countries represented at the Conference, with conclusions and suggestions regarding a system for controlling the observance of an agreement on the cessation of nuclear tests.

D. The Conference held 30 official sessions and completed its work on 21 August 1958. By prior agreement the Conference held its sessions in private.

E. The Conference of Experts considered the phenomena accompanying nuclear explosions set off under various conditions.

F. Some of these phenomena, namely the acoustic waves occurring when there are explosions in air and in water, the seismic oscillations that occur when there are explosions on the ground, under the ground, and under water, the radio pulses that are produced when there are explosions in the atmosphere, and the optical and gamma radiation when propagated over long distances, serve to indicate explosions and to estimate their time and place.

G. When nuclear explosion occur in the atmosphere the radioactive debris which is formed mixes in the atmosphere, and is dispersed over great distances. If a nuclear explosion is set off in the ocean or in the earth's crust, the radioactive debris will remain concentrated close to the site of the explosion for a considerable time.

H. The sensitivity of modern physical, chemical and geophysical methods of measurement makes it possible to detect nuclear explosions by the indications described above at considerable distances, as hereafter described. Thus it is known that explosions of high yield which are set off on the surface of the earth and in the lower part of the atmosphere can be detected without difficulty at points of the globe which are very remote from the site of the explosion. On the other hand, explosions which are of low yield (a few kilotons) can be detected with good reliability given the present state of observational techniques only if there is a specially set up control system such as that suggested in Section IV of this report.

I. A basic difficulty in detecting and identifying small explosions arises because many natural phenomena (earthquakes, thunder storms and others) give signals which are similar to those produced by explosions, or which by their presence hinder the detection of the signals sought.

J. The discrimination of the signals of natural events from signals of explosions is aided by a careful analysis of the recorded data, taking into account readings obtained at several points. Those remaining unidentified events which could be suspected as being nuclear explosions might be resolved by inspection of the site.

K. The Conference of Experts has considered the methods of detecting nuclear explosions by the acoustic, hydro-acoustic and seismic oscillations which they produce in the air, water, or in the earth's crust, and, also the detection of explosions by the electromagnetic oscillations which are propagated from them, and by the radioactive debris that the explosions cause.

L. The Conference has examined the effectiveness and limitations of each of these methods for the detection of nuclear explosions and it has agreed that the combined use of the various methods considerably facilitates the detection and identification of nuclear explosions.

M. After examining the separate methods, the Conference examined the question of the technical equipment of the control system necessary to detect and identify nuclear explosions, and, after that, it passed to the question of the control system as a whole.

N. As a result of the examination of these questions the Conference reached the conclusion that it is technically feasible to set up, with the capabilities and limitations indicated in Section IV of this report, a workable and effective control system for the detection of violations of an agreement on the worldwide cessation of nuclear weapons tests.

O. In the present report information is given about the various methods of detection and identification of nuclear explosions, about the technical equipment of a control system and about a control system as a whole. Copies of the individual documents containing the conclusions adopted by the Conference on each of the questions mentioned are attached to the present report. Verbatim records and working documents in the working languages of the Conference will follow as soon as they are available for attachment to the report.

II. BASIC METHODS FOR DETECTION AND IDENTIFICATION OF NUCLEAR EXPLOSIONS

A. *Conclusions as to the applicability of the Method of Recording Acoustic Waves for the Detection of Nuclear Explosions.*

The Conference of Experts examined the process of propagation of the acoustic waves caused by nuclear explosions and the methods of recording these waves with the aim of determining the possibility of using them for detecting nuclear explosions.

1. When there are explosions in air, a strong air acoustic wave is formed which propagates over large distances. An indication of the amplitude of the air pressure wave is given by a formula which is approximately valid for a homogeneous atmosphere and according to which this amplitude is proportional to the cube root of the yield and inversely proportional to the distance. However, the amplitude of this acoustic wave is strongly dependent upon meterological conditions and cannot be predicted accurately by a simple formula of such a kind. The observed amplitude in certain cases can be five times larger or smaller than that predicted by a formulation which includes only the energy release and the distance to detecting station.

2. Existing apparatus of special design can detect the air wave from a one kiloton explosion in the air above local background noise at relatively large distances.

The detection capability of a single station is strongly dependent upon the orientation of the propagation path to the station with respect to the upper winds. When the upper winds are mainly in one direction, a one kiloton explosion can be detected with a high degree of confidence downwind at a distance of 2,000 to 3,000 kilometres and upwind at a distance of 500 kilometres. When the upper winds are erratic and the average wind is small, such as frequently happens in the spring and fall, detection of a one kiloton explosion can be accomplished with a similar degree of confidence to a distance of approximately 1,300 kilometres independently of the direction. On the basis of the records from three stations, the location of the explosion can be determined with an accuracy of better than 100 kilometres.

3. The acoustic apparatus at control posts at the above distances from an explosion can detect explosions which occur between the surface and a height of 30 kilometres. A reasonable extrapolation of existing experience indicates that for explosions taking place up to an altitude of about 50 kilometres there should not be a great change in the detectability of the acoustic wave. Whether a substantial acoustic wave will be generated at higher altitudes is not well known from direct experiment or from any theoretical considerations so far discussed. Deep underground and underwater explosions do not produce air waves sufficiently intense for detection purposes.

An underwater explosion in the oceans generates very strong underwater sound waves (hydroacoustic), which even in the case of small explosions can be detected at distances of about 10,000 kilometres.

4. Acoustic waves which resemble in certain cases the acoustic signals of nuclear explosions may be produced by natural events (primarily meteoric, volcanic or submarine disturbances). In such cases the identification of the event as natural or as a nuclear explosion must be based on a comparison of acoustic data with those obtained by aid of other methods.

5. It is noted that methods of recording of pressure waves may be further improved to increase the precision and the sensitivity, and to eliminate background noise and spurious signals.

B. *Conclusions as to the Applicability of the Method of Using Radioactive Debris for Detecting and Subsequently Identifying Nuclear Explosions.*

The Conference of Experts has studied the process of the dissemination of radioactive debris resulting from a nuclear explosion and has considered the collection of samples of radioactive debris and its analysis as one of the methods for detecting and subsequently identifying nuclear explosions.

1. When an explosion occurs a considerable quantity of radioactive debris is produced. If the explosion is based on a fission reaction then this quantity amounts to 3×10^8 curies per 1 kt TNT equivalent of the energy of the explosion as of one hour after the reaction. Thermonuclear reactions will lead to the formation of Carbon 14, Tritium, and other radioactive substances which result from neutron irradiation and which, in principle, can also be used to detect an explosion.

2. When nuclear explosions occur between the earth's surface and a height of approximately ten kilometres the radioactive debris is thrown into the atmosphere where it is carried by winds to great distances. The concentration of this radioactive debris is greatly influenced by the vertical and horizontal distribution of the wind in the troposphere and in the lower layers of the stratosphere. The concentration is also decreased as a consequence of washing out by rain and gravitational deposition.

3. The distribution by height of the radioactive debris carried in the atmosphere will depend in the first place on the energy of the explosion, on the conditions in which the explosion took place (i.e. on the earth, under the earth, or in the air) and on the meteorological conditions at the moment of explosion. In the case of low energy explosions in the air up to a height of approximately ten kilometres the radioactive debris will initially concentrate in a small volume below the troposphere. This debris will gradually get disseminated both horizontally and vertically in the troposphere and in the course of a period of from one to thirty days (depending on the turbulence of the atmosphere, the wind structure, and the dimensions of the particles which carry the radioactive substances) it can be detected close to the earth's surface, as also at various heights up to the tropopause.

4. The spreading of the cloud in the atmosphere is determined by many meteorological processes. As a result of the action of these processes the cloud is bound to reach a stage when it is mixed in a vertical direction and spread in a horizontal direction in such a way as to afford the most convenient conditions for taking samples.

Calculations and experimental data give ground for considering that this stage will be reached in the period between the fifth and twentieth day of the existence of the cloud. Before that period the cloud may be too small, both in its horizontal and its vertical extent. After thirty days have expired a considerable part of the radioactive debris will decay and a sample will constitute a lesser proportion of the natural or other background, thereby making more difficult the detection and identification of an explosion.

5. Existing radiochemical techniques make it possible to detect and identify fresh decay products in a sample of radioactive debris containing about 10^8 fissions. The time of origin of this fresh debris can be determined within five to ten per cent of its age if the sample contains about 10^{10} fissions

and is not contaminated to any considerable extent by old fission products.

6. The taking of samples on the surface of the earth by a network of control posts makes it possible to carry out continual monitoring of the contamination of the air at many separate points by means of air filtration and also by collecting radioactive fallout and fallout in rain. If control posts are disposed at distances of the order of 2,000-3,000 kilometres then an explosion with an energy of 1 kt set off in the troposphere (0-10 kilometres above the surface of the earth) will be detected with a high degree of reliability in the period of five to twenty days although the place of explosion cannot be exactly determined and although the time of explosion will be determined with some error. Calculation shows that with favourable meterological conditions an explosion of even lesser energy can be detected in this way.

In the course of the period of time or from two to five days after an explosion of energy equivalent to 1 kt the collection of a sample of radioactive debris from the explosion which is suitable for analysis can be effected in the air by an aircraft if the area of the supposed location of the cloud is known approximately. The taking of such a sample will make it possible to establish approximately the point of the explosion by means of using meterological data for back-tracking the trajectory of movement of the cloud.

7. Underground or underwater explosions set off at shallow depths and accompanied by the throwing up of earth or water can also be identified by the method of collecting radioactive samples although with lesser reliability than for explosions of the same energy in the troposphere.

8. The Conference of Experts considers that systematic measurements of radioactive substances in the air and also the collection of radioactive aerosols deposited on the ground and measurements of the radioactivity of precipitation can be successfully used for the detection of nuclear explosions and also, in many cases, for assessing certain parameters relating to them even in the absence of other indications.

The utilisation for a regular control service, as a method for detecting nuclear explosions, of the taking of samples of the air by aircraft over oceans can be used for detecting nuclear explosions. For this purpose use should be made of existing aircraft flights over the oceans which are carried out by various countries for the purposes of meteorological observations.

9. The Conference of Experts considers that the method

of taking samples of radioactive debris can also be used successfully for subsequent investigation of the fact of a nuclear explosion in those cases when there are the appropriate indications from other methods.

For this purpose it is possible to use the detection of radioactive debris remaining at the point of the supposed explosion (on the earth's surface, under the earth, in the water) and also the determination of the presence of a radioactive cloud in the period between two and five days after a supposed explosion in the atmosphere in the area where the cloud is calculated to be by the time of investigation.

In such a case search for the radioactive cloud can be made on an aircraft having equipment for the taking of a sample of radioactive debris. To this end use should be made chiefly of the aircraft flights over the oceans made for the purposes of meteorological observations.

10. In some cases use can be made of aircraft flights over the territories of the USA, the USSR, the UK and other countries to collect air samples for the purpose of checking on data obtained by other methods of detection of nuclear explosions.

The Experts consider that to accomplish this task it would be quite sufficient to make use of the aircraft of the country being overflown and that in such cases it is sufficient that flights for the purpose specified should be made along routes laid down in advance. Representatives of the USSR, the USA, the UK or other States participating in the operation of the control system may be on board these aircraft in the capacity of observers.

11. The experts note that in the course of time the sensitivity and efficiency of the method of collecting radio-active debris will increase as a consequence of the atmosphere becoming cleared of the radioactive products it contains, and also as a result of the perfection of the techniques for collecting and analysing samples.

C. *Conclusions as to the Applicability of the Method of Recording Seismic Waves for the Detection of Nuclear Explosions.*

The Conference has considered the processes of propagation of seismic waves generated by nuclear explosions and the methods for recording these waves for the purpose of determining the possibility of using them for the detection of underground and underwater nuclear explosions.

1. When nuclear explosions occur under the ground or under the water, longitudinal transverse and surface waves are formed and get propagated to great distances. The first longitudinal wave is the most important, both for detecting an explosion and for determining the place of the explosion, and also for distinguishing an earthquake from explosions. Transverse and surface waves also help to define the nature of a seismic perturbation.

2. Longitudinal seismic waves caused by underground nuclear explosions set off under conditions analogous to those in which the Rainier[18] shot occurred can be detected and the direction of first motion of the longitudinal wave can be determined at a distance of approximately 1,000 kilometres, and also at distances of approximately 2,000-3,500 kilometres at sites which are considerably more quiet than the average for:

(a) explosions of the order of one kiloton recorded during periods of favourable noise conditions.

(b) explosions of the order of five kilotons recorded during periods of unfavourable noise conditions.

It must be noted that all seismic stations situated at thousands of kilometres from one another cannot have an identically high or identically low level of background at one and the same time.

3. Conditions for detection and identification of underwater explosions set off in shallow water but at a sufficient depth, are considerably more favourable than conditions for detecting underground explosions.

4. Control posts carrying out seismic observations should be put at sites with a minimal level of microseismic background, such as are possible in internal continental regions. Such stations, when provided with arrays of seismographs, can insure the obtaining of the data indicated above. However, at stations which are in unfavourable regions such as coastal and island regions the noise level will be higher than at quiet stations inside continents. In these cases for detection and determination of the sign of the first motion the energy of the explosion must increase in the ratio of the power of 3/2 with respect to the increase of background level. This is in part compensated by the fact that quiet stations inside con-

[18] The underground nuclear explosion "Rainier" with an energy of 1.7 kilotons (Nevada) was set off in unfavourable conditions for transferring energy to the ground. However, even worse conditions of coupling are possible. [Footnote in original.]

tinents will register more powerful explosions at distances of from 2,000 to 3,500 kilometres. Bursts with an energy of 5 kilotons and more will be detected by quiet stations placed at the distances named.

5. The majority of earthquakes can be distinguished from explosions with a high degree of reliability if the direction of first motion of the longitudinal wave is clearly registered at 5 or more seismic stations on various bearings from the epicentre. Thus not less than 90 per cent of all earthquakes taking place in continents can be identified. The remaining 10 per cent or less of cases will require the analysis of additional seismograms where this is possible; and for this purpose use must also be made of the data of the existing network of seismic stations. If required, these supplementary stations should be further equipped with improved apparatus. In relatively aseismic areas it is sufficiently merely to define the position of the epicentre. In this connection cases of detection of seismic events will be regarded as suspicious and will require further investigation with the help of other methods. For those cases which remain unidentified inspection of the region will be necessary.

In regions where the regular disposition of seismic stations in quiet conditions is not possible, the percentage of correct identification of earthquakes will be less.

With modern methods and making use of the data of several surrounding seismic stations the area within which an epicentre is localized can be assessed as approximately 100-200 square kilometres.

6. It is noted that the range and accuracy of recording and identifying underground nuclear explosions can be improved in the future by means of perfecting the methods of recording seismic waves, both by way of perfecting apparatus and also by way of perfecting the methods for differentiating an earthquake from explosions.

D. *Conclusions on the Applicability of the Method of Recording of Radio Signals for the Detection of Nuclear Explosions.*

The Conference of Experts considered the generation and propagation of radio pulses originating from a nuclear explosion and the methods of recording these signals in order to determine the possibility of using them for the detection of nuclear explosions.

1. In the case of a nuclear explosion in the atmosphere,

there arises a powerful electromagnetic radiation (radio signal), caused by the gamma radiation accompanying the explosion. In the case of underground, underwater, or specially shielded explosions radio emissions are not expected which can be recorded at great distances by modern techniques.

When the explosion is carried out on or above the surface of the earth (water) and without specially constructed layers to absorb gamma rays, the energy and spectral distribution of the radio signal are such that its essential components are propagated over the whole terrestrial globe. The strength of the radio signal depends upon certain features of the construction of the bomb and on the altitude of the explosion. An explosion of 1 kiloton yield can be detected by means of radio signals at distances exceeding 6,000 km assuming that in the neighbourhood of the receiving station there is no high noise level from local thunderstorms or other sources.

By radio direction finding methods, it is possible to determine the azimuth of the signal source with an accuracy of about 2°, i.e., about 30 km at a distance of 1,000 km. The time of production of the signal may be established with an accuracy of several milliseconds. The attainment of such accuracy depends on the choice of sufficiently flat location and on the absence of electrical interference at the receiving site.

2. Lightning flashes emit radio signals in the same frequency range and act as interference for the method of detection of a nuclear explosion by means of its radio signal.

Close to the source of radiation, the forms of radio signals from lightning and from nuclear explosions examined to date are quite different. However, at distances exceeding 1,000 kilometres, due to the distortion of the form of radio signals in the wave guide formed by the earth and the ionosphere, the form of radio signals from some individual lightning flashes is similar to the signal from nuclear explosions. The number of signals from lightning flashes recorded by apparatus without using special techniques of signal selection depends on the sensitivity of the apparatus and on the locality and can amount to from ten to several hundred signals per second. Existing techniques can be applied to exclude automatically the preponderant majority of signals from lightning. The distinction of the remaining signals due to atmospherics from those due to nuclear explosions requires the application of special methods of discrimination, including criteria on form of signal, spectral distribution and distance to source of radiation.

In the present state of the technique of the discrimination of signals in some individual cases the record of a signal cannot be identified either as coming from a nuclear explosion or from lightning.

3. The Conference of Experts recommends that further research should be carried out in order to understand more fully the physical properties of atmospherics involved in differentiating signals from nuclear explosions and atmospherics, by means of the development of the theory of this problem, the collection and systematization of data about atmospherics and the development of suitable automatic instruments. The Conference considers that there are good prospects for improvement of procedures of signal discrimination.

4. Theoretical considerations suggest that recording of radio signals can be used to detect nuclear explosions occurring at altitudes up to the order of 1,000 kilometres.

E. *Conclusions on the Methods of Detection of Nuclear Explosions Carried out at High Altitude (More than 30 to 50 Kilometres) Above the Earth*

The Conference of Experts has given theoretical consideration to the gamma radiation and neutrons resulting from a nuclear explosion and the conditions of recording them from earth satellites; and to optical phenomena and ionization of the air in the upper layers of the atmosphere in the case of a high altitude explosion (altitudes above 30-50 kilometres) and has arrived at the following conclusions:

1. A kiloton nuclear explosion produces at its source delayed gamma-rays from fission products, and prompt gamma-rays and neutrons. The number of prompt gamma-rays and neutrons depends upon the construction of the device and upon the materials surrounding it. The delayed gamma-rays are insignificantly affected by these factors. At a distance of 10^4 kilometres in vacuo, typical quantities of radiation from a one kiloton fission explosion are:

    (a) Delayed gamma-rays
           10^4 quanta/cm^2 during the first second
    (b) prompt gamma rays[19]
           10^2 quanta/cm^2

[19] Special shielding of the exploding device can considerably reduce the gamma-radiation accompanying the reaction, but cannot reduce the radiation from fission products. However, such shielding involves increasing by several times the weight of the whole device. [Footnote in original.]

distributed over a time of about 10^{-7} sec.
  (c) Neutrons
        10^4 neutrons/cm^2
distributed over a time of a few seconds.

The cosmic background at the height at which earth satellites orbit is under study at the present time, attention being paid to the quantity, nature and energy of the particles; however, on the basis of preliminary data, it can be considered that the detection of an explosion from an earth satellite is possible, by means of registering the gamma-rays accompanying the nuclear reaction, neglecting shielding, and also by means of registering the gamma rays of the fission products and the neutrons. If both prompt gamma rays and neutrons are registered, it is possible to get some idea of the distance to the explosion. The use of gamma-rays from a nuclear explosion will make it possible to detect the explosion in cosmic space at a distance of the order of hundreds of thousands of kilometres from the earth. Estimate of the maximum distance for the detection requires data concerning the magnitude of the cosmic radiation at the orbit of the earth satellite. If there is an explosion at a height of 30-50 km and above, and if the height at which the earth satellite orbits is some thousands of kilometres, one can neglect the absorption of gamma quanta in the upper layers of the atmosphere. The Conference of Experts considers that it is possible to use for the detection of nuclear explosions at high altitudes the registration of gamma-radiation and neutrons with properly instrumented earth satellites.

  2. In the case of an explosion at a great height light will be emitted at the point of the explosion and there will be luminescence in the upper layers of the atmosphere under the action of X-rays and fast atoms from the materials in the device. Light phenomena may be detectable from the surface of the earth in clear weather at night with the help of simple apparatus; in day time with the help of more sensitive apparatus. In cloudy weather the detection of optical phenomena from stations on the earth's surface would probably be extremely difficult.

  The radiation from a nuclear explosion creates in the upper layers of the atmosphere a region of increased ionization which is detectable by the absorption of cosmic radio-signals or by anomalies in the propagation of radio waves.
  Our knowledge of the absorption of cosmic noise by iono-

spheric phenomena is not sufficient to determine the number of natural events similar to those resulting from a nuclear explosion.

The Conference of Experts considers that it is possible to use the recording of ionospheric phenomena, using appropriate radio techniques, and of optical phenomena for the detection of nuclear explosions at high altitudes.

3. The Conference of Experts has not considered the problem of the detection of nuclear explosions which might be conducted in cosmic space at distances of millions of kilometres from the earth.

F. The Conference has recommended the inclusion of the first four of these methods in the number of basic methods for detecting nuclear explosions by means of a network of control posts, and considers it possible to use several methods for detection of nuclear explosions at high altitudes as stated in IIE1 and IIE2.

III. CONCLUSIONS ON THE QUESTION OF THE TECHNICAL EQUIPMENT OF THE CONTROL SYSTEM FOR THE DETECTION AND IDENTIFICATION OF NUCLEAR EXPLOSIONS

The Conference of Experts has considered the questions related to the technical equipment of a control net intended to detect and identify nuclear explosions, and has come to the following conclusions:

1. The posts of the control net situated in continents should regularly be equipped with apparatus for the detection of explosions by the acoustic and seismic methods and also by the methods of recording radio signals and of collecting radioactive debris.

2. Certain posts situated on islands or near the shores of oceans should be equipped, in addition to the methods just mentioned, with apparatus for hydroacoustic detection of explosions.

3. Posts located on ships stationed or drifting within specified ocean areas should be equipped with apparatus for the detection of explosions by the method of collecting radioactive debris and by the hydroacoustic method. The method of recording radio signals and the acoustic method might also be used on ships if suitable equipment is developed, but the effectiveness of these two methods, particularly the acoustic one, will be considerably less than on land.

4. The apparatus installed at posts of the control network

must be uniform and must satisfy the following basic technical requirements:

A. *Seismic apparatus*

The seismic apparatus of the control post should include:

(1) Approximately 10 short-period vertical seismographs dispersed over a distance of 1.5-3 kilometres and connected to the recording system by lines of cable. The seismographs should have a maximum magnification of the order of 10^6 at a frequency of 1 c.p.s. and a receiving band adequate to reproduce the characteristic form of the seismic signal;

(2) 2 horizontal seismographs with the parameters indicated in point (1);

(3) One three-component installation of long-period seismographs having a broad receiving band and a constant magnification of the order of $10^3 - 2 \times 10^3$ in the period range 1—10 seconds;

(4) One three-component installation of seismographs with a narrow receiving band and magnification of the order of 3×10^4 when $T = 2 - 2.5$ seconds;

(5) At certain posts one three-component installation of long-period seismographs with magnification of the order of $10^4 - 2 \times 10^4$ at periods of $T = 25$ seconds;

(6) Auxiliary equipment necessary in order to get precise records of the seismic signal; recording devices, chronometers, power supply units and apparatus for receiving automatic radio-signals giving correct time.

The seismic apparatus should be installed in places with a minimal level of micro-seismic background, away from industrial areas, and on outcrops of bedrock (where possible). The seismographs should be installed in suitable vaults.

The area required for installing the seismic apparatus should be about 3×3 kilometres.

B. *Acoustic apparatus*

(1) The infra-acoustic equipment for a control post should include not less than three sets of microbarographic units each of which should have: a system for averaging out turbulent noise, a pressure sensing unit, a transmission line and appropriate electronic amplifiers and automatic writing instruments;

(2) The sensitivity of the microbarographic stations must ensure recording of acoustic signals in the period range 0.5—40 seconds, with an amplitude of 0.1 dynes per cm^2;

(3) The pressure sensing units of the microbarographs should be dispersed at about 10 kilometres from one another in order to determine the direction of arrival of the acoustic signal and the speed of propagation of the signal;

(4) The hydroacoustic apparatus for a post, which is recommended for use only in oceanic zones, should include several hydrophones placed in the main submarine sound channel.

The hydrophones should be connected with the recording station on the coast by cables. Recordings of the hydroacoustic signal should be made in several frequency subranges, covering a general frequency range of from one cycle per second to several thousand cycles per second.

The infra-acoustic equipment operates best in areas of low surface winds and flat terrain covered with trees or shrubs.

C. *Apparatus for recording a radio signal*

The apparatus for recording a radio signal should consist of:

(1) A loop-shaped radio direction finder or a radio direction finder with vertical antennas dispersed 4-5 kilometres from one another, with a frequency range of 10-15 kilocycles per second which will detect signals as low as 2 millivolts per metre;

(2) A device for recording the form of the signal, the device to provide recording of the form of the radio-pulse in a frequency range 500 c.p.s.-200 kilocycles per second when the intensity of the field is 10 millivolts per metre and more;

(3) An automatic selecting device based on separating out the characteristic electromagnetic signals accompanying nuclear explosion by their form, by their spectral density and by their amplitude and a device for analysing the signal spectrum that provides display of the spectral density of the signal in the frequency range 6-100 kilocycles per second. Although existing techniques exclude the preponderant majority of signals from lightning, further advantage will be taken of information from the acoustic, seismic or other basic methods of detection to aid in further discrimination between signals from nuclear explosions and from lightning flashes;

(4) The requisite measuring and auxiliary apparatus and also power-supply units and means for obtaining correct radio time signals.

The site on which the antennas and the electromagnetic

recording apparatus are disposed should be on flat or rolling terrain with about 300 metres clear space around the antennas, and distant from sources of electrical interferences, power lines and communications lines.

D. *Apparatus for collecting and analysing radioactive debris*

The apparatus for collecting and analysing radioactive debris should include:

(1) A large filtering installation with a through-put capacity of 2×10^4 cubic metres of air over 10-24 hours, and which is used on a 24-hour basis;

(2) Equipment for collecting radioactive depositions— a surface with about 100 square metres area should be used. During dry weather, the surface can be washed down to collect dry fallout;

(3) A laboratory for simple radiochemical analysis.

Apparatus should be located in open areas, preferably on high ground, with high precipitation frequency. Apparatus should not be located in cut-off valleys or near regions with high natural background.

E. *Apparatus installed on aircraft for collecting radioactive debris and detection of a radioactive cloud*

(1) A filtering installation for aircraft should provide for the collection of the maximum quantity of the products of radioactive decay, the rate of filtering being about 3500 cubic metres an hour.

(2) The aircraft utilized for the collection of radioactive debris should have equipment for the comparatively fast determination of the presence of fresh radioactive debris.

(3) A small radiochemical laboratory will be located at each base for routine aircraft sampling flights.

Aircraft flights over ocean areas should be laid out as nearly as possible in approximately a north-south direction, and located near the sides of the major continents, as well as in the centre of oceans remote from continents.

5. All the apparatus of the control posts should be designed for reliable continuous operation.

6. Improved apparatus and techniques should be actively developed and expeditiously incorporated into the control system for the purpose of continuously improving the effectiveness for the detection and identification of nuclear explosions.

IV. CONCLUSIONS ON A CONTROL SYSTEM FOR DETECTING VIOLATIONS OF A POSSIBLE AGREEMENT ON THE SUSPENSION OF NUCLEAR TESTS

The Conference of Experts, having considered a control system for detecting violations of a possible agreement on the suspension of nuclear tests, has come to the conclusion that the methods for detecting nuclear explosions available at the present time, viz. the method of collecting samples of radioactive debris, the methods of recording seismic, acoustic, and hydroacoustic waves, and the radio-signal method, along with the use of on-site inspection of unidentified events which could be suspected of being nuclear explosions, make it possible to detect and identify nuclear explosions, including low yield explosions (1-5 kt). The Conference has therefore come to the conclusion that it is technically feasible to establish with the capabilities and limitations indicated below, a workable and effective control system to detect violations of an agreement on the worldwide suspension of nuclear weapons tests.

The Conference of Experts has come to the following conclusions regarding such a system:

1. The control system should be under the direction of an international control organ which would ensure the coordination of the activities of the control system in such a way that the system would satisfy the following technical requirements and perform the functions involved:

(a) The development, testing, and acceptance of the measuring apparatus and of the equipment, and stating the criteria for the siting, of the control posts;

(b) Carrying out at the control posts and on aircraft, mentioned in items 3 and 5 of the present Conclusions, of continuous and effective observations for the phenomena which make it possible to detect nuclear explosions by the use of the methods recommended by the Conference;

(c) Reliable communication, with the aid of existing channels where they are suitable for this purpose, between the international control organ on the one hand and, on the other hand, the control posts and the bases from which the regular aircraft flights are carried out; communications and transportation should ensure the speedy transmission of the results of observations, of data (including samples), of reports, and of necessary supplies;

(d) Means of transport of personnel of the control posts

in accordance with their duties and, so far as necessary, for the staff of the international control organ;

(e) Timely analysis and processing of the data from the observations of the control posts with the aim of speedily identifying events which could be suspected of being nuclear explosions, and in order to be able to report thereon in such manner as is considered by governments to be appropriate;

(f) Timely inspection of unidentified events which could be suspected of being nuclear explosions, in accordance with item 6 of the present Conclusions;

(g) Staffing of the control system (the network of control posts on land, on ships, and on aircraft, and also the staff of the international control organ) with qualified personnel having appropriate fields of specialization;

(h) Providing assistance in putting into effect a scientific research program, with the aim of raising the scientific standard of the system.

2. A network of control posts is characterized by three main parameters:

(a) The minimum yield adopted for the nuclear explosion or the natural events giving equivalent signals;

(b) The number of control posts;

(c) The probability of correct identification of natural events, particularly earthquakes.

The dependence between these parameters is such that with an increase in the yield of the explosion or the number of control posts the probability of detection and identification increases, and the number of unidentified events suspected of being a nuclear explosion decreases. On the other hand, for the identification of the increased number of unidentified events resulting from a smaller number of control posts it would be necessary to increase the number of on-site inspections or to make greater use of information coming from sources not subordinate to the international control organ or, if necessary, both.

The Conference considers that the problem of detecting and identifying underground explosions is one of the most difficult, and that, to a large extent, it determines the characteristics of the network of control posts.

3. The network of control posts would include from 160 to 170 land-based control posts (equipped in accordance with Section III of this report) and about 10 ships. Of these 160-170 control posts about 100-110 would be situated in continents, 20 on large oceanic islands, and 40 on small oceanic islands;

however, the exact number of control posts within the limits indicated above, can be determined only in the process of actually disposing them around the globe, taking into account the presence of noise at the sites at which they are located, and other circumstances.

The spacing between the control posts in continental aseismic areas would be about 1700 kilometres, and in seismic areas about 100 kilometres. The spacing between the control posts in ocean areas would vary between 2000 and more than 3500 kilometres; the spacing between island control posts in seismic areas would be about 1000 kilometres. This would lead to the following approximate distribution of control posts over the globe (with a network including 110 continental posts):

North America—24, Europe—6, Asia—37, Australia—7, South America—16, Africa—16, Antarctica—4; together with 60 control posts on islands and about 10 ships.

4. The tasks of the personnel of the control posts would include the ensuring of the normal functioning of apparatus, the preliminary processing of data received, and the forwarding of these data to the international control organ and to the government of the country on whose territory the control post is located in such a manner as may be considered appropriate by governments.

In order to carry out the tasks required one might need for each control post about 30 persons with various qualifications and fields of specialization, and also some persons for the auxiliary servicing staff.

5. In addition to the basic network described, air sampling would be accomplished by aircraft carrying out regular flights along north-south routes over the oceans along the peripheries of the Atlantic and Pacific Oceans, and also over areas of the oceans which are remote from surface control posts.

When it is necessary to investigate whether a radioactive cloud is present, in the case of detection of an unidentified event which could be suspected of being a nuclear explosion, special aircraft flights would be organized in order to collect samples of radioactive debris in accordance with Section II B 10.

6. When the control posts detect an event which cannot be identified by the international control organ and which could be suspected of being a nuclear explosion, the international control organ can send an inspection group to the site of this event in order to determine whether a nuclear

explosion had taken place or not. The group would be provided with equipment and apparatus appropriate to its task in each case. The inspection group would forward a report on the investigation it had carried out to the international control organ, and to the government of the country on the territory of which the investigation was made in such a manner as may be considered appropriate by governments.

7. The network of control posts disposed as described, together with the use of aircraft as described, would have the following effectiveness, subject to the qualifications discussed in items 8 and 9:

(a) Good probability of detecting and identifying nuclear explosions of yields down to about 1 kiloton, taking place on the surface of the earth and up to 10 kilometre altitude, and a good probability of detecting, but not always of identifying, explosions taking place at altitudes from 10 to 50 kilometre. In these cases the independent methods enumerated in Sections II A, II B and II D would be used.

(b) Good probability of detecting nuclear explosions of 1 kiloton yield set off deep in the open ocean. In this case use would be made of the independent hydroacoustic and seismic methods described in Sections II A and II C.

The identification of underwater explosions can, in comparatively rare cases, be made more difficult by natural events which give similar hydroacoustic and seismic signals.

(c) Good probability of recording seismic signals from deep underground nuclear explosions in continents equivalent to 1 kiloton and above. In this case use would be made of the seismic method described in Section II C.

The problem of identifying deep underground explosions is considered in item 8.

8. Along with the observation of signals of possible underground explosions the control posts would record at the same time a considerable number of similar signals from natural earthquakes. Although, with the present state of knowledge and techniques, the network of control posts would be unable to distinguish the signals from underground explosions from those of some earthquakes, it could identify as being of natural origin about 90 per cent of the continental earthquakes, whose signals are equivalent to 5 kiloton, and a small percentage of continental earthquakes equivalent to 1 kiloton.[21]

[21] The Conference notes that in order to increase the percentage of earthquakes of less than 5 kiloton yield which could be identified, it would be

It has been estimated on the basis of existing data that the number of earthquakes which would be undistinguishable on the basis of their seismic signals from deep underground nuclear explosions of about 5 kiloton yield could be in continental areas from 20 to 100 a year. Those unidentified events which could be suspected of being nuclear explosions would be inspected as described in item 6.

The capability of the control system to identify underground nuclear explosions of 1-5 kiloton yield depends on:

(a) The small fraction of earthquakes than can be identified on the basis of data obtained from the control posts alone;

(b) The fraction of earthquakes that can be identified with the aid of supplementary data obtained from existing seismic stations; and

(c) The fraction of events still left unidentified which could be suspected of being nuclear explosions and for which the international control organ carries out inspection in accordance with item 6.

Although the control system would have great difficulty in obtaining positive identification of a carefully concealed deep underground nuclear explosion, there would always be a possibility of detection of such a violation by inspection.

The on-site inspection carried out by the international control organ in accordance with item 6 would be able to identify with good probability underwater nuclear explosions with a yield of 1 kiloton and above.

9. The Conference notes that in certain special cases the capability of detecting nuclear explosions would be reduced; for instance, when explosions are set off in those areas of the ocean where the number of control posts is small and the meteorological conditions are unfavorable; in the case of shallow underground explosions; when explosions are set off on islands in seismic regions; and in some other cases when the explosion is carefully concealed. In some cases it would be impossible to determine exactly the area in which a nuclear explosion that had been detected took place.

However, the Conference considers that whatever the precautionary measures adopted by a violator he could not be

_____
appropriate to supplement the data from the control posts by trustworthy data from the best existing seismic stations. The results of the observations of these seismic stations should, for this purpose, be made available to the international control organ, and the equipment of the seismic stations suitable for this purpose could be improved by using the best modern apparatus. [Footnote in original.]

guaranteed against exposure, particularly if account is taken of the carrying out of inspection at the site of the suspected explosion.

10. The system described does not include specific means to detect and identify nuclear explosions at high altitudes (above 30-50 kilometres). The Conference has formulated its findings on the methods of detecting nuclear explosions set off at altitudes greater than 30-50 kilometres and has characterized these methods in Section II E.

11. The Conference of Experts recommends the control system described above for consideration by governments.

The following experts participated as delegates at the Conference:

Western Experts

Dr. James B. Fisk
Dr. F. Bacher
Sir John Cockcraft
Dr. Ernest O. Lawrence
Sir William Pennoy
Prof. Yves André Rocard
Dr. O. M. Solandt

Delegations of:

Union of Soviet Socialist Republics

E. K. Fedorov
N. N. Semenov
I. E. Tamm
M. A. Sadovski
O. I. Leipunski

I. P. Pasechnik
K. E. Gubkin
S. K. Tsarapkin

Polish People's Republic

M. Miesowicz
L. Jurkiewicz
M. Blusztajn

Czechoslovak Republic

C. Simáně
F. Běhounek
A. Zátopek
Z. Trhlik

People's Republic of Romania

H. Hulubei

3. *Exchange of Views on Negotiations for the Suspension of Nuclear Tests.*

(41) *Statement by the President, August 22, 1958.*[21]

The United States welcomes the successful conclusion of the Geneva meeting of experts who have been considering whether and how nuclear weapon tests could be detected. Their conclusions indicate that, if there were an agreement to eliminate such tests, its effective supervision and enforcement would be technically possible.

[21] *Department of State Bulletin,* v. 39 (September 8, 1958), pp. 378-379.

This is a most important conclusion, the more so because it is concurred in by the experts of the Soviet Union. Progress in the field of disarmament agreements depends upon the ability to establish effective international controls and the willingness of the countries concerned to accept those controls. The fact therefore of an agreement on technical possibilities of inspection and control opens up a prospect of progress in the vitally important field of disarmament.

The United States, taking account of the Geneva conclusions, is prepared to proceed promptly to negotiate an agreement with other nations which have tested nuclear weapons for the suspension of nuclear weapons tests and the actual establishment of an international control system on the basis of the experts' report.

If this is accepted in principle by the other nations which have tested nuclear weapons, then in order to facilitate the detailed negotiations the United States is prepared, unless testing is resumed by the Soviet Union, to withhold further testing on its part of atomic and hydrogen weapons for a period of one year from the beginning of the negotiations.

As part of the agreement to be negotiated, and on a basis of reciprocity, the United States would be further prepared to suspend the testing of nuclear weapons on a year-by-year basis subject to a determination at the beginning of each year that: (A) the agreed inspection system is installed and working effectively; and (B) satisfactorily progress is being made in reaching agreement on and implementing major and substantial arms control measures such as the United States has long sought. The agreement should also deal with the problem of detonations for peaceful purposes, as distinct from weapons tests.

Our negotiators will be instructed and ready by October 31 this year to open negotiations with other similarly instructed negotiators.

As the United States has frequently made clear, the suspension of testing of atomic and hydrogen weapons is not, in itself, a measure of disarmament or a limitation of armament. An agreement in this respect is significant if it leads to other and more substantial agreements relating to limitation and reduction of fissionable material for weapons and to other essential phases of disarmament. It is in this hope that the United States makes this proposal.

(42) *Soviet Note, August 30, 1958.*[22]

The Ministry of Foreign Affairs of the Union of Soviet Socialist Republics presents its compliments to the Embassy of the United States of America and referring to the Embassy's Note of 22 August this year has the honor to state that the Government of the Union of Soviet Socialist Republics is ready to start 31 October 1958 negotiations of representatives of the Union of Soviet Socialist Republics, the United States of America and Great Britain with the aim of concluding agreement on cessation forever of tests of atomic and hydrogen weapons by states with establishment of appropriate control for fulfillment of such agreement. In the opinion of the Soviet Government, the most convenient place for conducting such negotiations would be Geneva. To avoid the dragging out of negotiations it would be expedient to agree beforehand on limitation of their duration to a definite period. On its part, the Soviet Government purposes to set this period at two to three weeks.

Forwarded herewith is the text of the statement of the Chairman, Council of Ministers, Union of Soviet Socialist Republics, N. S. Khrushchev, in which the point of view of the Soviet Government is set forth on questions touched upon in the statement of President Eisenhower of 22 August.[23]

(43) *Statement by the President, October 25, 1958.*[24]

On August 22, 1958, the United States declared its willingness, in order to facilitate negotiations for the suspension of nuclear weapons tests and establishment of an international control system, to withhold testing of atomic and hydrogen weapons for a period of 1 year from the beginning of these negotiations on October 31. The sole condition for this voluntary 1-year suspension is that the Soviet Union should not itself conduct tests during this period.

The United Kingdom has similarly declared its willingness to suspend tests. It thus lies with the Soviet Union to decide whether on October 31st all countries which have tested nuclear weapons will have voluntarily suspended testing.

The United States regrets that the Soviet Union has not

[22] *Ibid.* (September 29, 1958), pp. 503-504.
[23] See *New Times*, no. 36 (September 1958), Supplement, pp. 2-4.
[24] *Department of State Bulletin*, v. 39 (November 10, 1958), p. 723.

accepted the offer of the United States and the United Kingdom, although we still hope that it will do so.[25]

4. Negotiations Concerning the Prevention of Surprise Attack.

(44) Letter from the Chairman of the Council of Ministers of the USSR (Khrushchev) to the President, July 2, 1958.[26]

(Excerpts)

DEAR MR. PRESIDENT: I am addressing this letter to you in order to make a proposal for joint steps toward solving the problem of preventing surprise attack.

The tension in present international relations and the continuing acceleration of the tempo of armament by states, especially in the production of ever more destructive types of weapons of mass destruction, makes it necessary, in our opinion, to reach agreement on the adoption of measures for preventing the possibility of surprise attack by one state against another, along with initial measures for restricting the armaments race such as, for example, the universal cessation of nuclear weapons tests. The Soviet Government, attaching great significance to this matter, proposed, as you know, ᵗhat it be included in the agenda for the meeting of heads of government.

*   *   *

The Government of the USA is familiar with the proposals of the Soviet Government regarding specific measures for preventing the possibility of surprise attack. The Soviet Union proposes that agreement be reached concerning the establishment of control posts at railway centers, large ports

[25] On October 28, 1958, the Secretary of State (Dulles) announced that the Soviet government has resumed testing nuclear weapons at "an intensive rate," having made "at least 14 test explosions" since September 30, 1958. Ibid. (November 17, 1958), p. 768. On November 7, 1958 the President confirmed that "continued testing by the Soviet Union has occurred despite the fact that negotiations for the suspension of testing of nuclear weapons have since October 31 been under way at Geneva. . . . This action by the Soviet Union relieves the United States from any obligation under its offer to suspend nuclear weapons tests. However, we shall continue suspension of such tests for the time being, and we understand that the United Kingdom will do likewise. We hope that the Soviet Union will also do so.

If there is not shortly a corresponding renunciation by the Soviet Union, the United States will be obliged to reconsider its position." Ibid. (November 24, 1958), p. 810.

[26] Ibid. (August 18, 1958), pp. 279-281.

and major highways in combination with specific disarmament measures and concerning aerial photography in areas that are of great significance from the standpoint of preventing the danger of surprise attack. In particular, we are prepared to reach agreement on reciprocal aerial photography in the zone of concentration of the main armed forces of the two grouping of states in Europe to a depth of 800 kilometers east and west of the line of demarcation between those forces. The Soviet Government also proposes, in addition to the zone in Europe, the establishment of a zone of aerial inspection which would include a portion of Soviet territory in the Far East and a corresponding portion of the territory of the USA.

*   *   *

Mindful of the importance that agreement on joint measures for the prevention of surprise attack by one state against another would have for the preservation of universal peace, I should like to propose to you, Mr. President, that the governments of our countries show practical initiative in this important matter. In the opinion of the Soviet Government it would be useful if in the near future the appropriate representatives—including those of the military agencies of both sides, e.g., at the level of experts—designated by the Governments of the USSR, the USA, and possibly by the governments of certain other states, met for a joint study of the practical aspects of this problem and developed within a definite period of time, to be determined in advance, recommendations regarding measures for the prevention of the possibility of surprise attack. The results of these negotiations could be considered at a meeting of heads of government. Such preliminary work would undoubtedly facilitate the adoption of a decision on this question at the meeting itself.

We hope that this proposal will meet with a favorable attitude on the part of the Government of the United States and that the joint efforts of our two countries will bring about a strengthening of trust between states, which is so necessary for ensuring peace throughout the world.[27]

With sincere respect,

N. KHRUSHCHEV

[27] For an exchange of notes preceding a meeting of experts at Geneva beginning November 10, 1958, see the *Department of State Bulletin* v. 39 (August 18, 1958), pp. 278-279; (September 29, 1958), p. 504; (October 27, 1958), pp. 648-649 and (November 24, 1958), pp. 815-816.

(45) *Department of State Announcement on the Adjournment of the Geneva Negotiations Sine Die, December 18, 1958.*[28]

The Geneva technical talks on surprise attack recessed today [December 18]. The recess occurred at the end of an anticipated duration of 5 weeks. No definite date has been set for resumption.

The United States believes further progress can best be made after a review by governments of the conference work to date. We consider such a review to be appropriate at this time. We look forward to an early resumption of the discussion of the surprise attack problem following a study of the conference records and accomplishments.

The United States experts at this conference, together with those of Canada, France, Italy and the United Kingdom, sought to lay a rational and technically sound foundation for dealing with the problem of increasing protection against surprise attack. Our experts sought to make a realistic technical assessment of the relative importance of the varying weapons which might be used in a surprise attack. They wished to determine, for example, how and to what degree it is possible to inspect and control missiles, airplanes, ground and naval forces to give warning in the event of their imminent use in surprise attack. The United States continues to believe that such work is necessary to assure successful political negotiations.

The United States regrets that the approach of the U.S.S.R. was to deal with this question on a political basis and to bypass the technical facts which need to be considered. This was not in keeping with Prime Minister Khrushchev's letter of July 2, 1958 to President Eisenhower which agreed on the desirability of "a joint study of the practical aspects" of the surprise attack problem. The introduction of political issues and proposals can only serve to prevent the achievement of the objectives of a meeting of experts.

Political negotiations on the complex problems inherent in disarmament have been under way for more than a decade. Despite our determined efforts to bring these earlier negotiations to a successful conclusion they resulted in little tangible progress. Accordingly, we proposed technical meet-

[28] *Ibid.,* v. 40 (January 5, 1958), p. 13.

ings in the belief that initial agreement could be reached on the technical aspects of the disarmament problem.

We are confident that technical discussions among experts can produce agreements on the technical facts about instruments of surprise attack and their control and that these results in turn can provide an agreed basis for subsequent political negotiations. We have repeatedly made clear that such technical discussions are not an end in themselves, and that the United States is ready to undertake political negotiations on disarmament matters at any time in the proper forum. We have consistently stated that meetings of experts would be undertaken without prejudice to respective positions of the governments concerned—either the Soviets or our own—on the timing and interdependence of various aspects of disarmament.

We urge the U.S.S.R. to review constructively their own proposals and the record of the conference. We expect such a review to lead to an early resumption of discussions on the increasingly urgent problems of reducing the danger of surprise attack.

E. European Security.

1. *The Rapacki Plan.*

(46) *Polish Note and Memorandum, February 14, 1958.*[1]

I wish to refer to the conversation which I had on December 9, 1957, with the Chargé d'Affaires of the Embassy of the United States in Warsaw. In this conversation I have presented the position of the Polish Government in respect to the tendencies to make the nuclear armaments in Europe universal and particularly towards the acceleration of armaments in Western Germany. The threat of further complications, primarily in Central Europe, where the opposing military groupings come into a direct contract and the apparent danger of an increase in the international tension have prompted the Polish Government to initiate at that time direct discussions through diplomatic channels on the Polish proposal submitted to the United Nations General Assembly on October 2, 1957, concerning the establishment of a denuclearized zone in Central Europe.

[1] *Ibid.*, v. 38 (May 19, 1958), pp. 822-823.

This proposal has evoked a wide interest in government and political circles as well as in the broad strata of public opinion in many countries.

Taking into account a number of opinions expressed in declarations made in connection with the Polish proposal and with the view to facilitate negotiations, the Polish Government has resolved to present a more detailed elaboration of its proposal. This finds its expression in the attached memorandum which is simultaneously being transmitted by the Polish Government to the governments of France, Great Britain and the Union of Soviet Socialist Republics as well as to the governments of other interested countries.

The Polish Government is conscious of the fact that the solution of the problem of disarmament on a world-wide scale requires, first of all, negotiations among the great powers and other countries concerned. Therefore, the Polish Government supports the proposal of the U.S.S.R. government concerning a meeting on the highest level of leading states men with the participation of heads of governments. Such a meeting could also result in reaching an agreement on the question of the establishment of a denuclearized zone in Central Europe, should an agreement among the countries concerned not be reached in the meantime. In any event the initiation at present of discussions on the question of a denuclearized zone in Central Europe would contribute to a successful course of the above mentioned meeting.

The Polish Government expresses the hope that the Government of the United States will study the attached memorandum and that the proposals contained in it will meet the understanding of the Government of the United States. The Polish Government on its part would be prepared to continue the exchange of views on this problem with the Government of the United States.

MEMORANDUM

On October 2, 1957, the Government of the Polish People's Republic presented to the General Assembly of the United Nations a proposal concerning the establishment of a denuclearized zone in Central Europe. The governments of Czechoslovakia and of the German Democratic Republic declared their readiness to accede to that zone.

The Government of the Polish People's Republic proceeded with the conviction that the establishment of the proposed denuclearized zone could lead to an improvement in the international atmosphere and facilitate broader discussions on disarmament as well as the solution of other controversial internal issues, while the continuation of nuclear armaments and making them universal could only lead to a further solidifying of the division of Europe into opposing blocks and to a further complication of the situation, especially in Central Europe.

In December 1957 the Government of the Polish People's Republic renewed its proposal through diplomatic channels.

Considering the wide repercussions which the Polish initiative has evoked and taking into account the propositions emerging from the discussion which has developed on this proposal, the Government of the Polish People's Republic hereby presents a more detailed elaboration of its proposal, which may facilitate the opening of negotiations and reaching of an agreement on this subject.

I. The proposed zones should include the territory of: Poland, Czechoslovakia, German Democratic Republic and German Federal Republic. In this territory nuclear weapons would neither be manufactured nor stockpiled, the equipment and installations designed for their servicing would not be located there; the use of nuclear weapons against the territory of this zone would be prohibited.

II. The contents of the obligations arising from the establishment of the denuclearized zone would be based upon the following premises:

1. The states include in this zone would undertake the obligation not to manufacture, maintain nor import for their own use and not to permit the location on their territories of nuclear weapons of any type, as well as not to install nor to admit to their territories of installations and equipment designed for servicing nuclear weapons, including missiles launching equipment.

2. The four powers (France, United States, Great Britain, and U.S.S.R.) would undertake the following obligations:

(A) Not to maintain nuclear weapons in the armaments of their forces stationed on the territories of states included in this zone; neither to maintain nor to install on the territories of these states any installations or equipment designed for servicing nuclear weapons, including missiles' launching equipment.

(B) Not to transfer in any manner and under any reason

whatsoever, nuclear weapons nor installations and equipment designed for servicing nuclear weapons—to governments or other organs in this area.

3. The powers which have at their disposal nuclear weapons should undertake the obligation not to use these weapons against the territory of the zone or against any targets situated in this zone.

Thus the powers would undertake the obligation to respect the status of the zone as an area in which there should be no nuclear weapons and against which nuclear weapons should not be used.

4. Other states, whose forces are stationed on the territory of any state included in the zone, would also undertake the obligation not to maintain nuclear weapons in the armaments of these forces and not to transfer such weapons to governments or to other organs in this area. Neither will they install equipment or installations designed for the servicing of nuclear weapons, including missiles' launching equipment, on the territories of states in the zone nor will they transfer them to governments or other organs in this area.

The manner and procedure for the implementation of these obligations could be the subject of detailed mutual stipulations.

III. In order to ensure the effectiveness and implementation of the obligations contained in Part II, paragraphs 1-2 and 4, the states concerned would undertake to create a system of broad and effective control in the area of the proposed zone and submit themselves to its functioning.

1. This system could comprise ground as well as aerial control. Adequate control posts, with rights and possibilities of action which would ensure the effectiveness of inspection, could also be established.

The details and forms of the implementation of control can be agreed upon on the basis of the experience acquired up to the present time in this field, as well as on the basis of proposals submitted by various states in the course of the disarmament negotiations, in the form and to the extent in which they can be adapted to the area of the zone.

The system of control established for the denuclearized zone could provide useful experience for the realization of broader disarmament agreement.

2. For the purpose of supervising the implementation of the proposed obligations an adequate control machinery

should be established. There could participate in it, for example, representatives appointed/not excluding additional personal appointments/by organs of the North Atlantic Treaty Organization and of the Warsaw Treaty. Nationals or representatives of states, which do not belong to any military grouping in Europe, could also participate in it.

The procedure of the establishment, operation and reporting of the control organs can be the subject of further mutual stipulations.

IV. The most simple form of embodying the obligations of states included in the zone would be the conclusion of an appropriate international convention. To avoid, however, implications, which some states might find in such a solution, it can be arranged that:

1. These obligations be embodied in the form of four unilateral declarations, bearing the character of an international obligation deposited with a mutually agreed upon depository state.

2. The obligations of great powers be embodied in the form of a mutual document or unilateral declaration/as mentioned above in paragraph 1/;

3. The obligations of other states, whose armed forces are stationed in the area of the zone, be embodied in the form of unilateral declarations/as mentioned above in paragraph 1/.

On the basis of the above proposals the government of the Polish People's Republic suggests to initiate negotiations for the purpose of a further detailed elaboration of the plan for the establishment of the denuclearized zone, of the documents and guarantees related to it as well as of the means of implementation of the undertaken obligations.

The government of the Polish People's Republic has reasons to state that acceptance of the proposal concerning the establishment of a denuclearized zone in Central Europe will facilitate the reaching of an agreement relating to the adequate reduction of conventional armaments and of foreign armed forces stationed on the territory of the states included in the zone.

(47) *United States Reply, May 3, 1958.*[2]

EXCELLENCY: I have the honor to acknowledge the receipt of Mr. Rapacki's note of February 14, 1958, enclosing a mem-

[2] *Ibid.*, pp. 821-822.

orandum elaborating on the Polish Government's proposals concerning the establishment of a denuclearized zone in Central Europe.

Recognizing that the initiative of the Polish Government stems from a desire to contribute to the attainment of a stable and durable peace, my Government has given these proposals serious and careful consideration. On the basis of this study it has concluded that they are too limited in scope to reduce the danger of nuclear war or provide a dependable basis for the security of Europe. They neither deal with the essential question of the continued production of nuclear weapons by the present nuclear powers nor take into account the fact that present scientific techniques are not adequate to detect existing nuclear weapons. The proposed plan does not affect the central sources of power capable of launching a nuclear attack, and thus its effectiveness would be dependent on the good intentions of countries outside the area. The proposals overlook the central problems of European security because they provide no method for balanced and equitable limitations of military capabilities and would perpetuate the basic cause of tension in Europe by accepting the continuation of the division of Germany.

An agreement limited to the exclusion of nuclear weapons from the territory indicated by your Government without other types of limitation would, even if it were capable of being inspected, endanger the security of the Western European countries in view of the large and widely deployed military forces of the Soviet Union. Unless equipped with nuclear weapons, Western forces in Germany would find themselves under present circumstances at a great disadvantage to the numerically greater mass of Soviet troops stationed within easy distance of Western Europe which are, as the Soviet leaders made clear, being equipped with the most modern and destructive weapons, including missiles of all kinds.

The considerations outlined above have caused the United States in association with other Western Powers to propose that nations stop producing material for nuclear weapons, cease testing such weapons and begin to reduce present stockpiles. The United States has further proposed broader areas of inspection against surprise attack, including an area in Europe, roughly from the United Kingdom to the Ural mountains. We remain willing to do this. You will recall, moreover, that the Western nations offered at the London disarmament negotiations to discuss a more limited zone in Europe. With regard to missiles you will recall that over a year and a half ago the United States proposed that we begin to study the inspection and control needed to assure the exclusive peaceful use of outer space now threatened by the development of such devices as intercontinental and intermediate range ballistic missiles.

The United States, in association with other Western Powers, has also proposed that a comprehensive and effective European security arrangement be established in conjunction with the reunification of Germany. The proposed arrangements would provide for limitations on both forces and armaments, measures for the prevention of surprise attack in the area, and assurances of reaction in the event of aggression.

Your note speaks of the existence of opposing military groupings in Central Europe as being responsible for tensions in the area. It should not be necessary for me to recall that the present division of Europe stems primarily from the decision of the Soviet Union not to permit Eastern European nations to participate in the European Recovery Plan. Nor need I repeat the many assurances given as to the defensive character of the North Atlantic Treaty Organization which is reflected in its entire organizational and command structure. The entire history of its creation and development testify to this, though persistent efforts are made in some quarters to portray it otherwise.

In the absence of effective arrangements either general or regional in character which would promote real security and in view of the present policies and armaments of the Soviet Union, the countries of Western Europe along with Canada and ourselves, joined in alliance with them, have no other recourse than to develop the required pattern of integrated NATO military strength and to utilize for defensive purposes modern developments in weapons and techinques.

The views which I have presented above on behalf of my Government point out the basic reasons why the United States considers that the Polish Government's proposals for establishing a denuclearized zone in Central Europe would not serve to advance their expressed objectives. Nevertheless, the United States appreciates the initiative of the Polish Government in seeking a solution to these problems.[3] It hopes that

[3] On November 4, 1958 the Polish Foreign Minister (Rapacki) introduced modifications of his proposal, in order to meet some of the objections of the United States.

this exchange of correspondence will enable the Polish Government better to understand American proposals in the fields of European security and disarmament. I trust that the improved relations between Poland and the United States will serve as a basis for a better understanding between our two countries on these problems, as well as on other matters.

2. Exchange of Notes Concerning a Friendship Treaty Proposed by the Soviet Union.

(48) Soviet Note, July 15, 1958.[4]

(Excerpts)

The Soviet Government considers it necessary to address itself to the Government of the United States of America on the following question.

The Government of the USSR considers that the situation unfolding on the European Continent obligates the Governments of all interested states to undertake efforts for working out joint measures which would halt the sliding of Europe toward war and to find roads toward the strengthening of peace on the basis of the growth of mutual trust and the broadening of multilateral cooperation between European states.

*   *   *

Being the largest state in Europe which twice in the course of one generation was subjected to invasion over its western borders, the Soviet Union, naturally, cannot but show unremitting concern over security in Europe which is inseparable from its own security. Millions of Soviet people did not give their lives on the field of battle during the Second World War in order that now the Soviet people could indifferently observe how in Europe inflammable material for a new war was being accumulated.

Like the other peace-loving states, the Soviet Union did and continues to do everything depending upon it to remove the danger of war and to establish peaceful cooperation based on trust among all the European states regardless of their social structure and membership in one or the other grouping of Powers.

The Soviet Union liquidated its military bases located in the territory of other states. Beyond the confines of its own

⁴ Department of State Bulletin, v. 39 (September 22, 1958), pp. 462-465.

borders the Soviet Union does not maintain stockpiles of atomic and hydrogen arms or missile launching sites. In the last three years the strength of the Soviet armed forces has been reduced unilaterally by a total of two million one hundred forty thousand persons. In this regard the armed forces of the USSR in the German Democratic Republic were reduced by more than ninety thousand persons. Military expenditures and armaments were correspondingly reduced. At the last session of the Supreme Soviet of the USSR a resolution was approved for the unilateral cessation by the Soviet Union of tests of all types of atomic and hydrogen arms.

At the meeting of the Political Consultative Committee of the states participating in the Warsaw Treaty, which took place at the end of May in Moscow, a decision was made concerning the withdrawal at a very early date from the Rumanian Peoples Republic of the Soviet armies which were there in conformity with that treaty and also concerning an additional reduction of the Soviet armies stationed in the territory of the Hungarian People's Republic.[5]

Desiring to weaken the split appearing between the two basic groupings of powers in Europe which are in military conflict and to exclude the danger of the growing contradictions between them, the participants in the meeting proposed the conclusion of a pact of non-aggression between the member-states of the Warsaw Treaty and the member-states of the North Atlantic Alliance. The Soviet Government is convinced that the conclusion of such a pact of non-aggression would be a reliable preventive measure, strengthening the peace in Europe.

In spite of the tremendous positive role of such a pact of non-aggression, it is impossible, however, not to take into consideration that this measure represents only an initial step, the minimum, that it is necessary to undertake under present conditions for the purpose of establishing in Europe an atmosphere of due trust among states. It would be an unforgivable omission if, along with this, no effort was made to establish additional transitional steps from the present dangerous situation toward the establishment of the conditions of a firm peace in Europe.

As is well known, in the period between the two world wars the plans of guaranteeing security in Europe and the organization of general European cooperation suffered ruin above all because agreement was not achieved among the

[5] Documents 64 and 65, below.

leading states which had the most powerful armed forces and whose united efforts would have made aggression impossible. In the opinion of the Soviet Government, it is necessary to study that period of history and not to repeat the serious errors of the past.

It is no longer necessary now to prove that the attempts to substitute for the solution of the tasks facing Europe as a whole the practice of founding on a narrow, closed basis different unions of individual European states, like the coal and steel community, the common market, EURATOM, and so on, lead only to a situation in which these states more and more are opposed to the other states of Europe, digging ever deeper the ditch dividing today the Western part of Europe from the Eastern.

The idea of cooperation of all European states, their drawing together in the interests of preserving the peace, of securing the well-being and flourishing of Europe, has deep roots in history and in the present life of European peoples. In the East as well as in the West of our continent, the striving for the development of mutual understanding and all round intercourse among European states is becoming stronger. The fact in particular that at the XII Session of the UN all European states and the USA voted for the resolution on peaceful and good neighborly relations among states testifies in particular to this.[6]

The Soviet Government considers that the governments of European states, and the Government of the United States, if they all wish to stop the dangerous development of events in Europe, should make efforts toward working out on a regional basis general European decisions, which in practice could be brought into existence at the present stage and which could be acceptable for all governments. In this connection it is introducing a proposal on concluding a treaty of friendship and cooperation by the European states and also by the United States.

*　　*　　*

[6] General Assembly Resolution 1236 (XII), Adopted December 14, 1957. (See United Nations, General Assembly, *Official Records, Twelfth Session,* Supplement No. 18 (A/3805), p. 5.)

(49) Text of Proposed "Treaty of Friendship and Cooperation of European States." [7]

The Signatories

Resolved to promote in every way the development of friendly relations and cooperation between European states and to resolve all questions arising between them exclusively by peaceful means: recognizing that the creation of an atmosphere of trust between them is the most important task of the peoples of the European states, of excluding the possibility of the outbreak of a new war on the European continent;

Animated by a desire to carry out the high principles of the UN and in development of the situation in keeping with the resolution concerning peaceful and good neighborly relations between states, approved by the XII Session of the General Assembly of the UN.

They have decided to conclude the present treaty on Friendship and Collaboration of the European states and to these ends have agreed as follows:

Article 1

The signatories of the treaty may be all European states and the United States of America which recognize the aims and accept for themselves the obligations set forth in the present treaty.

Article 2

The signatories will, in the spirit of genuine cooperation and mutual understanding, develop and strengthen good neighborly and friendly relations among their peoples on the basis of the principles of mutual respect for territorial integrity and sovereignty, non-aggression, non-interference in each other's internal affairs, equality and mutual advantage.

Article 3

The signatories obligate themselves to solve all disputes which may arise among them exclusively by peaceful means and in accordance with the principles of the United Nations Charter.

In case a situation arises which could lead to a deterioration of the friendly relations between states or create a threat to the peace in Europe, the signatories will consult at once with

[7] *Department of State Bulletin,* v. 39 (September 22, 1958), pp. 465-466.

one another for the purpose of taking such necessary mutual measures as are found appropriate for the elimination of the situation which has arisen.

Article 4

If one or more of the signatories is subjected to an attack on the part of any state, the other signatories to this treaty obligate themselves not to provide military and economic aid or moral support to the aggressor regardless of whether or not they are bound as allies or by some other commitments with the aggressor state.

Article 5

Until the conclusion of a general agreement on the limitations of arms and of armed forces and the banning of atomic weapons the signatories are obligated:

a) To reduce in the course of 1 to 2 years their armed forces and arms located in the territory of Germany by 1/3 or by another agreed amount, whereby the reduced contingents of armed forces must be withdrawn from the territory of Germany to within the confines of their own national borders.

After the aforesaid reduction of armed forces and armaments, to consider the question of the further reduction of foreign armed forces which are stationed on the territory of Germany and also the reduction of foreign armed forces located on the territory of other European states with the removal in both cases of the reduced contingents of the armed forces to the confines of their own national borders.

Regularly, and not less than twice yearly, to exchange information on the strength of armed forces and the quantity of armament of the signatories located on the territory of other states in Europe;

b) For the prevention of a possible surprise attack to provide for the conducting of aerial photography within a zone extending for 800 kilometers from the line demarking the armed forces of the member-countries of the North Atlantic Treaty and the participating states of the Warsaw Treaty. Such a zone will be established by agreement with the states whose territories are included in this zone.

The representatives of the signatories in the course of not more than 6 months after the signing of the present treaty will define the boundaries of the zones specified in paragraph

(b) and will also establish an appropriate system of control and inspection for the fulfillment of the obligations specified in the present Article.

Article 6

The signatories unanimously favor the creation of a zone in Central Europe, free from the production and presence of atomic, hydrogen, and missile weapons, as well as from the equipping and manning of the above mentioned types of arms. This zone ought to comprise with the agreement of the appropriate governments the territory of the German Democratic Republic, the Federal Republic of Germany, the Polish Peoples' Republic, and the Czechoslovak Republic.

The signatories are obligated to respect the status of this zone and consider the territory of the governments which comprise it as a sphere for the use of atomic, hydrogen, and missile weapons. They recognize as indispensable the establishment of an appropriate system of control and inspection for fulfillment of agreement concerning the creation of such a zone.

Article 7

Proceeding on the belief, that economic cooperation and contacts between states are the natural and stable foundation for the strengthening of peaceful and friendly relations between them, the signatories are obligated:

a) To develop economic cooperation and an exchange of experience; to extend the necessary cooperation to one another in the matter of solving the most urgent economic problems facing the most important significance for insuring the full employment of the population and the improvement of their well being;

To develop in every possible way cooperation in the field of trade between the countries participating in the agreement on the principles of full equality and mutual benefit.

b) To take measures toward the gradual elimination of the obstacles and limitations still existing in the field of the development of economic relations between states on the basis of bilateral and multilateral agreements, as well as within the framework and by means of the European economic commission of the UN;

c) To develop cooperation in the field of utilization of atomic energy for peaceful purposes, including exchange of experience in the construction of atomic energy, and the exchange of specialists, raw and other materials, and equipment.

Article 8

For the purpose of broadening international ties and cooperation in the field of science and culture, furthering mutual understanding between peoples, the signatories are obligated to develop and strengthen mutual ties in the field of science, culture, technology, and education. To these ends they express readiness to discuss in the near future concrete questions of cultural and scientific cooperation, having in view the conclusion of a bilateral or multilateral agreement on these questions.

Article 9

The present treaty is valid for a period of 10 years.

The treaty is subject to ratification in conformity with the legislative powers of the signatory states of the treaty.

Article 10

The treaty is open for the adherence of all European states.

Article 11

The present treaty, the Russian, English, French and German texts of which are authentic, will be submitted to the custody of the Secretary-General of the UN.

In witness thereof, the plenipotentiaries have signed the present treaty and have affixed their seals thereto.

DRAWN UP IN THE CITY _____ 1958.

(50) *United States Note, August 22, 1958.*[8]

The United States Government has examined the Soviet Government's note of July 15 and the draft Treaty attached to it. It does not propose at present to comment on the substance of either. This is not because it agrees with what is said or with the premise on which the Soviet Government bases its arguments. The reason is simply that the United States Government notes that the proposals embodied in the draft Treaty are largely a reflection of proposals already included in the Soviet Memorandum of May 5 about an agenda for

⁸ *Ibid.,* p. 462.

a meeting of Heads of Government, although surprisingly no mention is made of such meeting in the Soviet note of July 15. The Western powers have made their own suggestions for topics to be examined by Heads of Government. They are prepared to express their views about the Soviet proposals and to receive Soviet views about their own. For this purpose, the Western powers suggested, as long ago as May 31, a practical procedure for discussing the agenda which would be fair to both parties. They still await a reply to this and also to their letter of July 1.[9] In the meantime, to their regret, the preparatory discussions in Moscow are at a standstill. The United States Government believes that the first thing to be done, before the proposals of either party are discussed, is to resolve this question.

F. Germany.

1. *The Unification of Germany.*

(51) *Aide Memoire of the Federal Republic of Germany, September 9, 1958.*[1]

The German Federal Parliament (Bundestag) at its meeting July 2, 1958, unanimously passed the following resolution, which was endorsed by the German Federal Council (Bundesrat) at its meeting July 18, 1958:

In order to promote the reestablishment of German unity, the Federal Government is herewith directed to request the four powers, France, the Union of Socialist Soviet Republics, the United Kingdom, and the United States, to set up, either at a future international conference (summit conference) or independently thereof, a four-power group (at least at the level of an ambassadors' conference) with a mandate to prepare joint proposals for the solution of the German problem.

The Federal Government shares the desire expressed in the Bundestag resolution, that a group of the four powers responsible for the solution of the German problem be set up either at a future international conference (summit conference) or independently thereof. It hopes that this group will study proposals concerning the reestablishment of German unity, and carry out the preparatory work necessary for final negotiations to be held at a later date.

In compliance with the mandate given to it by the Bundes-

[9] Document 31, above.
[1] *Department of State Bulletin,* v. 39 (October 20, 1958), pp. 614-615.

tag and the Bundesrat, and in view of the talks in preparation for an international conference which have been taking place in Moscow between representatives of the four powers responsible for the reunification of Germany, the Federal Government begs to direct the attention of the Government of the United States of America to the desire expressed in the above resolution.

(52) *Soviet Note, September 18, 1958.*[2]

The Government of the Union of Soviet Socialist Republics presents its compliments to the Government of the United States of America and considers it necessary to transmit the following for its information.

On 5 September of this year the Soviet Government received the note of the Government of the German Democratic Republic in which disquiet is expressed in connection with the impermissibly delayed preparation of a peace treaty with Germany.[3] In the note a proposal is advanced about the urgent creation of a commission of representatives of the four great powers whose tasks would be the carrying out of consultations about the preparation of a peace treaty with Germany. As the Government of the G.D.R. communicated, notes to the same effect were addressed also to the Governments of the United States of America, Great Britain and the French Republic. Moreover, the G.D.R. Government made it known that it simultaneously proposed to the Government of the F.R.G. to create a commission of representatives of both German states which would examine from a German point of view all questions connected with the preparation of a peace treaty with Germany. According to the proposal of the G.D.R. Government, this commission will occupy itself also with questions relevant to the competence of the two German states, connected with the creation of a united peace-loving democratic Germany.

Taking into account that the question about preparing a peace treaty is that part of the German problem for the decision of which all states which participated in the war, and in the first place the four great powers, bear responsibility, the Soviet Government would like to express to the Government of the U.S.A. its considerations regarding the proposals advanced by the Government of the G.D.R. so that in the

[2] *Ibid.*, pp. 616-617.
[3] Not printed.

nearest future it might be possible to undertake joint steps in the interest of a peaceful settlement with Germany. The statement of the G.D.R. Government points out how acutely the German people feel that abnormal situation which already in the course of 13 years has been preserved in Germany as result of the absence of a peace treaty with this country. It is a new reminder to the great powers on whom lies the main responsibility for a peaceful settlement with Germany about the need at least to fulfill their duty before the German people. The proposal of the G.D.R. Government about the creation of a commission of representatives of the four powers and also of a corresponding German commission for the preparation of a peace treaty with Germany takes into account the concrete conditions which have arisen up to the present and opens the way for a practical solution of this long since matured problem.

The Soviet Government being an advocate of the basic solution of the German question has repeatedly come out in the past with proposals, directed toward an urgent conclusion of a peace treaty with Germany, which unfortunately have not at that time met support on the part of the Western powers. Recently it once more advanced this question in connection with the preparation for the convocation of a summit meeting considering it necessary to examine this as one of the important problems of the agenda of such a meeting.

The indisputable fact is evident to all that the absence of a peace treaty with Germany leaves open many questions which profoundly disturb the whole German people and affect important interests of the other European peoples who took part in the war with Germany, including the interests of their security. No one has the right in the course of such a long time to deprive the German people of a possibility of enjoying all the benefits of a peaceful situation, all the more since the solution of analogous questions in connection with all the countries drawn into the war on the side of Hitlerite Germany has long since been a passed stage.

The conclusion of a peace treaty with Germany would finally draw a line under the past war and its heavy consequences for the European peoples and would undoubtedly have important significance for reducing tension and guaranteeing security in Europe. At the same time it would permit the guarding from any outside interference the internal development of Germany and the restoring in full measure of its sovereignty and independence. Germany would be placed in all relations in a position of equality with other states and would receive access to the U.N. The working out of the draft of a peace treaty, which would define the political and economic conditions of the development of Germany and its military status, is dictated also by a real need to give the German people clear perspectives for the development of Germany in the future.

In supporting the initiative of the Government of the German Democratic Republic, the Soviet Government has also in mind that the preparatory work's concluding a peace treaty with the participation of the Governments of both German states would facilitate a rapprochment between them and the unification of their efforts for the purpose of restoring the state unity of Germany.

The Soviet Government hereby informs the Government of the U.S.A. that it has notified the G.D.R. Government about its agreement with its proposal to create a commission of representatives of the four powers with the aim of carrying out consultations about preparing a peace treaty with Germany.

It also supports the idea of the creation of a commission of representatives of both German states and declares its readiness to render any aid for the activity of such a commission. The Soviet Government expects that the Government of the United States of America, in accordance with the obligations lying on it in connection with the peaceful settlement with Germany, also will support the said proposals of the Government of the G.D.R. and will adopt the necessary steps for their realization. The Soviet Government would be grateful to the Government of the U.S.A. for the receipt in a short time of its considerations on the question touched upon.

Notes of identical content have been addressed by the Soviet Government also to the Governments of Great Britain and France.

(53) *United States Note to the Soviet Union, September 30, 1958.*[4]

The Embassy of the United States of America presents its compliments to the Ministry of Foreign Affairs of the Union of Soviet Socialist Republics and on instruction of its Government has the honor to state the following:

[4] *Department of State Bulletin,* v. 39 (October 20, 1958), pp. 615-616.

The United States Government wishes to refer to the Soviet Government's note of September 18. It regrets that the Soviet note ignores the proposals made by the Government of the Federal Republic of Germany, which were contained in an Aide Memoire of September 9 addressed to the Governments of France, the Soviet Union, the United Kingdom and the United States. These proposals, based on an unanimous resolution of the German Federal Parliament which was endorsed by the German Federal Council, also called for the establishment of a Four Power group to discuss the German problem. The United States Government observes that instead, the Soviet note is based on proposals made by the so-called "Government of the German Democratic Republic."

The United States Government fully shares the view expressed in the Soviet Government's note that "no one has the right to deprive the German people for such a long time of the opportunity to enjoy all the advantages of a state of peace."

It also notes with satisfaction the statement that the Soviet Government is "in favor of a fundamental settlement of the German question." It is well known to the Soviet Government that this has long been the aim of the United States Government. It is sufficient to recall the opening words of the Berlin Declaration which was made by the Governments of France, the Federal Republic of Germany, the United Kingdom and the United States on July 29, 1957;[5]

"Twelve years have elapsed since the end of the war in Europe. The hopes of the peoples of the world for the establishment of a basis for a just and lasting peace have nevertheless not been fulfilled. One of the basic reasons for the failure to reach a settlement is the continued division of Germany, which is a grave injustice to the German people and a major source of international tension in Europe."

The United States Government agrees that, as stated in the Soviet note, "the conclusion of a peace treaty with Germany would finally draw the line below the last war," and that the German people should themselves participate in the preparation of such a treaty. An essential prerequisite for the negotiation of a peace treaty is, however, the creation of a Government which truly reflects the will of the German people. Only a Government created on such a basis could undertake obligations which would inspire confidence on

[5] *Documents on American Foreign Relations, 1957,* pp. 142-147.

the part of other countries and which would be considered just and binding by the people of Germany themselves. Moreover, German representatives at any discussions about a peace treaty which were held in advance of the reunification of Germany would, as the Soviet Government must be aware, have no power to commit a future all-German Government to any of the conclusions reached. For these reasons, the United States Government considers that the first task in any discussion of the German problem must be the reunification of Germany and the formation of an all-German Government by means of free elections.

On the method by which such Government should be formed, the United States Government finds the proposals in the Soviet Government's note both unrealistic and unsatisfactory. According to these proposals, the question of the reunification of Germany is to be left to a commission composed of representatives of the Federal Republic and the Soviet Zone. The regime established in the Soviet Zone of Germany does not represent the will of the people of Eastern Germany. It is rightly regarded by the people of all parts of Germany as a regime imposed by a foreign power and maintained in power by foreign forces. Since his regime has no mandate from the people it purports to speak for, it would violate any genuine concern for the interests of the German people to allow such a regime to participate in any discussions involving their future Government.

In the Directive issued by the Four Heads of Government at Geneva in 1955, the Soviet Government recognized its responsibility for the reunification of Germany. The Directive provides *inter alia:* "The Heads of Government, recognizing their common responsibility for the settlement of the German question and the re-unification of Germany, have agreed that the settlement of the German question and the re-unification of Germany by means of free elections shall be carried out in conformity with the national interests of the German people and the interests of European security." The United States Government cannot accept that the Soviet Government has the right unilaterally to evade this responsibility or this agreement. In accordance with its similar responsibility the United States Government, in conjunction with the Governments of France and the United Kingdom, has on many occasions put forward proposals designed to achieve the restoration of German unity. These Western proposals recognize the right of the German people to determine their own way of life in freedom, to determine for themselves their own political, economic and social system, and to provide for their security with due regard to the legitimate interests of other nations. They provide for the exercise of this right through the holding of free elections throughout Germany, the establishment of an all-German Government, and the negotiation with this Government of the terms of a peace treaty.

The Government of the United States is ready at any time to enter into discussions with the Soviet Government on the basis of these proposals, or of any other proposals genuinely designed to insure the reunification of Germany in freedom, in any appropriate forum. It regards the solution of the German problem as essential if a lasting settlement in Europe is to be achieved. This problem has been included as one of the subjects which the Western Powers put forward on May 28 for examination at a conference of Heads of Government. Although the Soviet Government agreed that preparations for such a conference should be made between representatives of the Four Powers in Moscow, these preparations have been in suspense since the end of May because of the Soviet Government's failure to reply to the Western proposals of May 31 for overcoming the procedural difficulty caused by the divergence in the Soviet and Western sets of agenda proposals. The further Western communications of July 1 and August 22 have so far also remained unanswered. Since the Soviet Government has indicated in its note that it, too, attaches importance to the solution of the German problem, the United States Government hopes that the Soviet Government will now reply to the Western proposal so that the preparatory talks may continue.

In the interests of making progress on this subject, the Government of the United States is, however, prepared to discuss the German problem in a separate Four Power group to be set up in accordance with the desire of the Federal Government expressed in its Aide Memoire of September 9. The purpose of the group would be to discuss proposals connected with the German problem and to carry out the preparatory work necessary for final negotiations to be held at a later date either at a conference of Heads of Government, if one can be arranged, or otherwise.

The Government of the United States hopes that, in view of the importance of settling the German problem, not only for the German people but also as a contribution towards the relaxation of tension in Europe, the Soviet Government will agree to the procedure set out above.

A copy of the United States Government's reply to the Federal Government's Aide Memoire of September 9 is attached. The United States Government is also informing the Federal Government of the terms of this note.

(54) *United States Aide Memoire to the Federal Republic of Germany, September 30, 1958.*[6]

The Embassy of the U.S.A. has been instructed to inform the Federal Ministry of Foreign Affairs as follows:

The Government of the United States refers to the Aide Memoire of the Federal Government of September 9, 1958, which draws attention to a resolution passed by the German Federal Parliament and endorsed by the German Federal Council. This resolution calls for the establishment of a Four Power group composed of representatives of the powers responsible for solution of the German problem with a mandate to prepare joint proposals for the solution of the German problem. It also suggests that the group envisaged would be set up either at a future international conference of Heads of Government or independently thereof.

The Government of the United States notes that the Government of the Federal Republic shares the desire expressed in the resolution of the German Legislature and that it hopes that this group will study proposals concerning the reestablishment of German unity and carry out the preparatory work necessary for final negotiations to be held at a later date.

The Government of the United States welcomes the initiative of the Federal Government. As the latter is aware, the German problem is an important element in the proposals put forward by the Western Powers to the Soviet Government on May 28 for an agenda for a meeting of Heads of Government. The preparatory talks in Moscow for such a meeting, mentioned in the Federal Republic's Aide Memoire, have been in suspense since the end of May because of the Soviet Government's failure to reply to the Western proposal of May 31 for overcoming the procedural difficulty caused by the divergence in the Soviet and Western sets of agenda proposals. Additional efforts to obtain a response, made by the Western Powers on July 1 and August 22, have also so far been to no avail.

[6] *Department of State Bulletin,* v. 39 (October 20, 1958), pp. 613-614.

The Western Powers continue to hold that a summit meeting would be desirable if it would provide opportunity for serious discussions of major problems and if it would be an effective means of reaching agreement on significant subjects. The Government of the United States hopes that the Soviet Government will now reply to the Western proposal so that the preparatory talks which would cover the important question of Germany, may continue. At the same time, in view of the crucial importance of the settlement of the German problem to the relaxation of world tensions, the Government of the United States is also prepared to discuss the German problem in a separate Four Power group to be set up in accordance with the desire of the Federal Government expressed in its Aide Memoire of September 9.

The Government of the United States has constantly sought to bring about the creation of a freely-elected all-German government which would be truly representative of the German people and which could conclude a peace treaty. Until such a Government is created the continued division of Germany maintains a situation in which a segment of the German people is forced to suffer the oppression of a regime imposed on it from without.

For a long time, efforts to resolve German questions have been thwarted by the refusal of the Soviet Government to agree to any plan which would make reunification possible in a way which would insure the freedom of the whole German people. Once a freely-elected all-German Government truly representative of the German people has been created, it would be possible to proceed with such a Government to the conclusion of a peace treaty. The Government of the United States is informing the Soviet Government of its support of the initiative of the Federal Republic and urging the Soviet Government to give it favorable consideration.

2. The Problem of Berlin.

(55) Address by the Secretary of State (Dulles), Berlin, May 8, 1958.[7]

(Excerpts)

* * *

A first lesson of Berlin is taught by your environment. You live here encircled by a surrounding ring of Communist

[7] *Ibid.,* v. 38 (May 26, 1958), pp. 854-857.

rule. Your position in this respect is itself a tragic symbol of disregard for the pledged word. The Potsdam agreements of 1945 made it perfectly clear that the purpose of the military occupation was not to dismember Germany or permanently to divide it. And indeed until recently the Soviet Union admitted that it shared a responsibility to bring about the re-unification of Germany. At the Geneva summit meeting of July 1955 President Eisenhower, together with the Prime Ministers of France and the United Kingdom, obtained formal recognition by the heads of the Soviet Government, including Mr. Khrushchev, that the four powers had "common responsibility for the settlement of the German question and the re-unification of Germany," and they agreed that "the settlement of the German question and the re-unification of Germany by means of free elections" should be carried out. Those engagements, it now seems, are evaded by the Soviet Union.

This illustrates the great difficulty of dealing with the Soviet Union.

*   *   *

You yourselves here in Berlin, you who are a living exhibit of Soviet violations of international agreements, surely understand. And your plight ought to teach the world that it is reckless to make concessions in reliance on Soviet promises merely because those promises are alluring.

Also you here see about you the tragic results of the application of the Communist thesis that individuals are not spiritual beings but merely physical particles to be used to promote the glorification of the Soviet Communist state and the extension of its dominion throughout the world. The steady flow of refugees from East Germany which continues at the high level of about 20,000 per month is an indisputable demonstration of which our societies provides the most in the way of human opportunity, both in terms of economic livelihood and in terms of spiritual and cultural satisfaction. This steady flight from the East to West is the more significant because those who seek the West are in large part young people who throughout most of their mature lives have been subjected to the intense application of Communist doctrine and practice.

*   *   *

A third lesson of Berlin is that there is a vast potential in the spiritual unity and practical co-operation of those everywhere who love freedom. Free Berlin and free Germany would never have achieved their present advances without the faith and works of their own people. But equally indispensable was the support of other free peoples.

Americans are proud of the part they have been privileged to play in this connection. The first clearing of the city and the reestablishment of the basic facilities—light, heat, power, sewers, and transport—were all carried out with German labor and planning and with financial contributions from the United States.

The airlift which surmounted the Soviet blockade was conducted by the Western powers.

Following the end of the blockade there has been a well-planned development in the way of construction, both industrial and cultural, in all of which the United States has been glad to help. Here in Berlin cooperation has become real in stone and mortar, in halls of learning, in places of work and conference, in labor and in recreation.

Perhaps most important of all is the shield of power behind which these tasks of peace are carried forward. I recall here the declaration which the Foreign Ministers of the United Kingdom and France and I made on October 3, 1954.[8] We said: "The security and welfare of Berlin and the maintenance of the position of the Three Powers there are reguarded by the Three Powers as essential elements of the peace of the free world in the present international situation. Accordingly they will maintain armed forces within the territory of Berlin as long as their responsibilities require it. They therefore reaffirm that they will treat any attack against Berlin from any quarter as an attack upon their forces and themselves."

I went over that declaration with President Eisenhower an hour before I left. We read it together. He authorized me to say that it stands and can be reaffirmed as a declaration of the solemn determination of the United States.

I know that the people of Berlin realize how significant for them has been the military deterrent which has provided the shield behind which their works of peace have gone forward. I hope that you and others will realize that the peace and security of all the free world equally depend upon such a shield.

The Soviet Government is attempting by every device of propaganda to compel the abandonment of that shield. It

[8] *Documents on American Foreign Relations, 1954*, p. 117.

claims that those who create that shield are proved by that fact to be evil militarists. It claims that those who draw together to get protection from that shield are "aggressive groupings." It claims that those who seek only defense should prove it by renouncing all but inferior weapons, leaving modern weapons to be a monopoly of those who have a tragically long record of expansion by the use of violence.

It claims that certain of our aerial defense precautions are dangerous and frightening. But when we try to make it possible to revise them on the basis of reciprocal international inspection that will give a large measure of assurance against surprise attack, the Soviets say "nyet." They did so again at the United Nations Security Council last week.

The Soviet Union professes not to want to use nuclear weapons but insists upon continuing at a feverish pace to multiply such weapons in its own arsenals. It calls the free world to rely upon Soviet promises not to use its nuclear weapons in the event of war despite the long record of broken promises to which I have alluded.

This Communist propaganda line is designed to produce a world dominated by the military power of the Sino-Soviet bloc. Freedom would have no adequate defense. There is a duty to look behind words that sound alluring and to see and reject the underlying plot against freedom.

I hope that the lessons of Berlin—the lesson taught by its surroundings, the lesson taught by its faith, and the lesson taught by the cooperative action of the free—will be applied to the larger context of world affairs.

* * *

(56) Soviet Note, November 27, 1958.[9]

(Excerpts)

The Government of the Union of Soviet Socialist Republics addresses the Government of the United States of America as one of the signatory powers of Potsdam Agreement on the urgent question of the status of Berlin.

The problem of Berlin, which is situated in the center of the German Democratic Republic but the western part of which is cut off from the GDR as a result of foreign occupation, deeply affects not only the national interests of the

[9] Department of State Bulletin, v. 40 (January 19, 1958), pp. 181-189.

German people but also the interests of all nations desirous of establishing lasting peace in Europe. Here in the historic capital of Germany two worlds are in direct contact and at every turn there tower the barricades of the "cold war." A situation of constant friction and tension has prevailed for many years in this city, which is divided into two parts. Berlin, which witnessed the greatest triumph of the joint struggle of our countries against Fascist aggression, has now become a dangerous center of contradiction between the Great Powers, allies in the last war. Its role in the relations between the Powers may be compared to a smoldering fuse that has been connected to a powder keg. Incidents arising here, even if they seem to be of local significance, may, in an atmosphere of heated passions, suspicion, and mutual apprehensions, cause a conflagration which will be difficult to extinguish. This is the sad pass to which has come, after the 13 postwar years, the once joint and concerted policy of the Four Powers —the USSR, the USA, Great Britain and France—with regard to Germany.

* * *

When the peoples were celebrating victory over Hitlerite Germany a conference of the heads of government of the Soviet Union, the USA and Great Britain was held in Potsdam in order to work out a joint policy with respect to postwar Germany. The Potsdam Agreement, to which France acceded soon after it was signed, generalized the historical experience of the struggle waged by the peoples to prevent aggression by German militarism.

* * *

The Potsdam Agreement contained important provisions whereby Germany was to be regarded as a single economic entity, even during the occupation period. The agreement also provided for the creation of central German administrative departments. The Council of Foreign Ministers, established by a decision of the Potsdam Conference, was instructed to prepare a peace settlement for Germany.

The implementation of all these measures should have enabled the German people to effect a fundamental reconstruction of their life and to ensure the creation of a united, peaceloving, democratic German state.

* * *

The policy of the USA, Britain, and France with respect to West Germany has led to the violation of those provisions of the Potsdam Agreement designed to ensure the unity of Germany as a peace-loving and democratic state. And when a separate state, the Federal Republic of Germany, was set up independently [of the Soviet Union] in West Germany, which was occupied by the troops of the Three Powers, East Germany, where forces determined not to allow the German people to be plunged once again into disaster assumed the leadership, had no alternative but to create in its turn an independent state.

Thus, two states came into being in Germany. Whereas in West Germany, whose development was directed by the United States, Britain, and France, a government took office the representatives of which do not conceal their hatred for the Soviet Union and often openly advertise the similarity of their aspirations to the plans of the Hitlerite aggressors, in East Germany a government was formed which has irrevocably broken with Germany's aggressive past. State and public affairs in the German Democratic Republic are governed by a constitution fully in keeping with the principles of the Potsdam Agreement and the finest progressive traditions of the German nation. The rule of monopolies and Junkers has been abolished forever in the GDR. Nazism has been eradicated and a number of other social and economic reforms have been carried out, which have destroyed the basis for the revival of militarism and have made the German Democratic Republic an important factor of peace in Europe. The Government of the GDR has solemnly proclaimed that it will fulfill, to the letter, its commitments under the Potsdam Agreement, which, incidentally, the Government of the FRG obstinately evades.

The inclusion of the FRG in the North Atlantic bloc compelled the Soviet Union to adopt countermeasures, in as much as the commitments binding the Soviet Union, the United States, Great Britain, and France were broken by the Three Western Powers, which united with West Germany, and previously with Italy, against the Soviet Union, which had borne the brunt of the struggle against the Fascist aggressors. That closed military alignment created an equal threat to other countries as well. Such a situation compelled the Soviet Union, as well as a number of other European countries that were victims of aggression by German and Italian Fascism, to establish their own defensive organization, concluding for this purpose the Warsaw Treaty, to which the GDR also acceded.

There is only one conclusion to be drawn from the foregoing: The Potsdam Agreement has been grossly violated by the Western Powers.

* * *

Actually, of all the Allied agreements on Germany, only one is being carried out today. It is the agreement on the so-called quadripartite status of Berlin. On the basis of that status, the Three Western Powers are ruling the roost in West Berlin, turning it into a kind of state within a state and using it as a center from which to pursue subversive activity against the GDR, the Soviet Union, and the other parties to the Warsaw Treaty. The United States, Great Britain, and France are freely communicating with West Berlin through lines of communication passing through the territory and the airspace of the German Democratic Republic, which they do not even want to recognize.

The governments of the Three Powers are seeking to keep in force the long-since obsolete part of the wartime agreements that governed the occupation of Germany and entitled them in the past to stay in Berlin.

* * *

If the USA, Great Britain, and France are indeed staying in Berlin by virtue of the right stemming from the aforementioned international agreements and, primarily, from the Potsdam Agreement, this implies their duty to abide by these agreements. Those who have grossly violated these agreements have lost the right to maintain their occupation regime in Berlin or any other part of Germany. Furthermore, is it possible to insist on the occupation regime being maintained in Germany or in any part thereof for more than 13 years after the end of the war? For, any occupation is an event of limited duration, which is expressly stipulated in the Four-Power agreements on Germany.

It is well known that the conventional way to put an end to occupation is for the parties that were at war to conclude a peace treaty offering the defeated country the conditions necessary for the re-establishment of normal life.

The fact that Germany still has no peace treaty is the fault primarily of the governments of the USA, Britain, and France, which have never seemed to be in sympathy with the idea of drafting such a treaty. It is known that the governments of the Three Powers reacted negatively to every approach the Soviet Government has made to them regarding the preparation of a peace treaty with Germany.

At present, the USA, Great Britain, and France are opposed, as follows from their notes of September 30 of this year, to the latest proposals for a peaceful settlement with Germany put forward by the Soviet Union and the GDR, while making no proposals of their own on this question, just as they have made none throughout the postwar period. As a matter of fact, the last note of the US Government is a restatement of the position that proved to be utterly unrealistic, whereby Germany's national unity is to be re-established by the USSR, the USA, Great Britain, and France rather than by the German states that are to unite. It also follows from the US Government's note that it is once again avoiding negotiations with the Soviet Union and the other interested states for the purpose of preparing a peace treaty with Germany. The result is a veritable vicious circle: The US Government is objecting to the drafting of a German peace treaty by referring to the absence of a united German state while at the same time hampering the reunification of Germany by rejecting the only real possibility of solving this problem through agreement between the two German states.

Is it not because the Western Powers would like to prolong indefinitely their privileges in West Germany and the occupation regime in West Berlin that they take this position on the question of drafting a peace treaty? It is becoming increasingly clear that such is the actual state of affairs.

The Soviet Government reaffirms its readiness to participate at any time in negotiations to draft a peace treaty with Germany. However, the absence of a peace treaty can by no means be an excuse now for attempting to maintain the occupation regime anywhere in Germany.

* * *

The Four-Power status of Berlin came into being because Berlin, as the capital of Germany, was designated as the seat of the Control Council established for Germany's administration during the initial period of occupation. This status has been scrupulously observed by the Soviet Union up to the present time, although the Control Council ceased to exist as early as ten years ago and there have been two capitals in

Germany for a long time. As for the USA, Great Britain, and France, they have chosen to abuse in a flagrant manner their occupation rights in Berlin and have exploited the Four-Power status of the city for their own purposes to the detriment of the Soviet Union, the German Democratic Republic, and the other Socialist countries.

*   *   *

An obviously absurd situation has thus arisen, in which the Soviet Union seems to be supporting and maintaining favorable conditions for the Western Powers in their activities against the Soviet Union and its Allies under the Warsaw Treaty.

It is obvious that the Soviet Union, just as the other parties to the Warsaw Treaty, cannot tolerate such a situation any longer. For the occupation regime in West Berlin to continue would be tantamount to recognizing something like a privileged position of the NATO countries, for which there is, of course, no reason whatsoever.

*   *   *

In this connection, the Government of the USSR hereby notifies the United States Government that the Soviet Union regards as null and void the "Protocol" of the Agreement between the Governments of the Union of Soviet Socialist Republics, the United States of America, and the United Kingdom on the zones of occupation in Germany and on the administration of Greater Berlin," of September 12, 1944, and the related supplementary agreements, including the agreement on the control machinery in Germany, concluded between the governments of the USSR, the USA, Great Britain, and France on May 1, 1945, i.e., the agreements that were intended to be in effect during the first years after the capitulation of Germany.

It is easy to see that all the Soviet Government is doing by making this statement is to recognize the actual state of affairs, which consists in the fact that the USA, Great Britain, and France have long since rejected the essentials of the treaties and agreements concluded during the war against Hitler Germany and after its defeat. The Soviet Government is doing no more than drawing conclusions that inevitably ensue for the Soviet Union from this actual state of affairs.

Pursuant to the foregoing and proceeding from the principle of respect for the sovereignty of the German Democratic Republic, the Soviet Government will enter into negotiations with the Government of the GDR at an appropriate time with a view to transferring to the German Democratic Republic the functions temporarily performed by the Soviet authorities by virtue of the above-mentioned Allied agreements and under the agreement between the USSR and the GDR of September 20, 1955.[10] The best way to solve the Berlin problem would undoubtedly be to adopt a decision based on the enforcement of the Potsdam Agreement on Germany. But this is possible only in the event that the three Western Powers return to a policy in German affairs that would be pursued jointly with the USSR and in conformity with the spirit and principles of the Potsdam Agreement. In the present circumstances this would mean the withdrawal of the Federal Republic of Germany from NATO with the simultaneous withdrawal of the German Democratic Republic from the Warsaw Treaty [organization], and an agreement whereby, in accordance with the principles of the Potsdam Agreement, neither of the two German states would have any armed forces except those needed to maintain law and order at home and guard the frontiers.

*   *   *

An independent solution to the Berlin problem must be found in the very near future since the Western Powers refuse to take part in the preparation of a peace treaty with Germany and the Government of the FRG, supported by the same powers, is pursuing a policy hampering the unification of Germany. It is necessary to prevent West Berlin from being used any longer as a springboard for intensive espionage, sabotage, and other subversive activities against Socialist countries, the GDR, and the USSR or, to quote the leaders of the United States Government, to prevent its being used for "indirect aggression" against the countries of the Socialist camp.

*   *   *

Of course, the most correct and natural way to solve the problem would be for the western part of Berlin, now actually detached from the GDR, to be reunited with its eastern part and for Berlin to become a unified city within the state in whose territory it is situated.

[10] Documents on American Foreign Relations, 1955, pp. 108-111.

However, the Soviet Government, taking into account the present unrealistic policy of the USA as well as of Great Britain and France with respect to the German Democratic Republic, cannot but foresee the difficulties the Western powers have in contributing to such a solution of the Berlin problem. At the same time, it is guided by the concern that the process of liquidating the occupation regime may not involve any painful break in the established way of life of the West Berlin population.

One cannot of course fail to take into account the fact that the political and economic development of West Berlin during the period of its occupation by the three Western powers has progressed in a different direction from the development of East Berlin and the GDR, as a result of which the way of life in the two parts of Berlin are at the present time entirely different. The Soviet Government considers that when the foreign occupation is ended the population of West Berlin must be granted the right to have whatever way of life it wishes for itself. If the inhabitants of West Berlin desire to preserve the present way of life, based on private capitalistic ownership that is up to them. The USSR, for its part, would respect any choice of the West Berliners in this matter.

In view of all these considerations, the Soviet Government on its part would consider it possible to solve the West Berlin question at the present time by the conversion of West Berlin into an independent political unit—a free city, without any state, including both existing German states, interfering in its life. Specifically, it might be possible to agree that the territory of the free city be demilitarized and that no armed forces be contained therein. The free city, West Berlin, could have its own government and run its own economic, administrative, and other affairs.

The Four Powers which shared in the administration of Berlin after the war could, as well as both of the German states, undertake to respect the status of West Berlin as a free city, just as was done, for instance, by the Four Powers with respect to the neutral status which was adopted by the Austrian Republic.

For its part, the Soviet Government would have no objection to the United Nations also sharing, in one way or other, in observing the free-city status of West Berlin.

It is obvious that, considering the specific position of West Berlin, which lies within the territory of the GDR and is cut off from the outside world, the question would arise of some kind of arrangement with the German Democratic Republic concerning guarantees of unhindered communications between the free city and the outside world—both to the East and to the West—with the object of free movement of passenger and freight traffic. In its turn West Berlin would undertake not to permit on its territory any hostile subversive activity directed against the GDR or any other state.

The above-mentioned solution of the problem of West Berlin's status would be an important step toward normalizing the situation in Berlin, which, instead of being a hotbed of unrest and tension, could become a center for contacts and cooperation between both parts of Germany in the interest of her peaceful future and the unity of the German nation.

The establishment of a free-city status for West Berlin would firmly ensure the development of West Berlin's economy, due to its contacts on all sides with the states of the East and the West, and would ensure a decent standard of living for the city's population. For its part, the Soviet Union states that it would contribute in every way toward the achievement of these ends, in particular by placing orders for industrial goods and amounts that would fully ensure the stability and prosperity of the free city's economy, and by regular deliveries on a commercial basis of the necessary quantities of raw materials and food stuffs to West Berlin. Thus, by the liquidation of the occupation regime, not only would the more than two million people of West Berlin not be harmed but on the contrary they would have every opportunity to raise their living standard.

In case the Government of the USA and the governments of Great Britain and France express their agreement to consider the question of liquidating the present occupation regime in West Berlin by setting up a free city within its territory, the Soviet government would be willing on behalf of the Four Powers to enter into official contact on this matter with the government of the German Democratic Republic, with which it has already had preliminary consultations prior to the sending of the present note.

Naturally, it would also be realized that the GDR's agreement to set up on its territory such an independent political organism as a free city of West Berlin would be a concession, a definite sacrifice on the part of the GDR for the sake of strengthening peace in Europe, and for the sake of the national interest of the German people as a whole.

The Soviet Government, guided by a desire to normalize the situation in Berlin in the interest of European peace and in the interest of a peaceful and independent development of Germany, has resolved to effect measures on its part designed to liquidate the occupation regime in Berlin. It hopes that the Government of the USA will show a proper understanding of these motives and make a realistic approach to the Berlin question.

At the same time, the Soviet Government is prepared to enter into negotiations with the governments of the United States of America and with those of the other states concerned on granting West Berlin the status of a demilitarized free city. In case this proposal is not acceptable to the government of the USA then there will no longer remain any topic for negotiations between the former occupying powers on the Berlin question.

The Soviet Government seeks to have the necessary change in Berlin's situation take place in a cold atmosphere, without haste and unnecessary friction, with maximum possible consideration for the interests of the parties concerned. Obviously, a certain period of time will be necessary for the powers which occupied Germany after the defeat of Hitler's Wehrmacht to agree on proclaiming West Berlin a free city provided, naturally, that the Western powers display due interest in this proposal.

It should also be taken into consideration that the necessity may arise for talks between the municipal authorities of both parts of Berlin and also between the GDR and the FRG to settle any questions that may arise. In view of this, the Soviet Government proposes to make no changes in the present procedure for military traffic of the USA, Great Britain, and France from West Berlin to the FRG for half a year. It regards such a period as fully sufficient to provide a sound basis for the solution of the questions connected with the change in Berlin's situation and to prevent a possibility of any complications, provided, naturally, that the governments of the Western powers do not deliberately seek such complications. During the above-mentioned period the parties will have an opportunity to prove in practice their desire to ease international tension by settling the Berlin question.

If the above-mentioned period is not utilized to reach an adequate agreement, the Soviet Union will then carry out the planned measures through an agreement with the GDR. It is envisaged that the German Democratic Republic, like any other independent state, must fully deal with questions concerning its space, i.e., exercise its sovereignty on land, on water, and in the air. At the same time, there will terminate all contacts still maintained between representatives of the armed forces and other officials of the Soviet Union in Germany and corresponding representatives of the armed forces and other officials of the USA, Great Britain, and France on questions pertaining to Berlin.

Voices are raised in the capitals of some Western powers that those powers do not recognize the Soviet Union's decision to relinquish its part in the maintenance of the occupation status in Berlin. But how can one place the question on such a level? He who today speaks of nonrecognition of the steps planned by the Soviet Union obviously would like to talk with the latter not in the language of reason and well-founded arguments but in the language of brute force, forgetting that the Soviet people are not affected by threats and intimidation. If behind the words about "nonrecognition" there really lies the intention to resort to force and drag the world into a war over Berlin, the advocates of such a policy should realize that they assume a very grave responsibility for all its consequences before all nations and before history. Those who indulge in sabre-rattling in connection with the situation in Berlin are once again betraying their interests in preserving for aggressive purposes the occupation regime in Berlin.

The Government of the Soviet Union would like to hope that the problem of normalizing the situation in Berlin, which life itself raises before our states as a natural necessity, will in any case be solved in accordance with considerations of statesmanship, the interests of peace between peoples, without the unnecessary nervous strain and intensification of a "cold war."

Methods of blackmail and reckless threats of force will be least of all appropriate in solving such a problem as the Berlin question. Such methods will not help solve a single question, but can only bring the situation to the danger point. But only madmen can go to the length of unleashing another world war over the preservation of privileges of occupiers in West Berlin. If such madmen should really appear, there is no doubt that strait jackets could be found for them. If the statesmen responsible for the policy of the Western powers are guided by feelings of hatred for communism and the socialist countries in their approach to the

Berlin question as well as other international problems, no good will come out of it. Neither the Soviet Union nor any other small socialist state can or will deny its existence precisely as a socialist state. That is why, having united in an unbreakable fraternal alliance, they firmly stand in defense of their rights and their state frontiers, acting according to the motto—one for all and all for one. Any violation of the frontiers of the German Democratic Republic, Poland, or Czechoslovakia, any aggressive action against any member state of the Warsaw Treaty will be regarded by all its participants as an act of aggression against them all and will immediately cause appropriate retaliation.

The Soviet Government believes that it would be sensible to recognize the situation prevailing in the world and to create normal relations for the co-existence of all states, to develop international trade, to build relations between our countries on the basis of the well-known principles of mutual respect for one another's sovereignty and territorial integrity, nonaggression, non-interference in one another's internal affairs, equality and mutual benefit.

The Soviet Union and its people and government are sincerely striving for the restoration of good relations with the United States of America, relations based on trust, which are quite feasible as shown by the experience in the joint struggle against the Hitlerite aggressors, and which in peacetime would hold out to our countries nothing but the advantages of mutually enriched spiritual and material cooperation between our peoples, and to all other people the blessings of a tranquil life under conditions of an enduring peace.

Moscow, *November 27, 1958*

(57) *United States Statement, November 27, 1958.*[11]

The Soviet Government has today handed the United States Ambassador in Moscow a communication relating to Berlin. Apparently similar notes have been received by the Ambassadors of France, the United Kingdom, and the Federal Republic of Germany. The communication is a very long one and will of course receive careful study.

The Soviets seem to be proposing that, while they keep their grip on East Berlin, the three Western allies abandon their rights in West Berlin and retire in favor of what is

11 *Department of State Bulletin*, v. 39 (December 15, 1958), p. 948.

called a "free city." Their "free city" proposal is limited to West Berlin. The Soviet Government indicates that, unless the three Western allies accept this Soviet proposal within 6 months, the Soviet Union will consider itself free of its obligations to them in relation to Berlin.

It is clear that a number of fundamental considerations are raised which will have to be kept in mind while we study the Soviet note.

One of these is that the United States, along with Britain and France, is solemnly committed to the security of the Western sectors of Berlin. Two and a quarter million West Berliners in reliance thereon have convincingly and courageously demonstrated the good fruits of freedom.

Another consideration is that the United States will not acquiesce in a unilateral repudiation by the Soviet Union of its obligations and responsibilities formally agreed upon with Britain, France, and the United States in relation to Berlin. Neither will it enter into any agreement with the Soviet Union which, whatever the form, would have the end result of abandoning the people of West Berlin to hostile domination.

The Western allies have for years sought to negotiate with the Soviets for the freedom of all of Germany, of which Berlin is part, on the basis of free elections by the German people themselves. Indeed, the three Western powers are still awaiting a reply to their latest proposals presented on September 30, 1958, to the Soviet Government.

The United States Government will consult with the British and French Governments as well as with the Federal Republic of Germany and NATO in regard to the new Soviet note.

(58) *Four Power Western Communiqué, December 14, 1958.*[12]

The Foreign Ministers of France, the Federal Republic of Germany, the United Kingdom and the United States met on December 14, 1958 in Paris to discuss developments in the Berlin situation during the past month, including notes addressed to their several governments on November 27 by the Soviet Union. The four Foreign Ministers had the benefit of an oral statement on the situation in Berlin by Herr Brandt, Governing Mayor of that city.

[12] *Ibid.* (December 29, 1958), pp. 1041-1042.

The Foreign Ministers of France, the United Kingdom and the United States once more reaffirmed the determination of their governments to maintain their position and their rights with respect to Berlin including the right of free access.

They found unacceptable a unilateral repudiation by the Soviet Government of its obligations to the Governments of France, the United Kingdom and the United States in relation to their presence in Berlin and the freedom of access to that city or the substitution of the German authorities of the Soviet Zone for the Soviet Government insofar as those rights are concerned.

After further discussion of the Soviet notes of November 27, 1958 the four Ministers found themselves in agreement on the basic issues to be dealt with in the replies to those notes. They will consult with their allies in the NATO Council, following which the four governments will formulate their replies.

(59) *Declaration of the North Atlantic Council, December 16, 1958.*[13]

1. The North Atlantic Council examined the question of Berlin.

2. The Council declares that no state has the right to withdraw unilaterally from its international engagements. It considers that the denunciation by the Soviet Union of the interallied agreements on Berlin can in no way deprive the other parties of their rights or relieve the Soviet Union of its obligations. Such methods destroy the mutual confidence between nations which is one of the foundations of peace.

3. The Council fully associates itself with the views expressed on the subject by the Governments of the United States, the United Kingdom, France and the Federal Republic of Germany in their statement of 14th December.

4. The demands expressed by the Soviet Government have created a serious situation which must be faced with determination.

5. The Council recalls the responsibilities which each member state has assumed in regard to the security and welfare of Berlin and the maintenance of the position of the three powers in that city. The member states of NATO could

not approve a solution of the Berlin question which jeopardized the right of the three Western powers to remain in
Berlin as long as their responsibilities require it, and did
not assure freedom of communication between that city and
the free world. The Soviet Union would be responsible for
any action which had the effect of hampering this free communication or endangering this freedom. The two million
inhabitants of West Berlin have just reaffirmed in a free vote
their overwhelming approval and support for that position.

6. The Council considers that the Berlin question can only
be settled in the framework of an agreement with the U.S.S.R.
on Germany as a whole. It recalls that the Western powers
have repeatedly declared themselves ready to examine this
problem, as well as those of European security and disarmament. They are still ready to discuss all these problems.

(60) *United States Note, December 31, 1958.*[14]

The Government of the United States acknowledges the
note which was addressed to it by the Government of the
U.S.S.R. under date of November 27.

The note contains a long elaboration on the events which
preceded and followed the last war. It attempts to portray the
Western Powers—France, the United Kingdom and the
United States—as supporters of Hitlerism as against the
Soviet Union. This portrayal is in sharp contrast with the
actual facts. In this connection we refer to the contemporane-
ous statement made by the Soviet Minister of Foreign Affairs
to the Supreme Soviet of the U.S.S.R. on October 31, 1939.
In that statement he refers, among other things, to the "conclusion of the Soviet-German non-aggression pact of August
23" and points out "we now had a rapprochement and the
establishment of friendly relations between the U.S.S.R. and
Germany." The statement goes on to assail the British and
French Governments for their opposition to Hitlerism in
the following language: "The ruling circles of Britain and
France have been lately attempting to depict themselves as
champions of the democratic rights of nations against Hitlerism, and the British Government has announced that its aim
in the war with Germany is nothing more nor less than the
'destruction of Hitlerism' . . . everybody will understand
that an ideology cannot be destroyed by force, that it cannot be eliminated by war. It is therefore not only senseless,

[14] *Ibid.* (January 19, 1959), pp. 79-80.

but criminal to wage such a war—a war for the 'destruction of Hitlerism' camouflaged as a fight for 'democracy.' "

The situation of Berlin of which the Soviet Government complains and which it considers abnormal is a result of the very nature of the German problem such as it has existed since 1945. When the empire of Hitler collapsed the Western Allies were in military possession of more than one-third of what subsequently was occupied by the Soviet authorities.

The Soviet Union was in possession of Berlin. On the basis of the agreements of September 12, 1944 and May 1, 1945, the Western Allies withdrew, thereby permitting a Soviet occupation of large parts of Mecklenburg, Saxony, Thuringia and Anhalt, and concurrently, the three Western Powers occupied the western sectors in Berlin, then an area of rubble.

The Soviet Union has directly and through its puppet regime—the so-called German Democratic Republic—consolidated its hold over the large areas which the Western Allies relinquished to it. It now demands that the Western Allies should relinquish the positions in Berlin which in effect were the *quid pro quo*.

The three Western Powers are there as occupying powers and they are not prepared to relinquish the rights which they acquired through victory just as they assume the Soviet Union is not willing now to restore to the occupancy of the Western Powers the position which they had won in Mecklenburg, Saxony, Thuringia and Anhalt and which, under the agreements of 1944 and 1945, they turned over for occupation by the Soviet Union.

The agreements made by the Four Powers cannot be considered obsolete because the Soviet Union has already obtained the full advantage therefrom and now wishes to deprive the other parties of their compensating advantages. These agreements are binding upon all of the signatories so long as they have not been replaced by others following free negotiations.

Insofar as the Potsdam agreement is concerned, the status of Berlin does not depend upon that agreement. Moreover, it is the Soviet Union that bears responsibility for the fact that the Potsdam agreement could not be implemented.

The Soviet memorandum purports formally to repudiate the agreements of September 12, 1944 and May 1, 1945. This repudiation in fact involves other and more recent engagements. We refer in this connection to the Four Power agreement of June 20, 1949 whereby, among other things, the Soviet Union assumed "an obligation" to assure the normal functioning of transport and communication between Berlin and the Western Zones of Germany.[15] This "obligation" the Soviet Union now purports to shed. The United States also refers to the "summit" agreement of July 23, 1955[16] whereby the Four Powers recognized "their common responsibility for the settlement of the German question," a phrase which necessarily includes the problem of Berlin. Apparently the Soviet Union now attempts to free itself from these agreed responsibilities and obligations.

The United States Government cannot prevent the Soviet Government from announcing the termination of its own authority in the quadripartite regime in the sector which it occupies in the city of Berlin. On the other hand, the Government of the United States will not and does not, in any way, accept a unilateral denunciation of the accords of 1944 and 1945; nor is it prepared to relieve the Soviet Union from the obligations which it assumed in June, 1949. Such action on the part of the Soviet Government would have no legal basis, since the agreements can only be terminated by mutual consent. The Government of the United States will continue to hold the Soviet Government directly responsible for the discharge of its obligations undertaken with respect to Berlin under existing agreements. As the Soviet Government knows, the French, British and United States Governments have the right to maintain garrisons in their sectors of Berlin and to have free access thereto. Certain administrative procedures have been agreed with the Soviet authorities accordingly and are in operation at the present time. The Government of the United States will not accept a unilateral repudiation on the part of the Soviet Government of its obligations in respect of that freedom of access. Nor will it accept the substitution of the regime which the Soviet Government refers to as the German Democratic Republic for the Soviet Government in this respect.

In the view of the Government of the United States, there can be no "threat" to the Soviet Government or the regime which the Soviet Government refers to as the German Democratic Republic from the presence of the French, British and United States garrisons in Berlin. Nor can there be any military threat from Berlin to the Soviet Government and

---

[15] *Documents on American Foreign Relations, 1949*, p. 104.
[16] *Ibid., 1955*, pp. 225-227.

this regime. The forces of the three Western Powers in Berlin number about ten thousand men. The Soviet Government, on the other hand, is said to maintain some three hundred and fifty thousand troops in Eastern Germany, while the regime which the Soviet Government refers to as the German Democratic Republic is understood also to maintain over two hundred thousand men under arms. In these circumstances, the fear that the Western troops in Berlin may "inflict harm" appears to be wholly unfounded. If Berlin has become a focus of international tension, it is because the Soviet Government has deliberately threatened to disturb the existing arrangements at present in force there, arrangements to which the Soviet Government is itself a party. The inhabitants of West Berlin have recently reaffirmed in a free vote their overwhelming approval and support for the existing status of that city. The continued protection of the freedom of more than two million people of West Berlin is a right and responsibility solemnly accepted by the Three Western Powers. Thus the United States cannot consider any proposal which would have the effect of jeopardizing the freedom and security of these people. The rights of the Three Powers to remain in Berlin with unhindered communications by surface and air between that city and the Federal Republic of Germany are under existing conditions essential to the discharge of that right and responsibility. Hence the proposal for a so-called "free city" for West Berlin, as put forward by the Soviet Union, is unacceptable.

As is stated in the Soviet Government's note of November 27, it is certainly not normal that thirteen years after the end of the war there should still remain in a part of German territory a system of occupancy instituted in 1945. The United States deplores this fact and the fact that Germany has not yet been reunified so that Berlin might resume its rightful position as capital of a united Germany. If the treaty of peace, which alone can bring an end to this situation, has not been concluded with a reunited Germany, the responsibility in no way rests with the Three Western Powers which have not spared any effort to bring the Four Powers out of the impasse where they have so long found themselves. Pending the conclusion of a peace treaty, the present situation continues.

In reality, the form of government in Berlin, the validity of which the Soviet Government attempts to contest today, is only one aspect, and not the essential one, of the German problem in its entirety. This problem, which has often been defined, involves the well-known questions of reunification, European security, as well as a peace treaty. It has in the past been discussed without success in the course of numerous international meetings with the Soviets. The Government of the United States has always been and continues today to be ready to discuss it. The United States made clear this readiness in its note to the Soviet Union of September 30, 1958, in which it was stated:

"The Government of the United States is ready at any time to enter into discussions with the Soviet Government on the basis of these proposals [i.e., the Western proposals for free all-German elections and free decisions for an all-German Government], or of any other proposals genuinely designed to insure the reunification of Germany in freedom, in any appropriate forum. It regards the solution of the German problem as essential if a lasting settlement in Europe is to be achieved." The Soviet Union has not yet seen fit to reply to this note.

Public repudiation of solemn engagements, formally entered into and repeatedly reaffirmed, coupled with an ultimatum threatening unilateral action to implement that repudiation unless it be acquiesced in within six months, would afford no reasonable basis for negotiation between sovereign states. The Government of the United States could not embark on discussions with the Soviet Union upon these questions under menace or ultimatum; indeed, if that were intended, the United States would be obliged immediately to raise a protest in the strongest terms. Hence, it is assumed that this is not the purpose of the Soviet note of November 27 and that the Soviet Government, like itself, is ready to enter into discussions in an atmosphere devoid of coercion or threats.

On this basis, the United States Government would be interested to learn whether the Soviet Government is ready to enter into discussions between the Four Powers concerned. In that event, it would be the object of the Government of the United States to discuss the question of Berlin in the wider framework of negotiations for a solution of the German problem as well as that of European security. The United States Government would welcome the views of the Soviet Government at an early date.

G. Cultural, Technical and Educational Exchange.

(61) *Communiqué and Text of an Agreement between the United States and the USSR on Exchanges in the Cultural, Technical and Educational Fields, January 27, 1958.*[1]

The United States and the Union of Soviet Socialist Republics announced today that an agreement on exchanges had been reached. The agreement was signed by Ambassador William S. B. Lacy, Special Assistant to the Secretary of State, for the United States and by Georgi N. Zaroubin, Ambassador of the Union of Soviet Socialist Republics, for the Soviet Union. The agreement undertakes to provide for exchanges in such media as radio and television broadcasts and showing of films, as well as to arrange over the next two years for wider exchange in the cultural, technical, and educational field. In the academic area, exchanges of graduate students, instructors and professors of the universities of both countries will take place for the first time. Exchange of scientists for purposes of lecturing and research are to be worked out by the respective Academies of Science. In medicine and agriculture there are multiple exchange visits covering a two-year period. Other exchanges are to take place between athletic teams, while outstanding entertainment groups and artists are to visit each other's country.

Some of the exchanges are to begin in the near future. With respect to others—such as direct air flights between New York and Moscow—there was agreement "in principal" and further discussions will be held.

This Agreement is regarded as a significant first step in the improvement of mutual understanding between the peoples of the United States and the Union of Soviet Socialist Republics, and it is sincerely hoped that it will be carried out in such a way as to contribute substantially to the betterment of relations between the two countries, thereby also contributing to a lessening of international tensions.

The text of the Agreement follows:

AGREEMENT BETWEEN THE UNITED STATES OF AMERICA AND THE UNION OF SOVIET SOCIALIST REPUBLICS ON EXCHANGES IN THE CULTURAL, TECHNICAL AND EDUCATIONAL FIELDS

By agreement between the Governments of the United States of America and the Union of Soviet Socialist Republics,

[1] *Department of State Bulletin*, v. 38 (February 17, 1958), pp. 243-247.

delegations headed on the United States side by Ambassador William S. B. Lacy and on the Soviet side by Ambassador G. N. Zaroubin conducted negotiations in Washington from October 28, 1957 to January 27, 1958, with regard to cultural, technical, and educational exchanges between the United States of America and the Union of Soviet Socialist Republics. As a result of these negotiations, which have been carried on in a spirit of mutual understanding, the United States and the Soviet Union have agreed to provide for the specific exchanges which are set forth in the following Sections during 1958 and 1959 in the belief that these exchanges will contribute significantly to the betterment of relations between the two countries, thereby contributing to a lessening of international tensions.

SECTION I

General

(1) The visits and exchanges enumerated in the following Sections are not intended to be exclusive of others which may be arranged by the two countries or undertaken by their citizens.

(2) The exchanges provided for in the following Sections shall be subject to the Constitution and applicable laws and regulations in force in the respective countries. It is understood that both parties will use their best efforts to have these exchanges effected in accordance with the following Sections.

SECTION II

Exchanges of Radio and Television Broadcasts

(1) Both parties will provide for an exchange of radio and television broadcasts on the subjects of science, technology, industry, agriculture, education, public health, and sports.

(2) Both parties will provide for regular exchanges of radio and television programs, which will include the exchange of transcribed classical, folk and contemporary musical productions on magnetic tape and records; the exchange of filmed musical, literary, theatrical and similar television productions.

(3) For the purpose of strengthening mutual understanding and developing friendly relations between the United States and the Union of Soviet Socialist Republics, both

parties agree to organize from time to time an exchange of broadcasts devoted to discussion of such international political problems as may be agreed upon between the two parties. The details of the exchanges shall be agreed upon at the working level.

(4) Both parties will provide for an exchange of samples of equipment for sound-recording and telecasting and their technical specifications.

(5) Both parties will provide for an exchange of delegations of specialists in 1958 to study the production of radio and television programs, the techniques of sound recording, the equipment of radio and television studios, and the manufacture of films, recording tape, tape recorders, and records.

SECTION III

Exchange of Groups of Specialists in Industry, Agriculture and Medicine

(1) Both parties agree to provide for an exchange of delegations in 1958 in the fields of iron and steel, mining (iron ore), and plastics industry. Both parties agree as to the desirability of arranging additional exchanges in industry during 1958-1959.

(2) Both sides will provide for the exchange of delegations of specialists in agriculture, the American side receiving during 1958-1959 nine delegations of Soviet specialists in the following fields: mechanization of agriculture, animal husbandry, veterinary science, mixed feeds, cotton growing, agricultural construction and electrification, horticulture (including vegetable growing), hydro-engineering (irrigation) and reclamation, and forestry, lumbering and millwork. In 1958-1959 the Soviet side will receive nine American delegations of specialists in the following fields: the study of agricultural crops, veterinary science, soil use and the use of water resources (irrigation and drainage), mechanization of agriculture, agricultural economics (excluding distribution of agricultural products), cotton growing and plant physiology, sheep raising, biological control of agricultural pests, and forestry, lumbering and millwork.

Details of the exchanges will be agreed upon by representatives of the Department of State of the United States of America and of the Embassy of the Union of Soviet Socialist Republics in the United States of America.

(3) Both parties agree to provide for the exchange in 1958-

1959 of eight medical delegations of five to six specialists for periods of two to six weeks to become familiar with research and achievement in the following fields: new antibiotics, microbiology, physiology and pharmacology of the nervous system, radiobiology, biochemistry, metabolic diseases, endocrinology, community and industrial hygiene.

Both parties recognize the desirability of providing for an exchange of delegations in the field of the manufacture of medical apparatus and instruments.

(4) Both parties agree in principle to provide for an exchange in 1958 of delegations of specialists in fisheries.

SECTION IV

Visits by Representatives of Cultural, Civic, Youth and Student Groups

(1) For the purpose of establishing contacts, exchanging experiences, and becoming more familiar with the public and cultural life of both countries, the Soviet side will arrange to invite to the Union of Soviet Socialist Republics during 1958 groups of American writers (5-6 persons), composers (5-6 persons), painters and sculptors (3-4 persons). In 1958, the United States side reciprocally will arrange to invite similar Soviet groups to visit the United States.

(2) Both parties will provide for the exchange in 1958-1959 of delegations of representatives of youth and delegations of women in various professions.

(3) Both parties agree to provide for an exchange of delegations of student and youth newspaper editors in 1958-1959.

(4) Both parties will promote the development and strengthening of friendly contacts between Soviet and American cities.

SECTION V

Exchange of Visits of Delegations of Members of the United States Congress and Deputies of the Supreme Soviet of the U.S.S.R.

The proposal to exchange delegations of members of the United States Congress and deputies of the Supreme Soviet of the Union of Soviet Socialist Republics will be subject to further discussion between the two parties.

SECTION VI

Joint Conferences of U.S.A. and U.S.S.R. Organizations

The desirability of agreement to hold joint conferences of interparliamentary groups in 1958 and 1959 or meetings of representatives of the United States and Soviet associations for the United Nations and UNESCO is a matter for the organizations concerned.

SECTION VII

Cooperation in the Field of Cinematography

Recognizing the importance of developing mutual cooperation between the United States of America and the Union of Soviet Socialist Republics in the field of motion pictures, both parties have agreed to the following:

(1) To make provisions for the sale and purchase of motion pictures by the film industries of both countries on the principles of equality and on mutually acceptable financial terms. Toward this end, not later than January 1958, Sovexportfilm will enter into contact with representatives of the motion picture industry in the United States, to be approved by the Department of State of the United States, for the purpose of the sale and purchase of films in 1958.

(2) To arrange for the holding simultaneously in the United States of America and the Union of Soviet Socialist Republics of film premieres (American films in the Union of Soviet Socialist Republics and Soviet films in the United States of America, respectively), inviting to these premieres leading personalities of the film industries of both countries.

(3) To carry out in 1958 an exchange of 12 to 15 documentary films in accordance with a list to be mutually agreed upon by the two parties. On the Soviet side the exchange of documentary films will be carried out by Sovexportfilm, such films to be recorded in the English language, and for the United States of America by the United States Information Agency, such films to be recorded in the Russian language.

(4) In the second half of 1958 to provide for carrying out for a period of up to one month an interchange of delegations of leading motion picture personalities, scenario writers and technical personnel to be approved by each side for the purpose of becoming acquainted with experiences in the production of motion pictures in the respective countries.

(5) To recognize the desirability and usefulness of organizing joint production of artistic, popular-science and documentary films and of the conducting, not later than May 1958, of concrete negotiations between Soviet film organizations and United States film companies on this subject, such United States companies to be approved by the Department of State of the United States. The subject matter of the films will be mutually agreed upon by the two parties.

(6) To recommend to the appropriate United States organizations the making of arrangements for the holding of a Soviet Film Week in the United States in 1958 and to recommend to the appropriate motion picture organizations of the Soviet Union the making of arrangements for the holding of a United States Film Week in the Soviet Union in 1958, and to envision the participation in these Film Weeks of delegations from each side numbering 3 or 4 motion picture personalities for a period of two weeks.

(7) To recognize the desirability of producing feature films, documentary films and concert films for television or non-theatrical showing in the United States by Soviet motion picture organizations and the producing of similar films by appropriate United States organizations for television or non-theatrical showing in the Soviet Union. Additional concrete negotiations on this question will be carried on between the Department of State of the United States and the Soviet Embassy in the United States of America.

(8) To designate a standing committee of four members, two from the United States and two from the Soviet Union, the powers of which will be for a period of one year and which will meet once in Moscow and once in Washington during that year to examine problems which may arise in connection with the implementation of the provisions of this Section. The authority of this committee may be extended by mutual agreement.

SECTION VIII

Exchange of Theatrical, Choral and Choreographic Groups, Symphony Orchestras and Artistic Performers

(1) The Ministry of Culture of the Union of Soviet Socialist Republics will invite the Philadelphia Symphony Orchestra to visit the Soviet Union in May or June 1958 and will send the ballet troupe of the Bolshoi Theatre of the Soviet

Union, numbering 110-120 persons, to the United States in 1959 for a period of one month.

(2) The Ministry of Culture of the Union of Soviet Socialist Republics, on the basis of an existing agreement with Hurok Attractions, Inc., and the Academy of the National Theatre and Drama, will send two Soviet performers— E. Gilels, pianist, and L. Kogan, violinist—to the United States in January-April, 1958, and will invite two American soloists—B. Thebom, vocalist, and L. Warren, vocalist—to visit the Soviet Union.

(3) The Ministry of Culture of the Union of Soviet Socialist Republics will send Soviet vocalists I. Petrov, P. Lisitsian, and Z. Dolukhanova, as well as I. Bezrodni, violinist, and V. Ashkenazi, pianist, to the United States and will invite R. Peters, vocalist, L. Stokowski, conductor, and others to visit the Soviet Union.

(4) The Ministry of Culture of the Union of Soviet Socialist Republics, in accordance with an agreement with Hurok Attractions, Inc., will send the State Folk Dance Ensemble of the Union of Soviet Socialist Republics to the United States in April-May, 1958 and will consider inviting a leading American theatrical or choreographic group to the Soviet Union in 1959.

(5) The Soviet side will send the Red Banner Song and Dance Ensemble of the Soviet Army or the Choreographic Ensemble "Beriozka" to the United States in the fourth quarter of 1958 and invite one of the leading American choreographic groups to visit the Soviet Union.

SECTION IX

Visits by Scientists

(1) The Academy of Sciences of the Union of Soviet Socialist Republics and the National Academy of Sciences of the United States will, on a reciprocal basis, provide for the exchange of groups or individual scientists and specialists for delivering lectures and holding seminars on various problems of science and technology.

(2) The Academy of Sciences of the Union of Soviet Socialist Republics and the National Academy of Sciences of the United States will, on a reciprocal basis, provide for the exchange of scientific personnel and specialists for the purpose of conducting joint studies and for specialization for a period of up to one year.

(3) The details of exchanges mentioned in paragraphs (1) and (2) will be agreed upon directly between the presidents of the Academy of Sciences of the Union of Soviet Socialist Republics and the National Academy of Sciences of the United States in Moscow in the early part of 1958.

(4) The Ministry of Health of the Union of Soviet Socialist Republic will send in 1958 to the United States a group of Soviet medical scientists (3-4 persons) for a period of 2 to 3 weeks to deliver lectures and exchange experiences and will receive a similar group of United States medical scientists to deliver lectures and exchange experiences at the Institutes of the Academy of Medical Sciences of the Union of Soviet Socialist Republics and at medical institutes in Moscow, Leningrad, and Klev.

(5) In 1958 the Ministry of Agriculture of the Union of Soviet Socialist Republics will, on a reciprocal basis, invite United States scientists to visit the Union of Soviet Socialist Republics for the purpose of delivering lectures and exchanging experiences in the fields of biology, selection, pedigreed stockbreeding, agrotechny, mechanization of agriculture, stockbreeding, and others.

SECTION X

Exchange of University Delegations

(1) Both parties will provide for the exchange in 1958 of four delegations of university professors and instructors for a period of 2 to 3 weeks in the fields of natural sciences, engineering education, and liberal arts, and the study of the systems of higher education in the United States and the Soviet Union, each delegation to consist of from five to eight persons.

(2) Both parties will provide for an exchange of delegations of professors and instructors between Moscow and Columbia Universities and Leningrad and Harvard Universities. Further exchanges of delegations of professors and instructors of other universities of the United States of America and the Union of Soviet Socialist Republics, shall be decided upon as appropriate by both parties.

(3) Both parties will provide for an exchange of students between Moscow and Leningrad Universities, on the one hand, and United States universities, on the other, amounting to 20 persons on each side for the period of the academic year 1958-1959. For the academic year 1959-1960, the number

will be 30. The composition of the student groups shall be determined by each side.

(4) Both parties will provide for an exchange of delegations of educators (8-10 persons) for a period of 30 days in the latter part of 1958.

SECTION XI

Exchange of Individual Athletes and Athletic Teams

Both parties will provide for an exchange of individual athletes and athletic teams and in 1958-1959 will provide for the holding of the following contests in the United States and in the Union of Soviet Socialist Republics:

(1) Basketball games between representative men's and women's teams to be held in the Soviet Union in April 1958.

(2) Basketball games between representative men's and women's teams to be held in the United States in 1959.

(3) Wrestling matches between representative teams to be held in the United States in February 1958.

(4) Wrestling matches between representative teams to be held in the Soviet Union in 1959.

(5) Track and field contests between representative teams to be held in the Soviet Union in July 1958.

(6) Track and field contests between representative teams to be held in the United States in 1959.

(7) Weight lifting contests between representative teams to be held in the United States in May 1958.

(8) Canadian hockey games between representative teams to be held in the Soviet Union in March-April 1958.

(9) Chess tournaments between representative teams to be held in the United States in 1958.

The details of these exchanges of athletes and athletic teams as well as financial arrangements for these exchanges shall be discussed between appropriate American and Soviet sports organizations.

SECTION XII

Development of Tourism

Both parties will promote the development of tourism.

SECTION XIII

Exchange of Exhibits and Publications

(1) Both sides agree in principle on the usefulness of exhibits as an effective means of developing mutual understanding between the peoples of the United States and the Soviet Union. Toward this end both sides will provide for an exchange of exhibits on the peaceful uses of atomic energy in 1958.

(2) Both parties will promote the further development of exchange of publications and various works in the field of science and technology between scientific institutions and societies and between individual scientists and specialists.

(3) Provisions will be made for the Central Scientific Medical Library of the Ministry of Health of the Union of Soviet Socialist Republics and corresponding medical libraries in the United States to exchange medical journals.

(4) Both parties will promote the exchange of curricula, textbooks, and scientific pedagogical literature through the appropriate agencies of higher and secondary education and directly between educational institutions.

(5) The Ministry of Health of the Union of Soviet Socialist Republics will arrange to make available in 1958 from 8 to 10 medical films for presentation in the United States. On a reciprocal basis, the United States will arrange to make available the same number of American medical films for presentation in the Soviet Union.

(6) The Ministry of Agriculture of the Union of Soviet Socialist Republics and the Department of Agriculture of the United States are prepared to exchange in 1958 films on such agricultural subjects as stockbreeding, mechanization of agriculture, construction and utilization of irrigation and drainage systems, protection of plants from pests and blights, and fight against erosion.

(7) The representatives of the American and Soviet sides, having exchanged their views on the problems of distributing the magazines *Amerika* in the Soviet Union and *USSR* in the United States, have agreed on the desirability and necessity of promoting the distribution of these magazines on the basis of reciprocity. Examination of measures taken by both parties to achieve this end will continue at the ambassadorial level.

SECTION XIV

Establishment of Direct Air Flights

Both parties agree in principle to establish on the basis of reciprocity direct air flights between the United States and the Soviet Union. Negotiations on terms and conditions satisfactory to both parties will be conducted by appropriate representatives of each Government at a mutually convenient date to be determined later.

SECTION XV

Entry into Force

The present agreement shall enter into force on the date it is signed.

IN WITNESS WHEREOF, the undersigned, duly authorized, have signed the present agreement and have affixed their seals thereto.

DONE, in duplicate, in the English and Russian languages, both equally authentic, at Washington this twenty-seventh day of January, one thousand nine hundred fifty-eight.

FOR THE UNITED STATES OF AMERICA:

WILLIAM S. B. LACY

FOR THE UNION OF SOVIET SOCIALIST REPUBLICS:

ZAROUBIN

ADDITIONAL U.S. STATEMENT

With reference to the agreement on exchanges entered into with the Union of Soviet Socialist Republics today, it was noted that, on the United States side, the exchanges will, for the most part, be carried out by private persons and organizations. In the United States, private persons cannot, of course, be directed to participate in such activities. During the course of the negotiations the various persons, firms, and corporations concerned with the proposed exchanges were consulted, and they have expressed their willingness and desire to participate. The agreement is entered into subject to the applicable United States laws and regulations, including the availability of funds.

LETTERS OF UNDERSTANDING

Identical letters relating to paragraph 3 of section II of the U.S.—U.S.S.R. agreement on exchanges were exchanged as follows.

JANUARY 27, 1958

DEAR MR. AMBASSADOR: With respect to paragraph 3 of Section II of the Agreement signed this date, it is the understanding of both parties to the Agreement that the texts of such broadcasts shall be exchanged in advance and discussed at the working level. In the event that either party shall consider that the effect of any such broadcast will not contribute to a betterment of relations between the United States of America and the Union of Soviet Socialist Republics, the exchange of such broadcast shall not take place.

Sincerely yours,

WILLIAM S. B. LACY
(GEORGI N. ZAROUBIN)

His Excellency
GEORGI N. ZAROUBIN,
   Ambassador of the Union of Soviet Socialist Republics.

(His Excellency
WILLIAM S. B. LACY,
   Department of State.)

H. Trade Relations between the United States and the Soviet Union.

(62) *Letter from the Chairman of the Council of Ministers of the USSR (Khrushchev), June 2, 1958.*[1]

DEAR MR. PRESIDENT: I am addressing this letter to you in order to take up once again the question concerning which there has recently been a certain exchange of opinions between the Governments of our two countries and to which the Soviet Government attaches very great importance, namely, the question of the ways and means to improve and develop the relations between the Soviet Union and the United States of America. I must say that, in my opinion, there are great and so far unused opportunities to solve this problem.

[1] *Ibid.,* v. 39 (August 4, 1958), pp. 200-202.

The Soviet-American agreement on exchanges in cultural, technical, and educational fields that was signed recently was, in our opinion, a good practical step toward a rapprochement between our two countries. It is comforting to see that the conclusion of this agreement has met with the approval of large elements of the public both in the USSR and in the USA, as well as in other countries. I believe that it has met with such a reception primarily because peoples saw in this agreement concrete proof of the fact that Soviet-American relations can really improve, which makes it possible to hope also for a general improvement in the present unstable and troubled international situation.

If we want to justify these hopes of many millions of people, we should exert joint efforts both in finding a peaceful and concerted solution to urgent, common international problems, which, we are convinced, can be furthered by a meeting at the highest level of top government officials as proposed by the Soviet Union, and in further developing direct relations between the Soviet Union and the United States of America.

In considering possible further steps in this direction, the Soviet Government has come to the conclusion that the existing conditions permit taking important and far-reaching steps to develop trade relations between the USSR and the United States which will be of great mutual benefit to both our countries and will further the cause of world peace.

There is no need to dwell on the usefulness of developing economic and, above all, trade relations between countries. The importance of such relations is obvious and it has been repeatedly emphasized by government officials both of the USSR and the USA. We remember, for instance, the words of the late Secretary of State of the United States, Cordell Hull, to the effect that "commerce and association may be the antidote for war." You, I believe, will agree that now, in particular, as perhaps never before, the world is in need of such an antidote.

Extensive trade between the Soviet Union and the United States of America is nothing new for our countries. After all, there have been periods when economic relations expanded very successfully to the advantage of both sides. However, during the past ten years trade between the Soviet Union and the United States of America not only failed to attain further development, but, on the contrary, decreased to a negligible level for reasons beyond the control of the USSR. The United

States of America is now the only great power that has no
trade agreement with the Soviet Union. Individual trade
transactions concluded between American firms and Soviet
organizations for foreign trade are very insignificant and in
no way correspond to the economic potentials of the two
countries.

It appears to us that the time has come for the Governments of the USSR and the USA to take concerted action for
improving and widely developing Soviet-American trade relations and that such action on the part of our Governments
would satisfy the mutual interest of both States and would
be favorably received by the peoples of our countries.

Motivated by the sincere desire to improve relations between our countries, the Government of the Soviet Union
proposes to the Government of the United States of America
that they jointly take resolute steps to expand trade between
them.

The Soviet Union and the United States of America, as the
two strongest powers from the economic standpoint, can engage in trade with each other on a large scale. During the
last decade, the United States has considerably expanded its
production facilities and it is natural for American business
circles to be interested in a substantial expansion of foreign
trade. At the same time, the Soviet Union, at its present high
level of economic development, now has immeasurably
greater possibilities and resources for trade with other countries, including the United States, than ever before.

I should like, Mr. President, to emphasize particularly that
the Soviet Government, in advancing its proposal for the
expansion of Soviet-American trade, by no means has in mind
armaments or plant equipment for military production.

The Soviet Union is now engaged in carrying out a new
and extensive program for a further increase in the production of consumer goods. Along with an increase in the output
of products made of natural raw materials, this program
provides for considerable expansion of the production of
synthetic materials—fibers, plastics, leather, furs, and finished
articles made thereof. This program pursues exclusively
peaceful purposes and is directed toward further improving
the prosperity of the population.

The Soviet Union has all the possibilities and its own
resources for carrying out this program successfully. However, in order to expedite this program, the Government of
the Soviet Union could make large-scale purchases of appro-

priate equipment and materials in the United States. Thus, the United States would have the opportunity to expend the volume of orders placed with its industrial enterprises and increase the employment of its population, while the USSR would be able to expedite still further its program for the production of consumer goods.

In the opinion of the Soviet Government, cooperation between our countries in the field of the production of synthetic materials and finished articles thereof could be developed along the following lines:

Purchases by the Soviet Union of industrial equipment in the United States, including complete equipment for plants and factories;

Conclusion of agreements with firms for obtaining licenses in individual cases, for inviting American specialists to work in Soviet enterprises as consultants on the production of certain synthetic materials, and for acquainting Soviet specialists with production of these materials and finished articles thereof. The Soviet Union, for its part, is prepared to make it possible for American specialists to learn about the achievements of the USSR in this field;

Organization of meetings of American and Soviet scientists and specialists for discussing problems of production of synthetic materials, organization of exhibits of samples of materials, products made from them, etc.;

Mutual participation of Soviet scientists in the work of scientific research institutions of the USA, and of American scientists in the work of scientific research institutions of the USSR, both with a view to exchanging experience and also to developing jointly new types of synthetic materials and technological processes.

At the same time the Soviet Union could propose a broad program for placing orders in the USA also for other types of equipment for the production of consumer goods, and for housing and public construction. Orders could be placed for refrigeration equipment; installations for air conditioning; equipment for the cellulose, paper, and wood-processing industries, the textile, leather-footwear, and food industries; television equipment; equipment for the manufacture of packing materials; packing, packaging, and automatic vending machines; pumps and compressors; machinery for the mining industry, for the manufacture of building materials and the mechanization of construction; hoisting, transporting, and other equipment.

In addition to this, big orders could be placed for a number of industrial materials and finished products, including orders for equipment for rolling ferrous metals, pipes for city gas lines, various chemical products, medical equipment, medicines, and certain consumer goods.

The Soviet Government assumes that purchases of equipment and various materials in the USA under the corresponding agreement on the part of both sides might amount to several billion dollars in the next few years.

Naturally, there arises the question of payments for such large purchases of American goods. The Soviet Union is able to pay for its purchases through the delivery of Soviet goods which are of interest to the USA, and among such goods we might mention manganese and chromium ores, ferrous alloys, platinum, palladium, asbestos, potassium salts, lumber, cellulose and paper products, certain chemical products, furs, and other goods. If American firms manifest an interest, the Soviet Union could also consider the question of developing the extraction of iron ore for delivery to the USA. At the same time the Soviet Union could propose to the USA a number of types of modern machinery and equipment which could be of interest to American firms.

We realize that the break in commercial relations between our two countries has created certain difficulties in renewing American purchases of Soviet goods in considerable dimensions within a short period of time. Apparently this would require a certain amount of time. On the other hand, American firms are interested in obtaining orders now. If this is the case, we are prepared in the next few years to purchase more American goods than we sell of ours.

In this connection, in particular, the question arises concerning possible payments in installments and making available long-term credits on normal terms and conditions.

Of course, it is possible to begin the development of commerce on the basis of reciprocal deliveries, but because of the circumstances stated above, credit and payments in installments might create conditions for considerably larger immediate Soviet orders and purchases in the USA.

It is also obvious that the development of trade between the USSR and the USA will require the creation of the requisite contractual and legal basis. The question of creating such a basis, as well as that of implementing a program for purchases of American goods and deliveries of Soviet goods, and also payments for them, could, provided the

Government of the USA consents, be subject to intergovernmental negotiation. The reaching of an agreement on these problems would create favorable conditions for extensive trade operations between the American and Soviet organizations concerned.

We also believe that the successful development of Soviet-American trade would be an effective contribution to the general revival of international trade. This would be a good example for the normalization and expansion of economic ties of other countries. From such a course of events everyone would gain, including the USA, which might receive big and profitable orders not only from the Soviet Union but also from many other countries.

Such, Mr. President, are the considerations of the Soviet Government concerning the possibilities of developing trade between the USA and the Soviet Union. We hope that the Government of the USA will consider with due attention the proposals set forth in this letter. A positive solution of the question of Soviet-American trade would also be an important step toward a rapprochement between our two countries.

With sincere respect,

N. KHRUSHCHEV,
Chairman of the Council of Ministers of the Union of SSR

(63) *Letter from the President, July 14, 1958.*[2]

DEAR MR. CHAIRMAN: I have read with interest your letter of June 2, 1958, proposing a considerable increase in U.S.-Soviet trade. As I made clear at the Geneva Conference of Heads of Government in 1955 and more recently in my letter of January 12, 1958 to Premier Bulganin, the United States favors the expansion of peaceful trade with the Soviet Union. Expanded trade between our countries could, under certain conditions, be of mutual benefit and serve to improve our relations in general. This would especially be true if it were accompanied by broad contacts between our peoples and a fuller exchange of information and ideas aimed at promoting mutual understanding as a basis for lasting peace.

Americans believe that the economic welfare of each contributes to the economic welfare of all. Therefore they cannot but welcome the emphasis you place in your letter on

[2] *Ibid.,* p. 200.

striving to expand the supply of consumers goods and housing available to the Soviet people. Our people have done a great deal in recent years to promote higher standards of living through expanded trade with many countries. They would like to trade with the Soviet Union as well, for the same purpose.

As you know, United States export and import trade is carried on by individual firms and not under governmental auspices. There is no need, therefore, to formalize relations between United States firms and Soviet trade organizations. Soviet trade organizations are free right now, without any need for special action by the United States Government, to develop a larger volume of trade with firms in this country.

They may not be taking advantage of all available possibilities. In recent years, United States firms have bought far more from Soviet trade organizations than the latter have purchased from the United States. Furthermore, many of the more important Soviet trade items mentioned in your letter are accorded duty-free entry into the United States. Thus, the situation favors the expansion of Soviet purchases in this country. While the extension of long-term credits for Soviet purchases in the United States would raise complex legal and political questions, the normal commercial credit terms presently available to Soviet trade organizations permit the further expansion of trade between our two countries.

I am asking the Department of State to examine the specific proposals contained in your letter and to communicate further with your government.

Sincerely,

DWIGHT D. EISENHOWER

CHAPTER FOUR

THE COMMUNIST BLOC

A. The Warsaw Treaty.

(64) *Declaration of the Warsaw Treaty States, Moscow, May 27, 1598.*[1]

(Excerpts)

Guided by the interests of assuring peace in Europe and developing peaceful cooperation among states, which is the primary task of the Warsaw Treaty Organization, the governments of the Albanian People's Republic, the Bulgarian People's Republic, the Hungarian People's Republic, the German Democratic Republic, the Polish People's Republic, the Union of Soviet Socialist Republics and the Czechoslovak Republic called a conference of the Political Consultative Committee of the Warsaw Treaty member-states on May 24, 1958, to consider the international situation and work out new joint measures to reduce international tension.

The exchange of views—in which observers from the Chinese People's Republic also participated—confirmed the unanimity of the governments represented at the conference concerning both the assessment of the international situation and ways to strengthen peace.

* * *

At present, NATO military agencies are drawing up new plans for increasing the armed forces and military expenditures of these countries, and the NATO Defense Ministers' conference in April, 1958, discussed the question of doubling the armed forces under the American Supreme Commander of NATO. It is further known that on May 1, 1958, the permanent NATO Council adopted a decision on supplying atomic weapons to those members of the North Atlantic bloc that do not have such weapons at present. The governments of a number of NATO countries—Britain, France, Italy, Turkey and others—made land available for American launching sites for atomic-armed missiles and for atomic

[1] *Pravda*, May 27, 1958. Translation reproduced from *The Current Digest of the Soviet Press*, v. 10 (July 2, 1958), pp. 16-18.

weapons depots, despite the vigorous protests of the peoples of these countries.

Military preparations in the Federal German Republic, whose Bundestag passed a resolution authorizing the F.G.R. government to equip the West German armed forces with nuclear weapons and missiles, are becoming particularly dangerous. Thus, the most dangerous types of weapons are being placed in the hands of militarist and revanchist circles making territorial claims on other states.

By supporting the policy of arming the F.G.R. and undertaking to supply West Germany with nuclear weapons and missiles, the U.S. government is in fact encouraging these circles to pursue a policy jeopardizing peace and involving disastrous consequences for the German people themselves. At the same time, measures are being taken to enlist West Germany in the production and development of the latest types of weapons; one such measure is the tripartite agreement between France, Italy and the F.G.R. on cooperation in military research and arms production—an agreement that has been quite widely publicized.

These military preparations are provoking grave apprehension in West Germany itself and are encountering constantly increasing popular resistance there.

*   *   *

The participants in the conference express deep concern over the continuing attempts of the governments of the U.S.A., Britain, France and other colonial powers to interfere in the affairs of the countries of Asia and Africa and to set up regimes and governments in these areas that are alien to the people and that are prepared once again to sell out to the colonizers countries that have only recently embarked on the road of national independence.

*   *   *

The Warsaw Treaty member-states are convinced of the fact that depriving the Chinese People's Republic of the opportunity of taking its rightful place in the U.N. seriously damages the work of that organization. They are equally profoundly convinced that the participation of people's China in the work of the U.N. would have immense positive importance for the maintenance of peace in the Far East, and also of world peace.

*   *   *

The countries signatory to the Warsaw Pact resolutely condemn the policy of exacerbating international tension and preparing for atomic war which has been pursued in NATO by the leading states of that aggressive alignment. They call upon the governments of the countries of the North Atlantic alliance to take no steps at the present crucial moment that might increase the already tense situation in Europe and certain other parts of the world. In order to decrease the danger of war rather than increase it and to replace mistrust and suspicion between states with confidence and businesslike cooperation, it is necessary above all to refrain from such senseless actions as those engaged in by the American Air Force or as the decision to equip West Germany with atomic weapons, which amounts to a challenge to all the peoples of Europe.

The socialist countries of Europe and Asia have given many proofs of their good will and desire for cooperation with other states in the interests of strengthening peace among all peoples. All the Warsaw Treaty member-states have frequently made unilateral reductions in their armed forces. These forces have been reduced by a total of 2,477,000 men since 1955. These countries' armaments, military facilities and equipment and expenditures for defense were correspondingly reduced. During the same period the armed forces of the Soviet Union were reduced by 2,140,000 men, of the Polish People's Republic by 141,500 men, of the Czechoslovak Republic by 44,000 men, of the German Democratic Republic by 30,000 men, of the Rumanian People's Republic by 60,000 men, of the Bulgarian People's Republic by 18,000 men, of the Hungarian People's Republic by 35,000 men and of the Albanian People's Republic by 9000 men.

The conference participants declare that the peoples of the countries they represent, peoples determined to use every means to strengthen peace and avert a new world-wide war conflagration, are interested in establishing a zone free of atomic, hydrogen and rocket weapons in Central Europe, in an area including both German states—the G.D.R. and the F.G.R.—as well as Poland and Czechoslovakia.

In supporting the proposal of the Polish People's Republic to create a zone free of nuclear weapons and missiles, the participants seek no military advantages whatsoever for themselves.[2]

If comparison is made of the size of the territories of the

[2] Document 46, above.

states that would be included in the atom-free zone, it is seen that the area comprising the G.D.R., Czechoslovakia and Poland is more than twice as large as that of the fourth participant in this zone, West Germany. Moreover, the size of the population of the states to be included in this zone from among the Warsaw Treaty member-states also exceeds the size of the population of the NATO state to be included in this zone.

* * *

The implementation of this initiative, as an effort to arrive at a partial agreement, would smooth the way for broader disarmament agreements and would promote the chief aim of peoples—the elimination of the threat of atomic war in Europe, and consequently of war in general. It should be said that the proposal was understood in precisely this way by broad public circles and by diverse political circles in the West.

The ruling circles of certain NATO powers, declaring in words their desire to conduct successful negotiations, in actual fact do everything possible to complicate the calling of a summit meeting, if not to rule it out altogether.

For this purpose they advance the trumped-up question of the so-called situation in the countries of Eastern Europe, i.e., a question that in fact does not exist. The conference participants resolutely reject any discussion whatsoever of this question as an intolerable interference in the internal affairs of sovereign states incompatible with international law and the U.N. Charter.

As for the attempts to put the question of German unification on the agenda of a summit conference, such attempts can only be of use to those who oppose the convening of such a conference and who do not wish a successful settlement of this question.

* * *

Other states, regardless of the rights they might claim for themselves, are not competent to solve this problem over the heads of the German people and the representatives of their governments, the German Democratic Republic and the Federal German Republic.

* * *

The Warsaw Treaty member-states are in favor of doing away with all military blocs and alignments, since their existence leads to strained relations between states and creates a constant danger of military conflict between them. However, in view of the fact that the Western powers are not prepared to dissolve the military alignments which they have created and replace them with an effective system of collective security in Europe and in a number of other areas of the world, the conference participants consider it necessary to take precautionary measures to relax the tensions that arise and to prevent the contradictions between the two major alignments of powers from developing into a military conflict. To this end they propose the conclusion of a nonaggression pact between the member-states of the Warsaw Treaty and those of the North Atlantic pact to be based, tentatively, on the following mutual obligations:

1. Not to resort to force or the threat of force against each other;

2. To refrain from any sort of interference whatsoever in each other's internal affairs;

3. To resolve all disputes that might arise between them through negotiations between the interested parties;

4. To hold mutual consultations in the event of a situation arising that might comprise a threat to peace in Europe.

The conference drafted a nonaggression pact between the member-states of NATO and the Warsaw Treaty and has decided to submit the draft to the NATO countries.

*   *   *

(65) *Communiqué on the Conference of the Consultative Committee of Member States of the Warsaw Treaty of Friendship, Cooperation and Mutual Aid, Moscow, May 27, 1958.*[3]

A conference of the Political Consultative Committee of member-states of the Warsaw Treaty of Friendship, Cooperation and Mutual Aid was held in Moscow on May 24, 1958.

The following representatives took part in the conference of the Political Consultative Committee:

from the Albanian People's Rebublic—Mehmet Shehu, Chairman of the Council of Ministers; Enver Hoxha, First Secretary of the Albanian Labor Party Central Committee; Behar Shtylla, Minister of Foreign Affairs; and Maj. Gen. Arif Hasko, Chief of the General Staff of the People's Army of the Albanian People's Republic;

[3] *Pravda*, May 27, 1958. Translation reproduced from *The Current Digest of the Soviet Press*, v. 10 (July 2, 1958), pp. 18-19.

from the Bulgarian People's Republic—Anton Yugov, Chairman of the Council of Ministers; Todor Zhivkov, First Secretary of the Bulgarian Communist Party Central Committee; Karlo Lukanov, Minister of Foreign Affairs; General of the Army Peter Panchevski, Minister of National Defense;

from the Hungarian People's Republic—Janos Kadar, Minister of State and First Secretary of the Hungarian Socialist Workers' Party Central Committee; Endre Sik, Minister of Foreign Affairs; and Col. Gen. Geza Revesz, Minister of Defense;

from the German Democratic Republic—Otto Grotewohl, Chairman of the Council of Ministers; Walter Ulbricht, First Secretary of the German Socialist Unity Party Central Committee; Col. Gen. Willi Stoph, Minister of National Defense; Bruno Leuschner, Vice-Chairman of the Council of Ministers; and Otto Winzer, Deputy Minister of Foreign Affairs;

from the Polish People's Republic—Josef Cyrankiewicz, Chairman of the Council of Ministers; Wladyslaw Gomulka, First Secretary of the Polish United Workers' Party Central Committee; Adam Rapacki, Minister of Foreign Affairs; and Col. Gen. Marian Spychalski, Minister of National Defense;

from the Rumanian People's Republic—Chivu Stoica, Chairman of the Council of Ministers; Gheorghe Gheorghiu-Dej, First Secretary of the Rumanian Workers' Party Central Committee; Emil Bodnaras, Vice-Chairman of the Council of Ministers; Avram Bunaciu, Minister of Foreign Affairs; and Col. Gen. Leontin Salajan, Minister of the Armed Forces;

from the Union of Soviet Socialist Republics—N. S. Khrushchev, Chairman of the Council of Ministers and First Secretary of the C.P.S.U. Central Committee; A. A. Gromyko, Minister of Foreign Affairs; Marshal of the Soviet Union R. Ya. Malinovsky, Minister of Defense;

from the Czechoslovak Republic—Viliam Siroky, Chairman of the Government; Vaclav David, Minister of Foreign Affairs; Col. Gen. Bohumir Lomsky, Minister of National Defense.

Chen Yun and Li Fu-chun, Deputy Premiers of the Chinese People's Republic State Council, participated as observers for that country.

Anton Yugov, Chairman of the Bulgarian People's Republic Council of Ministers, presided over the meetings.

In accord with Article 3 of the Warsaw Treaty, which calls for consultations between member-states of the treaty on all important international questions affecting their common

interests, there was an exchange of opinions on the present
international situation at the conference of the Consultative
Committee. The Political Consultative Committee noted
with satisfaction the complete unanimity of the socialist
countries participating at the conference both in their
analysis of the international situation and on their common
tasks in the struggle for peace and the security of nations.
The Political Consultative Committee unanimously adopted
a declaration of the member-states of the Warsaw Treaty,
which is published in the press.

The Political Consultative Committee heard a report by
Marshal of the Soviet Union I. S. Konev, Commander-in-Chief
of the Joint Armed Forces of the Warsaw Treaty member-
states, on a new reduction in the armed forces of the member-
states of the Warsaw Treaty and on the withdrawal of Soviet
troops from the territory of the Rumanian People's Republic.

In addition to the Soviet Union's further reduction of its
armed forces by 300,000 men in 1958, which has already been
announced,[4] the Warsaw Treaty member-states have decided
to cut their armed forces by a total of 119,000 men in 1958 in
addition to the significant reductions that have already been
made; this reduction will be effected by cuts of 55,000 men in
the Rumanian People's Republic, 23,000 in the Bulgarian
People's Republic, 20,000 in the Polish People's Republic,
20,000 in the Czechoslovak Republic and 1000 in the Albanian People's Republic. Thus in 1958 the Warsaw Treaty
member-states will cut their armed forces by 419,000 men.

The Political Consultative Committee approved a proposal by the government of the Soviet Union, agreed upon
by the government of the Rumanian People's Republic, on
the withdrawal in the near future of Soviet troops stationed
in the Rumanian People's Republic under the provisions of
the Warsaw Treaty.

By agreement with the Hungarian government, the Soviet
government has decided to reduce the number of Soviet
troops stationed in Hungary by an additional division, which
is to be withdrawn from Hungarian territory in 1958.

The Political Consultative Committee approved this decision by the Soviet government.

Decisions were also taken on certain organizational questions concerning the activities of the joint armed forces of
the member-states of the Warsaw Treaty.

[4] *Pravda*, January 7, 1958. For an English text of the announcement see *The
Current Digest of the Soviet Press*, v. 10 (February 12, 1958), p. 31.

The Political Consultative Committee adopted a resolution to propose to the member-states of the North Atlantic Treaty Organization the conclusion of a nonaggression pact between the member-states of the Warsaw Treaty and the member-states of NATO. The text of this nonaggression pact is published separately.

The work of the conference of the Political Consultative Committee of the Warsaw Treaty member-states demonstrated the complete unanimity and indestructible fraternal friendship and cooperation of the socialist countries. These countries are making every effort to ease international tension, create an atmosphere of mutual confidence and businesslike cooperation among all states, and to further strengthen peace.

B. Communist Bloc Economic Cooperation.

(66) *Communiqué on the Conference of Representatives of Communist and Workers' Parties of Member States of the Economic Mutual Aid Council, Moscow, May 25, 1958.*[1]

A conference of representatives of Communist and Workers' Parties of Economic Mutual Aid Council member-states was held in Moscow May 20-May 23, 1958.

Participating in the conference were representatives of the Albanian Labor Party, the Bulgarian Communist Party, the Hungarian Socialist Workers' Party, the German Socialist Unity Party, the Polish United Workers' Party, the Rumanian Workers' Party, the Communist Party of the Soviet Union and the Czechoslovak Communist Party. Also participating in the conference by invitation were representatives of the Vietnam Workers' Party, the Chinese Communist Party, the Korean Labor Party and the Mongolian People's Revolutionary Party.

The conference discussed questions connected with the further development of economic cooperation among the socialist countries on the basis of gradual implementation of an international socialist division of labor and of rational specialization and coordination of production; it also heard reports on the work done by the socialist countries' state planning agencies in the drawing up of long-range plans for the development of basic branches of the economy.

[1] *Pravda*, May 25, 1958. Translation reproduced from *The Current Digest of the Soviet Press*, v. 10 (July 2, 1958), pp. 19-21.

The conference participants unanimously noted that the economic ties among the socialist countries are being steadily strengthened and becoming increasingly far-reaching. In recent years there has been a considerable development in specialization and coordination of production, particularly in machine building. The Economic Mutual Aid Council and its permanent commissions have worked hard to prepare recommendations in connection with the drafting of long-range plans for the economic development of the socialist countries.

Multifaceted cooperation among the socialist countries, based on principles of complete equality, mutual respect for national interests and socialist mutual aid, successfully serves the cause of building socialism and communism and permits maximum use of the advantages of the world socialist system of economy in developing the productive forces of each of the socialist countries and in strengthening the economic might of the socialist camp as a whole.

The conference considers that at the present time, when economic ties among the socialist countries have been greatly strengthened and have taken on a comprehensive character, further development and perfecting of the forms of economic cooperation among them and more intense specialization and coordination of the production of interrelated branches of the economies of the socialist camp countries is of particular importance.

The correct organization of production coordination and specialization within the socialist camp ensures a savings in material resources, an increase in socialized labor productivity and a more rational use of the natural resources and economic conditions of the socialist countries in accelerating the rates of expansion of socialist reproduction. The conference devoted attention to the need for all-round development of the power industry and the raw materials branches of the economy, and also to the further development and introduction of the most modern technology. The need for further intensification of coordination and specialization in machine building received particular attention. The latter would make it possible to shift to better large-scale serial production and mass production and to reduce unit production costs sharply.

The representatives of the Communist and Workers' Parties unanimously endorsed the need for fuller utilization of the vast opportunities of the socialist countries and for an all-round consideration of their mutual interests in drawing up long-range plans and also for broadening mutually advantageous forms of cooperation in order to raise the level of industrialization of the least highly developed countries.

The conference recognized the need for further increasing the role of the Economic Mutual Aid Council and its agencies in organizing economic cooperation.

Concerted recommendations on questions of the further development of economic cooperation among the socialist countries, the coordination and specialization of production and also on the question of working out long-range plans for the development of the national economies of the countries were drawn up and approved at the conference. The conference decided to turn over these recommendations to the Economic Mutual Aid Council for elaboration of the requisite practical measures.

The representatives of the Parties of countries not belonging to the Economic Mutual Aid Council expressed their readiness to participate actively in the economic cooperation among the socialist countries and also to strengthen this mutual cooperation in appropriate forms by implementing measures corresponding to the concrete conditions of their own countries.

The discussion of the questions on the conference's agenda took place in a cordial, friendly atmosphere and in the spirit of fraternal mutual understanding and showed the complete unanimity of the Party representatives' views on all questions discussed.

C. Sino-Soviet Consultations.

(67) *Joint Statement on Talks Held between the Chairman of the Chinese People's Republic (Mao) and the Chairman of the Council of Ministers of the USSR (Khrushchev), Peking, August 3, 1958.*[1]

Mao Tse-tung, Chairman of the Central Committee of the Communist Party of China and Chairman of the People's Republic of China, and N. S. Khrushchov, First Secretary of the Central Committee of the Communist Party of the Soviet Union and Chairman of the Council of Ministers of the

---

[1] *Peking Review*, v. 1 (August 12, 1958), pp. 6-7. For a full translation of the Russian text of the joint statement published in *Pravda*, August 4, 1958, see *The Current Digest of the Soviet Press*, v. 10 (September 10, 1958), pp. 3-4.

U.S.S.R., met and held talks in Peking from July 31 to August 3, 1958.

Also taking part in the talks on the side of China were:

Chou En-lai, Premier of the State Council,
Marshal Peng Teh-huai, Vice-Premier of the State Council and Minister of National Defence,
Chen Yi, Vice-Premier of the State Council and Minister of Foreign Affairs,
Wang Chia-hsiang, Member of the Secretariat of the Central Committee of the Communist Party of China.

Also taking part in the talks on the side of the U.S.S.R. were:

Marshal R. Y. Malinovsky, Minister of Defence,
V. V. Kuznetsov, Acting Minister of Foreign Affairs,
B. N. Ponomarev, Member of the Central Committee of the Communist Party of the Soviet Union.

In an atmosphere of perfect sincerity and cordiality, the two parties to the talks held all-round discussions on urgent and important questions of the present international situation, on the further strengthening of the relations of friendship, alliance and mutual assistance between China and the Soviet Union, and on the common struggle for the peaceful settlement of international issues and maintenance of world peace, and reached complete unity of views.

The two parties agreed that the Soviet Union and China, together with the other countries in the socialist camp and all other peace-loving countries and peoples, have achieved great successes in the struggle to ease international tension and maintain peace. The policy of peace of China and the Soviet Union has won the increasingly widespread sympathy and support of the peoples of the world. India, Indonesia, the United Arab Republic and the other countries and people of Asia, Africa, America and Europe who uphold peaceful co-existence are playing an ever more important part in consolidating peace. The forces of peace have already grown to an unprecedented extent.

In contrast to this clear and unalterable policy which is in the vital interests of the peoples of our two countries as well as of those of the other countries of the world, the aggressive imperialist bloc headed by the United States monopoly groups persistently opposes peaceful co-existence and co-operation, stubbornly refuses to ease international tension, obstructs a meeting of the heads of government of the big powers, steps up preparations for a new war and threatens the peace and the security of all peoples. The imperialist forces are the enemy of peace, democracy, national independence and socialism. They have patched together aggressive military and political blocs and dotted the world with their military bases; they are interfering more and more brazenly in the internal affairs of other countries.

The armed aggression recently carried out by the United States and Britain against the Lebanon and Jordan and the armed threat they pose to the Republic of Iraq and the United Arab Republic have greatly increased the tension in the Near and Middle East and aggravated the danger of war; they have aroused widespread protest and condemnation of all peoples of the world.[2]

China and the Soviet Union sternly denounce the flagrant aggression carried out by the United States and Britain in the Near and Middle East; they firmly maintain that a conference of heads of government of the big powers should be called at once to discuss the situation in the Near and Middle East and resolutely demand that the United States and Britain withdraw their forces immediately from the Lebanon and Jordan.

China and the Soviet Union give firm support to the just struggles of the peoples of the United Arab Republic, the Republic of Iraq and the other Arab countries, as well as to the national independence movements of the peoples of Asia, Africa and Latin America.

The events in the Near and Middle East and in other parts of the world prove that the national liberation movement is an irresistible tide, that the age of colonialism is gone for ever, and that any attempt to maintain or restore colonial rule, which goes against the trend of historical development, is harmful to the cause of peace and is foredoomed to fail.

The two parties had a full exchange of views on a series of major questions confronting the two countries in Asia and Europe in the present international situation, and reached complete agreement on measures to be taken to oppose aggression and safeguard peace.

China and the Soviet Union will continue to do their utmost in working for the easing of international tension and the prevention of the disaster of a new war. The two parties reaffirmed that the right of every people to choose its own

2 Documents 81-84, below.

social and political system must be respected, that countries with different social systems must co-exist peacefully in accordance with the famous Five Principles which are widely accepted internationally, that all international disputes should be settled through peaceful negotiation, and that the development of economic and cultural relations among nations on the principles of mutual benefit and peaceful competition should be encouraged, as such relations will increase mutual understanding between peoples and are in full accord with the aim of easing international tension and safeguarding peace.

In order to maintain and consolidate peace, the primary task at the moment is to bring about agreement among nations on the reduction of armaments, discontinuance of the testing of atomic and hydrogen weapons and prohibition of their use, elimination of all military blocs and all military bases on foreign soil, and the conclusion of pacts of peace and collective security.

But whether war can be avoided does not rest with the good wishes and one-sided efforts of the peace-loving peoples alone. The aggressive bloc of the Western powers has up to now refused to take any serious steps to save peace, but on the contrary is aggravating international tension unscrupulously, thus bringing mankind to the brink of the catastrophe of war. It should know, however, that if the imperialist war maniacs should dare to impose war on the people of the world, all the countries and peoples who love peace and freedom will unite closely to wipe out clean the imperialist aggressors and so establish an eternal world peace.

The two parties noted with great satisfaction that fraternal relations of friendship, all-round co-operation and mutual assistance are being developed successfully and steadily strengthened between the Communist Parties and governments of China and the Soviet Union as well as between our two peoples. The economies of both countries are developing by leaps and bounds. Their strength is growing mightier from day to day. And there is a great vitality in their solidarity and co-operation based on complete equality and comradely mutual help, which conduces not only to accelerating their progress along the road of socialism and communism but also to reinforcing the strength of the entire socialist camp.

The two parties decided to continue their all-out efforts to develop all-round co-operation, to further strengthen the solidarity of the socialist camp and their solidarity with all other peace-loving countries and peoples, and reached full agreement on all the questions discussed.

The two parties fully agreed in their appraisal of the tasks faced in common by the Communist Parties of China and the Soviet Union. The unshakable unity of these Marxist-Leninist Parties is always the reliable guarantee for the victory of our common cause.

The Communist Parties of China and the Soviet Union will spare no effort to uphold this sacred unity, to safeguard the purity of Marxism-Leninism, to uphold the principles of the Moscow Declarations of the Communist and Workers' Parties of various countries,[3] and to wage uncompromising struggle against revisionism, the chief danger in the communist movement, which is clearly manifested in the Programme of the League of Communists of Yugoslavia.

The two parties expressed full confidence that the daily growing forces of peace and socialism will certainly be able to overcome all obstacles in their way and win great victory.

MAO TSE-TUNG	N. S. KHRUSHCHOV
Chairman of the Central Committee of the Communist Party of China	*First Secretary of the Central Committee of the Communist Party of the Soviet Union*
Chairman of the People's Republic of China	*Chairman of the Council of Ministers of the U.S.S.R.*

Peking, August 3, 1958

D. Poland.

(68) *Department of State Announcement on the Conclusion of Economic Talks between Government Delegations of the United States and the Polish People's Republic, February 15, 1958.*[1]

Representatives of the Governments of the United States and Poland on February 15 issued a joint statement announcing the results of the economic discussions between the two countries which began on October 31, 1957.

As indicated in the joint statement,[2] the United States

[3] *Documents on American Foreign Relations, 1957*, pp. 150-157.
[1] *Department of State Bulletin*, v. 38 (March 3, 1958), pp. 349-350.
[2] *Ibid.*, pp. 350-351. For a text of the agreement and notes covering the rate of exchange between the dollar and the zloty, see *ibid.*, pp. 351-353.

and Poland have entered into credit and sales arrangements providing for the shipment to Poland of agricultural commodities, other raw materials, and various types of machinery and equipment. An amount of $25 million will be extended to Poland in the form of a line of credit, to be administered by the Export-Import Bank of Washington. In addition, an amount of $73 million is provided for in the agreement for the sale to Poland of wheat, animal feed grains, cotton, vegetable oils, and nonfat dry milk for local currency (Polish zlotys) pursuant to the Agricultural Trade Development and Assistance Act (Public Law 480).

Polish zlotys received by the United States under the surplus agricultural commodities agreement will be deposited at the rate of 24 zlotys to $1, the most favorable prevailing rate of exchange, in a special dollar-denominated account. Such zlotys will be available for U.S. uses, including expenses of the American Embassy in Warsaw. The agreement provides that, beginning March 1, 1963, the Polish Government will repurchase for dollars, at a rate not to exceed $2,810,000 per year, such zlotys as the United States does not use.

The Polish Government has expressed its desire to make additional purchases of agricultural commodities, other raw materials, and agricultural and industrial machinery and equipment in the United States under credit or local-currency sales arrangements. The U.S. Government has indicated its willingness to discuss such additional purchases with the Polish Government at a mutually convenient date and, in connection therewith, to consider in particular the steps which are required to enable Poland to finance such purchases in the United States. Since it has not been possible, under the terms of the present agreement, to meet fully the immediate needs of the Polish agricultural economy with respect to supplies of bread grains, and in recognition of the possibility that decisions of the Polish Government as to its grain policy in 1958-59 may have to be made within the relatively near future, the U.S. Government is prepared, if requested by the Polish Government, to discuss the possibility of the future sale by the U.S. Government of an additional quantity of bread grains under the provisions of title I of Public Law 480.

The two sides have also agreed to discuss, through normal diplomatic channels, additional ways and means of facilitating the expansion of trade between the United States and Poland, including the possibility of the extension to Poland of most-favored-nation treatment by the United States.

Previous agreements between the United States and Polish Governments, concluded on June 7, 1957, and August 14, 1957,[3] provided for credit and sales arrangements covering the shipment to Poland of commodities with an export market value of $95 million. Most of these commodities have now been purchased and shipped to Poland. Under the P.L. 480 agreements concluded in 1957, which provided for $65 million export market value of agricultural commodities, the U.S. Government has shipped to Poland about 407,000 tons of wheat, 41,300 tons of cotton, 17,200 tons of tallow, and 1,000 tons of soybean oil, and an additional 6,000 tons of cotton will be shipped shortly. Under the $30 million line of credit established under the agreement of June 7, 1957, and administered by the Export-Import Bank, an additional 111,-000 tons of wheat, 57,000 tons of soybeans, and 2,000 tons of cotton have been shipped to Poland. Purchases of the coal-mining equipment included under this line of credit in the amount of $4 million have been almost completed, and the equipment will be shipped soon.

The delivery in Poland of the commodities provided under the agreements concluded in 1957 has contributed to the improvement of stocks of grain in Poland as well as to improvement in the supplies of raw materials needed for certain Polish industries.

The U.S. and Polish Governments will shortly begin negotiations for a lump-sum settlement by the Polish Government of American property claims. The U.S. Government is now examining the information as to the estimated value of claims based upon the nationalization or other taking of American property by Polish authorities, and negotiations with the Polish Government for the lump-sum settlement will be initiated as soon as these claims have been analyzed.

The economic discussions were conducted for the U.S. and Polish Governments by the following representatives:

For the U.S. Government

Wilson T. M. Beale, Jr., Deputy Assistant Secretary of State for Economic Affairs

Marshall M. Smith, Deputy Assistant Secretary of Commerce for International Affairs

Horace J. Davis, Department of Agriculture

[3] *Documents on American Foreign Relations, 1957*, pp. 170-181.

David Richardson, International Cooperation Administration

Frederick M. Cone, Export-Import Bank

For the Polish Government

Tadeusz Lychowski, Economic Minister, Embassy of Polish People's Republic

Stanislaw Raczkowski, Financial Counselor, Embassy of Polish People's Republic

Edward Iwaszkiewicz, Director, Polish Purchasing Agency, Embassy of Polish People's Republic

(69) *Joint Declaration on Talks held between Party and Government Delegations of the Soviet Union and the Polish People's Republic, Moscow, November 10, 1958.*[4]

(Excerpts)

At the invitation of the C.P.S.U. Central Committee, the Presidium of the U.S.S.R. Supreme Soviet and the Soviet government, a delegation from the Polish People's Republic paid a friendship visit to the Soviet Union Oct. 24, 1958, to Nov. 12, 1958.

* * *

During the talks, which were held in a cordial atmosphere and in a spirit of complete mutual understanding, there was a thorough-going discussion of the question of further consolidating friendly relations, cooperation and mutual understanding between the U.S.S.R. and the P.P.R., as well as of problems of interest to both sides relative to the present international situation and questions flowing from the common struggle of both countries in defense of peace. Both delegations found that their views on all the questions discussed fully coincided.

I.

Both sides, after a broad exchange of views on major international issues, emphasized the steadily growing influence of the socialist system and its countries and the forces of socialism and peace on the development of international con-

[4] *Pravda*, November 12, 1958. Translation reproduced from *The Current Digest of the Soviet Press*, v. 10 (December 17, 1958), pp. 12, 13 and 32.

ditions. The ideas of socialism are increasingly taking hold among the broad masses. The countries of the socialist camp do not threaten anyone and strive for the peaceful settlement of all disputes; they uphold the principle of peaceful co-existence among countries with different social and political systems and favor peaceful competition between the socialist and capitalist systems. They are convinced that in this competition the victor will be the socialist system, which is demonstraing in practice its superiority over the capitalist system.

*　　*　　*

U.S. imperialist circles, in striving to subordinate to their rule the majority of countries, are rallying around themselves all the reactionary forces of the capitalist world.

The position taken by the government of the Federal German Republic is the main buttress of this policy in Europe. The imperialist circles are using for their own ends the revanchist policy of the F.G.R. government. The rapid move to remilitarize this country, the accelerated arming of the Bundeswehr with atomic weapons and missiles, the desire of the Federal German Republic to occupy the leading place among the European members of the Atlantic pact, the support given the Adenauer government by militarist and revanchist elements, who openly make territorial claims on other countries—all of this represents a threat to the peace and security of the European countries, which will be the first to suffer the consequences of such a policy.

Both sides emphasize the growing role of the German Democratic Republic, the first workers' and peasants' state in the history of Germany, as a major factor for peace in Europe. They support the German Democratic Republic's proposal designed to pave the way to the conclusion of a German peace treaty, which would substantially facilitate the reduction of the present tension in Europe.

In view of the increased arming of the F.G.R., the Polish People's Republic's proposal for the establishment of an atom-free zone in Central Europe, a proposal which has the full support of the Warsaw Pact member-states and which met with broad response in various Western circles, has assumed even more importance.[5]

*　　*　　*

[5] Document 46, above.

The Polish delegation resolutely supports the Soviet proposal for a summit conference, at which the most pressing problems of disarmament and measures to strengthen security in Europe and throughout the world could be examined and decided. However, the tactics of delaying and evading negotiations, employed above all by the ruling circles of the United States, hinder the achievement of agreements which would settle the questions on which world peace depends.

Under these conditions both delegations consider it necessary to strengthen the defensive Warsaw Pact, which safeguards the general security of all the countries of the socialist camp. In addition, they will continue their efforts to reduce international tension, including efforts by way of partial agreements, and stand ready to cooperate with all states and forces pursuing the same goal.

The Polish delegation, supporting the measures taken by the Soviet Union aimed at the complete cessation of nuclear weapons tests, shares the view that the most urgent task of today should be the achievement of agreement among the great powers on the immediate and universal cessation of these tests for all time, particularly since the Geneva conference of experts on atomic matters confirmed the complete feasibility of establishing controls over experimental explosions.

* * *

II.

The leaders of the Communist Party of the Soviet Union and the Polish United Workers' Party have exchanged information on the work of their parties and discussed questions of relations between the Parties, as well as pressing problems of the international workers' movement.

Both Parties attach considerable importance to the comprehensive development and strengthening of fraternal relations among the states belonging to the great family of socialist countries, which are united by the common ideas of Marxism-Leninism and the common goal of building socialism and communism.

* * *

A necessary condition for success in the building of socialism is an uncompromising struggle against revisionism, which represents the main danger at the present stage and which seeks to undermine the fundamental principles of the ideology of Marxism-Leninism and to weaken the unity of the great family of socialist countries and the international workers' movement.

The cause of socialism requires further creative development of Marxist-Leninist doctrine, observance of the general laws governing the building of socialism and bold application of these laws through methods that accord with the conditions of each country; it also requires a struggle against manifestations of dogmatism.

Concrete measures for the further exchange of experience in Party work and for expanding contacts between the Communist Party of the Soviet Union and the Polish United Workers' Party were discussed. It was noted with satisfaction that the Communist Party of the Soviet Union and the Polish United Workers' Party are cooperating even more closely, as is evidenced, in particular, by the reciprocal visits of Party delegations for the purpose of joint discussion of a number of major questions and by the exchange of delegations between individual cities and regions of the Soviet Union and the Polish People's Republic.

The Communist Party of the Soviet Union and the Polish United Workers' Party are fully determined to continue developing and broadening fraternal cooperation between the two Parties and the exchange of experience in Party work, convinced that this serves the cause of the successful development of both countries and their advance toward socialism and communism and at the same constitutes a contribution to the theory and practice of Marxism-Leninism.

Both Parties will combat any attempts to disrupt the unity of the socialist camp. They will continue to expand and strengthen international ties with all Communist and Workers' Parties and with the entire international revolutionary movement for the victory of peace, progress and socialism.

III.

* * *

Soviet-Polish friendship and the alliance between the U.S.S.R. and the Polish People's Republic, which are supported by the will of the peoples and today constitute a powerful material force, are an important factor of peace in Europe and the best guarantee of the inviolability of Poland's western boundary along the Oder and Neisse

Luzycka. This is particularly important in view of the growing activity of the West German revanchist forces and also in view of the Western powers' continued refusal to take a clear-cut stand on this indisputable issue.

The hopes and calculations of certain reactionary and imperialist circles to set the Polish people and the peoples of the U.S.S.R. against each other and to weaken their fraternal friendship have proved futile. The Soviet and the Polish people are well aware that any weakening of the bonds that unite them, as of the bonds uniting both their peoples with the entire great socialist family, could only damage the cause of socialism and peace and would be exploited by the imperialist forces hostile to both peoples, particularly by the revanchist and chauvinist elements in West Germany. The Soviet-Polish Joint Declaration of Nov. 8, 1956,[6] the purpose of which was to strengthen and further develop relations between the U.S.S.R. and Poland on the immutable Leninist principle of proletarian internationalism, has fully passed the test of life and has helped to deepen the indestructible solidarity and friendship uniting the two countries.

This friendship, based on the most reliable principles of proletarian internationalism, respect for each other's sovereignty, mutual fraternal aid and solidarity and on common interests and aspirations is today stronger than ever before.

The common class foundations of the state systems of the two countries—one of which, the Polish People's Republic, has been building socialism for 14 years and the second of which, the Soviet Union, has successfully completed the building of socialism and is building a communist society—and the common theoretical principles of the immortal teachings of Marxism and Leninism are the firm foundation on which Soviet-Polish friendship and cooperation are developing.

Both countries are supporting each other in the international arena with respect to measures having the single aim of averting the threat of war and establishing firm peaceful international cooperation.

* * *

The delegation of the Polish People's Republic proposed to the Soviet government that the Soviet Union render technical aid to the Polish People's Republic in developing certain important branches of the Polish national economy,

[6] Paul E. Zinner, ed., *National Communism and Popular Revolt in Eastern Europe* (New York, Columbia University Press, 1956), pp. 306-314.

specifically, in prospecting for new oil and natural gas deposits and preparing them for exploitation, building an oil refinery, expanding the Lenin Metallurgical Combine and developing the copper industry. The U.S.S.R. government, with a view to further expanding economic cooperation between the two countries, agreed to assist the Polish People's Republic in the above matters.

*   *   *

Both sides expressed their firm resolve to continue expanding political, economic and cultural cooperation between the two countries in every way, to develop and strengthen the inviolable fraternal friendship and alliance between the U.S.S.R. and the Polish People's Republic on the principles of Marxism-Leninism and on the principles of proletarian internationalism.

The friendship visit of the delegation of the Polish People's Republic to the U.S.S.R. will help to further expand brotherhood and friendship between the peoples of both countries, will be a new contribution to the unity of the great family of socialist states and will promote the cause of strengthening peace throughout the world.

During its stay in the Soviet Union the Polish People's Republic delegation invited N. S. Khrushchev, First Secretary of the C.P.S.U. Central Committee and Chairman of the U.S.S.R. Council of Ministers, together with other Party and state leaders of the Soviet Union, to visit the Polish People's Republic.

This invitation was accepted with pleasure.

N. KHRUSHCHEV   W. GOMULKA
Moscow, Nov. 10, 1958.

E. Hungary.

> (70) *Announcement by the Ministry of Justice of the Hungarian People's Republic on the Trial of Imre Nagy and His Associates, Budapest, June 16, 1958.*[1]

(Excerpts)

Budapest, June 16. The Hungarian Telegraph Agency has transmitted the following bulletin of the Hungarian People's Republic Ministry of Justice:

[1] *Pravda,* June 17, 1958. Translation reproduced from *The Current Digest of the Soviet Press,* v. 10 (July 23, 1958), pp. 14-16.

The organs of justice of the Hungarian People's Republic have completed the trial of the high-ranking group of persons who on October 23, 1956, with the active cooperation of the imperialists, unleashed an armed counterrevolutinary uprising designed to overthrow the lawful regime in the Hungarian People's Republic.

In his indictment the prosecutor general of the Hungarian People's Republic accused Imre Nagy and his accomplices Ferenc Donath, Miklos Gimes, Zoltan Tildy, Pal Maleter, Sandor Kopacsi, Jozsef Szilagyi, Ferenc Janosi, and Miklos Vasarhelyi of organizing a conspiracy aimed at overthrowing the people's democratic state regime in Hungary and, in addition, accused Imre Nagy of treason and Sandor Kopacsy and Pal Maleter of ogranizing a military uprising. The case against the accused Geza Losonczy was dropped as a result of his death following an illness.

*   *   *

The court established that by the end of 1955 Imre Nagy had already created a close underground group from among his closest supporters for the purpose of forcible seizure of power. This underground group carried out its hostile activity, using both legal and illegal ways and means. To accomplish their goal of overthrowing the people's regime, they mobilized and enlisted on their side any and all enemies of the people's democratic state regime. At the same time, in a demagogic and false manner, concealing their true purposes, proclaiming "socialist" slogans, they temporarily led astray trusting people as well and used them for their antigovernment ends.

The group of conspirators, particularly Imre Nagy, the leader of the group, worked out in detail a political platform, the immediate tasks and methods and the future aims of the movement directed against the people's democracy. The indictment presented to the court secret documents in large measure written by Imre Nagy himself.

*   *   *

The infamous demonstration of Oct. 23 was begun at the iniatiative of Imre Nagy and his group, who used their ties with the Petofi circle and with higher educational institutions for this purpose. For example, at a meeting held at the Polytechnical Institute on the night of Oct. 22, Jozsef Szilagyi, on instructions of Imre Nagy, issued a personal appeal for the demonstration. The Oct. 23 demonstration was directed by the Imre Nagy group through Gabor Tanczos and his accomplices.

* * *

For direct guidance of the armed uprising, which was unleashed at the same time as, and under cover of, the demonstration, the conspirators created several underground centers. One of these centers, the members of which were Sandor Kopacsi, Jozsef Szilagyi, Miklos Gimes, Gyorgy Fazekas and Tamas Aczel, was organized in the Budapest Police Department. Sandor Kopacsi, breaking his oath, abusing his office as head of the Budapest Police Department and misleading his subordinates, carried out the tasks worked out by the underground center. In order to arm the forces hostile to the people's democracy and at the same time to disrupt the armed forces, which were loyal to socialism, he ordered the regional police departments not to oppose the rebels but, on the contrary, to hand over their weapons and police buildings to them. In this way Sandor Kopacsi distributed to the rebels more than 20,000 firearms from the police arsenals. This group worked in close cooperation with another group, set up Oct. 24, 1956; an auxiliary center whose members were Geza Losonczy, Ferenc Donath and Ferenc Janosi. This center, in particular, directed subversive activity in the ranks of the army and at the same time issued regularly to the rebels the military plans of the armed forces which were defending the people's republic.

Long before the October uprising Imre Nagy and his accomplices had established secret ties and held talks with the proponents of a bourgeois restoration, with whom they concluded an alliance for the forcible seizing of power.

* * *

In order to secure its power the conspiratorial group of Imre Nagy concluded an alliance with other extreme reactionary groups as well. It "rehabilitated" even the legally condemned former Cardinal Jozsef Mindszenty and enabled him to come out against the people's republic.

* * *

While Premier, breaking the oath which he had sworn, Imre Nagy abolished the constitutional administrative organs of the country—the National Assembly, the H.P.R.

Presidium and the government—and illegally created a so-called "cabinet" as his personal administrative organ. This cabinet was even then organized in such a manner that reactionary forces had the upper hand, although in order to deceive the masses Imre Nagy also included in it people devoted to socialism.

* * *

After the dissolution and elimination of the central organs of the people's republic Imre Nagy and his conspiratorial group set about liquidating the local agencies of authority. They dissolved the legal organs of state power, the local councils and the economic administrative agencies, and replaced them with the so-called "revolutionary committees," formed for the most part from bourgeois, fascist elements, and with the so-called workers' councils, designed to deceive the working class.

By means of treasonous and subversive activity, Imre Nagy and his accomplices, having obtained a cease-fire, finally succeeded in paralyzing the armed forces, which were defending the people's republic. At the same time they organized, equipped with arms and ultimately legalized the counterrevolutionary forces of the rebels. They recruited war criminals and criminals against the people, convicts released from prisons, and all possible enemies of the people's republic in their so-called "national guard."

To accomplish their aims and to open the door wide for imperialist interference, Imre Nagy and his traitorous group tried unlawfully to denounce the Warsaw Pact, a defensive alliance of which the H.P.R. is a member. This attempt was made in a radio broadcast of Nov. 4, 1956, by Imre Nagy; in this broadcast he called on the imperialists to open an armed attack against the Revolutionary Workers' and Peasants' Government and against the Soviet troops called upon by that government for aid.

After the counterrevolutionary armed uprising was crushed, certain groups of conspirators of the Imre Nagy brand sought refuge where they had earlier found support. Bela Kiraly, Anna Kethly, Jozsef Kovago and others who took part in overthrowing the state fled to the West to escape responsibility. Jozsef Mindszenty, as the Hungarian authorities know, hid in the American Embassy. Istvan B. Szabo tried to hide in the British Consulate in Budapest. The Imre Nagy group, who had come forth earlier under the pirated banner of "national communism," escaped responsibility by fleeing to the Yugoslav Embassy in Budapest.

It is characteristic that the threacherous conspirators continued to carry on their counterrevolutionary activity without interruption even after the Hungarian people, under the direction of the Revolutionary Workers' and Peasants' Government, had set about re-establishing the lawful regime, ensuring a peaceful life for the people and liquidating the grave damage done by the counterrevolutionaries. Anna Kethly, Bela Kiraly, Jozsef Kovago and their accomplices—from the West—and Imre Nagy, Geza Losonczy and others—from the Yugoslav Embassy—gave instructions on continuing armed resistance, organizing strikes to paralyze the life of the country and reorganizing underground subversive activities.

* * *

At the trial the accused Ferenc Donath, Miklos Gimes, Zoltan Tildy, Sandor Kopacsi, Ferenc Janosi and Miklos Vasarhelyi, expressing their remorse, made a full confession of their guilt. Imre Nagy, Jozsef Szilagyi and Pal Maleter denied their guilt. However, during the course of the trial they were proved guilty by the testimony of their accomplices and of witnesses as well as by material evidence, and in their testimony they partially acknowledged the facts of their crimes.

The collegium of the people's court under the Hungarian People's Republic Supreme Court, considering the seriousness of the crimes and the aggravating and extenuating circumstances, declared on the basis of the materials of the trial that the accused were guilty of the crimes with which they were charged and sentenced Imre Nagy to death, Ferenc Donath to 12 years in jail, Miklos Gimes to death, Zoltan Tildy to six years in jail, Pal Maleter to death, Sandor Kopacsi to life imprisonment, Dr. Jozsef Szilagyi to death, Ferenc Janosi to eight years in jail, and Miklos Vasarhelyi to five years in jail.

The sentence is not subject to appeal. The death sentences have been carried out.

(71) United States Statement on the Execution of Hungarian Patriots, June 17, 1958.[2]

The execution of Imre Nagy and Pal Maleter and other Hungarian patriots, first publicly anounced last night [June 16] by Radio Moscow, can only be regarded by the civilized world as a shocking act of cruelty. The preparation of this act, beginning with the Soviet abduction of Imre Nagy from the Yugoslav Embassy in Budapest in violation of assurances of safe conduct pledged by the Soviet puppet, Kadar, was by stealth and secrecy. It follows, significantly, on Mr. Khrushchev's April visit to Budapest. It has also come at a time when the Soviet Union has been attempting to persuade the world that international discussion of the plight of Hungary and Eastern Europe generally should not take place because it would constitute unwarranted intervention in the internal affairs of these countries.

The Soviet Union, which has pursued a policy of terror toward the peoples of Hungary and of the other dominated countries of Eastern Europe for over 12 years, must bear fundamental responsibility for this latest crime against the Hungarian people and all humanity. The murder of these two Hungarian leaders, who chose to serve the interests of their nation rather than those of Soviet communism, brings to a tragic culmination the Soviet-Communist betrayal of the Hungarian people. It is the executioners of Imre Nagy and Pal Maleter, and not the executed patriots, who have committed treason against the Hungarian nation. By this act the Soviet Union and the Soviet-imposed regime in Hungary have once more violated every principle of decency and must stand in judgment before the conscience of mankind.

(72) United States Note Refuting Hungarian Charges Alleging Hostile and Improper Activities by the United States against the Hungarian People's Republic, November 21, 1958.[3]

The Legation of the United States of America presents its compliments to the Ministry for Foreign Affairs of the Hungarian People's Republic and, with reference to the Ministry's note No. 00941/5/1958 of September 20,[4] has the honor

[2] *Department of State Bulletin*, v. 39 (July 7, 1958), p. 7.
[3] *Ibid.* (December 8, 1958), pp. 910-913.
[4] Not printed.

under instructions from the United States Government to communicate the following:

The Note of the Hungarian Government is largely concerned with the issue of foreign interference in the internal affairs of Hungary. The Government of the United States accordingly avails itself of the opportunity to set forth in the clearest terms its views on this issue.

I

For well over a century, the Government and people of the United States have had strong feelings of friendship and good will for the people of Hungary. In conjunction with these sentiments, the Government and people of the United States have viewed with sympathy and understanding the long struggle of the Hungarian people to realize their right of national independence and to decide for themselves their way of life and form of government. In addition to these ties of sympathy and interest, however, the United States bears clear responsibilities toward the Hungarian people under the terms and as one of the principal signatories of the United Nations Declaration, the Yalta Declaration on Liberated Europe, the Charter of the United Nations, and the Treaty of Peace with Hungary. The Hungarian Government, on its part, is specifically obligated under Article 2 of the Treaty of Peace to secure to all persons under its jurisdiction the enjoyment of human rights and the fundamental freedoms and under Articles 1, 55, and 56 of the United Nations Charter to promote and encourage respect for and observance of these rights and freedoms without distinction as to race, sex, language, or religion.

The Hungarian Government speaks, in its note, about United States "interference" in the internal affairs of Hungary. This charge is without foundation, as has been proved in the United Nations, and is wholly misdirected. The United States Government has not intervened politically, militarily, or in any other way in the internal affairs of Hungary and has neither the intention nor the desire to do so. In keeping with its international obligations, however, the United States recognizes and supports the inalienable right of the Hungarian people to live in freedom under institutions of their own choosing. United States policy toward Hungary is accordingly aimed at encouraging respect for the independence of Hungary and supporting the right of the Hungarian people, in friendly association with all other peoples, to work out their own destiny free of any foreign domination.

The incongruity of the Hungarian Government's charges of United States "interference" is revealed by the development of events in Hungary since the close of World War II. The fact of repeated acts of Soviet interference in Hungarian internal affairs is incontrovertible. The Soviet Union has continued its armed occupation of Hungary long after its right to do so terminated under the provisions of the Treaty of Peace. It is the Soviet Union which in 1956 committed an act of massive armed aggression against the Hungarian people which had as its object the perpetuation of Soviet domination and which clearly has served this aim. It is the Soviet Union, in flagrant violation of its international pledges and willful defiance of the decisions of the United Nations, which persists in its efforts to maintain its domination of Hungary.

The Hungarian Government has acquiesced in this Soviet domination. Indeed, it has actively supported the Soviet objectives. This is demonstrated most notably by the recent reprisals against many leaders, especially Imre Nagy, of the Hungarian people's heroic fight for independence in 1956 and by the fact that the Hungarian Government has actively joined the Soviet Union in flouting the decisions of the United Nations.

The United States fully recognizes the necessity of friendly relations between the Soviet Union and Hungary in the interest of a stable and constructive peace in Eastern Europe. At the same time it supports the right of the Hungarian people to national independence, and to have institutions of their own choosing, free from both the threat and the fact of foreign interference.

II

The Hungarian Government alleges that the United States Government "employs" the United Nations and other international bodies to "launch attacks against the Hungarian People's Republic" and "to force other countries also to adopt a similar conduct." This charge is not only false but it also reflects a grave distortion of the nature and functioning of the United Nations. It misrepresents United States relations with the member states of the United Nations and impugns the sovereignty of these states. The attitude and actions of the United Nations toward any of its members is essentially determined by their conduct and sincerity in honoring their obligations, not by the expression by the United States or any other state of its views in the forum of the General Assembly.

It is clearly within the competence and it is precisely the function of the United Nations to discuss situations and problems which concern the well-being of the international community of nations, involve violations of international obligations, and disturb or threaten the peace of the world. The Soviet and Hungarian Delegations at the United Nations have repeatedly set forth the point of view of their Governments on the Hungarian question. The fact that this point of view has found acceptance on the part of only a conspicuously few member states speaks for itself and echoes the authoritative findings of the Special Committee on the Problem of Hungary concerning the facts relating to the Hungarian revolution of 1956 as well as the secret trials and executions of Imre Nagy, Pal Maleter, and other leaders and participants in the national uprising.

Moreover, both the Hungarian Government and the Soviet Government have refused to comply with the terms of the various resolutions on Hungary adopted by overwhelming majorities in the General Assembly and have persistently refused to cooperate in any way with the United Nations Special Committee on the Problem of Hungary and with the United Nations Special Representative on the Hungarian Problem.[5] The conduct of the Soviet and Hungarian Governments in these matters is clearly not such as to inspire confidence on the part of other member states in their willingness to fulfill their international obligations under the United Nations Charter.

III

The note of the Hungarian Government states that relations between the United States and Hungary are not "normal." This statement is correct, for the Hungarian Government has not permitted the development of normal relations. For more than a decade, the Hungarian Government, supported by the Soviet-Government, has sought to obstruct friendly interchange and understanding between the Hungarian and American peoples. It has tried persistently to isolate the people of Hungary from other peoples with whom

[5] Documents on American Foreign Relations, 1956, pp. 267-268, and ibid., 1957, pp. 182-193.

they have traditional ties of friendship. This policy has involved not only attempts to deny freedom of expression and association to the Hungarian people, but also systematic efforts to obstruct the legitimate diplomatic operations of the American Legation in Budapest through the harassment and slandering of American diplomatic officers and the intimidation, arrest, and deportation of Hungarian employees of the Legation. The Hungarian Government's reckless and malicious charges of American espionage and other improper activities have been proved in the United Nations and in other public and diplomatic forums to be without foundation. This absence of truth in the allegations put forward by the Hungarian Government is not remedied by spurious displays of radio receivers, pistols, and other equipment of undetermined origin, or by the stated "testimony" of agents of the Hungarian Government.

Among other charges, the Hungarian Government accuses the United States Government of giving moral and material support to "fascist Hungarian refugees." This charge is patently false, but its assertion reveals that the Hungarian Government is quite prepared to apply the epithet "fascist" indiscriminately to all Hungarians who have fled from the oppression that exists in their homeland and have found refuge in foreign countries. The United States Government is proud that it, together with many other nations, has been able to assist thousands of these refugees in finding new homes where they may enjoy freedom.

Again, the Hungarian Government accuses the Voice of America of transmitting "subversive propaganda" directed against the Hungarian People's Republic. The radio broadcasts which are beamed to Hungary by the Voice of America are factual reports and commentary on the national and international events and developments such as free men throughout the world have the opportunity to read and listen to daily in their local newspapers and news broadcasts. To those who believe that the free exchange of information and ideas is essential for the kind of peaceful coexistence and competition which the Hungarian Government itself professes to desire, it is entirely logical and justifiable that such broadcasts should be directed to the Hungarian people in view of the practice of the Hungarian Government of erecting artificial barriers against normal communication and contacts between peoples. In this connection, it must be noted that the Hungarian Government continues to devote what must be very considerable resources to jamming American and other Free World radio programs.

The Government of the United States desires to contribute in every possible way to the removal of barriers to mutual understanding and friendly co-operation between all peoples. It is obvious, however, that the development of normal and constructive relations between governments must rest on the secure foundations of respect for truth, willingness to fulfill international obligations, and enlightened regard for the rights and the will of the peoples governed. The Hungarian Government in its note of September 20 has complained at length concerning various matters such as passport and visa problems and the difficulties of commercial and cultural intercourse under existing circumstances. It is true that such difficulties exist, for the restrictive and repressive policies which the Hungarian Government has pursued for many years have afforded the United States Government no alternative other than to institute on a reciprocal basis such limitations on activities in these fields as are required by its national interest and security. These manifestations of the lack of normal relations are symptoms, however, rather than basic causes. The real issues which exist between the United States Government and the Hungarian Government are of a more fundamental character.

The United States Government considers that any real improvement in its relations with the Hungarian Government depends primarily and basically upon the Hungarian Government's manifesting a willingness to live up to its international obligations under the United Nations Charter and the Treaty of Peace. It is most unfortunate in this respect that the Hungarian Government's note under reference appears to indicate that the Hungarian Government is determined to do everything in its power to frustrate such a development. The United States Government observes with deep regret this further expression of a policy which can only prevent, so long as it obtains, the growth of that friendly relationship which is so earnestly desired by both the Hungarian and American peoples.

The Legation of the United States of America avails itself of this opportunity to renew to the Ministry for Foreign Affairs the assurances of its high consideration.

(73) *General Assembly Resolution 1312 (XIII), Adopted December 12, 1958.*[6]

The General Assembly,

Having considered the supplementary report, dated 14 July 1958, of the United Nations Special Committee established by resolution 1132 (XI) of 10 January 1957 to report on the problem of Hungary,

Having considered the report, dated 9 December 1957, of the Special Representative of the General Assembly, His Royal Highness Prince Wan Waithayakon, who was appointed by Assembly resolution 1133 (XI) of 14 September 1957 to take steps to achieve the objectives of Assembly resolutions 1004 (ES-II) of 4 November 1956, 1127 (XI) of 21 November 1956, 1131 (XI) of 12 December 1956 and 1132 (XI) of 10 January 1957,

1. *Expresses its appreciation* to its Special Representative, Prince Wan Waithayakon, for the efforts he has made to enter into consultation with the appropriate authorities with a view to achieving the objectives of the resolutions referred to above;

2. *Endorses* the unanimous report of the Special Committee on the Problem of Hungary, dated 14 July 1958, and expresses its thanks to the Committee for its objective and efficient discharge of the tasks entrusted to it;

3. *Deplores* the continued refusal of the Government of the Union of Soviet Socialist Republics and the régime in Hungary to co-operate with the Special Representative and with the Committee in their efforts to achieve the objectives of the United Nations in accordance with the pertinent resolutions of the General Assembly;

4. *Deplores* the continuing repression in Hungary of fundamental rights of the Hungarian people and of their freedom of political expression under the shadow of the continuing presence of Soviet armed forces;

5. *Denounces* the execution of Mr. Imre Nagy, General Pál Maléter and other Hungarian patriots;

6. *Condemns* this continued defiance of the resolutions of the General Assembly;

7. *Again calls upon* the Union of Soviet Socialist Repub-

[6] United Nations, General Assembly, *Official Records, Thirteenth Session,* Supplement No. 18 (A/4090), pp. 59-60. The resolution was adopted by a vote of 54-10 (Soviet bloc and Yugoslavia)-15. Israel and Yemen were absent.

lics and the present authorities in Hungary to desist from repressive measures against the Hungarian people and to respect the liberty and political independence of Hungary and the Hungarian people's enjoyment of fundamental human rights and freedoms;

8. *Declares* that the United Nations will continue to be seized of the situation in Hungary in view of the fact that the Government of the Union of Soviet Socialist Republics and the present authorities in Hungary are disregarding the above-mentioned resolutions of the General Assembly;

9. *Decides* to appoint Sir Leslie Munro to represent the United Nations for the purpose of reporting to Member States or to the General Assembly on significant developments relating to the implementation of the Assembly resolutions on Hungary;

10. Requests the Secretary-General to provide the necessary facilities to assist Sir Leslie Munro in the performance of his duties.

CHAPTER FIVE

THE NEAR AND MIDDLE EAST

A. The Eisenhower Doctrine.

(74) *Message of the President Transmitting the Second Progress Report on Activity under the American Doctrine for the Middle East, March 5, 1958.*[1]

To the Congress of the United States:

I am transmitting herewith the second report to the Congress covering activities through December 31, 1957, in furtherance of the purposes of the joint resolution to promote peace and stability in the Middle East.[2] This report supplements the first one forwarded to the Congress on July 31, 1957, concerning activities through June 30, 1957.[3]

The resolution continues to be an important element in United States foreign policy relating to the Middle East. Communist opposition to it is clearly revealed by the fact that over the past 6 months Communist propaganda and its adherents in the Middle East have intensified their efforts to distort the purposes of the resolution and to depreciate the contribution it has made to the creation of more stable conditions in this important part of the world. I am convinced that we must continue to devote major attention in our Middle East policy to assisting the states of the area, on a cooperative basis, in maintaining their independence and integrity. The resolution forcefully embodies the purpose of promoting these means of achieving international peace and stability in the Middle East.

DWIGHT D. EISENHOWER.

THE WHITE HOUSE, *March 5, 1958.*

PROGRESS IN FURTHERANCE OF THE RESOLUTION, JULY 1 TO DECEMBER 31, 1957

The policy embodied in Joint Resolution 117 to promote peace and stability in the Middle East, approved by the

[1] House Document 349, 85th Cong., 2d Sess.
[2] *Documents on American Foreign Relations, 1957,* pp. 206-207.
[3] *Ibid.,* pp. 211-218.

President on March 9, 1957, continues to be a cornerstone of United States foreign policy in this vital area.

The resolution proclaims the intention of the United States to assist nations in the general area of the Middle East to maintain their independence. Its continuing, central purpose is to leave no possibility of miscalculation in the minds of potential Communist or Communist-controlled aggressors as to the results of aggressive action on their part.

In the 15 countries of the Middle East which Ambassador Richards and his delegation visited in March and April of 1957,[4] and where the Ambassador expounded the principles and motives of the policy and answered many probing questions, a broader understanding of, and a greater confidence in, the aims and purposes of the United States has been achieved. The commitments for assistance made by Ambassador Richards reinforced the internal strength of the nations which welcomed our assistance.

The determination of the United States, explicit in the resolution, that it is prepared to use armed forces, if requested, to render assistance in the event of armed Communist aggression in the Middle East, has been particularly heartening to the nations which have joined together in the Baghdad Pact. It has unquestionably contributed to the steadfastness with which they, and other states of the Near East, resisted the campaign of intimidation and disruption conducted by the Soviet Union and its agents.

The full force of the Communist propaganda apparatus has been brought to bear throughout the Middle East in an attempt to portray the resolution as an effort by the United States to extend its domination over the area, to split the Arab world, and to reinstate a form of colonialism. Misunderstanding concerning the specific purposes of the resolution, and of United States policy in general, have been created affecting the attitudes of even non-Communist elements. The recent Afro-Asian Conference in Cairo, where the Communists played such a major role, asserted, in a resolution on "Imperialism," that "both the Baghdad Pact and the Eisenhower doctrine interfere with the independence of the Arab countries, infringe on their sovereignty, and endanger their security."

This propaganda assault has been coupled with a more tangible campaign on the part of the Soviet Union and its satellites to penetrate and expand their influence in the area

[4] *Ibid.*, pp. 208-210.

through economic and military assistance. By seeking to create the impression, through initially generous offers, that Soviet aid is free from all conditions and political "strings," the Soviet bloc has attempted to discredit the constructive efforts of the United States and other free nations and to pose as the disinterested partisan of the legitimate economic and political aspirations of the countries of the Middle East.

The task of those in the Middle East who courageously strive to preserve their freedom, independence, and security in the face of these Soviet activities is not an easy one. The political, social, and economic needs and problems of the area are manifold and complex. The new nations of the Middle East are sensitive to the echoes of the past colonial relationships. By the exercise of diplomatic skill, by patient and persistent efforts to reach understanding on the common objective, and by imaginative and vigorous action through our assistance programs, we can hope, with the continuing support of the Congress, to achieve the resolution's goal of promoting peace and stability in the Middle East.

ECONOMIC AND MILITARY ASSISTANCE EXTENDED IN FURTHERANCE OF THE RESOLUTION

The joint resolution authorized the President to cooperate in programs of economic and military assistance with any nation or group of nations in the general area of the Middle East desiring such aid to develop the strength necessary to preserve their integrity and national independence. Section 3 of the resolution contained special authorization to utilize not to exceed $200 million from funds previously appropriated to carry out the provisions of the Mutual Security Act of 1954, as amended, in furtherance of the purposes of the resolution.

Section 3 of the resolution was particularly useful to Ambassador Richards in initiating action in behalf of those countries desiring assistance, and enabled effective use to be made of appropriated funds. During the 6 months ending December 31, 1957, the regular authorities of the Mutual Security Act, and funds appropriated pursuant thereto, were used to implement further the general purposes of sections 1 and 2 of the resolution.

1. *Economic Assistance*

A total of $123 million of funds available under the Mutual Security Act for the fiscal year of 1957 was committed for nonmilitary-aid programs in implementation of the joint resolution. Of this amount, $67.9 million was committed by Ambassador Richards, $23.4 million being obligated under the special authority of section 3, and $44.5 million[5] under the regular authority of the Mutual Security Act. In addition, economic assistance in the amount of $55.1 million was obligated by ICA for Middle East programs not arranged by Ambassador Richards but which required the authority of section 3. If this special authority had not been available, most of these Middle East programs could not have been initiated. The details of these various commitments have previously been reported to the appropriate committees of the Congress.

During the 6 months ending December 31, 1957, prompt and positive action was taken to carry out all commitments for economic assistance made under the resolution. Materials have already been delivered or are in process of delivery; and new projects have been undertaken or existing ones advanced.

2. *Military Assistance*

Although there was a marked intensification of the Soviet Communist effort, during the second half of 1957, to penetrate and subvert states of the Middle East, it was not necessary to invoke the final provision of section 2 of the resolution. This enables the United States, upon determination by the President of the necessity thereof, to render armed assistance to any nation requesting it in the defense of its independence and integrity against aggression from any country controlled by international communism. The existence of this provision undoubtedly constituted a strong deterrent to overt Communist aggression.

In addition to the broad psychological reassurance imparted by the resolution, the expeditious and tangible fulfillment of the special military assistance commitments, totaling $51.1 million, made by Ambassador Richards contributed not only to the material ability, but to the determination of the nations of the Middle East to resist both internal subversion and external aggression. During the period of July 1

[5] $20 million of this amount, which could not be obligated prior to the end of fiscal 1957 because of unforeseen legal and technical difficulties, was reappropriated under the fiscal year 1958 mutual security program and is currently in process of obligation following successful negotiations with the country concerned. [Footnote in original.]

to December 31, 1957, virtually all of the items of equipment represented by these commitments, with the exception of some long lead-time items and certain material being provided under offshore procurement, were delivered, and have already been integrated into the armed forces of the recipient countries. The authority of section 2 of the resolution made rapid military aid of this kind feasible, while the underlying sense of purpose and urgency conveyed by the promulgation of the resolution as a whole lent renewed impetus to the current fiscal year 1958 military assistance program. Indeed, in certain urgent cases it resulted in a considerable acceleration of this program.

The decisive role played by the joint resolution in strengthening the nations of the Middle East, through the provision of special and selective military assistance, to resist the insidious and everpresent threat of international communism was of crucial importance during the past year.

ACTION PURSUANT TO SECTION 4 OF THE RESOLUTION

Section 4 of the resolution enjoins the President to continue to furnish facilities and military assistance to the United Nations Emergency Force in the Middle East with a view to maintaining the peace in that region. This assistance has been rendered.

The value of the supplies and equipment made available to the force by the United States on a reimbursable basis through 1957 has totaled approximately $4.5 million. These were financed with funds appropriated to the Department of Defense.

Early in 1957 the United States contributed, as its share of the UNEF assessment of $10 million, some $3.3 million. This was provided out of funds appropriated to the Department of State for contributions to international organizations. The United States has also indicated its willingness to contribute on a matching basis one-half of the $6.5 million of the UNEF's 1957 costs for which the General Assembly had requested contributions, using funds under section 401 (b) of the Mutual Security Act of 1954, as amended. Of this sum, the United States has paid $920,850 to match contributions received from other members of the United Nations. In response to an urgent request from the Secretary General of the United Nations for special assistance to meet the deficit incurred for UNEF's 1957 costs, the United States has made a special contribution of $12 million, using $2.25

million of funds under section 401 (b) of the Mutual Security
Act of 1954, as amended, and $9.75 million of funds under
section 400 (a) of the same act.

B. Crisis in the Middle East.

1. *The Threat to the Security of Lebanon.*

(75) *News Conference Comments by the Secretary
of State (Dulles), May 20, 1958.*[1]

* * *

*Q. Mr. Secretary, during the earlier phases of the Lebanese
crisis there seemed to be some non-understanding as to
whether the Eisenhower doctrine applied in this case. However, it seems that later we came to feel that we liked Lebanon, although the Eisenhower doctrine probably did not
specifically apply, and therefore would aid her if requested.
I wonder if you could clear up this confusion that some of
us have, sir?*

A. I suppose that by the Eisenhower doctrine you refer
to the Middle East resolution that was adopted by the Congress. That resolution contains several provisions. It is not
just one thing. It authorizes the United States to assist economically and militarily nations which want such assistance
in order to preserve their independence. It says that the independence and integrity of these nations of the Middle
East is vital to world peace and the national interest of the
United States. It says that, if they are attacked from a country
under the control of international communism, then the
President is authorized, upon request, to send forces to resist
that attack.

Now we do not consider under the present state of affairs
that there is likely to be an attack, an armed attack, from
a country which we would consider under the control of
international communism. That doesn't mean, however, that
there is nothing that can be done. There is the provision of
the Middle East resolution which says that the independence
of these countries is vital to peace and the national interest
of the United States. That is certainly a mandate to do something if we think that our peace and vital interests are endangered from any quarter.

There is the basic right, and almost duty, at the request or

[1] *Department of State Bulletin*, v. 38 (June 9, 1958), pp. 945 and 948.

with the consent of a government, to assist in the protection of American life and property. There is the program of military assistance which we render to many countries, including Lebanon, in terms of giving them equipment and certain measures of military training and techniques and helping them train technicians to use this equipment. So that there are a number of areas of possible action if the situation calls for it.

I would say that we are not anxious to have a situation which would be in any sense a pretext for introducing American forces into the area. We hope and believe that that will not be called for, and the situation, to date, does not suggest that it would be called for.

* * *

Q. Mr. Secretary, the last part of our 1950 Tripartite Declaration on the Middle East also mentions the independence and territorial integrity of the nations of the area.[2] Do you regard that as applicable also as part of the Eisenhower doctrine?

A. We do regard it as applicable. We don't regard it as powerful, you might say, as the phrase in the Middle East resolution that I referred to, because that Tripartite Declaration has never had specific congressional approval. We have always considered that whether action under that, or another declaration that President Eisenhower made, I think, in '56, dealing with these problems, that the constitutional power of the President to act under those was not as great as though they had received express congressional approval.[3] The Middle East resolution has received congressional approval, and therefore we consider that it is a stronger mandate and it gives the President a greater authority than if it would purely have been a declaration by the President himself.

* * *

Q. You spoke about what the Government of Lebanon considers serious evidence that there has been interference by the U.A.R. And yet there has been no appeal at this time, sir, to the Security Council. Could you tell us whether, in view of this outside interference, we are suggesting to the Government of the United Arab Republic that it should stop this outside interference?

[2] *Documents on American Foreign Relations, 1950,* pp. 659-662.
[3] *Ibid., 1956,* pp. 282-283.

A. My impression is that the United States considers that it is up to the Government of Lebanon to try to get the U.A.R. to stop. And while the Government of Lebanon has talked with us about the matter and about possible action in the United Nations, it has made no decision on that point as yet.

* * *

(76) *Letter from the Representative of Lebanon to the United Nations (Azkoul) to the President of the Security Council, May 22, 1958.*[4]

Upon instructions from my Government, I have the honour to request you, in your capacity as President of the Security Council, to call an urgent meeting of the Council to consider the following question:

"Complaint by Lebanon in respect of a situation arising from the intervention of the United Arab Republic in the internal affairs of Lebanon, the continuance of which is likely to endanger the maintenance of international peace and security."

The said intervention consists *inter alia* of the following acts: the infiltration of armed bands from Syria into Lebanon, the destruction of Lebanese life and property by such bands, the participation of United Arab Republic nationals in acts of terrorism and rebellion against the established authorities in Lebanon, the supply of arms from Syria to individuals and bands in Lebanon rebelling against the established authorities, and the waging of a violent radio and press campaign in the United Arab Republic calling for strikes, demonstrations and the overthrow of the established authorities in Lebanon, and through other provocative acts.

Please accept, etc.

(Signed) Karim Azkoul
Permanent Representative of
Lebanon to the United Nations

(77) *Resolution of the United Nations Security Council, Adopted June 11, 1958.*[5]

The Security Council,

Having heard the charges of the representative of Lebanon concerning interference by the United Arab Republic in the

[4] United Nations Document S/4007, dated May 23, 1958.
[5] United Nations Document S/4023, dated June 11, 1958.

internal affairs of Lebanon and the reply of the representative of the United Arab Republic,

Decides to dispatch urgently an observation group to proceed to Lebanon so as to ensure that there is no illegal infiltration of personnel or supply of arms or other materiel across the Lebanese borders;

Authorizes the Secretary-General to take the necessary steps to that end;

Requests the observation group to keep the Security Council currently informed through the Secretary-General.[6]

(78) *News Conference Comments by the Secretary of State (Dulles), June 17, 1958.*[7]

Q. Mr. Secretary, can you give us your assessment of the situation in Lebanon, and whether or not any action seems to be required under the circumstances?

A. The situation in Lebanon is, obviously, one which causes very considerable anxiety to those who believe in the independence and integrity of the countries in the Middle East. That, as you will recall, was proclaimed as of vital interest to the United States by a Middle East resolution. I would also recall the fact that, even though at the moment the disturbance assumes, in part at least, the character of a civil disturbance, it is covered by the United Nations resolution of 1949 on indirect aggression.[8] This denounces the fomenting from without of civil strife. Therefore we watch the situation with concern.

The events are moving on a day-to-day, hour-to-hour basis, and I would not feel that it was wise, or I would be on solid ground, in discussing them in detail at this time.

Q. Can you say, sir, what our attitude is toward a larger U.N. force in the area, possibly on the Syrian-Lebanese border?

A. I believe that the representatives of the United Nations who have already arrived there have come to the conclusion that it would be necessary to have a force somewhat larger in number and somewhat different in composition than had been anticipated at first. It may have to be larger, and it may

---

[6] For the reports of the United Nations observation group in Lebanon (UNOGIL) see United Nations Documents S/4040, dated July 3, 1958; S/4051, dated July 16, 1958; S/4052, dated July 17, 1958; S/4069, dated July 30, 1958; S/4085, dated August 14, 1958; S/4100, dated September 29, 1958.

[7] *Department of State Bulletin*, v. 39 (July 7, 1958), p. 8.

[8] *Documents on American Foreign Relations, 1949*, pp. 306-307.

also have to have greater elements of mobility than had been originally contemplated. I believe that that is being sympathetically considered by the Secretary-General. He himself, I think, plans to go out to the area today. The United States would be disposed to support, as a member of the United Nations, any action along those lines which commended itself to the Secretary-General.

(79) News Conference Comments by the Secretary of State (Dulles), July 1, 1958.[9]

*   *   *

Q. Mr. Secretary, Mr. Chamoun of Lebanon is quoted this morning as saying that, if the United Nations action fails, he would appeal to friends of Lebanon and the West for direct military assistance under article 51 of the United Nations Charter. Could you define for us under what circumstances the United States would be willing to render direct military assistance to Lebanon?

A. I will make a reply to your question, although I am not going to attempt to define in detail all the circumstances under which we might respond. I would say this: The normal way to deal with these problems is through the processes of the United Nations, and the Government of Lebanon initiated such a process when it took its case to the Security Council and obtained the resolution for observation under which the Secretary-General is now acting and under which, I believe, some results at least are being obtained.

Now we have never believed that you could only act under such processes; indeed, article 51 was put into the charter to meet the contingency that it might be impractical, because of the veto power or otherwise, to obtain appropriate action from the United Nations. Article 51, as you will recall, talks about collective defense if an armed attack occurs. Now we do not think that the words "armed attack" preclude treating as such an armed revolution which is fomented from abroad, aided and assisted from abroad. Indeed you will recall perhaps in the report on the North Atlantic Treaty that the Senate Foreign Relations Committee indicated that that kind of a civil disturbance could be treated as an armed attack. In our Japanese security treaty that is expressly spelled out. However, we believe that the best way to deal with these things is through the processes of the United Nations. We do

[9] *Department of State Bulletin,* v. 39 (July 21, 1958), pp. 105-106.

not think it is proper yet to conclude that those processes have failed or will fail. If and when we had to reach that conclusion, then there would be a new situation which we would have to deal with in the light of the new circumstances at the time.

Q. Mr. Secretary, have the United Nations observers in Lebanon any authority or power to halt, to arrest, to seize, or to otherwise physically interfere with the infiltrations?

A. No. They are there to observe and to report. It is believed that the very fact that they are there in that capacity will have a practical effect in stopping movements across the border. Of course that is somewhat diminished by the fact that the borders are not readily accessible at the present time, and it is hard to know just exactly what is going on. But to answer your precise question—it is not my understanding that the present force there is in any sense a police force where they use armed force. That may be a second stage.

Q. Mr. Secretary, the Lebanese Government, through Mr. Chamoun and through its Foreign Minister, has in a variety of cases said it would be desirable for the United Nations to put enough people into Lebanon to seal off the border. What is our view toward such an operation?

A. I doubt whether it is practical to carry on an operation of that magnitude, and I think that perhaps that is not required. But I would not want to pass any final judgment on that until I saw what kind of case the Government of Lebanon could make if they were to make such a request of the Security Council. So far they haven't made it, and I would not want to prejudge our action before we knew just what kind of case they could make out.

Q. Mr. Secretary, keeping in mind the role we played in discouraging, at least, the invasion of Suez, is it realistic to think that we would participate in any kind of military intervention in Lebanon except under the most extreme circumstances?

A. I don't think that there is any analogy whatsoever between the situation in Lebanon, where the lawful Government is calling for assistance, and the Suez case where the armed intervention was against the will of the government concerned. There is no parallel whatever between the two cases. We do believe that the presence in Lebanon of foreign troops, however justifiable—and it is thoroughly justifiable from a legal and international-law standpoint—is not as good a solution as for the Lebanese to find a solution themselves. It would be, as you put it, a sort of measure of last resort.

2. Revolution in Iraq.

(80) Proclamation by the Revolutionary Government, July 14, 1958.[10]

With the aid of God Almighty and the support of the people and the armed services, we have liberated the country from the domination of a corrupt group which was installed by imperialism to lull the people.

The army is yours. It has already achieved your wish and got rid of tyrants who played with the rights of the people. It is your duty to support it. Victory can be achieved only through the organization of the army, and by defending it against imperialist conspiracies.

We appeal to the people to inform the authorities of all traitors and corrupt persons so that we may get rid of them. We ask you to be united in an effort to destroy those criminals and to rid the country of their evils.

We call on you to be calm and to uphold discipline, unity and cooperation in the interests of the country.

Be confident that we shall continue to work for you. Power will be given to a government inspired by the people.

There will be an Iraqi republic which will preserve Iraqi unity and maintain brotherly ties with the other Arab countries and fulfill all obligations and treaties which are in the interests of the country and will carry out the principles of the Bandung conference and the United Nations Charter.

This new national government will now be called the Iraqi Republic.

A council of sovereignty will carry out presidential duties until there is a general plebiscite.

3. Dispatch of United States Troops to Lebanon.

(81) Statement by the President, July 15, 1958.[11]

Yesterday morning, I received from President Chamoun of Lebanon an urgent plea that some United States forces be stationed in Lebanon to help maintain security and to evidence the concern of the United States for the integrity and independence of Lebanon. President Chamoun's appeal was

[10] New York Times, July 15, 1958.
[11] Department of State Bulletin, v. 39 (August 4, 1958), pp. 181-182.

made with the concurrence of all of the members of the Lebanese Cabinet.

President Chamoun made clear that he considered an immediate United States response imperative if Lebanon's independence, already menaced from without, were to be preserved in the face of the grave developments which occurred yesterday in Baghdad whereby the lawful government was violently overthrown and many of its members martyred.

In response to this appeal from the government of Lebanon, the United States has dispatched a contingent of United States forces to Lebanon to protect American lives and by their presence there to encourage the Lebanese government in defense of Lebanese sovereignty and integrity. These forces have not been sent as any act of war. They will demonstrate the concern of the United States for the independence and integrity of Lebanon, which we deem vital to the national interest and world peace. Our concern will also be shown by economic assistance. We shall act in accordance with these legitimate concerns.

The United States, this morning, will report its action to an emergency meeting of the United Nations Security Council.[12] As the United Nations charter recognizes, there is an inherent right of collective self-defense. In conformity with the spirit of the charter, the United States is reporting the measures taken by it to the Security Council of the United Nations, making clear that these measures will be terminated as soon as the Security Council has itself taken the measures necessary to maintain international peace and security.

The United States believes that the United Nations can and should take measures which are adequate to preserve the independence and integrity of Lebanon. It is apparent, however, that in the face of the tragic and shocking events that are occurring nearby, more will be required than the team of United Nations observers now in Lebanon. Therefore, the United States will support in the United Nations measures which seem to be adequate to meet the new situation and which will enable the United States forces promptly to be withdrawn.

Lebanon is a small peace-loving state with which the United States has traditionally had the most friendly relations. There are in Lebanon about 2,500 Americans and we cannot, consistently with our historic relations and with the principles of the United Nations, stand idly by when Lebanon

[12] *Ibid.*, pp. 186-188.

appeals itself for evidence of our concern and when Lebanon may not be able to preserve internal order and to defend itself against indirect aggression.

(82) Message of the President to the Congress, July 15, 1958.[13]

To the Congress of the United States:

On July 14, 1958, I received an urgent request from the President of the Republic of Lebanon that some United States forces be stationed in Lebanon. President Chamoun stated that without an immediate showing of United States support, the Government of Lebanon would be unable to survive. This request by President Chamoun was made with the concurrence of all the members of the Lebanese Cabinet. I have replied that we would do this and a contingent of United States Marines has now arrived in Lebanon. This initial dispatch of troops will be augmented as required. United States forces will be withdrawn as rapidly as circumstances permit.

Simultaneously, I requested that an urgent meeting of the United Nations Security Council be held on July 15, 1958. At that meeting, the permanent representative of the United States reported to the Council the action which this Government has taken. He also expressed the hope that the United Nations could soon take further effective measures to meet more fully the situation in Lebanon. We will continue to support the United Nations to this end.

United States forces are being sent to Lebanon to protect American lives and by their presence to assist the Government of Lebanon in the preservation of Lebanon's territorial integrity and independence, which have been deemed vital to United States national interests and world peace.

About 2 months ago a violent insurrection broke out in Lebanon, particularly along the border with Syria which, with Egypt, forms the United Arab Republic. This revolt was encouraged and strongly backed by the official Cairo, Damascus, and Soviet radios which broadcast to Lebanon in the Arabic language. The insurrection was further supported by sizable amounts of arms, ammunition, and money and by personnel infiltrated from Syria to fight against the lawful authorities. The avowed purpose of these activities was to overthrow the legally constituted Government of Lebanon

[13] House Document 422, 85th Cong., 2d Sess.

and to install by violence a government which would subordinate the independence of Lebanon to the policies of the United Arab Republic.

Lebanon referred this situation to the United Nations Security Council.[14] In view of the international implications of what was occurring in Lebanon, the Security Council on June 11, 1958, decided to send observers into Lebanon for the purpose of insuring that further outside assistance to the insurrection would cease. The Secretary General of the United Nations subsequently undertook a mission to the area to reinforce the work of the observers.

It was our belief that the efforts of the Secretary General and of the United Nations observers were helpful in reducing further aid in terms of personnel and military equipment from across the frontiers of Lebanon. There was a basis for hope that the situation might be moving toward a peaceful solution, consonant with the continuing integrity of Lebanon, and that the aspect of indirect aggression from without was being brought under control.

The situation was radically changed, however, on July 14, when there was a violent outbreak in Baghdad, in nearby Iraq. Elements in Iraq strongly sympathetic to the United Arab Republic seem to have murdered or driven from office individuals comprising the lawful Government of that country. We do not yet know in detail to what extent they have succeeded. We do have reliable information that important Iraqi leaders have been murdered.

We share with the Government of Lebanon the view that these events in Iraq demonstrate a ruthlessness of aggressive purpose which tiny Lebanon cannot combat without further evidence of support from other friendly nations.

After the most detailed consideration, I have concluded that, given the developments in Iraq, the measures thus far taken by the United Nations Security Council are not sufficient to preserve the independence and integrity of Lebanon. I have considered, furthermore, the question of our responsibility to protect and safeguard American citizens in Lebanon of whom there are about 2,500. Pending the taking of adequate measures by the United Nations, the United States will be acting pursuant to what the United Nations Charter recognizes is an inherent right—the right of all nations to work together and to seek help when necessary to preserve their independence. I repeat that we wish to withdraw our

[14] Document 76, above.

forces as soon as the United Nations has taken further effective steps designed to safeguard Lebanese independence.

It is clear that events which have been occurring in Lebanon represent indirect aggression from without, and that such aggression endangers the independence and integrity of Lebanon.

It is recognized that the step now being taken may have serious consequences. I have, however, come to the considered and sober conclusion that despite the risks involved this action is required to support the principles of justice and international law upon which peace and a stable international order depend.

Our Government has acted in response to an appeal for help from a small and peaceful nation which has long had ties of closest friendship with the United States. Readiness to help a friend in need is an admirable characteristic of the American people, and I am, in this message, informing the Congress of the reasons why I believe that the United States could not in honor stand idly by in this hour of Lebanon's grave peril. As we act at the request of a friendly government to help it to preserve its independence and to preserve law and order which will protect American lives, we are acting to reaffirm and strengthen principles upon which the safety and security of the United States depend.

Dwight D. Eisenhower

The White House, *July 15, 1958.*

(83) *Radio-TV Address by the President, July 15, 1958.*[15]

Yesterday was a day of grave developments in the Middle East. In Iraq a highly organized military blow struck down the duly constituted Government and attempted to put in its place a committee of Army officers. The attack was conducted with great brutality. Many of the leading personalities were beaten to death or hanged and their bodies dragged through the streets.

At about the same time there was discovered a highly organized plot to overthrow the lawful Government of Jordan.

Warned and alarmed by these developments, President Chamoun of Lebanon sent me an urgent plea that the United States station some military units in Lebanon to evidence our

[15] *Department of State Bulletin,* v. 39 (August 4, 1958), pp. 183-186.

concern for the independence of Lebanon, that little country which itself has for about 2 months been subjected to civil strife. This has been actively fomented by Soviet and Cairo broadcasts and abetted and aided by substantial amounts of arms, money, and personnel infiltrated into Lebanon across the Syrian border.

President Chamoun stated that without an immediate show of United States support the Government of Lebanon would be unable to survive against the forces which had been set loose in the area.

The plea of President Chamoun was supported by the unanimous action of the Lebanese Cabinet.

After giving this plea earnest thought and after taking advice from leaders of both the executive and congressional branches of the Government, I decided to comply with the plea of the Government of Lebanon. A few hours ago a battalion of United States Marines landed and took up stations in and about the city of Beirut.

The mission of these forces is to protect American lives—there are about 2,500 Americans in Lebanon—and by their presence to assist the Government of Lebanon to preserve its territorial integrity and political independence.

The United States does not, of course, intend to replace the United Nations, which has a primary responsibility to maintain international peace and security. We reacted as we did within a matter of hours because the situation was such that only prompt action would suffice. We have, however, with equal promptness moved in the United Nations. This morning there was held at our request an emergency meeting of the United Nations Security Council. At this meeting we reported the action which we had taken. We stated the reasons therefor. We expressed the hope that the United Nations would itself take measures which would be adequate to preserve the independence of Lebanon and permit of the early withdrawal of the United States forces.

The Situation in Lebanon

I should like now to take a few minutes to explain the situation in Lebanon.

Lebanon is a small country, a little less than the size of Connecticut, with a population of about 1½ million. It has always had close and friendly relations with the United States. Many of you no doubt have heard of the American University at Beirut, which has a distinguished record. Lebanon has been a prosperous, peaceful country, thriving on trade largely with the West. A little over a year ago there were general elections, held in an atmosphere of total calm, which resulted in the establishment, by an overwhelming popular vote, of the present Parliament for a period of 4 years. The term of the President, however, is of a different duration and would normally expire next September. The President, Mr. Chamoun, has made clear that he does not seek reelection.

When the attacks on the Government of Lebanon began to occur, it took the matter to the United Nations Security Council, pointing out that Lebanon was the victim of indirect aggression from without. As a result, the Security Council sent observers to Lebanon in the hope of thereby insuring that hostile intervention would cease. Secretary-General Hammarskjold undertook a mission to the area to reinforce the work of the observers.

We believe that his efforts and those of the United Nations observers were helpful. They could not eliminate arms or ammunition or remove persons already sent into Lebanon. But we believe they did reduce such aid from across the border. It seemed, last week, that the situation was moving toward a peaceful solution which would preserve the integrity of Lebanon and end indirect aggression from without.

Those hopes were, however, dashed by the events of yesterday in Iraq and Jordan. These events demonstrate a scope of aggressive purpose which tiny Lebanon could not combat without further evidence of support. That is why Lebanon's request for troops from the United States was made. That is why we have responded to that request.

Some will ask, does the stationing of some United States troops in Lebanon involve any interference in the internal affairs of Lebanon? The clear answer is "no."

First of all, we have acted at the urgent plea of the Government of Lebanon, a Government which has been freely elected by the people only a little over a year ago. It is entitled, as are we, to join in measures of collective security for self-defense. Such action, the United Nations Charter recognizes, is an "inherent right."

Pattern of Conquest by Indirect Aggression

In the second place what we now see in the Middle East is the same pattern of conquest with which we became familiar during the period of 1945 to 1950. This involves taking over a nation by means of indirect aggression; that is, under the cover of a fomented civil strife the purpose is to put into domestic control those whose real loyalty is to the aggressor.

It was by such means that the Communists attempted to take over Greece in 1947. That effort was thwarted by the Truman Doctrine.

It was by such means that the Communists took over Czechoslovakia in 1948.

It was by such means that the Communists took over the mainland of China in 1949.

It was by such means that the Communists attempted to take over Korea and Indochina, beginning in 1950.

You will remember at the time of the Korean war that the Soviet Government claimed that this was merely a civil war, because the only attack was by north Koreans upon south Koreans. But all the world knew that the north Koreans were armed, equipped, and directed from without for the purpose of aggression.

This means of conquest was denounced by the United Nations General Assembly when it adopted in November 1950 its resolution entitled "Peace Through Deeds." [16] It thereby called upon every nation to refrain from "fomenting civil strife in the interest of a foreign power" and denounced such action as "the gravest of all crimes against peace and security throughout the world."

We had hoped that these threats to the peace and to the independence and integrity of small nations had come to an end. Unhappily, now they reappear. Lebanon was selected to become a victim.

Last year the Congress of the United States joined with the President to declare that "the United States regards as vital to the national interest and world peace the preservation of the independence and integrity of the nations of the Middle East."

I believe that the presence of the United States forces now being sent to Lebanon will have a stabilizing effect which will preserve the independence and integrity of Lebanon. It will also afford an increased measure of security to the thousands of Americans who reside in Lebanon.

We know that stability and well-being cannot be achieved purely by military measures. The economy of Lebanon has been gravely strained by civil strife. Foreign trade and tourist traffic have almost come to a standstill. The United States

[16] *Documents on American Foreign Relations, 1950,* p. 187.

stands ready, under its mutual security program, to cooperate with the Government of Lebanon to find ways to restore its shattered economy. Thus we shall help to bring back to Lebanon a peace which is not merely the absence of fighting but the well-being of the people.

The Purpose of the United States

I am well aware of the fact that landing of United States troops in Lebanon could have some serious consequences. That is why this step was taken only after the most serious consideration and broad consultation. I have, however, come to the sober and clear conclusion that the action taken was essential to the welfare of the United States. It was required to support the principles of justice and international law upon which peace and a stable international order depend.

That, and that alone, is the purpose of the United States. We are not actuated by any hope of material gain or by any emotional hostility against any person or any government. Our dedication is to the principles of the United Nations Charter and to the preservation of the independence of every state. That is the basic pledge of the United Nations Charter.

Yet indirect aggression and violence are being promoted in the Near East in clear violation of the provisions of the United Nations Charter.

There can be no peace in the world unless there is fuller dedication to the basic principles of the United Nations Charter. If ever the United States fails to support these principles, the result would be to open the floodgates to direct and indirect aggression throughout the world.

In the 1930's the members of the League of Nations became indifferent to direct and indirect aggression in Europe, Asia, and Africa. The result was to strengthen and stimulate aggressive forces that made World War II inevitable.

The United States is determined that that history shall not now be repeated. We are hopeful that the action which we are taking will both preserve the independence of Lebanon and check international violations which, if they succeeded, would endanger world peace.

We hope that this result will quickly be attained and that our forces can be promptly withdrawn. We must, however, be prepared to meet the situation, whatever be the consequences. We can do so, confident that we strive for a world in which nations, be they great or be they small, can preserve their independence. We are striving for an ideal which is close to the heart of every American and for which in the past many Americans have laid down their lives.

To serve these ideals is also to serve the cause of peace, security, and well-being, not only for us but for all men everywhere.

4. Dispatch of United Kingdom Troops to Jordan.

(84) Statement by the Prime Minister of the United Kingdom (Macmillan), July 17, 1958.[17]

* * *

Within a matter of minutes after the end of the debate yesterday I was given a telegram from Her Majesty's representative in Jordan. This contained the first news we had had that King Hussein and the Prime Minister of Jordan had made a request for the immediate dispatch of British forces to Jordan.

In making this request the King and the Prime Minister said that Jordan was faced with an imminent attempt by the United Arab Republic to create internal disorder and to overthrow the present regime on the pattern of recent events in Iraq.

They went on to say that Jordan's territorial integrity was threatened by the movement of Syrian forces toward her northern frontier and by the infiltration of arms across it. They had information that a *coup* organized by the United Arab Republic would be attempted today.

I asked the Cabinet to meet late last night to consider this request.

From our own sources, we have received up-to-date intelligence which clearly showed that the apprehensions of the Jordan Government were well founded and that an attempt indeed was being organized for today.

The Government accordingly decided to accede to Jordan's request, and British forces are in fact being sent by air to Jordan from Cyprus.

The purpose of this military assistance is to stabilize the situation in Jordan by helping the Jordanian Government to resist aggression and threats to the integrity and independence of their country.

Our troops will be under the orders of the local British

[17] House of Commons, Parliamentary Debates, *Weekly Hansard*, July 11-17, 1958, cols. 1448-1449.

commander, who will act with the agreement of the King and Government of Jordan.

The Jordan Government have made a similar request for help to the United States Government, who are considering it urgently in the light of their other commitments in the area. The British Government decision was taken after full consultation with the United States Government, and our action has the full support and approval of the United States Government.

The decision of the British Government is being reported to the United Nations, and we are making it clear to the United Nations that if arrangements can be made by the Security Council to protect the lawful government of Jordan from the external threat, and so maintain international peace and security, the action which we have taken will be brought to an end.

We have informed the other Commonwealth countries and also the North Atlantic Treaty Organization Council of the action we have taken and the reasons which have led to the Government's decision.

* * *

5. Action by the United Nations Security Council.

(85) *United States Draft Resolution, Vetoed July 18, 1958.*[18]

The Security Council,

Recalling its resolution of 11 June 1958 establishing an Observation Group "to insure that there is no illegal infiltration of personnel or supply of arms or other material across the Lebanese borders,"

Commending the efforts of the Secretary-General and noting with satisfaction the progress made to date and the encouraging achievements reported by the United Nations Observation Group in Lebanon,

Recalling that the "Essentials of Peace" resolution of the General Assembly of 1 December 1949 calls upon States to "refrain from any threats or acts, direct or indirect, aimed at impairing the freedom, independence or integrity of any State, or at fomenting civil strife and subverting the will of the people in any State,"

[18] United Nations Document S/4050/Rev.1, dated July 17, 1958. The resolution was rejected by a vote of 9-1 (USSR)-1 (Sweden).

Recalling that the "Peace Through Deeds" resolution of the General Assembly of 18 November 1950 condemned "intervention of a State in the internal affairs of another State for the purpose of changing its legally established government by the threat or use of force" and solemnly reaffirms that "whatever weapons used, any aggression, whether committed openly, or by fomenting civil strife in the interest of a foreign Power, or otherwise, is the gravest of all crimes against peace and security throughout the world,"

Noting the statement of the representative of Lebanon that infiltration of arms and personnel is continuing and the territorial integrity and independence of Lebanon are being threatened, that the Government of Lebanon in the exercise of the right of self-defence had temporarily requested direct assistance of friendly countries, and that the Government of Lebanon requested further assistance from the Security Council to uphold its integrity and independence,

Noting the statement of the representative of the United States regarding the provision of assistance by the United States to the Government of Lebanon at its request to help maintain the territorial and political independence of Lebanon,

Noting further the statement of the United States representative that United States forces will remain in Lebanon "only until the United Nations itself is able to assume the necessary responsibility to ensure the continued independence of Lebanon" or the danger is otherwise terminated,

1. *Invites* the United Nations Observation Group in Lebanon to continue to develop its activities pursuant to the Security Council resolution of 11 June 1958;

2. *Requests* the Secretary-General immediately to consult the Government of Lebanon and other Member States as appropriate with a view to making arrangements for additional measures, including the contribution and use of contingents, as may be necessary to protect the territorial integrity and independence of Lebanon and to ensure that there is no illegal infiltration of personnel or supply of arms or other material across the Lebanese borders;

3. *Calls upon* all Governments concerned to co-operate fully in the implementation of this resolution;

4. *Calls* for the immediate cessation of all illegal infiltration of personnel or supply of arms or other material across the Lebanese borders, as well as attacks upon the Govern-

ment of Lebanon by government-controlled radio and other information media calculated to stimulate disorders;

5. *Requests* the Secretary-General to report to the Security Council as appropriate.

(86) *Japanese Draft Resolution, Vetoed July 22, 1958.*[19]

The Security Council,

Having further heard the charges of the representative of Lebanon concerning interference by the United Arab Republic in the internal affairs of Lebanon and the reply of the representative of the United Arab Republic,

1. *Request* the Secretary-General to make arrangements forthwith for such measures, in addition to those envisaged by the resolution of 11 June 1958, as he may consider necessary in the light of the present circumstances, with a view to enabling the United Nations to fulfill the general purposes established in that resolution, and which will, in accordance with the Charter, serve to ensure the territorial integrity and political independence of Lebanon, so as to make possible the withdrawal of United States forces from Lebanon;

2. *Requests* the Secretary-General to report to the Security Council on the arrangements made;

3. *Calls upon* the Governments concerned to co-operate fully in the implementation of this resolution.

6. Exchange of Correspondence between the President and the President of Lebanon (Chamoun).

(87) *Letter from the President of Lebanon (Chamoun), July 21, 1958.*[20]

DEAR MR. PRESIDENT: I wish to express to you on my own personal behalf and on behalf of Lebanon, and through you to the Government and people of the United States, our profound gratitude for responding to my call for help, based on a decision by the legitimate Government of Lebanon, through the landing of United States forces in Lebanon to help us defend our independence and integrity in conformity with Aricle 51 of the United Nations Charter.

I want to assure you, Mr. President, that we are both happy and honored to find ourselves side by side with the

[19] United Nations Document S/4055/Rev.1, dated July 21, 1958.
[20] *Department of State Bulletin*, v. 39 (August 11, 1958), p. 235.

great American nation defending not only our independence and integrity against direct aggression, but the high principles in which the free world believes and by which it lives.

Faithfully yours,

CAMILLE CHAMOUN

(88) *Letter from the President, July 25, 1958.*[21]

JULY 25, 1958

DEAR MR. PRESIDENT: I wish to thank you for your message of July 21 in which you express personally and on behalf of Lebanon gratitude for the United States' affirmative response to Lebanon's call for assistance. The purpose of our action was to help your country preserve its independence, in accord with the inherent right of nations to cooperate for self-defense. Our countries have long enjoyed close and friendly relations, and I look forward to further cooperation between the American people and the people of Lebanon in furthering the principles and purposes of the United Nations Charter.

Sincerely,

DWIGHT D. EISENHOWER

7. *Exchange of Correspondence Among the Heads of Government of the US, UK, France and the USSR Concerning the Convocation of a Summit Meeting on Middle East Problems.*

(89) *Letter from the Chairman of the Council of Ministers of the USSR (Khrushchev) to the President, July 19, 1958.*[22]

DEAR MR. PRESIDENT: The course of the recent events shows that we are now living through one of the most responsible moments of history, that the world has been placed on the brink of a catastrophe. Alarm is gripping the minds of people in all continents, popular masses are coming into motion, realizing as they do that a war conflagration, wherever it begins, may spread to all the world.

As allies in past battles, we know, although in different degrees, what the blood and ruins of the past world war were like. We realize what horrors a new war can bring to mankind, and we have no moral right to play with fire in the

[21] *Ibid.*
[22] *Ibid.*, pp. 231-233.

powder magazine into which the world has been turned because of the arms race.

Under these conditions the armed intervention started by the United States in Lebanon, and then by Britain in Jordan, and the danger of an intervention looming large over Iraq and all the states of the Arab world, may bring about extremely dangerous and unpredictable consequences, can set off a chain reaction which it would be impossible to arrest.

We address you not from positions of intimidation, but from positions of reason. If there can be any talk of intimidation, it should be referred to the irresponsible military leaders of the United States, such as the commander of the American Sixth Fleet, who are now diligently engaged in it. With a zest worthy of a better cause, he pronounces such provocative speeches that if he were a citizen of countries which have prohibited military propaganda, he would have been arraigned before a court, or submitted to a medical check-up and placed in a madhouse because such statements can be made only by a criminal or a person out of his senses. The laurels of this naval commander have deprived of sleep the Secretary for Defense also.

We know that the United States has atomic and hydrogen bombs, we know that you have an air force and navy. But you are also well aware that the Soviet Union, too, possesses atomic and hydrogen bombs, an air force and a navy, plus ballistic missiles of all types, including intercontinental ones. However, we believe that at this momentous hour it would be more reasonable not to bring the heated atmosphere to a boiling point, it is sufficiently inflammable as it is. The statesmen of countries must seek for solutions not by means of fanning war psychosis, but reasonably and calmly, so as to rule out war and insure world peace.

What do the United States and Great Britain want to achieve by landing their forces in Lebanon and Jordan?

You explain the armed intervention in Lebanon by President Chamoun's request to help him combat aggression. But an internal struggle is under way in Lebanon, and the events in that country prior to the landing of the American troops could in no way be classed as direct or indirect aggression by other states, a fact confirmed by the United Nations observers and the United Nations Secretary General. An internal struggle was going on there and you yourself have confirmed this.

The principle of noninterference of other states in the internal strife going on in this or that country is a generally recognized standard of international law. It is not for me to tell you that the American people and their government categorically objected in the past to foreign interference in the American civil war, in the struggle between the South and the North. I do not even mention the fact that in the case of Lebanon, the Lebanese President's appeal to the United States was not supported by the Parliament of that country, and the speaker of Parliament strongly protested against the American armed intervention. Consequently, the "invitation" sent by Chamoun has no constitutional power.

The same situation prevails in Jordan, where the British troops have been sent not to uphold the interests of the people and the country, but to save the monarchy. The rulers of Lebanon and Jordan, who have lost the support of the people in their countries, and who cannot rely on their armies which refuse to support anti-national regimes, have decided to look for cover in the shadow of the Anglo-American guns, to lean back on the interventionist forces. But history still does not know any case when the throne and government could be propped up by bayonets, particularly foreign ones. The twentieth century leaves no illusions on this score.

The military intervention of the United States and Britain in Lebanon and Jordan has been undertaken at the request of irresponsible rulers who do not enjoy the support of their peoples and act against their will. And such a request was enough for American and British troops to be sent to Lebanon and Jordan in circumvention of the United Nations, which was informed post factum of this aggressive act.

It is also said that the American and British troops have invaded Lebanon and Jordan to defend the lives and property of American and British citizens there. But this is a very old trick of the colonialists. It will mislead no one, the more so because everyone knows that no foreigners, including Americans and Britons, were hurt or threatened either in Lebanon or Jordan.

You, Mr. President, often make public statements in support of the United Nations, but by their actions in Lebanon and Jordan the governments of the United States and Great Britain are dealing a body blow at this international organization. At such a momentous hour in the life of the peoples, the United Nations has actually been pushed out of the way with the bayonets of the American and British forces.

The aggressors are now playing with fire. It is always easier to start a fire than to put it out. But once kindled, it is better put out at the very beginning than when the flame flares up and sets afire the neighboring homes. The most correct solution in the present conditions would be to withdraw the occupationist forces immediately from the Middle East and to give the peoples of this area an opportunity to decide their destiny for themselves.

At this grim period of history, when we cannot afford to wait another minute, the Soviet Union which has always come out for world peace, against war, for peaceful coexistence, cannot remain indifferent to what is happening in the Middle East, next to its borders. The Soviet Union cannot keep aloof when the question of war or peace is being decided.

This is why the Government of the Soviet Union proposes to call immediately a conference of the heads of government of the U.S.S.R., the United States, Britain, France and India, with the participation of the United Nations Secretary General, to take urgent measures to stem the beginning military conflict.

We propose to meet on any day, at any hour, the sooner the better. You are perfectly aware that history has left us a small margin in which to avert war, to prevent the annihilation of many millions of people, to prevent the destruction of great material and cultural values.

In its statements the Government of the Soviet Union has set forth sufficiently clearly its views regarding the peaceful solution of urgent Middle Eastern problems. The Soviet Union believes that a solution can and must be found conforming to the vital interests of the Middle Eastern peoples, insuring their sovereign rights, and with due regard for the interests of all states associated with the countries of this area.

The Western governments say that they are interested in using oil and other raw material resources in this area of the world. But the nations of this area do not deny this opportunity to the Western powers. They demand only one thing; that this problem should be solved on an equitable and mutually profitable commercial basis which is the most reasonable principle.

The Soviet Government believes that the conference of the heads of government of the U.S.S.R., the United States, Britain, France and India could consider also the question of discontinuing arms deliveries to the Middle East, as earlier proposed by the U.S.S.R.

We deem it necessary that this summit conference should work out concrete recommendations to end the military conflict in the Middle East and submit them to the Security Council so that this United Nations body would study them with the participation of representatives from the Arab states.

The question of the conference's date and place cannot be an obstacle to its convocation. The Soviet Government is prepared to agree to any place, including Washington, if for some reason Geneva or another capital of a neutral country will not suit the Western powers. The main thing is not to wait, not to waste priceless time because cannons are already starting to speak. We propose to meet at Geneva on July 22.

The most reasonable act of our governments in the prevailing conditions would be to convene a summit conference to settle the military conflict which has broken out in the Middle East. This would be a priceless contribution to the cause of consolidating peace and international security. This would be an irrefutable proof that the idea of peaceful and not military solution of questions can and must triumph throughout the world. The ending of the aggression in the Middle East would be wholeheartedly greeted by all the peoples irrespective of color, religious convictions or political views.

In conclusion I wish to lay special emphasis on the fact that the question of whether the conflict in the Middle East will be settled through war or peace now depends on your Government, on you personally, Mr. President.

The Soviet Government expects that the Government of the United States and you, Mr. President, will understand this appeal correctly, that it will meet with your positive response and readiness to turn the course of events radically from the road of war to the road of peace.

I have simultaneously approached on the above question the Prime Minister of Great Britain, Mr. Macmillan, the President of the Council of Ministers of France, Mr. de Gaulle, and the Prime Minister of India, Mr. Nehru.

Respectfully yours,

N. KHRUSHCHEV

(90) *Reply of the President, July 22, 1958.*[23]

DEAR MR. CHAIRMAN: I have received your comunication of July 19.

[23] *Ibid.*, pp. 239-241.

May I assure you that the establishment and maintenance of a just peace is the dominant influence in American policy. I cannot agree that the United States has acted in Lebanon in a manner calculated to disturb the peace. Rather it is motivated by the purpose of helping stop acts of violence, fomented from without, designed to destroy the genuine independence and integrity of that small nation. Such a process, if unchecked, would have grave implications for all small nations everywhere.

The manner in which you have chosen to express yourself is hardly calculated to promote the atmosphere of calm reasonableness which, you correctly say, should replace the presently overheated atmosphere.

I am not aware of any factual basis for your extravagantly expressed fear of the danger of general war.

What has happened in regard to Lebanon is this:

On Monday, July 14, the lawful Government of Iraq was violently overthrown. On the same day a comparable plot against the Kingdom of Jordan was discovered and barely thwarted. The Government of Lebanon, which had already for some months been subjected to indirect aggression from without, appealed to the United States for instant assistance. In the light of the developments in neighboring Iraq and Jordan, it felt that nothing less than immediate help would make it possible to preserve the independence and integrity of Lebanon. The United States responded to this appeal. We knew that the plea was based upon solid facts that showed that Lebanon was gravely menaced.

Surely, it is not "aggression" thus to help a small nation maintain its independence.

You speak of "armed conflict in the Near or Middle East." There has been the bloody coup in Iraq, the plot to assassinate those who compose the Government of Jordan, and the civil strife in Lebanon fomented from without. Otherwise, I know of no "armed conflict." Unless those of aggressive disposition are far gone in folly, they would not start war because Lebanon, with a population of about $1\frac{1}{2}$ million, is helped to maintain its integrity and independence. The real danger of war would come if one small nation after another were to be engulfed by expansionist and aggressive forces supported by the Soviet Union.

We do not want to see a repetition of the progressive destruction of the independence of small nations which occurred during the 1930s and which led to the Second World

War. To be acquiescent in aggression, be it direct or in-direct, is not the road to peace.

This does not mean that the United States is dedicated to a perpetuation of the status quo in the Arab world. The United States recognizes and sympathizes with the yearning of the Arab peoples for a greater nationalistic unity. For example, the United States promptly recognized the United Arab Re-public,[24] bringing together Egypt and Syria, as soon as it was apparent that the change was accepted by the people con-cerned and after the new government had undertaken to meet the normally applied international standards.

But it is one thing to change the international status quo by orderly and peaceful processes, and another thing to change it by indirect aggression. Such processes cannot be reconciled with a peaceful world or with the ideals of the United Nations which recognizes the equal rights of nations large and small and the dignity and worth of the human person.

The action of the United States in relation to Lebanon was fully in accord with the accepted principles of international law and with the Charter of the United Nations. The Gov-ernment of Lebanon was one which had been chosen by freely held, peaceful, nationwide elections only a little over a year ago. The appeal to the United States was made by the President of Lebanon with the full approval of the Cabinet. When last week the Soviet Union introduced in the United Nations Security Council a Resolution condemning our action in Lebanon, that Resolution received only one vote— that of the Soviet Union itself. I also note that efforts were made within the Security Council to provide Lebanon with increased protection from the United Nations so as to pre-serve its integrity and independence, thus permitting United States forces promptly to be withdrawn. There were two such proposals, each defeated by the one vetoing vote of the Soviet Union.[25]

How does the Soviet Union reconcile its allegation that United States forces in Lebanon endanger world peace with the veto of these two proposals?

Am I to conclude, Mr. Chairman, that the Soviet Union seeks by imputing to others war motives and itself boasting of its nuclear and ballistic missile power, to divert attention from the steady erosion of the independence of small na-

[24] Document 108, below.
[25] Documents 85 and 86, above.

tions? Are we, as civilized peoples, to accept the increasing use of violence, murder and terrorism as instruments of international policy? If so, this constitutes the real danger to peace. The United States will steadfastly oppose that danger and seek to strengthen the established processes of international law and order.

The Soviet Union, by its constant abuse of its veto power in the Security Council—its veto of today was the 85th—would tear down, and not strengthen, the orderly processes which the nations have established for the maintenance of international peace and security.

Your present proposal seems further calculated to derogate from the authority and prestige of the United Nations. What you propose amounts in effect to five nations, without sanction of the United Nations and without conformity with its Charter, reaching what you call "recommendations" regarding the Near and Middle East which would then be submitted to the United Nations Security Council. But in reality such so-called "recommendations" would be decisions and the process would in effect make the United Nations into a "rubber stamp" for a few great powers.

Furthermore, Mr. Chairman, when procedures are sought to be improvised to meet what is alleged to be a situation of great urgency, this can scarcely be expected to save time. It raises a whole series of new problems which must be considered by the various nations that might consult together, and by others which might feel that they were improperly omitted and which are deeply concerned with the Near and Middle East.

If, indeed, the Soviet Union seriously believes that there is an imminent threat to world peace, it is bound by the United Nations Charter to take the matter to the Security Council. By Article 24 of the United Nations Charter, the Soviet Union, with other members of the United Nations, has conferred on the Security Council "primary responsibility for the maintenance of international peace and security," and all the members have agreed that, in these matters, it "acts on their behalf." It is also agreed that that Council has the responsibility to "determine the existence of any threat to the peace" and to "decide what measures shall be taken . . . to maintain or restore international peace and security." Surely this solemn undertaking ought to be respected.

The Security Council is already dealing with certain phases of the problem alluded to by your note. If you or we believe that other aspects of this problem or other problems should be urgently dealt with in the interest of peace, then it lies open to any of us to enlarge the scope of the Security Council consideration. Furthermore, under the Charter, members of government, including Heads of Government and Foreign Ministers, may represent a member nation at the Security Council. If such a meeting were generally desired, the United States would join in following that orderly procedure.

I do not, of course, exclude the discussion, outside the United Nations, of world or regional problems, not posing alleged imminent threats to the peace. I cannot but deplore the persistent refusal of your Government for so many months to agree to the adequate preparation of a "summit" meeting at which we could exchange considered views on the great problems which confront the world. The Ambassadors of France, the United Kingdom and the United States were negotiating at Moscow with your Foreign Minister to develop a list of topics which might lend themselves to considered and useful discussion at a summit meeting. These negotiations were broken off by your Government on June 16th.[26]

In conclusion, I venture to express in most earnest terms my hope that the Soviet Government will unite with us for real peace. The longing of mankind for peace is too precious to be used for ulterior purposes. I hope that ways can be found to act for peace in accordance with the standards prescribed by the Charter of the United Nations. All the world, I believe, knows that peace with justice is the dedication of the American nation. We have in the past sacrificed greatly for that devotion. We have loyally complied with the pledge we made, by the United Nations Declaration of January 1, 1942, to renounce any aggrandizement for ourselves. Just as we shall resist any efforts to use love of peace to mask aggression, so we shall equally never fail to take any step, at any sacrifice, which will genuinely promote the cause of peace and justice in the world.

Sincerely,

DWIGHT D. EISENHOWER

[26] Document 31, above.

(91) *Reply of the Prime Minister of the United Kingdom (Macmillan), July 22, 1958.*[27]

I am now able to send you a considered reply to your message of July 19 about the situation in the Middle East.[28] As I explained in my interim reply which will have reached you earlier today this is a matter which Her Majesty's Government have considered in consultation with our allies.

I shall come quickly to the point of your letter. First, however, I wish to make it plain that I do not share your judgement that the world is on the verge of a military catastrophe. I say this in full and certain knowledge of the pacific intentions of the Western Powers and in the belief that the Soviet Government would not themselves take a step which would lead to world war.

I also wish to forestall any misunderstanding by saying at once that I cannot accept in any particular your description of the action which we have taken in sending troops to Jordan, of our motives, or of the situation in Jordan itself. As has been made abundantly clear, the sole reason for our action in Jordan was to protect a small and independent country which had appealed for help against the threat of aggression and subversion stimulated from without.

However, although I reject your premises, it by no means follows that I reject your conclusion. Indeed I agree with you that it would be useful if Heads of Government could find an early opportunity to meet and discuss the Middle East. I should certainly be glad to explain to you face to face how Her Majesty's Government view the problems which beset the area.

I was glad to see that in your message you referred, with marked disapproval, to the idea of "circumventing the United Nations." As you know, the Security Council already has under consideration certain questions concerning the Middle East. I hope that you will agree that the proceedings in the Security Council should not be circumvented but that the discussions for which you have asked should take place in that forum thus providing continuity. Article 28 (2) of the United Nations Charter enables the Security Council to hold meetings at which each of its members may, if it so desires, be represented by a member of the Government or by some

[27] United Nations Document S/4071, dated August 1, 1958, pp. 2-3.
[28] Not printed.

other specially designated representative. I would certainly be ready to go to New York for such a meeting if you would also go: and I take it from the terms of your message that you would.

It would not be the intention of Her Majesty's Government that any resolutions should be put forward at this special meeting of the Security Council unless they arose out of previous agreement. In other words, the object would be to reach fruitful agreements rather than to register differences by votes. I hope that this spirit will prevail.

You hoped that we might meet in Geneva today. I hope that we may meet soon in New York in accordance with the plan I have suggested.

(92) *Reply of the President of the Council of Ministers of France (de Gaulle), July 22, 1958.*[29]

Sir,

I have studied with the greatest care, in both substance and form, the letter which you addressed to me on 19 July proposing that I should take part in an immediate meeting of heads of Governments on the subject of the Middle East.[30]

As you know, the French Government has always considered it desirable that the Powers should undertake a serious discussion of the problems which divide them and which constitute a potential threat to peace. Hence it is favourably disposed at this time towards the principle of a meeting on the Middle East.

Nevertheless I must tell you frankly, Sir, that some of the reasons which you invoke and some of the terms which you employ do not appear to me to be those most conducive to the success of your proposal.

It is my feeling that a "summit meeting" held against the background of a world plunged in anxiety and fear can be successful only if it is conducted in an atmosphere of objectivity and serenity.

Yet I am constrained to observe that many passages in your letter are not such as to promote the necessary easing of tension and spirit of understanding among those who might participate.

Why, for example, compare the presence of United States forces in Lebanon and United Kingdom forces in Jordan,

[29] United Nations Document S/4075, dated August 1, 1958, pp. 2-3.
[30] Not printed.

requested by the Governments of those States following the events which took place in Iraq, to the aggression committed not so long ago by Hitler against Poland? (Hitler, unfortunately, was not alone). Can it honestly be said that such a comparison is realistic?

Why tell me that France has "tried to undertake a military demonstration on the shores of Lebanon" when France is not participating in the United States-United Kingdom enterprise and the mission of the French forces is simply to assist French nationals if need be?

Why assert that "the sad and unfortunate experience which France has acquired in Algeria and during the unprovoked attack of British, French and Israel forces on Egypt has left deep traces in the heart of every Frenchman?" Algeria is exclusively the concern of France and the Suez Canal undertaking was clearly provoked.

For my own part, I shall refrain from emphasizing in turn the traces which certain undertakings have left in the soul of the Russian people.

Having stated the foregoing, Sir, I wish to confirm to you my intention to take part in the direct contacts which you favour between the heads of the Governments of the principal Powers to discuss the Middle East, provided that they can be organized in an atmosphere of "reason and calm," as you yourself have written.

The United Nations is currently seized of the problem. I think that for the moment it would be best to allow it to continue its discussions. If these produce no result, the idea of a "summit" meeting could then, in my opinion, be pursued. In that event the French Government would be ready to discuss immediately the most appropriate composition, date and place of the proposed meeting.

I have the honour to be, etc.

(Signed) Charles de Gaulle

(93) Letter from the Chairman of the Council of Ministers of the USSR (Khrushchev) to the President, July 23, 1958.[31]

Sir,

I have received your answer to my message of 19 July. I have also received replies from Mr. Nehru, Mr. Macmillan and Mr. de Gaulle to my messages of 19 July addressed to them.

[31] United Nations Document S/4064, dated July 23, 1958, pp. 2-4.

At the present time, we have no wish to enter into polemics about the causes of the tension and the threat to peace in the Near and Middle East. The views of the Soviet Government on all these matters were set forth in my message of 19 July. I should only like to repudiate most emphatically the assertion in your message that the Soviet Union is encouraging expansionist and aggressive forces in the world. At this time, especially after the armed intervention of the United States in Lebanon and that of the United Kingdom in Jordan, no one can have any doubts, if doubts there ever were, as to who in actual fact is pursuing an expansionist and aggressive policy which is threatening the peace and security of the peoples.

The Soviet Government considers that at the present time the threat to general peace is so serious that all possible steps must be taken, and at the earliest possible date, without wasting time on polemics which can only delay the reaching of agreement, to prevent the outbreak of a world conflict. The danger of such a conflict cannot be minimized, for there are forces which are in favor of widening the area of aggression and, in particular, are fomenting plans for an armed attack on Iraq.

It is for this very purpose, to prevent the outbreak of a world conflict, that we proposed the immediate calling of a meeting of the heads of the Goverments of the USSR, the United States, the United Kingdom, France and India, with the participation of Mr. Hammarskjold, the Secretary-General of the United Nations. We note with satisfaction that the Soviet Government's proposal for a meeting of the heads of Governments has met with a favourable response on your part. Mr. Macmillan, the Prime Minister of the United Kingdom, Mr. de Gaulle, The President of the Council of Ministers of France and Mr. Nehru, the Prime Minister of India have also expressed the view that such a meeting would be desirable, and we are grateful to them for this response.

We take no exception to the views expressed by Mr. Macmillan, the Prime Minister of the United Kingdom, as regards the calling of the meeting of the heads of Governments within the framework of the Security Council. The Soviet Government pointed out in its message of 19 July that the Security Council should not be circumvented.

Bearing in mind the need for urgent solutions with a view to the maintenance of peace, we consider that the formalities of the meeting of the heads of Governments can have no decisive significance in the present case. The important thing is that the meeting should take place as soon as possible, so that we can rapidly arrive at a correct solution calculated to promote the maintenance and strengthening of peace, to bring tranquillity to the Near and Middle East and to help bring about a relaxation of tension in relations between States.

We also agree with the approach proposed by Mr. Macmillan to the work of such a special meeting of the Security Council. We agree that at this special meeting of the Security Council no resolutions should be submitted unless they arise from previous agreement, and that the purpose of the meeting will be to reach agreement rather than to register differences by votes.

In this connexion the Soviet Government assumes that the heads of Governments, with a view to achieving as rapidly as possible constructive solutions designed to promote the maintenance and strengthening of peace, will have the opportunity to consult together not only officially, but unofficially as well.

In view of the fact that the Security Council will in the present instance be dealing not with ordinary current matters but with questions of special importance for the maintenance of peace and security, we consider that it would be useful in this case to invite India, a very large Asian country which has won universal recognition as a State which strives for the strengthening of peace, to take part in the Security Council's proceedings. India's participation would be genuinely useful, unlike that of one of the so-called permanent members, which in fact represents no one. We consider it essential that India should be represented in the work of the Security Council through Mr. Nehru, its Prime Minister, who has agreed to participate in the meeting of heads of Governments.

In your message, Sir, you state that if a special meeting of the Security Council including heads of Governments were generally desired, the United States would join in following that orderly procedure.

So far as the Soviet Union is concerned, since Mr. Macmillan, Prime Minister of the United Kingdom, Mr. de Gaulle, President of the Council of Ministers of France, Mr. Nehru, Prime Minister of India and you, Sir, as is evident from your message, are prepared to take part personally in the work of the special meeting of the Security Council, the Soviet Union will be represented at that meeting by the Chairman of the Council of Ministers of the USSR.

It is self-evident that the Governments of the interested Arab States should be brought into the discussion in the Security Council to be participated in by the heads of the Governments of the five Powers referred to.

The Soviet Government would like to learn as soon as possible the United States Government's views as to the date of meeting of the Security Council with the participation of the heads of Governments. For our part, we would propose that the work should be begun in the Security Council on 28 July in New York.

I have the honour to be, etc.

(*Signed*) N. Khrushchev

(94) *Reply of the President, July 25, 1958.*[32]

DEAR MR. CHAIRMAN: I have studied your letter of July 23. I find in it apparent misunderstandings of the views expressed in my letter of July 22, which I would request you to read again more carefully.

I then said that if, despite the facts established in the recent meetings of the Security Council, your Government still desires to allege that the situation in Lebanon constitutes an imminent danger to peace in the Middle East, the proper forum for appropriate discussion is the United Nations Security Council. I am glad that you now recognize the responsibility of the United Nations and have withdrawn your original proposal which would have gravely undermined the prestige and authority of the United Nations.

My letter pointed out that the Charter of the United Nations authorizes members of government, and that of course includes Heads of Government and Foreign Ministers, to represent a member nation at the Security Council and that if such a meeting were generally desired, the United States would join in following that orderly procedure. It is, of course, not yet certain that such a meeting is in fact "generally desired," although that may prove to be the case.

You now make specific suggestions dealing with the composition of the Security Council and the conditions under which nations other than members of the Council may participate in discussions of the Council. My letter to you of July 22 urged that one of the advantages of proceedings in the Security Council is that there are established rules on these matters and it is accordingly not necessary to rely on

[32] *Department of State Bulletin*, v. 39 (August 11, 1958), pp. 233-234.

improvising. I pointed out that when rules of this kind are sought to be improvised, there is raised a whole series of new problems, notably as to the participation and non-participation of various states. The United States will adhere, in these respects, to the Charter, which lays down the conditions under which nations which are not members of the Council may participate in the discussions of the Council.

As to the agenda, we agree that it should be limited to a discussion of the problems of the Middle East, including the causes of those problems. I would, however, be lacking in candor if I did not make clear that to put peace and security on a more stable basis in the Middle East requires far more than merely a consideration of Lebanon and Jordan. These situations are but isolated manifestations of far broader problems. In my opinion the instability of peace and security is in large measure due to the jeopardy in which small nations are placed. It would be the purpose of the United States to deal with the specific incidents you raise within that broad context. To do otherwise would be to be blind to the teaching of history.

You will recall, Mr. Chairman, that World War II was brought about by a series of acts of direct and indirect aggression against small nations. In March 1939 the then head of the Soviet Communist Party pointed out that the failure of nonaggressive nations, among which he named Britain and France, to check direct or indirect aggression against small countries meant "giving free rein to war and, consequently, transforming the war into a world war." That forecast unhappily proved true.

You will also recall the 1950 "Peace through Deeds" Resolution of the General Assembly which condemns the "fomenting of civil strife in the interest of a foreign power" as among "the gravest of all crimes."

It is my earnest hope that through the United Nations Security Council steps can be taken in regard to the Middle East which, by making peace more secure there, will help promote it elsewhere.

In conclusion, I suggest that the Permanent Representatives of the members of the United Nations Security Council in New York should exchange views, under arrangements made by the Secretary General, to ascertain that a meeting of the kind and under conditions I suggest is generally acceptable. If so they should also agree upon a date which would

be generally satisfactory. The date of July 28 would be too
early for us.

I am today authorizing our own Permanent Representative
to act in this sense.

Sincerely,

DWIGHT D. EISENHOWER

(95) *Letter from the Chairman of the Council of
Ministers of the USSR (Khrushchev) to the
President, July 28, 1958.*[33]

Sir,

I have received your message of 25 July in reply to my
message of 23 July concerning the calling of a meeting of
heads of Governments.

To my regret, I note from your reply that the Government of the United States is retreating from the position
which it took on 22 July concerning the calling of an urgent
special meeting of the Security Council with the participation
of the heads of Governments to consider the situation in the
Near and Middle East.

It is now evident that the United States Government is
trying to delay the calling of a meeting of heads of Governments, and does not want such a meeting to take urgent steps
for the peaceful settlement of the hostilities which have
broken out in the Near and Middle East.

It must be pointed out that the agreement to the calling
of a meeting of heads of Governments within the framework of the Security Council which you indicated in your
letter of 22 July met with a favourable reception in all
countries. The agreement between the USSR, the United
States, the United Kingdom, France and India concerning
a meeting of heads of Governments had some tranquillizing
effect, and the peoples of the world believed, with every
justification, that the meeting would take place in the very
early future and would ensure the maintenance and strengthening of peace in the Near and Middle East.

The Soviet Government stated that it was in agreement
with Mr. Macmillan's proposal, inasmuch as the Prime
Minister of the United Kingdom, in suggesting that the
meeting of heads of Governments should be held within
the framework of the Security Council, expressly indicated

[33] United Nations Document S/4067, dated July 28, 1958, pp. 2-8.

that at this meeting no resolutions should be submitted unless they arose from previous agreement and that the object of our work together should be to reach fruitful agreements rather than register differences by votes.

Your present reply is a step backwards from the agreement reached, and will inevitably give rise to serious concern among the peoples of the world. The United States Government now proposes that the situation in the Near and Middle East, a situation which constitutes a threat to peace, should not be taken up by the heads of the Governments of the five Powers but should instead be referred again to a regular meeting of the United Nations Security Council. That proposal is now also being supported by Mr. Macmillan, Prime Minister of the United Kingdom. But what results can that bring? You are fully aware that the Security Council has been dealing with the situation in Lebanon and Jordan for a considerable time, but has so far reached no solution.

The question of putting an end to the armed aggression in the Near and Middle East has now become so acute that the Security Council, as the experience of these recent meetings has shown, is unable to take a prompt and effective decision on the matter at its regular meetings.

A continuous build-up of armed forces is going on in this region, which is more and more being turned into a powder-keg the smallest spark could explode, bringing about a world-wide catastrophe. In these circumstances it is essential that the heads of the Governments of the five Powers—the USSR, the United States, the United Kingdom, France and India—should meet at the earliest possible date, with the participation of the Secretary-General of the United Nations, since they particularly, vested as they are with high powers, would be able to reach agreement on the immediate cessation of the military conflict in the Near and Middle East and on measures for the maintenance and strengthening of world peace.

Quite obviously, anyone who genuinely wishes to find a way to reduce tension must agree that in the present case it is particularly these five Powers which must first reach agreement on the measures necessary for the maintenance and strengthening of peace. There can hardly be any doubt that if these Powers were to succeed in reaching agreement on the immediate cessation of the armed conflict in the Near and Middle East all other States which are truly interested in the strengthening of peace would welcome and support such a solution.

Mr. Macmillan's proposal of 22 July that the heads of Governments should meet within the framework of the Security Council did in fact envisage a meeting of this kind. But as I have already pointed out, you, Mr. President, and the Prime Minister of the United Kingdom are now retreating from this proposal. It is self-evident that in this way steps are being taken to bury the agreement reached to hold a meeting at the earliest possible date between the heads of Governments of the USSR, the United States, the United Kingdom, France and India.

We cannot accept this.

The Soviet Government stands steadfastly for the maintenance and strengthening of peace and for peaceful coexistence between States, irrespective of their social and economic systems. The Soviet Government has consistently stood for the settlement of conflicts by peaceful means, through negotiation. That is why we insist on the immediate ending of aggression and on the prompt withdrawal of the interventionist forces from the territories of Lebanon and Jordan.

We are deeply convinced that a meeting of the heads of the Governments of the five Powers would in fact help to find ways and means to end the military conflict and to bring tranquillity to the Near and Middle East, given a genuine desire on the part of all sides to bring about those ends.

In this connexion, the Soviet Government expresses its satisfaction at the statement made by Mr. de Gaulle, the head of the Government of France, in his message of 26 July, that he supports the proposal to call a meeting of the heads of the Governments of the five Powers, with the participation of the Secretary-General of the United Nations, without delay.[34] As we understand it, this view does not differ from the Soviet Government's proposal on the question. We consider, as we have stated earlier, that this would be the most correct course and one which might ensure an early solution of the urgent problem of putting an end to the military conflict in the Near and Middle East.

In order to delay still further the holding of a meeting of heads of Governments you state in your message that there

[34] Not printed. See United Nations Document S/4075, dated August 1, 1958, pp. 4-5.

has apparently been some misunderstanding of the views on such a meeting expressed by the United States Government. If that is the case, it can only be wondered whether those views were not deliberately worded so as to be open to varying interpretation and to cause loss of time in correspondence to clarify their meaning. Since you agreed in your message of 22 July to take part in a special meeting of the Security Council with the participation of the heads of Governments, we could only, in the circumstances, interpret your statement to mean that you were in agreement that such a meeting should be held as soon as possible. Now, retreating from the idea of calling such a meeting as soon as possible, you recommend us to read your letter of 22 July again. It is difficult to interpret these words of yours otherwise than as evidence that the United States Government clearly does not want measures to be taken at the earliest possible date to put an end to armed intervention in Lebanon and Jordan.

I feel obliged to point out, Sir, that the position taken by the Governments of the United States and the United Kingdom, which amounts to a refusal to call a meeting of heads of Governments, will necessarily cause concern among the peoples of the world who are impatiently awaiting an end to the armed conflict in the Near and Middle East and the initiation of measures for the maintenance and strengthening of world peace.

Representatives of public opinion in all countries are anxiously asking whether the Governments of the States responsible for the existing tension in the Near and Middle East are not seeking to lull the vigilance of the peoples while preparing secretly for new acts of aggression. The United States Government is fully aware that American troops are still being landed in Lebanon, where with the support and protection of United States bayonets Mr. Murphy, the special emissary of the State Department, has been carrying on his suspicious activities, and high-handedly interfering in the domestic affairs of Lebanon; that United States naval forces are being concentrated in the eastern Mediterranean and that United States reinforcements are being air-lifted from Europe to the Near and Middle East, particularly to the Adana area in Turkey. In this connexion, special attention must be drawn to the extensive preparations which have recently been made in Turkey itself for armed intervention in the affairs of the countries of the Arab East. King Hussein of Jordan, who has lost the support of his people and depends on help from abroad, has the audacity to rattle his sabre and threaten a march on Baghdad. He is acting as a pliant instrument in the hand of certain Western Powers which are plotting against the peoples of the Arab East. There is a marked tendency to widen the area of aggression. The threat of armed attack hangs over the Republic of Iraq.

Thus, the delay in the negotiations for a meeting of the heads of the Governments of the five-Powers, accompanied as it is by the increasing concentration of armed forces in the Near and Middle East, is resulting in a further aggravation of the situation and a spread of the conflict, and is liable to plunge mankind into catastrophe.

Today more than ever before, urgent and energetic measures are needed to ensure the immediate withdrawal of foreign troops from Lebanon and Jordan and to prevent the widening of the area of military conflict in the Near and Middle East. There is no time to lose.

It must be pointed out, however, that instead of helping to bring about a meeting of heads of Governments at an early date with a view to putting an immediate end to the armed conflict in the Near and Middle East, the United States Government has sent its Secretary of State to London for a meeting of members of the Baghdad Pact.[35] Hasty attempts are being made to shore up that Pact, the withdrawal from which of Iraq, its only Arab member, serves to emphasize once again the failure of the Western Powers' policy of "position of strength"—a policy of building up aggressive blocs. At the same time the United States Government is trying by every means at its command to hinder the solution —a solution awaited by all mankind—of the main problem of the present day, which is to put an end to armed intervention by the United States, and the United Kingdom in the Near and Middle East; it is trying to embroil the negotiations on a meeting of heads of Governments in a maze of endless discussion on the form and procedure for such a meeting.

The meeting in London of representatives of the Governments of the United Kingdom, the United States, Turkey, Pakistan and Iran at a time when, instead of foreign troops being withdrawn from Lebanon and Jordan, preparations are proceeding apace for armed intervention in the affairs of the Republic of Iraq, has the appearance of a plot against the

[35] Documents 105 and 106, below.

Arab countries. Is not all this being done in furtherance of a conspiracy to perpetrate new acts of aggression and to confront the world, by pursuing the policy of the *fait accompli*, with an increasing expansion of military conflict?

But can the serious consequences of such a policy, particularly for its initiators, be ignored? For today the peoples of the world are vigilant, and will not approve acts of aggression.

The United States Government is doing everything possible to frustrate the possibility of a meeting of the heads of the Governments of the five Powers, the purpose of which would be to put an end to armed aggression in Lebanon and Jordan and to take urgent steps for the maintenance and strengthening of world peace.

Thus, you are not pursuing a policy of bringing about a settlement of the military conflict which has begun in the Near and Middle East, with a view to the maintenance and strengthening of peace, but are in fact widening the area of military conflict and exposing mankind to the threat of world catastrophe. In so doing you above all are assuming a serious responsibility before mankind and history for the consequences of such a policy on the part of the United States Government. A serious responsibility also rests with Mr. Macmillan, Prime Minister of the United Kingdom, who, although he is trying to manoeuvre, is in fact pursuing the same policy of frustrating the adoption of any measures for the settlement of the military conflict in Jordan and Lebanon.

The Soviet Government, in view of the extremely tense situation that has come about in the Near and Middle East, still considers it essential that a meeting of the heads of the Governments of the USSR, the United States, the United Kingdom, France and India, with the participation of the Secretary-General of the United Nations, should be called without delay.

With regard to the place of meeting, we have noted the statement made by Mr. de Gaulle, the head of the Government of France, in his message of 26 July, to the effect that he would prefer the meeting to be held in Europe. The Soviet Government had even earlier expressed the view that the meeting should be held in Europe, and supports Mr. de Gaulle's proposal.

The possibility of holding the meeting of heads of Governments in a European city is particularly deserving of study in view of suggestions among United States diplomats and in the

American press that the authorities of the United States might find it difficult to ensure the security of the heads of Governments if the meeting were held in that country. We have no wish to place the United States Government in a difficult position in this respect. Accordingly, the Soviet Government while it still has no objection to meeting in New York, would agree to meet at Geneva, Vienna or Paris, or in any other place acceptable to all the participants.

We should also be happy if agreement were reached to hold the meeting of heads of Governments in Moscow, where the Soviet Government would guarantee delegations absolute security and the necessary conditions for fruitful work. We are confident that the Soviet people would welcome any envoys who came in order to take prompt measures to put an end to the conflict in the Near and Middle East and to strengthen world peace, thereby demonstrating its steadfast adherence to the cause of peace.

Your message evades the question of the participation of the Prime Minister of India in the meeting of heads of Governments. In this connexion, I feel obliged to stress once again that India's participation in the meeting would be highly important for the attainment of constructive decisions on a settlement of the situation in the Near and Middle East.

With regard to the date of the meeting of heads of Governments with the participation of the Secretary-General of the United Nations, we suggested 28 July. Since you have stated that this date is too early for the United States Government, we are prepared to agree to any other early date, and would appreciate a clear answer to the question when the United States would be prepared to participate in a meeting of the heads of the Governments of the five Powers.

I should be grateful, Sir, for a reply to my message at the earliest possible date.

I have the honour to be, etc.,

(*Signed*) N. KHRUSHCHEV

(96) *Reply of the Prime Minister of the United Kingdom (Macmillan), July 31, 1958.*[36]

I have received your letter of July 28.[37] I will not reply to its many accusations against allied policy in the Middle East. None of these has any foundation in fact.

[36] United Nations Document S/4071, dated August 1, 1958, pp. 2-3.
[37] Not printed. See United Nations Document S/4067, dated July 28, 1958, pp. 9-15.

In my letter of July 22 I proposed a special meeting of the Security Council to be attended by Heads of Government. On July 26 I elaborated this proposal.[38] I said that I was glad that it was acceptable to you and I suggested that the necessary arrangements should at once be made through the permanent representatives of members of the Security Council. I hope that on reflection you will agree that this is the best course; I am encouraged in this hope by the passage in your last letter where you call for a return to my original proposal. From this proposal I have never departed.

In addition to meetings of the whole Council under Article 28 it would of course be possible to arrange less formal meetings of Heads of Government on the questions which the Security Council is considering. The procedure would thus be flexible and should promote the chances of making progress. As I said in my message of July 22 it would not be our intention that any resolutions should be put forward at this special meeting of the Security Council unless they arose out of previous agreement.

Of course this meeting would not preclude the holding of the Summit Meeting for which we have been working for some time.

I am now instructing the United Kingdom permanent representative at the United Nations to propose to the President of the Security Council a special meeting to take place under Article 28 on August 12. Meanwhile the permanent representatives should discuss arrangements for the special meeting and decide where it will take place. If this meeting is agreed I shall be there on August 12. I hope you will be there too. So far as I am concerned New York, Geneva or any other place generally agreeable will do.

(97) *Reply of the President of the Council of Ministers of France (de Gaulle), July 31, 1958.*[39]

Sir,

Your letter of 29 [sic] July stresses once again the importance and urgency which you attach to a meeting of the heads of the Governments of the USSR, the United States of America, the United Kingdom, France and India to study the problems of the Middle East.[40] You feel that this meet-

[38] Not printed. See United Nations Document S/4071, dated August 1, 1958, p. 2.
[39] United Nations Document S/4075, dated August 1, 1958, pp. 6-7.
[40] Not printed. See United Nations Document S/4067, dated July 28, 1958, pp. 16-20.

ing should take place in Europe. You state that its object should be "to secure the immediate withdrawal of foreign troops from Lebanon and Jordan and to prevent any widening of the area of military conflict."

As far as the principle of a meeting of heads of Governments is concerned, I confirm that the French Government agrees, provided that such a meeting take place in the necessary atmosphere of objectivity and serenity. If the other Governments are agreed that such a meeting should take place and if they can ensure that it will be held in such an atmosphere, I will be ready to proceed to any city in Europe at any date which the participants consider suitable. I myself should like to propose that such a meeting might be held at Geneva on 18 August next.

With regard to the purpose of the meeting, I think that it should not be limited to the problems raised by the presence of United States troops in Lebanon and United Kingdom troops in Jordan, which is only the consequence of a general situation, or to the possible widening of the area of military conflict, since no such conflict is in progress. In my view, the meeting should deal frankly and fully with the whole subject of the Middle East and the continual state of crisis which prevents that area of the world from living and developing in normal conditions.

Following the consultations which it is holding with certain States, France will make specific proposals, as appropriate, on these subjects.

Pending a decision by the Governments concerned with regard to the plan for a summit meeting, the French Government has no objection to a new meeting of the Security Council as suggested by the Governments of the United Kingdom and the United States. Such a meeting, however, in view of the composition of the Council, the number of States which would have to be invited to take part in it, the nature of its agenda and the character of its discussions, would obviously not be the same thing as a meeting of heads of Governments.

In any case, I feel that we should now pursue through normal diplomatic channels such discussions as may yet be necessary before agreement can be reached with regard to the principle, the place, the date and the purpose of the meeting which you yourself originally proposed.

I have the honour to be, etc.

(*Signed*) CHARLES DE GAULLE

(98) *Reply of the President, August 1, 1958.*[41]

DEAR MR. CHAIRMAN: For several centuries personal correspondence between Heads of Government and Heads of State has been an extremely valuable channel of communication when the normal diplomatic channels seemed unable to carry the full burden. However, it has always been recognized —not just as a matter of diplomatic form but as a requirement of efficacy—that the essential ingredient in such correspondence, whether confidential or public, was a tone of serious purpose and an absence of invective.

It is in this tradition that I reply to your letter of July 28.

I consider it quite inaccurate for you, both implicitly and explicitly, to convey the impression that the Government of the United States has embarked on a policy of delay based on niggling procedural argument. The fact is that the differences between us are not procedural but basic.

Very simply, the two basic points which the United States has stated many times in the past, and which I repeat now, are (a) do all of us, the Charter Members of the United Nations, agree that the United Nations Security Council has the principal responsibility for the maintenance of international peace and security; and (b) shall small nations as well as a few so-called "great powers" have a part in the making of decisions which inevitably involve them?

As to my first point—What of the United Nations? It was created out of the travail of World War II to establish a world of order and of justice. It embodied and still embodies the hopes of mankind. At this juncture, when you claim peace is endangered, you would push it aside—we would invoke its processes.

This leads to my second point—What of the small powers of this world? Shall they be ignored or shall the small nations be represented in the making of decisions which inevitably involve them? History has certainly given us ample proof that a nation's capacity to contribute to the advancement of mankind is not to be measured by the number of divisions it can put in the field. You must be aware, as I am, of the many very specific proposals made these last years by the so-called smaller powers which have been of great value to all of us.

The stated assumption in your letter that the decisions of

five great powers will be happily accepted by all other interested powers seems to indicate an attitude on your part which could have dangerous consequences in the future for the smaller powers of this world.

Your position, which means that the desires, the dignity, in fact the security, of the smaller nations should be disregarded, is one which the United States has consistently opposed and continues to oppose today. Essentially you are proposing that we should join you in a policy reminiscent of the system of political domination you imposed in Eastern Europe. The United States cannot accept that point of view.

The problem of the Middle East is not one of a threat of aggression by the United States but rather the threat, by others, of further indirect aggression against independent states. This problem is clearly the responsibility of the United Nations Security Council.

I am, therefore, instructing the United States Permanent Representative to the Security Council to seek a special meeting on or about August 12 of the Security Council under Article 28 (2), which would permit direct discussions among Heads of Governments and Foreign Ministers. I would hope that you would similarly instruct your Permanent Representative. Such a meeting will make it possible for the Council to discharge its responsibilities in the manner contemplated by the Charter.

As for the place of the meeting, the United States agrees that the meeting might be held elsewhere than New York City but we could not agree to the meeting being held in Moscow. The memory of the well-organized mass demonstration and serious damage to the United States Embassy in Moscow is too fresh in the minds of the American people.

If such a meeting is arranged, I expect to attend and participate and I hope that you would do likewise.

Sincerely,

DWIGHT D. EISENHOWER

8. Further Exchange of Views between the Chairman of the Council of Ministers of the USSR (Khrushchev) and the President.

(99) Letter from the Chairman of the Council of Ministers of the USSR (Khrushchev), August 5, 1958.[42]

(Excerpts)

Sir,

I have received your message of 1 August. I fully agree with the views you express regarding the value of personal correspondence between heads of Governments. In present circumstances it is essential that such personal correspondence should contribute to the fundamental objective of the peoples —the preservation of peace and peaceful co-existence between States irrespective of their social systems.

I also agree with you that our present correspondence is unusual. I should like to make it quite clear that this unusual correspondence is the result of the unusual steps which the United States and the United Kingdom have taken in the Near and Middle East. The United States and the United Kingdom have committed a breach of the peace in that area by invading Lebanon and Jordan with their forces.

*   *   *

If we consider the present composition of the Security Council, we are forced to conclude that, under pressure from the United States, this organ has in effect developed into a sort of committee which is mainly composed of countries belonging to NATO, the Baghdad Pact and SEATO and on which the seat of the lawful representative of the great Chinese People's Republic is occupied by the representative of Chiang Kai-shek, a political ghost.

The policy of ignoring the People's Republic of China does not make sense. This great Power exists, is growing and is developing, whether certain States recognize it or not. If common sense prevailed and the Chinese People's Republic took its rightful place in the United Nations, this would be duly appreciated by all peoples, for the peoples understand that without the Chinese People's Republic the Security Council and the United Nations cannot be the fully effective

[42] United Nations Document S/4079, dated August 5, 1958, pp. 10-19.

organ for preserving peace and security which the United Nations Charter requires.

Thus a situation has arisen in which the Security Council is virtually paralysed and is unable to take any decision which would effectively promote the preservation of peace throughout the world, independently of the will of the United States of America.

* * *

No State which is genuinely concerned to protect the independence and security of the small countries can arrogate to itself the right to intervene in those countries' affairs and proclaim this or that "doctrine" with such an end in view. This being so, however, what is the justification for the proclamation by the United States Government of the doctrine which bears your name and for its intervention in the affairs of the countries of the Near and Middle East? For example, when the people of Lebanon, incensed at the policy of its President who had become the servant of the United States of America instead of the servant of his own people, demanded his removal, that President, who had lost his people's confidence, only had to appeal to you, in violation of his country's Constitution, for the United States Government to set the United States Sixth Fleet in motion, to throw its assault units into Lebanon, and to begin introducing "order" there in accordance with the aforementioned doctrine. The United Kingdom Government headed by Mr. Macmillan used an appeal by the King of Jordan, who has no following whatever among his people, as a pretext for intervention by its armed forces in Jordan's domestic affairs.

There are still those in the United States of America who boast of the fact that the United States Government intervened in the affairs of Guatemala and expelled the lawfully elected Government and President. Surely this is not another illustration of what you mean by concern for small countries and respect for their independence and dignity?

If this is so, Mr. President, our ideas evidently differ regarding the rights of the small nations. In the generally accepted language of politics, such actions on the part of the United States Government constitute a violation of the rights of the small nations and the imposition on them of its own domination, against which the peoples of all countries whose independence is infringed by the United States of America and the United Kingdom are waging an unre-mitting struggle.

If we were to quote other similar instances, without even going far back into the past—the very recent landing of United States troops in Cuba is a case in point—we should have a great deal to say, and our message would be much lengthier.

I am compelled to refer to your assessment of events in the Near and Middle East. You assert that the problems of the Middle East is not one of aggression by the United States but rather of indirect aggression. The fact that you refer to indirect aggression of some kind, Mr. President, means that, in common with us and the overwhelming majority of other countries, you apparently regard the introduction of foreign troops into the territory of others as an act of direct aggression. This is not open to question. That is why, throughout the world, the introduction of United States troops into Lebanon and United Kingdom troops into Jordan is rightly regarded as direct aggression. With regard to the allusions in your message to some sort of indirect aggression, reference to such an imaginary danger can only be regarded as an attempt to mask the direct aggression of the United States.

And indeed the allegations of indirect aggression threaten-ing Lebanon are refuted by the two well-known reports of the United Nations observers specially sent to Lebanon by the Security Council.

In these circumstances, Mr. President, we do not under-stand by what right the United States Government assumes the mantle of the arbiter and judge, and maintains that there has been some kind of indirect aggression in Lebanon. It is evident from this that you do not recognize the right of the peoples of the Near and Middle East to handle their own affairs and to organize their States along lines which serve their own interests. Thus, Mr. President, you are guilty of direct contradiction of your own assertions concerning regard for the desires, the dignity and the security of the smaller countries.

The whole world knows that domestic events in Lebanon, Iraq and Jordan reflect the wrath of the peoples of those countries, who have revolted against the system imposed on them by the imperialist colonizers. In Iraq the people re-belled when they could no longer endure the oppression and excesses of the lackeys of foreign States. Now the United

States and other Western Powers have recognized the Republican Government of Iraq.[43] Hence you, Mr. President, and your allies have recognized that the Iraqi people have the right to change the existing order.

Thus your assertions about some form of indirect aggression are wholly without foundation, and merely divert attention from the real aggression in the Near and Middle East which was committed by the United States and the United Kingdom.

We regret, Mr. President, that you do not agree to the holding of a meeting of the heads of Governments at Moscow, and that you referred in this connexion to the angry demonstration by the inhabitants of Moscow near the United States Embassy against United States armed intervention in Lebanon. This demonstration was a completely spontaneous expression of the Soviet people's sympathy for a victim of aggression. Your reference to this occurrence is particularly unconvincing in view of the fact that the United States Government itself so far refuses to take steps to ensure normal working conditions for the Permanent Soviet Mission to the United Nations and has not put a stop to the systematic acts of provocation against that Mission on the part of certain elements in New York which, it stands to reason, inevitably influenced the feelings of the Soviet people who took part in the demonstration.

Mr. President, it is not our people that started such demonstrations. It would be desirable to call a halt to such occurrences in the United States. Our people would attach due weight to this.

I should like to point out that our people assess events correctly and are well able to distinguish between the acts of hired hooligans against the Permanent Soviet Mission in New York and the genuine feelings of the American people. We entertain the most friendly feelings for the people of the United States and are anxious to develop broad cultural and economic ties between our countries. We want our respective peoples to know each other better, and to join forces to preserve and strengthen peace and to end the estrangement between countries, so that all States may live with one another on a basis of genuine good-neighbourliness. The Soviet people's attitude to the American people is well known. We

[43] On August 2, 1958 the United States extended recognition to the government of the Republic of Iraq. *Department of State Bulletin*, v. 39 (August 18, 1958), p. 273.

might point out that, at the time when irresponsible elements, paid out of certain funds set up for the purpose of subversive activity against States that do not belong to the aggressive blocs in which the United States plays a leading part, were creating an uproar outside the building of the Permanent Soviet Mission in New York, American scientists, specialists, sportsmen, tourists and even Mr. Adlai Stevenson, a well-known public figure in the United States, were being received in the USSR with the Soviet people's usual cordiality and hospitality.

I wish now to return to the main point, to what at this juncture should have been the only subject of our present correspondence: namely the adoption, as speedily as possible, of effective measures to end the armed intervention of the United States and the United Kingdom in the Near and Middle East. You consider it essential that the consideration of this question should be entrusted to the United Nations Security Council. Unhappily, as I have already pointed out, the present situation of the Security Council, in which it is to all intents and purposes subordinated to United States foreign policy and most of the representatives of countries who attend its meetings are not free to take any action which deviates from the United States position, prevents us from regarding your proposal as the right one. The policy of the United States in regard to the Security Council is undermining its chances of adopting effective measures to protect peace and to halt aggression. It is destroying the effectiveness of the Security Council as an instrument of peace.

The United Nations and its Security Council are essential international organs and should reflect the peace-loving aspirations of the peoples. However, the United States Government is using the Council for its own selfish interests, through the representatives of countries belonging to military blocs in which the United States occupies the dominant position. In reality the United States of America is trying to reduce the Security Council to the position of a subsidiary organ of the United States Department of State. How can we close our eyes to the true position and ignore the fact that the Security Council, as now composed, is in no position to reach objective conclusions on the situation in the Near and Middle East?

No, Mr. President; for the sake of preserving world peace and strengthening security, we need a sane approach which

would pave the way for a positive decision and would ensure
that peace prevailed.

Since the very start of the United States and United Kingdom intervention in the Near and Middle East, the Soviet
Union has advocated the adoption of immediate measures
to check the aggression, to secure the withdrawal of foreign
forces from Lebanon and Jordan, to prevent the intervention
from spreading, and to eliminate the dangerous tension
caused by the actions of the United States and the United
Kingdom. To that end, we proposed to call a meeting of the
heads of the Governments of the five Powers, the USSR,
the United States, the United Kingdom, France and India,
with the participation of Mr. Hammarskjold, the Secretary-
General of the United Nations. We regret that you and Mr.
Macmillan have not found it possible to accept this proposal
and that a positive decision has not therefore been taken on
calling a meeting of the heads of the Governments of the
five Powers with the participation of the Secretary-General
of the United Nations.

Although the Governments of the United States and the
United Kingdom have made it impossible to convene a meeting of the five Powers and are directly responsible for this
state of affairs, it is now clearly apparent that the demands
of the peoples for the immediate convening of such a meeting in order to end the armed intervention in Lebanon and
Jordan and the determination of peace-loving States to halt
aggression in the Near and Middle East have forced those who
embarked on this armed intervention to refrain at the present
juncture from extending the aggression to other countries
and primarily to the Republic of Iraq and the United Arab
Republic. It is no accident, therefore, that the Western
Powers, including the United States and the United Kingdom, have been obliged to recognize the Republic of Iraq,
whose establishment the aggressors originally alleged to be
a threat to peace in the Near and Middle East. This does
not mean, however, that the danger of the extension and
aggravation of the conflict in that area has been eliminated
or that the security of the Republic of Iraq and the other
Arab States has been ensured. The forces of the interven-
tionists have not yet been withdrawn from Lebanon and
Jordan. Furthermore, fresh contingents of foreign troops
are arriving in that area and further military measures are
being taken in the countries of the Baghdad Pact.

The question of the complete cessation of armed intervention in the Near and Middle East and of the establishment of conditions which would protect the peoples of that
area against foreign intervention still calls for speedy settlement. The foreign forces must be withdrawn from Lebanon
and Jordan without delay, as their presence constitutes a
continuing threat to peace and to the independence of the
peoples concerned and a flagrant violation of the United
Nations Charter, which cannot be condoned by a single
Member of the United Nations.

In these circumstances, the Soviet Government considers
it essential to pursue its efforts to maintain and strengthen
peace in the Near and Middle East. Since the Governments
of the United States and the United Kingdom have abandoned the idea of calling a meeting of the heads of the Governments of the five Powers and since, as we have already
pointed out, the Security Council has shown itself unable
to achieve a peaceful solution of the problem of the Near and
Middle East, the Government of the Soviet Union, with a
view to ensuring that the necessary steps to halt aggression
are taken without delay, has instructed its representative
to the United Nations to request the convening of a special
session of the General Assembly of the United Nations to
discuss the question of the withdrawal of United States forces
from Lebanon and United Kingdom forces from Jordan.
The Soviet Government hopes that consideration of this
question in the General Assembly, where large and small
States alike are represented, will make it possible to find
means of removing the military danger that has arisen in the
Near and Middle East as a result of the actions of the United
States and the United Kingdom and will bring tranquillity
to that region.

I think that you will agree with me, Sir, that the events
in the Near and Middle East, which have confronted the
world with the threat of general war with all the untold
miseries it would inflict on the peoples, lend particular
urgency to the question of establishing conditions for the
peaceful co-existence of States and for putting an end to the
"cold war," which is contaminating the whole international
atmosphere. The Soviet Union and all peace-loving countries
are working for the day when no great Power will be able
to commit aggression, even against a small country. Aggression by a small country against a great Power is quite out
of the question. A small country does not possess the di-

visions you mention, Mr. President, in your message. We have to take account of realities and practical possibilities. A world war can be unleashed by a great Power with large numbers of divisions and many atomic and hydrogen weapons, rockets, bombers and other means of destruction, but not by a small country. Accordingly, it is precisely the great Powers which must agree to refrain from any action that would bring the world to the brink of military catastrophe.

The Soviet Government considers that all possible steps should be taken to develop contacts and relations between the statesmen of all countries. Personal meetings between the leaders of States can lessen the existing tension, promote the growth of confidence and mutual understanding among States and hasten the thawing of the ice of the "cold war."

We attach particular importance to such contacts and, as you know, as early as December 1957, we proposed a meeting of statesmen at the highest level. We are convinced that, given the efforts of all participants, such a summit meeting, with the composition we proposed earlier, would help to find ways and means to banish the "cold war" and to make impossible the outbreak of a shooting war.

Let us do everything within our power to see that this meeting, for which all peoples of the world are waiting, is not postponed indefinitely. We await your agreement to our proposal for a summit meeting and are prepared to take part in such a meeting at any time. It is in the interests of all States, great and small, that a summit meeting should be convened at the earliest opportunity.

In conclusion, I should like to express the hope that the United States Government will support the proposal to convene a special session of the General Assembly of the United Nations, which might be a useful step towards the relaxation of tension and would pave the way for a summit meeting at an earlier date.

I have the honour to be, etc.

(*Signed*) N. KHRUSHCHEV

(100) *Statement by the President, August 5, 1958.*[44]

I welcome Mr. Khrushchev's agreement that the problems we have had under discussion in our recent exchange of letters should be placed again before the United Nations. I regret that he did not accept the Security Council with the

[44] *Ibid.* (September 1, 1958), p. 342.

Heads of Government present as the appropriate forum in view of his alleged concern over the threats to the peace. However, the General Assembly is completely acceptable, particularly since the United States previously proposed on July 18th such a procedure to the Security Council.

I am therefore instructing the United States Permanent Representative to the Security Council to move the previously presented United States resolution requesting that this matter be put before the General Assembly. This resolution has been held in abeyance in order to permit consideration of Mr. Khrushchev's proposals of July 19th, 23rd, and 28th.[45]

9. Third Emergency Session of the United Nations General Assembly, August 8-21, 1958.

(101) Address by the President, August 13, 1958.[46]

Mr. President, Mr. Secretary-General, members of the General Assembly, and guests:

First, may I express my gratitude for the generosity of your welcome.

It has been almost 5 years since I had the honor of addressing this Assembly. I then spoke of atomic power and urged that we should find the way by which the miraculous inventiveness of man should not be dedicated to his death but consecrated to his life. Since then great strides have been taken in the use of atomic energy for peaceful purposes. Tragically little has been done to eliminate the use of atomic and nuclear power for weapons purposes.

That is a danger.

That danger in turn gives rise to another danger—the danger that nations under aggressive leadership will seek to exploit man's horror of war by confronting the nations, particularly small nations, with an apparent choice between supine surrender or war.

This tactic reappeared during the recent Near East crisis. Some might call it "ballistic blackmail."

In most communities it is illegal to cry "fire" in a crowded assembly. Should it not be considered serious international misconduct to manufacture a general war scare in an effort to achieve local political aims?

Pressures such as these will never be successfully practiced against America, but they do create dangers which could

45 Documents 89, 93 and 95, above.
46 Department of State Bulletin, v. 39 (September 1, 1958), pp. 237-242.

affect each and every one of us. That is why I have asked for the privilege of again addressing you.

The immediate reason is two small countries—Lebanon and Jordan.

The cause is one of universal concern.

The lawful and freely elected Government of Lebanon, feeling itself endangered by civil strife fomented from without, sent the United States a desperate call for instant help. We responded to that call.

On the basis of that response an effort has been made to create a war hysteria. The impression is sought to be created that, if small nations are assisted in their desire to survive, that endangers the peace.

This is truly an "upside down" portrayal. If it is made an international crime to help a small nation maintain its independence, then indeed the possibilities of conquest are unlimited. We will have nullified the provision of our charter which recognizes the inherent right of collective self-defense. We will have let loose forces that could generate great disasters.

The United Nations has, of course, a primary responsibility to maintain not only international peace but also security. But we must not evade a second fact, namely, that in the circumstances of the world since 1945 the United Nations has sometimes been blocked in its attempt to fulfill that function.

Respect for the liberty and freedom of all nations has always been a guiding principle of the United States. This respect has been consistently demonstrated by our unswerving adherence to the principles of the charter, particularly in its opposition to aggression, direct or indirect. Sometimes we have made that demonstration in terms of collective measures called for by the United Nations. Sometimes we have done so pursuant to what the charter calls "the inherent right of collective self-defense."

I recall the moments of clear danger we have faced since the end of the Second World War—Iran, Greece and Turkey, the Berlin blockade, Korea, the Straits of Taiwan.

A common principle guided the position of the United States on all of these occasions. That principle was that aggression, direct or indirect, must be checked before it gathered sufficient momentum to destroy us all—aggressor and defender alike.

It was this principle that was applied once again when

the urgent appeals of the Governments of Lebanon and Jordan were answered.

I would be less than candid if I did not tell you that the United States reserves, within the spirit of this charter, the right to answer the legitimate appeal of any nation, particularly small nations.

I doubt that a single free government in all the world would willingly forgo the right to ask for help if its sovereignty were imperiled.

But I must again emphasize that the United States seeks always to keep within the spirit of the charter.

Thus, when President Truman responded in 1947 to the urgent plea of Greece, the United States stipulated that our assistance would be withdrawn whenever the United Nations felt that its action could take the place of ours.

Similarly, when the United States responded to the urgent plea of Lebanon, we went at once to the Security Council and sought United Nations assistance for Lebanon so as to permit the withdrawal of United States forces.

United Nations action would have been taken, and United States forces already withdrawn, had it not been that two resolutions, one proposed by the United States, the other proposed by the Government of Japan, failed to pass because of one negative vote—a veto.

But nothing that I have said is to be construed as indicating that I regard the status quo as sacrosanct. Change is indeed the law of life and of progress. But when change reflects the will of the people, then change can and should be brought about in peaceful ways.

In this context the United States respects the right of every Arab nation of the Near East to live in freedom without domination from any source, far or near.

In the same context, we believe that the charter of the United Nations places on all of us certain solemn obligations. Without respect for each other's sovereignty and the exercise of great care in the means by which new patterns of international life are achieved, the projection of the peaceful vision of the charter would become a mockery.

The Problem of Lebanon

Let me turn now specifically to the problem of Lebanon.

When the United States military assistance began moving into Lebanon, I reported to the American people that we had immediately reacted to the plea of Lebanon because the situation was such that only prompt action would suffice.

I repeat to you the solemn pledge I then made. Our assistance to Lebanon has but one single purpose—that is the purpose of the charter and of such historic resolutions of the United Nations as the "Essentials of Peace" resolution of 1949 and the "Peace Through Deeds" resolution of 1950. These denounce, as a form of aggression and as an international crime, the fomenting of civil strife in the interest of a foreign power.

We want to prevent that crime—or at least prevent its having fatal consequences. We have no other purpose whatsoever.

The United States troops will be totally withdrawn whenever this is requested by the duly constituted Government of Lebanon or whenever, through action by the United Nations or otherwise, Lebanon is no longer exposed to the original danger.

It is my earnest hope that this Assembly, free of the veto, will consider how it can assure the continued independence and integrity of Lebanon. Thus the political destiny of the Lebanese people will continue to lie in their own hands.

The United States delegation will support measures to this end.

Jordan, Another Urgent Problem

Another urgent problem is Jordan.

If we do not act promptly in Jordan, a further dangerous crisis may result, for the method of indirect aggression discernible in Jordan may lead to conflicts endangering the peace.

We must recognize that peace in this area is fragile, and we must also recognize that the end of peace in Jordan could have consequences of a far-reaching nature. The United Nations has a particular responsibility in this matter, since it sponsored the Palestine armistice agreements upon which peace in the area rests and since it also sponsors the care of the Palestine refugees.

I hope that this Assembly will be able to give expression to the interest of the United Nations in preserving the peace in Jordan.

Question of Inflammatory Propaganda

There is another matter which this Assembly should face in seeking to promote stability in the Near East. That is the question of inflammatory propaganda. The United Nations Assembly has on three occasions—in 1947, 1949, and 1950—passed resolutions designed to stop the projecting of irresponsible broadcasts from one nation into the homes of citizens of another nation thereby "fomenting civil strife and subverting the will of the people in any state." That was stated in the language of the resolution. We all know that these resolutions have recently been violated in many directions in the Near East.

If we, the United States, are one of those who have been at fault, we stand ready to be corrected.

I believe that this Assembly should reaffirm its enunciated policy and should consider means for monitoring the radio broadcasts directed across national frontiers in the troubled Near East area. It should then examine complaints from these nations which consider their national security jeopardized by external propaganda.

United Nations Peace Force

The countries of this area should also be freed from armed pressure and infiltration coming across their borders. When such interference threatens, they should be able to get from the United Nations prompt and effective action to help safeguard their independence. This requires that adequate machinery be available to make the United Nations presence manifest in the area of trouble.

Therefore I believe that this Assembly should take action looking toward the creation of a standby United Nations Peace Force. The need for such a force is being clearly demonstrated by recent events involving imminent danger to the integrity of two of our members.

I understand that this general subject is to be discussed at the 13th General Assembly and that our distinguished Secretary-General has taken an initiative in this matter.[47] Recent events clearly demonstrate that this is a matter for urgent and positive action.

Arab Development Institution

Now I have proposed four areas of action for the consideration of the Assembly—in respect to Lebanon, to Jordan, to subversive propaganda, and a standby United Nations force. These measures, basically, are designed to do one thing: to preserve the right of a nation and its people to

[47] See United Nations Document A/3943, dated October 9, 1958.

determine their own destiny, consistent with the obligation to respect the rights of others.

This clearly applies to the great surge of Arab nationalism.

Let me state the position of my country unmistakably. The peoples of the Arab nations of the Near East clearly possess the right of determining and expressing their own destiny. Other nations should not interfere so long as this expression is found in ways compatible with international peace and security.

However, here as in other areas we have an opportunity to share in a great international task. That is the task of assisting the peoples of that area, under programs which they may desire, to make further progress toward the goals of human welfare they have set for themselves. Only on the basis of progressing economies can truly independent governments sustain themselves.

This is a real challenge to the Arab people and to all of us.

To help the Arab countries fulfill their aspirations, here is what I propose:

First—that consultations be immediately undertaken by the Secretary-General with the Arab nations of the Near East to ascertain whether an agreement can be reached to establish an Arab development institution on a regional basis.

Second—that these consultations consider the composition and the possible functions of a regional Arab development institution, whose task would be to accelerate progress in such fields as industry, agriculture, water supply, health, and education, among others.

Third—other nations and private organizations which might be prepared to support this institution should also be consulted at an appropriate time.

Should the Arab states agree on the usefulness of such a soundly organized regional institution, and should they be prepared to support it with their own resources, the United States would also be prepared to support it.

The institution would be set up to provide loans to the Arab states as well as the technical assistance required in the formulation of development projects.

The institution should be governed by the Arab states themselves.

This proposal for a regional Arab development institution can, I believe, be realized on a basis which would attract international capital, both public and private.

I also believe that the best and quickest way to achieve the most desirable result would be for the Secretary-General to make two parallel approaches: first, to consult with the Arab states of the Near East to determine an area of agreement; then, to invite the International Bank for Reconstruction and Development, which has vast experience in this field, to make available its facilities for the planning of the organizational and operational techniques needed to establish the institution on its progressive course.

I hope it is clear that I am not suggesting a position of leadership for my own country in the work of creating such an institution. If this institution is to be a success, the function of leadership must belong to the Arab states themselves.

I would hope that high on the agenda of this institution would be action to meet one of the major challenges of the Near East, the great common shortage—water.

Much scientific and engineering work is already under way in the field of water development. For instance, atomic isotopes now permit us to chart the courses of the great underground rivers. The new horizons are opening in the desalting of water. The ancient problem of water is on the threshold of solution. Energy, determination, and science will carry it over that threshold.

Another great challenge that faces the area is disease.

Already there is substantial effort among the peoples and governments of the Near East to conquer disease and disability. But much more remains to be done.

The United States is prepared to join with other governments and the World Health Organization in an all-out, joint attack on preventable disease in the Near East.

But to see the desert blossom again and preventable disease conquered is only a first step. As I look into the future, I see the emergence of modern Arab states that would bring to this century contributions surpassing those we cannot forget from the past. We remember that Western arithmetic and algebra owe much to Arabic mathematicians and that much of the foundation of the world's medical science and astronomy was laid by Arab scholars. Above all, we remember that three of the world's great religions were born in the Near East.

But a true Arab renaissance can only develop in a healthy human setting. Material progress should not be an overriding objective in itself. It is an important condition for achieving higher human, cultural, and spiritual objectives.

But I repeat, if this vision of the modern Arab community is to come to life, the goals must be Arab goals.

Arms-Control Arrangements

With the assistance of the United Nations, the countries of the Near East now have a unique opportunity to advance, in freedom, their security and their political and economic interests. If a plan for peace of the kind I am proposing can be carried forward, in a few short years we may be able to look back on the Lebanon and Jordan crises as the beginning of a great new prosperous era of Arab history.

But there is an important consideration which must remain in mind today and in the future.

If there is an end to external interference in the internal affairs of the Arab states of the Near East—

If an adequate United Nations Peace Force is in existence—

If a regional development institution exists and is at work on the basic projects and programs designed to lift the living standards of the area—

Then with this good prospect, and indeed as a necessary condition for its fulfillment, I hope and believe that the nations of the area, intellectually and emotionally, will no longer feel the need to seek national security through spiraling military buildups. These lead not only to economic impotence but to war.

Perhaps the nations involved in the 1948 hostilities may, as a first step, wish to call for a United Nations study of the flow of heavy armaments to those nations. My country would be glad to support the establishment of an appropriate United Nations body to examine this problem. That body would discuss it individually with these countries and see what arms-control arrangements could be worked out under which the security of all these nations could be maintained more effectively than under a continued wasteful, dangerous competition in armaments. I recognize that any such arrangements must reflect these countries' own views.

Six-Point Program for Peace and Progress

I have tried to present to you the framework of a plan for peace in the Near East. It would provide a setting of political order responsive to the rights of the people in each nation; which would avoid the dangers of a regional arms race; which would permit the peoples of the Near East to devote their energies wholeheartedly to the tasks of development and human progress in the widest sense.

It is important that the six elements of this program be viewed as a whole. They are:

(1) United Nations concern for Lebanon.

(2) United Nations measures to preserve peace in Jordan.

(3) An end to the fomenting from without of civil strife.

(4) A United Nations Peace Force.

(5) A regional economic development plan to assist and accelerate improvement in the living standards of the people in these Arab nations.

(6) Steps to avoid a new arms-race spiral in the area.

To have solidity, the different elements of this plan for peace and progress should be considered and acted on together, as integral elements of a single concerted effort.

Therefore, I hope that this Assembly will seek simultaneously to set in motion measures that would create a climate of security in the Near East consonant with the principles of the United Nations Charter and at the same time create the framework for a common effort to raise the standard of living of the Arab peoples.

Foreign Economic Development Activities

But the peoples of the Near East are not alone in their ambition for independence and development. We are living in a time when the whole world has become alive to the possibilities for modernizing their societies.

The American Government has been steadily enlarging its allocations to foreign economic development in response to these worldwide hopes. We have joined in partnership with such groupings as the Organization of American States and the Colombo Plan; and we are working on methods to strengthen these regional arrangements. For example, in the case of the Organization of American States, we are consulting now with our sister Republics of this hemisphere to strengthen its role in economic development. And the Government of the United States has not been alone in supporting development efforts. The British Commonwealth, the countries of Western Europe, and Japan have all made significant contributions.

But in many parts of the world both geography and wise economic planning favor national rather than regional development programs. The United States will, of course, continue its firm support of such national programs. Only where the desire for a regional approach is clearly manifested and where the advantage of regional over national is evident will the United States change to regional methods.

The United States is proud of the scope and variety of its development activities throughout the world. Those who know our history will realize that this is no sudden, new policy of our Government. Ever since its birth the United States has gladly shared its wealth with others. This it has done without the thought of conquest or economic domination. After victory in two world wars and the expenditure of vast treasure, there is no world map, either geographic or economic, on which anyone can find that the force of American arms or the power of the American Treasury has absorbed any foreign land or political or economic system. As we cherish our freedom, we believe in freedom for others.

A World Community of Open Societies

The things I have talked about today are real and they await our grasp. Within the Near East and within this Assembly are the forces of good sense, of restraint, and of wisdom to make, with time and patience, a framework of political order and of peace in that region.

But we also know that all these possibilities are shadowed, all our hopes are dimmed, by the fact of the arms race in nuclear weapons—a contest which drains off our best talents and vast resources, straining the nerves of all our peoples.

As I look out on this Assembly, with so many of you representing new nations, one thought above all impresses me.

The world that is being remade on our planet is going to be a world of many mature nations. As one after another of these new nations moves through the difficult transition to modernization and learns the methods of growth, from this travail new levels of prosperity and productivity will emerge.

This world of individual nations is not going to be controlled by any one power or group of powers. This world is not going to be committed to any one ideology.

Please believe me when I say that the dream of world domination by one power or of world conformity is an impossible dream.

The nature of today's weapons, the nature of modern communications, and the widening circle of new nations make it plain that we must, in the end, be a world community of open societies.

And the concept of the open society is the ultimate key to a system of arms control we all can trust.

We must, then, seek with new vigor, new initiative, the path to a peace based on the effective control of armaments, on economic advancement, and on the freedom of all peoples to be ruled by governments of their choice. Only thus can we exercise the full capacity God has given us to enrich the lives of the individual human beings who are our ultimate concern, our responsibility, and our strength.

In this memorable task there lies enough work and enough reward to satisfy the energies and ambitions of all leaders everywhere.

Thank you very much for your kind attention.

(102) *General Assembly Resolution 1237 (ES-III), Adopted August 21, 1958.*[48]

The General Assembly,

Having considered the item entitled "Questions considered by the Security Council at its 838th meeting on 7 August 1958";

Noting the Charter aim that States should practice tolerance and live together in peace with one another as good neighbours,

Noting that the Arab States have agreed, in the Pact of the League of Arab States to strengthen the close relations and numerous ties which link the Arab States, and to support and stabilize these ties upon a basis of respect for the independence and sovereignty of these States, and to direct their efforts toward the common good of all the Arab countries, the improvement of their status, the security of their future and the realization of their aspirations and hopes,

Desiring to relieve international tension,

I

1. *Welcomes* the renewed assurances given by the Arab States to observe the provision of Article 8 of the Pact of the League of Arab States that each member State shall respect the systems of government established in the other member States and regard them as exclusive concerns of these States, and that each shall pledge to abstain from any action calculated to change established systems of government;

[48] United Nations, General Assembly, *Official Records, Third Emergency Special Session,* Supplement No. 1 (A/3905), p. 1.

2. *Calls upon* all States Members of the United Nations to act strictly in accordance with the principles of mutual respect for each other's territorial integrity and sovereignty, of non-aggression, of strict non-interference in each other's internal affairs, and of equal and mutual benefit, and to ensure that their conduct by word and deed conforms to these principles;

II

Requests the Secretary-General to make forthwith, in consultation with the Governments concerned and in accordance with the Charter, and having in mind section I of this resolution, such practical arrangements as would adequately help in upholding the purposes and principles of the Charter in relation to Lebanon and Jordan in the present circumstances, and thereby facilitate the early withdrawal of the foreign troops from the two countries;

III

Invites the Secretary-General to continue his studies now under way and in this context to consult as appropriate with the Arab countries of the Near East with a view to possible assistance regarding an Arab development institution designed to further economic growth in these countries;

IV

1. *Requests* Member States to co-operate fully in carrying out this resolution;
2. *Invites* the Secretary-General to report hereunder, as appropriate, the first such report to be made not later than 30 September 1958.

(103) *Report of the United Nations Secretary-General (Hammarskjold), September 29, 1958.*[49]

(Excerpt)

*   *   *

Practical Arrangements: General Considerations

21. The practical arrangements for the purposes mentioned in the resolution, as explained above, must be adjusted to the development of the good neighbour policy to which Member Governments have pledged themselves in the resolution. The implementation of the joint pledge is still at an early stage

[49] United Nations Document A/3934, dated September 29, 1958.

and it is therefore premature to pass a judgement on the degree of success with which it may meet. From all the Governments contacted, I have heard firm expressions of an intention to translate the terms of the resolution into a living reality. At the same time, however, most of the Governments found reasons, although in varying degree, to complain about the way in which, so far, the joint pledge to a good neighbour policy had been implemented by others.

22. It is undoubtedly true that, so far, we have not reached the stage in which mutual confidence is restored and departures from the desirable line of action are such rare occurrences as to make it possible to disregard them. However, it seems reasonable to work on the assumption that the impact of the intention of all Governments to translate the words of the resolution into deeds will increasingly be felt and that, therefore, the implementation of the good neighbour policy will meet with growing success. Regarding developments which have taken place after the consultations, I wish to mention, especially, encouraging contacts about the supply of oil to Jordan through the Syrian region and the supply of oil from Iraq on a commercial basis.

23. For the present, practical arrangements made by the Secretary-General may be developed on the aforementioned assumption and with a view to strengthening the forces working in the desirable direction. Were the assumption later to prove unwarranted, a reconsideration of the practical arrangements would become necessary. In the ultimate case of a failure of the good neighbour policy they would have to be so developed as to present a more solid guarantee for the line of action which they are intended to support.

24. On the basis of this assumption it seems reasonable to conclude that the practical arrangements should, on the one hand, provide means for the United Nations to keep the implementation of part I, and the policy it establishes, continuously within its purview and, on the other hand, provide means for the United Nations, in case of departures from a good neighbour policy, as set out in the resolution, to take appropriate diplomatic or political action. The two sets of arrangements, although naturally closely related, should be kept strictly apart so that neither the arrangements for the purview may come to be used also for diplomatic purposes, nor the character of the diplomatic arrangements may be distorted by their being used also for the purpose of the purview. The natural link between the two sets of

arrangements is the office of the Secretary-General which would receive reports on the findings, made in the course of the purview, and decide on the political or diplomatic action to be taken through the means created for that purpose.

25. It should be noted that in the case of Lebanon, the United Nations has already extensive arrangements for keeping within its purview one aspect of the implementation of the good neighbour policy, that is, possible infiltration or smuggling of arms across the border. In considering the practical arrangements to be made, the work of this organization, the United Nations Observation Group in Lebanon (UNOGIL), has had to be re-evaluated with a view to deciding on its possible role within the new set of practical arrangements to be made.

Practical Arrangements in Relation to Jordan

26. The representative of the Government of Jordan stated in the debate of the General Assembly at the Emergency Special Session that his Government did not accept the stationing of a United Nations force in Jordan nor the organization of a border observation group in the country for purposes similar to those served by UNOGIL in Lebanon. This view was restated to me in the consultations in Amman.

27. As from the beginning it had been also my view that neither a United Nations force nor a border observation group would adequately serve the purposes of the resolution in relation to Jordan, I accepted this stand of the Government of Jordan. Consequently the consultations in Jordan were limited of co-operation to which all Arab States, in co-sponsoring the resolution, had pledged themselves. It was felt that by working in that direction, the United Nations would most adequately further all the purposes of the resolution. The spirit and direction of the consultations in Jordan thus corresponded fully to the interpretation of the resolution which I have given in this report.

28. With the wide area of agreement existing from the beginning, the consultations regarding a formula under which the United Nations could assist in relation to Jordan did not present any problems of principle. The basis for the consideration was the need to provide, as explained above, both for keeping current developments under the resolution in relation to Jordan within purview and for proper diplomatic arrangements for any subsequent action by the United Na-

tions which might be rendered necessary by the findings made.

29. It was agreed that the most practical location of a United Nations organ, designed to keep under purview the adherence of all to the principles set out in part I of the resolution in relation to Jordan, would be Jordan itself. In recognition of this, Jordan stated its willingness to serve as host country for a United Nations representative, properly staffed, to serve "as a special representative of the Secretary-General to assist in the implementation of the resolution, specifically with a view to help in upholding the purposes and principles of the Charter in relation to Jordan in the present circumstances."

30. The stationing in Jordan of a United Nations organ, for the purposes mentioned, gave rise to a practical problem because the new organ with this location would require an established and guaranteed line of communication. For practical reasons this would involve also the Governments of Lebanon and the U.A.R. However, as both these Governments have undertaken to grant all the facilities, including liaison offices in Beirut and Damascus, needed in support of the establishment of a United Nations organ in Jordan, I have concluded that the practical problems can be resolved and that the new organ can be stationed in Amman.

31. In the light of this conclusion, based on the stands taken by the Governments of Jordan, Lebanon and the U.A.R., Ambassador Spinelli, Under-Secretary in charge of the European Office of the United Nations in Geneva, has been assigned to go to Amman in order to work out the necessary practical arrangements for the new operation with the Governments concerned. He proceeded to Amman on 27 September. In the course of his stay there he will also, on a preliminary basis, serve as special representative with the terms of reference mentioned above. When his duties in Geneva make a replacement necessary, a new representative will be appointed on a more definite basis.

32. Pending a study of the situation by Ambassador Spinelli and his report on that matter, it is premature to say how large a staff would be needed and how it might best be composed. In deciding on the size and nature of the staff, decisive importance will have to be given to the wide range of tasks the representative and his staff will have to perform, concerned as they are with any relevant departures from the principles set out in part I of the resolution in relation to Jordan.

33. Regarding the parallel diplomatic arrangements which are necessary in order to give the organ stationed in Jordan its full value, the Government of Jordan expressed a preference for diplomatic representatives of the Secretary-General in the capitals of the Arab neighbour countries. However, the stationing of such diplomatic representatives in Baghdad and Cairo was not considered desirable, for the present, by the Governments of Iraq and the U.A.R. This question has not been raised with the Governments of Lebanon and Saudi Arabia.

34. In my own view the necessary diplomatic arrangements could either take the form suggested by the Government of Jordan or else be achieved through the designation for the purpose, by the Secretary-General, of an official stationed at Headquarters but going, as necessary, to the capitals concerned for consultations and negotiations. Although the more extensive arrangements envisaged by the Government of Jordan might best help to unburden the office of the Secretary-General, I have concluded that, irrespective of the stands taken by the Governments of Iraq and U.A.R., the last-mentioned arrangement, that is to say, the designation of a high-level representative at Headquarters for the diplomatic actions that may be called for in various capitals, is the more adequate one. One reason for this conclusion is that there is a considerable likelihood that diplomatic representatives on the senior level stationed in various capitals would not have current work to do of a sufficient scope and regularity to render possible the recruitment of men of the desirable standing and experience or to justify the considerable costs involved. Another consideration of great importance is that the arrangement would lend itself to misunderstandings as it might be viewed as indicating an intention of the United Nations to establish a "presence" in various parts of the area going beyond the purposes of the resolution. The arrangement might therefore introduce an element of friction and suspicion in the relations between the States concerned and the United Nations.

35. Were a local diplomatic representation to be established, it should obviously cover the whole area. It would, therefore, be impossible to reduce the weight of the objections mentioned by a compromise, limiting the representation to only some of the capitals concerned. In these circumstances the most satisfactory arrangement has seemed to me to be the assignment for the purpose of a special representative at

Headquarters, who would proceed to the area and visit the various Governments on behalf of the Secretary-General, as need be. The Government of Jordan, recognizing the reasons for my conclusion, has accepted it while maintaining its stand that local diplomatic representation in all the capitals from its viewpoint would have been preferable. The other Governments concerned have assured me of their willingness to receive a diplomatic representative of the Secretary-General from Headquarters, as I might find it necessary.

36. Under the planned practical arrangements there will thus be two officials assigned to assist the Secretary-General, for purposes of the resolution: one keeping within his purview the implementation of the principles of the resolution by all nations in relation to Jordan; one serving as a special representative of the Secretary-General in such direct contacts of a diplomatic nature with the Governments concerned as the Secretary-General may find called for in the light of the findings of the representative charged with the purview. The last mentioned representative would for practical reasons be stationed in Jordan, while the diplomatic spokesman would be at Headquarters.

37. It follows from the principles reflected in the planned arrangements that the representative in Amman would be in contact with the Government of Jordan as host Government and with the Secretary-General, but not directly with any other Government in the area, while on the other hand the diplomatic representative would be entitled to take up discussions with those other Governments on behalf of the Secretary-General, but would not be in direct contact with the Government of Jordan. The liaison offices in Beirut and Damascus would be directly subordinated to the representative stationed in Amman, with the task of assisting him in questions relating to the line of communication to be established.

38. The reports to the Secretary-General from the representative stationed in Amman would not be public documents unless the situation were found to call for their circulation as official documents of the United Nations. Such circulation, which might serve as a basis for action by the General Assembly or the Security Council, represents obviously an alternative line of action open to the Secretary-General in such cases as would seem to him to call for stronger measures than diplomatic démarches. Were the findings to be of a serious nature, they may, under present

circumstances, be regarded as indicating a threat to peace and security in the sense of Article 99 of the Charter. This fact, and the possibilities for action which it opens for the Secretary-General, lends added weight to the planned arrangements as a means to help in upholding the purposes of the Charter in relation to Jordan.

Practical Arrangements in Relation to Lebanon

39. During his stay in Lebanon, the Secretary-General had the privilege of getting the views of the Lebanese authorities on practical arrangements which, in their view, would adequately help in upholding the purposes of the Charter in relation to Lebanon. It was felt that the United Nations Observation Group, set up under a resolution of the Security Council, 11 June 1958, while continuing to serve the general purposes mentioned in that resolution, presents a practical arrangement in the sense of the resolution of the General Assembly, 21 August 1958, and in present circumstances, with the further development of it envisaged, adequately helps in upholding the purposes of the Charter in relation to Lebanon.

40. It was found unnecessary for the time being to consider any additional practical arrangements under the General Assembly resolution. Decisive significance was, in this context, attached to the successful implementation of part I of the resolution, that is, to the development of the good neighbour policy in the area, to which the Arab Governments have pledged themselves in the resolution. The United Nations operation, now organized in Lebanon, was considered as helpful in the development of such a policy. After the withdrawal of foreign troops from Lebanon, the question of the Observation Group and of alternative or additional practical arrangements under the resolution would have to be considered in the light of the degree of success with which the implementation of part I of the resolution of 21 August 1958 had met.

41. In the finding that no additional arrangements were needed in Lebanon, with the Observation Group to be developed as envisaged, it was recognized that the terms of reference of the Group precluded it from reporting on all the possible departures from a satisfactory implementation by Arab States of the principles of the resolution in relation to Lebanon. This marks a basic difference between the Observation Group in Lebanon and the planned arrangement in re-

lation to Jordan. The Observation Group must follow any infiltration and smuggling of arms, and its reports are public. The special representative in relation to Jordan should follow any departures from the principles of the resolution and report to the Secretary-General, for further action, but his findings would not be public unless their nature would seem to call for a circulation of a report in the United Nations. One reason why no additional arrangement in Lebanon, similar to the one organized in relation to Jordan, has been found to be necessary, is that in the cases not covered by the UNOGIL it is felt that the matters may be drawn directly to the attention of the Secretary-General, who can follow them up, using the official assigned to assist him with the diplomatic action necessary under the resolution. This stand may have to be reconsidered in the light of experience at a stage when the withdrawal has taken place.

Withdrawals of United States and British Forces

The Governments of Lebanon and of the United States have been fully informed about the conclusions drawn after my consultations in the region and about the arrangements made or planned regarding the United Nations Observation Group in Lebanon. In view of the information thus conveyed, the Government of Lebanon and the United States Government are at present discussing a schedule for the completion of the withdrawal of the United States forces. I am informed that it is the intention of the two Governments that the total withdrawal of the forces shall begin in the near future and be completed as expeditiously as possible, they hope by the end of October, provided the international security situation with respect to Lebanon continues to improve in the framework of a successful implementation of part I of the resolution of 21 August 1958. The two Governments concerned plan to announce their decision shortly. A memorandum received by me from the Government of the United States is annexed to this report (Annex 1).

I have informed the Governments of Jordan and of the United Kingdom about these conclusions and the arrangement in relation to Jordan set out in this report, including the designation of a Special Representative who is now in Amman to elaborate, in consultation with the Government of Jordan, the organizational details of the arrangement. I have further informed them about the situation, as known to me, regarding the resumption of oil deliveries to Jordan and related matters. Taking this information into account, the Governments of Jordan and of the United Kingdom are discussing the fixing of dates for the beginning and the completion of the withdrawal of British forces. It is their intention that, provided satisfactory progress is being made, the withdrawal shall begin during the month of October and that it shall be completed as quickly as the situation in the area allows. The two Governments concerned hope to be able to announce their decision on 1 October. A memorandum on the matter which I have received from the Government of the United Kingdom, is annexed to this report (Annex 2).

Assistance in Economic Co-operation

In the course of the consultations in the Middle East I had an opportunity to touch also upon the question of possible assistance regarding an Arab development institution referred to in part III of the resolution of 21 August 1958.

In the light of these preliminary contacts, I have, after my return, on 26 September 1958, addressed identical letters to the ten co-sponsoring Arab Governments in which I have set out in what respects, at various stages of the development, the United Nations might be of assistance, were the Governments to wish to avail themselves of the services of the Organization in their joint economic efforts. In the letter, I mentioned that the Governments would be welcome to study the results of certain studies undertaken jointly by the International Bank and the United Nations Secretariat. The preliminary results of these studies, to which I referred in my intervention in the General Assembly of 8 August 1958, had been summarized in an internal memorandum dated 26 March 1958. This memorandum would be put at the disposal of interested Arab Governments if they so desired.

From my contacts, I drew the conclusion that, while there was a widespread interest in a constructive approach to the development problem along the lines on which the Arab League had already embarked, it was felt that a successful re-activation of economic co-operation might require that some further progress should be made in the political field, and also that financial surpluses should become available from national sources beyond what, in view of imperative domestic needs which have to be met, seemed likely within the immediate future.

In the circumstances, I believe that the information given in the letter referred to above, represents what for the moment the United Nations can usefully contribute in furtherance of the aim mentioned in part III of the resolution. On the basis of this information, the Arab Governments may now themselves evaluate what assistance they might wish to seek in pursuance of the letter and of this part of the resolution of 21 August 1958.

MEMORANDUM
[Annex 1]

In view of improvements in the international aspects of the Lebanese security situation owing to the steps which have been taken with respect to the situation in Lebanon, it has already been possible for the United States Government, in agreement with the Lebanese authorities, to withdraw a portion of its forces. The United States Government has now been informed by the Secretary-General of his view, shared by the Lebanese authorities, that the United Nations Observation Group set up under the resolution of the Security Council of 11 June 1958 presents a satisfactory practical arrangement within the meaning of the resolution of the General Assembly of 21 August 1958, and in present circumstances is, or can be made, adequate to uphold the purposes and principles of the Charter in relation to Lebanon. The United States Government has also been informed by the Secretary-General of the planned augmentation of the United Nations observation group in Lebanon and of his view, likewise shared by the Lebanese authorities, that for the time being it is unnecessary to consider any additional practical arrangements under the General Assembly resolution of 21 August with regard to Lebanon.

In view of the above information conveyed to the United States Government by the Secretary-General, the United States Government has informed the Secretary-General that it is discussing with the Government of Lebanon a schedule for the completion of the withdrawal of United States forces. It is the intention of the United States and Lebanese governments that the total withdrawal of United States forces shall begin in the near future and be completed as expeditiously as possible, we hope by the end of October, provided the international security situation with respect to Lebanon continues to improve in the framework of successful implementation of part I of General Assembly resolution of 21

August 1958. The Governments of the United States and Lebanon plan to announce their decision shortly.[50]

27 September 1958

MEMORANDUM
[Annex 2]

1. Her Majesty's Government in the United Kingdom have taken note of the arrangements which the Secretary-General is making, in agreement with the Governments directly concerned, for the stationing of a United Nations Representative in Amman, for the establishment of Liaison Offices in Beirut and Damascus and for the appointment of a diplomatic agent to maintain such contact as may be necessary between the Secretary-General and the Arab capitals other than Amman. The United Kingdom Government understand that the object of these measures is to keep under continuous review the implementation of the Resolution of 21 August in relation to Jordan under present circumstances, and to provide means, in the event of a failure to implement the resolution, for the United Nations to take appropriate action.

2. The United Kingdom Government have been informed by the Secretary-General that the Governments concerned have again expressed their intention to conduct their relations with Jordan in accordance with the Resolution of 21 August, and in particular have expressed their willingness to restore Jordan's normal communications by land and air across their territories.

3. The United Kingdom Government have accordingly informed the Secretary-General that, taking this information into account, they are discussing with the Government of Jordan the fixing of dates for the beginning and completion of the withdrawal of British forces. It is the intention of the United Kingdom and Jordanian Governments that, provided satisfactory progress is being made on the lines set out in paragraphs 1 and 2 above, the withdrawal shall begin during the month of October and that it shall be completed as quickly as the situation in the area allows. The Governments of the United Kingdom and Jordan hope to be able to announce their decision on 1 October.

28 September 1958

[50] On October 8, 1958 the Department of State announced that "by agreement with the government of the Republic of Lebanon it has now been decided to complete withdrawal of U.S. forces . . . by the end of October." *Department of State Bulletin*, v. 39 (October 27, 1958), pp. 650-651.

C. The Baghdad Pact.

1. Baghdad Pact Council Meeting, Ankara, January 27-30, 1958.

(104) Final Communiqué, January 31, 1958.[1]

The Fourth Session of the Baghdad Pact Council was held in the new Grand National Assembly Building in Ankara from January 27 to January 30, 1958. His Excellency Mr. Adnan Menderes, Prime Minister of Turkey was in the Chair. The Delegations from the member countries were led by:—

(i) His Excellency Dr. Manouchehr Eghbal—Prime Minister—Iran

(ii) His Excellency Sayid Nuri Al-Said—Iraq

(iii) Malik Firoz Khan Noon—Prime Minister—Pakistan

(iv) His Excellency Mr. Adnan Menderes—Prime Minister—Turkey

(v) The Right Honourable Selwyn Lloyd—Secretary of State for Foreign Affairs—United Kingdom.

The United States participated through a delegation led by the Honourable John Foster Dulles, Secretary of State. The Council noted with satisfaction the presence of Mr. Dulles at the session.

The Council, during its four day session, reviewed the work of the Baghdad Pact Organisation and after discussions adopted the reports and recommendations of:—

(i) The Economic Committee;

(ii) The Liaison Committee;

(iii) The Counter Subversion Committee; and

(iv) The Military Committee.

The Council recalled that the Baghdad Pact arose from the desire of the peoples of the area for security from Communist imperialism or Communist-inspired domination in any shape or form, and noted with satisfaction that despite attacks on the Pact and its members, the Pact had developed into a strong and cohesive organisation representing the best hope for the safeguard of peace, liberty and independence in the area.

The purpose of the Pact, a free alliance between equal partners, is the defence and security of the area. This is as vital to world peace as it is to constructive cooperation for

[1] Ibid., v. 38 (February 17, 1958), pp. 255-257.

the benefit of the 135 million people of the Pact region who are predominantly Muslim.

The Council recognised that attempts at subversion in the area must be defeated and peaceful conditions maintained.

The Council reaffirmed that the economic progress of the Pact area and the promotion of the social well-being of its people require a speedy implementation of its programme of economic development.

Political

The Council reviewed the international situation in a series of meetings. A number of these meetings were of a private nature in which heads of delegations were able to exchange views and information with that frankness which befits the equal and intimate association of member countries within the Pact. The Council recognised the usefulness of full and candid discussions which have become an invaluable feature of the Baghdad Pact Organisation.

The Council recognised the need for the constant exposure of the familiar Communist technique of subversive penetration falsely presented as friendly co-existence and help for underdeveloped countries.

While the free world has taken bold and important steps in the liberation and granting of independence to many nations in recent years; and while it is striving to settle the problems of the area in a spirit of justice and equality, the Council noted with regret that in pursuit of its aims, the International Communist movement attempts to exploit nationalism, fear of war, economic distress, the plight of Arab refugees, "colonialism," and Afro-Asian sentiment through propaganda and Communist controlled and influenced organisations. Communist efforts to penetrate the region by means of indirect aggression such as infiltration and subversion continue to be a menace and call for constant vigilance and increased solidarity.

The Council further noted that since its last meeting in Karachi in June, 1957,[2] Communist imperialism had increased its efforts to dominate the Middle East. These efforts, in the form of pressure, threats and false accusations, were particularly directed by the Soviet Union against Turkey, whose calm and courageous stand evoked the admiration of her associates in the Council.

The Council expressed the desirability of cooperation

[2] *Documents on American Foreign Relations, 1957,* pp. 253-257.

between the Pact and other free world regional collective security organisations, in the belief that closer contacts among free world nations would contribute to their common cause of promoting security and social well-being for their peoples.

The Council noted with concern that areas of conflict which offer a rich opportunity for exploitation by Communist Imperialism and constitute a potential threat to international peace continue to exist in various parts of the world. It devoted considerable time to discussing the situations in the Mediterranean region, the Middle East and South Asia and emphasised that situations which imperil the security of the Pact area should be resolved in accordance with the principles of justice and the United Nations Charter.

The Council was of the opinion that the indiscriminate use of the Veto in the Security Council should be given up as an instrument of cold war so that the United Nations can function as an effective force for the pacific settlement of disputes.

The Council believed that the concept of the United Nations Emergency Force as an instrument of the United Nations and its use in areas of disturbance should be recommended for acceptance to members of the United Nations.

While recognising the continuing need for vigilance and therefore for constant improvement in the security and defence of the Pact area, the Council reaffirmed their earnest desire for peace and their determination to spare no efforts to seek it.

Economic

The Council reviewed the work of the Economic Committee and approved resolutions containing recommendations in the fields of health, agriculture, communications, public works, trade and the financing of joint projects.

The Council noted with satisfaction that a firm basis of economic cooperation had been established on which the Pact could continue to build and that, as a result of the work done by the sub-committees, there is now a promising programme of technical assistance which is developing on a cooperative basis. This will be of great benefit to the living standards in the Region.

Technical Assistance already provided or planned covers the following fields:—

Health; Agriculture; Pest-Control; Animal Health; and Animal Production.

In the field of technical assistance the Government of Iran has allocated 10,000,000 rials, the Government of Turkey TL750,000 over a period of 5 years. These are in addition to the offers made at Karachi (namely £1,000,000 over five years by the United Kingdom and RS.500,000 by Pakistan).

The Council noted that progress had been made in the implementation of approved joint projects. It approved the resolution of the Economic Committee for further implementation of these projects. This resolution recommends that the donor governments, members of the Baghdad Pact Economic Committee, give early and favourable consideration to providing assistance for such projects; and that member countries of the region continue their present efforts to implement them.

The Council recognised the need for specific action on approved projects and was pleased to note that the survey for the telecommunications network linking the capitals of the area members was already under way. It received with appreciation the announcement by the United States that it expected to provide an additional $10,000,000, thus ensuring that most of the funds needed for the construction of this network will be available. The United States referred also to the possibility of obtaining additional financing for joint projects from the World Bank, the Export-Import Bank and the recently established Development Loan Fund.

Scientific Cooperation:

The Council noted that cooperation among members of the Economic Committee and the sub-committees and in the Nuclear Centre and its Scientific Council is already making a contribution to the raising of standards of technical and scientific knowledge in the Pact countries. It decided that their Deputies should examine the possibilities of extending the present programme into wider fields.

Military

The Council noted that "The Combined Military Planning Organisation" had been set up in Baghdad last autumn. This gave considerable impetus to defensive military planning, increased the effectiveness of the defence efforts of the signatory states of the Pact and marked a significant step forward in the determination of member nations by international cooperation to uphold their sovereignty.

The Council approved the designation of the permanent planning organisation as the "Combined Military Planning Staff," and approved a charter for the Director and his staff. Among the duties of the Combined Military Planning Staff are the planning and coordination of combined staff training exercises.

The Council also accepted a recommendation of the Military Committee to hold combined staff training exercises in the near future.

The Council also accepted the Military Committee's recommendation to appoint Lt. General Ekrem Akalin of the Turkish Army to be Director of the Combined Military Planning Staff for the year 1958. He will be assisted by Major General Daniel S. Campbell of the United States Air Force, who has been the Deputy Director of the Combined Military Planning Staff since September 1957.

The Council commended the work in 1957 of the first Director of the Combined Military Planning Staff, Major General M. Habibullah Khan of the Pakistan Army.

Next Meeting of the Council

The Council decided to hold its next meeting at the Ministerial level in London in July, 1958. Meanwhile the Council will continue to meet regularly at the Deputy level.

2. Baghdad Pact Council Meeting, London, July 28-29, 1958.

(105) Declaration, July 28, 1958.[3]

1. The members of the Baghdad Pact attending the Ministerial meeting in London have re-examined their position in the light of recent events and conclude that the need which called the Pact into being is greater than ever. These members declare their determination to maintain their collective security and to resist aggression, direct or indirect.[4]

2. Under the Pact collective security arrangements have been instituted. Joint military planning has been advanced and area economic projects have been promoted. Relationships are being established with other free world nations associated for collective security.

[3] Department of State Bulletin, v. 39 (August 18, 1958), p. 273.
[4] Iraq was not represented at the meeting, although the revolutionary government did not formally withdraw from the Pact.

3. The question of whether substantive alterations should be made in the Pact and its organization or whether the Pact will be continued in its present form is under consideration by the Governments concerned. However, the nations represented at the meeting in London reaffirmed their determination to strengthen further their united defence posture in the area.

4. Article I of the Pact of Mutual Co-operation signed at Baghdad on February 24, 1955[5] provides that the parties will co-operate for their security and defence and that such measures as they agree to take to give effect to this co-operation may form the subject of special agreements. Similarly, the United States, in the interest of world peace, and pursuant to existing Congressional authorisation, agrees to co-operate with the nations making this Declaration for their security and defence, and will promptly enter into agreements designed to give effect to this co-operation.

MANOUCHEHR EGHBAL
Prime Minister of Iran
MALIK FIROZ KHAN NOON
Prime Minister of Pakistan
ADNAN MENDERES
Prime Minister of Turkey
HAROLD MACMILLAN
Prime Minister of the United Kingdom
JOHN FOSTER DULLES
Secretary of State, United States of America

(106) *Final Communiqué, July 29, 1958.*[6]

The Baghdad Pact Council met, as previously scheduled, in London on July 28 and July 29. The delegations from member countries present were led by:

(i) His Excellency Dr. Manouchehr Eghbal, Prime Minister, Iran.

(ii) His Excellency Malik Firoz Khan Noon, Prime Minister, Pakistan.

(iii) His Excellency Mr. Adnan Menderes, Prime Minister, Turkey.

(iv) The Right Honourable Harold Macmillan, Prime Minister, United Kingdom.

The United States delegation was led by Secretary of State, the Honourable John Foster Dulles.

[5] *Documents on American Foreign Relations, 1955,* pp. 342-344.
[6] *Department of State Bulletin,* v. 39 (August 18, 1958), p. 273.

Mr. Harold Macmillan, Prime Minister of the United Kingdom, was in the chair.

A significant Declaration was signed on July 28. The member governments represented welcomed the new initiative of the United States as set out in paragraph 4 of the Declaration, whereby the United States agreed to cooperate with the other nations making the Declaration for their security and defence.

The Ministers exchanged views on the world situation with particular reference to the Middle East. They expressed their concern at the recent examples of aggression by indirect means. This represents a spreading and dangerous threat to the independence and territorial integrity of sovereign states and should be combatted by all possible legitimate means including action by the United Nations. In this connection, the Ministers appreciated the recent prompt action taken in accordance with the principles of international law and in conformity with the United Nations Charter, by the United Kingdom and the United States of America in responding to the call for help of the lawful governments of Lebanon and Jordan.

The Ministers agreed to maintain the close contact existing between their Governments in order to achieve the aims and purposes of their association for mutual cooperation and to strengthen their ability to resist direct or indirect aggression.

D. The United Arab Republic.

(107) *Proclamation on the Merger of Syria and Egypt into the United Arab Republic, February 1, 1958.*[1]

On February 1, 1958, in a historic session held at Kubbah Palace in Cairo, His Excellency President Shukry El-Kuwatly of Syria and President Gamal Abdel Nasser of Egypt met the representatives of the Republics of Syria and Egypt: El Sayed Sabry El-Assaly, El Sayed Abdel Latif El-Baghdady, El Sayed Khaled El-Azm, El Sayed Zakaria Mohieddin, El Sayed Hamed El-Khoga, El Sayed Anwar El-Sadat, El Sayed Fakher El-Kayyaly, El Sayed Maamoun El-Kozbary, El Sayed Hussein El-Shaffei, El Sayed Assaad Haroun, General Abdel Hakim Amer, El Sayed Salah Eddin El-Bitar, El Sayed Kamaleddin Hussein, El Sayed Khalil El-Kallas, El Sayed Noureddin

[1] *Current History*, v. 34 (April 1958), p. 239.

Tarraf, El Sayed Saleh Akeil, El Sayed Fathy Radwan, General Afif El-Bizry, El Sayed Mahmoud Fawzi, El Sayed Kamal Ramzi Stino, El Sayed Aly Sabri, El Sayed Abdel Rahman El-Azm, and El Sayed Mahmoud Riad.

The purpose of this meeting was to discuss the final measures to be taken for the realization of the Arab people's will, and the execution of what the Constitutions of both Republics stipulate, namely that the people of each of them form a part of the Arab nation. They, therefore, discussed the decisions unanimously approved by the National Assembly of Egypt and the Syrian House of Representatives that unity should be established between the two countries as a preliminary step towards the realization of complete Arab unity. They also discussed the clear signs manifest in the past few years, that Arab nationalism was the inspiring spirit that dominated the history of Arabs in all their different countries, their common present and the hoped-for future of every Arab.

They came to the conclusion that this unity which is the fruit of Arab nationalism is the Arabs' path to sovereignty and freedom, that it is one of humanity's gateways to peace and cooperation, and that it is therefore their duty to take this unity with persistence and determination staunch and unwavering out of the circle of wishes and aspirations to where it can be converted into a reality. They came out of this with the conviction that the elements conducive to the success of the union of the two Republics were abundant, particularly recently after their joint struggle which had brought them even closer to one another and made the meaning of nationalism considerably clearer. They stressed the fact that it was a movement for liberation and rehabilitation and that it was a faith in peace and cooperation.

For all this, the participants declare their total agreement, complete faith and deeply rooted confidence in the necessity of uniting Egypt and Syria into one state to be named "The United Arab Republic." They have likewise decided to declare their unanimous agreement on the adoption of a presidential democratic system of government for the Arab Republic. The executive authority shall be vested in the head of the state assisted by the ministers appointed by him and responsible to him. The legislative authority shall be vested in one legislative house. The new Republic shall have one flag, one army, one people who shall remain joined in a unity where all will share equal rights and duties, where all will call for the protection of their country with heart and soul, and complete in the consolidation of its integrity and the insurance of its invulnerability.

His Excellency President Shukry El-Kuwatly and President Gamal Abdel Nasser will each deliver a statement to the people in the Syrian and the Egyptian Parliaments respectively on Wednesday, February 5, 1958, in which they will announce the decision reached in this meeting and explain the principles of the unity on which this rising young republic shall stand. The peoples of Egypt and Syria shall be called upon to participate in a general plebiscite on the principles of this unity and the choice of the head of the state within thirty days.

In proclaiming these decisions, the participants feel great pride and overwhelming joy in having assisted in taking this positive step on the road to Arab unity and solidarity, a unity which had been for many an epoch and many a generation the Arabs' much cherished hope and greatly coveted objective.

In deciding on the unity of both nations, the participants declare that their unity aims at the unification of all the Arab peoples and affirm that the door is open for participation to any Arab state desirous of joining them in a union or federation for the purpose of protecting the Arab peoples from harm and evil, strengthening Arab sovereignty, and safeguarding its existence.

May God protect this step we have taken and those which are to follow with His ever vigilant care and benevolence so that the Arab people under the banner of unity may live in dignity and peace.

(108) *United States Recognition of the United Arab Republic, February 25, 1958.*[2]

STATEMENT ON RECOGNITION

The United States Government has been officially informed of the proclamation of the United Arab Republic following the plebiscite conducted in Egypt and Syria on February 21. The United States Government, having taken note of the assurances of the United Arab Republic that it intends to respect and observe its international obligations, including all international obligations of Egypt, and Syria, respectively, existing at the time of the formation of the United Arab Republic, extended recognition [today] to the

[2] *Department of State Bulletin*, v. 38 (March 17, 1958), p. 418.

Government of the United Arab Republic, with the expression of its good wishes.

(109) *Joint Statement on Talks Held between the President of the United Arab Republic (Nasser) and the Chairman of the Council of Ministers of the USSR (Khrushchev), Moscow, May 15, 1958.*[3]

(Excerpts)

President of the United Arab Republic Gamal Abdel Nasser made an official visit to the Soviet Union at the invitation of the Presidium of the U.S.S.R. Supreme Soviet and the Soviet government.

During his visit to the U.S.S.R., statesmen of both countries held friendly talks in an atmosphere of trust and friendship.

*   *   *

As a result of the talks, both governments reached the following conclusions:

Both governments express their profound satisfaction with the development of close and constantly expanding relations between the two countries; they will work for a further development and strengthening of these relations on the basis of the following principles:

mutual respect for the sovereignty and territorial integrity of all states;

noninterference of any sort whatsoever in the internal affairs of any other state;

settlement of international problems solely by peaceful means and rejection of the use of force or threat of force against the sovereignty or independence of any other state;

inadmissibility of the use of political or economic pressure;

equality of rights among states and among peoples in their relations.

Both governments adhere to the principles of the peaceful co-existence of states regardless of their social systems and consider that this principle is the cornerstone for the development of friendly relations among states and is in keeping with the interests of peace among peoples.

They consider that putting an end to the "cold war,"

[3] *Pravda*, May 16, 1958. Translation reproduced from *The Current Digest of the Soviet Press*, v. 10 (June 25, 1958), p. 3.

which is doing serious harm to the relations among peoples, is in keeping with the vital interests of all peoples and will facilitate the development of friendly and good-neighbor relations among them and the strengthening of mutual trust in the relations among states.

They condemn colonialism in all its manifestations and forms and uphold the right of all peoples to self-determination and independence. Both governments condemn the existence of the military bases of one country on the territory of another. Such bases are a serious threat to international peace and violate the independence of those states in which they are situated; these bases must be liquidated.

Both governments have considered the question of the rights of the Palestine Arabs and their expulsion from their homeland. They have also considered the question of the violation of human rights and the threat to peace and safety in this area that has resulted from their expulsion. Both governments affirm their full support of the legitimate rights of the Palestine Arabs.

Both governments condemn the colonial aggression against Yemen and attempts to interfere in Yemen's internal affairs. Both governments fully support the independence, sovereignty and territorial integrity of Yemen.

Both governments condemn the barbarous war that France is waging against the Algerian people and the crimes that the French Armed Forces are committing against this heroic Arab country.

* * *

Both governments express their profound concern over acts of interference by certain foreign states in the internal affairs of Indonesia. They see this interference as a threat to world peace and safety and a violation of the U.N. Charter; they declare that a stop must be put to this interference and that the independence and sovereignty of Indonesia must be respected.

* * *

Both governments feel equally strongly that the Chinese People's Republic must be represented in the United Nations to rectify the existing abnormal situation and in the interests of international cooperation and a reduction of tensions in the Far East and the world as a whole.

Both governments assert their support of the principles

enunciated at Bandung,[4] principles that continue to unite the peoples of Asia and Africa, that have attracted ever-growing attention from world public opinion and that were reaffirmed by the Afro-Asian Solidarity Conference, held in Cairo in 1957,[5] which gave expression to the hopes and dreams of these two continents. Both governments also proclaim their support for the principles enunciated by the Conference of Independent States of Africa, which was held in Accra in April, 1958.[6]

Both governments express their profound concern over the armaments race, which is one of the greatest dangers to world peace and which could lead to a devastating nuclear war. Both governments proclaim that testing of atomic and hydrogen weapons must be stopped by all states that possess such weapons, pending the conclusion of the necessary agreement or agreements on the final and unconditional prohibition of all types of nuclear weapons, including termination of their production, their removal from the armaments of all states and the destruction of existing stockpiles of these weapons.

Both governments proclaim that atomic and hydrogen energy must be used solely for peaceful purposes and that all states must cooperate in this field in order to raise the standard of living of all peoples, especially the peoples of the underdeveloped countries.

Both governments feel that all states must multiply their efforts to reach eventual agreement on a sizeable reduction in armed forces and armaments.

* * *

Both governments are firmly convinced that the development of economic and cultural relations among states should be encouraged both as a means of establishing mutual understanding among peoples and reducing tension and as a means serving the aims of preserving peace. Such relations should not be accompanied by any conditions or motives directed at establishing the dominance of one country over another.

Both governments proclaim that the economic and cultural agreements between the Soviet Union and the United Arab Republic meet these conditions and are based on sound principles. They also proclaim their complete satisfaction

[4] *Documents on American Foreign Relations, 1955*, pp. 332-341.
[5] Document 112, below.
[6] Document 113, below.

with the development of economic and cultural cooperation between their countries and the exchange of goods between them. In this connection the government of the United Arab Republic has expressed its gratitude to the Soviet Union for its important contribution to the United Arab Republic's program of industrialization. Both governments affirm their determination to promote a further development of economic and cultural cooperation between the two countries for their common good.

Both governments feel that artificial barriers to international trade must be eliminated.

Both governments express their complete satisfaction with the results of the present talks.

*   *   *

N. S. KHRUSHCHEV,
Chairman of U.S.S.R.
Council of Ministers
Moscow, May 15, 1958.

GAMAL ABDEL NASSER,
President of United
Arab Republic

E. Afghanistan.

(110) *Joint Statement on Talks Held between the President and the Prime Minister of Afghanistan (Daud), June 27, 1958.*[1]

The President of the United States and His Royal Highness Sardar Mohammad Daud, Prime Minister of Afghanistan, today concluded friendly and fruitful discussions on various matters of mutual interest. These discussions have been supplemented by talks between the Prime Minister and his advisers and the Secretary of State and other American officials.

The Prime Minister, who is visiting the United States upon the invitation of the President, has also been introduced to both Houses of the United States Congress and has met with the Justices of the United States Supreme Court. At the conclusion of his Washington stay, the Prime Minister will tomorrow begin a 12-day coast-to-coast tour of the United States during which he will meet with various civic, cultural and business leaders.

In their review of the world situation, as well as of developments in various areas of the globe, the President and Prime Minister were conscious of the universal desire of all peoples that war be eliminated and peace based on international justice be established. They reaffirmed their deter-

[1] *Department of State Bulletin*, v. 39 (July 21, 1958), pp. 127-128.

mination to work for peace and security in the world. In behalf of their respective governments, they reasserted their firm attachment to the principles of the United Nations Charter and their determination to continue to cooperate in advancing the objectives of that vital instrument for peace.

Throughout the discussions between the Prime Minister and American representatives there was emphasis on the cordiality and genuine friendship which characterize Afghan-American relations. The President explained the principles and goals of the United States in the field of international affairs and the Prime Minister similarly described the attitude of the Government of Afghanistan in the field of international affairs including its traditional policy of neutrality and independence. It was agreed that both nations share beliefs in mutual respect for the sovereignty and independence of nations, in non-interference in the affairs of others, in social and economic progress for all peoples, and in the dignity of the human individual.

In this spirit, which underlay the examination of specific aspects of the relationship between the two countries, the Prime Minister was assured of the continuing readiness of the United States to be of assistance to Afghanistan in its high objective of developing the resources of the country for the welfare of the people. It was agreed that cooperation which already exists in the development of Afghan civil aviation, the Helmand Valley, surface transportation projects, and the Afghan educational system will be continued with a view toward making each of these projects as efficient and effective as circumstances permit.

As a symbol of the warm relations existing between the two countries and as an indication of a desire of the two nations to base their relations on mutual understanding, a cultural agreement between the Government of Afghanistan and the Government of the United States was signed on June 26.[2]

In concluding their discussions, the President and the Prime Minister agreed that the exchanges of views between Afghan and United States representatives have been most useful. They expressed their desire to maintain and strengthen the cordial understanding between the two countries, which was so manifest during the Prime Minister's visit.

SARDAR MOHAMMAD DAUD
DWIGHT D. EISENHOWER

[2] *Ibid.*, p. 128.

CHAPTER SIX

AFRICA

A. United States Policy.

(111) *Address by the Assistant Secretary of State for African Affairs (Satterthwaite) before the Western Regional Assembly, Lake Arrowhead, October 9, 1958.*[1]

Since last May, when the American Assembly held its seminar at Arden House, much has happened on the African scene. In fact the available topics one might consider are too numerous to consider adequately in a single talk. Consequently I shall limit my discourse tonight to sketching the current status of African nationalism, Africa's struggle for economic development, and our policies relating to these two basic topics.

The Status of Nationalism in Africa Today

As has been said again and again, the urge to create a national entity and to exercise the prerogatives of self-government is clearly the major political, social, and economic force at work in most of Africa today. This great drive—this dynamic force of nationalism—is weaving profound changes in the pattern of African society and is of direct and fundamental importance, first, to Europe and, of course, to the United States, the Americas, and Asia.

Political observers predict that within the next few years nearly 75 percent of the 140 million Africans still living in dependent territories will be governing themselves. Yet this great sociopolitical drama is taking place largely without the glare of publicity, for the spotlight of world attention is focused on more spectacular developments in the Near and Far East.

African nationalism, like the continent itself, is diverse. We cannot therefore expect to find many generalizations that will clearly interpret all the national dramas unfolding on

[1] *Department of State Bulletin,* v. 39 (October 27, 1958), pp. 641-648.

this great continent. Let us, then, survey some recent developments there and analyze their significance.

In northwest Africa, for example, dynamic nationalism is expressing itself among the independent states in strenuous efforts to realize a fuller sense of independence and complete sovereignty—in a word, to consolidate the gains of the last few years.

In the continent's oldest independent states, Ethiopia and Liberia, the prevailing spirit today can be described as that of awakening fervor, a growing sense of belonging to a new Africa on the move, and an increasing desire for national progress on all fronts—social, economic, and political.

In vast sub-Sahara Africa the trend is toward regional cooperation in quest of a greater unity of purpose in the nationalist movement, which, however, has still not reached every territory in the region.

The first conference of independent African states was held at Accra last April 15 to 22 on the invitation of Prime Minister Nkrumah.[2] This conference made clear that a major objective of the eight independent states of Africa participating is the rapid end of the continent's colonial system and the strengthening of their own independence.

Perhaps the most ambitious effort since World War II to revitalize the pan-African movement will be the All-African Peoples Conference, which has been called by the Convention Peoples Party of Ghana to convene in Accra from December 5 to 12 of this year.[3] Its sponsors report they are inviting all known African political parties to attend. About 60 such parties and organizations from countries and territories throughout the continent are already associated with the project, and the sponsors hope to have delegates from 100 organizations on hand by the time the conference convenes.

The main purpose of this assemblage, in the words of its hosts, is ". . . to formulate concrete plans and work out the Gandhian tactics and strategy of the African non-violent revolution in relation to colonialism and imperialism; racialism and discriminatory laws and practices; tribalism and religious separatism; and the position of chieftaincy under colonial rule and under a democratic society."

The United States will not be alone in watching with great interest the outcome of this conference.

[2] Document 113, below.
[3] The Conference was actually held from December 8 to 13, 1958.

It is clear that the majority of Africans today are seeking political unity of purpose, energy, and endeavor. The evolving European Community and other European efforts to achieve unity are in themselves examples for such endeavor. We may ask, then, where are the militant forces of nationalism leading Africa?

To answer this question, we need first to examine African objectives as stated by the continent's leaders themselves.

For example, Prime Minister Nkrumah of Ghana wrote in an article entitled "African Prospect" in the October issue of *Foreign Affairs* that, despite the diversity of Africa and the divergences, differences, and varying points of emphasis one finds in the continent, there are currently three traits common to all Africa. In his own words these are:

"1. Our desire to see Africa free and independent.

2. Our determination to pursue foreign policies based upon non-alignment.

3. Our urgent need for economic development."

In short, responsible and articulate Africans today seek equality, dignity, and justice for themselves and their fellow countrymen. They seek to bridge as rapidly as possible the great gulf between conditions on their continent and in the Western World. They are clearly determined to eliminate old-fashioned colonialism and racial discrimination from the African Continent. They seek to play an important and expanding role in world affairs—to project the new "African personality" on the world scene. As indicated by the various all-African conferences to which I have just referred, they seek to gain their objectives by achieving a greater unity of purpose among their diverse and disparate peoples.

What should the United States attitude toward these African nationalist objectives be?

Insofar as these objectives are progressive, just, and constructive, insofar as the methods employed to achieve the objectives are nonviolent and equitable, our attitude—in accordance with our national history, character, and tradition —should obviously be one of sympathy and support.

Secretary Dulles in his personal message to Prime Minister Nkrumah delivered at the opening of the Accra conference of independent states last April, declared: "Through you, I wish to assure the African nations that they can count on the sympathetic interest of the people and Government of the United States. The United States will continue to stand ready to support the constructive efforts of the states of

Africa to achieve a stable, prosperous community, conscious of its interdependence within the family of nations and dedicated to the principles of the United Nations Charter."

What should be our policy toward the diverse dependent territories now emerging toward varying forms of self-government and aspiring for independence?

Having long recognized that traditional colonialism is coming to an end, the United States supports the principle of orderly transition to self-government and eventual self-determination in the interests of all parties and peoples involved. The speed of this evolution, we believe, should be determined by the capacity of the African populations concerned to assume and discharge the responsibilities of self-government.

The United States supports European measures designed to provide self-government and eventual autonomy to dependent African territories. Insofar as we are able to do so, we also encourage moderate African leaders who recognize the benefit to their own people of evolutionary rather than revolutionary progress. In this connection the United States believes that all concerned should consider seriously the dangerous pitfalls that confront a newly independent state today. Economic viability, established and stable political, social, and cultural institutions, trained cadres of civil servants, and at least a modicum of experienced technicians are generally regarded as essential to a modern nation.

I should also like to point out that many Africans now look with gratitude and appreciation on their associations with the European powers, and we believe that the time may well come when most Africans will do so. For it is these powers which have brought Africa advanced administrative techniques, modern economic-development methods, needed public-health and educational measures, and great capital investment and construction.

The U.N. Trusteeship System

And speaking of constructive assistance in development, let us turn now to a consideration of one of the most important systems for political advancement in operation on the African Continent, the United Nations trusteeship system, which is designed to bring about "independence by orderly evolution."

This system is responsible for six trust territories: French Togo, British and French Cameroons, Ruanda-Urundi,

Tanganyika, and Somalia. A seventh territory—British Togo —joined the newly independent state of Ghana in March of 1957 in accordance with the will of the Togo population expressed in a popular plebiscite supervised by the United Nations.

Provision is made under this system for periodic visiting missions to the territories under trusteeship and also for hearing petitioners in person at sessions of the Trusteeship Council and the United Nations General Assembly.

A U.N. Trusteeship Council visiting mission will leave later this month for the British and French Cameroons, under the chairmanship of Mr. Benjamin Gerig of the United States. Representatives from Haiti, India, and New Zealand complete the mission, which has been requested to include in its report on the British Cameroons its views on the methods of consultation which should be adopted when the time comes for the people to express their wishes concerning their future. The mission will subsequently also examine conditions in French Cameroun, where important constitutional advances have been made in the past 2 years.

We are encouraged by a recent statement from French official sources to the effect that agreement has been reached between the French and Togo governments on plans which it is hoped will result in independence for Togo within the framework of the U.N. Charter.[4] Progress is also being made toward this same objective in negotiations between the French and Cameroun governments, an agreement having been drafted which now awaits approval of the two governments.

In accordance with the trusteeship agreement entered into by Italy and the General Assembly of the United Nations in 1950, the Trust Territory of Somaliland under Italian administration is scheduled to become the independent state of Somalia in 1960. Elections will probably be held early next year for a new legislative assembly which will be authorized to prepare the constitution for the new state. Although Somalia is faced with a large budgetary deficit and has a disputed border with Ethiopia, there is no reason to doubt that the orderly transition of this country to full independence will unfold as expected. The Trusteeship Council is concerned with exploring the possibilities of providing the

[4] See United Nations, General Assembly, *Official Records, Thirteenth Session,* Supplement No. 18 (A/4090), p. 31.

necessary economic assistance when independence is achieved, and the disputed border problem has been submitted to arbitration.

Tanganyika, a British East African trust territory, the largest and most populous of all African trust territories, held its first national elections in 5 of its 10 electoral districts last month. It will hold elections in the remaining 5 districts next spring to complete its new 67-member Legislative Council. The Council is formed on the multi-racial principle, with representatives from the African, Indian, and European communities. These elections have been held on the basis of a common roll, with each voter voting for three candidates— one each from the African, Asian, and European communities.

Following completion of these elections next year, the Constitutional Committee of the Tanganyika Legislative Council will be established to consider further constitutional steps to take, such as a review of the parity system of equal communal representation and of the possibility of increasing African representation on the Council. The Trusteeship Council at its 21st session this spring expressed the hope that the Tanganyika government would review its national electoral qualifications with a view to introducing universal suffrage with the least possible delay.

A 1957 visiting mission to the Belgian Trust Territory of Ruanda-Urundi reported that that territory was making encouraging progress toward the goals of the trusteeship system. Steps are being taken to eliminate the remaining vestiges of feudalistic society and to install institutions more in keeping with the principles of modern democracy; public opinion is making a greater effort to express itself, and the ultimate development of Ruanda-Urundi into a modern African state can now be envisaged.

Reviewing the progress of trust areas toward self-government or independence over the past 10 years, I believe we can fairly conclude that these areas are not only keeping pace with the non-trust territories emerging into independent states in Africa but will develop toward fuller autonomy at least as well-organized and experienced as those areas which have not had the benefits of the trusteeship system.

The United States is proud of the role it has played in the trusteeship process and will continue, where appropriate, to assist those African leaders who, during the trusteeship period, have sought to bring their countries into independence through the full exercise of democratic principles and practices.

Before I turn to other aspects of African nationalist development, I feel that I also should mention the constructive work of a less publicized and nonpermanent United Nations body that has concerned itself with conditions in African dependent areas—the Committee on Information from Non-Self-Governing Territories. The United Nations, of course, has no responsibility for the supervision of dependent areas other than trust territories. However, all governments having dependent territories are obligated by the charter of the United Nations to report regularly to the United Nations on the economic, social, and educational conditions in these areas.

The 14-member Committee on Information from Non-Self-Governing Territories, of which the United States has been a member since its inception, was created by the United Nations to review these reports and to make general recommendations on economic, social, and educational conditions. These recommendations can be very useful to governments which are engaged in promoting the orderly social and political evolution of the dependent territories under their jurisdiction.

Turning to developments in other parts of Africa, our attention first logically focuses on the recent constitutional referendum held in the 14 African territories of France (including Madagascar) on September 28. This single, dramatic action was one of the most significant and far-reaching developments in the political evolution of Africa this year and should result in a new and mutually beneficial association between France and French African territories.

As a result of this election, held on the basis of universal suffrage for all over 21, the territory of French Guinea, which voted in favor of its independence, is taking steps to withdraw from the French West African Federation.[5] The 13 other African territories of France will presumably be organized into the new French Community within the next 6 months. Each territory will apparently have full local autonomy. Matters common to members of the Community, such as defense, foreign relations, and currency, will be

[5] Guinea became an independent Republic on October 2, 1958. See *Department of State Bulletin*, v. 39 (December 15, 1958), p. 966.

handled by special federal institutions in which the French Government will have the dominant voice.

The executive of the new Community will be the President of the French Republic, assisted by a government composed of the French and territorial premiers and French ministers dealing with matters of community interest. A senate and a court of arbitration to settle disputes between territories are also provided.

According to the constitution, those territories which choose to join the Community may subsequently leave it and become independent. This independence, however, is to be negotiated between the territory and metropolitan France. It is hoped that a continuing close and profitable relationship will be maintained between France and these areas.

Developments in British African territories are equally encouraging. Forty-five delegates from Nigeria are currently holding a constitutional conference in London to determine the steps to be taken to lead the giant West African Federation of some 35 million people to independence in 1960. The conferees are struggling to settle such problems as the question of creating new states within the Federation, which now is divided into three large regions, the problem of the allocation of revenues between the regional and federal governments, the control of police, and electoral laws. In 1957, at another constitutional conference held in London, the Eastern and Western Regions requested internal self-government and have since achieved it. The Northern Region— the most populous and predominantly Muslin—wants self-government by March of 1959, and the southern Cameroons, a British trust territory which is represented in the federal Nigerian government, seeks internal self-government by October 1959.

Next year federal elections will be held throughout Nigeria, and the new House of Assembly will be asked to approve a motion formally requesting the British to grant independence to the Federation in 1960. Great Britain indicated last year that it would receive such a resolution sympathetically and be prepared to fix the date for ending the colonial rule which began about 100 years ago.

British Sierra Leone in west Africa and Uganda in east Africa are also making important strides toward autonomy and self-government. Kenya has held elections to fill the larger representation accorded Africans in the Legislative Council.

Pressure for still greater African participation in the multi-racial crown colony's government continues very strong, however.

The Search for a Just Racial Policy

The major political problem of east and central Africa, of course, is that of working out equitable policies to govern relations between the many races living side by side there.

Prime Minister Sir Roy Welensky of the Federation of Rhodesia and Nyasaland, in an article in the October edition of *Western World* published in Paris on September 24, said: "It is my firm belief that the regime of friendship, of cooperation between the races which we endeavor to practice in the Federation of Rhodesia and Nyasaland, does the most for the people of Africa."

The Federation, in effect, hopes to settle the race problem through a policy of racial partnership.

On the other hand, in such regions as west Africa, where white settlers are few or come almost exclusively as missionaries, traders, teachers, administrators, or technicians, racial problems have been relatively minor.

One can conclude then that contact between Africans and Europeans alone does not give rise to serious race problems, but social and economic competition between two permanently established racial groups—such as in settler areas—does seem to do so. The problem resolves essentially around the African aspiration to approximate more nearly the higher European living standard and to increase his share of his country's great natural resources and production.

Although we cannot ignore the many dangers inherent in any failure to meet the problem of harmonious relationships between the several races inhabiting Africa's dependent and independent territories, we must recognize that at the present time—in view of our own domestic problems—we must in humility avoid proposing specific solutions. We can and must, however, continue to stand steadfastly for the universal principle of nondiscrimination and racial equality.

Insofar as we are able to solve this knotty problem of harmonious race relationships within our own borders we will be in a better moral position to exercise greater influence for moderate solutions of racial problems in Africa and elsewhere in the world.

Alien Pressures: Communism

In addition to the disturbing influence of racial friction, the nationalist movement in Africa is further harassed by the machinations of international communism, forever seeking to turn fluid situations to advantage for the Communist bloc.

At the Cairo Afro-Asian Solidarity Conference held last December and January, the Communists notified the world that Africa was to be the next arena of their anticolonial subversion.[6]

In recent months the Communists have vigorously continued their work of penetrating individual African labor organizations, youth groups, and nationalist organizations. They continue working overtime in Egypt and western Europe to influence the thousands of African students now studying there, bringing many either to bloc countries or the Soviet Union on scholarships or "guided" tours. They are devoting greatly increased study and research to African subjects and training more specialists in African affairs both in the Soviet Union and its satellites. In the last 2 years they have signed trade agreements with most of the independent African states. They are pressing to exchange diplomatic representatives with those independent states with which they have not yet done so.

Although the current Soviet economic, cultural, and diplomatic offensive has not shown important results in Africa, no one can afford to be complacent. Persistent and ingenious Communists, skilled in subversive and revolutionary tactics, must be reckoned with. Success in meeting the Communist challenge in Africa will directly depend on success in helping Africans realize their legitimate political and economic aspirations in a progressive manner.

The Struggle for Economic Development

Africa's economic and social needs, closely related to her political and racial problems, are numerous and pressing. Among them are the need for more public and private capital for investment and development; for more technical, executive, and organizational skills and abilities; for more transportation and communication facilities; and for diversification of one-crop economies.

Constituting a major challenge to our wisdom, good will, and generosity, these economic problems require prompt

[6] Document 112, below.

remedial action. They are so numerous that no one nation can possibly solve them alone. Africa must have and deserves the cooperative support of all nations of the free world in this endeavor. Much is already being done.

The United Nations is contributing in numerous ways to assisting Africa's development. One-sixth of all loans made by the International Bank for Reconstruction and Development since 1951 have gone to African states and territories. Mr. Eugene R. Black, bank president, estimates that the International Bank's lending in Africa this year will be approximately $100 million. He has indicated, further, that he foresees a growing amount of bank activity there. The United States, it should be stressed, contributes at least 40 percent of the funds of the bank. The Soviet Union, it is equally important to note, is not even a member.

The United Nations Technical Assistance Program has been devoting more than $3 million annually to African development and is expected to expand this sum considerably in the years ahead.

This spring the Economic and Social Council of the United Nations created a new Economic Commission for Africa, which will establish its headquarters in Addis Ababa. The first session of this body will be held in December of this year. The United States is not a member of the Commission but will be represented by observers at its opening session.

We believe this new United Nations organ will be able to bring into focus Africa's many economic problems as well as its opportunities. It will be in a position to help the states of Africa find effective answers to their problems. It will also provide a forum for a broad exchange of views and ideas as well as for the more detailed consideration of future plans and new techniques for accelerating African economic development.

Side by side with economic development, of course, must come social progress. Both the United Nations and the countries of the free world must contribute to Africa's social advancement, for the advancement of African agriculture and its progress in industrialization must take into account available human resources and the social patterns within which economic development takes place. This is particularly true since social patterns in Africa range from primitive tribal organizations to highly developed urban societies.

In this connection we can note happily the important contributions to African social as well as economic development of the United Nations technical agencies—the World Health Organization (WHO), the Food and Agriculture Organization (FAO), the United Nations Children's Fund (UNICEF), the International Labor Organization (ILO), and the United Nations Educational, Scientific and Cultural Organization (UNESCO). The newly created Economic Commission for Africa will also consider social questions insofar as they are related to economic development.

United States and European private investments are of growing significance to African economic development. Our investment in the continent now totals about $624 million, one-half of which is in the Union of South Africa. European investment is many times that sum. European governments are expending between $600 and $700 million annually in African areas, principally for economic assistance to their dependent territories.

The United States reciprocal trade agreement and mutual security programs, which have been in effect for some years now, demonstrate clear recognition of our interdependence and mutuality of interest with other nations of the free world, including the African nations. For the last 2 fiscal years, the mutual security program alone has provided more than $70 million annually in economic and technical assistance to Morocco, Tunisia, Libya, Ethiopia, Somalia, Ghana, Liberia, and British African territories. Our 1959 fiscal year aid level will be greater than that of last year.

The United States Export-Import Bank has been providing African countries $10 to $15 million annually in development loans. The new Development Loan Fund is now beginning to announce approval of loans for African states. It is hoped that the volume of these loans can be increased, providing sufficient capital is made available by Congress.

In order to build sound and enduring economies in African territories, investment and expanding trade are necessary. Here private investment must play its part. In this connection it is of interest to note that the Stanford Research Institute has just recently announced a program to stimulate private overseas investment in Africa. This new program, made possible by funds from private industries and foundations, will compile information on investment opportunities throughout the continent.

In his address before the United Nations General Assembly on September 18,[7] Secretary Dulles outlined eight steps that

[7] *Department of State Bulletin*, v. 39 (October 6, 1958), pp. 525-530.

the United States would be prepared, subject to action by Congress as appropriate, to take or support in the coming year for worldwide economic-development purposes.

These steps, which bear repeating at this time because of their applicability to African needs, would include:

1. Pressing vigorously and effectively forward with existing development financing programs;

2. Increasing efforts to emphasize the constructive role that private initiative can play in economic development;

3. Considering how the United States might cooperate with regional development programs, where desired by the countries of the region and where the advantage of the regional over the bilateral approach would be evident;

4. Considering the advisability of increasing the capital of the International Bank for Reconstruction and Development and the quotas of the International Monetary Fund;

5. Considering the feasibility of creating an International Development Association, as an affiliate of the International Bank, under conditions likely to assure broad and effective support;

6. Supporting vigorously technical assistance through our own programs, through the expanded United Nations technical assistance programs, and through a substantial initial contribution to the new United Nations Special Projects Fund;

7. Enlisting the assistance of United States universities and scientific institutions, joining with those of other cooperating countries to achieve scientific and technological breakthroughs on problems of particular concern to less developed countries; and

8. Seeking funds from the Congress for health programs.

It is anticipated that in the months ahead the administration will set forth fuller details of these programs.

Conclusions

I have spoken at some length on Africa's political, economic, and social problems and developments and our relationship thereto. Let us summarize our conclusions.

First, the United States must properly evaluate the dynamic political forces currently at work in Africa. Recognizing the vital interdependence of Africa and Europe, we must also support constructive African political evolution and work for mutual understanding of our own policies and support for our common ideals as set forth in the United Nations Charter.

Africa is generally friendly to the West, although independent African states have evinced no apparent desire to formulate formal alliances. The threatening this basic attitude of friendliness, however, is the insidious international Communist force, which would deny the area to the West and ensnare it into the political and socioeconomic slavery of communism. We of the West have no time to lose. We must anticipate events, sympathetically understand African aspirations, and help to meet them.

Second, as it is clear that a basic African need is for timely help in economic and social development and the eradication of disease, ignorance, and poverty, the United States must act promptly, generously, and wisely with adequate economic and technical assistance to this vast underdeveloped continent. To do so we must have the full understanding and support of the American people.

The opportunity to develop a sound base for enduring friendly relations and mutual cooperation with an emerging Africa is ours today. We must make the most of this opportunity without delay.

B. The Afro-Asian People's Solidarity Conference, Cairo, December 26, 1957—January 1, 1958.

(112) *Declaration, Cairo, January 1, 1958.*[1]

We, Afro-Asian peoples, who met in Cairo from December 26, 1957, to January 1, 1958, to discuss international problems that concern Afro-Asian peoples in particular, reviewed the political, economic, social and cultural problems which face our peoples.

We have been animated with one feeling only—co-operation and unity among our peoples and close friendship with all the peoples of the world.

After seven days of harmonious discussion our Conference has reached unanimous agreements on proposals for the solution of various problems. This proves that the Afro-Asian peoples in the task of supporting peace have reached unity on a higher level and have arrived at a common program of action. The Conference has unanimously agreed to set up a permanent organization in Cairo for the purpose of promoting the realization of its resolutions.

We declare that the principles adopted by the Bandung Conference of April 1955 should remain the basis of international relations. We renew our absolute support for the

[1] *New Times*, January 16, 1958. Supplement, pp. 3-4.

following ten principles which have had the backing of our peoples during the past years:

1. Respect for the fundamental rights of man and the principles and objectives of the U.N. Charter.

2. Respect for the sovereignty of all peoples and the integrity of their territories.

3. Recognition of equality among all races and all nations, big and small.

4. Abstention from all intervention into the affairs of our countries.

5. Respect for the right of nations to defend themselves individually or collectively according to the U.N. Charter.

6. a) Abstention from the use of collective defence organizations for the private ends of any Great Power.

b) Abstention of any Power from applying pressure on other countries.

7. Avoidance of aggressive actions and threats and of the use of force against the regional security or the political independence of any country.

8. Settling of all international disputes by peaceful methods, such as negotiations, conciliation, arbitration, judicial measures or any other peaceful methods chosen by the parties concerned according to the U.N. Charter.

9. Development of our common interests and mutual cooperation.

10. Respect for justice and international obligations.

We are fully convinced that if these ten principles are accepted, the present world tension will definitely relax and the deadly fear of annihilation that now grips the hearts of the millions can be lifted.

We declare that the foundations of peace cannot be firmly established until we dissipate this tension. We welcome every step taken in this direction. We call upon the peoples of the world to use every possible means for the creation of areas of agreement and understanding which will inevitably lead to disarmament, to the banning of the production of nuclear weapons, their experiments and use. We call upon the peoples of the world to direct their scientific efforts and the use of nuclear energy towards peaceful purposes and the service of humanity and for the realization of prosperity and complete cooperation among the peoples on the basis of equality and according to the U.N. Charter.

The Afro-Asian peoples believe that imperialist domination, foreign exploitation and the other evils which result from the subjugation of peoples are a denial of the fundamental rights of man and a violation of the U.N. Charter apart from the other harmful effects on both the governments and the governed which impede the development of peace and international cooperation. The continued existence of imperialism is not compatible with the new era the world is now passing through. The Afro-Asian peoples firmly believe in the right of every people to their freedom and independence.

The Afro-Asian peoples desire unity in working together, to help each other in the struggle for the welfare of the Afro-Asian peoples, as well as of the whole of mankind. We will devote our relentless efforts to the achievement of enduring peace in the world.

Peace will surely be victorious.

Humanity can face its future with hope and confidence. This is the New Year message of the Afro-Asian Peoples Solidarity Conference in Cairo to the whole world.

The threat to make use of atomic weapons in a new war will indeed bring the world to a general catastrophe. This makes it encumbent on you, shapers of the future, to prevent this calamity by every possible means.

It is precisely for these reasons that the Afro-Asian Conference assembled in Cairo appeals to the conscience of the world at large, to you who are responsible for the invention of this destructive weapon, to take every possible step to bring pressure to bear upon all the governments concerned to prohibit the use of nuclear weapons and to destroy those in stock.

Let the scientists all over the world compete not in inventing new mass-destruction weapons but in fathoming the secrets of nature and making new discoveries that would serve the cause of progress of nations and peoples.

C. Conference of Independent African States, Accra, April, 15-22, 1958.

(113) *Declaration, Adopted April 22, 1958.*[1]

WE, the African States assembled here in Accra, in this our first Conference, conscious of our responsibilities to humanity and especially to the peoples of Africa, and desiring to assert our African Personality on the side of peace, hereby proclaim and solemnly reaffirm our unswerving loyalty to

[1] *Ghana Today*, London, v. 2 (May 14, 1958), p. 1.

the Charter of the United Nations, the Universal Declaration of Human Rights and the Declaration of the Asian-African Conference held at Bandung.

WE further assert and proclaim the unity among ourselves and our solidarity with the dependent peoples of Africa as well as our friendship with all nations. We resolve to preserve the unity of purpose and action in international affairs which we have forged among ourselves in this historic Conference, and to safeguard our hard-won independence, sovereignty and territorial integrity, and to preserve among ourselves the fundamental unity of outlook on foreign policy so that a distinctive African Personality will play its part in co-operation with other peace-loving nations to further the cause of peace.

WE pledge ourselves to apply all our endeavours to avoid being committed to any action which might entangle our countries to the detriment of our interests and freedom; to recognise the right of the African people to independence and self-determination and to take appropriate steps to hasten the realisation of this right; and to affirm the right of the Algerian people to independence and self-determination and to exert all possible effort to hasten the realisation of their independence; to uproot for ever the evil of racial discrimination in all its forms wherever it may be found; to persuade the Great Powers to discontinue the production and testing of nuclear and thermo-nuclear weapons, and to reduce conventional weapons.

FURTHERMORE, mindful of the urgent need to raise the living standard of our peoples by developing to the fullest possible advantage the great and varied resources of our lands, we hereby pledge ourselves to co-ordinate our economic planning through a joint economic effort and study the economic potentialities, the technical possibilities and related problems existing in our respective States; to promote co-ordinated industrial planning either through our own individual efforts and/or through co-operation with Specialised Agencies of the United Nations; to take measures to increase trade among our countries by improving communications between our respective countries and to encourage the investment of foreign capital and skills provided they do not compromise the independence, sovereignty and territorial integrity of our States.

DESIROUS of mobilising the human resources of our respective countries in furtherance of our social and cultural aspirations, we will endeavour to promote and facilitate the exchange of teachers, professors, students, exhibitions, educational and cultural and scientific material which will improve cultural relations between the African States and inculcate greater knowledge amongst us through such efforts as joint youth festivals, sporting events, etc.; will encourage and strengthen studies of African culture, history and geography in the institutions of learning in the African States; will take all measures in our respective countries to ensure that such studies are correctly orientated.

WE have charged our Permanent Representatives at the United Nations to be the permanent machinery for coordinating all matters of common concern to our States, for examining and making recommendations on concrete practical steps for implementing our decisions, and for preparing the grounds for future Conferences.

FAITHFUL to the obligations and responsibilities which history has thrown upon us as the vanguard of the complete emancipation of Africa, we do hereby affirm our dedication to the causes which we have proclaimed.

D. Algeria.

(114) *United Nations General Assembly Draft Resolution, Failed of Adoption, December 13, 1958.*[1]

The General Assembly,

Having discussed the question of Algeria,

Recalling its resolution 1012 (XI) of 15 February 1957, by which the General Assembly expressed the hope that a peaceful, democratic and just solution would be found through appropriate means, in conformity with the principles of the Charter of the United Nations,

Recalling further its resolution 1184 (XII) of 10 December 1957, by which the General Assembly expressed the wish that *pourparlers* would be entered into, and other appropriate means utilized, with a view to a solution, in conformity with the purposes and principles of the Charter of the United Nations,

Recognizing the right of the Algerian people to independence,

[1] United Nations Document A/4075, dated December 13, 1958, pp. 3-4. The penultimate paragraph (in square brackets) was deleted in plenary session by a vote of 38-0-43, after which the resolution as amended failed of adoption by a vote of 32-18-30, representing less than the required two-thirds majority.

Deeply concerned with the continuance of the war in Algeria,

Considering that the present situation in Algeria constitutes a threat to international peace and security,

[*Taking note* of the willingness of the Provisional Government of the Algerian Republic to enter into negotiations with the Government of France,]

Urges negotiations between the two parties concerned with a view to reaching a solution in conformity with the Charter of the United Nations.

E. Ghana.

(115) *Joint Statement on Talks Held between the President and the Prime Minister of Ghana (Nkrumah), July 26, 1958.*[1]

The visit to Washington of the Prime Minister of Ghana has afforded the opportunity for a full and friendly exchange of views between the Prime Minister and the President, the Secretary of State and other high Government officials. These conversations have had as their objective the further strengthening of the close ties of friendship and mutual respect which have characterized the relationship between the two countries since Ghana attained its independence last year.

The Prime Minister explained the importance that his government attaches to the Volta River project and also to the development plan which is being drawn up for the further economic and social development of Ghana. He hoped the Government of the United States would find it possible to assist the Government of Ghana with respect to both programs.

In subsequent conversations, representatives of the two governments explored the types and scope of assistance which the United States Government might be able to extend to the Government of Ghana. With regard to the Volta River project, the United States expressed its appreciation of the contribution this project could make to the economic development of Ghana. It agreed to continue to explore with private American interests the aluminum manufacturing phase of the project and to consider how it might assist with loans if the required private financing were assured. The United States also expressed willingness to examine any proposals which the Government of Ghana might advance

[1] *Department of State Bulletin,* v. 39 (August 18, 1958), pp. 283-284.

for the use of power from the Volta River for purposes other than the manufacture of aluminum. The two governments agreed that it would be desirable to bring up to date the engineering reports which were prepared in 1955 and to share the cost of this undertaking.

With respect to the new development plan now in the course of preparation, the Government of the United States indicated willingness to examine the plan with the Government of Ghana and to consider particular fields in which it might be able to cooperate through development loans. The United States Government further agreed to continue and expand its technical cooperation with the Government of Ghana through programs designed to aid in the gradual diversification and strengthening of the economy of that country.

The conversations included an exchange of views concerning the situation in the Middle East. The two governments were in agreement that the solution for the urgent problems of that area should be found within the framework of the United Nations in a manner which will preserve the independence and territorial integrity of all member nations, whether large or small. With respect to the particular situation in Lebanon, the United States emphasized its desire to withdraw its forces just as soon as the United Nations can act effectively to assure the independence and territorial integrity of that state. The Prime Minister noted that this position coincided with the views of his Government.

The representatives of the two governments emphasized their determination to work for the strengthening of the United Nations in the interests of establishment of world peace, prosperity and stability based upon international justice. It was apparent that both countries share the same beliefs with respect to mutual respect for the sovereignty and independence of nations, non-interference in the internal affairs of other nations, social and economic progress for all peoples, and the rights and dignity of the individual.

The two Governments also exchanged views on the emergence of new African states and the growing importance of the African continent in the realm of international affairs. The Prime Minister took the opportunity to explain the aspirations of the African states as they were expressed at the recent meeting of those nations at Accra and in his subsequent visits to each of the capitals of the states concerned. The President noted with deep interest the Prime Minister's explanations regarding the development of a distinctive African personality, emphasizing in this connection the sincere interest of the Government of the United States in the orderly political, economic and social advancement of the peoples of the African continent.

KWAME NKRUMAH
DWIGHT D. EISENHOWER

F. The Union of South Africa.

(116) *Statement by United States Representative to the United Nations General Assembly (Harrison) in the Special Political Committee, October 16, 1958.*[1]

(Excerpt)

*   *   *

We in the United States are especially aware of the problems that arise from the transition of economically and socially disparate groups into a community. We are actively engaged in the complex process of eliminating racial segregation, and we are learning that the adjustments are difficult. They sometimes lead to resistance and even violence. Nevertheless, there can be no question as to the direction in which we are moving. Despite the problems involved we will continue in this direction. To do otherwise would be to disregard our national ideals and way of life.

Several speakers have referred sympathetically to the energetic measures being taken in the United States. We appreciate that understanding of our problems and of our efforts.

In my lifetime I have seen a revolution in human relationships in my own country. I witnessed tremendous changes in the direction of recognizing inherent rights and human dignity of all our citizens. There was a time when one part of our nation suffered under a complex of racial inferiority, with consequent discrimination from another part. Today we find the members of our racial groups holding political office, practicing in our professions, and enjoying the same political and economic opportunities. In my time I have seen the United States trade-union movement take a firm stand that all its member organizations should eliminate

[1] *Ibid.* (November 24, 1958), pp. 842-844.

every vestige of racial discrimination. We will soon enjoy that objective.

Many of our unions in the United States who have discriminated against nonwhites have completely removed all restrictions and their organizations now consist of multiracial memberships with equality of membership privileges. There are many nonwhite trade-union officials. Our skilled trades are open to the members of all races, and they are employed without discrimination or restriction. This advancement is based on the recognition of the majority of our citizens that our nation is genuinely enriched in all aspects of life as we take advantage of an increasing contribution by our nonwhite millions in the activities of our society.

Policies of racial separation breed discontent and noncooperation, thus weakening the total effort any enlightened society must make to meet its responsibilities in a democratic civilization.

I have been speaking of my own country and my own experiences.

We in the United States consider that in working toward a solution of our own racial problems we are fulfilling part of our obligations under the charter. The imperfect observance of human rights is not a phenomenon peculiar to any one nation. Each member of the United Nations, as it strives to overcome inequalities of rights and freedoms, is fulfilling its international human-rights obligations. To the extent that it is not, it is shirking or avoiding those obligations, and that is a matter of concern to all of us.

The United States finds it difficult to equate a policy based on segregation with the obligations assumed under article 56 of the charter. It is our belief that a multiracial and multireligious society cannot be based on segregation or separation. The history of the United States proclaims its opposition to concepts based on segregation. In our view men of all races and religions are the product of a common creation. We all share a common creation. We all share a common destiny. In our view separation on the basis of race is inconsistent with the principles of equal rights of peoples to which we have all subscribed.

There are those who believe that the United Nations should condemn the Union of South Africa for not following the recommendations that this committee has seen fit to make over the past years. The United States does not share that view. Nevertheless, we believe the Assembly should express its regret and concern that the Government of the Union of South Africa has not responded to the appeals of the Assembly concerning its racial policies.

We believe that the only way in which a problem of this nature can be approached constructively is in a spirit of cooperation rather than through condemnation. In this connection we rely upon the force of world public opinion. Just as hostile public opinion can serve to isolate those who reject the standards of the community, so an informed and sympathetic public opinion serves to help a member overcome a problem. It is in this spirit that the United States will support the resolution embodying these principles which we understand will be introduced by a large number of cosponsors later today.

(117) *General Assembly Resolution 1248 (XIII), Adopted October 30, 1958.*[2]

The General Assembly,

Recalling its previous consideration of the question of race conflict in South Africa resulting from the policies of *apartheid* of the Government of the Union of South Africa,

Recalling in particular paragraph 6 of its resolution 917 (X) of 6 December 1955 calling upon the Government of the Union of South Africa to observe its obligations under the Charter of the United Nations,

1. *Declares again* that, in a multiracial society harmony and respect for human rights and freedoms and the peaceful development of a unified community are best assured when patterns of legislation and practice are directed towards ensuring equality before the law of all persons regardless of race, creed or colour, and when economic, social, cultural and political participation of all racial groups is on a basis of equality;

2. *Affirms* that governmental policies of Member States which are not directed towards these goals, but which are designed to perpetuate or increase discrimination, are inconsistent with the pledges of the Members under Article 56 of the Charter of the United Nations;

[2] United Nations, General Assembly, *Official Records, Thirteenth Session,* Supplement No. 18(A/4090), p. 7. The resolution was adopted by a vote 70-5 (Australia, Belgium, France, Portugal, and the U.K.) -4 (Dominican Republic, Luxembourg, Netherlands, Spain). Two delegations (Bolivia and the Union of South Africa) were absent.

3. *Solemnly calls upon* all Member States to bring their policies into conformity with their obligation under the Charter to promote the observance of human rights and fundamental freedoms;

4. *Expresses its regret and concern* that the Government of the Union of South Africa has not yet responded to appeals of the General Assembly that it reconsider governmental policies which impair the right of all racial groups to enjoy the same rights and fundamental freedoms.

CHAPTER SEVEN

THE FAR EAST AND SOUTH EAST ASIA

A. The Manila Pact.

(118) *Final Communiqué on the Fourth Annual Meeting of the SEATO Council, Manila, March 13, 1958.*[1]

The Fourth Annual Meeting of the SEATO Council was held in Manila from 11th to 13th March 1958 under the Chairmanship of the Acting Secretary of Foreign Affairs of the Philippines, the Honourable Felixberto M. Serrano.

The Council reviewed the world situation with special attention to the Treaty Area, approved the work of the Organization since the meeting in Canberra a year ago,[2] and considered reports by the Council Representatives, the Military Advisers and the Secretary-General.[3]

The Council welcomed the appointment of H. E. Nai Pote Sarasin of Thailand as Secretary-General of the Organization. This position was created at last year's meeting.

Security of the Region

The Council considered the continuing Communist threat to the region. The Ministers reaffirmed their determination to maintain national and collective defence against the possibility of Communist and Communist-inspired armed aggression, while at the same time earnestly working for international disarmament with adequate safeguards covering both nuclear and conventional elements.

SEATO has become a bulwark which has enabled the countries protected hereby to proceed in peace with their programmes of national development.

Members of SEATO recognized that a threat to security or to freedom in any region of the world was a threat to security and freedom everywhere.

Some criticism of the aims and objectives of SEATO continues to be heard. The Council agreed that every country

[1] *Department of State Bulletin*, v. 38 (March 31, 1958), pp. 504-506.
[2] *Documents on American Foreign Relations, 1957*, pp. 315-319.
[3] *Department of State Bulletin*, v. 38 (March 31, 1958), pp. 509-516.

has the right to follow the policy it prefers. The Council noted with regret that some countries nevertheless continue to criticise the collective security arrangements of the free world, though such arrangements are in accordance with the United Nations Charter.

Subversion

The problems of Communist subversion in the Treaty Area were discussed at length. It was recognized that this represented the most substantial current menace.

The Council was of the opinion that collective security measures had resulted in the diversion of the emphasis of Communist activities from the military to the non-military field.

Communist and Communist-inspired activity has continued within the Treaty Area. In countries protected by the Treaty there has been a noticeable change of emphasis by the Communists to activity in the economic, political and cultural fields and also to activity within youth and labour organizations.

The Council welcomed the counter subversion measures being taken by the members and noted particularly the success of the Seminar on Countering Communist Subversion held in Baguio in the Philippines last November.[4]

The Council recognized that in view of the insidious character of Communist subversion there was particular danger arising from some non-Communist governments failing to distinguish between the aims and ideals of the free world and the purposes of international communism.

Economic Activities

The Council heard statements on the economic progress and problems of the Treaty Area and on what further steps could be taken inside and outside SEATO to attain the economic objectives set forth in the Manila Treaty.

A principal means of attaining these objectives continues to be through extensive bilateral and other economic arrangements between the SEATO countries. During the past year over $700,000,000 for economic purposes was provided for countries covered by the Manila Treaty, principally by the United States. This aid is a major factor in preserving peace and genuine independence for countries of the region.

[4] *Ibid.*, v. 37 (December 23, 1957) , p. 993.

Australia announced that it would make available to the Asian members of SEATO a further £A1,000,000 ($2,240,000) for purposes generally related to SEATO defence; this is in addition to £A2,000,000 previously contributed by Australia for these purposes.

The United States announced that $2,000,000 was being made available to the Asian members of SEATO for vocational and on-the-job training. Australia, France, New Zealand and the United Kingdom also offered to help on various aspects of skilled labour training.

The United States also announced that the major portion of its economic aid was now being directed to the region of Asia.

The Council approved in principle a project submitted by Thailand to establish a SEATO Graduate School of Engineering in Bangkok and several members announced that they would be pleased to participate in providing the necessary funds.

Cultural Activities

The Council agreed to continue and expand its programme of cultural activities.

The Council expressed its satisfaction at the holding in Bangkok under SEATO auspices of a Round Table on the impact of modern technology upon traditional cultures in South East Asia. A number of SEATO Fellowships have been awarded and some Members are conducting bilateral cultural exchanges.

The Council agreed to continue its fellowships programmes and to initiate new cultural projects, the most important being a scholarship programme and the appointment of professors at universities of the Asian members and of travelling lecturers.

Relations with other Organizations and Countries

The Council expressed its interest in the development of relations with other collective defence organizations of the Free World as well as the facilitation of an exchange of information and opinion between these organizations on a mutually agreeable basis. The Council authorized the Secretary General to enter into contact with the Secretaries General of other collective security organizations of the Free World.

The Council considered that contacts between SEATO

and non-member States had proved useful in many respects and directed that, as circumstances permitted, such contacts be continued and expanded in the coming years.

Work of Military Advisers

The Council noted with approval the work of their Military Advisers and of the Military Planning Office, which has completed its first year's work. Plans in fulfillment of the defensive role of SEATO have been developed to resist aggression in the Treaty Area. Since the last Council meeting four major SEATO military exercises have been held as well as three multilateral or bilateral exercises. These have served effectively to increase the degree of cooperation between the forces of the SEATO powers and to make them more ready for speedy action in the event of any sudden attack. The Council authorized a further programme of combined exercises.

The Council learned with regret the news of the relief of Brigadier General Alfredo M. Santos, who has been the first Chief of the SEATO Military Planning Office. He is returning for reassignment in the Philippines.

The United States and the Philippines announced that they intend to co-sponsor a defence college to be located in the Philippines. This would be open to members and non-members of SEATO. The Council took note of this announcement with particular interest.

1958/59 Budget

The Council approved Budget Estimates totalling $850,360 for the financial year 1958/59, to cover the cost of the Secretariat-General and Military Planning Office in Bangkok and to finance certain joint programmes.

Next Meeting

The Council accepted with pleasure the invitation of the New Zealand Government to hold its next annual meeting in Wellington.

Conclusion

The Council considered that the work of the present meeting had helped to consolidate the work already achieved by SEATO. They placed on record their determination to continue to work together for the security and progress of South-East Asia in accordance with the principles and purposes of the Charter of the United Nations. The Council Members again emphasized the defensive character of SEATO and reaffirmed the principle that international disputes be settled peacefully in accordance with the principles of the United Nations Charter.

The Representatives attending the Fourth SEATO Council Meeting were—Australia—Rt. Hon. R. G. Casey; France —M. Christian Pineau; New Zealand—Rt. Hon. Walter Nash; Pakistan—Hon. Nawab Mozaffar Ali Khan Qizilbash; Philippines—Hon. Felixberto M. Serrano; Thailand— H. R. H. Prince Wan Waithayakon Krommun Naradhip Bongsprabandh; United Kingdom—Rt. Hon. Selwyn Lloyd; United States—Hon. John Foster Dulles.

B. The ANZUS Pact.

(119) Agreed Statement on the Meeting of the ANZUS Council, Washington, October 1, 1958.[1]

(Excerpt)

A meeting of the ANZUS Council was held at Washington October 1, 1958. Australia was represented by The Right Honorable Richard G. Casey, Minister for External Affairs; New Zealand was represented by The Right Honorable Walter Nash, Prime Minister and Minister of External Affairs; and the United States was represented by The Honorable John Foster Dulles, Secretary of State.

The Ministers reviewed events over the last year which were of interest and concern to the three countries. They agreed that militant and subversive Communist expansionism remains the greatest threat to the peaceful progress of the free world. The Ministers expressed their satisfaction with the opportunities presented by this meeting to strengthen further their close relationships in matters affecting the maintenance of international peace and security.

The Council noted that the Southeast Asia Treaty Organization, to which all three nations adhere, continues to grow in its capacity to promote the security and well-being of the peoples of the countries of Southeast Asia.

The members of the ANZUS Council have discussed the Chinese Communist attacks on the Quemoy and Matsu

[1] *Ibid.*, v. 39 (October 20, 1958), pp. 612-613.

islands and threats to seize Taiwan.[2] They agreed that the resort to force and threat of force constitute a serious menace to the peace of the area and is a matter in which they are therefore deeply concerned.

The representatives of Australia and New Zealand, noting that the United States is now engaged in bilateral negotiations with the Chinese Communists in Warsaw in an effort to resolve the crisis and arrive at an arrangement whereby its recurrence might be avoided, affirmed their resolution to support the bringing of these negotiations to a peaceful conclusion.[3] They joined the United States in calling on the Chinese Communists at once to discontinue their attacks on the Quemoy and Matsu islands in the interests of the peace of the area and as a first step to a peaceful settlement.

They hold that, regardless of the merits of claims and counter-claims, the use of aggressive force is a violation of the basic principle on which world order depends. Armed force should not be used to achieve territorial ambitions.

* * *

C. The Colombo Plan.

(120) *Address by the President before the Tenth Meeting of the Consultative Committee on Cooperative Development in South and South East Asia, Seattle, November 13, 1958.*[1]

(Excerpts)

* * *

Our task is a great one. It will take many years to fulfill. Yet if we undertake it boldly, with wisdom and determination, we can and will succeed.

* * *

The United States stands ready to play its full part in this great peaceful crusade to achieve continuing growth in freedom.

I should like to dwell briefly on the measures that the United States is prepared to take to this end, subject of course to appropriate action by the United States Congress.

[2] Documents 125-138, below.
[3] Documents 123 and 124, below.
[1] *Department of State Bulletin*, v. 39 (December 1, 1958), pp. 853-857.

Taken together, I believe that these measures constitute a comprehensive program for assisting economic development, one in which not only the United States but many other free countries might participate.

The United States will press these measures energetically, consistent with the maintenance of a sound domestic economy. Our country's outlays must never outrun the levels justified by the continuing growth of our economic strength, if this nation is to sustain the long-term effort that is required. Fortunately, the United States economy is forging ahead as it emerges from a brief period of readjustment. Its expanding resources should permit a vigorous prosecution of the program for progress I wish to outline today.

That program is addressed to the five major requirements for economic growth:

1. For expanded international trade.
2. For technical skills.
3. For private investment.
4. For normal bankable loans.
5. For financing to cover other sound projects which will afford the borrower flexibility regarding terms of repayment.

Expanded Trade

First, then, as to expanded trade.

The larger part of the capital goods required for economic development must, of course, be financed through international trade. I believe that great benefits should be realized by all, if all our countries cooperate in assuring the expansion of trade and in relaxing the restrictions which have hindered its flow.

For many of the less developed countries, export trade is concentrated in a few primary commodities. To maintain a healthy world demand for these commodities, we must have a high and expanding level of economic activity throughout the free world. Where special difficulties may arise with respect to particular primary commodities, the United States is prepared to join in a discussion of such problems to see whether or not a solution can promptly be found.

Technical Assistance Programs

The second major requirement is for technical skills.

These skills are the bedrock of economic development. Unless they are more widely shared in the free world, no amount of capital flow will bring about the desired growth. Indeed, without competent management, supplemented by satisfactory levels of skills in the professions and in the trades, the most efficiently constructed factory would represent nothing but a wasteful and useless expenditure.

Now what should be done to create this sharing of competence?

National programs of technical assistance should be carried forward. The United States will press its own program, through our International Cooperation Administration, even more vigorously than in the past. I hope that other countries will act in the same spirit.

The work of the United Nations is of great importance in this field. The United States will continue to participate in the Expanded Technical Assistance Program of that organization. We have pledged a contribution to its new Special Projects Fund.

Regional discussion of these technical assistance programs can be very helpful. An outstanding example is the work of the Colombo Plan association itself.

Private Investment

A third major requirement is for private investment.

Americans are particularly conscious of the importance of private investment for two reasons.

The continuing growth of their own country is due largely to private efforts and to private initiative. Our citizens have confidence in free enterprise as a means of achieving economic growth because we have seen it work. We know what it can do.

Secondly, the resources of American private capital are far larger than the amounts which our Government can possibly provide. Most of the productive talent and resources of our society are in private hands. Our strength lies in the diversity of private individuals, organizations, and interests, and in the quality of their technical skills, their imagination, and their initiative. If this country is to be of greatest help to less developed countries, therefore, its private resources will need to be drawn upon to the greatest extent possible.

The United States Government is studying how best to help bring this about. I am confident that we will discover methods of enhancing the constructive role of private investment in promoting the growth of less developed areas.

It would seem desirable that the less developed nations will also explore the full potentialities of private initiative. To create a favorable climate for outside investment, one of the things most needed is assurance to prospective private investors that their capital will be respected and allowed to work productively. Thus these countries will not only encourage the flow of needed capital and technical skills but will provide an added and helpful stimulus to the development of their own business enterprises.

Bankable Public Loans

The fourth requirement is for public loans on normal bankable terms.

These loans are usually made for projects, like the building of a new road system, which are not attractive to direct private investment. These loans are made to borrowers who will be able to repay in foreign exchange and on banking terms.

Such loans are now being extended by the International Bank for Reconstruction and Development. The recent meeting of the bank's Board of Governors in New Delhi decided that the Executive Directors would promptly consider an increase in the bank's capital subscriptions.[2] Without requiring the bank's members to make new payment, such an increase would enable the bank to obtain greater funds in the private market. The United States believes that this should be done.

At New Delhi it was also agreed to consider the advisability of an increase in the quotas of the International Monetary Fund. The fund has greatly helped the development of many countries through timely assistance in meeting their balance-of-payments difficulties and by providing valuable advice on fiscal and monetary policies. The United States believes that such an increase is important if the International Monetary Fund is to continue to carry out its vital role in furthering the economic growth of the free world.

The United States extends bankable loans for development also through the United States Export-Import Bank. Its operations and those of the International Bank complement and reinforce each other.

The Export-Import Bank has made an outstanding contribution to economic development. Other countries' lending agencies can also play an increasingly effective part in

[2] *Ibid.* (November 17, 1958), pp. 793-798.

providing bankable loans for sound development projects and programs.

Development Financing on Flexible Terms

I now turn to the fifth vital requirement: for development financing which will afford the borrower flexibility regarding terms of repayment.

Many sound projects which are essential to development cannot qualify for bankable loans. If these projects are not carried out, economic growth will not go forward at the rate that is required.

It was to help finance such projects on a businesslike basis that the United States Congress last year established the Development Loan Fund.[3]

The fund is authorized to make loans which can be repaid in the currency of the borrowing country, not only in dollars. It is intended to provide a basis for increasingly effective longterm programs to hasten growth in less developed areas. It enables these countries to utilize better their own resources for such programs. It works closely with our Export-Import Bank and with the International Bank to stimulate an increased flow of bankable loans for such programs. It furnishes increased loans for private projects and assists the growth of private enterprise in the less developed regions.

The Colombo Plan countries have already received more than half of the Development Loan Fund's loans.[4] Your response to this new instrument of development policy has underscored the importance of its operations.

Colombo Plan nations have requested further loans for key projects which exceed the available resources of the fund. Additions to the fund are needed if the Development Loan Fund is to carry forward these operations effectively.

I hope that the Congress will from time to time provide adequate resources for the Development Loan Fund. This will enable the fund to continue to serve as an effective instrument of United States policy in meeting the vital needs which exist for development financing with flexible repayment terms.

If other more developed countries should also act vigor-

[3] *Documents on American Foreign Relations, 1957*, p. 59.
[4] Of a total of $572 million in development loans approved by the Fund between January, 1958 when it began operations and November, 1958, $333 million were for projects in Colombo Plan countries.

ously to meet these growing needs, progress would be hastened. The United States would welcome the contributions of other countries to this end. The possibility of creating an International Development Association for this purpose, as an affiliate of the International Bank, was discussed at my suggestion by Secretary of the Treasury Anderson at the New Delhi meeting.[5] These discussions were encouraging. Possibly an International Development Association can be brought into being as one way of effectively mobilizing financial resources contributed by the free world as a whole.

Period of Stocktaking and Planning Ahead

This then is the five-part program for progress which I hope will be carried out by the United States and other countries: to expand international trade, to provide technical assistance, to encourage private investment and initiative, to support bankable lending, and to furnish financing on flexible terms of repayment for other sound projects.

The measures to expand trade and to provide increased technical assistance and bankable loans are already charted or under way. The vital measures to provide both greater private investment and expanded development financing on flexible terms remain to be carried out. It is these two important types of measures that will require special and increasing emphasis by all our countries in the period of stocktaking and planning that lies ahead.

If this is done and if sound measures of selfhelp are also charted by the less developed countries, this period of review could prove to be a turning point in the development efforts of free men.

*   *   *

(121) Communiqué on the Tenth Meeting of the Colombo Plan Consultative Committee, Seattle, November 13, 1958.[6]

The Consultative Committee of the Colombo Plan for Cooperative Economic Development in South and Southeast Asia met in Seattle, Washington, from November 10 to 13, 1958. This was the Tenth Meeting of the Consultative Committee, created at Colombo, Ceylon, in 1950 to "survey the needs, to assess the resources available and required, to focus

---

[5] Document 6, above.
[6] Department of State Bulletin, v. 39 (December 1, 1958), pp. 860-861.

world attention on the development problems of the area, and to provide a framework within which an international cooperative effort could be promoted to assist the countries of the area to raise their living standards."

Each year the Consultative Committee reviews the progress made, the problems encountered, and the tasks that lie ahead in the effort to accelerate economic development. The basic concept of the Colombo Plan is cooperation. Each country does what it can to further the long-run development of the area through its own development or economic assistance programs, for which the separate countries retain full responsibility.

The Tenth Meeting of the Consultative Committee was attended by Ministerial representatives of the 18 member countries: Australia, Burma, Cambodia, Canada, Ceylon, India, Indonesia, Japan, Laos, Malaya, Nepal, New Zealand, Pakistan, the Philippines, Thailand, the United Kingdom, together with Singapore, Sarawak and North Borneo, the United States and Viet-Nam. At the inaugural session the Consultative Committee was addressed by the President of the United States, who outlined a "Program for Progress" in the field of economic development.

During the Seattle meeting it was evident that the consultative technique of the Colombo Plan has proved its worth. The periodic discussion of national economic development programs and of bilateral economic assistance arrangements between member countries has contributed greatly to the development of South and Southeast Asia. As a cooperative international association the Colombo Plan is well designed to meet the economic needs and national desires of the member countries. It has become a symbol of the economic aspirations of hundreds of millions of people.

The Annual Report of the Consultative Committee prepared and approved at the Seattle Conference will be released in full in the capitals of the member countries on or after December 29, 1958. The introductory paragraphs of Chapter I, reviewing economic progress during the last year, and the full text of Chapter II, indicating the tasks ahead, are, however, being annexed to this communique.[7]

During the year reviewed in the report, significant progress continued to be made in furthering the development of the Colombo Plan region. The rate of progress was, however, somewhat less than in previous years. It appears that the

[7] *Ibid.,* pp. 861-865.

rate of growth in per capita real income in the region mentioned in previous reports was not maintained. In some countries of the region, adverse weather and a decline in food production, inflationary pressures and heavy imports accompanied by a decline in export earnings, and other factors, occasioned setbacks. This Conference, however, was confident that these setbacks would not reverse the forward movement of economic development as a whole. Progress continued to be made at a substantial rate in such vital economic sectors as industrial capacity and improvement of basic facilities, including roads, irrigation and land reclamation.

In the region as a whole public investment is playing a substantial role in development activities. However, the predominant position of the small cultivator and small businessman in these underdeveloped areas underlines the importance of private initiative and of widening the opportunities for private enterprise. The committee noted that member countries in the area have increasingly recognized the importance of private investment and have encouraged the growth of the private sector. Important also in this growth is the role of foreign private investment which can provide capital together with the technical and managerial skills so needed by the countries of the region. There is an increasing awareness of the need to attract foreign investment.

The Committee noted that by far the greater part of the economic resources devoted to the development of South and Southeast Asia has come from the countries of the area and would continue to do so. The Committee emphasized the importance of sound fiscal and monetary policies in further encouraging, wherever practicable, savings for developmental purposes. These public and private resources from within the area have been supplemented by important aid from outside. In the past year over $1,000 million in economic assistance have been made available by contributing members of the Colombo Plan to the countries of South and Southeast Asia. Since the inception of the plan about $5,000 million of external aid has been made available to help promote the development and economic stability of these countries. The variety of forms and sources of this aid is impressive. The Committee also noted that of the total training awards under the Colombo Plan Technical Cooperation Scheme the proportion provided by countries within the area increased from 11 percent to 20 percent during the year under review.

The Committee stressed the growing importance of technical assistance to the development progress of South and Southeast Asia. Unless the scope and variety of skills in the area are expanded, growth will be retarded. Increasing availability of external capital emphasizes even more the importance of meeting the requirements for training and skills in order to assure effective utilization of such capital.

The economic development of the less developed areas is a major challenge of our times. The peaceful evolution of world civilization requires that this challenge be met. In South and Southeast Asia the Colombo Plan is a major international instrument for attacking these problems on a cooperative basis. As a result of their ministerial meeting in Seattle, the representatives are confident that the members of the Colombo Plan will bring renewed vigor and determination to the tasks ahead, to the end that for hundreds of millions of human beings material progress may be achieved and the dignity of the individual enhanced.

The Committee agreed that its next meeting would be held in Indonesia in 1959.

D. The People's Republic of China.

1. *United States Policy on Nonrecognition.*

(122) *Department of State Memorandum, August 11, 1958.*[1]

Policy toward Communist China has been an important issue since the Communists came to power there, and it is of critical significance to the United States and the free world today. In the United States the issue is a very real one to the vast majority of the people. As a result of Korean and Chinese Communist aggression in Korea, the United States suffered 142,000 casualties, bringing tragedy to communities all over the country. Nevertheless, despite the emotions thus engendered and the abhorrence of the American people for the brutality and utter lack of morality of Communist systems, the policy of the United States Government toward China has necessarily been based on objective considerations of national interest. It also reflects a continuing appraisal of all available facts.

Basically the United States policy of not extending diplomatic recognition to the Communist regime in China pro-

[1] *Ibid.* (September 8, 1958), pp. 385-390.

ceeds from the conviction that such recognition would produce no tangible benefits to the United States or to the free world as a whole and would be of material assistance to Chinese Communist attempts to extend Communist dominion throughout Asia. It is not an "inflexible" policy which cannot be altered to meet changed conditions. If the situation in the Far East were so to change in its basic elements as to call for a radically different evaluation of the threat Chinese Communist policies pose to United States and free-world security interests, the United States would of course readjust its present policies. However, the course of events in the Far East since the establishment of the Chinese Communist regime in 1949 has thus far confirmed the United States view that its interests and those of the free world are best served by withholding diplomatic recognition from the regime in Peiping.

The basic considerations on which United States policy toward China rests are twofold. First, the Soviet bloc, of which Communist China is an important part, is engaged in a long-range struggle to destroy the way of life of the free countries of the world and bring about the global dominion of communism. The Chinese Communist regime has made no secret of its fundamental hostility to the United States and the free world as a whole nor of its avowed intention to effect their downfall. Today its defiance of and attacks on the non-Communist world have reached a level of intensity that has not been witnessed since the Korean war. The second basic factor is that East Asia is peculiarly vulnerable to the Communist offensive because of the proximity of the free countries of that area to Communist China, the inexperience in self-government of those which have recently won their independence, their suspicions of the West inherited from their colonial past, and the social, political, and economic changes which inevitably accompany their drive toward modernization.

The Chinese Communists see the victory of communism in Asia as inevitable; and now that they control the vast population and territory of mainland China they are utilizing the advantages these give to encompass their ends. Chinese Communist leaders have shown by their words and their acts that they are not primarily interested in promoting the welfare of their people while living at peace with their neighbors. Their primary purpose is to extend the Communist revolution beyond their borders to the rest of Asia and thence to the rest of the world. Liu Shao-chi, the second-ranking member of the Chinese Communist Party has said: "The most fundamental and common duty of Communist Party members is to establish communism and transform the present world into a Communist world." Mao Tse-tung himself has said that his regime's policy is "to give active support to the national independence and liberation movements in countries in Asia, Africa, and Latin America." That these are not empty words was shown by Chinese Communist aggression in Korea and provision of arms and other assistance to the Communist rebels in Indochina.

United States policy in Asia, as elsewhere in the world, is to promote the domestic welfare and to strengthen the independence of free nations. Because of the proximity of many Asian nations to mainland China and the disparity in size and power between them and Communist China, this can be done only if the Communist threat is neutralized. The first need of United States policy in the Far East is to deter Communist aggression, else the free nations would be in grave danger of succumbing to Communist pressures before they had gathered the strength with which to resist them. The United States has sought to accomplish this by military assistance to the nations directly in the path of Chinese Communist expansion—Korea, Taiwan, and Viet-Nam— and by a system of mutual defense arrangements with other nations of the area. We have been successful in this effort, and since 1954 the Chinese Communists have not been able to make further gains through the open use of military force.

The measures the United States and its allies in Asia have taken to preserve the security of the free nations of the area are of vital interest to the other free nations of the world. Loss of the rest of East Asia to communism could have a disastrous effect on the free world's ability to resist effectively the encroachments of communism elsewhere. The consequences for Australia and New Zealand would be especially serious. Loss of the islands of the West Pacific and of the Southeast Asian peninsula would isolate these countries and place them in a strategically exposed and dangerous position.

Efforts to halt further Communist expansion cannot be confined to military deterrence alone. Countermeasures against Chinese Communist subversion and political infiltration are equally necessary. This is especially so as, since 1955, Peiping has increasingly resorted to propaganda, subversion, "people's diplomacy," and political maneuvering in its dealings with its Asian neighbors. Peiping seeks to win by this means what it apparently does not dare attempt through military conquest. The United States therefore considers that in preserving the peace and security of Asia it is as important to be alert to the threat of subversion as to that of open military attack.

In the effort to block Peiping's attempts to extend Communist rule in Asia the withholding of diplomatic recognition is an important factor. The extension of diplomatic recognition by a great power normally carries with it not only increased access to international councils but enhanced international standing and prestige as well. Denial of recognition on the other hand is a positive handicap to the regime affected and one which makes it that much the more difficult for it to pursue its foreign policies with success. One basic purpose of United States nonrecognition of Communist China is to deny it these advantages and to that extent limit its ability to threaten the security of the area.

In the case of China there are special considerations which influence United States policy with regard to recognition. For one thing, although the Chinese Communists have seized the preponderant bulk of China, they have not completed their conquest of the country. The generally recognized legitimate Government of China continues to exist and in Taiwan is steadily developing its political, economic, and military strength. The Government of the Republic of China controls the strategic island of Taiwan and through its possession of a sizable military force—one of the largest on the side of the free world in Asia—presents a significant deterrent to renewed Chinese Communist aggression. Recognition of Communist China by the United States would seriously cripple, if not destroy altogether, that Government. On the other hand, continued United States recognition and support of the Republic of China enables it to challenge the claim of the Chinese Communists to represent the Chinese people and keeps alive the hopes of those Chinese who are determined eventually to free their country of Communist rule.

Recognition of Communist China by the United States would have an adverse effect on the other free governments of Asia which could be disastrous to the cause of the free world in that part of the world. Those nations which are closely allied to the United States and are striving to maintain their independence on the perimeter of Chinese Communist power, especially Korea and Viet-Nam, would be profoundly confused and demoralized. They would interpret such action as abandonment of their cause by the United States. They might reason that their only hope for survival lay in desperate measures, not caring whether these threatened the peace of the area and the world. Governments further removed from the borders of China would see in American recognition of Communist China the first step in the withdrawal of the United States from the Far East. Without the support of the United States they would be unable long to defy the will of Peiping; and some would probably conclude that their wisest course would be speedily to seek the best terms obtainable from Peiping. Needless to say, these developments would place the entire free world position in Asia in the gravest peril.

Another special consideration in the case of China is that large and influential "overseas" Chinese communities exist in most of the countries of Southeast Asia. The efforts of these countries to build healthy free societies and to develop their economies would be seriously retarded if these communities were to fall under the sway of the Chinese Communists; and a grave threat of Communist subversion through these overseas communities would arise. Recognition of Communist China by the United States and the decline in the fortunes of the Republic of China which would inevitably result would have such a profound psychological effect on the overseas Chinese that it would make inevitable the transfer of the loyalties of large numbers to the Communist side. This in turn would undermine the ability of the most countries to resist the pressures tending to promote the expansion of Chinese Communist influence and power.

Still another factor which must be considered in the case of China is the effect which recognition of the Communist regime would have on the United Nations. Recognition of Peiping by the United States would inevitably lead to the seating of Peiping in that body.[2] In the view of the United States this would vitiate, if not destroy, the United Nations as an instrument for the maintenance of international peace. The Korean war was the first and most important effort to halt aggression through collective action in the United Nations. For Communist China, one of the parties against which the effort of the United Nations was directed, to be seated in

[2] On September 23, 1958, the United Nations General Assembly rejected an Indian proposal to consider the question of Chinese representation in the United Nations. United Nations, General Assembly, *Official Records, Thirteenth Session*, Supplement No. 18(A/4090), p. 57.

the United Nations while still unpurged of its aggression and defying the will of the United Nations in Korea would amount to a confession of a failure on the part of the United Nations and would greatly reduce the prospects for future successful action by the United Nations against aggression. Moreover, the Republic of China is a charter member in good standing of the United Nations, and its representatives there have contributed importantly to the constructive work of that organization. If the representatives of the Chinese Communist regime were to be seated in their place and given China's veto in the Security Council, the ability of that body in the future to discharge the responsibility it has under the charter for the maintaining of international peace and security would be seriously impaired.

Those who advocate recognition of the Chinese Communists often assume that by the standards of international law applied to such cases the Peiping regime is "entitled" to diplomatic recognition. In the view of the United States diplomatic recognition is a privilege and not a right. Moreover, the United States considers that diplomatic recognition is an instrument of national policy which it is both its right and its duty to use in the enlightened self-interest of the nation. However, there is reason to doubt that even by the tests often cited in international law the Chinese Communist regime qualifies for diplomatic recognition. It does not rule all China, and there is a substantial force in being which contests its claim to do so. The Chinese Communist Party, which holds mainland China in its grip, a tiny minority comprising less than 2 percent of the Chinese people, and the regimentation, brutal repression, and forced sacrifices that have characterized its rule have resulted in extensive popular unrest. To paraphrase Thomas Jefferson's dictum, this regime certainly does not represent "the will of the populace, substantially declared." Finally, it has shown no intention to honor its international obligations. One of its first acts was to abrogate the treaties of the Republic of China, except those it chose to continue. On assuming power it carried out a virtual confiscation without compensation of the properties of foreign nationals, including immense British investments notwithstanding the United Kingdom's prompt recognition of it. It has failed to honor various commitments entered into since, including various provisions of the Korean armistice and the Geneva accord on Viet-Nam and Laos, as well as the agreed announcement of September 1955 by which it pledged itself to permit all Americans in China to return home "expeditiously." [3]

The United States policy toward recognition of Communist China is then based on a carefully considered judgment of the national interest. Nonrecognition of Peiping coupled with continued recognition and support of the Republic of China facilitates the accomplishment of United States policy objectives in the Far East. Recognition of Peiping would seriously hinder accomplishment of these objectives and would facilitate the advance of Communist power in Asia.

In the process of determining its policy toward China the United States has taken into account the various statements and arguments advanced by proponents of extending diplomatic recognition to Peiping. One of the most commonly advanced reasons for recognition is that reality must be "recognized" and 600 million people cannot be "ignored." While superficially appealing, both statements themselves overlook the realities of the situation. United States policy is, of course, based on full appreciation of the fact that the Chinese Communist regime is currently in control of mainland China. However, it is not necessary to have diplomatic relations with a regime in order to deal with it. Without extending diplomatic recognition the United States has participated in extended negotiations with Chinese Communist representatives, in the Korean and Indochina armistice negotiations, and more recently in the ambassadorial talks in Geneva.[4] Similarly, United States policy in no sense "ignores" the existence and the aspirations of the Chinese people. Its attitude toward the the people of China remains what it historically has been, one of friendship and sympathetic understanding. It is nonetheless clear that our friendship for the Chinese people must not be permitted to blind us to the threat to our secuirty which the Communist regime in China now presents. Moreover, the United States is convinced that the Chinese Communist regime does not represent the true will or aspirations of the Chinese people and that our policy of withholding recognition from it is in actuality in their ultimate interest.

It is sometimes contended that by recognition of Communist China it would be possible to exert leverage on the Peiping regime which might ultimately be successful in weakening or even breaking the bond with Moscow. Un-

[3] *Documents on American Foreign Relations, 1955*, pp. 316-317.
[4] *Ibid.*, pp. 316-322, also *ibid.*, *1956*, pp. 405-412.

fortunately there is no evidence to support this belief, and there are important reasons why it is unlikely. The alliance between Moscow and Peiping is one of long standing; it traces its origin to the very founding of the Chinese Communist Party in 1921, in which representatives of the Comintern played an important role. It is based on a common ideology and on mutually held objectives with respect to the non-Communist world. All recent evidence points to the closeness of the tie between the Chinese Communists and the U.S.S.R. rather than in the other direction. The Chinese Communists were outspoken in championing the armed intervention of the Soviets in Hungary and have given unqualified endorsement to the execution of Nagy and the other leaders of the Hungarian revolt.[5] They were also leaders in the recent Communist-bloc attack on Yugoslavia for its attempts to pursue national policies independent of Kremlin control.[6] These and other facts make it apparent that the two partners in the Sino-Soviet alliance clearly realize their mutual dependence and attach great importance to bloc unity vis-a-vis the free world.

Furthermore, the alliance with the U.S.S.R. has a special importance for the Chinese Communists since it provides them with a dependable source of arms and military supplies. The Chinese Communist leaders, including Mao Tse-tung himself, came to power through their command of military force. They are therefore keenly conscious of the importance of military force to keep themselves in power against domestic and external opposition and to achieve the goals of their foreign policy. It is scarcely credible that they would dare risk any course of action which could lead to loss of their source of military supplies. For this reason alone it would seem unrealistic to believe that recognition of Peiping by the United States or any other leading nation would have the effect of tempting the Chinese Communists to play a "Titoist" role.

In fact, the opposite is quite likely to be the result. Were the United States to grant diplomatic recognition to Peiping —with all that this would entail by way of enhanced international prestige—its leaders would most likely feel confirmed in the correctness of their policies and the advantages of continued close cooperation with Moscow.

It is often alleged that recognition of Communist China

[5] Documents 70 and 71, above.
[6] Document 67, above.

is a necessary step in expanding trade relations with that country. For the United States this is of course not a consideration, since the United States embargoes trade with Peiping under the Trading With the Enemy Act as a result of the Korean war. But even for countries which do desire to expand trade with mainland China the facts do not support the contention that trade is dependent on recognition. To the contrary, Great Britain, which recognized Communist China in 1950, has found that she buys more goods from Communist China than Communist China buys from her. West Germany on the other hand does not recognize Peiping and enjoys a favorable trade balance with the mainland China. In any case, trade opportunities with Communist China are severely limited by a shortage of foreign exchange which is likely to persist for many years to come. Moreover, such trade would always be at the mercy of Communist policies. Peiping uses trade as a means of exerting pressure on the trading partner whenever it deems this to be expedient. A striking example is the case of Japan, where the Chinese Communists recently retaliated against Japanese refusal to make certain political concessions by cutting off all trade and even canceling contracts which had already been entered into. It would therefore seem that over the long run the advantages of trade with Peiping will prove more ephemeral than real.

An argument often heard is that the Chinese Communists are here "to stay"; that they will have to be recognized sooner or later; and that it would be the course of wisdom to bow to the inevitable now rather than be forced to do so ungracefully at a later date. It is true that there is no reason to believe that the Chinese Communist regime is on the verge of collapse; but there is equally no reason to accept its present rule in mainland China as permanent. In fact, unmistakable signs of dissatisfaction and unrest in Communist China have appeared in the "ideological remodeling" and the mass campaign against "rightists" which have been in progress during the past year. Dictatorships often create an illusion of permanence from the very fact that they suppress and still all opposition, and that of the Chinese Communists is no exception to this rule. The United States holds the view that communism's rule in China is not permanent and that it one day will pass. By withholding diplomatic recognition from Peiping it seeks to hasten that passing.

In public discussions of China policy one of the proposals

that has attracted widest attention is that known as the "two
Chinas solution." Briefly, advocates of this arrangement propose that the Chinese Communist regime be recognized as
the government of mainland China while the Government at
Taipei remains as the legal government of Taiwan. They
argue that this approach to the Chinese problem has the merit
of granting the Communists only what they already control
while retaining for the free world the militarily strategic
bastion of Taiwan. However, it overlooks or ignores certain
facts of basic importance. The Republic of China would not
accept any diminution of its sovereignty over China and could
be expected to resist such an arrangement with all the means
at its disposal. If a "two Chinas solution" were to be forcefully imposed against its will, that Government's effectiveness
as a loyal ally to the free-world-cause would be destroyed.
Peiping, too, would reject such an arrangement. In fact,
over the past year Chinese Communist propaganda has repeatedly and stridently denounced the "two Chinas" concept
and, ironically, has been accusing the United States Government of attempting to put it into effect. Peiping attaches great
importance to the eventual acquisition of Taiwan and has
consistently reserved what it calls its "right" to seize Taiwan
by force if other means fail. There is no prospect that it
would ever acquiesce in any arrangement which would lead
to the permanent detachment of Taiwan from China.

The "two Chinas" concept is bitterly opposed by both
Peiping and Taipei. Hence, even if such a solution could be
imposed by outside authority, it would not be a stable one.
Constant policing would be required to avert its violent overthrow by one side or the other.

It is sometimes said that nonrecognition of Peiping tends
to martyrize the Chinese Communists, thereby enabling them
to pose, especially before Asian neutralists, as an innocent and
injured party. It would be impossible to deny that there is
some truth in this. But this disadvantage is far outweighed
by the disadvantages that would result from following the
opposite course. It is surely better that some neutralists, who
are either unable or unwilling to comprehend the threat
inherent in Chinese Communist policies, mistakenly consider Peiping unjustly treated than that the allies of the
United States in Asia, who are the first line of defense against
Chinese Communist expansion, should be confused and demoralized by what to them could only appear to be a betrayal
of the common cause.

2. Ambassadorial Talks.

(123) Chinese Communist Statement on the Suspensions of Talks, April 12, 1958.[7]

It is four months since the 73rd meeting of the Sino-American ambassadorial talks held on December 12, 1957. During this period, in spite of repeated prodding by the Chinese side, the United States has used its customary Panmunjom tactics to drag on, so that the Sino-American ambassadorial talks have been suspended for a long time. This state of affairs has caused dissatisfaction among the people of our country and concern among the peace-loving people of the world. To set forth the truth, the Ministry of Foreign Affairs has decided to make public the facts behind the prolonged suspension of the Sino-American ambassadorial talks.

(1) At the 73rd meeting of the Sino-American ambassadorial talks, Ambassador U. A. Johnson, representative of the American side, informed our representative, Ambassador Wang Ping-nan, that he had been transferred to a new post and would henceforth be unable to participate in the talks, and that the U.S. Government had designated his assistant Mr. Edwin W. Martin as the U.S. representative.

Ambassador Wang Ping-nan pointed out at the time that, as the Sino-American ambassadorial talks were being held as a result of consultations between China and the United States, no alteration must be made by either party at will, and that designation by the U.S. Government of Mr. Martin, who is not of the rank of ambassador, as representative was evidently inconsistent with the agreed arrangement between China and the United States.

Thus, no date was fixed or published for the next meeting.

(2) In his letter to Ambassador Johnson dated January 14, 1958, Ambassador Wang Ping-nan pointed out that the American side had long been preventing progress in the talks by various means, and that now, in attempting to relegate the talks to a lower level, it was trying to create the false impression that the Sino-American talks continue, while actually it had no intention to settle any problem. Ambassador Wang was authorized to state that the Chinese Government could not agree to a unilateral alteration by the U.S. Government of the result of consultations between the Chinese and the American sides, and that if the U.S. Government has still any intention to carry on the Sino-American ambassadorial

[7] Peking Review, v. 1 (April 22, 1958), pp. 22-23.

talks, it should designate as soon as possible a representative of the rank of ambassador.

After a delay of nearly two months, Mr. Martin, on behalf of Ambassador Johnson, wrote to Ambassador Wang Ping-nan in reply on March 12, 1958. In his letter, Mr. Martin repeated statements made by Ambassador Johnson at the 73rd meeting, and indicated that the U.S. Government would continue to postpone the designation of a representative of ambassadorial rank. Moreover, Mr. Martin attempted to lay the blame on our side for the past failure of the Sino-American ambassadorial talks to fulfil the hopes placed in them.

(3) Mr. Martin's reply on behalf of the U.S. Government was disappointing. Ambassador Wang Ping-nan's assistant, Mr. Lai Ya-li, was therefore instructed to reply on March 26, 1958 to Mr. Martin that the Chinese Government cannot agree to a unilateral change of the level of the Sino-American ambassadorial talks, nor can it agree to suspending the talks for long and reducing them to an empty name on the pretext of administrative reasons; and that if the U.S. Government still has any intention of continuing the Sino-American ambassadorial talks, it should not delay further the designation of a representative of the rank of ambassador.

(4) It can be seen clearly from the above correspondence that, while the Chinese side has abided by the agreement and taken a just attitude, the United States has done everything to drag out the talks and go back on its promise in violation of agreement. In the face of the world's strong demand for relaxation of international tension, the United States dares not openly break up the Sino-American talks. On the other hand, it is afraid that such relaxation will further discomfit its cold-war policy. That is why it has prevented any progress in the talks and, moreover, tried to incapacitate the talks. Here lies the root cause why, for the past four months, the United States has been playing fraudulent tricks to stall the Sino-American talks.

(5) We now make public the letters from Ambassador Wang Ping-nan to Ambassador Johnson dated January 14, 1958, from Mr. Martin to Ambassador Wang Ping-nan dated March 12, 1958, and from Mr. Lai Ya-li to Mr. Martin dated March 26, 1958.

[*The annexed letters, referred to in the statement, were published in full in "Hsinhua News Agency Release," April 13, 1958—Editor.*] [8]

[8] Note in original.

(124) *Chinese Communist Statement on Resuming Talks, June 30, 1958.*[9]

More than half a year has passed since the U.S. Government suspended the Sino-American ambassadorial talks. The Chinese Government considers that this state of affairs should not continue. The U.S. ruling circles have been playing all sorts of tricks in an attempt to create the false impression that the Sino-American talks are still continuing in order to cover up its continued occupation of China's territory of Taiwan and its activities to create world tension. Such sinister designs must not be allowed to bear fruit. The Chinese Government agreed to hold the Sino-American ambassadorial talks with the aim of settling questions. The U.S. Government must answer clearly whether it is sincere about the talks.

Since December 12, 1957, when the U.S. Government broke the agreement between China and the United States on holding talks on an ambassadorial level by refusing to designate a representative of ambassadorial rank, thereby suspending the talks, the Chinese side, on January 14 and March 26, 1958 repeatedly urged the U.S. Government to designate a representative with the rank of ambassador to resume the talks. The U.S. Government, however, not only refused to do this but did not even consider it necessary to reply to the March 26 letter of the Chinese side. Moreover, a spokesman of the State Department of the United States recently even remarked nonchalantly that a First Secretary of its foreign service was ready to hold talks with us at any time, as if there had never been an agreement between China and the United States on the holding of talks on an ambassadorial level. This cannot but rouse the indignation of the Chinese people.

The imperialistic attitude consistently maintained by the United States is proven by the record of nearly three years of the Sino-American ambassadorial talks. The U.S. occupation of China's territory of Taiwan created tension in the Taiwan area. This is a naked act of aggression against China and the Chinese people have every right to take any measures to repulse it. Nevertheless, the Chinese side, in order to relax the tension in the Taiwan area, expressed its willingness to sit down and talk matters over with the United States and, during the Sino-American ambassadorial talks, put forward a

⁹ *Peking Review,* v. 1 (July 8, 1958), pp. 21-22.

series of reasonable proposals for the peaceful settlement of
the international disputes between China and the United
States in the Taiwan area. But the American side rejected all
these proposals. They attempted to confuse China's domestic
affair, a matter between the Chinese Government and the
Taiwan local authorities, with the international disputes between China and the United States in the Taiwan area, and
demanded that China give up its right of exercising sovereignty over its own territory and recognize the right of "self-
defence" for the United States on China's territory. This
demonstrates clearly that the aim of the United States is not
to relax the tension in the Taiwan area at all, but to insist
that China recognize the status quo of U.S. occupation of
Taiwan and to maintain and heighten tension. It is due to
the imperialist policy of the United States that discussion on
this crucial question of Sino-American relations has bogged
down since the latter part of 1956.

In order to break the deadlock and gradually improve
Sino-American relations, the Chinese side further put forward a series of proposals on certain questions that are comparatively easy to settle, such as removing the trade barriers
between the two countries, eliminating the obstacles in the
way of mutual contacts and cultural exchange between the
two peoples, exchanging correspondents for news coverage
on an equal and reciprocal basis and rendering judicial assistance between the two countries. Although questions such
as the entry of correspondents for news coverage and judicial
assistance were first raised by those concerned on the American side to those concerned on the Chinese side, and all the
proposals of the Chinese side were fully in accord with the
principles of equality and mutual benefit, the U.S. Government nonetheless rejected them. What is even more intolerable is the fact that the United States, in disregard of the
agreement reached in 1955 on the return of civilians of both
sides, continues to detain thousands upon thousands of Chinese civilians in the United States and prevent them from
returning to their motherland.

Irrefutable facts show that what the United States was
after in the Sino-American ambassadorial talks was by no
means a peaceful settlement of the international disputes
between China and the United States on the basis of equality
and mutual respect for territorial integrity and sovereignty,
but to impose its imperialist will on the Chinese people and,

failing that, to make use of the ambassadorial talks to deceive
the people of the world and cover up its sinister designs to
continue its aggression against China and to create international tension. During the past three years, the United States'
has been intensifying its interference and control of all
aspects of life in Taiwan, establishing on it bases for guided
missiles to threaten the Chinese people and utilizing the reactionary clique in Taiwan to carry out subversive activities
and armed intervention against Southeast Asian countries.
At the same time, the United States is endeavouring to bring
about, at many international conferences and organizations,
a situation of "two Chinas," to create eventually such a *fait
accompli* in the international arena, and thereby to prolong
its occupation of Taiwan. This is the crux of the reason for
the failure of the Sino-American ambassadorial talks to make
progress. U.S. Secretary of State Dulles recently declared that
it is in the best interests of the United States to persist in its
policy of enmity towards the People's Republic of China but
that it will deal with China when its interest so demands.
This demonstrates most clearly that, in the minds of the U.S.
ruling circles, the Sino-American ambassadorial talks are but
a means serving the imperialist policy of the United States.
The reason China agreed to hold the ambassadorial talks was
to try by peaceful means to eliminate armed aggression and
the threat of force in the Taiwan area on the part of the
United States. However, the Chinese people are by no means
afraid of U.S. aggression, and there is no reason whatsoever
why they should pine for talks with the United States. Building socialism with lightning speed, the Chinese people are
perfectly strong enough to liberate their territory of Taiwan.
No force on earth can stop the great cause of the Chinese
people in building up and uniting their motherland. The
handful of U.S. imperialists can only suffer isolation and
defeat from their policy of enmity towards the 600 million
Chinese people.

The Chinese Government hereby declares once again that
it can neither agree to the unilateral changing of the level of
the Sino-American ambassadorial talks, nor can it agree to
the continued suspension of the talks on any administrative
pretext. The Chinese Government demands that the United
States Government designate a representative of ambassadorial rank and resume the talks within fifteen days counting
from today, otherwise, the Chinese Government cannot but

consider that the United States has decided to break off the Sino-American ambassadorial talks.[10]

3. Crisis in the Taiwan Strait.

a. Renewal of Hostilities.

(125) Statement by the Secretary of State (Dulles), Newport, September 4, 1958.[11]

I have reviewed in detail with the President the serious situation which has resulted from aggressive Chinese Communist military actions in the Taiwan (Formosa) Straits area. The President has authorized me to make the following statement.

1. Neither Taiwan (Formosa) nor the islands of Quemoy and Matsu have ever been under the authority of the Chinese Communists. Since the end of the Second World War, a period of over 13 years, they have continuously been under the authority of Free China, that is, the Republic of China.

2. The United States is bound by treaty to help to defend Taiwan (Formosa) from armed attack[12] and the President is authorized by Joint Resolution of the Congress to employ the armed forces of the United States for the securing and protecting of related positions such as Quemoy and Matsu.[13]

3. Any attempt on the part of the Chinese Communists now to seize these positions or any of them would be a crude violation of the principles upon which world order is based, namely, that no country should use armed force to seize new territory.

4. The Chinese Communists have, for about 2 weeks, been subjecting Quemoy to heavy artillery bombardment and, by artillery fire and use of small naval craft, they have been harassing the regular supply of the civilian and military population of the Quemoys, which totals some 125 thousand persons. The official Peiping radio repeatedly announces the purpose of these military operations to be to take by armed force Taiwan (Formosa), as well as Quemoy and Matsu. In virtually every Peiping broadcast Taiwan (Formosa) and the

[10] For an additional Chinese Communist statement on resuming the ambassadorial talks see document 126, below. For comments by the Secretary of State (Dulles), see the *Department of State Bulletin*, v. 39 (July 21, 1958), pp. 106-107; (September 29, 1958), p. 488 and (October 20, 1958), pp. 599-600.
[11] *Ibid.* (September 22, 1958), pp. 445-446.
[12] *Documents on American Foreign Relations, 1954*, pp. 360-362.
[13] *Ibid., 1955*, pp. 298-299.

offshore islands are linked as the objective of what is called the "Chinese Peoples Liberation Army."

5. Despite, however, what the Chinese Communists say, and so far have done, it is not yet certain that their purpose is in fact to make an all-out effort to conquer by force Taiwan (Formosa) and the offshore islands. Neither is it apparent that such efforts as are being made, or may be made, cannot be contained by the courageous, and purely defensive, efforts of the forces of the Republic of China, with such substantial logistical support as the United States is providing.

6. The Joint Resolution of Congress, above referred to, includes a finding to the effect that "the secure possession by friendly governments of the Western Pacific Island chain, of which Formosa is a part, is essential to the vital interests of the United States and all friendly nations in and bordering upon the Pacific Ocean." It further authorizes the President to employ the Armed Forces of the United States for the protection not only of Formosa but for "the securing and protection of such related positions and territories of that area now in friendly hands and the taking of such other measures as he judges to be required or appropriate in assuring the defense of Formosa." In view of the situation outlined in the preceding paragraph, the President has not yet made any finding under that Resolution that the employment of the Armed Forces of the United States is required or appropriate in insuring the defense of Formosa. The President would not, however, hesitate to make such a finding if he judged that the circumstances made this necessary to accomplish the purposes of the Joint Resolution. In this connection, we have recognized that the securing and protecting of Quemoy and Matsu have increasingly become related to the defense of Taiwan (Formosa). This is indeed also recognized by the Chinese Communists. Military dispositions have been made by the United States so that a Presidential determination, if made, would be followed by action both timely and effective.

7. The President and I earnestly hope that the Chinese Communist regime will not again, as in the case of Korea, defy the basic principle upon which world order depends, namely, that armed force should not be used to achieve territorial ambitions. Any such naked use of force would pose an issue far transcending the offshore islands and even the security of Taiwan (Formosa). It would forecast a widespread use of force in the Far East which would endanger vital free world

positions and the security of the United States. Acquiescence therein would threaten peace everywhere. We believe that the civilized world community will never condone overt military conquest as a legitimate instrument of policy.

8. The United States has not, however, abandoned hope that Peiping will stop short of defying the will of mankind for peace. This would not require it to abandon its chains, however ill-founded we may deem them to me. I recall that in the extended negotiations which the representatives of the United States and Chinese Communist regime conducted at Geneva between 1955 and 1958, a sustained effort was made by the United States to secure, with particular reference to the Taiwan area, a declaration of mutual and reciprocal renunciation of force, except in self-defense, which, however, would be without prejudice to the pursuit of policies by peaceful means. The Chinese Communists rejected any such declaration. We believe, however, that such a course of conduct constitutes the only civilized and acceptable procedure. The United States intends to follow that course, so far as it is concerned, unless and until the Chinese Communists, by their acts, leave us no choice but to react in defense of the principles to which all peace-loving governments are dedicated.

(126) *Statement by the Prime Minister of the People's Republic of China (Chou), September 6, 1958.*[14]

(Excerpts)

*   *   *

(1) Taiwan and the Penghu Islands [Pescadores] have been China's territories from ancient times. Following the Second World War, they were restored to China after being occupied by Japan for a period of time. It is entirely China's internal affair for the Chinese people to exercise their sovereign right to liberate these areas. This is the Chinese people's sacred and inviolable right. The United States Government itself also declared formally that it would not get involved in China's civil conflict in the Taiwan area. Were it not for the fact that the United States Government later went back on its own statement and carried out armed intervention, Taiwan and the Penghu Islands would have long been liber-

14 *Peking Review*, v. 1 (September 9, 1958), pp. 15-16.

ated and placed under the administration of the Government of the People's Republic of China. These are undeniable facts recognized by fair-minded world public opinion unanimously.

(2) United States support of the Chiang Kai-shek clique entrenched on Taiwan and the Penghu Islands, which has long been repudiated by all the Chinese people, and its direct occupation of Taiwan and the Penghu Islands by armed force constitute unlawful interference in China's internal affairs and infringement of China's territorial integrity and sovereignty, and are in direct conflict with the United Nations Charter and all codes of international law. All so-called treaties concluded between the United States and the Chiang Kai-shek clique and all related resolutions adopted by the United States Congress are null and void as far as the Chinese people are concerned. They can never legalize United States aggression, much less can they be used as pretexts by the United States for expanding its aggression in the Taiwan Straits area.

*   *   *

(5) In pursuance of its foreign policy of peace, the Chinese Government has always stood for peaceful coexistence of countries with different social systems in accordance with the Five Principles and for the settlement of international disputes by the peaceful means of negotiation. Despite the fact that the United States has by armed force invaded and occupied China's territory . . . the Chinese Government proposed to sit down to negotiate with the United States Government to seek relaxation and elimination of the tension in the Taiwan area.

In the Sino-American ambassadorial talks which started in August, 1955, the Chinese side has time and again proposed that the two parties should . . . issue a statement declaring their intention to settle the dispute between China and the United States in the Taiwan area . . . through peaceful negotiation and without resorting to the threat or use of force against each other. But contrary to Dulles' assertion in his September 4 statement, it is precisely the United States that has refused to issue such a statement and, moreover, has later suspended unilaterally the talks themselves. After the Chinese Government demanded in July this year that the talks be resumed within a set time limit, the United States Government did not make a timely reply, but it has ultimately designated a representative of ambassadorial rank. Now, the United States Government again indicates its desire to settle the Sino-American dispute in the Taiwan area through peaceful negotiation. To make a further effort to safeguard peace the Chinese Government is prepared to resume the ambassadorial talks between the two countries. . . .

*   *   *

(127) *White House Statement, Washington, September 6, 1958.*[15]

The President discussed the Taiwan Straits situation with the Secretary of State. the Secretary of the Treasury, the Secretary of Defense, and the Chairman of the Joint Chiefs of Staff—members of the National Security Council. Also present were the Director of the United States Information Agency, the Director of the Office of Civil and Defense Mobilization, and the Acting Director of the Central Intelligence Agency. The Vice President, because of a long-standing out of town engagement, was unable to be present.

Consideration was given to measures which would conform to the policy enunciated on September 4 by the Secretary of State on the authority of the President. But particular note was taken of the reported radio statement of Mr. Chou En-lai indicating that the Chinese Communists were prepared to resume ambassadorial talks with the United States "in order to contribute further to the safeguarding of peace." These talks, which had been conducted in Europe for several years, were recently interrupted by the Chinese Communists.

So far the United States has not received any official word on this subject. We hope, however, that the reported statement of Mr. Chou En-lai is responsive to the urging, contained in our September 4 policy statement, that "armed force should not be used to achieve territorial ambitions," although such renunciation of force need not involve renouncing claims or the pursuit of policies by peaceful means. This is the course that the United States will resolutely pursue in conforming with our vital interests, our treaty obligations, and the principles on which world order is based.

The United States has sought to implement that policy in its past talks at the ambassadorial level with the Chinese

[15] *Department of State Bulletin*, v. 39 (September 22, 1958), pp. 446-447.

Communists. On July 28, 1958, and subsequently, we have sought a resumption of these talks.

If the Chinese Communists are now prepared to respond, the United States welcomes that decision. The United States Ambassador at Warsaw stands ready promptly to meet with the Chinese Communist Ambassador there, who has previously acted in this matter.

Naturally, in these resumed talks the United States will adhere to the negotiating position which it originally took in 1955, namely, that we will not in these talks be a party to any arrangement which would prejudice the rights of our ally, the Republic of China.

(128) *Letter from the Chairman of the Council of Ministers of the USSR (Khrushchev) to the President, September 7, 1958.*[16]

MR. PRESIDENT: I am addressing myself to you on a question of great importance which, we are sure, is now occupying the minds of all to whom the cause of peace is dear.

As a result of the policy being carried on by the USA in regard to China, and especially of the actions being undertaken at the present time by American Government in the area of the Chinese island of Taiwan and of the Taiwan Straits, a dangerous situation has arisen in the Far East. Humanity has again been put before the direct threat of the beginning of a military conflagration.

In this responsible moment, the Government of the Soviet Union has decided to turn to the Government of the USA with an appeal to show sense, not to permit steps which could entail irreparable consequences.

You well know, Mr. President, that the Soviet Union stands firmly on the position of the peaceful coexistence of all states, regardless of their social or state structure, and is in favor of not allowing the beginning of military conflicts, in order to assure conditions for a peaceful life for peoples on the whole globe. I think no one will dispute that the principles of peaceful coexistence have already received broad international recognition, and it can be said that for the overwhelming majority of states, they are the basis of their relations with other countries.

Nevertheless, in the postwar years, as a result of the policy of the USA, a deeply abnormal situation has been continu-

[16] *Ibid.* (September 29, 1958), pp. 499-503.

ously maintained in the Far East, the cause of which is the aggressive policy of the Government of the USA, a policy of war. The main reason for the tense and, it must be directly said, very very dangerous situation which has arisen is that the USA has seized age-old Chinese territory—the island of Taiwan with the Pescadores Islands—by force, is continuing to occupy these territories, cloaking this occupation with references to its support of the traitor of the Chinese people, Chiang Kai-shek, and is also trying to extend its aggression to the offshore Chinese islands.

As the Soviet Government has already stated many times in the organization of the United Nations, as well as in correspondence with the Government of the USA and governments of other powers, the situation is also inadmissible that a great state—The Chinese People's Republic—as a result of the position taken by the Government of the USA, is deprived of the opportunity to participate in the work of the organization of the United Nations, and is not represented in that organization, although it has a legitimate right to this.

You also know as well as I do that the Chinese state is one of the founders of the UN and that by force of that circumstance alone the existing situation is absolutely abnormal and deeply unjust in regard to the Chinese people.

The situation which has now arisen as a result of the actions of the USA in the area of the island of Taiwan and of the Taiwan Straits seriously disturbs the Soviet Government and the people. Indeed, I think, it will not be an exaggeration to say that it disturbs the whole world, every country, regardless of at what distance it is located from the Taiwan area. If you look squarely at the truth, you must acknowledge that the USA is trying to assume the functions of some sort of world gendarme in this area too. We think that for any state, regardless how strong and influential it is, to take such a role on itself is an unworthy affair for a civilized state and quite risky.

The Government of the USA is carrying out military demonstrations trying to prevent the liberation of Taiwan and to keep this Chinese island as its military base, aimed above all against the Chinese People's Republic, and also to hinder the lawful actions of the CPR directed at the liberation of the offshore island on which Chiang Kai-shekists have ensconced themselves.

In the area of the Taiwan Straits, there is one of the strongest naval units of the American Navy—the Seventh Fleet of the USA. Hasty measures are being taken to strengthen this fleet, and military vessels and aviation are being transferred to the Far East from the USA, the Mediterranean Sea, and other areas. More than that, it has been announced that in the next few days "joint maneuvers" of the naval forces and marines of the USA and Chiang Kai-shek clique will be carried out in the Taiwan area, and that new contingents of American troops are being transferred to Taiwan on this pretext. The question arises whether such actions in the present situation can be assessed as other than an open provocation. It seems to us that with the most indulgent approach no other evaluation can be given to these actions.

It must be said that, in general, the practice of urgently transferring naval vessels of the USA from one place to another has become a frequent phenomena recently. In truth, by the direction of movement of the American Naval Fleet one can now judge almost without error to what place will be directed the spearhead of the next blackmail and provocations.

Very recently the world was a witness to similar demonstrations of the American Navy in the Mediterranean Sea when the armed intervention of the USA into Lebanon was carried out and when the Sixth Fleet of the USA held the capital of Lebanon, and indeed that whole country, under the muzzles of its guns. When today attempts are being made to rattle the saber and threaten China, then, it seems to us, one should not forget that China is not small Lebanon which recently fell victim to foreign intervention, which has met universal condemnation at the just concluded special session of the UN General Assembly. The great 600 million Chinese people are powerful and unconquerable not only for their inexhaustible resources, but also for their solidarity in support of the government, and are confidently and firmly moving on the path of the further development and strengthening of their country, the raising of their welfare, at which we, Soviet people, are truly happy and at which all those who wish the Chinese people well cannot but be happy. But I would want to emphasize not only this side of the matter, but also that China is not alone; it has true friends ready to go to its aid at any moment in case of aggression against China, since the interests of the security of People's China are inseparable from the interests of the security of the Soviet Union.

In connection with the practice of transporting war fleets and air units from one end of the globe to another, for example, the regions of the Near and Middle East, the Far East, Latin America etc. in order to bring pressure to bear here on some, there on other states and to attempt to dictate one's will on them, in general the question arises—isn't it time to finish with such actions which, it goes without saying, can in no way ever be recognized as normal methods in international relations. There arises the legitimate question— ought this not be discussed in the UN and a decision be adopted forbidding powers from employing such movement of its naval and air forces for purposes of blackmail and intimidation and to the effect that these forces would be held within the limits of their national frontiers. At the same time, in connection with the application of this kind of methods in the foreign policy of the USA, I would like to make one more remark. Does it not seem to you, Mr. President, that such transferring of military vessels now in one, now in another direction to a significant degree is now deprived of any sense—at least in the relations of states which have modern types of weapons at their disposal? I do not know what your military advisers tell you but it seems to us it must also not be unknown to them that the epoch of the flourishing of the power of surface naval fleets is over, has gone into the past. In the century of nuclear and rocket weapons of hitherto unheard of power and speed of action, these once threatening naval vessels are fit, in essence, only for paying courtesy visits, giving salutes, and can still serve as targets for appropriate types of missiles. Perhaps this will wound the self-esteem of people who are closely connected with fleets but what can you do, it is impossible not to reckon with indisputable facts.

Nearly every day political and military leaders of the USA come out with threats addressed to People's China. Such and only such a meaning have the repeated statements of USA Secretary of State Dulles about the activities of the USA in the region of the Taiwan Straits and in particular the statement which he made in your and his name on 4 September. This statement cannot but evoke the most decisive condemnation. It represents an open attempt of crude and unceremonious trampling of the sovereign rights of other states. The Government of the USA having no rights for this permits itself arbitrarily to establish some kind of boundary of its interests and the sphere of operations of its armed forces on the territory of China. Such activities it is impossible to qualify otherwise than as aggressive, which undoubtedly will be condemned by all peoples.

It is impossible to evaluate differently as well the statement of the Government of the USA of 6 September.

The inciting statement of Minister of Defense McElroy draws special attention to itself in which are contained frank threats addressed to the Chinese People's Republic, and in which attempts are made to justify the aggressive activities of American armed forces in the Far East and in which the Chiang Kai-shek clique is taken under protection. And the commander of American armed forces on Taiwan Vice-Admiral Smoot has let himself go entirely and states the intention of the USA together with the Chiang Kai-shekists to inflict a defeat on Communist China.

Military leaders in the USA try even, with the tacit agreement of the American Government, to resort to atomic blackmail in relation to China, acting evidently still on inertia under the impression of the moods governing in Washington in that short period in the course of which the USA had at its disposal a monopoly of the atomic weapons. As is known, even at that time the policy of atomic blackmail did not have and could not have any success. Is it necessary to say that in present conditions when the USA has long not been the possessor of a monopoly in the field of atomic armaments, attempts to intimidate other states by atomic weapons are a completely hopeless business.

I speak about this because, as it seems to me, in the USA there are still people who do not want to part with the policy of threats and atomic blackmail although, it would seem, each day gives no little evidence that such a policy henceforth is doomed to failure.

One can with full confidence say that threats and blackmail cannot intimidate the Chinese people. This clearly follows also from the statement of the Premier of the State Council of the CPR Chou En-Lai of 6 September.

The Chinese people wants peace and defends peace but it does not fear war. If war will be thrust on China, whose people are full of determination to defend its rightful cause, then we have not the slightest doubt that the Chinese people will give a worthy rebuff to the aggressor.

The aggressive preparations of the USA in the Far East, judging by everything, are not limited only to the region of the Taiwan Straits. There are facts to the effect that encouraged and instigated by the United States Syngman Rhee again is preparing military provocations and declaring his intention to move "in a march to the North." Evidently someone in the US has definite plans once more to turn Korea into a field of bloody battle. It is not because, by the way, the Government of the USA so stubbornly refuses to withdraw its troops from South Korea? But it is impossible to permit a repetition of the Korean tragedy, and the criminal plots of the Syngman Rhee-ites must be stopped. There can be no doubts that if the Syngman Rhee-ites risk a repetition of their "march," then there awaits them the same fate which befell them when the Korean people and the Chinese people's volunteers inflicted a complete defeat on the aggressor and frustrated his plans. Of course responsibility for the provocation of Syngman Rhee lies entirely on the Government of the USA.

At the recently concluded special session of the UN General Assembly, you, Mr. President, spoke about indirect aggression.[17] Allegedly threatening certain Arab states of the Near East on the part of other Arab states, and called for the condemnation of this non-existent indirect aggression. At the same time the United States itself is carrying out in the Far East not only indirect but also direct aggression, by having seized the Chinese island of Taiwan and by supporting the anti-national clique of betrayers of the Chinese people, harbored on this island under the protection of American weapons and making from there bandit sorties against China.

The dispatch of its armed forces to the region of Taiwan and the waters of the Pacific Ocean adjacent to it the Government of the USA usually seeks to justify with reference to some kind of "obligations" undertaken by it in relation to the "defense" of this region. But did the Chinese people ask the American Government to take on itself such an obligation, by referring to which it permits itself to hamper the realization by China of its sovereign rights in relation to Taiwan and other Chinese islands?

The American people in the past itself had to beat off attempts of foreign powers to interfere in its internal affairs and by force of arms to impose their will on it. It is well known that these attempts ended lamentably for those who undertook them. Would it not be right to draw the appropriate conclusions from this historical experience of the United States and end the policy of interference in the inter-

[17] Document 101, above.

nal affairs of China? Indeed if national independence is dear to the American people, then why should it be less dear to the Chinese people, as well as to any other people?

It is possible you will find what I have said above as harsh. But I do not permit myself to agree with this. In this letter to you, as also on other occasions, I simply wish to express myself frankly and to emphasize the whole danger of the situation developing in the region of Taiwan and the Chinese offshore islands as result of actions of the USA. If we were to hide our thoughts behind outwardly polite diplomatic formulations, then, I think it would be more difficult to understand each other. Moreover, we desire, that you, the Government of the USA and the whole American people with whom we wish only good relations and friendship should have a correct idea about those consequences which the present actions of the USA in the Far East might have. It would be a serious miscalculation if in the United States the conclusion were drawn that it was possible to deal with China in accordance with the example as it was done by certain powers in the past. Such kind of miscalculation might have serious consequences for the cause of peace in the whole world. Therefore let us introduce into the question full clarity because reservations and misunderstandings in such affairs are most dangerous.

An attack on the Chinese People's Republic, which is a great friend, ally and neighbor of our country, is an attack on the Soviet Union. True to its duty, our country will do everything in order together with People's China to defend the security of both states, the interests of peace in the Far East, the interest of peace in the whole world.

Nothing would be further from the truth than an attempt to assess this, my message to you, as an intention to exaggerate unnecessarily and even more to utter some kind of threats. We desire only to draw your attention to the situation from which no one can escape—neither you nor we— if in the Far East the fire of war breaks out. We wish to find a common language with you with which to cease the present movement downward on the inclined slope, with which by the common efforts of the USSR, the USA, the Chinese People's Republic and other countries to remove the tension arising in the Far East, with which it might be possible to say that through united efforts a useful contribution was made in the interest of peace in the whole world. Of course to decide to "recognize" or "not to recognize" the Chinese

People's Republic is an affair of the Government of the USA itself. In this connection it is possible only to remark that neither the very fact of the existence of the CPR as one of the great powers of the world, nor the role which this government plays in our time in international relations, is changed because of that. But at the present time in view of the policy which the Government of the United States follows in relation to China such a situation has arisen that the question of the relationship of the United States to China obviously extends beyond the framework of purely internal affairs of the United States.

A situation has arisen which involves the interests of many countries. The tension artificially maintained in view of the policy of the USA in the relations between the United States and China and even more such actions which the United States is undertaking at the present moment in the Far East will lead also to a straining of relations between all great powers—the founders of the UN. It is possible without exaggerating to say that the present policy of the USA in relation to China complicates the solution of many important international questions and in a serious form hampers the normal activity of the UN as an international organization called upon to guard the cause of peace. There is one Chinese state and it is located in China and nowhere else and Taiwan and the other Chinese islands where at the moment the Chiang Kai-shekists have ensconced themselves—these are a part of China.

Only the Government of China—in the capital of China— Peking and to which the many million Chinese people have entrusted the leadership of their country has the right and the real possibility to represent China in international relations. And only the unrealistic position of the Government of the USA which still prefers to close its eyes to the actual state of affairs in China, is a stumbling block, prevents the states members of the UN from taking the only correct decision—to throw out of this organization the political corpse of the Chiang Kai-shekist imposter and to grant the representatives of Great China their legal place in the UN. Who will deny that China is attempting to free its own territory which has been transformed into a military base of a foreign power and which has become a source of continual threat for peaceful life of the Chinese people?

China has the full legal right to take all necessary measures against the traitor Chiang Kai-shek. It is taking these measures on its own soil and is not sending its armed forces on the territory of other countries. These actions of the Chinese People's Republic represent only legitimate measures of self-defense, foreseen also by the Charter of the United Nations organization. Quite otherwise acts the Government of the USA which is trying to confer upon itself the right to send its armed forces thousands and thousands of kilometers from the USA for the retention of the Chinese islands seized by it. It is not by accident that even the allies of the United States in the military blocs quite loudly censure American policy in relation to China as unrealistic and dangerous.

I think that every person who displays a real anxiety for the fate of peace cannot but speak out for having an end put to that abnormal and dangerous situation which has developed as a result of the current political course of the Government of the USA in the Far East. For that, according to the conviction of the Soviet Government, above all it is necessary to give up the narrow and alien-to-all-reality approach to the great historical changes which have taken place in China, it is necessary to recognize the legitimate rights and interests of the Chinese People's Republic and once and for all to cease the policy of provocation and blackmail in connection with the Chinese people.

In the Far East there can not be a stable peace until such time as the American Navy Fleet will be withdrawn from the Taiwan Straits, until American soldiers will leave the Chinese island of Taiwan and will go home. We are convinced that such an opinion is shared not only by the Soviet Union and other socialist states but also by all other countries for whom the cause of peace is dear in the Far East and in the whole world. Mr. President, concluding my present message to you, dictated by a sense of the great responsibility which lies upon our countries for the preservation of peace in the whole world, I wish with all force to emphasize that whether peace will reign in the Far East or whether this region will continue to remain a dangerous hotbed of war will depend fully on the further actions of the Government of the USA. I should like to hope that you with the necessary understanding will apprehend the present message to you from the side of the Soviet Government. I permit myself to express also the confidence that this message will be correctly understood by all the American people which—we are convinced of this—like other peoples desire peace and do not desire war.

If the Government of the USA will take the road of respect for the legitimate sovereign rights of the great Chinese people then this doubtless will be regarded with satisfaction by all peoples as a serious contribution of the people of the United States of America to the cause of strengthening of universal peace.

Sincerely,

N. KHRUSHCHEV

(129) *News Conference Comments by the Secretary of State (Dulles), September 9, 1958.*[18]

Q. Mr. Secretary, after the passage of the Formosa resolution, did this country do anything to encourage the Chinese Nationalists to build up their forces on the Quemoys in a formal or an informal way?

A. I think not. My distinct impression is that the decision to build up the defensive strength on Quemoy and Matsu was taken by the Chinese Nationalist Republic—the Republic of China—and that that was not urged or encouraged by the United States.

Q. Mr. Secretary, does this then mean that the Chinese Nationalist Government violated the intent of the exchange of notes between yourself and Foreign Minister Yeh?[19]

A. Not at all.

Q. It provides that there will be no significant depletion of the defensive strength on Formosa and the Pescadores of the forces which jointly support it.

A. There was no violation there. It is one thing to say did we encourage it or promote it, and it is another thing to say did we oppose it. After all, the Republic of China is a sovereign Government. It is not a puppet of ours. It has a normal right to take decisions of its own. It is one thing to say, as I did, that we did not promote or encourage this thing. It is a different thing again to say that we did not actively oppose it.

Q. Mr. Secretary, do you think it was wise to have stood by while the buildup occurred on these islands?

A. Yes; I think it was.

Q. In what respect?

A. That the attempt by the United States to impose its will in that respect upon the Republic of China would have had very unfortunate consequences. It would have weakened the

18 *Department of State Bulletin*, v. 39 (September 29, 1958), pp. 486-493.
19 *Documents on American Foreign Relations, 1954*, pp. 363-364.

defensive posture of the United States in the entire area. I must emphasize that this situation in that part of the world is not an isolated situation. You cannot isolate it and say that the only problem involved here is Quemoy and Matsu. What is involved, and what is under threat, is the entire position of the United States and that of its free-world allies in the Western Pacific, extending from Japan, Korea, Okinawa, Formosa, the Philippines, on down to Southeast Asia. That is what is under attack. That is of vital interest to the United States. And we have to conduct ourselves in relation to that situation, not as though little bits of it could be segregated and treated as isolated problems to be dealt with entirely on their own. We have to maintain good will and good relations and the morale of the governments that are our friends and allies in that part of the world. Those factors have to be taken into account and not purely military dispositions.

Q. Mr. Secretary, the U.S. warships in the Formosa Straits are convoying the Nationalist ships to within 3 miles of Quemoy. Can you tell us, sir, what the significance of this 3-mile limit is? Is it the Nationalist Chinese limit or the Red China limit?

A. That decision was taken while I was away, and I was not a participant in the discussions which led up to it. My understanding is that there were two elements that were involved in the decision. One was that to conduct what might appear to be combat activities within the 3-mile limit around Matsu and Quemoy might involve a decision, or require a decision, under the joint resolution. The other was that as a practical matter, I believe, our ships can operate on that basis without any material risk of coming under the fire of the shore batteries.

Q. Sir, on the point about whose 3-mile limit it is, then, you are not paying any attention, I gather, to the territorial claims of the Red Chinese or even to the use of a limit around Quemoy and Matsu.

A. No, the 3-mile limit referred to is the 3-mile limit which represents the territorial waters of the Republic of China around Quemoy and Matsu. We do not accept from the Chinese Communists or anybody else, for that matter, the extension of territorial waters to 12 miles.[20] That is what you might

[20] For a declaration by the Government of the People's Republic of China extending the "breadth of the territorial sea of the People's Republic of China" to twelve nautical miles and applying this principle to Taiwan and the Penghu islands, see the *Peking Review*, v. 1 (September 16, 1958), p. 21.

call a "grab." It cannot be effected unilaterally by any nation any more than it can grab territory.

Q. Mr. Secretary, your big argument for the Formosa resolution 2 years ago was that past wars had been caused by the failure of great powers to make absolutely clear where they would fight. In the light of that would you explain to us why you think it is still wise not to make our intentions crystal clear about the offshore islands and to continue the guessing game?

A. The position which I took, I think, at the time of the resolution and, indeed, the terms of the resolution itself make perfectly clear that the United States is to defend Taiwan and then Penghus. It also makes clear that it was the wish of the Congress that, if the President found that related areas should be defended as part of that effort, then he should defend them. Now in the nature of the case the President cannot, under the terms of the resolution, and, indeed, under the terms of our treaty, make an absolute decision in that respect. You may recall that the treaty that we have covers only Taiwan (Formosa) and the Penghus (the Pescadores). At the time of the ratification of that treaty we pointed out that ,if further area was to be brought under that treaty, we would go back to Congress—the Senate—and ask for an amendment of the treaty. Therefore, it is quite clear, and, I think, had been made clear from the beginning of this affair, that the offshore islands are not to be defended as such by the United States. If they are involved in what is in effect an attack upon areas which we are bound to defend, namely, Taiwan and the Penghus, then we will meet that attack at that point. But we cannot just say, through Presidential action, that we will defend, come what may, under any and all circumstances, an area which is beyond that to which we are committed by the treaty. This can be done only if there is an actual relationship between the two at the time in question. I think that was made very clear at the time of the adoption of the resolution. I made it clear in many press conferences back in 1955, and it is the same situation today as it was at that time.

Q. Mr. Secretary, in view of the fact that the Chinese Comnists' radio, in talking about Quemoy and Formosa, makes no distinction separating Quemoy from the eventual plan to liberate Formosa, if there were to be an attack, say today, would you think that everything added up to a decision to go ahead and help defend Quemoy on the grounds that it is essential to the defense of Formosa?

A. I think you can guess the answer to that if you read the statement of September 4. I don't want to add to or subtract from that statement, but I think it is pretty clear in that respect. The statement pointed out the reasons why the President could not now make a decision. It implied that, if those reasons no longer existed, then he would not hesitate to make the decision. But there could be changes in the situation, and I don't want to read into that statement more than is there, because I think there is plenty there.

* * *

(130) Radio-TV Address by the President, September 11, 1958.[21]

My friends: Tonight I want to talk to you about the situation, dangerous to peace, which has developed in the Formosa Straits in the Far East. My purpose is to give you its basic facts and then my conclusions as to our Nation's proper course of action.

To begin, let us remember that traditionally this country and its Government have always been passionately devoted to peace with honor, as they are now. We shall never resort to force in settlement of differences except when compelled to do so to defend against aggression and to protect our vital interests.

This means that, in our view, negotiations and conciliation should never be abandoned in favor of force and strife. While we shall never timidly retreat before the threat of armed aggression, we would welcome in the present circumstances negotiations that could have a fruitful result in preserving the peace of the Formosa area and reaching a solution that could be acceptable to all parties concerned, including, of course, our ally, the Republic of China.

Bombardment of Quemoy and Matsu

On the morning of August 23d the Chinese Communists opened a severe bombardment of Quemoy, an island in the Formosan Straits off the China coast. Another island in the same area, Matsu, was also attacked. These two islands have always been a part of Free China—never under Communist control.

This bombardment of Quemoy has been going on almost continuously ever since. Also, Chinese Communists have been

[21] Department of State Bulletin, v. 39 (September 29, 1958), pp. 481-484.

using their naval craft to try to break up the supplying of Quemoy with its 125,000 people. Their normal source of supply is by sea from Formosa, where the Government of Free China is now located.

Chinese Communists say that they will capture Quemoy. So far they have not actually attempted a landing, but their bombardment has caused great damage. Over 1,000 people have been killed or wounded. In large part these are civilians.

This is a tragic affair. It is shocking that in this day and age naked force should be used for such aggressive purposes.

But this is not the first time that the Chinese Communists have acted in this way.

In 1950 they attacked and tried to conquer the Republic of Korea. At that time President Truman announced the intention of protecting Formosa, the principal area still held by Free China, because of the belief that Formosa's safety was vital to the security of the United States and the free world. Our Government has adhered firmly ever since 1950 to that policy.

In 1953 and 1954 the Chinese Communists took an active part in the war in Indochina against Viet-Nam.

In the fall of 1954 they attacked Quemoy and Matsu, the same two islands they are attacking now. They broke off that attack when, in January 1955, the Congress and I agreed that we should firmly support Free China.

Since then, for about 4 years, Chinese Communists have not used force for aggressive purposes. We have achieved an armistice in Korea which stopped the fighting there in 1953. There is a 1954 armistice in Viet-Nam; and since 1955 there has been quiet in the Formosa Straits area. We had hoped that the Chinese Communists were becoming peaceful—but it seems not.

So the world is again faced with the problem of armed aggression. Powerful dictatorships are attacking an exposed, but free, area.

What should we do?

Shall we take the position that, submitting to threat, it is better to surrender pieces of free territory in the hope that this will satisfy the appetite of the aggressor and we shall have peace?

Do we not still remember that the name of "Munich" symbolizes a vain hope of appeasing dictators?

At that time the policy of appeasement was tried, and it

failed. Prior to the Second World War, Mussolini seized Ethiopia. In the Far East Japanese warlords were grabbing Manchuria by force. Hitler sent his armed forces into the Rhineland in violation of the Versailles Treaty. Then he annexed little Austria. When he got away with that, he next turned to Czechoslovakia and began taking it bit by bit.

In the face of all these attacks on freedom by the dictators, the powerful democracies stood aside. It seemed that Ethiopia and Manchuria were too far away and too unimportant to fight about. In Europe appeasement was looked upon as the way to peace. The democracies felt that, if they tried to stop what was going on, that would mean war. But, because of these repeated retreats, war came just the same.

If the democracies had stood firm at the beginning, almost surely there would have been no World War. Instead they gave such an appearance of weakness and timidity that aggressive rulers were encouraged to overrun one country after another. In the end the democracies saw that their very survival was at stake. They had no alternative but to turn and fight in what proved to be the most terrible war that the world has ever known.

I know something about that war, and I never want to see that history repeated. But, my fellow Americans, it certainly can be repeated if the peace-loving democratic nations again fearfully practice a policy of standing idly by while big aggressors use armed force to conquer the small and weak.

Let us suppose that the Chinese Communists conquer Quemoy. Would that be the end of the story? We know that it would not be the end of the story. History teaches that, when powerful despots can gain something through aggression, they try, by the same methods, to gain more and more and more.

Also, we have more to guide us than the teachings of history. We have the statements, the boastings, of the Chinese Communists themselves. They frankly say that their present military effort is part of a program to conquer Formosa.

It is as certain as can be that the shooting which the Chinese Communists started on August 23d had as its purpose not just the taking of the island of Quemoy. It is part of what is indeed an ambitious plan of armed conquest.

This plan would liquidate all of the free-world positions in the Western Pacific area and bring them under captive governments which would be hostile to the United States and the free world. Thus the Chinese and Russian Communists would come to dominate at least the western half of the now friendly Pacific Ocean.

So aggression by ruthless despots again imposes a clear danger to the United States and to the free world.

In this effort the Chinese Communists and the Soviet Union appear to be working hand in hand. Last Monday I received a long letter on this subject from Prime Minister Khrushchev. He warned the United States against helping its allies in the Western Pacific. He said that we should not support the Republic of China and the Republic of Korea. He contended that we should desert them, return all of our naval forces to our home bases, and leave our friends in the Far East to face, alone, the combined military power of the Soviet Union and Communist China.

Does Mr. Khrushchev think that we have so soon forgotten Korea?

I must say to you very frankly and soberly, my friends, the United States cannot accept the result that the Communists seek. Neither can we show, now, a weakness of purpose—a timidity—which would surely lead them to move more aggressively against us and our friends in the Western Pacific area.

If the Chinese Communists have decided to risk a war, it is not because Quemoy itself is so valuable to them. They have been getting along without Quemoy ever since they seized the China mainland 9 years ago.

If they have now decided to risk a war, it can only be because they, and their Soviet allies, have decided to find out whether threatening war is a policy from which they can make big gains.

If that is their decision, then a Western Pacific "Munich" would not buy us peace or security. It would encourage the aggressors. It would dismay our friends and allies there. If history teaches anything, appeasement would make it more likely that we would have to fight a major war.

Security of Western Pacific Vital to U.S.

Congress has made clear its recognition that the security of the Western Pacific is vital to the security of the United States and that we should be firm. The Senate has ratified, by overwhelming vote, security treaties with the Republic of China covering Formosa and the Pescadores, and also the Republic of Korea. We have a mutual security treaty with the Republic of the Philippines, which could be next in line for conquest if Formosa fell into hostile hands. These treaties commit the United States to the defense of the treaty areas. In addition, there is a joint resolution which the Congress passed in January 1955 dealing specifically with Formosa and the offshore islands of Free China in the Formosa Straits.

At that time the situation was similar to what it is today.

Congress then voted the President authority to employ the armed forces of the United States for the defense not only of Formosa but of related positions, such as Quemoy and Matsu, if I believed their defense to be appropriate in assuring the defense of Formosa.

I might add that the mandate from the Congress was given by an almost unanimous bipartisan vote.

Today, the Chinese Communists announce, repeatedly and officially, that their military operations against Quemoy are preliminary to attack on Formosa. So it is clear that the Formosa Straits resolution of 1955 applies to the present situation.

If the present bombardment and harassment of Quemoy should be converted into a major assault, with which the local defenders could not cope, then we would be compelled to face precisely the situation that Congress visualized in 1955.

I have repeatedly sought to make clear our position in this matter so that there would not be danger of Communist miscalculation. The Secretary of State on September 4th made a statement to the same end. This statement could not, of course, cover every contingency. Indeed, I interpret the joint resolution as requiring me not to make absolute advance commitments but to use my judgment according to the circumstances of the time. But the statement did carry a clear meaning to the Chinese Communists and to the Soviet Union. There will be no retreat in the face of armed aggression, which is part and parcel of a continuing program of using armed force to conquer new regions.

I do not believe that the United States can be either lured or frightened into appeasement. I believe that, in taking the position of opposing aggression by force, I am taking the only position which is consistent with the vital interests of the United States and, indeed, with the peace of the world.

Some misguided persons have said that Quemoy is nothing to become excited about. They said the same about South Korea—about Viet-Nam, about Lebanon.

Now I assure you that no American boy will be asked by

me to fight *just* for Quemoy. But those who make up our armed forces—and I believe the American people as a whole —do stand ready to defend the principle that armed force shall not be used for aggressive purposes.

Upon observance of that principle depends a lasting and just peace. It is that same principle that protects the Western Pacific free-world positions as well as the security of our homeland. If we are not ready to defend this principle, then indeed tragedy after tragedy would befall us.

Prospect for Negotiation

But there is a far better way than resort to force to settle these differences, and there is some hope that such a better way may be followed.

That is the way of negotiation.

That way is open and prepared because in 1955 arrangements were made between the United States and the Chinese Communists that an ambassador on each side would be authorized to discuss at Geneva certain problems of common concern. These included the matter of release of American civilians imprisoned in Communist China and such questions as the renunciation of force in the Formosa area. There have been 73 meetings since August 1955.

When our ambassador, who was conducting these negotiations, was recently transferred to another post, we named as successor Mr. [Jacob D.] Beam, our Ambassador to Poland. The Chinese Communists were notified accordingly the latter part of July, but there was no response.

The Secretary of State, in his September 4th statement, referred to these Geneva negotiations. Two days later, Mr. Chou En-lai, the Premier of the People's Republic of China, proposed that these talks should be resumed "in the interests of peace." This was followed up on September 8th by Mr. Mao Tse-tung, the Chairman of the People's Republic of China. We promptly welcomed this prospect and instructed our Ambassador at Warsaw to be ready immediately to resume these talks. We expect that the talks will begin upon the return to Warsaw of the Chinese Communist Ambassador, who has been in Peiping.

Perhaps our suggestion may be bearing fruit. We devoutly hope so.

Naturally, the United States will adhere to the position it first took in 1955, that we will not in these talks be a party to any arrangements which would prejudice rights of our ally, the Republic of China.

We know by hard experiences that the Chinese Communist leaders are indeed militant and aggressive. But we cannot believe that they would now persist in a course of military aggression which would threaten world peace, with all that would be involved. We believe that diplomacy can and should find a way out. There are measures that can be taken to assure that these offshore islands will not be a thorn in the side of peace. We believe that arrangements are urgently required to stop gunfire and to pave the way to a peaceful solution.

If the bilateral talks between ambassadors do not fully succeed, there is still the hope that the United Nations could exert a peaceful influence on the situation.

In 1955 the hostilities of the Chinese Communists in the Formosa area were brought before the United Nations Security Council. But the Chinese Communists rejected its jurisdiction. They said that they were entitled to Formosa and the offshore islands and that, if they used armed force to get them, that was purely a "civil war" and that the United Nations had no right to concern itself.

They claimed also that the attack by the Communist north Koreans on south Korea was "civil war" and that the United Nations and the United States were "aggressors" because they helped south Korea. They said the same about their attack on Viet-Nam.

I feel sure that these pretexts will never deceive or control world opinion. The fact is that Communist Chinese hostilities in the Formosa Straits area do endanger world peace. I do not believe that any rulers, however aggressive they may be, will flout efforts to find a peaceful and honorable solution, whether it be by direct negotiations or through the United Nations.

My friends, we are confronted with a serious situation. But it is typical of the security problems of the world today. Powerful and aggressive forces are constantly probing, now here, now there, to see whether the free world is weakening. In the face of this there are no easy choices available. It is misleading for anyone to imply that there are.

However, the present situation, though serious, is by no means desperate or hopeless.

There is not going to be any appeasement.

I believe that there is not going to be any war.

But there must be sober realization by the American people that our legitimate purposes are again being tested by those who threaten peace and freedom everywhere.

This has not been the first test for us and for the free world. Probably it will not be the last. But as we meet each test with courage and unity, we contribute to the safety and the honor of our beloved land—and to the cause of a just and lasting peace.

(131) *Letter from the President to the Chairman of the Council of Ministers of the USSR (Khrushchev), September 12, 1958.*[22]

DEAR MR. CHAIRMAN: I have your letter of September 7. I agree with you that a dangerous situation exists in the Taiwan area. I do not agree with you as to the source of danger in this situation.

The present state of tension in the Taiwan area was created directly by Chinese Communist action, not by that of the Republic of China or by the United States. The fact is that following a long period of relative calm in that area, the Chinese Communists, without provocation, suddenly initiated a heavy artillery bombardment of Quemoy and began harassing the regular supply of the civilian and military population of the Quemoys. This intense military activity was begun on August 23rd—some three weeks after your visit to Peiping.[23] The official Peiping radio has repeatedly been announcing that the purpose of these military operations is to take Taiwan (Formosa) as well as Quemoy and Matsu, by armed force. In virtually every Peiping broadcast, Taiwan (Formosa) and the offshore islands are linked as the objective of what is called the "Chinese Peoples Liberation Army."

The issue, then, is whether the Chinese Communists will seek to achieve their ambitions through the application of force, as they did in Korea, or whether they will accept the vital requisite of world peace and order in a nuclear age and renounce the use of force as the means for satisfying their territorial claims. The territory concerned has never been under the control of Communist China. On the contrary, the Republic of China—despite the characterizations you apply to it for ideological reasons—is recognized by the majority of the sovereign nations of the world and its government has been and is exercising jurisdiction over the territory concerned. United States military forces operate in the Taiwan area in fulfillment of treaty commitments to the Republic of China to assist it in the defense of Taiwan (Formosa) and the Penghu (Pescadores) Islands. They are there to help resist ag-

[22] *Ibid.*, pp. 498-499.
[23] Document 67, above.

gression—not to commit aggression. No upside down presentation such as contained in your letter can change this fact.

The United States Government has welcomed the willingness of the Chinese Communists to resume the Ambassadorial talks, which were begun three years ago in Geneva, for the purpose of finding a means of easing tensions in the Taiwan area. In the past, the United States representative at these talks has tried by every reasonable means to persuade the Chinese Communist representative to reach agreement on mutual renunciation of force in the Taiwan area but the latter insistently refused to reach such agreement. The United States hopes that an understanding can be achieved through the renewed talks which will assure that there will be no resort to the use of force in the endeavor to bring about a solution of the issues there.

I regret to say I do not see in your letter any effort to find that common language which could indeed facilitate the removal of the danger existing in the current situation in the Taiwan area. On the contrary, the description of this situation contained in your letter seems designed to serve the ambitions of international Communism rather than to present the facts. I also note that you have addressed no letter to the Chinese Communist leaders urging moderation upon them. If your letter to me is not merely a vehicle for one-sided denunciation of United States actions but is indeed intended to reflect a desire to find a common language for peace, I suggest you urge these leaders to discontinue their military operations and to turn to policy of peaceful settlement of the Taiwan dispute.

If indeed, for the sake of settling the issues that tend to disturb the peace in the Formosa area, the Chinese Communist leaders can be persuaded to place their trust in negotiation and a readiness to practice conciliation, then I assure you the United States will, on its part, strive in that spirit earnestly to the same end.[24]

Sincerely,

DWIGHT D. EISENHOWER

[24] On September 20, 1958 the White House announced at Newport that the President had received a second communication from the Chairman of the Council of Ministers of the USSR (Khrushchev) dealing with the situation in the Taiwan Strait. Because it was replete with false accusations, was couched in abusive and intemperate language, indulged in personalities and contained inadmissible threats, the communication was rejected and the United States Chargé d'Affaires in Moscow was instructed to return it to the Soviet Government. Department of State Bulletin, v. 39 (October 6, 1958), p. 530.

(132) *Letter from the Chairman of the Senate For-*
eign Relations Committee (Green) to the
President, September 29, 1958.[25]

DEAR MR. PRESIDENT: There are many indications of a real
danger that the United States may become involved in military hostilities in defense of Quemoy and Matsu. These indications comprise newspaper reports from the Far East, communications which I have received from very many Americans, dispatches from friendly nations throughout the world,
as well as concern expressed publicly by many prominent
Americans well informed in the field of foreign policy, and
your own statements to the American people.

Recently I have expressed my own views stating that "it
does not appear to me that Quemoy is vital to the defense of
either Formosa or the United States." I have suggested that
military action in the area should not be ordered unless you,
Mr. President, are sure beyond any reasonable doubt that the
security of Formosa itself is in fact directly threatened. Subsequent to your address of September 11, I proposed that if
there is danger of military involvement in this area—a danger which you indicated existed—Congress should be called
immediately into session.

The purpose of this letter, Mr. President, is to bring to
your attention my deep concern that the course of events in
the Far East may result in military involvement at the wrong
time, in the wrong place, and on issues not of vital concern
to our own security, and all this without allies either in fact
or in heart. Furthermore, it is my impression, confirmed by
the press and by my own mail, that United States military involvement in defense of Quemoy would not command that
support of the American people essential to successful military action.

My decision to send this letter to you has involved a great
deal of soul-searching on my part. At one point, I seriously
contemplated calling the Committee on Foreign Relations
back to Washington so that it might meet with cabinet members to learn fully the nature of our possible involvement.
That course was rejected for the present because I felt such
a public act might interfere with the conduct of negotiations
in which your representatives are now engaged. I also contemplated the advisability of seeking in advance of this letter the

[25] *Ibid.* (October 20, 1958), pp. 605-606.

consensus of views of the members of the Committee so that our joint views might be brought to your attention. But that action was rejected because it would be time consuming and because of the possibility that such action might be construed as a political maneuver.

It is not my intention to make this letter to you public at this time. I am sending copies of it, however, to each member of the Committee on Foreign Relations with the thought that he may wish to provide you independently with his views, particularly with reference to those I have set forth in this letter. I am sending a copy also to Senator Lyndon Johnson.

With respect and deep concern, I remain
   Sincerely yours,
     THEODORE FRANCIS GREEN
      Chairman
    Committe on Foreign Relations

(133) *News Conference Comments by the Secretary of State (Dulles), September 30, 1958.*[26]

* * *

Q. Mr. Secretary, in referring to the previous question on the renunciation of force, is it the position of this Government that the United States expects or supports the idea that the Nationalist Chinese Government is someday going to return to the mainland either by force or some other means?

A. Well, that is a highly hypothetical matter. I think it all depends upon what happens on the mainland. I don't think that just by their own steam they are going to get there. If you had on the mainland a sort of unrest and revolt, like, for example, what broke out in Hungary, then the presence of a free China with considerable power a few miles away could be a very important element in the situation. I think that we would all feel that, if there had been a free government of Hungary in existence within a few miles of Hungary at the time when that revolt took place, the situation might have developed in a different way from what it did.

So I wouldn't want to exclude any possibility of a situation developing on the mainland of China, or on parts of the mainland of China, which might not lead to reunification of some sort between mainland China, or that part of mainland China, and the free Government of China, the Republic of China, now on Formosa. I do not exclude it.

[26] *Ibid.*, pp. 599-604.

Q. Would that have to be entirely on the strength of the Government on Formosa, or is there any American commitment, explicit or implied, to aid in the kind of situation that you have described?

A. No. There is no commitment of any kind to aid in that. As I think you know, the only commitment that there is in this connection is the agreement involved in the exchange of letters between the Chinese Foreign Minister and myself which says that no force will be used from the treaty areas except in agreement between us. So neither of us is free to use force from the areas of the treaty against the mainland except, I think it says, in the case of emergency requirements of self-defense. But that exception would not cover the kind of a situation that you are speaking of.

Q. Mr. Secretary, if there were a rebellion or revolt in China, would you expect its leaders to, if they wanted to, turn over their mandate to Chiang Kai-shek?

A. Well, I really don't think that is a question that I can answer very well. It all—it depends upon the nature of the revolution. I would think that it would probably be primarily under local auspices and local leadership. And while outside cooperation and assistance might be sought, it would be hypothetical and problematical as to whether or not it would involve the going back of Chiang as the head of the government. I don't exclude that as a possibility. On the other hand, the situation is so hypothetical at the present time that it is almost unwise, I think, to try to guess about it.

*   *   *

Q. Mr. Secretary, inasmuch as you say you do not think it was sound for the Nationalist Chinese to have built up their forces on Quemoy and Matsu, I would like to ask you if you now think it would be sound to work out some arrangement for the withdrawal of those forces from those two islands?

A. It all depends upon the circumstances under which they would be withdrawn. I think to withdraw as a retreat under fire would not be a wise step to take because of the probable impact of that upon other peoples, other countries, and upon the morale, indeed, on Formosa itself.

Q. Would you state, sir, the circumstances under which you think a withdrawal could be achieved?

A. If there were a cease-fire in the area which seemed to be reasonably dependable, I think it would be foolish to keep these large forces on these islands. We thought that it was rather foolish to put them there, and, as I say, if there were a cease-fire it would be our judgment, military judgment even, that it would not be wise or prudent to keep them there.

Q. *Mr. Secretary, you seem to emphasize the need for a dependable cease-fire. Could you tell us how you can get a dependable cease-fire with the Communists, whose promises you don't like to accept?*

A. That is certainly a fair question and a difficult one to answer. I believe that promises of the Communists are never dependable merely because they are promises. They are only dependable if there are unpleasant consequences in case the Communists break their promises. And I believe that circumstances could be created where it would be felt that the consequences of breaking this promise would be so undesirable to the Communists that we could assume that they would probably live up to their promise, not because of the sanctity of the given word—which they do not believe in—but because of expediency.

Q. *Mr. Secretary, would it be necessary for a cease-fire to be written or unwritten? Could it be a de facto cease-fire gained simply by the cessation of shooting without anything being written?*

A. I think it could be *de facto.*

Q. *Mr. Secretary, some Senators seem to believe that the administration is extending the area of the security treaty with the Republic of China, and they are recalling that in February when you went before the Senate Foreign Relations Committee and said if you had any intention of extending the area you would return to the Senate. Is this a proper construction, you think, that is being put upon our activity there?*

A. No, I do not. The situation is that we do not have any legal commitment to defend the offshore islands. We do not want to make any such commitment. We do not have it today. What we are acting under is the authority of the joint resolution, which is equally the law of the land, which says that, if the President believes that the defense of those offshore islands is necessary or appropriate for the defense of the treaty area, then he can use the forces of the United States for that purpose. And that is the way it was understood, and that is the way we want it. I would say today, if the United States believed that these islands could be abandoned without its having any adverse impact upon the potential defense of Formosa and the treaty area, we would not be thinking of using forces there. It's because there is that relationship, under present conditions, conditions primarily of the Communists' making, that there is the tie-in there.

They say this is a push which is designed not merely to push the Chinese Nationalists out of Quemoy and Matsu but to push the United States out of Formosa. And when you have the edge, the front edge, of a wedge that is driving in, and where they say they are not going to stop at the first obstacle but to go on, then you have to decide whether by allowing the wedge to gather momentum and go on you are strengthening or weakening the defense of the area you are committed to defend. That is the problem we have to think about.

Q. Mr. Secretary, do you see any progress so far in a little more than 2 weeks of negotiation and crisis that now has gone on for more than a month? Do you see any progress at all toward a peaceful settlement either on an agreed basis or on a de facto basis?

A. I feel that there is a slight tendency toward a stabilization of the situation, and I feel on the whole that there is less likelihood of the hostilities intensifying and enlarging than I thought was the case a couple of weeks ago.

Q. Mr. Secretary, what do you have in mind when you say you think the circumstances could be created which would make breaking a cease-fire commitment by the Communists unpleasant? Were you talking about some joint allied commitment for Formosa itself, or something else?

A. I am thinking of sanctions that might be applied, perhaps by other nations in addition to the United States. For example, possible trade sanctions and the like.

Q. Have you made any effort with other nations to work out something like that?

A. I would not think that what we have done could be elevated to the role of what you might call an effort. There have been very widespread general discussions that have taken place between me and the Foreign Ministers of 15 or 20 countries about this whole situation. There are very few ideas that have not been batted back and forth on a tentative basis. I would not say that there has been any real effort to organize such a program because so far the premise of it does not seem to be sufficiently likely as to make it worth while. But we have a good many thoughts in our minds about such possibilities.

Q. Mr. Secretary, you said that the renunciation of force, if it occurs, should be reciprocal. Would you consider that under this reciprocal agreement would come renunciation by Chiang to intervene in a Hungarian-type revolt, or would you

say that the reciprocal agreement to renounce force ceases the
minute there is a revolution in China?

A. Well, you see, in Hungary you had, at least for a time, a government which sought assistance from outside and which asked the Soviet Union to withdraw. If there should be a recognized government in China which called for help, I would not consider that that involved an armed intervention in China.

Q. Under Secretary Herter said in a speech yesterday that the Quemoy and Matsu Islands are "not defensible in the defense of Formosa" and that the Chinese Nationalists' very devotion to them is "almost pathological." [27] *Do you subscribe to those views?*

A. I didn't hear the first sentence that you read. Are not defensible?

Q. Are not defensible in the defense of Formosa. It is phrased rather awkwardly, but it is a direct quote.

Q. In the New York Times *it says, "not strategically defensible in the defense of Formosa."*

A. Well, I don't like to comment on isolated quotations from a speech. I'd rather see what the full text said. I'm not familiar with it.

Q. Mr. Secretary, you said twice at the outset this morning that the United States policy has not changed. Yet during the course of the news conference you have seemed to clarify at least two major points that, so far as I know, have not been publicly clarified by the Department before, to wit: the reciprocal aspect of renunciation of force and the fact that the United States considered it foolish to build up military force on the islands and that under certain circumstances they should be withdrawn. If these two points are major and important, as they seem to be, why haven't they been expressed publicly before?

A. Well, there is nothing really new in our attitude on either of those propositions. I think, if you will go back, for example, to study the record of our prior talks with the Chinese Communists, we have assumed that the renunciation of force should be reciprocal if it occurs and that it would be obviously quite impractical and quite wrong to ask the Chinese Communists to abandon use of force if they were being attacked by the Chinese Nationalists. I might

---

[27] On September 29, 1958 the Under Secretary of State (Herter) addressed the National Guard Association at Atlantic City. *New York Times,* September 30, 1958.

say that when we speak about renunciation of force it has always been a renunciation of force except for purposes of self-defense. Perhaps I did not make that clear before. So that if anybody is attacked, then the renunciation of force would, of course, not apply.

Q. Mr. Secretary, is it fair to say that, while United States policy has not changed as of now, there is a possibility of some important changes, provided there is some give on the Chinese Communist side?

A. Yes, I would say so. Our policy in these respects is flexible and adapted to the situation that we have to meet. If the situation we have to meet changes, our policies change with it.

Q. Mr. Secretary, the Chinese Communists say that to renounce force in what they considered an internal affair is practically to renounce sovereignty and is tantamount, if one considered an American example, to renouncing the right of the United States Government to use, say, troops in Little Rock to prevent disorder. Is there any way that you think you could put this renunciation of force so that the Chinese Communists do not feel they are thereby renouncing their claim on Formosa?

A. Well, we have always made clear that renunciation of force, except for self-defense, on a reciprocal basis did not involve a renunciation of claims. You have comparable situations, I might say, all around the world. This is not a unique situation. In Korea, Viet-Nam, India, Pakistan, and Indonesia you might say that certain governments claim that a territory held by others is rightfully theirs. They could claim that to take it is purely a civil-war operation.

Now you have got to use, you might say, a rule of reason in trying to decide whether, in fact, a situation is a civil war or whether it involves a threat to international peace. And the Communists, as you know, made the argument in the case of Korea that that was purely a civil war, an effort by the north Koreans to reunite their country, that they had a right to do it, and that the United Nations and the United States were aggressors when they came in there to stop this effort of the Korean people to reunite their own country. Similar positions could be made in the case of other countries. You could say if the Federal Republic of Germany tried to reunite Germany that it was a civil operation. But none of us treat it that way.

You have a very practical situation to take into account, which is, will it, in fact, involve world peace? When you apply that test, I think there is no possible doubt but what this effort to take not just the offshore islands but Formosa and the Penghu Islands (the Pescadores) that that will involve world peace.

Here you have the Chinese Communists, with a treaty alliance with the Soviet Union, making these claims, and the Soviet Union saying they are prepared to back them up to the hilt. Here you have the Republic of China, which has a treaty of collectvie self-defense with the United States, which we are prepared to live up to. Now when those two forces come to clash, nobody in his senses could say, "This is purely a civil war and doesn't affect international peace." It does. And therefore it is properly a matter to be dealt with from the standpoint of international peace and the welfare of the world. You cannot treat it purely as a civil-war matter. You can say, "Well, the United States should stop helping the Nationalists, and the Soviet Union should stop helping Communist China." That is quite impractical. As far as we can tell, every plane, every piece of artillery, and practically all the ammunition that is being shot there today is of Soviet origin.

Q. Mr. Secretary, Chiang Kai-shek yesterday made statements about a cease-fire and the importance of Quemoy and Matsu which would seem to be quite different from some that you have made here this morning. My question is: Have you discussed your ideas about the cease-fire and possible withdrawal of the bulk of the forces from Quemoy and Matsu with the Nationalist Chinese?

A. Yes. We keep in pretty close touch with each other. We express our views. I wouldn't want to imply that they accept our views. And we don't accept their views in all respects, just as they don't accept ours. But we have a friendly exchange, and I think that, if it ever came down to a point where it was important practically to carry out these things, we would find a way to agree. At least I hope so.

(134) Letter from the President to the Chairman of the Senate Foreign Relations Committee (Green), October 2, 1958.[28]

DEAR SENATOR GREEN: I acknowledge your letter of September twenty-ninth with reference to the situation in the Far East. I note that you are concerned that the United States might become involved in hostilities in defense of Quemoy and Matsu; that it does not appear to you that Quemoy is

[28] *Department of State Bulletin*, v. 38 (October 20, 1958), pp. 605-606.

vital to the defense of Formosa or the United States; that in such hostilities we would be without allies, and, finally, that military involvement in the defense of Quemoy would not command that support of the American people essential to successful military action.

Let me take up these points in order:

1. Neither you nor any other American need feel that the United States will be involved in military hostilities merely in defense of Quemoy or Matsu. I am quite aware of the fact that the Joint Resolution of Congress, which authorized the President to employ the armed forces of the United States in the Formosa area, authorized the securing and protection of such positions as Quemoy and Matsu only if the President judges that to be required or appropriate in assuring the defense of Formosa and the Pescadores.

I shall scrupulously observe that limitation contained in the Congressional authority granted me.

2. The Congressional Resolution had, of course, not merely negative but positive implications. I shall also observe these. I note that it does not appear to you that Quemoy is vital to the defense of Formosa or the United States. But the test which the Congress established was whether or not the defense of these positions was judged by the President to be required or appropriate in assuring the defense of Formosa. The Congressional Resolution conferring that responsibility on the President was adopted by almost unanimous vote of both Houses of the Congress. Since then the people of the United States reelected me to be that President. I shall, as President and Commander-in-Chief of the Armed Forces of the United States, exercise my lawful authority and judgment in discharging the responsibility thus laid upon me.

I welcome the opinions and counsel of others. But in the last analysis such opinions cannot legally replace my own.

The Chinese and Soviet Communist leaders assert, and have reason to believe, that if they can take Quemoy and Matsu by armed assault that will open the way for them to take Formosa and the Pescadores and, as they put it, "expel" the United States from the West Pacific and cause its Fleet to leave international waters and "go home."

I cannot dismiss these boastings as mere bluff. Certainly there is always the possibility that it may in certain contingencies, after taking account of all relevant facts, become necessary or appropriate for the defense of Formosa and the

Pescadores also to take measures to secure and protect the related positions of Quemoy and Matsu.

I am striving to the best of my ability to avoid hostilities; to achieve a cease-fire, and a reasonable adjustment of the situation. You, I think, know my deep dedication to peace. It is second only to my dedication to the safety of the United States and its honorable discharge of obligations to its allies and to world order which have been assumed by constitutional process. We must not forget that the whole Formosa Straits situation is intimately connected with the security of the United States and the free world.

3. You say that in the event of hostilities we would be without allies "in fact or in heart." Of course, no nation other than the Republic of China has a treaty alliance with us in relation to the Formosa area. That is a well known fact—known to the Congress when it adopted the Formosa Joint Resolution and known to the Senate when it approved of our Treaty of Mutual Security with the Republic of China. But if you mean that the United States action in standing firm against armed Communist assault would not have the approval of our allies, then I believe that you are misinformed. Not only do I believe that our friends and allies would support the United States if hostilities should tragically, and against our will, be forced upon us, I believe that most of them would be appalled if the United States were spinelessly to retreat before the threat of Sino-Soviet armed aggression.

4. Finally, you state that even if the United States should become engaged in hostilities, there would not be "that support of the American people essential to successful military action."

With respect to those islands, I have often pointed out that the only way the United States could become involved in hostilities would be because of its firm stand against Communist attempts to gain their declared aims by force. I have also often said that firmness in supporting principle makes war less, rather than more, likely of occurrence.

I feel certain, beyond the shadow of a doubt, that if the United States became engaged in hostilities on account of the evil and aggressive assaults of the forces of Communism, the American people would unite as one to assure the success and triumph of our effort.

I deeply deplore the effect upon hostile forces of a statement that if we became engaged in battle, the United States would be defeated because of disunity at home. If that were believed, it would embolden our enemies and make almost inevitable the conflict which, I am sure, we both seek to avoid provided it can be avoided consistently with the honor and security of our country.

Though in this letter I have explained the facts and the principles that guide the government in dealing with the critical Formosa Straits situation, I cannot close without saying that our whole effort is now, and has always been, the preservation of a peace with honor and with justice. After all, this is the basic aspiration of all Americans, indeed of all peoples.

Inasmuch as there have been public reports on the essence of your letter, I feel I should make this reply public.[29]

With great respect and best wishes,

Sincerely,

DWIGHT D. EISENHOWER

b. *The Prospects of a Cease-Fire.*

(135) *Statement by the Minister of Defense of the People's Republic of China (Peng), October 6, 1958.*[30]

All compatriots, military and civilian, in Taiwan, Penghu, Quemoy and Matsu!

We are all Chinese. Of all choices, peace is the best. The fighting round Quemoy is of a punitive character. For quite a long time, your leaders have been far too wild. They have ordered aircraft to carry out wanton raids on the mainland, dropping leaflets and secret agents, bombing Foochow and harassing Kiangsu and Chekiang, reaching as far as Yunnan, Kweichow, Szechuan, the Kangting area and Chinghai. How can this be tolerated? Hence the firing of a few shells, just to call your attention. Taiwan, Penghu, Quemoy and Matsu are

[29] On October 5, 1958, Senator Green issued the following statement:

"On receipt of the President's reply dated October 2, 1958, to my letter to him of last September 29, I am making public my letter so that the opposing points of view may be compared.

It is worth noting, however, that during the past week both the President and Secretary Dulles have shown a more realistic attitude than before toward the situation in the Far East. This is encouraging and may be attributable in part to various expressions of the kind to which I have given voice.

There has been widespread public concern lest our position in the Far East has been too aggressive and I welcome the President's letter which shows a more realistic present approach to the problems in that area."

[30] *Peking Review,* v. 1 (October 7, 1958), Supplement.

Chinese territory. To this you agree, as proved by documents issued by your leaders, which confirm that they are decidedly not territory of the Americans. Taiwan, Penghu, Quemoy and Matsu are part of China, they do not constitute another country. There is only one China, not two, in the world. To this, you also agree, as proved by documents issued by your leaders. The military agreement signed between your leaders and the Americans is unilateral; we do not recognize it. It should be abrogated. The day will certainly come when the Americans will leave you in the lurch. Do you not believe it? History will bear witness to it. The clue is already there in the statement made by Dulles on September 30.[31] Placed in your circumstances, how can you help but feel dismayed? In the last analysis, the American imperialists are our common enemy. It is hard for the 130,000 troops and civilians in Quemoy to stand for long the lack of supplies and the pestering hunger and cold. Out of humanitarian considerations, I have ordered the bombardment to be suspended on the Fukien front for a tentative period of seven days, starting from October 6. Within this period, you will be fully free to ship in supplies on condition that there be no American escort. This guarantee will not stand if there should be American escort. It is not good that fighting between you and us have been in progress for 30 years and have not yet ended. We propose that talks be held to effect a peaceful settlement. You were notified of this by Premier Chou En-lai several years ago. This is China's internal problem involving your side and our side; it is no issue between China and the United States. The issue between China and the United States is U.S. invasion and occupation of Taiwan, Penghu and the Taiwan Straits, and this should be settled through negotiations between the two countries, which are now being held in Warsaw. The Americans will have to pull out. It won't do if they don't. For the United States, the sooner they go the better, because in this way it can have the initiative. Otherwise, it will be to its disadvantage, because it will then be always on the defensive. Why should a country in the East Pacific have come to the West Pacific? The West Pacific belongs to the people in this region, just as the East Pacific belongs to the people over there. This is common sense which the Americans should have understood. There is no war between the People's Republic of China and the United States of America, and so the question of cease-fire does not arise. Is it not a farce to talk about a

[31] Document 133, above.

cease-fire when there is no fire? Friends in Taiwan! There are flames of war between us. They should be stopped and extinguished. To achieve this talks are needed. Of course, it would not matter so much even if the fighting should continue for another 30 years. It is, however, better to secure an early peaceful settlement. The choice is up to you.

(136) *Order of the Ministry of National Defense of the People's Republic of China, October 13, 1958.*[32]

Comrades of the People's Liberation Army at the Fukien front:

Suspend the shelling of Quemoy for another two weeks starting from today, so as to see what the opposite side is going to do and to enable our compatriots on Quemoy, both military and civilian, to get sufficient supplies, including food and military equipment, to strengthen their entrenchment. Nothing is too deceitful in war. But this is no deceit. This is directed against the Americans. This is a noble national cause, and a clear-cut line must be drawn between the Chinese and the Americans. Taken as a whole, this action on our part does ourselves no harm, but benefits others. Whom does it benefit? It benefits the 10 million Chinese in Taiwan, Penghu, Quemoy and Matsu; it benefits the 650 million people of our whole nation; it only hurts the Americans. Some Communists may not yet understand this for the time being. How comes such an idea? We don't understand! We don't understand! Comrades! You will understand after a while. The Americans in Taiwan and the Taiwan Straits must go home. They have no reason to hang on there; refusing to go will not do. Among the Chinese in Taiwan, Penghu, Quemoy and Matsu, the majority are patriots, only a few are traitors. Therefore, political work must be done to enable the great majority of the Chinese over there to wake up gradually, and to isolate the handful of traitors. The effect will be felt with the accumulation of hours and days of work. So long as the Kuomintang in Taiwan has not yet entered into peaceful negotiations with us and a reasonable solution has not been worked out, the civil war still continues. The spokesman of Taiwan said that stop-fight-stop-fight . . . is but a trick of the Communists. It is quite true that fighting has been going off and on. But this is no trick. If you are not willing to hold peace talks, fighting is unavoidable. So long as you take such a stubborn attitude as you are doing at present, we are free to fight when we want to fight and stop when we want to stop. The Americans want to take a hand in our civil war. They call it cease-fire. This cannot but make one laugh in one's sleeve. What right have the Americans got to raise this question? Whom do they represent, it may be asked. They represent none. Do they represent the Americans? There is no war between China and the United States, and hence no fire to cease. Do they represent the people in Taiwan? The Taiwan authorities have not given them any credentials. The Kuomintang leaders are completely opposed to the Sino-American talks. The American nation is a great nation, and American people are well-meaning. They don't want war. They welcome peace. But among the U.S. government workers, there are some people, like Dulles and his ilk, who are indeed not so smart. Take, for instance, the talk about a cease-fire. Is this not lacking in common sense? To recover Taiwan, Penghu, Quemoy and Matsu as a whole and complete the unification of the motherland is the sacred task of our 650 million people. This is China's internal affair, and no foreigner has any right to meddle with. The United Nations has no right to meddle with, either. The time is not far away when the aggressors and their running dogs in the world will all of them be buried. There can be no escape for them. It won't do even if they take to hiding in the moon. Where the enemy can go, we also can go, and drag them back anyway. In a word, victory belongs to the people of the world. The Americans must not conduct escort operations in the Quemoy water area. If there should be any escort, shelling shall start at once. This order is to be strictly observed.

(137) News Conference Statement by the Secretary of State (Dulles), October 14, 1958.[33]

The United States welcomes the Chinese Communist decision of October 12 to continue to suspend the shelling of Quemoy. We hope that this suspension will in fact be for more than the 2 weeks mentioned. Short suspensions of armed attack do not provide a solid foundation upon which to stabilize the situation in the interest of peace.

The Peiping cease-fire order says that the American nation is a "great nation" and that its people "do not want war. They welcome peace." That is very true. So we shall strive for peace

[33] *Department of State Bulletin*, v. 39 (November 3, 1958), p. 681.

consistently with honorable performance of our obligations to our allies and to world order.

It is, however, not easy to reconcile these basic obligations of ours with the announced Chinese Communist objectives. The Chinese Communists' statement again makes it crystal clear that their objective in the Far East goes far beyond the offshore islands and has as its primary, if not exclusive, purpose to take over Taiwan (Formosa).

The offshore islands are treated as a matter of indifference. Indeed, the statement says that the suspension of shelling is "to enable our compatriots on Quemoy, both military and civilian, to get sufficient supplies, including food and military equipment, to strengthen their entrenchment."

The main theme constantly reiterated is that the Americans must abandon Taiwan and their alliance with the Republic of China made for the defense of Taiwan and "go home."

The United States remains loyal to its treaty of mutual security with the Republic of China. It believes that this treaty is not just an intergovernmental arrangement but one that is responsive to the aspirations of all Chinese who cherish freedom.

c. Resumption of Firing on the Offshore Islands.

(138) *News Conference Comments by the Secretary of State (Dulles), October 28, 1958.*[34]

Q. Mr. Secretary, what do you think of the idea of having war every other day? [35]

A. Well, it is part of this upside-down acting and talking to which we have had to grow accustomed, or try to grow accustomed. It seems to me the most shocking aspect of it is the complete demonstration that this shooting is not for military purposes but merely for the purpose of promiscuous killing. If you have a military purpose, you carry on your

[34] *Ibid.* (November 17, 1958), pp. 769-770.
[35] On October 25, 1958 the Ministry of National Defense of the People's Republic of China addressed a "Second Message to Compatriots in Taiwan" in which it stated *inter alia* that it had "ordered . . . troops at the Fukien front not to shell the airfield in Quemoy and the wharf, beach and ships at Liaolo Bay on even days of the calendar, so that the compatriots, both military and civilian, on the big and small islands of Greater Quemoy, Lesser Quemoy, Tatan, Erhtan and other may all get sufficient supplies, including . . . military equipment, to facilitate your entrenchment for a long time to come." The message warned, however, that "your ships and aircraft should not come on odd days. We will not necessarily conduct shelling on odd days. But you should refrain from coming, to avoid possible losses." *Peking Review*, v. 1 (October 28, 1958), p. 5.

shooting for military objectives and your purpose is to destroy the capacity of your enemy to resist. When you do it only every other day and say, in between times you can bring in supplies—indeed, we will give them to you, so as to increase your capacity to resist—and the next day you do your shooting, that shows the killing is done for political purposes and promiscuously. It is only designed to kill primarily the civilians, who are the ones most exposed. It is an extremely repugnant procedure according to our standards.

Q. *Do you recall any precedent for any ceasefire arrangement such as this?*

A. No, I think it has no precedent. I think it can be explained. My own interpretation of it is this: For 7 weeks they carried on a very extensive bombardment, together with interference by naval craft, to try to interdict the resupplying of the islands. At the end of that 7 weeks it became apparent that the techniques that had been developed jointly between the Chinese Nationalists and ourselves, and carried out primarily by the Chinese, were such that the island could not be cut off and made to wither on the vine, so to speak, through this level of fire. Therefore they had to confront a new situation. They knew that we could resupply the island; so in order to save face they said, "We will let you resupply the island every other day." Thus what we had demonstrated, the ability to do so against their will, they now made to appear as something that we did at their will. In that way they are trying to save themselves from a loss of face and a defeat in the effort which they had initiated but had been unable to conclude successfully.

Q. *Mr. Secretary, do you suggest, then, that they will allow the firing to just wither away one of these days and be done with it?*

A. That is a possibility. I wouldn't ever bank heavily, put all your bets, on just one theory of the Chinese Communists' action, because they can reverse themselves overnight. But it seems as though, at least for the moment, they do not want to raise up the level of their military effort, as by bringing in large amounts of airpower and the like; also they did not want to be exposed as having failed in the present level of effort. So, as I say, to save their face they seemed to devise this somewhat outlandish and rather uncivilized way of dealing with it. What they will do in the future I don't know. My belief is that they will not engage in a level of military effort which is likely to provoke a general war. I do not think they want that, and I think they know that that would not be a profitable enterprise for them to engage in.

Furthermore it has been made apparent beyond any possibility of doubt that their real objective in this affair is not Quemoy and Matsu but is Taiwan itself. They are now concentrating for a time, at least, how long I don't know, on propaganda efforts which are designed to try to split the inhabitants of Taiwan away from cooperation with the Americans. In effect they say, "Let's have a coprosperity sphere of Asia for the Asians. Let us work together and get rid of these Americans—they are the cause of all our trouble." They now seem to be concentrating on propaganda aspects of the matter.

E. The Republic of China.

> (139) *Joint Communiqué on Talks Held between the Secretary of State (Dulles) and the President of the Republic of China (Chiang), Taipei, October 23, 1958.*[1]

Consultations have been taking place over the past three days between the Government of the United States and the Government of the Republic of China pursuant to Article IV of the Mutual Defense Treaty.[2] These consultations had been invited by President Chiang Kai-shek. The following are among those who took part in the consultations:

For the Republic of China:

President Chiang Kai-shek
Vice President-Premier Chen Cheng
Secretary General to the President Chang Chun
Minister of Foreign Affairs Huang Shao-ku
Ambassador to the United States George K. C. Yeh

For the United States of America:

Secretary of State John Foster Dulles
Assistant Secretary of State Walter S. Robertson
Ambassador to the Republic of China Everett F. Drumright

The consultations had been arranged to be held during the two weeks when the Chinese Communists had declared they would cease fire upon Quemoy. It had been hoped that, under

[1] *Department of State Bulletin*, v. 39 (November 10, 1958), pp. 721-722.
[2] *Documents on American Foreign Relations, 1954*, pp. 360-364.

these circumstances, primary consideration could have been given to measures which would have contributed to stabilizing an actual situation of non-militancy. However, on the eve of the consultations, the Chinese Communists, in violation of their declaration, resumed artillery fire against the Quemoys. It was recognized that under the present conditions the defense of the Quemoys, together with the Matsus, is closely related to the defense of Taiwan and Penghu.

The two Governments recalled that their Mutual Defense Treaty had had the purpose of manifesting their unity "so that no potential aggressor could be under the illusion that either of them stands alone in the West Pacific Area." The consultations provided a fresh occasion for demonstrating that unity.

The two Governments reaffirmed their solidarity in the face of the new Chinese Communist aggression now manifesting itself in the bombardment of the Quemoys. This aggression and the accompanying Chinese Communist propaganda have not divided them, as the Communists have hoped. On the contrary, it has drawn them closer together. They believe that by unitedly opposing aggression they serve not only themselves but the cause of peace. As President Eisenhower said on September 11, the position of opposing aggression by force is the only position consistent with the peace of the world.

The two Governments took note of the fact that the Chinese Communists, with the backing of the Soviet Union, avowedly seek to conquer Taiwan, to eliminate Free China and to expel the United States from the Western Pacific generally, compelling the United States to abandon its collective security arrangements with free countries of that area. This policy cannot possibly succeed. It is hoped and believed that the Communists, faced by the proven unity, resolution and strength of the Governments of the United States and the Republic of China, will not put their policy to the test of general war and that they will abandon the military steps which they have already taken to initiate their futile and dangerous policy.

In addition to dealing with the current military situation, the two Governments considered the broad and long-range aspects of their relationship.

The United States, its Government and its people, have an abiding faith in the Chinese people and profound respect for the great contribution which they have made and will continue to make to a civilization that respects and honors the individual and his family life. The United States recognizes that the Republic of China is the authentic spokesman for Free China and of the hopes and aspirations entertained by the great mass of the Chinese people.

The Government of the Republic of China declared its purpose to be a worthy representative of the Chinese people and to strive to preserve those qualities and characteristics which have enabled the Chinese to contribute so much of benefit to humanity.

The two Governments reaffirmed their dedication to the principles of the Charter of the United Nations. They recalled that the treaty under which they are acting is defensive in character. The Government of the Republic of China considers that the restoration of freedom to its people on the mainland is its sacred mission. It believes that the foundation of this mission resides in the minds and the hearts of the Chinese people and that the principal means of successfully achieving its mission is the implementation of Dr. Sun Yat-sen's three people's principles (nationalism, democracy and social well-being) and not the use of force.

The consultations which took place permitted a thorough study and reexamination of the pressing problems of mutual concern. As such they have proved to be of great value to both Governments. It is believed that such consultations should continue to be held at appropriate intervals.

F. Japan.

(140) *Joint Statement on Talks Held between the Foreign Minister of Japan (Fujiyama) and the Secretary of State (Dulles), September 11, 1958.*[1]

The Secretary of State and the Foreign Minister of Japan met together at the Department of State this afternoon and had a constructive exchange of views in an atmosphere of cordiality and mutual understanding. They reviewed the international situation, discussed Japanese-American security arrangements and took up other matters pending between their two countries. Others present at the meeting included Ambassador Asakai, Ambassador MacArthur, Assistant Secretary Robertson, Assistant Secretary (Defense) Sprague and General Lemnitzer.

[1] *Department of State Bulletin*, v. 39 (October 6, 1958), pp. 532-533.

Security problems facing the two countries were the principal subjects of the discussion today. It was agreed that the Japanese-American Committee on Security, whose establishment was agreed upon in the talks between President Eisenhower and Prime Minister Kishi last year, had been successful in strengthening mutual cooperation and understanding in the security field. Foreign Minister Fujiyama pointed out at the same time that seven years have passed since the United States-Japan Security Treaty was signed. He stated that with the re-established position of Japan in the intervening years the situation has now evolved to the point where it would be advantageous to re-examine the present security arrangements with a view to adjusting them on a basis entirely consistent with the new era in relations between the two countries affirmed by Prime Minister Kishi and President Eisenhower in the Joint Communique of June 21, 1957.[2] It was agreed that the two governments will consult further on this matter through diplomatic channels following Mr. Fujiyama's return to Tokyo.[3]

With respect to the Ryukyu Islands, Foreign Minister Fujiyama welcomed the current discussions taking place between the United States authorities and Ryukyuan representatives looking toward a satisfactory resolution of the land problem.[4] Secretary Dulles expressed his understanding of Japanese interest in the Ryukyus and it was agreed that on Ryukyuan matters the two governments would continue to exchange views through diplomatic channels.

The Foreign Minister also touched upon specific issues among which was included the Japanese desire for compensation of former inhabitants of the Bonin Islands who are unable to return to their former homes. The Secretary assured Mr. Fujiyama that the United States is sympathetically aware of the problem and is studying it carefully in the hope of achieving a reasonable solution.

Discussions will be continued tomorrow.

[2] *Documents on American Foreign Relations, 1957*, pp. 320-324.
[3] For a reaction of the Chinese Communist authorities to the proposed revisions of the security treaty see a statement issued by the Foreign Minister of the People's Republic of China (Chen) on November 19, 1958. *Peking Review*, v. 1 (November 25, 1958), pp. 10-11.
[4] *Documents on American Foreign Relations, 1957*, p. 323.

(141) *Joint Statement on Talks Held between the Foreign Minister of Japan (Fujiyama) and the Under Secretary of State for Economic Affairs (Dillon), September 12, 1958.*[5]

Foreign Minister Fujiyama met today with Secretary Dulles and Under Secretary Dillon to discuss a wide range of subjects of interest to Japan and the United States. Topics discussed included United States-Japan trade relations, Asian economic development, and the actions and intentions of Communist China, with specific reference to the Taiwan Straits.

In connection with trade between the United States and Japan, the Foreign Minister pointed out the importance of trade with the United States and other industrial nations. He noted that, in relation to trade with the United States, particular attention would be paid to orderly trade and marketing procedures to avoid sudden changes in volume and prices which might have damaging effects. Mr. Dillon expressed appreciation of Japan's efforts in connection with orderly trade and marketing procedures. He referred to the recent extension of the Trade Agreements Act as evidence of United States interest in pursuing liberal trade policies.[6]

The question of the need for increasing the rate of economic growth in South and Southeast Asia was discussed, and opinions were exchanged with a view to achieving such economic growth in the interest of the free world.

In their discussion of the international situation, the Secretary and the Foreign Minister agreed that international Communism remains the major threat to peace in the world. They also exchanged views on the forthcoming session of the General Assembly of the United Nations, and recent developments in the Taiwan Straits. With respect to the latter they agreed that the use of force by Communist China created grave tension in the Far East. They also agreed that the situation in the Taiwan Straits should be settled by peaceful means and without recourse to force.

The Secretary and the Foreign Minister agreed that their talks during the past two days have been most helpful in achieving closer understanding and in enabling a higher degree of coordination in fields of mutual interest.

Today's meetings concluded the Washington talks.

[5] *Department of State Bulletin,* v. 39 (October 6, 1958), p. 533.
[6] Document 3, above.

G. Korea.

(142) *United Nations General Assembly Resolution 1264 (XIII), Adopted November 14, 1958.*[1]

The General Assembly,

Having received the report of the United Nations Commission for the Unification and Rehabilitation of Korea,[2]

Reaffirming its resolutions 112 (II) of 14 November 1947, 195 (III) of 12 December 1948, 293 (IV) of 21 October 1949, 376 (V) of 7 October 1950, 811 (IX) of 11 December 1954, 910 A (X) of 29 November 1955, 1010 (XI) of 11 January 1957 and 1180 (XII) of 29 November 1957,

Noting the exchange of correspondence between the communist authorities and the United Kingdom of Great Britain and Northern Ireland on behalf of the Governments of countries which have contributed forces to the United Nations Command in Korea,[3] in which these Governments expressed their wish to see a genuine settlement of the Korean question in accordance with United Nations resolutions, their willingness at all times to further the consideration of measures designed to effect reunification on this basis, and stated that, in accordance with the existing recommendations of the General Assembly of the United Nations, the Governments concerned are prepared to withdraw their forces from Korea when the conditions for a lasting settlement laid down by the General Assembly have been fulfilled,[4]

Noting further that in this exchange the Governments concerned, observing that the greater part of the forces sent to Korea in accordance with resolutions of the United Nations have already been withdrawn, welcomed the announcement that the Chinese communist troops were also to be withdrawn from North Korea.

1. *Calls to the attention* of the communist authorities concerned the continued determination of the United Nations to bring about by peaceful means establishment of a unified,

[1] United Nations, General Assembly, *Official Records, Thirteenth Session,* Supplement No. 18(A/4090), pp. 4-5. The resolution was adopted by a vote of 54-9-17.
[2] *Ibid.,* Supplement No. 13 (A/3865) [Footnote in the Original.]
[3] See the *Peking Review,* v. 1 (May 13, 1958), pp. 21-22; (November 18, 1958), pp. 15-16; United Nations Documents A/3821, dated April 10, 1958; A/3845 dated July 7, 1958; and the *Department of State Bulletin,* v. 39 (December 22, 1958), p. 1004.
[4] United Nations Document A/3845. [Footnote in the Original.]

independent and democratic Korea under a representative form of government, and the full restoration of international peace and security in the area;

2. *Calls upon* these authorities to accept the established United Nations objectives in order to achieve a settlement in Korea based on the fundamental principles for unification set forth by the nations participating on behalf of the United Nations in the Korean Political Conference held at Geneva in 1954, and reaffirmed by the General Assembly;

3. *Urges* these authorities to agree at an early date on the holding of genuinely free elections in accordance with the principles endorsed by the General Assembly;

4. *Requests* the United Nations Commission for the Unification and Rehabilitation of Korea to continue its work in accordance with the relevant resolutions of the General Assembly;

5. *Requests* the Secretary-General to place the Korean question on the provisional agenda of the fourteenth session of the General Assembly.

H. The Republic of the Philippines.

1. *Establishment of a Mutual Defense Board.*

(143) *Joint United States-Philippines Announcement, Manila, May 15, 1958.*[1]

The Philippine and United States Governments today announced agreement on the establishment of a Philippine-United States Mutual Defense Board and the assignment of a Philippine military liaison officer to the staff of the Base Commander in major United States military bases in the Philippines.

One of a continuing series of actions implementing existing security and defense agreements between the two countries, today's exchange of notes marks a major step in securing effective collaboration between the two countries in the joint effort to improve and enhance the common defense.

As stated in the Exchange of Notes "the purpose of this (Mutual Defense) Board is to provide continuing inter-governmental machinery for direct liaison and consultation between appropriate Philippine and United States authorities on military matters of mutual concern so as to develop and improve,

[1] *Department of State Bulletin*, v. 38 (June 2, 1958), p. 913.

through continuing military cooperation, the common defense of the two sovereign countries." The Board will have Philippine and United States co-chairmen.

The Philippine military liaison officer, who will be assigned to a major United States military base, will cooperate with the Base Commander by advice, suggestion and/or other appropriate action to assure observance of Philippine law and regulations within the base, will advise the Base Commander concerning problems involving Philippine nationals and residents on the base, and the day-to-day relationships between the base, Base Commander and such nationals and residents. These officers will be appointed by the Chief of Staff, Armed Forces of the Philippines, will be under the Administration of the Philippine Co-Chairman of the Mutual Defense Board, and will submit reports to the Board.

The agreements announced today are designed to enable the two governments to carry out more effectively the specified purposes and objectives of the Mutual Defense Agreement, and are part of the continuing effort of both governments to further strengthen their mutual defense and to contribute to international peace and security.

2. Visit of the President of the Philippines.

(144) *Joint Statement on Talks Held between the President and the President of the Republic of the Philippines (García), June 20, 1958.*[2]

The President of the United States and the President of the Republic of the Philippines today concluded the valuable discussions they have held over the past few days on matters of interest to both countries. These talks centered chiefly on United States-Philippines relations, but they also included an exchange of views on matters of international significance to both countries with special emphasis on Asia.

During his three-day visit President García addressed a Joint Meeting of both houses of the Congress, and he and members of his Party conferred with the Vice President, the Secretary of State, individual Members of Congress, and other United States Government officials. After leaving Washington President García will visit other parts of the United States and will meet governmental, cultural, and business leaders.

[2] *Ibid.*, v. 39 (July 21, 1958), pp. 120-121.

I.

The two Presidents reviewed the long history of friendship and cooperation between their countries and they expressed confidence that their respective peoples will continue to benefit from this close association in the future. Moreover, they recognized that similar cooperation among the nations of the Free World had been effective in recent years in preventing overt aggression in the Far East and elsewhere in the world. The two Presidents pledged themselves to maintain the unity of strength and purpose between their countries and the other countries of the Western Pacific in order to meet any threats to peace and security that may arise.

The two Presidents reaffirmed their adherence to the principles and purposes of the United Nations Charter. They recognized that through dedication to that Charter the nations of the world can progress toward the attainment of the universal ideal of peace with justice based on the dignity of the individual. With this objective they will continue to support and encourage the activities of the United Nations organization.

They noted that great progress has been achieved under SEATO in the strengthening of the Free World's defenses against communist imperialism in Southeast Asia. They concurred that in the light of the continued threat of communist military power in Asia, SEATO's defensive capability must be carefully maintained. Toward this end the United States will continue to assist in the development of the Armed Forces of the Philippines, in accordance with mutual security programs jointly approved with the Republic of the Philippines.

They reviewed, in this connection, the important role played by the Mutual Defense Pact between the Philippines and the United States. They agreed that the aggressive intentions and activities of communism in the Far East and in Southeast Asia render the maintenance and strengthening of these defensive arrangements an absolute necessity. President Eisenhower made clear that, in accordance with these existing alliances and the deployments and dispositions thereunder, any armed attack against the Philippines would involve an attack against United States forces stationed there and against the United States and would instantly be repelled.

In the spirit of these alliances, and with particular reference to the problems affecting the military bases operated by the United States in the Philippines, they expressed mutual confidence that these questions would be resolved to the satisfaction of the two countries, having regard to the principle of sovereign equality and the vital requirements of an effective common defense.

II.

The two Presidents reviewed progress toward economic development made in the Philippines over the past several years and examined the current economic problems with which that nation is faced. Economic discussions were also held between Philippine officials and representatives of the State and Treasury Departments, the Export-Import Bank and the International Cooperation Administration. The Philippine officials outlined a long-term program for economic development. In view of the inability of the United States to anticipate accurately financial availabilities and relative requirements beyond the next twelve months, immediate emphasis was placed on meeting the initial requirements of the Philippine program.

For these initial requirements the Export-Import Bank informed the Philippine Government that it will establish a new line of credit of $75 million for financing private and public development projects in the Philippines.

The Philippine Government was also informed that, subject to Congressional action on the additional appropriations being requested, the Development Loan Fund would examine specific projects submitted to it to determine whether they would merit Development Loan Fund financing in an amount not to exceed $50 million.

III.

In the course of their talks, the two Presidents were deeply aware of the special significance of their meeting as the Heads of State of two countries, one of which through the evolutionary process and by mutual agreement obtained its independence from the other. They realized that, in the context of present events, their meeting would provide a valuable object lesson on the relations of mutual respect and equal justice most appropriate to two countries, great or small, which share a common faith in freedom and democracy.

IV.

President Eisenhower and President García concluded that the understandings reached, as well as the personal relationships established during this visit, will contribute significantly to the mutual good will and friendship which traditionally support Philippines-United States relations.

C. P. GARCÍA
DWIGHT D. EISENHOWER

CHAPTER EIGHT

THE WESTERN HEMISPHERE

A. Canada.

1. *Joint Arrangements Concerning the North American Air Defense Command (NORAD).*

(145) *Canadian Note, May 12, 1958.*[1]

WASHINGTON, D.C.
12th May 1958

No. 263

SIR, I have the honour to refer to discussions which have taken place between the Canadian and the United States authorities concerning the necessity for integration of operational control of Canadian and United States air defences and, in particular, to the study and recommendations of the Canada-United States Military Study Group. These studies led to the joint announcement on August 1, 1957, by the Minister of National Defence of Canada and the Secretary of Defense of the United States indicating that our two Governments had agreed to the setting up of a system of integrated operational control for the air defences in the continental United States, Canada and Alaska under an integrated command responsible to the Chiefs of Staff of both countries.[2] Pursuant to the announcement of August 1, 1957, an integrated headquarters known as the North American Air Defence Command (NORAD) has been established on an interim basis at Colorado Springs, Colorado.

For some years prior to the establishment of NORAD, it had been recognized that the air defence of Canada and the United States must be considered as a single problem. However, arrangements which existed between Canada and the United States provided only for the coordination of separate Canadian and United States air defence plans, but did not provide for the authoritative control of all air defence weapons which must be employed against an attacker.

The advent of nuclear weapons, the great improvements in

[1] *Department of State Bulletin*, v. 38 (June 9, 1958), pp. 979-980.
[2] *Documents on American Foreign Relations, 1957*, p. 375.

the means of effecting their delivery, and the requirements of the air defence control systems demand rapid decisions to keep pace with the speed and tempo of technological developments. To counter the threat and to achieve maximum effectiveness of the air defence system, defensive operations must commence as early as possible and enemy forces must be kept constantly engaged. Arrangements for the coordination of national plans requiring consultation between national commanders before implementation had become inadequate in the face of the possible sudden attack, with little or no warning. It was essential, therefore, to have in existence in peacetime an organization, including the weapons, facilities and command structure, which could operate at the outset of hostilities in accordance with a single air defence plan approved in advance by national authorities.

Studies made by representatives of our two Governments led to the conclusion that the problem of the air defence of our two countries could best be met by delegating to an integrated headquarters the task of exercising operational control over combat units of the national forces made available for the air defence of the two countries. Furthermore, the principle of an integrated headquarters exercising operational control over assigned forces has been well established in various parts of the North Atlantic Treaty area. The Canada-United States region is an integral part of the NATO area. In support of the strategic objectives established in NATO for the Canada-United States region and in accordance with the provisions of the North Atlantic Treaty, our two Governments have, by establishing the North American Air Defence Command (NORAD), recognized the desirability of integrating headquarters exercising operational control over assigned air defence forces. The agreed integration is intended to assist the two Governments to develop and maintain their individual and collective capacity to resist air attack on their territories in North America in mutual self-defence.

The two Governments consider that the establishment of integrated air defence arrangements of the nature described increases the importance of the fullest possible consultation between the two Governments on all matters affecting the joint defence of North America, and that defence cooperation between them can be worked out on a mutually satisfactory basis only if such consultation is regularly and consistently undertaken.

In view of the foregoing considerations and on the basis of the experience gained in the operation on an interim basis of the North American Air Defence Command, my Government proposes that the following principles should govern the future organization and operations of the North American Air Defence Command.

1. The Commander-in-Chief NORAD (CINCNORAD) will be responsible to the Chiefs of Staff Committee of Canada and the Joint Chiefs of Staff of the United States, who in turn are responsible to their respective Governments. He will operate within a concept of air defence approved by the appropriate authorities of our two Governments, who will bear in mind their objectives in the defence of the Canada-United States region of the NATO area.

2. The North American Air Defence Command will include such combat units and individuals as are specifically allocated to it by the two Governments. The jurisdiction of the Commander-in-Chief, NORAD, over those units and individuals is limited to operation control as hereinafter defined.

3. "Operational control" is the power to direct, coordinate, and control the operational activities of forces assigned, attached or otherwise made available. No permanent changes of station would be made without approval of the higher national authority concerned. Temporary reinforcement from one area to another, including the crossing of the international boundary, to meet operational requirements will be within the authority of commanders having operational control. The basic command organization for the air defence forces of the two countries, including administration, discipline, internal organization and unit training, shall be exercised by national commanders responsible to their national authorities.

4. The appointment of CINCNORAD and his Deputy must be approved by the Canadian and United States Governments. They will not be from the same country, and CINCNORAD staff shall be an integrated joint staff composed of officers of both countries. During the absence of CINCNORAD, command will pass to the Deputy Commander.

5. The North Atlantic Treaty Organization will continue to be kept informed through the Canada-United States Regional Planning Group of arrangements for the air defence of North America.

6. The plans and procedures to be followed by NORAD in wartime shall be formulated and approved in peacetime by appropriate national authorities and shall be capable of rapid

implementation in an emergency. Any plans or procedures recommended by NORAD which bear on the responsibilities of civilian departments or agencies of the two Governments shall be referred for decision by the appropriate military authorities to those agencies and departments and may be the subject of intergovernmental coordination.

7. Terms of reference for CINCNORAD and his Deputy will be consistent with the foregoing principles. Changes in these terms of reference may be made by agreement between the Canadian Chiefs of Staff Committee and the United States Joint Chiefs of Staff, with approval of higher authority as appropriate, provided that these changes are in consonance with the principles set out in this note.

8. The question of the financing of expenditures connected with the operation of the integrated headquarters of the North American Air Defence Command will be settled by mutual agreement between appropriate agencies of the two Governments.

9. The North American Air Defence Command shall be maintained in operation for a period of ten years or such shorter period as shall be agreed by both countries in the light of their mutual defence interests, and their objectives under the terms of the North Atlantic Treaty. The terms of this agreement may be reviewed upon request of either country at any time.

10. The Agreement between parties to the North Atlantic Treaty regarding the status of their forces signed in London on June 19, 1951, shall apply.[3]

11. The release to the public of information by CINC-NORAD on matters of interest to Canada and the United States will in all cases be the subject of prior consultation and agreement between appropriate agencies of the two Governments.

If the United States Government concurs in the principles set out above, I propose that this note and your reply should constitute an agreement between our two Governments effective from the date of your reply.

Accept, Sir, the renewed assurances of my highest consideration.

N. A. ROBERTSON

The Honourable JOHN FOSTER DULLES,
Secretary of State of the United States,
Washington, D.C.

[3] *Department of State Bulletin,* v. 25 (July 2, 1951), p. 16.

(146) *United States Note, May 12, 1958.*[4]

EXCELLENCY: I have the honor to refer to your Excellency's note No. 263 of May 12, 1958 proposing on behalf of the Canadian Government certain principles to govern the future organization and operation of the North American Air Defense Command (NORAD).

I am pleased to inform you that my Government concurs in the principles set forth in your note. My Government further agrees with your proposal that your note and this reply shall constitute an agreement between the two Governments effective today.

Accept, Excellency, the renewed assurances of my highest consideration.

For the Secretary of State:
CHRISTIAN A. HERTER

His Excellency
NORMAN ROBERTSON,
   Ambassador of Canada.

2. Visit of the President to Canada, July 8-11, 1958.

(147) *Address by the President before a Joint Session of the Canadian Houses of Parliament, Ottawa, July 9, 1958.*[5]

(Excerpt)

*   *   *

This is my fourth visit to your beautiful capital. I recall well when your gracious Queen came to Washington from Ottawa we spoke together of the beauty of this city and of the greatness of Canada.

It is good to return—to see old friends and to make new ones.

I came here first in 1946 to congratulate the Canadian people on the brilliant role played by the Canadian forces that you placed under my command in the World War which had then recently ended in victory.

My next visit was made as Commander of NATO forces in Europe. In 1953 I returned as President and talked in this House of some aspects of the relationship between our two countries.

[4] *Ibid.,* v. 38 (June 9, 1958), p. 980.
[5] *Ibid.,* v. 39 (August 4, 1958), pp. 204-208.

I then spoke of the Saint Lawrence Seaway in prospective terms. Today it is near completion, and next year it will be open. This is truly a great joint accomplishment. It will open up important regions of both Canada and the United States to ocean traffic. It will ever stand as a monument to what can be achieved by the common effort of two sovereign nations.

On that same occasion I spoke of the need to devise ways to protect our North America from any surprise attack. Since then we have made great strides. The Distant Early Warning (DEW) Line has been built and placed in operation.[6] In the process of its construction I am sure much has been learned which will contribute to the more rapid development of the northern reaches of Canada and of our new State, Alaska.

Last month an agreement was concluded between our two Governments to establish a combined air defense headquarters for this continent. We have also—both of us—striven, as we will continue to strive, for the Soviet Union's agreement to a system of inspection to protect against surprise attack through the Arctic. Recent Soviet communications have strengthened the hope that they will come to see that by such a system any basis for their professed fears of an attack across the Pole will be removed. For Canada and for the United States such a system in operation would add measurably to our security against a sudden attack. Possibly it might also pave the way for still further measures of arms control and permit some reduction of the burden and danger of modern armaments.

Both of these developments, the Seaway—a broadened, deepened road for peaceful commerce—and the strengthening of our common defense of this continent strikingly illustrate two things.

The first is that change is the law of life and of relations between nations. When two great peoples such as ours, energetic and optimistic, live side by side in all the diversity that freedom offers, change is rapid and brings in its wake problems, sometimes frictions.

The second lesson that I see in these common achievements in diverse fields is that by mutual respect, understanding, and with good will we can find acceptable solutions to any problems which exist or may arise between us.

It is important to remember this. Such differences as are from time to time expressed never affect the similarity of purpose which binds our two countries together.

[6] *Documents on American Foreign Relations, 1955*, pp. 379-381.

Of course, each of us possesses a ditinctive national character and history. You won your independence by evolution, the United States by revolution. Our forms of government—though both cast in the democratic pattern—are greatly different. Indeed, sometimes it appears that many of our misunderstandings spring from an imperfect knowledge on the part of both of us of the dissimilarities in our forms of government.

And yet, despite these dissimilarities in form, our two Governments are developing and are increasingly using effective ways to consult and act together. This we do to meet the problems that confront us in our relations with each other and in the relations of both with all other nations of the world.

Similarity in Basic Beliefs

We share the basic belief that only under free institutions, with government the servant and not the master, can the individual secure his life, his liberty, and the pursuit of happiness. We are both determined to frame and follow policies which safeguard the lives and homes of our people, their peace of mind, their material well-being, and, above all things, their ideals. True to these ideals, both our countries, for example, are determined that the great decisions of peace and war will remain always under civilian control.

Moreover, we both recognize a design of aggressive Communist imperialism which threatens every free nation. Both of us face a military threat and political attack. Our system of free enterprise is challenged throughout the world by a state-directed, state-controlled economic system. Indeed, my friends, this could well be the area in which the competition will be most bitter and most decisive between the free world and Communist imperialism. We must never allow ourselves to become so preoccupied with any differences between our two nations that we lose sight of the transcendent importance of free-world cooperation in the winning of the global struggle.

Now, acting in accordance with our common dedication, the two of us, with others, have drawn together in collective-security arrangements. The most notable of these in the North Atlantic Treaty Organization, in which both Canada and the United States are equal partners. We are both determined to maintain what George Washington described as "a respectable military posture." We are equally determined to maintain our institutions in good repair and to insure that our own economies function well.

Thus we seek not only to meet the expanding needs of our people but also to set an example of free men's accomplishments which will encourage and attract those less fortunate. And, finally, we are agreed that we shall never cease striving for a just and lasting peace to be achieved by negotiation with those who challenge us. We overlook no opportunity to settle the issues which divide the world and under safeguarded conditions to reduce the burden of armaments.

U.S.-Canadian Problems

Now, against this background of similarity in basic factors and policy, let me now point to some of the matters which it seems to me are troublesome between us. Among some examples are the surplus-wheat disposal policies of the United States, the imbalance in our mutual trade, certain aspects of United States private investment in Canada, and Canadian fears of a trend in the United States away from forward-looking policies in the field of trade.

I am sure you agree that we should talk frankly to each other. Frankness, in good spirit, is a measure of friendship. It should be the practice, I believe, on both sides so to speak, when either feels that important interests are adversely affected by actions contemplated or taken by the other. Happily, these instances are rare. Now, in mentioning today the specific problems on which we do not see eye to eye, I am doing so as an American, expressing an American viewpoint. I can assure you that your Prime Minister, in discussing these problems with my associates and me—most loyally and eloquently, I might add—expresses the viewpoint of Canada.

It is my conviction, which I believe he fully concurs in, that for all our present problems and all our future ones we will find acceptable solutions. It will take understanding, common sense, and a willingness to give and take on both our parts. These qualities we have always found in our dealings with Canada. I hope that you have not found them lacking in us.

First, then, in some detail, I would like to comment briefly on our surplus-wheat disposal policies. I think that no one can quarrel with our purpose though some of our methods may seem unorthodox by traditional standards. Simply stated, our wheat disposal program has three aspects.

In times of local famine or disaster we give wheat away. We have also bartered it for strategic materials. Finally, we sell wheat for local currency to countries which cannot afford to purchase it commercially. In these cases our policy is to lend back to the government in question most of the proceeds for local economic development. Our intent is not to damage normal commercial markets, and in this I think we have been generally successful.

I know that in the past there was criticism of certain aspects of these programs and particularly of our barter arrangements. I believe that the basis of these objections has been largely removed. Increasingly close consultation between officials of our two Governments has ironed out many misunderstandings respecting our surplus disposals. Your Government knows in detail what we plan. I assure you that it is our desire and intention to keep the doors of consultation always and fully open. There must never be a final word between friends.

In several respects, despite inconvenience and even occasional damage in the past, Canada stands to benefit from our moving some surplus agricultural commodities into consumption overseas. First and most evident of all, many hungry people around the world have had food which they otherwise would not have had. Secondly, had these products remained in dead storage, they would have had a depressing influence on the world market and on world prices. Finally, the funds which we have been enabled to make available to recipient countries should in the long run help to raise standards of living, which in turn will create enlarged markets for all of us.

I come next to the question of the imbalance of trade between our two countries. You buy more from the United States than you sell to us. This fact is of concern to many thoughtful Canadians. There are a few basic points which should be noted in this connection.

First of all, the United States and Canada are not state traders. All the products of industry manufactured in the United States and sold to customers abroad are sold through the enterprise of the private seller. These articles come to you here in Canada only because of the desire of the individual Canadian consumer to buy a particular piece of merchandise. The United States Government does not place goods in Canada as part of a state-directed program. This aspect of our trade with each other is the natural consequence of two private-enterprise economies working side by side and trading with each other.

Then we should also remember that the free world represents a multilateral trading community. To try to balance our books once a month or once a year with every nation with which we trade would stifle rather than expand trade. I assume that Canada is as interested as we are in the expansion of world trade rather than in its artificial redirection. Both our peoples want to buy and sell in a climate of economic vigor and expansion. An imbalance in trade with one country, in such a climate, is usually balanced or largely offset by the state of the accounts with other trading nations.

This is the case with Canadian trade. Your export deficit to the United States is offset by export surpluses to other countries and by the flow of investments to Canada. The promotion of healthy multilateral trade, as opposed to artificial bilateral balancing, is an important objective of the International Monetary Fund and the General Agreement on Tariffs and Trade, to which both Canada and the United States belong.

Other Side of the Trade Equation

For a moment I want to address myself as well to the other side of the trade equation, namely, your exports to the United States. Here you can rightly say that, through quotas and tariffs, our governmental policies can either expand or restrict your opportunities to sell to us. The same is, of course, true of actions taken by your Government which can affect the volume of our exports to Canada.

Neither of our countries is a "free trader" in the classical economic sense. Each of us feels a responsibility to provide some protection to particular sectors of our economies which may be in distress or are for other reasons deserving of governmental assistance. We have taken some actions of this sort. So has Canada.

Oil imports into our country contribute a case in point. We believe that to insure adequate supplies of oil in an emergency it is necessary that exploration to develop oil reserves be carried forward with vigor. This means a healthy oil industry to the continent. A healthy domestic oil-producing industry is vital to our national security. And we recognize that our security and yours are inseparable. We have been keenly sensitive to that fact in considering the nature of the voluntary restrictions on oil imports that have been put into effect by oil companies in the United States and have minimized their impact on your economy.

Our restrictive action with respect to oil is not in any sense reflective of a change in the fundamental trade policy of the United States. Such actions must be viewed in perspective.

For example, since the so-called "escape clause" was incorporated in our trade agreements legislation in 1951, there have come from industry in the United States a number of requests for the imposition of quotas or higher tariffs. In about a dozen cases Presidential approval for some relief has been granted. In only one of these cases was Canada directly affected as an exporter. We have always conscientiously sought to take account of your interests as well as our own in seeking the best remedy to these intricate problems. I believe that a study of the record will bear out the truth of this statement.

Next, the flow of investment funds from the United States into Canada has led to expressions of concern on your part. These funds have been attracted to your country by the business opportunities Canada has offered. Though they may raise questions in specific cases respecting control of an industry by American citizens, these industries are, of course, subject to Canadian law. Moreover, these investments have helped you to develop your resources and to expand your industrial plant at a far faster rate than could have been possible had you relied wholly on your own savings. They have thereby helped to provide employment, tax revenues, and other direct benefits. These funds have also helped Canada to finance with ease its recent surplus of imports from the United States, a fact that is testified to by the premium of the Canadian dollar over the United States dollar.

I am confident that, if there are some defects in this investment process, ways will be found to correct them, because this is the interest of both our countries.

One final word on the foreign trade policy of the United States. In 1934 the United States took an historic decision to embark on a positive policy of fostering trade with the launching of the reciprocal trade agreements program. This policy we continue to support and to practice. The Government of the United States, after a public searching of soul at times of renewal of the Trade Agreements Act, has consistently reaffirmed this policy. Have no fear that the United States will abandon a policy so well established. The problems I have been discussing concern our economic lives. Our points of economic contact are varied and numerous, as they of necessity must be under our chosen system of private enterprise.

Our Governments have a responsibility to help compose

difficulties, but we must not forget that thousands of individual citizens of Canada and the United States must themselves find in their diversified activities the answers to many of these problems.

Finally, there is no cause to be surprised or disturbed to discover that occasionally differences arise between us. The distinguishing character of the peoples of the free world lies in the fact that differences between them can develop, can be expressed, and then amicably resolved.

We in the United States have no more desire than you have to seek in our relations with others the silent, sullen unity that elsewhere has been purchased or imposed. The hallmark of freedom is the right to differ as well as the right to agree.

I have spoken to you in the knowledge that through you I address a nation strong in the tradition of freedom and vigilant in its defense. You and we are alike convinced, by our history, by our religious faith, and our common heritage of freedom, that economic well-being and political liberty both depend upon the efforts of individuals and on their willingness to accept the responsibilities of freedom. Today I assure you once more of the pride and of the gratification that we of the United States feel in our long and friendly association with you, our sturdy northern neighbor.

We stand together at a pivotal point in history. All that we Canadians and Americans, and those who went before us, have built, all that we believe in, is challenged as it has never been challenged before. The new horizons of competition range from the polar areas and extend to the infinity of outer space.

It is for us—all of us—to bring to the challenge a response worthy of ourselves and our two nations. As we do, we shall know the satisfaction of having built, in friendship, a safer and ampler home here on the earth for this generation and those that shall come after us.

I thank you for your kind attention.

(148) *Statement on Safeguards against Surprise Attack, July 9, 1958.*[7]

The President and the Prime Minister discussed today questions concerning disarmament and, in particular, proposals for safeguards against surprise attack. This discussion reaffirmed the closeness of the views of the two Governments

[7] *Department of State Bulletin,* v. 39 (August 4, 1958), p. 208.

on a suitable approach to these questions. Particularly they emphasized the great importance which both countries attach to a system of control which would cover the Arctic and related areas.

The President and the Prime Minister exchanged views on the recent letter from Chairman Khrushchev to President Eisenhower with reference to expert examination of possible systems of supervision and control to prevent surprise attack.[8] Although they recognized that certain aspects of Mr. Khrushchev's recent letter were unacceptable, they were nevertheless encouraged by certain elements of responsiveness to the earlier Western proposals on this matter. Mr. Diefenbaker indicated Canada's willingness to make a constructive contribution to study of control methods, and it was agreed that the experts of both countries would work together, and in cooperation with those of other free-world countries concerned, in study of this problem.

(149) *Statement on United States Export Policies, July 9, 1958.*[9]

The Canadian and United States Governments have given consideration to situations where the export policies and laws of the two countries may not be in complete harmony. It has been agreed that in these cases there will be full consultations between the two Governments with a view to finding through appropriate procedures satisfactory solutions to concrete problems as they arise.

(150) *Statement on the Establishment of a Joint Cabinet Committee on Defense, July 10, 1958.*[10]

The Prime Minister and the President have taken note of the intimate cooperation which exists between their two Governments in matters relating to continental defense. In furtherance of the policy of both Governments that such matters shall be subject to civilian decision and guidance, they have agreed that there will be established a Cabinet Committee to be known as the Canada-United States Committee on Joint Defense. This Committee will consist, for Canada, of the Secretary of State for External Affairs, the Minister of

[8] Document 44, above.
[9] *Department of State Bulletin*, v. 39 (August 4, 1958), p. 209.
[10] *Ibid.*, pp. 208-209.

National Defense, and the Minister of Finance; and for the United States, of the Secretary of State, the Secretary of Defense, and the Secretary of the Treasury. Other ministers may participate on an *ad hoc* basis as requested by the Committee.

The Committee will consult on matters bearing upon the common defense of the North American continent which lies within the North Atlantic Treaty area. It will, in a supervisory capacity, supplement and not supplant existing joint boards and committees.

The Committee will normally meet alternately in Washington and Ottawa. The chairman of each meeting will be the Secretary of State of the country in whose capital the meeting is held.

B. The American Republics.

1. *The Eisenhower Mission.*

(151) *Statement by the Representative of the President (Milton Eisenhower), August 1, 1958.*[1]

MR. PRESIDENT: My associates and I are deeply moved by your personal reception of us this evening; we recognize that your generous action is inspired by more than brotherly affection; it is also your unmistakable notice to all the world that you, as we, consider firm, abiding relations among the nations of this Hemisphere to be essential to our common future. You sent us on a mission of good will and fact-finding.

At once, upon our return from three weeks in Panama, the five Central American countries,[2] and Puerto Rico, we wish to express our deep appreciation to the Presidents and peoples of the area visited for their friendly reception of us. Everywhere we experienced the warm friendliness which the peoples of this hemisphere have for the United States.

The absence of any unfriendly incident may have confounded those who were looking for sensational headlines, but this very circumstance enabled us, calmly and rationally, to accomplish precisely what we set out to do—to gain a new perspective of the problems, progress, attitudes, and aspirations of the nations visited, as a basis for determining whether new approaches in our own policies and programs might strengthen relations among us.

I re-affirm now all I reported to you, Mr. President, in No-

[1] *Ibid.*, v. 39 (August 25, 1958), pp. 309-310.
[2] Honduras, Costa Rica, Nicaragua, El Salvador and Guatemala.

vember 1953 following the fact-finding trip I made to the ten republics of South America.[3]

Now, however, I must add a note of urgency to what I then recommended. I shall make additional suggestions for policy and program improvements which I hope will be found acceptable.

I shall even this evening make a preliminary report. My suggestions will deal with:

1. The imperative need for bankable loans—not grants—in every country visited;

2. The response which I believe the United States should make to the appeal of the Latin American nations for more stable relationships between raw-commodity prices and the prices of manufactured products;

3. The urgent and immediate need to bring about throughout the hemisphere a clear, accurate understanding of United States policies, purposes, programs, and capabilities.

My associates and I met with some 1,200 leaders of government, industry, agriculture, labor, commerce, finance, education, health and social and cultural institutions. We had candid conversations with all of them. They submitted to us some 1,000 pages of data and suggestions.

Now I shall want to hold a series of conferences with numerous individuals and agencies, as I study and integrate this evidence—especially with the Vice President, who recently returned from a trip to South America; officials of the International Bank; the Board of the Export-Import Bank and the Board of Directors of the Development Loan Fund. I shall also want to consult with high officials in the State, Treasury, Labor, Agriculture, Commerce and other Departments.

Since I must do this without neglecting my University duties, I cannot predict when a final brief report will be ready, but the sense of urgency I feel about the problems in the great Central area of this Hemisphere—indeed, about the situation in all the Americas—will impel me to conclude my assignment at the earliest possible moment.

My confidence in the unity, common purpose, and common destiny of the Americas has been strengthened by all I have learned on this trip. The vast majority of the leaders and peoples of Latin America are firm friends of the United States. They do not intend to permit a tiny minority of conspirators and a few misguided associates of such conspirators to confuse and divide us.

[3] *Department of State Bulletin*, v. 29 (November 23, 1953), pp. 695-717.

May I say in all candor that while, of course, I believe the United States must shore up its policies and programs with respect to Latin America, it is just as essential that all our neighbors to the South re-examine—as I know they will—their policies with respect to the United States. Good relations are never the result of unilateral action. They are the outcome of mutual understanding, mutual respect, shared goals, and a common determination to live, work, and progress together. We are partners in the quest for independence, freedom, democracy, and peace with justice.

I repeat the final words of my 1953 report: "Working together, the nations of this Hemisphere can, if history should so decree, stand firmly against any enemy in war, and prosper mightily together in times of peace."

(152) Report by the Representative of the President (Milton Eisenhower), December 27, 1958.[4]

(Excerpts)

I recommend that the United States take the leadership in urging the Organization of American States to place high on its program effective efforts to develop among the governments and peoples of the American Republics that genuine understanding on which fruitful cooperative action must be based.

*　　*　　*

I also recommend that each of the twenty-one governments be urged to assume a large measure of responsibility for promoting the relevant understanding within its own country.

*　　*　　*

I recommend that the information facilities of the State Department be increased, that the State Department cooperate continuously with the United States National Commission for Latin American Affairs (as recommended above) and that special efforts be made to induce the mass media of the United States to maintain competent correspondents in Latin America and to carry a steady flow of news and interpretive material from all twenty republics.

[4] Ibid., v. 40 (January 19, 1959), pp. 89-105.

I also recommend that leadership, student, and other exchanges of persons be encouraged by every means.

* * *

I further recommend that the activities of the United States Information Agency in Latin America be increased:

* * *

I recommend that the projected Inter-American development institution subsequently discussed herein, be so organized and staffed as to assist the American Republics in development planning, in the assignment of priorities, and in the preparation of loan projects, and that the United States International Cooperation Administration assist in the financing of this section of the development agency through its technical cooperation funds.

* * *

I recommend that the proposed inter-American development institution exercise leadership in this field; that it promote more specific planning by Latin America in the utilization of existing credit facilities; that it have broad responsibility for achieving greater understanding and coordination in the whole field of loans to the Republics of Latin America.

* * *

I recommend that United States lending institutions, with the help of IBRD if possible, inform the Republics of Latin America that they stand ready, as a cooperative group, to consider sympathetically the extension of sound, well-timed loans in support of practical development plans, and that they will meet jointly with delegations from each applicant country to determine how credit resources may best be employed to help that nation proceed effectively with its economic program.

* * *

I urge that the United States proceed as rapidly as possible to cooperate with leaders of the Latin American Republics in creating an Inter-American bank. Such a new institution should coordinate its operations closely with those of the World Bank, United States lending institutions and private lending agencies to the end that the total flow of development capital into Latin America may be increased.

*   *   *

I recommend that, after careful preparation through appropriate channels, the United States participate with the five republics of Central America, and Panama if possible, in a regional conference, either at the Ministerial or technical level, to stimulate public and private lending institutions, and private industrial enterprises, to take a positive approach in helping Central America and Panama to the end that new industries, guaranteed free access to the entire market of the participating countries, would be established; that every effort be made to have this development serve as a model for all of Latin America; and that such steps as may be deemed appropriate be taken to encourage the northern group of South American countries, and the southern group of South American countries, to consider the creation of common regional markets in those areas.

*   *   *

I recommend that the United States, if requested to do so, cooperate to the extent of furnishing such information as laws and regulations permit to assist the producing countries in enforcing agreed-upon marketing quotas.

*   *   *

I recommend that the United States, when requested by producing nations, participate in single-commodity study groups, giving every possible technical assistance, but always making clear that our participation in no way implies subsequent cooperation in plans the producing nations might develop to stabilize prices.

*   *   *

I recommend that the technical cooperation program for Latin America be under the direct supervision of the Ambassador in each country.

I further recommend that the Assistant Secretary of State for Inter-American Affairs be given authority under the general guidance of the Under Secretary of State for Economic Affairs, to coordinate the technical cooperation programs in

Latin American nations with the diplomatic, social, cultural and other activities over which he has cognizance.

* * *

I recommend that you establish a Council on Inter-American Affairs, whose task would be to advise with the Secretary of State on all matters of hemispheric importance, bringing to him creative ideas for strengthening relations, and constantly emphasizing by its very existence and public statements the importance which the Government and people of the United States attach to good partnership among the American Republics.

* * *

Everywhere Vice President Nixon went in South America,[5] and everywhere I went in Central America this year, the charge arose that while the United States treasures freedom and democracy for itself, it is indifferent about these in Latin America—indeed, that we support Latin American dictators. I have previously mentioned this as a serious misunderstanding. It is just that. But I now wish to recommend a change in policy which may seem slight, but I think it is important.

In my visits with Panamanian and Central American leaders this summer, I pointed out with candor that from the beginning of our history until 1933, we had not been very consistent in our policies toward Latin America and that some of our actions in that period had clearly strengthened the hands of dictators. But I also pointed out that at Montevideo in 1933, we agreed to a vital change in policy. We agreed thereafter not to intervene in the internal affairs of our sister republics.

Now, obviously, we cannot at one and the same time refrain from intervention and express judgments regarding the degree of democracy our sister republics have achieved.

We had a few months of optimism regarding this knotty problem in 1945 and 1946 when the Foreign Minister of Uruguay proposed that the American nations collectively encourage the development of democratic governments by withholding recognition from those which did not measure up to democratic norms. It seemed logical to maintain that the collective judgment could not be construed as internal intervention, at least by a single nation. The United States

[5] *Ibid.*, v. 38 (June 9, 1958), pp. 950-951.

supported the proposal. But our neighbors overwhelmingly defeated it.

Since the policy of non-intervention was adopted in 1933, dictatorships in Latin America have steadily declined. Whether this is a result of the policy or a coincidence, I leave to others to argue. My own belief is that one is at least partly the result of the other. Today, only a third as many dictators are in power as were in 1933.

What then, other than constantly reaffirming our hope that all peoples may enjoy the blessings of democracy, can we do about the matter?

I believe the suggestion of Vice President Nixon is sound and would be applauded by Latin America itself—that we have an "abrazo" for democratic leaders, and a formal handshake for dictators. Trivial as this may sound, I recommend that it be our official policy in relations with Latin American leaders and nations.

We have made some honest mistakes in our dealings with dictators. For example, we decorated several of them. Most Latin American nations did the same, and in grander style. Whatever reason impelled them and us to take those actions, I think, in retrospect, we were wrong.

I recommend that we refrain from granting special recognition to a Latin American dictator, regardless of the temporary advantage that might seem to be promised by such an act.

I most emphatically do not believe that we should withdraw our programs from Latin American countries which are ruled by dictators. We should not withdraw or diminish our technical assistance programs, diplomatic missions, loans, or other activities. Reasoning which caused one to feel that we should do so would lead logically to the conclusion that throughout the world we should cease cooperating with any nation in which democracy is not complete. Patently, such a policy would paralyze the conduct of all foreign relations.

Non-recognition and non-cooperation would not help another nation achieve democracy. Most people want freedom, though many have never experienced it. By cooperating with them, even through dictators—by keeping open the lines of communication—one may hope that a growing understanding of the strength, glory, and basic morality of democracy will enable the people of a harshly ruled country to achieve and maintain democratic institutions of their own design.

We must be careful in deciding which leader deserves a

mere handshake and which an "abrazo." In Latin America one finds widely varying degrees of freedom. At least one nation which today is labeled by some a "dictatorship" has greater freedom of the press, of assembly, of speech, of worship, and of research and teaching, than do several others which are generally conceived to be democratic.

An important consideration, it seems to me, is the direction a nation is taking. Throughout Latin America, a strong and irresistible trend toward freedom and democracy is evident. We should watch this trend in each country, and encourage it in any way that may be appropriate, without violating the fundamental policy of non-intervention.

Finally, I may say I do not know of a single act the United States has taken since 1954 that could be construed as granting special or even friendly favors to a dictator in this hemisphere. I state this in fairness to our many diplomatic officials who are on the firing line in international affairs, and who, dedicated to democratic ideals, sometimes must suffer quietly under unjustified criticism. It is true that one dictator has fled to the United States since 1954. What is not generally known, apparently, is that the successor government of his country issued him a diplomatic passport and requested permission for him to enter the United States. By such small acts very great misunderstandings are encouraged.

* * *

2. *Meeting of the Foreign Ministers of the American Republics, Washington, September 23-24, 1958.*

(153) *Communiqué, Washington, September 24, 1958.*[6]

The Foreign Ministers of the 21 American Republics met informally in Washington on September 23 and 24, at the invitation of the Secretary of State of the United States, and discussed important current questions of common interest. In three sessions, the Foreign Ministers exchanged views regarding inter-American relations and problems, particularly those of an economic nature, and also reviewed the international scene.

The Ministers recognize that in the history of the world, the solidarity of the American States has been of great importance, and that at the present time it acquires special sig-

[6] *Ibid.,* v. 39 (October 13, 1958), pp. 575-576.

nificance. They reaffirm that solidarity, which is founded on
the principles of the Charter of the Organization [of American
States]. The present period of evolutionary change in the
political, economic and social structure of society calls for a
renewed dedication to the inter-American ideals of independence, political liberty, and economic and cultural progress,
and for a reaffirmation of the faith of the American nations in
their capacity to proceed dynamically toward the realization
of those high ideals.

The Ministers are confident that their exchange of views
and informal conversations will have fruitful results. They
agree to recommend that their governments instruct their
representatives on the Council of the Organization of American States to consider the desirability of holding more frequently similar informal meetings of Foreign Ministers and
other high-ranking government representatives.

The Ministers are of the opinion that, in keeping with the
aspirations and needs of the peoples of America expressed on
numerous occasions, action to promote the greatest possible
economic development of the continent must be intensified.
They are certain that a harmonious and carefully planned
joint effort to that end will contribute enormously to strengthening the solidarity of the hemisphere and to the well-being of
all Americans.

The Foreign Ministers are deeply gratified at the affirma-
tion made by President Eisenhower, that the Government of
the United States is prepared to lend its full cooperation in
achieving concrete results in the common effort to promote
the economic development of the American countries, for it
considers that peace, prosperity and security are in the end,
indivisible.

They furthermore consider that this is the proper time to
review and strengthen inter-American cooperation in the economic field, as has been suggested by President Kubitschek[7]
and in the proposals of various American Governments. The
Ministers recommend that, during the coming period before
the Eleventh Inter-American Conference, special attention
be given to working out additional measures of economic cooperation taking as the point of departure the six topics proposed by the Government of Brazil in its memorandum of
August 9, 1958 concerning the plan known as "Operation Pan
America," [8] any other specific topics that the other govern-

[7] *Ibid.,* v. 38 (June 30, 1958), pp. 1090-1091.
[8] *Operación Panamericana,* Compilación de Documentos (Rio de Janeiro,
1958), v. 2, pp. 97-106.

ments of the Republics of the hemisphere may wish to submit in connection with the general topic under consideration, namely, the promotion of economic development, and the following topic proposed by the Foreign Minister of Argentina:

Preparation and immediate execution of a broad hemispheric program to train experts for economic development, chiefly in the fields of engineering, agronomy, industrial engineering, economics, public administration, and business administration.

For this purpose and to facilitate other informal talks, the Ministers are of the opinion that the Council of the Organization of American States should set up a Special Commission of the Council on which the governments of the 21 American Republics would be represented. As the Commission reaches conclusions regarding measures that might be taken, it should submit its reports to the Council of the Organization. Then the necessary action may be taken to have those proposals or measures carried out through the organs of the Organization, or directly by the governments, as may be appropriate.

Also, the Ministers are of the opinion that practical measures may be taken now in connection with certain specific proposals. These are:

1. The establishment of an inter-American economic development institution in which all the American countries would participate.[9] For this purpose the Inter-American Economic and Social Council should convene as soon as possible a specialized committee of government representatives, as recommended in Resolution XVIII of the Buenos Aires Economic Conference. It is recommended that this committee meet in continuous session until it completes draft articles of the agreement for the proposed institution, which will be signed at a later date.

2. Intensification of efforts to establish regional markets in Latin America. It would be well for the governments directly concerned and the international organizations directly interested, chiefly the Organization of American States, the Economic Commission for Latin America, and the Organization of Central American States, to expedite their studies and con-

[9] The Under Secretary of State for Economic Affairs (Dillon) stated before the Inter-American Economic and Social Council of the OAS on August 12, 1958 that the United States "is prepared to consider the establishment of an inter-American regional development institution which would receive support from all its member countries." Department of State Bulletin, v. 39 (September 1, 1958), pp. 347-348.

crete measures directed toward the establishment of regional markets in Central and South America. The Ministers suggest that a report on this important project be submitted to the members of the OAS not later than the Eleventh Inter-American Conference. In this connection the Ministers note that the United States Government has made known that it is prepared to assist financially in the establishment of solvent industries, through appropriate agencies, under suitable conditions, with a view to promoting enjoyment of the benefits of regional markets through public and private investment.

The Ministers again express their constant concern about the problems of markets for basic products. They are in agreement that the economic structure of the majority of the American Republics requires that solutions to these problems be sought urgently, for which purpose consultations should be carried out between the interested members of the Organization of American States, on bilateral and multilateral bases, as well as with the producer and consumer countries of other geographic areas.

In concluding this communiqué, the Ministers expressed that there prevailed at this meeting an atmosphere of frankness, sincerity, and understanding which contributed greatly to the establishment of a feeling of confidence that the important tasks being started at this time will be completed successfully.

(154) News Conference Comments by the Secretary of State (Dulles), September 30, 1958.[10]

*   *   *

Well, I will tell you this—I know it won't be popular for me to say it—but I would say one of the reasons why this conference was such a success was that it was understood at the beginning that nobody was talking for the record. I am quite sure that, if it had been the kind of a conference where people made speeches that were going to be publicized and so forth, we would not have accomplished nearly what we did holding the conference on an informal basis. I may say that the Foreign Ministers were, I think, on the whole amazed that there was so much that could be actually accomplished, so much practical work actually gotten under way, within a meeting which lasted roughly for a day and a half. (The second half day was a little long; it lasted until five o'clock.) But we did

[10] Ibid. (October 20, 1958), p. 601.

accomplish a great deal, and we could not possibly have gotten the accomplishments done that we did, I think, if we had not said at the beginning, "This is going to be an entirely informal meeting. It is going to be off the record. People can say anything that is on their minds, and there is not going to be any record kept of what takes place." And there was no record kept. You know that it is human nature with all of us that, when there is a record kept, when speeches are made which are going to be published in the home papers, and so forth, we all want to talk quite a bit more than we do when we are talking where there is no record being kept.

I believe that the meeting did achieve very extraordinary results in the short span of time, largely because it was operated on this quite informal basis.

* * *

. . . it would have been very difficult to have briefed the press in advance about this meeting because, frankly, when we went into it we didn't know where we were going to come out. I may say in all frankness that I went into this meeting with very considerable trepidation. The auguries were not entirely good. I knew we were going to make this announcement about lead and zinc the day before the meeting was held, and I didn't know what the result of that would be.[11] Some people are critical of the fact that we made that announcement just the day before. But I felt that, as long as the decision had been taken that we had to go in for quotas, it was more honorable and straightforward to put it on the table before the meeting took place rather than to keep it up our sleeve—to have the meeting and then to pull it immediately after the meeting. But I say very frankly that I went into the meeting with trepidation, with worriment as to what would come out of the meeting. And what came out of the meeting was nothing that could have been foreseen. It gathered a momentum as it went along largely because, as I say, people did speak with perfect frankness. The Minister of Peru didn't spare any words at all in what he said about what he thought about our quotas. We talked very frankly with each other, and there was an atmosphere of real comradeship in that meeting which was quite unusual [laughter] and

[11] Pursuant to section 7 of the Trade Agreements Extension Act of 1951, as amended, the President issued a proclamation on September 22, 1958 limiting imports of lead and zinc by an annual quota equivalent in amount to 80 percent of average annual commercial imports during the five-year period 1953-1957. *Ibid.* (October 13, 1958), pp. 579-583.

which, I think, was an eye opener to all of us. But we couldn't
have briefed all that in advance.

3. *Meeting of the Special Committee of the Council of
   the Organization of American States to Study the
   Formulation of New Measures for Economic Cooperation, Washington, November 17-December 12,
   1958.*

(155) *Address by the Under Secretary of State for
   Economic Affairs (Dillon), November 18,
   1958.*[12]

It is an honor and a great pleasure for me to welcome you
to Washington. We are meeting here to examine the whole
range of economic problems facing the American states with
one objective in mind: to attain sound, stable, expanding
economies in Latin America with steadily rising standards of
living. The United States is prepared to cooperate fully in
a combined effort to achieve this goal.

To succeed we will need to address ourselves to three major
questions:

First, how can we enlarge the flow of capital into sound
development projects in Latin America?

Second, how can we step up our joint activities in the field
of technical cooperation, which is so essential to the development process?

And third, how can we improve and expand international
trade, upon which the good health of all our economies is increasingly dependent?

I would like to say a few words on each of these matters.

Enlarging the Flow of Capital

First, there is the proposal to establish a new lending institution which would concentrate all its efforts in promoting
the development of Latin America. We have agreed that a
special committee of government representatives will meet
early in January of next year to negotiate and draft a charter
for this institution.

The eventual success or failure of this institution will depend greatly on the wisdom with which its foundations are
established. We have therefore given much serious thought to
various alternatives regarding its nature and functions. There
are many questions on which decisions will have to be reached

[12] *Ibid.* (December 8, 1958), pp. 918-922.

by the special committee. For example, what sort of projects should this institution finance? Should it be devoted solely to productive development projects, or should its resources be available also to help meet such needs as housing, schools, and hospitals? Again, for example, should it make loans to cover some or all of the local-currency costs of projects, and, if so, what limitations should there be on this type of lending?

Obviously, another major question to be decided is the capital structure of the institution. What is to be its authorized capital? In what form are the capital subscriptions to be made? Should there be some arrangement for spreading out the payment of this subscribed portion or should payment be made in one lump sum? Should there be any limitations on the free use of any of the currencies received by the bank as subscriptions, and, if so, what should such limitations be? Under what conditions should the unpaid portion of the authorization be callable? How should the subscription quotas be allocated among the various member countries?

Finally, a very important question will be whether the institution should be authorized to make loans repayable in the currency of the borrower and, if so, to what extent and under what limitations or conditions.

I have tried to indicate some of the issues to which our Government and, I am sure, your respective governments are giving serious consideration. Of course this is not the time or place to reach conclusions on these issues. This will be done at the January meeting. In the meantime we expect to explore these matters in a preliminary way through consultations.

I would like to suggest that this new institution should be organized and operated so that it will work in the closest collaboration and harmony with existing lending institutions, both public and private. If this is done, it should make it possible for these existing institutions to increase their participation in development.

The Export-Import Bank has played a primary role in Latin America. Over the past decade about 40 per cent of all Export-Import Bank loans have been made in Latin American countries. To date, the Export-Import Bank has authorized in excess of $3.5 billion in loans to Latin America, while presently outstanding commitments total $1.8 billion. This year the Congress authorized an increase of the lending authority of the Export-Import Bank from $5 billion to $7 billion. As a result the bank now has $2.2 billion available for lending. The factor of fundamental importance to Latin America is that the bank is now in a position to continue a program of vigorous lending activity in Latin America in the period immediately ahead.

No one, I believe, has seriously suggested that the Export-Import Bank should expand its activity by lowering the economic standards applied to its loans. However, there have been some requests for loans to meet the local-currency costs of projects and for loans in dollars which could be repaid in local currencies. The United States has recognized the need for loans of this type, which are not suitable to the Export-Import Bank. Accordingly, it has established a new lending institution—the Development Loan Fund—with authority broad and flexible enough to make loans of this kind. We need to consider carefully how the Development Loan Fund can best be used to help and support the new Inter-American Development Institution.

Another source for public loans to the countries of Latin America is the International Bank for Reconstruction and Development, or World Bank. Its loans to Latin America are currently running over $150 million a year, and the total of such loans now approaches $1 billion.

The United States has recently made two proposals for strengthening the World Bank and enlarging its sphere of operations. Last month, at the annual meeting of the bank's Governors in New Delhi, Secretary of the Treasury Anderson suggested, and it was agreed, that consideration be promptly given to the desirability of an increase in the capitalization of the bank, so that it will have the resources needed to achieve a high rate of lending over the years ahead. He also proposed that consideration be given to establishing, as an affiliate of the World Bank, a new International Development Association which would be authorized to make loans repayable in whole or in part in the currency of the borrower in much the same way as our own Development Loan Fund.

The adoption of these suggestions will depend upon the attitude of other countries which are members of the World Bank, and, in the United States, upon the approval of our Congress. The bank is ready and willing to play an active role in Latin America, and the proposed enlargement of its capital would assure it adequate resources for the purpose.

The United States, then, is taking important forward steps to increase the flow of public lending to Latin America both through existing institutions and through the establishment of new ones.

But public lending, no matter what our efforts may be, can never substitute for private initiative and private capital. Fortunately the capital resources at the disposal of private enterprise are far larger than the amount which governments can ask their taxpayers to provide.

During the past 3 years the flow of new private capital from the United States to Latin America has averaged more than $600 million annually. However, it is clear that more needs to be done if private foreign capital is to make its full contribution to the development of Latin America. We need to clear away the obstacles to the entry of private capital into countries desiring investment. And we need to provide, in greater degree, positive incentives to increased investment.

The removal of obstacles to investment is within the control of the Latin American countries themselves. What is required is the maintenance of a hospitable atmosphere in which private enterprise can operate with confidence.

Turning to the question of fresh incentives to the flow of private capital, we in the United States are earnestly searching for new methods. We have asked a group of leading businessmen associated with our Department of Commerce to look at the problem and tell us what they, as businessmen, would like to see done in order to make foreign investment more attractive. We hope to get concrete and useful suggestions from their study. There is one new incentive, in the field of taxation, which we are already prepared to adopt, and which we hope may yield constructive results. Let me explain.

Under United States law, if a foreign government grants a special income-tax reduction in order to attract the United States investor, that investor has to pay to the United States Government whatever has been waived by the foreign government. We are seeking to correct this situation so that tax benefits granted to induce investment abroad can retain their full effect. To accomplish this the United States Government is prepared to consider conventions which, with proper safeguards and restrictions, would contain a tax-sparing provision that would cure this situation. The only way to accomplish this result is by treaty. We invite negotiations.

There also are other kinds of agreements which help to improve the climate of investment and establish confidence. Among these are investment guaranty agreements and treaties of friendship, commerce, and navigation. The United States would also welcome negotiations on these subjects with Latin American countries.

It will do little good to provide larger amounts of capital for development purposes if that capital is dissipated through unrestrained inflation. Inflation both wastes economic resources and leads to serious balance-of-payments difficulties.

There needs to be a better public understanding of the fact that inflation does not create resources; it simply transfers them from one group to another. In the process it hurts those with fixed incomes and the poorer classes. It also kills the incentive to save and hence is the deadly enemy of economic development.

During the past year inflationary pressure was one of the causes of the acute balance-of-payments difficulties which confronted many countries in Latin America. In cooperation with the International Monetary Fund, the United States assisted a number of the Latin American countries to bring these problems under control.

The International Monetary Fund was designed specifically to help member governments in temporary balance-of-payments difficulties through stabilization loans and effective technical advice. The fund has a fine staff which is expert in analyzing fiscal and monetary problems and suggesting appropriate remedies.

Last month at New Delhi the Government of the United States proposed that consideration be given to the desirability of an increase in the quotas of the International Monetary Fund in order that it might be even more effective in the future in helping its member countries. This proposal was accepted and the Executive Directors of the fund were asked to submit recommendations in the very near future.

Expansion of Technical Cooperation

Technical cooperation is the second major area in which we must all step up our activities if the development of Latin America is to be hastened. Surely it must be obvious that as economies grow and become more complex there will be a steadily increasing need for skills of all kinds. Economic development requires more than capital and modern machinery. It also requires technical and managerial personnel who know how to operate business and agricultural enterprises. It requires a literate and healthy population. It requires intelligent public administration.

For its part, the United States is prepared to intensify its participation in technical assistance programs in Latin America—through its own bi-lateral programs, through the Organization of American States, and through the United Nations programs.

There is, however, one aspect of technical cooperation to which I believe we should give special attention. This is the role which might be played by the proposed Inter-American Development Institution in the field of technical advice. In the past many development projects have failed to go forward either because they were not adequately prepared and engineered or because they were not well designed in relation to the overall development needs of the country concerned. We believe that the proposed Inter-American Development Institution should be so staffed that it will be able to render its member countries technical assistance of this kind. If desired, the United States, through its technical assistance program, would be prepared to support an effort of this nature by the new institution.

Expanding International Trade

The third major area in which we need to intensify our cooperative economic endeavor is that of international trade. All of us in the community of American states live in an interdependent world. If we are to achieve a richer life for our people we must continuously enlarge the opportunities for international trade, both among ourselves and between ourselves and the rest of the free world. As a result of the recent action of our Congress in extending our Reciprocal Trade Agreements Act for a longer period than ever before, the United States is prepared to participate in negotiations to reduce further the barriers to international trade.

In our discussions of international trade I know that there are two subjects which are uppermost in your minds. One of these relates to trade in primary commodities and the other to the possibilities for regional markets in Latin America. I would like to speak briefly to each of these.

Because the economies of the countries of Latin America are heavily dependent on exports of one or a few primary commodities, they can be placed in serious difficulties by sharp price declines for these commodities in world markets. The United States recognizes the importance of this problem. It understands and sympathizes with the concern expressed by Latin American countries on this subject. We are ready to join in the study of individual commodity problems which are creating difficulties to see whether cooperative solutions can be found. We have already done so in the case of coffee and more recently in the case of lead and zinc. We believe that effective international cooperation to avoid acute and recurring imbalances between supply and demand in these commodities can make an important contribution to our objectives.

This does not mean that we feel that easy solutions can be found. It does not mean that we have altered our view regarding the impracticality of rigid price-stabilization schemes. It does mean that we feel that real gains can be made whenever we sit down together in good faith and discuss our common problems.

During the past year or so there has been increasing discussion about the possibility of establishing a regional market or markets in Latin America. It has been the policy of the United States to encourage arrangements to achieve economic integration between two or more countries because it has believed that such arrangements, if correctly designed, can lead to increased competitive opportunities, greater productivity, and a higher level of trade both within the area concerned and with other countries, including our own. In short we have encouraged integration measures of a forward-looking, trade-creating nature, while at the same time opposing narrower arrangements which would serve to divert and restrict trade. Thus we have supported the European Common Market and the proposed European Free Trade Area, while endeavoring to assure that the interests of outside countries, including those in Latin America, are adequately protected. We have also supported a free-trade area in Central America. We have also made it clear that we are prepared, through the Export-Import Bank, to consider the dollar financing required by sound regional industries in Latin America.

I think I can say with confidence that, if proposals for regional markets in Latin America seem likely to result in genuine economic benefit for the countries directly concerned and in the long-run development of international trade, the United States will give careful study to them in relation to its commercial policies and trade agreements. We are also prepared to do what we can to help interested Latin American countries in framing arrangements for economic integration which would be economically sound. It is in this spirit that we have expressed our willingness to participate in the committee of experts which the executive secretary of GATT has suggested should meet in Washington to examine and discuss specific proposals in the field of regional economic integration in Latin America.

A Cooperative Effort for Development

Throughout their history the American Republics have shared the conviction that free peoples who respect the dignity of the individual and the equality of nations can, through cooperation, not only preserve their liberties and cultures but also build a better and fuller life for themselves and their children. Today we live in a time of great danger to our way of life. It is also a time of great opportunity that challenges us to prove that our system of democratic freedom can yield the greatest material benefit to the individual as well as the greatest spiritual benefits.

Here on the American continent we have great resources and great determination. We have already accomplished much. In Latin America as in the United States we have experienced a dynamic economic expansion. If we all set ourselves resolutely to our task, if each does his share, and if we work cooperatively for an integrated program of development —not for just one part of it, omitting other parts essential to success—we can demonstrate that free peoples can outproduce enslaved peoples and can do so without sacrificing their way of life.

(156) Declaration, Approved December 12, 1958.[13]

At the close of the first meeting, at which the governments of all twenty-one American republics were represented, the Special Committee of the Council of the Organization of American States deems it fitting to state that, from the start of its deliberations on November 17, 1958, the representatives of the member states have had full opportunity, in the course of the sessions, to express with all frankness and clarity the views of their governments on the pressing need for strengthening inter-American cooperation.

Opinions were freely exchanged, always in an atmosphere of extreme cordiality and mutual understanding. The members of the committee unanimously reaffirmed their faith in the Organization of American States and their common determination to strengthen the harmonious relations uniting their countries in bonds of brotherhood. They also recognized the

[13] Ibid., v. 40 (January 12, 1959), pp. 49-50.

urgent necessity of making the best possible use of all the means and the facilities available within the regional system for promoting the economic development of the hemisphere in a way that will bring positive benefits to each and every one of the American republics.

There was a full discussion of each of the topics accepted at the Informal Meeting of American Foreign Ministers, held in Washington last September 23 and 24, and of many other proposals that were presented by the various delegations during the sessions.

Special attention was given the problem of financing the economic development of Latin America, and a draft resolution was adopted endorsing the proposal to establish an inter-American institution for economic development and expressing the hope that the Committee of Experts convoked by the Inter-American Economic and Social Council and scheduled to meet next January 8 will, in the shortest possible time, draw up the draft conventions that are to bring this new instrument of inter-American cooperation into existence.

In regard to the need for creating new incentives to the flow of private capital, all the representatives agreed that it was necessary to supplement such measures as the countries interested in attracting and receiving foreign capital have adopted, or will in the future adopt, by concluding agreements with capital-exporting countries so that the special tax rates that are now offered, or may later be offered, by the former will not be negated by the absence of counterpart measures in those countries in a position to furnish capital.

This matter is one in which the initiative is left to the interested governments, and with respect to which the willingness of the United States Government to conclude the necessary agreements, as expressed on the very first day of the meeting, can be counted on.

There was general agreement that the heavy reliance of the Latin American economies on the export trade in one or a few primary products poses a serious problem, since abrupt fluctuations and sudden drops in the prices of those commodities give rise to serious disturbances and impair the entire economic and financial outlook.

In this respect, the representatives of all the American countries displayed a willingness to participate in the study of the problems connected with each product in an effort to find satisfactory solutions within a spirit of hemisphere solidarity and an awareness of the mutual benefits that spring from the many and varied relationships linking the countries of the American regional community.

All the representatives at the meeting placed special emphasis on the need for intensifying technical cooperation and providing a new and greater stimulus to the campaigns directed toward increasing technical ability and productivity, which are the principal requirements for economic development.

In this connection, highly constructive suggestions, inspired by a proposal of Argentina, were made. These suggestions are aimed at expanding and intensifying the pertinent programs now being conducted by the OAS and at awakening the interest of and obtaining assistance in this field from other public and private organizations.

The committee is about to suspend its sessions because it feels that, now that the general viewpoints have been expounded, the time has come to proceed without loss of time to the stage of preparing concrete formulas and specific proposals. In order to carry out this technical work, which is essential if useful results are to be obtained, the committee has appointed a working group that will develop the practical arrangements for arriving at the aforesaid objectives. The working group will meet at the Pan American Union beginning January 15, 1959, and will enlist the effective and indispensable services of the IA-ECOSOC and the General Secretariat of the OAS. When it completes its task, which should be no later than April 1, 1959, the Group will report its conclusions and recommendations to the Special Committee. Thus, the new measures required for more effective inter-American cooperation are already in progress.

When the Special Committee meets again in April, it will examine these specific proposals and submit them to the Council of the Organization of American States, so that the governments may arrive at final agreements and decisions.

Strongly evident was a feeling of gratitude on the part of all the governments to President Juscelino Kubitschek of Brazil for his timely proposal for setting in motion what has come to be known as "Operation Pan America."

The Special Committee is fully aware of the far-reaching importance of the tasks assigned to it by the American governments; in view of what has already been said and done, the Committee feels confident that it will be possible to advance toward the goal set by the governments, namely: the promotion of economic development in their respective countries with a view to raising the standard of living of their peoples, thus paving the way for progress and strengthening democracy in the hemisphere.

C. Brazil.

(157) *Joint Communiqué on Talks Held between the Secretary of State (Dulles) and the President of Brazil (Kubitschek) on Multilateral Subjects, Brasilia, August 6, 1958.*[1]

At the conclusion of the talks between President Juscelino Kubitschek de Oliveira and Secretary of State John Foster Dulles and Foreign Minister Francisco Negrao de Lima, the following Joint Communique was approved:

On the occasion of his visit to Brazil on August 4 and 5 Secretary of State John Foster Dulles was received by the President of Brazil Juscelino Kubitschek de Oliveira and by Foreign Minister Francisco Negrao de Lima. They held extensive conversations, exchanging views about the international situation and those problems relating to the movement for hemispheric unity which President Juscelino Kubitschek de Oliveira has called Operation Pan America.[2] At the end of these frank and cordial talks, held within the general framework of the exchange of views now taking place among the American Republics, the two governments:

I. Reaffirm their determination in carrying out all obligations under the Charter of the Organization of American States. They emphatically declared that the exchange of letters between the President of Brazil, Juscelino Kubitschek de Oliveira, and the President of the United States of America Dwight D. Eisenhower[3], was most timely and useful in that it advocates the rededication of the Pan-American ideals with a view to strengthening continental unity and preserving peace.

II. Declare that we are in complete agreement to seek formulation of policies designed not only to strengthen the defense of the value of western civilization but also to give a greater creative momentum toward the attainment of this goal.

III. Agree that Latin America has an important role to play among the nations of the world. It is highly desirable

[1] *Ibid.*, v. 39 (August 25, 1958), pp. 301-302.
[2] *Operación Panamericana*, Compilación de Documentos (Rio de Janeiro, 1958), 2 v.
[3] *Department of State Bulletin*, v. 38 (June 30, 1958), pp. 1090-1091.

that Latin America take an even more active part in formulating those broad international policies which guide the free world.

IV. Reiterate their convictions that the strengthening of the American community requires, among other measures, dynamic efforts to overcome the problems of underdevelopment. They believe that this principle—this fight for greater development which is inseparable from the collective security of the hemisphere—will be supported throughout the hemisphere.

V. Reaffirm that it has become necessary to fight with determination for religious and democratic principles, for the right of nations to freedom, and for respect for man's individuality and dignity. These values which constitute the heritage of western civilization and the culture and the spirit and soul of the Americas, are now challenged by the greed of atheistic Communism. Urgent measures should therefore be taken to assure in an effective manner a defense of these ideals.

VI. Reaffirm their purpose of continuing along the line of broader contact and consultation already successfully started among the American Republics. The American Republics will be best able to attain their common goal: a coordinated and harmonious effort to develop the economies of the countries in the hemisphere.

VII. Agreed that the time has come for the American Republics to organize to meet together not just to deal with problems of immediate urgency but to discuss on a regular basis any and all problems of mutual concern, bearing in mind their common responsibilities when peace and freedom are threatened. To this end it was agreed that both governments would suggest to the other American Republics that their Foreign Ministers should meet at regular intervals in the framework of the Organization of American States.

VIII. Agreed that consultation between their two countries shall be continued.

IX. Details of their conversations will be promptly communicated to the other American Republics.

(158) *Joint Communiqué on Talks Held between the Secretary of State (Dulles) and the President of Brazil (Kubitschek) on Bilateral Subjects, Brasilia, August 6, 1958.*[4]

In addition to discussions on the international situation and on Inter-American unity, the Foreign Minister, Negrao de Lima, the Minister of Finance, Lucas Lopes, and the United States Secretary of State, John Foster Dulles, with members of their respective staffs, discussed a number of problems of bilateral concern.

Satisfaction was expressed at the fact that the Governmental measures now being undertaken in Brazil to promote financial equilibrium, complemented by the outcome of negotiations conducted with the competent agencies in Washington, the International Monetary Fund and the Export-Import Bank, and the private banks will allow the Brazilian Government to pursue its efforts to foster a balanced economic development.

Both groups reviewed the coffee situation and the steps already taken towards a better general understanding on the matter and towards bringing a greater degree of stability to the coffee market. It was agreed to continue to support the coffee study group, where producers and consumers are represented. Full acknowledgement was also given to the helpful participation of the United States Representatives in the discussions of the special group. This represents a formal recognition on the part of the United States Government of the vital importance of coffee for the economy of many coffee producing countries and the need for an international approach to the problem.

Both groups believe that the contacts here renewed should represent an important contribution towards urgent and orderly solutions of the serious problem affecting the Brazilian economy as a result of the imbalance between supply and demand of coffee.

The groups reviewed the efforts made by Brazil to increase its domestic production of petroleum and the relationship of this problem to the questions of balance of payments and foreign exchange reserves. This review was held within the principle that the different countries have their own ways of developing their petroleum resources and, while no decisions

[4] *Ibid.*, v. 39 (August 25, 1958), p. 302.

were made, it was agreed to continue discussions in the same friendly atmosphere.

Some connected problems relating to specified products of importance to certain regions of Brazil were examined. It was agreed that mutually satisfactory solutions would be sought through diplomatic channels.

The goals of the Government of Brazil and its program of economic development and the related question of long-term financing of foreign currency costs were discussed and it was agreed that the subject would continue to be reviewed in the context of the joint statement issued by the Brazilian Financial Mission to Washington and the Export Import Bank of July 1956.

D. Argentina

(159) *Joint Announcement Concerning the Conclusion of a Stabilization and Loan Agreement with the Republic of Argentina, Washington, December 29, 1958.*[1]

A $329 million program to assist the Republic of Argentina in its efforts to achieve stabilization and economic development was announced on December 29 by 3 U.S. Government agencies and 11 private financial institutions in cooperation with the International Monetary Fund.

(Simultaneously, a far-reaching program of financial reform for Argentina was announced by the Argentine Government at Buenos Aires and the International Monetary Fund at Washington.)

The United States participation, said Deputy Under Secretary of State Robert Murphy, represents "one of the most comprehensive operations ever undertaken by the United States in Latin America."

The arrangements were concluded following negotiations at Washington and New York between Argentina's Minister of Economy, Emilio Donato Del Carril; the Secretary of the Treasury, Robert B. Anderson, the Under Secretary of State for Economic Affairs, Douglas Dillon; the President of the Export-Import Bank of Washington, Samuel C. Waugh; the Managing Director of the Development Loan Fund, Dempster McIntosh; and officials of the following commercial banks: Bank of America N.T. & S.A., the Chase Manhattan Bank, the First National Bank of Boston, the First National

[1] *Ibid.*, v. 40 (January 19, 1959), pp. 105-106.

City Bank of New York, Grace National Bank, Guaranty Trust Company of New York, the Hanover Bank, Manufacturers Trust Company, J. P. Morgan & Company, Inc., the Philadelphia National Bank, the Royal Bank of Canada (N. Y. Agency).

The U.S. Government agencies and private banks will make available approximately $250 million. The International Monetary Fund announced simultaneously the conclusion of a $75-million standby arrangement with Argentina. Details of the conditions of availability of the standby arrangements are contained in a separate International Monetary Fund release.

The U.S. credits and other arrangements include: $54 million by 11 private banks; approximately $125 million by the Export-Import Bank; about $25 million by the Development Loan Fund; and a $50-million exchange agreement with the U.S. Treasury. U.S. assistance involves new economic development credits to help Argentina reverse the faltering private investment trend of recent years, increase economic output, develop new exports, and reduce certain major import requirements.

These major development loans for industrial free enterprise, a vital part of the Argentine recovery programs, include a $10-million credit to the Argentine Industrial Bank for allocation to small business. Under the new Argentine financial program, it is hoped that foreign private investment will be attracted in amounts considerably in excess of these government development loans.

Commenting upon these announcements, Mr. Waugh said:

"Argentina's efforts to regain full financial health and economic vigor are important to the entire Western community. The magnitude as well as the complexity of Argentine problems, and the extent of the new Argentine program, required the farflung and cooperative actions taken today. The financial arrangements announced today to support the Argentine effort recognize the courageous initiative being undertaken by the Government and people of that country."

Credits from the 11 private banks are intended for short-term Argentine requirements, as are the agreements with the Treasury and the International Monetary Fund. The long-range necessity in Argentina, however, is for expansion of fundamental sources of production.

To help meet this necessity, Eximbank expects to devote up to $100 million of its $125-million credit to implement loans on a case-by-case basis—with participation of investment from U.S. private sources—to finance U.S. purchases in connection with the following types of projects: a substantial electric power expansion program; development of industries such as cement, pulp and paper, and rubber manufacturing; petrochemicals; expansion of the meat industry; and other types of industrial expansion.

The remaining $25 million of Export-Import Bank credit will be used to maintain essential imports from the United States during the next year.

The Development Loan Fund credit of about $25 million will be used to finance importation of capital items in connection with projects contributing to economic development in the fields of transportation, electric power, and waterworks.

Under the Treasury's $50-million agreement Argentina may request the U.S. Exchange Stabilization Fund to purchase Argentine pesos. Any pesos acquired by the U.S. Treasury would subsequently be repurchased by Argentina with dollars.

CHAPTER NINE

THE UNITED NATIONS: MILITARY, SCIENTIFIC AND LEGAL PROBLEMS

A. Disarmament.

1. *Proposed Resumption of Disarmament Talks in the United Nations Disarmament Commission.*

(160) *United States Statement, March 15, 1958.*[1]

The United States seeks early resumption of disarmament talks. To this end, the United States suggested privately to the Soviet representative at the United Nations early this month certain procedures designed to lead to an early resumption of disarmament talks and at the same time maintain the continuing responsibility of the United Nations.

Yesterday's [March 14] statement by the U.S.S.R. Foreign Ministry distorts the U.S. position and casts doubt that the Soviet Union wants serious discussions on the disarmament question or that it is really seeking a relaxation of tension. Our doubts were confirmed by the fact that the U.S.S.R. made public its statement before Ambassador Arkady Sobolev, Soviet representative to the United Nations, conveyed his Government's position officially to Ambassadors Lodge and Wadsworth yesterday.

Specifically, the United States proposed to the U.S.S.R., after consultation with a number of other U.N. members, that a meeting of the enlarged Disarmament Commission be held pursuant to the resolution adopted overwhelmingly by the General Assembly last year.[2] Despite the fact that the Soviets have indicated an intention to boycott such a meeting, we believe the Disarmament Commission should meet in light of the action of the General Assembly.

The United States also informed the U.S.S.R. that, if it was found that owing to Soviet nonparticipation the Disarmament Commission could not usefully pursue serious discus-

[1] *Department of State Bulletin*, v. 38 (March 31, 1958), p. 516.
[2] *Documents on American Foreign Relations, 1957*, pp. 446-449.

sions, the Security Council should hold a purely procedural meeting in order to provide a proper link between the United Nations and any subsequent disarmament discussions.

Under the charter the Security Council has an important responsibility to bring about the regulation of armaments. The purpose of Council consideration would be to give this body the opportunity to take procedural action designed to lead to an early resumption of disarmament discussions through other channels. Rather than creating obstacles in the way of future disarmament discussions, this procedure would ease the way to and enhance the possibility of meaningful talks.

The U.S.S.R.'s reiteration of its unwillingness to participate in the Disarmament Commission constitutes a continued flouting of the resolution adopted overwhelmingly by the General Assembly. In opposing Security Council consideration of disarmament, even on a procedural basis, the U.S.S.R. seems to be implying that it no longer recognizes the responsibility of the Council to deal with disarmament. The United States is not prepared to disregard the United Nations in its efforts to resume disarmament talks.

The U.S.S.R. purports to favor a heads-of-government meeting to consider urgent international problems, including disarmament. We are prepared to participate in a high-level meeting, provided prior preparations indicate that it would result in reaching agreements. The United States seeks meaningful agreements which will, in fact, resolve issues, reduce tensions, and respond to the hopes of mankind. The recent Soviet statement in the field of disarmament is hardly calculated to achieve these ends. Nevertheless, the United States will continue to take every feasible step to bring about a resumption of serious disarmament negotiations.

2. Action by the United Nations General Assembly.
(161) General Assembly Resolution 1252 (XIII), Adopted November 4, 1958.[3]

A

The General Assembly,
Reaffirming the continuing interest and responsibility of the United Nations in the field of disarmament, which have found expression in the Charter of the United Nations and in previous resolutions of the General Assembly.

[3] United Nations, General Assembly, *Official Records, Thirteenth Session,* Supplement No. 18(A/4090), pp. 3-4.

Welcoming the agreement which has been achieved in the Conference of Experts to Study the Possibility of Detecting Violations of a Possible Agreement on the Suspension of Nuclear Tests,[4]

Noting that negotiations on the suspension on nuclear weapons tests and on the actual establishment of an international control system on the basis of the report of the Conference of Experts will begin on 31 October 1958,

Noting further that qualified persons are expected to meet soon to study the technical aspects of measures against the possibility of surprise attack,

Recognizing that these developments are encouraging steps in the direction of progressive openness of information concerning technologies and armaments, which may assist in promoting the fundamental aims of the United Nations in the field of disarmament,

I

1. *Urges* that in the negotiations between states that have tested nuclear weapons the parties make every effort to reach early agreement on the suspension of nuclear weapons tests under effective international control,

2. *Urges* the parties involved in these negotiations not to undertake further testing of nuclear weapons while these negotiations are in progress,

II

3. *Calls attention* to the importance and urgency of achieving the widest possible measure of agreement in the forthcoming study of the technical aspects of measures against the possibility of surprise attack,

III

4. *Expresses determination* that the trend of the recent encouraging initiatives, including the technical approach, should continue with a view to contributing to a balanced and effectively controlled world-wide system of disarmament,

IV

5. *Invites* the conferences on nuclear weapons tests and on surprise attack to avail themselves of the assistance and services of the Secretary-General and requests them to keep the United Nations informed,

6. *Invites* the Secretary-General, in consultation with the

⁴ Document 40, above.

Governments concerned to render whatever advice and assistance may seem appropriate to facilitate current developments or any further initiatives related to problems of disarmament,

7. *Requests* that the records of the meetings of the First Committee at which various aspects of disarmament were discussed be transmitted by the Secretary-General to the participants in the conferences on nuclear weapons tests and on surprise attack;

V

8. *Reiterates* to the States concerned the invitation made in General Assembly resolution 1148 (XII), of 14 November 1957, to devote, out of the funds made available as a result of disarmament, as and when sufficient progress is made, additional resources to the improvement of living conditions throughout the world and especially in the less developed countries.

B

The General Assembly,

Welcoming the report of the Conference of Experts to Study the Possibility of Detecting Violations of a Possible Agreement on the Suspension of Nuclear Tests,

Welcoming further the decision of the States which have tested nuclear weapons to meet in a conference at Geneva commencing 31 October 1958, concerning the question of nuclear weapons tests,[5]

1. *Expresses the hope* that the conference will be successful and lead to an agreement acceptable to all;

2. *Requests* the parties concerned to report to the General Assembly the agreement that may be the result of their negotiations;

3. *Requests* the Secretary-General to render such assistance and provide such services as may be asked for by the conference commencing at Geneva on 31 October 1958.

C

The General Assembly,

Noting the agreement among certain States to meet to study the technical aspects of measures against the possibility of surprise attack,[6]

1. *Expresses the hope* that the widest possible measure of agreement will be achieved in the forthcoming study;

[5] Documents 41-43, above.
[6] Documents 44 and 45, above.

2. *Requests* the Secretary-General to render such assistance and provide such services as may be asked for and required by this conference;

3. *Requests* the States participating in the study to inform the United Nations of the progress achieved.

D

The General Assembly,
Having regard to the universal desire for the establishment of genuinely peaceful conditions in the world and therefore for taking steps to avoid the destruction that would result from a major armed conflict,

Reaffirming the responsibility of the United Nations for seeking a solution of the disarmament problem,

Expressing its determination that all Members of the United Nations should be in a position to contribute to a solution of this problem on a continuing basis,

1. *Decides* that the Disarmament Commission shall, for 1959 and on an *ad hoc* basis, be composed of all the Members of the United Nations;

2. *Transmits* to the Disarmament Commission all the documents, proposals and records of discussions relating to disarmament at the thirteenth session of the General Assembly;

3. *Requests* the Disarmament Commission to convene as appropriate and to submit to the Security Council and the General Assembly, at a special session if necessary, constructive proposals and recommendations in the field of disarmament;

4. *Decides* that the first meeting of the Disarmament Commission shall be convened by the Secretary-General after consultation with the Member States and that the Commission, having begun its activities under rule 162 of the rules of procedure of the General Assembly and taking that rule into account, shall adopt its own rules of procedure.

3. United States Proposal Concerning the Establishment of an Inspection Zone in the Arctic against Surprise Attack.

(162) News Conference Comments by the Secretary of State (Dulles), May 1, 1958.[7]

I should like to make some observations regarding the United States resolution before the United Nations Security

[7] *Department of State Bulletin,* v. 38 (May 19, 1958), pp. 804-805.

Council, which calls for the establishment of an Arctic inspection zone.

The establishment of international inspection in an Arctic
zone is proposed by the United States not as a maneuver, not
as propaganda, but in a sincere effort to meet the admitted
problems of a particular area. The United States, not only
publicly but privately, has done its best to make clear to the
Soviet Government the sincerity of its purpose and its desire
to avoid turning this grave matter into a propaganda battle.

The Soviet Government has said that it is worried by the
flights of United States aircraft in this area. We have said that
we need to keep planes aloft because we are fearful that the
Soviets may launch a nuclear attack against us over the top
of the world.[8] It seemed to us that, if both sides are animated
by really peaceful intentions, there is a natural solution—
that is to have international inspection which would allay the
fears on both sides. If the Soviets do not have bomber and
missile bases in the north of their country available for a sudden surprise attack upon the United States, then our own
problem of security is greatly altered. Perhaps we would then
feel it safe greatly to minimize the flights of which the Soviet
Union complains. In any event the Soviet Union would know
that any United States flights are so safe-guarded, beyond risk
of misadventure, that they cannot be a threat to the Soviet
Union unless the Soviet Union first attacks.

The establishment of one important zone of international
inspection, as proposed by the United States, would be a constructive first step toward easing world tensions. It is a step
that can be taken at once without awaiting any high-level conference. The United States believes that an addition, along
the lines proposed by Sweden, is totally consistent with this
initiative. It is also consistent with the position taken by the
United States regarding a possible heads-of-government meeting.

We continue to believe that the present situation requires

[8] On April 21, 1958 the United Nations Security Council met to consider a
question submitted by the USSR concerning "urgent measures to put an
end to flights by United States military aircraft armed with atomic and
hydrogen bombs in the direction of the frontiers of the Soviet Union". The
representative of the USSR introduced a draft resolution calling upon the
United States "to refrain from sending its military aircraft . . . towards
the frontiers of other States for the purpose of creating a threat to their
security or staging military demonstrations." (United Nations Document
S/3993, dated April 21, 1958). At the close of the debate the representative
of the USSR withdrew the draft resolution. For a statement by the United
States Representative to the United Nations (Lodge) see ibid. (May 12,
1958), pp. 760-763.

that every attempt be made to reach agreement on the main problems affecting the maintenance of peace and stability in the world. In the circumstances a summit meeting would be desirable if it would provide opportunity for conducting serious discussions of major problems and would be an effective means of reaching agreement on significant subjects. Before a summit meeting can take place, however, preparatory work is required so that some assurance can be given that meaningful agreements can be achieved.

We believe the discussions initiated by certain governments in Moscow can constitute a useful prior preparatory phase before any possible summit meeting. Similarly, we believe that the steps contemplated by the United States resolution before the Council, in addition to their intrinsic merit, could also serve, as the Swedish Government suggests, as a useful prelude for the discussion of the disarmament problem at any possible summit meeting. We therefore hope that the U.S.S.R. will agree to sit down with the interested states at once to begin the necessary technical discussions looking toward the establishment of an Arctic inspection zone.

Q. Mr. Secretary, if the Russians were to accept an Arctic inspection system, would we abandon or modify our present "fail safe" system?

A. I say in this statement that the question of what we would do would depend upon what we learn as a result of inspection. I cannot tell you in advance what that would be.

Q. Mr. Secretary, the reason I ask the question—if there were an inspection system, it would seem to be inconsistent with the takeoff flights of planes in the Arctic at a time when the inspector would be there, and it would be difficult to see how the present system of unilateral flights, based on our radar installations, could be continued if there were international inspection.

A. I have the strong belief that, if there were established this international inspection system, it would, in fact, lead to a considerable modification of our practices. That assumes that we do not find, or the international inspection system does not find, something that is so alarming that it makes it necessary to continue. On that assumption, and the assumption the inspection system would give us a more effective notice of a possible attack than we get now when we are dependent on radar information, which is not always reliable in the first instance—then I would think the other precautions would be moderated.

Q. Mr. Secretary, the Russian reaction—Mr. Gromyko's reaction—the other day was, in part, that it did not include any of the United States excluding Alaska whereas it includes part of the Soviet Union. Is the area described by Mr. Lodge in the United Nations negotiable, or is it that area of the Arctic and nothing else?

A. Well, I don't think it is anything that we would haggle about in detail. A few changes or variations here and there, I suppose, would not be objectionable. But, broadly speaking, this is the area which we think should be covered now, and we do not want to get into areas which are remote from that particular area and which carry with them a whole new set of political problems.

This area was thought of as a useful beginning place for two reasons: first because it is an area of very high strategic importance, second because it is relatively free from the political complications that exist, for example, in Europe; so, consistently with that principle, we would want to stick at this stage to that particular area.

I don't say that the particular details are sacrosanct. For instance, our resolution suggests that we would be glad to include the portions of Sweden and of Finland and, I think, a little bit of Iceland, which are not in the zone as was originally proposed. That indicates that we are not totally inflexible on the subject.

Q. Mr. Secretary, to clarify one point, you said our flights would depend on whether we found something so alarming as to warrant their continuation. Is it likely the Russians would leave, in an area to be inspected, something so alarming as to warrant continuation of the American flights?

A. I think it unlikely. I think it almost certain that, if there were inspection, that would allay the fears of sudden surprise attack to a degree that might make these flights unnecessary.

(163) United States Draft Resolution, Vetoed in the Security Council, May 2, 1958.[9]

The Security Council,
Considering further the item of the U.S.S.R. of 18 April 1958,
Noting the development, particularly in the Soviet Union and the United States of America, of growing capabilities of massive surprise attack,

[9] United Nations Document S/3995, dated April 28, 1958. The vote on the resolution was 10-1 (USSR).

Believing that the establishment of measures to allay fears of such massive surprise attack would help reduce tensions and would contribute to the increase of confidence among States,

Noting the statements of certain members of the Council regarding the particular significance of the Arctic area,

Recommends that there be promptly established the Northern zone of international inspection against surprise attack, comprising the area north of the Arctic Circle with certain exceptions and additions, that was considered by the United Nations Disarmament Sub-Committee of Canada, France, the U.S.S.R., the United Kingdom and the United States during August 1957;

Calls upon the five States mentioned, together with Denmark and Norway, and any other States having territory north of the Arctic Circle which desire to have such territory included in the zone of international inspection, at once to designate representatives to participate in immediate discussions with a view to agreeing on the technical arrangements required;

Expresses the view that such discussions might serve as a useful basis for the deliberations on the disarmament problem at a summit conference on the convening of which talks are in progress;

Decides to keep this matter on its agenda for such further considerations as may be required.

B. The Peaceful Uses of Atomic Energy.

(164) *Department of State Announcement Concerning Further United States Assistance to the International Atomic Energy Agency, January 18, 1958.*[1]

The United States Government on January 18 made three new offers of assistance to speed the work of the new International Atomic Energy Agency and to insure the future supply of nuclear scientists available to the Agency and its members.

In three separate actions, announced at the Agency headquarters in Vienna by Robert McKinney, the U.S. representative to the IAEA, the U.S. Government:

1. offered to make available to the Agency, on a cost-free

[1] *Department of State Bulletin,* v. 38 (February 19, 1958), pp. 237-238.

basis, the services of 20 to 30 expert consultants in the field of peaceful uses of atomic energy;

2. offered to provide approximately 120 fellowships over the next 2 years for training in nuclear sciences in the United States; and

3. indicated that it would contribute up to $125,000 toward a $250,000 Agency fellowship fund for similar training in member states throughout the world. This contribution from the United States would be limited to 50 percent of the total contributions to this fund.

Mr. McKinney estimated that these proposals involve about one million dollars worth of training.

The offer of technical consultants is intended to permit the Agency to provide the services of experts or teams of experts to countries desiring Agency assistance in the evaluation of their national programs, particularly those countries less advanced in nuclear development. The program is designed to permit immediate availability of consultative service before the Agency is sufficiently staffed to carry out such work with its own personnel.

The variety of skills represented among the consultants would permit the composition of teams, where necessary, to provide expert advice in the various peaceful fields of atomic science, such as its application to medicine, agriculture, industry, and nuclear power.

Such services would facilitate the preparation of projects by countries desiring further Agency assistance. Mr. McKinney expressed the hope of the U.S. Government that other member states possessing the technological capability would find it possible likewise to make specialists available to the Agency, thus permitting the organization of international teams.

The U.S. representative added that the United States was gratified at the progress being made by the newly created Agency. The actions of the Board of Governors and the Director General and his staff since the first general conference in October have been heretofore primarily concerned with organizational problems. However, the current session is the first to take up the Agency's future substantive program. Mr. McKinney noted that the new United States contribution to the Agency constituted further confirmation of the United States desire to see the Agency play a major role in the world-wide development of atomic energy for peaceful purposes.

The United States Government has previously offered to the Agency, on terms to be agreed, 5,000 kilograms of enriched uranium and to match similar contributions of materials by other countries through June 1960. It has already announced the matching of the contributions made at the IAEA general conference last October by the Soviet Union, Great Britain, and Portugal. In addition, the United States has indicated its intention to make available to the Agency a research reactor, a technical atomic-energy library, and isotope laboratories.

C. The Peaceful Uses of Outer Space.

(165) *Statement by the Legal Adviser of the Department of State (Becker) before the Special Senate Committee on Space and Astronautics, May 14, 1958.*[1]

(Excerpts)

* * *

The most immediate problem in the field of space foreign policy is how to insure that outer space is used for peaceful purposes only. As your chairman [Senator Lyndon B. Johnson] put it in his opening statement before this committee:

"The challenge of the atomic age, at the beginning, was to harness a vast destructive power to prevent its use in war.

The challenge of the space age, at the beginning now, is to open a new frontier to permit its use for peace."

* * *

. . . this new venture into our universe opens a vast area for programs of scientific study and exploration.

At this time I have in mind certain projects from which every nation in the world can benefit: radio-relay satellites which will provide for near-perfect worldwide radio; TV and radio-telephone service; weather-charting satellites which will afford early warning against natural catastrophe; aids to navigation which will enable aircraft and ships to chart their way over the surface of the earth with great accuracy and speed; construction of space platforms as takeoff points for further outer-space exploration; and manned moon-rocket flights to the moon and other planets. These are but a few of the many valuable programs we can anticipate.

[1] *Ibid.* (June 9, 1958), pp. 962-967.

These programs can have far-reaching international implications. Without proper international coordination and cooperation such activities could lead to involved international problems and could project narrow rivalries into this new field.

Here, however, as with the military implications, one significant fact is readily apparent. The national programs of the two nations now having the technological capability to carry out outer-space exploration are still in their early developmental stage. This limitation will not long exist. Thus, early action is essential if we are to thwart narrow national objectives.

There are, moreover, certain technological relationships between areas of potential international cooperation and the military programs which involve outer space. A most obvious illustration of this is the close relationship between the missile-propulsion systems and the means of putting scientific satellites into orbits. Yet it makes clear that an international program of scientific study and exploration is related to efforts to assure the use of outer space for peaceful purposes. There are many other highly technical considerations of this order involved here. Such considerations at the present time are under very active study within the Government.

The Department of State feels, however, that there are possible arrangements for international cooperation in the peaceful scientific and technological areas of outer-space activity. These arrangements could be pursued independently of control arrangements over military uses of outer space. Such cooperation would avoid conflicts of exclusively national programs. It would allow for necessary coordination of activities, thus assuring the most productive efforts. It would facilitate progress through a combination of efforts which would greatly accelerate scientific discoveries. It would provide a means by which many nations would participate in this new venture. It would insure that the scientific study of outer space is carried on in the classic tradition of scientific openness. Finally, such cooperation would set the pattern for further space activities, thus assuring the world of a logical and peaceful progression into the reaches of outer space.

To foster and guide the cooperative efforts that are possible, we believe it to be axiomatic that some appropriate international machinery should be created. Its principal responsibility would be to promote and to coordinate efforts in the field of outer space. Its functions might include, among other things, the establishment of certain international space regulations, the collection and exchange of information, and appropriate planning and coordinating of outer-space research and exploration. To undertake these functions properly, the agency might well be established under the auspices of the United Nations but, in any event, should have a suitable and necessary relationship with the United Nations and with other international organizations such as the World Meteorological Organization. In this respect a precedent has already been set. I refer specifically to the International Atomic Energy Agency. As you are aware, this Agency has the task of both promoting international exchange and scientific cooperation, as well as assuring that nuclear materials in its possession are used exclusively for peaceful purposes. There is no reason to believe that a space organization formulated along similar lines could not be just as effective—or more effective, since we have this IAEA experience from which to draw.

At this time we envisage no obstacles, political or technical, which would preclude the establishment of such an international system of cooperation and coordination. We, in fact, believe that only through the creation of such an international organization will the interests of science and humanity be amply protected and assured. I should add that international space cooperation is already imbued with some encouraging possibilities of collective action. In March of this year the Soviet Union placed on the provisional agenda of the 13th General Assembly an item calling for, among other things, "the establishment of a United Nations agency for international cooperation in the study of cosmic space." This could mean that the first imperative step has been taken—recognition of the need for international cooperation in this field. If this is so, it allows for an initial atmosphere of hope. Yet, even here, there remain initial problems. This proposal I have just quoted is tied to a broad international agreement which includes, among other things, a provision for the elimination of foreign military bases. That is an old Soviet proposal and one we are not prepared to accept. Further, we see no link between international space cooperation and elimination of foreign bases. Thus, it is clear that a number of other steps must be taken before we can gain the staggering opportunities and benefits which await a peaceful, international venture into this new world.

We have yet to reach a practical agreement which offers assurance that space shall be devoted to peaceful purposes and that there shall be international cooperation in exploring its infinite bounds. Until a satisfactory agreement has been reached, we in the State Department shall maintain and preserve every national right of the United States in the atmosphere and in space.

INTERNATIONAL LAW AFFECTING OUTER SPACE

a. Article 51 of the United Nations Charter

I have read a number of articles in which it is stated that the only international agreement relating to space or to the atmosphere is the Chicago Convention of 1944, relating to civil aviation matters. I have seen it asserted that there is no international law with respect to space outside the atmosphere.

I regard such statements as incorrect because of the specific provisions of article 51 of the United Nations Charter, to which I have previously referred. Under that provision each of the members of the United Nations reserved its "inherent right" of individual or collective self-defense against armed attack.

Now the origin of an armed attack against the United States, or the particular point in space through which it would have to pass in order to reach the United States or one of its collective-security partners, is completely immaterial. The United States is prepared at all times to react to protect itself against an armed attack, whether that attack originates in outer space or passes through outer space in order to reach the United States.

If and when the United States takes such action, it will be exercising a right which it has under international law, because that law in the last analysis is what nations will agree to. And the inherent right of individual and collective self-defense has been recognized as a fundamental principle of international law in the United Nations Charter.

b. Implications of the International Geophysical Year

There is another misconception with respect to the rights of the United States in this sphere that I should like to correct. I have several times seen it stated that we do not have any right to protest or take any action with respect to satellites because of the events relating to the International Geophysical Year. Now, the facts are these:

The arrangements with respect to the International Geophysical Year were not made on an intergovernmental basis. They were arrangements made between scientific bodies in a private capacity. It is true that certain governments, including the Soviet Union and the United States, announced in advance that during the International Geophysical Year they intended to place objects in orbit around the earth. And it was also stated in connection with these announcements that, the purpose of these satellites would be for scientific investigation. No nation protested these announcements.

It follows, therefore, that the only conclusion that can be reached with respect to the arrangements regarding the International Geophysical Year is that there is an implied agreement that, for the period of the International Geophysical Year, it is permissible to put into orbit satellites designed for scientific purposes. Once the year is over, rights in this field will have to be determined by whatever agreement may be reached with respect to such objects.

c. Is There Any Agreed Upper Limit of Sovereignty?

The next question of international law which I would like to mention is the position of the United States regarding its sovereignty upwards. There are those who have argued that the sovereignty of the United States ends with the outer limits of the atmosphere and that space outside the atmosphere is either free to all or should possibly be conceded to be within the sovereignty of one or another international organization.

The United States Government has not recognized any top or upper limit to its sovereignty. This position has been taken entirely aside from article 51 of the United Nations Charter and any limitations that may be inherent in that, such as "armed attack."

It is true that, in such international agreements as the Chicago Convention of 1944, the parties thereto recognize that each of them "has complete and exclusive sovereignty of the airspace above its territory." But it is important to note that there is nowhere in the Chicago Convention of 1944 or other international agreements comparable thereto any definition of what is meant by the term "airspace."

I do not wish to take, nor has the State Department ever officially taken, a definitive position as to how this term "airspace" should be defined. I think it important to note, however, that one of the suggestions that has been made in this regard is that the airspace should be defined to include that portion of space above the earth in which there is any atmosphere. I am informed that astronomically the earth's atmosphere extends 10,000 miles above its surface.

It follows that it would be perfectly rational for us to maintain that under the Chicago Convention the sovereignty of the United States extends 10,000 miles from the surface of the earth, an area which would comprehend the area in which all of the satellites up to this point have entered. At any rate, that type of definition would afford us enough elbowroom for discussion.

Furthermore, although the United States, in its domestic law as well as agreements such as the Chicago Convention, has plainly asserted its complete and exclusive sovereignty over the airspace above its territory, at no time have we conceded that we have no rights in the higher regions of space. One rationale for this position which seems to me self-sufficient was that the United States had no need to define its position with respect to what rights, if any, it might possess outside the earth's atmosphere until such time as mankind had demonstrated a capability of existing outside the atmosphere.

Even after such a capability is demonstrated, there will be no imperative requirement in international law that the United States make any claims of sovereignty in order to protect its rights.

A very apt analogy is afforded by the Antarctic. There, for many, many years, the United States has been engaged in activities which under established principles of international law, without any question whatsoever, created rights upon which the United States would be justified in asserting territorial claims, that is to say, claims to sovereignty over one or more areas of the Antarctic. Notwithstanding this fact the United States has not asserted any claim of sovereignty over any portion of Antarctica, although the United States has, at the same time, made it plain that it did not recognize any such claims made by other states.

Nonetheless, the United States has been consistent in asserting that under international law and practice its activities in the Antarctic Continent have entitled it to rights in that area which it has at all times expressly reserved. It is the position of the United States Government, and one well founded in international law, that the fact that the United States has not based a claim of sovereignty over one or more areas of Antarctica, upon the basis of the activities it has engaged in there, in no way derogates from the rights that were established by its activities.

So, too, in outer space the United States has already engaged in activities which, it could be asserted, have given to it certain rights as distinguished from those states who have not engaged in such activities. Up to this time the United States has made no claims of sovereignty based upon such activities.

As in the situation with respect to Antarctica, this should not be interpreted as any concession of any kind whatsoever on the part of the United States that its activities have not given it certain rights in space which, in turn, could be relied upon as the basis of a claim of sovereignty.

d. Should Space Law Be Codified at This Time?

I would like now to turn to the question of whether or not the law of space should be codified at this time.

As you know, the development or the tendency of development of the common law as it is applied in the United Kingdom and the United States and a number of other countries has been on a case-to-case basis. Speaking very generally, it has been felt that the soundest way to progress in the extremely complex field of the law is by means of specific decisions on specific questions presented by specific-fact situations. Even in those states which applied the principles of the civil law, it is recognized that a body of law can only be created upon a broader body of ascertained fact.

Moreover, there are very great risks in attempting to transmute a body of law based upon one determined set of facts into a body of law with respect to which the basic facts have not been determined.

Accordingly, we are inclined to view with great reserve any such suggestions as that the principles of the law of space should be codified now or that the principles of the law of the sea should be applied in space, until we ascertain many more facts with respect to conditions in space. Basically, it is the position of our Government that the law of space should be based upon the facts of space and that there is very much more that we have to learn about the conditions existing in space before we shall be in a position to say what shall be the legal principles applicable thereto.

*　　*　　*

(166) *Statement by the Chairman of the Special Senate Committee on Space and Astronautics (Johnson) in the General Assembly of the United Nations, November 17, 1958.*[2]

I come today with one purpose. I am here to express to you the essential unity of the American people in their support of the goals of the resolution offered now in their name.

This resolution is presented, as our system requires, by the representative of the executive branch of our Government. I speak here today at its request.

The executive position in the United States is held by the Republican Party through the mandate of the people. I am here as a member of one house of the legislative branch, in which the majority position is held, also at the mandate of the people, by the Democratic Party, of which I am a member.

These are distinctions. They are not, on this resolution, differences. On the goal of dedicating outer space to peaceful purposes for the benefit of all mankind there are no differences within our Government, between our parties, or among our people. The executive and the legislative branches of our Government are together. United we stand.

There need be no differences among us here.

The very opportunity of the issue before this Assembly is to erase the accumulated differences of our earth's long and troubled history and to write across the vastness of space a proud new chapter of unity and peace.

Men have not faced such a moment of opportunity before. Until now our strivings toward peace have been heavily burdened by legacies of distrust and fear and ignorance and injury.

Those legacies do not exist in space. They will not appear there unless we send them on ahead.

To keep space as man has found it and to harvest the yield of peace which it promises, we of the United States see one course—and only one—which the nations of earth may intelligently pursue. That is the course of full and complete and immediate cooperation to make the exploration of outer space a joint adventure.

There is, I emphasize, no other course.

In saying this I express no personal belief alone, but rather I convey to you the conviction of my countrymen and the

[2] *Ibid.*, v. 39 (December 15, 1958), pp. 977-980.

force of the American decision which has already been established.

Record of Bipartisan Congressional Support

The American people, through their elected representatives in the Congress, have spoken their aims and their purposes. The will of the people is now fixed in our laws and our policies.

The end is peace. The means to that end is international cooperation. This is—and this will remain—the American decision.

Eleven months ago the Senate Preparedness Subcommittee submitted to the full Senate a report on an exhaustive inquiry into the satellite and missile program of the United States. In that report the bipartisan membership of the subcommittee made this unanimous declaration: "The immediate objective is to defend ourselves, but the equally important objective is to reach the hearts and minds of men everywhere so that the day will come when the ballistic missile will be merely a dusty relic in the museums of mankind and men everywhere will work together in understanding."

On July 29 of this year the Congress in an act signed by the President established in the executive branch an agency under civilian control to guide and direct our national efforts in the exploration of space.[3] By the act creating this agency, Congress embedded in the permanent law of the United States the following declaration of policy: "The Congress hereby declares that it is the policy of the United States that activities in space should be devoted to peaceful purposes for the benefit of all mankind."

Further, in the same section of that act, Congress stated as a firm objective of the national efforts the following: "Cooperation by the United States with other nations and groups of nations in work done pursuant to this act and in the peaceful application of the results thereof."

Subsequent to that, the majority leader of the House of Representatives, the Honorable John McCormack, introduced before that body a resolution expressly requesting the President of the United States to submit to the United Nations the question of international cooperation in dedicating outer space to peaceful purposes only. That resolution received the earnest support of the full membership of the

[3] *Public Law* no. 85-568, 85th Cong. 2d Sess. (National Aeronautics and Space Act of 1958, July 29, 1958).

Foreign Affairs Committee of the House, and it was adopted unanimously by the full membership of the House of Representatives.

In the Senate the Foreign Relations Committee, under the chairmanship of the Honorable Theodore Green, likewise accorded to the resolution the most serious study and recommended without dissent that it be adopted. The Senate of the United States, like the House of Representatives, gave to the resolution the unanimous support of the Senators of both parties. Thus it is a matter of record that the sense of the full membership of the Congress of the United States is that this question should be here on the agenda of the nations of the world. It is also the congressional view that this organization should assume the responsibility of leadership in promoting international cooperation in the exploration of outer space.

This is the American decision, expressed firmly in the resolutions of policy by the elected representatives of the people and established solidly by them in the cornerstone law of our nation's space effort.

Adoption of U.S. Resolution Urged

The resolution before this Assembly now embodies fully the will of the Congress and the will of the people whom the Members of the Congress serve. Thus I can—and I do—commend it to you for adoption. The record already made assures you the continuing support of the Congress for the cooperative endeavors toward peaceful uses of outer space which the resolution contemplates.

The full dimensions of the promise of space are now beyond the scope of our knowledge and our imagination. To presume that we have more now than merely a glimpse of those dimensions would be both a vain and perhaps ultimately a fatally limiting error.

At this moment the nations of the earth are explorers in space, not colonizers. Hence it is proper that this Assembly should provide—first—the means for the United Nations to encourage and inspire that exploration. That is contemplated in the form of this resolution, which would create an exploratory *ad hoc* committee of representatives of member nations to carry out the following tasks:

First, to inventory the activities and resources of the United Nations, its specialized agencies, and other international bodies relating to peaceful uses of outer space;

Second, to determine areas of international cooperation

and programs which could be undertaken under auspices of this organization by member nations without regard to their present stage of economic or scientific advancement;

Third, to consider the future form of internal organization in the United Nations which would best facilitate full international cooperation in this field; and

Fourth, to survey the nature of the legal problems which may arise in implementation of this joint adventure among the nations of the earth.

These are essential first steps. Until these explorations are conducted, orderly procedure to the broader horizons beyond will not be possible. Thus to impede this first step is to impede all progress toward the goals of peace which men of faith believe exist in the realms of space.

While these are first steps, they are decisive steps, and we cannot be unmindful of the precedents which, if established now, may influence or even control the longer steps ahead.

The Case Against Unilateral Action

We of the United States have recognized and do recognize, as must all men, that the penetration into outer space is the concern of all mankind. All nations and all men, without regard to their roles on earth, are affected alike by what is accomplished over their heads in outer space.

If nations proceed unilaterally, then their penetrations into space become only extensions of their national policies on earth. What their policies on earth inspire—whether trust or fear—so their accomplishments in outer space will inspire also. For nations given to aggression and war and tyranny on earth, unilateral success in space technology would only multiply many times over their threat to peace. Thus it is the interest of nations dedicated to peace and freedom that the opportunity of space not be perverted to the end of aggression and control over earth by the aggressors.

Recognizing this as true, men of peace will recognize fully the necessity to proceed without delay on the first step which is here proposed.

Today outer space is free. It is unscarred by conflict. No nation holds a concession there. It must remain this way.

We of the United States do not acknowledge that there are landlords of outer space who can presume to bargain with the nations of the earth on the price of access to this new domain. We must not—and need not—corrupt this great opportunity by bringing to it the very antagonisms which we may, by courage, overcome and leave behind forever through a joint adventure into this new realm.

What man has done thus far has been the result directly of international cooperation on an informal basis by men of science through the years. The success, further, of the formal cooperation undertaken in observance of the International Geophysical Year foretells the high promise offered by enlargement of our goals and intensification of our support and efforts.

We know the gains of cooperation. We know the losses of failure to cooperate. If we fail now to apply the lessons we have learned or even if we delay their application, we know that the advances into space may only mean adding a new dimension to warfare. If, however, we proceed along the orderly course of full cooperation, we shall by the very fact of cooperation make the most substantial contribution yet made toward perfecting peace. Men who have worked together to reach the stars are not likely to descend together into the depths of war and desolation.

It is the American vision, I believe, that, out of this fresh start for humankind which space affords, man may at last free himself of the waste of guarding himself against his ignorance of his neighbors.

Barriers between us will fall as our sights rise to space. Secrecy will cease to be. Man will come to understand his fellow man—and himself—as never he has been able to do. In the infinity of the space adventure, man can find growing richness of mind, of spirit, and of liberty.

The promise of this moment of opportunity is great. We of the United States believe that this Assembly will honor the moment and fulfill the opportunity—and all mankind will be the beneficiary of your courage.

(167) *General Assembly Resolution 1348 (XIII), Adopted December 13, 1958.*[4]

The General Assembly,

Recognizing the common interest of mankind in outer space and recognizing that it is the common aim that outer space should be used for peaceful purposes only,

Bearing in mind the provision of Article 2, paragraph 1, of

---

[4] United Nations, General Assembly, *Official Records, Thirteenth Session,* Supplement No. 18(A/4090), pp. 5-6. The resolution was adopted by a vote of 53-9-19.

the Charter of the United Nations, which states that the Organization is based on the principle of the sovereign equality of all its Members,

Wishing to avoid the extension of present national rivalries into this new field,

Desiring to promote energetically the fullest exploration and exploitation of outer space for the benefit of mankind,

Conscious that recent developments in respect of outer space have added a new dimension to man's existence and opened new possibilities for the increase of his knowledge and the improvement of his life,

Noting the success of the scientific co-operative programme of the International Geophysical Year in the exploration of outer space and the decision to continue and expand this type of co-operation,

Recognizing the great importance of international co-operation in the study and utilization of outer space for peaceful purposes,

Considering that such co-operation will promote mutual understanding and the strengthening of friendly relations among peoples,

Believing that the development of programmes of international and scientific co-operation in the peaceful uses of outer space should be vigorously pursued,

Believing that progress in this field will materially help to achieve the aim that outer space should be used for peaceful purposes only,

Considering that an important contribution can be made by the establishment within the framework of the United Nations of an appropriate international body for co-operation in the study of outer space for peaceful purposes,

Desiring to obtain the fullest information on the many problems relating to the peaceful uses of outer space before recommending specific programmes of international co-operation in this field,

1. *Establishes* an *ad hoc* Committee on the peaceful uses of outer space consisting of the representatives of Argentina, Australia, Belgium, Brazil, Canada, Czechoslovakia, France, India, Iran, Italy, Japan, Mexico, Poland, Sweden, the Union of Soviet Socialist Republics, the United Arab Republic, the United Kingdom of Great Britain and Northern Ireland and the United States of America and requests it to report to the fourteenth General Assembly on the following:

(a) The activities and resources of the United Nations, of its specialized agencies and of other international bodies relating to the peaceful uses of outer space;

(b) The area of international co-operation and programmes in the peaceful uses of outer space which could appropriately be undertaken under United Nations auspices to the benefit of States irrespective of the state of their economic or scientific development, taking into account the following proposals, *inter alia:*

(i) Continuation on a permanent basis of the outer space research now being carried on within the framework of the International Geophysical Year;

(ii) Organization of the mutual exchange and dissemination of information on outer space research; and

(iii) Co-ordination of national research programmes for the study of outer space, and the rendering of all possible assistance and help towards their realization;

(c) The future organizational arrangements to facilitate international co-operation in this field within the framework of the United Nations;

(d) The nature of legal problems which may arise in the carrying out of programmes to explore outer space;

2. *Requests* the Secretary-General to render appropriate assistance to the above-named Committee and to recommend any other steps that might be taken within the existing United Nations framework to encourage the fullest international co-operation for the peaceful uses of outer space.

D. The United Nations Conference on the Law of the Sea, Geneva, February 24–April 28, 1958.

(168) *Statement by the Chairman of the United States Delegation (Dean), March 11, 1958.*[1]

(Excerpts)

* * *

Mr. Chairman, my delegation considers that two matters before Committee I are of such importance as to be the key to the general success of this conference. They are, *first,* the breadth of the territorial sea and, *second,* the contiguous zone.

[1] *Department of State Bulletin,* v. 38 (April 7, 1958), pp. 574-581.

Solutions of the problems implicit in these articles 3 and 66 would make the work of this committee a milestone in the development of international law.[2]

*   *   *

The position of the United States of America concerning the breadth of the territorial sea is determined by its attitude toward the doctrine of the freedom of the seas. There is no doctrine of international law more universally recognized than the principle that the high seas are the common property of all and that no part of them can be unilaterally appropriated by any state to its own use without the concurrence of other states.

In this day of improved methods of transportation and communication, which have served to bring countries ever closer together, it is vitally important that the international highways of the sea and of the superjacent air should not be brought under the restrictive domination or control of individual states, however worthy their motives. I repeat, any such proposals which would result in restricting the freedom of the seas would not be progress but rather retrogression.

We sincerely believe that this doctrine, in its widest impli-

[2] For the text of the "articles concerning the law of the sea," adopted by the Eighth Session of the International Law Commission, Geneva, April 23–July 4, 1956, see United Nations, General Assembly, *Official Records, Eleventh Session,* Supplement No. 9 (A/3159). The articles specifically referred to by Mr. Dean read as follows:

Article 3

1. The Commission recognizes that international practice is not uniform as regards the delimitation of the territorial sea.
2. The Commission considers that international law does not permit an extension of the territorial sea beyond twelve miles.
3. The Commission, without taking any decision as to the breadth of the territorial sea up to that limit, notes, on the one hand, that many States have fixed a breadth greater than three miles and, on the other hand, that many states do not recognize such a breadth when that of their own territorial sea is less.
4. The Commission considers that the breadth of the territorial sea should be fixed by an international conference.

Article 66

1. In a zone of the high seas contiguous to its territorial sea, the coastal State may exercise the control necessary to
   (a) Prevent infringement of its customs, fiscal or sanitary regulations within its territory or territorial sea;
   (b) Punish infringement of the above regulations committed within its territory or territorial sea.
2. The contiguous zone may not extend beyond twelve miles from the baseline from which the breadth of the territorial sea is measured.

cation, is the principle fairest to all, large and small. The doctrine of the freedom of the seas is not a mere historical relic of the so-called time when maritime law was developed by the great powers.

There have been suggestions here that the interests of small and large states in these matters are different.

The history of the United States and of the 3-mile limit is a living refutation of such suggestions.

* * *

It is the view of my Government, without elaboration or citation of authorities or making an extended legal argument at this time, that the 3-mile rule is established international law; that it is the only breadth of territorial waters on which there has ever been anything like common agreement; and that unilateral acts of states claiming greater territorial seas are not only not sanctioned by any principle of international law but are indeed in conflict with the universally accepted principle of the freedom of the seas.

There is universal agreement that each state is entitled to a territorial sea of a breadth of 3 miles, or 1 marine league. But this cannot be said of any claim to a greater breadth, each of which claims has been protested by many states. This fact was recognized in the report of the International Law Commission covering the work of its seventh session when it stated that "international law does not require states to recognize a breadth [of territorial sea] beyond three miles." [3]

The United States regards this to be the true legal situation. Further, it considers that there is no obligation on the part of states adhering to the 3-mile rule to recognize claims on the part of other states to a greater breadth of territorial sea.

Since the right of states to a 3-mile territorial sea is universally recognized, and since in its view the greatest freedom of the seas is in the interest of all states, large and small, the delegation of the United States of America proposes that article 3 of the ILC draft be changed to an unequivocal declaration of restraint that the breadth of the territorial sea shall not exceed 3 miles or 1 marine league.

* * *

[3] United Nations, General Assembly, *Official Records, Tenth Session,* Supplement No. 9 (A/2934).

Contiguous Zone

I said at the start of this statement that the United States of America attached the utmost importance to article 66 relating to the contiguous zone.

My Government is not unmindful of and, indeed, is highly sympathetic with the problems which concern a large number of the coastal states and which have led them in the past to certain unilateral actions in high-seas areas for the primary purpose of conservation of the fish stocks off their coasts.

We submit that these needs, which have been so eloquently expressed by some of our friends from Latin America, may be fully and adequately met by means other than through extensions of the territorial sea, which extensions violate the rights and freedoms of all countries. We are prepared to be helpful in working out a constructive solution.

It is to take care of the legitimate needs of many countries that the United States attaches deep significance to article 66 and also to the articles on fishery conservation which are under the jurisdiction of the Third Committee.

We also attach significance to the problem of the continental shelf, which is under the jurisdiction of the Fourth Committee, and to the problems of landlocked countries, under the jurisdiction of the Fifth Committee, and shall make appropriate statements in each of these several committees.

It is the belief of the United States that these rules set down by the International Law Commission may be molded to give full and sufficient remedy to the genuine needs and to make possible a more fruitful exploitation of the resources of the sea for the benefit of all mankind.

*   *   *

Testing of Nuclear Weapons on High Seas

Now let me turn for just a moment to another problem. Since the problem of the testing of nuclear weapons on the high seas has been raised in the debate in this committee, as well as in other committees, I should like very briefly to clarify the United States position on this matter at this conference.

Now the real danger to the world lies in the possible use of nuclear weapons and not in some slight addition to the natural forces of radioactivity. While the United States of America conducts its tests in a manner recognized as being consonant with international law, it should also be abundantly clear to this conference that we have repeatedly offered to enter into arrangements embodying meaningful and effective measures for the control of nuclear weapons.

Unfortunately no agreement has yet been reached which would make this possible.

Because of its paramount importance to all mankind, this subject should continue to be dealt with in the established United Nations organs created specifically to deal with the problems of weapons control.

We must all hope that further negotiations on disarmament, of which the nuclear testing problem is but one element, will produce satisfactory results in the interests of humanity. But in line, I trust, with the position the distinguished representative of India tentatively indicated here the other day, I question whether we are a proper body to intervene in this negotiating process.

* * *

(169) *Statement by the Chairman of the United States Delegation (Dean), April 28, 1958.*[4]

In putting before this conference the United States proposal relating to the breadth of the territorial sea and to exclusive fishing rights in a contiguous zone constituting a part of the high seas, under certain limitations recognizing certain rights of others than the coastal state, I made it clear that the United States regarded this as a realistic compromise and that it was made at considerable sacrifice to United States interests.[5]

[4] *Department of State Bulletin,* v. 38 (June 30, 1958), pp. 1110-1111.
[5] The U.S. compromise proposal provided:
"1. The maximum breadth of the territorial sea of any state shall be six miles.
"2. The coastal state shall in a zone having a maximum breadth of twelve miles, measured from the applicable baseline, determined as provided in these rules, have the same rights in respect of fishing and the exploitation of the living resources of the sea as it has in its territorial sea; provided that such rights shall be subject to the right of the vessels of any state whose vessels have fished regularly in that portion of the zone having a continuous baseline and located in the same major body of water for the period of five years immediately preceding the signature of this Convention, to fish in the outer six miles of that portion of the zone, under obligation to observe therein such conservation regulations as are consistent with rules on fisheries adopted by this Conference and other rules of international law.
"3. Any dispute with respect to the interpretation or application of this article shall, at the request of any party to the dispute, be submitted to arbitration unless the parties agree to another method of peaceful solution.
"4. For the purposes of this Convention the term 'mile' means a nautical

Our proposal was made in a sincere effort to meet other countries' points of view with the sole purpose of achieving international agreement on these important matters. It was an effort to reconcile the diverse and often conflicting interests of those coastal states desiring a larger share in the resources of the seas off their coasts and the interests of those states desiring the broadest possible freedom of the seas.

We greatly appreciate and wish to thank all those who supported our proposal, which received 45 votes, or some 7 votes short of the two-thirds majority required and yet considerably greater support than any other proposal on this subject. Every country must be the judge of its own position and needs, and, while we are disappointed, we have nothing to say about the decision made here.

Our offer to agree on a 6-mile breadth of territorial sea, provided agreement could be reached on such a breadth under certain conditions, was simply an offer and nothing more. Its nonacceptance leaves the preexisting situation intact.

We are happy with the 3-mile rule. In our judgment it is the principle giving the greatest opportunity to all nations, large and small, new and old, coastal and landlocked, because it is the doctrine most consistent with freedom of the seas, a time-tested and universally recognized principle.

We have made it clear from the beginning that in our view the 3-mile rule is and will continue to be established in-

mile (which is 1,852 meters), reckoned at sixty to one degree of latitude.

"5. As respects the parties thereto, the provisions of paragraph 2 of this article shall be subject to such bilateral or multilateral arrangements, if any, as may exist or be entered into.

"NOTE: It is proposed that this article be entered into with the express understanding that each party to the Convention undertakes to consider sympathetically the request of another party to consult on the question of whether the rights granted by this article are being exercised in such manner as to work an inequity upon one or more of the other parties and, if so, what measures should and can be taken to remedy the situation."

While this proposal indicated the United States was prepared to depart from its traditional adherence to the 3-mile limit in order to achieve conference agreement, Mr. Dean made it clear that the United States would continue to adhere to the 3-mile limit unless the conference agreed on a change in the traditional rule. He stated, for example:

"My government stands firmly upon the view that the three-mile limit is fully established as a principle of international law and that this principle can only be changed by agreement. If we do not agree, our work here will be a nullity and no statement, or proposal or argument, will have any effect whatsoever to extend the breadth of the territorial sea beyond three miles."

The vote on the U.S. compromise proposal was 45 for and 33 against, with 7 abstaining. (The Yemen delegation was absent.) While the U.S. proposal narrowly missed obtaining the necessary two-thirds majority, it was the only proposal on the subject which obtained the affirmative vote of an absolute majority of the 86 conference participants.

ternational law, to which we adhere. It is the only breadth of the territorial sea on which there has ever been anything like common agreement. Unilateral acts of states claiming greater territorial seas are not only not sanctioned by any principle of international law but are, indeed, in conflict with the universally accepted principle of freedom of the seas.

Furthermore we have made it clear that in our view there is no obligation on the part of states adhering to the 3-mile rule to recognize claims on the part of other states to a greater breadth of territorial sea. And on that we stand.

While we consider that the 3-mile rule is existing international law, nevertheless we are still optimistic that upon reflection the great majority of our good friends in the international community will come to realize that international agreement on the breadth of the territorial sea and on fishing rights is necessary in order that a regime of law may be effected and that the diverse and often conflicting interests of national states may not jeopardize the peace of the international community.

To this end we pledge our cooperation.

We sincerely believe that such international agreement is possible, and we shall continue to lend our efforts to that end.[6]

E. The International Geophysical Year: United States Proposal for Continuing Scientific Cooperation in the Antarctic.

(170) *United States Note, May 1, 1958.*[1]

EXCELLENCY: I have the honor to refer to the splendid example of international cooperation which can now be observed in many parts of the world because of the coordinated efforts of scientists of many countries in seeking a better understanding of geophysical phenomena during the current International Geophysical Year. These coordinated efforts of the scientists of many lands have as their objective a greatly increased knowledge of the planet on which we live and will

[6] The conventions, protocol and resolutions adopted by the conference are printed in the *Department of State Bulletin*, v. 38 (June 30, 1958), pp. 1111-1125. On December 10, 1958 the United Nations General Assembly adopted a resolution requesting, among other things, that the Secretary General convoke a second conference on the law of the sea "at the earliest convenient date in March or April 1960, at the European Office of the United Nations in Geneva." United Nations, General Assembly, *Official Records, Thirteenth Session*, Supplement No. 18 (A/4090), pp. 54-55.
[1] *Department of State Bulletin*, v. 38 (June 2, 1958), pp. 911-912.

no doubt contribute directly and indirectly to the welfare of the human race for many generations to come.

Among the various portions of the globe where these cooperative scientific endeavors are being carried on with singular success and with a sincere consciousness of the high ideals of mankind to which they are dedicated is the vast and relatively remote continent of Antarctica. The scientific research being conducted in that continent by the cooperative efforts of distinguished scientists from many countries is producing information of practical as well as theoretical value for all mankind.

The International Geophysical Year comes to a close at the end of 1958. The need for coordinated scientific research in Antarctica, however, will continue for many more years into the future. Accordingly, it would appear desirable for those countries participating in the Antarctic program of the International Geophysical Year to reach agreement among themselves on a program to assure the continuation of the fruitful scientific cooperation referred to above. Such an arrangement could have the additional advantage of preventing unnecessary and undesirable political rivalries in that continent, the uneconomic expenditure of funds to defend individual national interests, and the recurrent possibility of international misunderstanding. It would appear that if harmonious agreement can be reached among the countries directly concerned in regard to friendly cooperation in Antarctica, there would be advantages not only to those countries but to all other countries as well.

The present situation in Antarctica is characterized by diverse legal, political, and administrative concepts which render friendly cooperation difficult in the absence of an understanding among the countries involved. Seven countries have asserted claims of sovereignty to portions of Antarctica, some of which overlap and give rise to occasional frictions. Other countries have a direct interest in that continent based on past discovery and exploration, geographic proximity, sea and air transportation routes, and other considerations.

The United States for many years has had, and at the present time continues to have, direct and substantial rights and interests in Antarctica. Throughout a period of many years, commencing in the early eighteen-hundreds, many areas of the Antarctic region have been discovered, sighted, explored and claimed on behalf of the United States by nationals of the United States and by expeditions carrying the flag of the United States. During this period, the Government of the United States and its nationals have engaged in well-known and extensive activities in Antarctica.

In view of the activities of the United States and its nationals referred to above, my Government reserves all of the rights of the United States with respect to the Antarctic region, including the right to assert a territorial claim or claims.

It is the opinion of my Government, however, that the interests of mankind would best be served, in consonance with the high ideals of the Charter of the United Nations, if the countries which have a direct interest in Antarctica were to join together in the conclusion of a treaty which would have the following peaceful purposes:

A. Freedom of scientific investigation throughout Antarctica by citizens, organizations, and governments of all countries; and a continuation of the international scientific cooperation which is being carried out so successfully during the current International Geophysical Year.

B. International agreement to ensure that Antarctica be used for peaceful purposes only.

C. Any other peaceful purposes not inconsistent with the Charter of the United Nations.

The Government of the United States is prepared to discuss jointly with the Governments of the other countries having a direct interest in Antarctica the possibility of concluding an agreement, which would be in the form of a treaty, for the purpose of giving legal effect to these high principles. It is believed that such a treaty can be concluded without requiring any participating nation to renounce whatever basic historic rights it may have in Antarctica, or whatever claims of sovereignty it may have asserted. It could be specifically provided that such basic rights and such claims would remain unaffected while the treaty is in force, and that no new rights would be acquired and no new claims made by any country during the duration of the treaty. In other words, the legal status quo in Antarctica would be frozen for the duration of the treaty, permitting cooperation in scientific and administrative matters to be carried out in a constructive manner without being hampered or affected in any way by political considerations. Provision could likewise be made for such joint administrative arrangements as might be necessary and desirable to ensure the successful accomplishment of the agreed objectives. The proposed treaty would be deposited with the United Nations, and the cooperation of the specialized technical agencies of the United Nations would be sought. Such an arrangement would provide a firm and favorable foundation for a continuation of the productive activities which have thus far distinguished the International Geophysical Year; would provide an agreed basis for the maintenance of peaceful and orderly conditions in Antarctica during years to come; and would avoid the possibility of that continent becoming the scene of international discord.

In the hope that the countries having a direct interest in Antarctica will agree on the desirability of the aforesaid high objectives, and will work together in an effort to convert them into practical realities, the Government of the United States has the honor to invite the Government of _____ to participate in a Conference for this purpose to be convened at an early date at such place as may be mutually agreeable.

Accept, Excellency, the renewed assurances of my highest consideration.

(171) *Statement by the President, May 3, 1958.*[2]

The United States is dedicated to the principle that the vast uninhabited wastes of Antarctica shall be used only for peaceful purposes. We do not want Antarctica to become an object of political conflict. Accordingly, the United States has invited 11 other countries, including the Soviet Union, to confer with us to seek an effective joint means of achieving this objective.[3]

We propose that Antarctica shall be open to all nations to conduct scientific or other peaceful activities there. We also propose that joint administrative arrangements be worked out to insure the successful accomplishment of these and other peaceful purposes.

The countries which have been invited to confer are those which have engaged in scientific activities in Antarctica over the past 9 months in connection with the International Geophysical Year. I know of no instance in which international cooperation has been more successfully demonstrated.

[2] *Ibid.*, pp. 910-911.
[3] The countries invited were Argentina, Australia, Belgium, Chile, France, Japan, New Zealand, Norway, the Union of South Africa, the USSR, and the United Kingdom.

However, the International Geophysical Year terminates on December 31, 1958. Our proposal is directed at insuring that this same kind of cooperation for the benefit of all mankind shall be perpetuated after that date.

I am confident that our proposal will win the wholehearted support of the peoples of all the nations directly concerned, and indeed of all other peoples of the world.

INDEX

This is a selective index intended to supplement the detailed table of contents which appears at the head of this volume. Listings are restricted to the names of personalities who are connected with major documents in the text and to a small number of topical entries covering subjects that are either not independently listed elsewhere or may be difficult to locate through the table of contents.

566